PHOTOSHOP CS
at YourFingertips

PHOTOSHOP CS
at Your Fingertips

Get In, Get Out, Get Exactly What You Need™

JASON CRANFORD TEAGUE AND WALT DIETRICH

SYBEX®

San Francisco • London

Associate Publisher: Dan Brodnitz

Acquisitions Editor: Bonnie Bills

Developmental Editor: Pete Gaughan

Editor: Pat Coleman

Production Editor: Lori Newman

Technical Editor: Stephen Burns

Compositor: Happenstance Type-O-Rama

Proofreaders: Laurie O'Connell, Nancy Riddiough

Indexer: Ted Laux

Cover Designer: Daniel Ziegler

Cover Illustrator/Photographer: Daniel Ziegler

Interior Designer: Franz Baumhackl

Library of Congress Card Number: 2003115439

ISBN: 0-7821-4289-3

The artwork throughout the pages of this book were used with the permission of the following:

Teodoru Badiu; www.apocryph.net

Philip Baca; www.pixeldelic.org

Ian Rogers; www.greynotgrey.com

Maggie Taylor; www.maggietaylor.com

Michelle Kwajafa; www.soulsabyss.net

Manufactured in the United States of America

10 9 8 7 6 5 4 3 2 1

Dear Reader,

Thank you for choosing *Photoshop CS at Your Fingertips*. This book is part of a new wave of Sybex graphics books, all written by outstanding authors—artists and teachers who really know their stuff and have a clear vision of the audience they're writing for.

Founded in 1976, Sybex is the oldest independent computer book publisher. More than twenty-five years later, we're committed to producing a full line of consistently exceptional graphics books. With each title, we're working hard to set a new standard for the industry. From the paper we print on, to the writers and photographers we work with, our goal is to bring you the best graphics books available.

I hope you see all that is reflected in these pages. I'd be very interested to hear your comments and get your feedback on how we're doing. To let us know what you think about this, or any other Sybex book, please visit us at `www.sybex.com`. Once there, go to the product page, click on Submit a Review, and fill out the questionnaire. Your input is greatly appreciated.

Please also visit www.sybex.com to learn more about the rest of our growing graphics line.

Best regards,

Daniel A. Brodnitz
Associate Publisher
Sybex Inc.

For Johnny, who sparked my love of the arts at an early age.
—Jason Cranford Teague

For Rebecca, who gave me my first set of keys to Photoshop.
—Walt Dietrich

Acknowledgments

We are extremely thankful to the good folks at Sybex. Thanks to Dan Brodnitz, who listened to us with great patience. Thanks to Bonnie Bills, who nurtured this project from infancy. Thanks to Pete Gaughan, Lori Newman, and Pat Coleman, who edited out our mistakes and helped direct us toward a better book. We're grateful to Stephen Burns for his technical review. Thank you to compositors Maureen Forys and Kate Kaminski at Happenstance Type-O-Rama and all the proofreaders: Laurie O'Connell and Nancy Riddiough.

Thanks to the many talented artists who contributed their work to the book: Maggie Taylor, Philip Baca, Ian Rogers, Michelle Kwajafa, and Teodoru Badiu.

We also want to thank Adobe for making such great software to write about. Specifically, we want to thank Stacey Strehlow, who ran the beta program.

From Jason

First, I want to thank my family for their unwavering support. Thanks to my wife, Tara, who has put up with my mad tantrums and my dashing around taking photographs at odd times. Thanks to my daughter, Jocelyn, and son, Dashiel, for lifting my spirits and inspiring me with their smiles. Thanks to my parents and parents-in-law for helping take care of my family during the thick of writing this book.

A special thank you to Neil Salkind and Studio B, for representing me and my better interests.

I am always thankful to Ms. Rhodes, Judy, Sue, Boyd, Dr. G, and the Teachers of America.

Finally, I'd like to thank the people whose art, film, music, theater, and writings inspire me daily: The The, Gustav Klimt, Woody Guthrie, Tim Burton, Charles Dodgson, Neil Gaiman, Miles Davis, Cindy Sherman, Nine Inch Nails, ZBS Studios (for the *Ruby* series), Bad Religion, H.P. Lovecraft, Graham Greene, The Sisters of Mercy, Frank Miller, The Hollies, Dashiell Hammett, New Model Army, The Smiths, Marcel Duchamp, Mojo Nixon, William Gibson, James, John William Waterhouse, Phillip K. Dick, Siouxsie & the Banshees, Carl Sagan, and, of course, Douglas Adams.

From Walt

Thanks to my family for their love and support over the years. It has surely been a long and bumpy road. Thanks to the many teachers who have encouraged me in creative exploration, especially Rebecca, Pam, and Dotty, who were there for me at the last fork in the road. I'll be forever grateful for the support and encouragement of the gang at the office, without your help none of this would have been possible.

To Bonnie and Jason especially: thanks, this has been an amazing experience. To the folks at Adobe: wow, what a thrill you have provided me through this product. Last, but not least, my thanks go out to my online community for their support, just for being there; without you all, none of this would have come to pass. To all my online collaborators and friends, from unmondo to the Battle Domes—much love and respect.

About the Authors

Jason Cranford Teague has been working in digital media design since 1994. Over the years, his clients have included Bank of America, Coca-Cola, Virgin, CNN, Kodak, Siemens, The European Space Agency, and WebMD. A graduate of Rensselaer Polytechnic Institute, where he spent a very cold year getting his M.S. in Technical Communication, Jason is regularly asked to speak at conferences about design for Web, print, and video. An internationally recognized writer and columnist, Jason is the author of numerous books and articles including the best selling *DHTML and CSS for the World Wide Web*, *Final Cut Pro 4 and the Art of Filmmaking*, *SVG for Web Designers*, and *Final Cut Express Solutions*. In addition, he has written for the *Apple Developers Connection*, *Computer Arts Magazine*, *Macworld Magazine*, and *C\Net* as well as appearing on *TechTV's* "The Screen Savers." Jason is currently running Bright Eye Media (www.brighteyemedia.com), which specializes in Web sites for education and entertainment.

Walt Dietrich is a graphic designer, digital artist, and Photoshop enthusiast. He admits he's hooked on the experience of online digital imaging and collaboration, sometimes called Photoshop Tennis. He has been a part-time Photoshop instructor for the past several years and has been an active member of several online design communities supporting digital collaboration. Walt is also among the artists featured in *Photoshop Secrets of the Pros: 20 Top Artists and Designers Face Off* by Mark Clarkson.

Contents

UNIVERSAL

TASKS

PHOTO AND
VIDEO TASKS

**PRINT
TASKS**

439

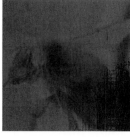

**WEB
TASKS**

475

Introduction

More than a decade ago, Photoshop revolutionized the way images are edited using the computer. Image-editing programs were around before Photoshop, and many more programs have come after it, but Photoshop reigns supreme as the workhorse image-editing tool of choice for photographers, designers, and artists around the world. The reason for Photoshop's success is easily explained: versatility. Despite its name, Photoshop does much more than simply allow you to edit photographs. Over the years, Adobe has added functionality and tools to Photoshop for print, art, web, and video design.

Now, with the release of Photoshop CS, the toolset is yet further refined and expanded to meet the needs of today's designers.

Who Is This Book For?

If you are reading this, most likely you are standing in a bookstore or a library, surrounded by dozens of other books about Photoshop, trying to select the one that will best suit your needs. If you are looking for a complete resource for Photoshop, one that will help you learn new skills and improve existing ones, you have picked up the right book.

When you're faced with a particular job, would you like to be able to find out quickly how to accomplish just that task? Would you like to know the shortcuts and secrets that help you work faster and better in Photoshop? If you are a photographer, a graphic artist, a print designer, or a web designer looking for a complete resource for Photoshop, you need this book.

The concept behind writing *Photoshop CS at Your Fingertips* was to give Photoshop users a well-organized, comprehensive, and visual resource.

Regardless of your skill level, this book provides immediate access to the program.

Beginning If you are new to Photoshop, use this book to get acquainted with the Photoshop interface and get step-by-step instruction in fundamental tasks so you can get right to work on your images.

Intermediate Once you master the basic Photoshop skills, you can use this book to discover shortcuts and more efficient ways of doing routine tasks. You can use it as a springboard to specialize your skills for particular uses such as print, web, photography, and video.

Advanced Photoshop has undergone a lot of changes in the last several years, and staying ahead of the curve is never easy. This book is a comprehensive reference manual, with thorough cross-referencing to help you find the detailed information you need to stay up-to-date.

How This Book Is Organized: A Task-Based Reference

When you're working in Photoshop, you're trying to *do* something. That's why *Photoshop CS at Your Fingertips* is organized around the many tasks you perform and breaks these down to explain the various ways to perform them.

Photoshop is a complex piece of software. It has dozens of commands, hundreds of features, and thousands of options. Yet most experienced Photoshop users tend to stick with what they know. That is, once they learn how to do a particular task in Photoshop, they rarely think to try it a different way. This is unfortunate, because they often overlook not only easier ways to do the same thing, but ways that might produce slightly different results for them to play with.

One of the great strengths of Photoshop is its ability to conform to your needs, providing functionality as you need it, rather than trying to force you to follow some set process. Although this flexibility gives you maximum creative freedom, it makes it meaningless to organize information around the program's interface. This book does have sections covering the options and features of each and every tool, preference setting, and dialog box. But the majority of the book is divided into the broad tasks users call upon Photoshop to accomplish, with one major section devoted to the universal tasks that all Photoshop users need to know.

Photoshop Workspace Chapters 1–5 introduce you to the Photoshop interface and detail all the different parts you will be using. Here is general information about menus, tools, palettes, and preferences, with references to where in the book you can find more information for using them.

Universal Tasks Chapters 6–18 provide the skills that every Photoshop user needs to master, regardless of how they use the program.

Photo and Video Tasks Chapters 19–22 deal with the specific issues involved in producing high-quality photographic and video images.

Print Tasks Chapters 23–25 deal with specific skills for those using Photoshop to create high-end printed pieces.

Web Tasks Chapters 26–29 deal not only with using Photoshop for creating web output but also include extensive information about ImageReady, the stand-alone application that can be used with Photoshop to provide further web design capabilities.

A Book for All Users

Although this book includes information about all the most recent Photoshop features in version CS, we will always specify that a feature is new when explaining it so that those of you with older versions of Photoshop should be able to follow along with no difficulty. (The Appendix lists the new CS features and where they can be found in the book.) In addition, you can use this book with any of the operating systems on which Photoshop CS is available:

Windows Photoshop CS runs on Windows 2000 (Service Pack 3) and Windows XP and works the same in both versions, although the appearance of certain interface objects (such as the title bar) varies from version to version.

Mac OS X Photoshop CS runs natively in Apple's next-generation operating system starting with version 10.2.4. If you are using version 10.2.4, however, it's recommended that you upgrade to version 10.3, which offers a significant speed boost.

We've illustrated the book with screens from both Windows and Mac operating systems. When there's a significant difference in the options or function between Windows and Macintosh, you'll see both interfaces represented.

Photoshop CS at Your Fingertips also supplies keyboard shortcuts using both operating systems' conventions. In the margins, you'll see both the Macintosh and the Windows versions, on separate lines in that order. In text, we've run them together a bit, but still provide you with both: Command-Option/Ctrl-Alt means the Command and Option keys on a Mac, the Ctrl and Alt keys in Windows.

Using This Book

Each section in this book is organized around the idea of letting you quickly scan the information to find if a page has what you need or sending you to another section in the book to look there. Rather than burying cross-references and keyboard shortcuts in the text, we placed these in their own column, along with general tips and warnings relevant to the topic at hand.

In addition, this book makes extensive use of lettered "callout" labels on the figures to help you identify the various parts of the Photoshop interface and how they work. These are generally integrated with step-by-step instructions or bulleted lists, which refer to particular dialogs or palettes, with the callouts explaining how to set the various options.

Numbered section head Each new section in a chapter starts at the top of a page and is numbered for quick reference.

Quick cross-references Each topic points you to other sections that relate to the subject or offer alternative or more detailed information.

Keyboard shortcuts We provide the keyboard commands relevant to the section's subject.

Tips Additional notes and warnings are included about the task or tool presented in the section.

Callouts Hundreds of images in the book provide detailed labeling to eliminate the guesswork of figuring out how the Photoshop interface works.

Sidebars You'll find additional information that can be applied to the tasks presented in the chapter.

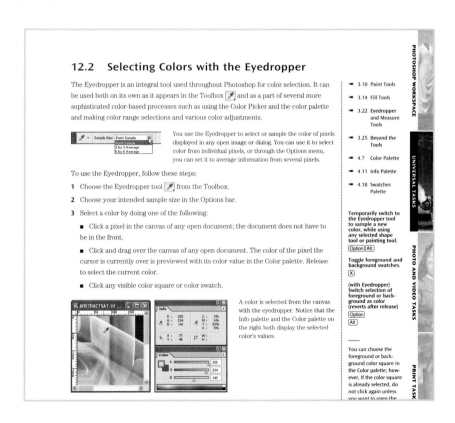

Photoshop CS at Your Fingertips on the Web

Sybex strives to keep you supplied with the latest tools and information you need for your work. Please check our website at www.sybex.com for additional content and updates that supplement this book. Enter the book's ISBN (4289) in the Search box, or type "photoshop and fingertips," and click "Go" to get to the book's update page.

Contacting the Authors

Jason and Walt are always happy to answer any questions that you have about Photoshop that you can't find answers for in this book. E-mail them with your questions at photoshop@webbedenvironments.com.

PHOTOSHOP WORKSPACE

UNIVERSAL TASKS

PHOTO AND VIDEO TASKS

PRINT TASKS

WEB TASKS

CHAPTER 1

Interface Overview

PHOTOSHOP CS IS AVAILABLE FOR Windows (2000 and XP) and for Mac OS X (version 10.2.4). Regardless of which operating system you happen to be using, Photoshop works much the same. There may be a few operating system–specific buttons, controls (especially with printing), shortcut keys (of course), and even the occasional additional menu; but understanding Photoshop in Windows is the same as understanding Photoshop on the Mac.

The first thing you notice when you open Photoshop are the controls. They are everywhere, allowing you to adjust just about anything you can possibly imagine in the images you edit. There are thousands of buttons, controls, menu options, and other objects, and each has a specific purpose. Learning all these may seem a Herculean task, and mastering them nigh impossible. Yet all the controls in Photoshop follow a similar logic, and once you get the hang of a few controls, understanding the entire interface will quickly follow.

- 1.1   **The Macintosh interface**
- 1.2   **The Windows interface**
- 1.3   **The document window**
- 1.4   **Interface objects**

1.1   The Macintosh Interface

Hide all controls
[Tab]

**Hide all controls
except Toolbox and
tool options bar**
[Option] [Tab]

Since standard Mac
mice do not have a
right button (as do PC
mice), use Control-click
whenever right- clicking
is indicated. If your
mouse does have a
right mouse button,
you can use either
method.

Photoshop CS is the first
version of Photoshop
that is *not* available for
the "classic" versions
of the Macintosh oper-
ating system. In fact,
Photoshop CS is not
compatible with early
versions of the Mac OS X
operating system. If you
are using any version of
the Mac operating sys-
tem before 10.2.4, you
will need to upgrade.

To run Photoshop CS on a Macintosh, your system will need to meet the following minimum requirements: Mac OS 10.2.4 or later; G3 or higher processor; 192 MB RAM, although 256 MB is recommended; 320 MB of available hard disk space; 1024×768 resolution monitor with 16-bit or better color; CD-ROM drive (for installation).

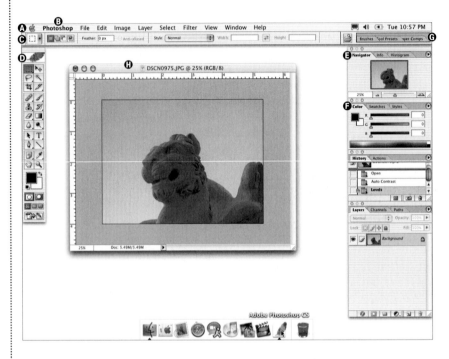

ⓐ Menu bar Click any of the menu headings to view a list of menu options.

ⓑ Application menu (Photoshop) This menu is available in Mac OS X to provide access to appli-cation-specific options such as About Photoshop and Preferences. Use can also use this menu to hide Photoshop or other applications.

ⓒ Tool Options bar This part of the interface provides options for the currently selected tool.

ⓓ Toolbox Click an icon to select a particular tool to use in the canvas.

ⓔ Palettes Through the Window menu, you can access 17 floating palettes that contain controls and options for the various tools and the canvas. A palette is distinguished by a tab with its name.

ⓕ Palette group You can group palettes and then bring an individual palette to the front of a group by clicking its tab.

ⓖ Palette Well This space holds palettes for quick access. Simply drag and drop a palette's tab into the area to add it to the well.

ⓗ Document window The document window displays the image currently being edited (also called the image window). Multiple document windows can be open at a given time, but only one is on top and can be edited.

1.2 The Windows Interface

To run Photoshop CS on a Windows machine, you will need the following: Windows 2000 (Service Pack 3), Windows XP, or a later version of Windows; Pentium III or 4 processor (or equivalent) or higher; 192 MB RAM, although 256 MB is recommended; 280 MB of available hard disk space; 1024×768 resolution monitor with 16-bit or better color; CD-ROM drive (for installation)

A Menu bar Click a menu heading to view a list of menu options.

B Tool Options bar This part of the interface provides options for the currently selected tool.

C Toolbox Click to select a particular tool to use in the canvas.

D Palettes Through the Window menu, you can access 17 floating palettes that contain controls and options for the various tools and the canvas. A tab with the palette name distinguishes a palette.

E Palette group You can group palettes, and then you can bring an individual palette to the front of a group by clicking its tab.

F Palette Well This space holds palettes for quick access. To add a palette to the well, drag and drop its tab into this area.

G Document window This window displays the image currently being edited (also called the image window). Multiple document windows can be open at a given time, but only one is on top and able to be edited.

H Image magnification This space displays the current magnification of the canvas. Click and enter a new magnification.

I Document information This space displays document information as chosen in the drop-down immediately to the right. Option/Alt-click to view width, height, channels, and resolution.

J Document information selection Click to select the information displayed.

K Action Much like the Tool Tip, this area displays the action possible with the current tool.

Hide all controls
[Tab]

Hide all controls except Toolbox and tool options bar
[Shift] [Tab]

The primary differences between Photoshop on the Mac and Photoshop in Windows are the placement of the menu bar, the ability to enlarge the application to fill the entire window using the application buttons in the top-right corner of the screen, and the placement of the status bar at the bottom of the application window (rather than in the document window).

1.3   The Document Window

**Minimize window
(Windows only)**
⌘ M

**Close front document
window**
⌘ W
Ctrl W

**Close all document
windows**
Option ⌘ W
Shift Ctrl W

New document
⌘ N
Ctrl N

Open document
⌘ O
Ctrl O

Browse for document
Shift ⌘ O

Shift Ctrl O

**Open document as
(Windows only)**
Alt Ctrl O

─────

You can have multiple
document windows
open at the same
time and juggle these
documents using the
Window > Documents
submenu. You can tile
the open document
windows in a variety
of ways, or you can
choose the document
you want to work with
and bring it to the
front.

When you open an image or start a new image, it is placed in its own document window. The document window not only displays the image, allowing you to edit it in a variety of ways in the canvas, but also displays important information about the document and some controls for the image file.

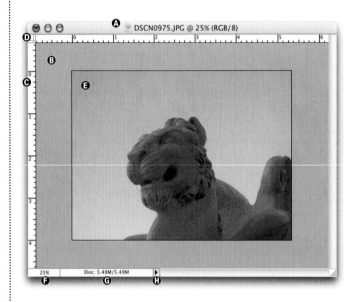

ⓐ Title bar Displays the filename, the magnification, and the color mode of the document in the window. Mac users can ⌘-click the title to view the saving path.

ⓑ Image Mat Surrounds the area around the canvas with a gray frame to the edge of the window. Shift-click in the image mat with the Paint Bucket to change the color to the selected foreground color.

ⓒ Rulers Displays the measurement of the image in selected units. Click and drag to set a guideline. Double-click to open Rulers & Units preferences.

ⓓ Adjust Ruler Origin Click and drag to adjust the origin point for the ruler in the display area. Double-click to reset the origin to the top-left corner of the image.

ⓔ Canvas Edit the image in this work area. The canvas area in the document window depends on the dimensions, resolution, and magnification of the image. If the canvas is too large for the display area of the document window, scroll bars are added so that you can "move" the image around.

ⓕ Image Magnification (Mac only) Displays the current magnification of the canvas. Click and enter a new magnification.

ⓖ Document Information (Mac only) Displays document information as chosen in the dropdown. Option/Alt-click to view width, height, channels, and resolution.

ⓗ Document Information Selection (Mac only) Click to select the document information displayed in G.

1.4 Interface Objects

Regardless of which operating system you are using to run Photoshop, several "widgets" are used in the interface. Although they look slightly different in the two operating systems, for the most part, they behave identically.

The various controls are context specific. That is, when you use them to control something (color, percentage, size), you have to look at surrounding labels to see what the control is specifically affecting. Many controls (although not all) will have a brief text label in the general vicinity of the control, or you can use Tool Tips for a more detailed explanation.

One other important, but often overlooked, fact about the Photoshop interface has to do with text labels. Many interface objects will have a text label in close proximity to identify what the object is for. Often, clicking the text label will either select the object or, in the case of form fields, select the content of the field, allowing you to start typing to replace it.

A text label is used to identify the data field to its right (in this case width and height). Click the text label to quickly select the text in the field.

Tool Tip

Although not technically a control, a Tool Tip is available with almost all controls in the Photoshop interface. Simply place your cursor over any control or control label in the interface and wait less than a second. A small yellow box appears, displaying a brief description of the control.

Place the mouse pointer over an object to display a Tool Tip describing the object.

If you do not see the Tool Tip, open the Photoshop General preferences (Command/Ctrl-K) and check the Show Tool Tips option. If you still do not see the Tool Tip, this object may not have one. Try a different object.

➡ 2   Menus

➡ 3   Tools

➡ 4   Palettes

Hide all controls
[Tab]

Hide all controls except Toolbox and tool options bar
[Option] [Tab]
[Shift] [Tab]

Toggle between fields (when cursor is in field)
[Tab]

Contextual menu
[Ctrl] **one-button mouse click**
Left-click

Text labels next to data fields can prove very useful. Double-click to select the value, click and slide to increase or decrease the value, and Shift-click and slide to increase or decrease the value by 10.

Interface Menus

Although Photoshop comes well equipped with the menu bar across the top of the screen (Mac) or window (Windows), additional menus are available throughout the interface that fall into four basic categories: palette menus, footer menus, contextual menus, and dialog menus.

Palette Menu   Click the circular arrowhead button in the top-right corner of the palette or (when in the Palette Well) the arrowhead on the left side of the tab to open the Palette menu. This menu contains palette-specific options as well as the Dock To Palette Well option. For example, the Color palette includes various options that you can use to choose how colors are set.

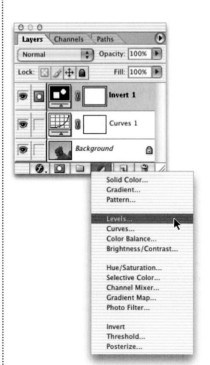

Footer Menu   Click to view a list of options. The icons for footer menus come in all shapes and sizes and can be found at the bottoms of palettes in the interface. They are identified by a small arrowhead next to the icon pointing down. For example, the Layers palette includes a Footer menu that you can use to quickly add adjustment layers.

1.4　Interface Objects (Continued)

Contextual Menu　Control/right-click anywhere in the document window, a palette, or a dialog window to open a contextual menu that contains options which affect the object being clicked. These options depend on what was clicked, where it was clicked, and the currently selected tool. For example, if you select the Zoom tool, clicking in the canvas displays a contextual menu that contains zooming options.

If you are looking for a quicker way to get something done, check to see if an option in the contextual menu will save you time.

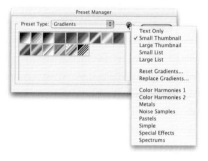

Dialog Menu　Many dialog windows in Photoshop have one or more menus embedded in them. These menus generally provide window-specific options. Most of these menus are distinguished by an arrowhead in a circular button. For example, in the Preset Manager dialog, the menu provides ways to save and load gradient presets into the current list or to replace gradient presets in the current list.

Selection Controls

Photoshop uses check boxes, radio buttons, menus, and palettes to let you make choices. Check boxes represent on/off decisions; radio buttons let you choose between two or more mutually exclusive options. Generally, a select menu is used for three or more options.

Check Box　You use check boxes to select or deselect a particular option. A text label always immediately follows the check box. Click the check box or text label to toggle the option on and off. For example, you can turn Auto-Select Layer on and off for the Move tool.

Radio Button　Click the radio button or its text label to select that option. All radio buttons for related options are grouped together. For example, you can choose between using Sampled and Pattern for the Healing Brush tool. Choosing Pattern activates the Pattern menu.

1.4   Interface Objects *(Continued)*

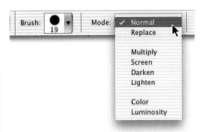

Select Menu   Like the radio button, the select menu allows you to choose between two or more mutually exclusive options. Click the menu and then click the desired option again or use the Up and Down arrow keys to navigate the list, and then press Enter to choose an option. For example, you can select the blending mode used by a Brush tool.

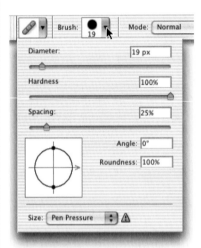

Drop-Down   Some menus are not truly menus but a set of controls used to set additional options. Click the drop-down control, make adjustments, and then click anywhere outside the control or press Enter to close it. For example, some brushes allow you to set various options to define the brush.

Data Fields

You use data fields to enter numbers in control options. Data fields, located in the tool options bar or in palettes, allow you to click in the field and then type the number directly from the keyboard, click in the field and use the arrow keys to increase or decrease values, or click the text label and slide left or right to increase or decrease the value.

Data fields can be combined with select menus so that you can either enter a value directly or click the menu arrow (on the right side) to select an option.

In addition, some data fields are accompanied by a slider control, which is helpful when a wide range of values is possible or when you need to quickly change the value for comparison purposes.

Data Field   Click in the field to edit its content; double click in the field or click the field's label to select its content; click on the label and move left or right to adjust the value, using a conceptual slider as shown in the image. For example, you can enter the number of pixels to feather a selection.

1.4 Interface Objects *(Continued)*

Data Field with Drop-Down Click in the data field to enter a value directly, click the drop-down arrow (on the right) to choose a value from the list, or use the slider. For example, you can use the slider to set the opacity, or you can select a font size directly from a list in the drop-down.

Slider Click and drag the slider to the left or right to change the value in the data field. You can also click the slider line to move the slider to that point. Sliders are sometimes next to the data field but can also be included as a drop–down. For example, the Navigator palette has a slider at the bottom of the window that controls the magnification of the image. (The field is to the left.)

Buttons

A wide variety of buttons are used in the Photoshop interface.

Action Button Click to perform a specific action. Click again to repeat the action. For example, every time you click the Create A New Layer button in the Layers palette, a new blank layer is added to the image.

Text Button Click to perform a specific action. Click again to repeat the action. These buttons are similar to the action buttons, but do not use an icon to represent functionality. For example, in the Zoom tool options bar, three text buttons allow you to magnify the image for a variety of purposes.

Select Button Click to select a single option from a group of related options, much like a radio button. However, rather than using a text label, select buttons use icons to indicate what they do. The various options are usually touching each other. For example, text allows you to select one of three justifications: left, center, or right.

Most data fields have units associated with them (such as pixels, points, or a percentage). Photoshop usually inserts the unit or percent sign if you do not include it. However, some fields have select menus next to them to specify the unit used in the data field.

1.4   Interface Objects *(Continued)*

Generally, sliders work in "real time," meaning that as you make a change, you see the effect of the change.

Select Button with Drop-Down Click the drop-down menu on the right side of a select button group to view additional controls or a menu of options. The menu is context sensitive to the button selected in the group. For example, if you select the Line Draw tool, the drop-down provides additional options for using that tool.

Toggle Button Click to turn an option on (highlighted) or off, much like a check box. However, rather than using text labels, toggle buttons use icons to indicate what they do. For example, the Airbrush button allows you to turn Airbrush mode on or off for the selected brush.

Color Squares

You can select two general colors for use while working: foreground and background. However, any time you see a color square in the interface (a small rectangle or a square of color), you can double-click it to open the Color Picker. This is true virtually anywhere you see color, not only in the Toolbox and Color palette, but also in the Text Options bar and the Gradient Editor.

Double-click to open the Color Picker. For example, click the annotation color square to select the highlight color for a note.

Toggles

Several palettes, most notably the Layers palette, include one or more columns on the left side of a list of elements (layers, history states, channels) that allow you to toggle a specific option about that list element.

Click in the square next to the list item to toggle an option on or off for that item. Some toggles work like radio buttons, meaning that only one list item can have that option at a time. For example, you can select only one history state at a time to be used for the History Brush tool.

chapter 2

Menus

YOU USE MENUS TO PERFORM a variety of actions with the software being run. In Photoshop CS, you use menus to do everything from opening images to changing image format to manipulating the image content. This chapter takes a look at each of the Photoshop CS menus and the actions they can perform:

2.1   Menu Overview

➡ 5.2 Setting
       Keyboard
       Shortcuts

➡ 5.4 General
       Preferences

———

Like most software, many Photoshop menu options have keyboard shortcuts that let you quickly activate them without using the mouse. If a shortcut is available for a menu option, it is given across from the menu option. In this book, keyboard shortcuts are listed in the margins underneath page cross-references.

———

You can adjust the keyboard shortcuts by choosing Edit > Keyboard Preferences.

Photoshop CS has nine menus (10 in Mac OS X) at the top of the screen (Mac) or window (Windows). These menus give you access to hundreds of options that you use to create your images. On the Mac, the menu bar is always at the very top of the screen. In Windows, the menu bar is always at the top of the application window.

The menu bars for Mac OS X and Windows are much the same. Notice, however, that the Mac OS X version includes an extra menu called Photoshop, which collects all the Photoshop-specific options into one menu. (See Section 2.2 for more details.)

Photoshop menu options can be classified into six types:

Submenus A menu option with a triangle to the left contains a submenu of further options from which you must choose. *Example*: Layer > New is a submenu of options for creating a new layer.

Commands An action is performed immediately after you choose a menu option. *Example:* Edit > Cut immediately removes the selected object and places it in memory.

Dialogs These menu options end with an ellipsis (…), which indicates additional steps that are presented through one or more dialogs. *Example:* View > New Guide… opens a dialog that asks you to specify the orientation and location of the guide you are adding to the canvas.

Show/Hide Several menu options control the appearance of the Photoshop interface, allowing you to show and hide interface items as needed. When the option is set to Show, a check appears next to it in the menu. *Example:* View > Rulers shows or hides the rulers that appear around the top and left sides of the document window.

On/Off Several menu options allow you to turn certain Photoshop features on or off. When a feature is on, a check appears next to the menu option. *Example:* View > Snap turns snapping on or off.

Pseudotools Although not in the Toolbox, these menu options work much like tools in that they allow you to use the mouse cursor to change the image manually. *Example:* Edit > Free Transform allows you to rotate and resize the current layer or a selected object using the mouse.

Wizards These menu options open dialogs that guide you through a particular multistep process. *Example:* Help > Resize Image aids you while making decisions about the image size above and beyond using the Image > Image Size command.

2.2   Photoshop Menu (Mac Only)

One of the most noticeable differences between Photoshop CS for Mac and Windows is the Application menu in Mac OS X, which appears on the left side of the screen next to the Apple menu and uses the name of the currently running application, in this case Photoshop. This menu contains options to view information about Photoshop in addition to controls for the program.

Ⓐ Displays the opening splash screen detailing information about this version of Photoshop. Click to close the splash screen. Windows places this option in the Help menu.

Ⓑ Displays a submenu with a list of all installed plug-ins. Choosing one of the plug-ins displays its information panel. Click the panel to close it. Windows places this option in the Help menu.

Ⓒ Opens a dialog that contains options to control program-wide color settings. Windows places this option in the Edit menu.

Ⓓ Displays a submenu of Photoshop preferences. Preferences allow you to control how Photoshop looks and behaves. Windows places this option in the Edit menu.

Ⓔ Displays a submenu of systemwide actions in some applications. However, Photoshop CS does not use this submenu.

Ⓕ Choose one of these options to hide Photoshop, hide all other running applications, or display all other running applications.

Ⓖ Quits Photoshop, allowing you to save changes to open documents first.

➡ 5.3   Setting Photoshop Preferences

➡ 8.4   Choosing a Color Working Space

➡ 14.1 Filter Basics

Color Settings dialog
Shift ⌘ K

General Preferences dialog
⌘ K

Hide Photoshop
Ctrl ⌘ H

Hide all other applications
Option ⌘ H

Quit Photoshop
⌘ Q

———

In the About Photoshop screen, additional Photoshop credits will begin to scroll by if you wait a few seconds. If you can hold out, you'll see some amusing messages at the end.

———

Your serial number (except for the last four numbers) is displayed in the About Photoshop screen.

———

If you quit with unsaved changes, you will be asked to save changes. You can select to save changes, discard changes, or cancel. Canceling stops the Quit process.

2.3　File Menu

The File menu contains all the options for opening, acquiring, and outputting files used in Photoshop. The Windows version of this menu includes a few options for managing Photoshop that the Mac places in the Photoshop menu.

New File dialog
⌘ N

Ctrl N

Open File dialog
⌘ O
Ctrl O

Image Browser
Shift ⌘ O
Shift Ctrl O

Close top window
⌘ W
Ctrl W

Close all windows
Option ⌘ W
Alt Ctrl W

Save changes to document
⌘ S
Ctrl S

Save As dialog
Shift ⌘ S
Shift Ctrl S

Save For Web dialog
Option Shift ⌘ S
Alt Shift Ctrl S

| Photoshop | File | Edit | Image | Layer | Select | Filter | View | Window | Help |

Ⓐ New...　⌘N
Ⓑ Open...　⌘O
Ⓒ Browse...　⇧⌘O
Ⓓ Open Recent　▶
Ⓔ Edit in ImageReady　⇧⌘M
Ⓕ Close　⌘W
Ⓖ Close All　⌥⌘W
Ⓗ Save　⌘S
Ⓘ Save As...　⇧⌘S
Ⓙ Save a Version...
Ⓚ Save for Web...　⌥⇧⌘S
Ⓛ Revert　F12
Ⓜ Place...
Ⓝ Online Services...
Import　▶
Export　▶
Automate　▶
Scripts　▶
File Info...　⌥⌘I
Versions...
Page Setup...　⇧⌘P
Print with Preview...　⌥⌘P
Print...　⌘P
Print One Copy　⌥⇧⌘P
Jump To　▶

Ⓐ Opens a dialog you can use to start a new Photoshop file.

Ⓑ Opens a dialog in which you can open a Photoshop or compatible file from any available drive.

Ⓒ Displays the File Browser window. This is the same as choosing the Window **>** File Browser option.

Ⓓ Displays a submenu that lists recently opened files.

Ⓔ Opens the current document in Adobe ImageReady.

Ⓕ Closes the active document window, giving you a chance to save changes first.

Ⓖ Closes all open files giving you a chance to save changes first.

Ⓗ Updates the saved version of the file with any changes made since the last save.

Ⓘ Opens a dialog to save a file by specifying file format, name, location to be saved on the hard drive, and other options.

Ⓙ Works like Save As, but immediately takes you to saving the file to a shared computer over a local network or the Internet that is set up for Version Cue projects.

Ⓚ Opens a dialog to specify how to save an image for display on the Web.

Ⓛ Restores the previously saved version of the file. You cannot undo this action, and you are warned before the action is performed.

Ⓜ Imports an EPS or PDF image file into the current Photoshop file.

Ⓝ Starts a wizard used to send files directly to online service bureaus for ordering prints, books, and other material.

2.3 File Menu (Continued)

Photoshop **File** Edit Image Layer Select Filter View Window Help

New...	⌘N
Open...	⌘O
Browse...	⇧⌘O
Open Recent	▶
Edit in ImageReady	⇧⌘M
Close	⌘W
Close All	⌥⌘W
Save	⌘S
Save As...	⇧⌘S
Save a Version...	
Save for Web...	⌥⇧⌘S
Revert	F12
Place...	
Online Services...	
Ⓞ Import	▶
Ⓟ Export	▶
Ⓠ Automate	▶
Ⓡ Scripts	▶
Ⓢ File Info...	⌥⌘I
Ⓣ Versions...	
Ⓤ Page Setup...	⇧⌘P
Ⓥ Print with Preview...	⌥⌘P
Ⓦ Print...	⌘P
Ⓧ Print One Copy	⌥⇧⌘P
Ⓨ Jump To	▶

Ⓞ Displays a submenu that includes options to acquire images from a variety of sources (including scanners and digital cameras). The exact options listed depend on your operating system and plug-ins.

Ⓟ Opens a dialog to output parts of the document (such as paths) to be used by other applications.

Ⓠ Displays a submenu of options to automate your work flow by allowing you to script repetitive tasks.

Ⓡ Includes various multipart actions for outputting parts of a file.

Ⓢ Opens a dialog that you can use to view and edit information saved with the file such as its title, author, and copyright notice.

Ⓣ Opens a dialog that allows you to view and edit information about different versions of the document saved to a shared computer using a local network or the Internet that is set up for Version Cue projects.

Ⓤ Opens a dialog in which you can set general printing options.

Ⓥ Opens a dialog that you can use to preview the document being printed and set Photoshop-specific printing options.

Ⓦ Opens a dialog in which you can set printing options and send the document to be printed.

Ⓧ Instantly sends the document to the printer, bypassing the Print dialog.

Ⓨ Displays a submenu primarily used to move the current file to ImageReady or other Adobe software.

Open As... (Windows only) Opens a dialog in which you can open a file as a specific file type, for example, to open a TIF file as a JPEG. On the Mac, this operation is handled directly in the Open dialog.

Exit (Windows only) Closes all open documents in Photoshop (allowing you to save changes first) and quits Photoshop. OS X places this option in the Photoshop menu as Quit.

Revert
F12

File Info
Option ⌘ I
Alt Ctrl I

Page Setup dialog
Shift ⌘ P
Shift Ctrl P

Print With Preview dialog
⌘ P
Ctrl P

Print dialog
Option ⌘ P
Alt Ctrl P

Print one copy
Option Shift ⌘ P
Alt Shift Ctrl P

Jump image to ImageReady
Shift ⌘ M
Shift Ctrl M

Quit/Exit Photoshop
⌘ Q
Ctrl Q

The Versions commands replace the Workgroup commands introduced in Photoshop 7 for creating shared files distributed over the Internet.

The number of items in the Open Recent list is set in the File Handling preferences. The default is 10, and the maximum is 30.

2.4 Edit Menu

The Edit menu contains options used to work with a layer or a selection. In addition, the Edit menu contains several options for editing Photoshop tools. The Edit menu in Windows has Color Settings and Preferences options, which in OS X are in the Photoshop menu.

➥ 5.2 Setting Keyboard Shortcuts

➥ 5.3 Setting Photoshop Preferences

Undo/Redo last action
⌘ Z
Ctrl Z

Step forward in document history
Shift ⌘ Z
Shift Ctrl Z

Step backward in document history
Option ⌘ Z
Alt Ctrl Z

Fade last filter or adjustment
Shift ⌘ F
Shift Ctrl F

Copy selection on all layers as merged layer
Shift ⌘ C
Shift Ctrl C

Paste contents of Clipboard into selected layer
⌘ V
Ctrl V

Paste contents of Clipboard into center of selection
Shift ⌘ V
Shift Ctrl V

Free transform selected or layers content
⌘ T
Ctrl T

Repeat previous transform
Shift ⌘ T
Shift Ctrl T

Ⓐ Reverts a file to its previous appearance.

Ⓑ Moves forward and backward in the file's history.

Ⓒ Opens a dialog that allows you to control the strength of the previously applied filter and adjustments.

Ⓓ Removes the selection and places it in the Clipboard.

Ⓔ Copies the selected area of the image in the selected layer to the Clipboard.

Ⓕ Copies the selected area of the image from all layers to the Clipboard as a merged image.

Ⓖ Places a copy of the image on the Clipboard in the selected layer.

Ⓗ Places a copy of the image on the Clipboard into the selected area of the selected layer.

Ⓘ Clears the content in the selected area of the current layer.

Ⓙ Opens a dialog that you can use to check the spelling of text layers in the image.

Ⓚ Opens a dialog that you can use to locate text in text layers and replace it if desired.

Ⓛ Opens a dialog that you can use to fill a layer or a selected area with a color or a pattern.

Ⓜ Opens a dialog that you can use to add a solid line around a selected area.

Ⓝ Displays a pseudotool that you can use to resize, rotate, skew, and distort to a selected area.

Ⓞ Displays a submenu that lists pseudotools you can use to scale, rotate, skew, distort, add perspective to, and flip a selection.

Ⓟ Opens dialogs that you can use to define brushes, patterns, and custom shapes.

Ⓠ Displays a submenu with options to clear the memory storing Undo, Clipboard, and history.

Ⓡ Opens a dialog to change the keyboard shortcuts used in Photoshop.

Ⓢ Opens a dialog that you can use to adjust presets for brushes, swatches, gradients, styles, patterns, contours, custom shapes, and tools.

Color Settings... (Windows only) Opens a dialog that you can use to control program-wide color settings. Mac OS X places this option in the Photoshop menu.

Preferences (Windows only) Displays a submenu of Photoshop preferences. You set preferences to control how Photoshop looks and behaves. Mac OS X places this option in the Photoshop menu.

2.5 Image Menu

You use the items in the Image menu to control options that will be applied to the entire canvas area, except for adjustments that are applied to the current layer or the current selection.

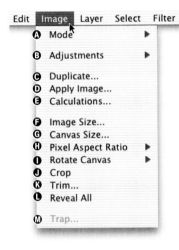

Ⓐ Displays a submenu that contains options you can use to specify the image's color modes and other color table options.

Ⓑ Displays a submenu that contains options you can use to change the image's properties, including color, contrast, saturation, brightness, and levels.

Ⓒ Opens a dialog that you can use to create a new file, duplicating the open file as it currently appears (not its saved version). The new file is unsaved.

Ⓓ Opens a dialog that you can use to blend layers and channels of an image file (including itself) into the current file if the two were duplicated from a common image.

Ⓔ Opens a dialog that you can use to blend the layers and/or channels of two image files into the current image file if all three files were duplicated from a common source.

Ⓕ Opens a dialog that you can use to change the width, height, and resolution of the image.

Ⓖ Opens a dialog that you can use to change the width and height of the canvas. Changing the dimensions of the canvas does *not* change the size of the image, but may clip parts of the image if the sizes are smaller than the original.

Ⓗ Opens a submenu that allows you to view the image in various video aspect ratios.

Ⓘ Displays a submenu that contains options to rotate the canvas (all layers). This menu also contains options to flip the canvas horizontally or vertically.

Ⓙ Reduces the canvas size to the selected area.

Ⓚ Opens a dialog that you can use to crop the canvas based on specific color criteria.

Ⓛ Disables masks showing all the image.

Ⓜ Opens a dialog to add a trap width to a CMYK image used when printing the image on a four-color press.

➡ 7.1   Canvas Basics

➡ 8.2   Understanding Image Modes

➡ 10.1   Layer Basics

➡ 20.3   Viewing for Video

➡ 21.1   Compositing Basics

➡ 22.1   Adjustment Basics

Levels dialog
⌘ L
Ctrl L

Auto Levels
Shift ⌘ L
Shift Ctrl L

Auto Contrast
Option Shift ⌘ L
Alt Shift Ctrl L

Auto Color
Shift ⌘ B
Shift Ctrl B

Curves dialog
⌘ M
Ctrl M

Color Balance dialog
⌘ B
Ctrl B

Hue/Saturation dialog
⌘ U
Ctrl U

Desaturate Colors
Shift ⌘ U
Shift Ctrl U

Invert Image Colors
⌘ I
Ctrl I

2.6 Layer Menu

New layer
Shift ⌘ N
Shift Ctrl N

Copy to create new layer
⌘ J
Ctrl J

Cut to create new layer
Shift ⌘ J
Shift Ctrl J

Create Clipping Mask
⌘ G
Ctrl G

Release Clipping Mask
Shift ⌘ G
Shift Ctrl G

Bring layer to front
Shift ⌘]
Shift Ctrl]

Bring layer forward one level
⌘]
Ctrl]

Send layer to back
Shift ⌘ [
Shift Ctrl [

Send layer back one level
⌘ [
Ctrl [

The Layer menu contains options for creating and working with individual layers in an image. The Layer menu is contextual, so the options it contains depend on the properties of the active layer in the Layers palette: whether it is visible, linked to other layers, grouped with other layers, or in a layer set.

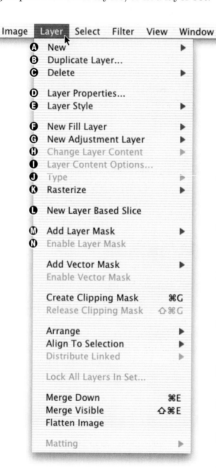

Ⓐ Displays a submenu that contains options to create a new layer or layer set.

Ⓑ Opens a dialog that you can use to make an exact copy of a selected layer.

Ⓒ Displays a submenu that contains options to delete the selected layer, the selected layer and layers linked to it, or hidden layers.

Ⓓ Opens a dialog that you can use to set the layer name and highlight color of the layer in the Layers palette.

Ⓔ Displays a submenu that contains options for adding and working with layer styles such as blending modes, drop shadows, and glows.

Ⓕ Displays a submenu that contains options to add a layer with a solid color, gradient, or pattern fill.

Ⓖ Displays a submenu that contains options to adjust a layer's blending options or add an adjustment layer.

Ⓗ Displays a submenu that contains options to control the content in the selected layer.

Ⓘ Opens a dialog in which you can set options for a layer's content.

Ⓙ Displays a submenu that contains options for working with Type layers.

Ⓚ Displays a submenu that contains options for turning layers containing vector images into bitmap images.

Ⓛ Turns the content in a selected layer into a slice for use in web designs.

Ⓜ Displays a submenu that contains options to add/remove layer masks.

Ⓝ Disables or enables a layer mask if it has been added to the selected layer. This will not delete the layer mask, but shows what the layer looks like without it.

2.6   Layer Menu *(Continued)*

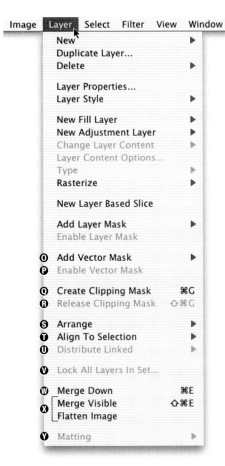

| Image | Layer | Select | Filter | View | Window | Help |

New ▶
Duplicate Layer...
Delete ▶

Layer Properties...
Layer Style ▶

New Fill Layer ▶
New Adjustment Layer ▶
Change Layer Content ▶
Layer Content Options...
Type ▶
Rasterize ▶

New Layer Based Slice

Add Layer Mask ▶
Enable Layer Mask

Ⓞ Add Vector Mask ▶
Ⓟ Enable Vector Mask

Ⓠ Create Clipping Mask ⌘G
Ⓡ Release Clipping Mask ⇧⌘G

Ⓢ Arrange ▶
Ⓣ Align To Selection ▶
Ⓤ Distribute Linked ▶

Ⓥ Lock All Layers In Set...

Ⓦ Merge Down ⌘E
Ⓧ Merge Visible ⇧⌘E
Flatten Image

Ⓨ Matting ▶

Ⓞ Opens a submenu with options to add/remove vector masks from a layer.

Ⓟ Disables or enables a vector mask if it has been added to the selected layer. Selecting this option does not delete the vector mask, but shows what the layer looks like without it.

Ⓠ Creates a knockout using the linked layers with the bottommost layer or (if no layers are linked) with the layer beneath it.

Ⓡ Ungroups the layers used in clipping masks layers grouped with the selected layer.

Ⓢ Displays a submenu that contains options to adjust the stacking order of layers.

Ⓣ Aligns the active and linked layers with the top, left, right, bottom, or center of a selection *or* the content of two or more linked layers with their top, left, right, bottom, or center.

Ⓤ Distributes the content of three or more linked layers based on their top, left, right, bottom, or center.

Ⓥ Locks all the layers linked to the current layer or in the selected set, preventing them from being moved.

Ⓦ Merges linked layers, merges the current layer down into the layer beneath, or merges all visible layers to turn two or more layers into one layer.

Ⓧ Flattens the entire image into the Background layer.

Ⓨ Displays a submenu that contains options for working with a layer's matte.

Merge layer down
⌘ E
Ctrl E

Merge visible layers into one layer
Shift ⌘ E
Shift Ctrl E

When you arrange layers using the menu, you are actually moving them up or down in the Layers palette.

When layers are merged, text, styles, blending modes, and opacity changes are rasterized to create the new layer.

Align and Distribute will not work if the background layer is one of the linked layers.

2.7 Select Menu

➡ 9.1 Selection
    Basics

You use the Select menu to work with and modify a selection in the canvas.

Select All
⌘ A
Ctrl A

Deselect
⌘ D
Ctrl D

Reselect
Shift ⌘ D
Shift Ctrl D

Inverse selected area
Shift ⌘ I
Shift Ctrl I

Feather selection
Option ⌘ D
Alt Ctrl D

Ⓐ Selects the entire canvas area.

Ⓑ Removes the selection. (The content of the selected area is unaffected.)

Ⓒ Reinstates the last selection.

Ⓓ Swaps the selected and unselected areas.

Ⓔ Opens a dialog in which you can select a particular range of colors throughout an image, a layer, or an existing selection.

Ⓕ Opens a dialog in which you can set the existing selection to gradually soften the selection edges rather than using a hard edge.

Ⓖ Displays a submenu that contains options to change the existing selection to a border of a certain width, smooth the edges of the selection, expand the selection, or contract the selection.

Ⓗ Enlarges the selection to include pixels with a similar color in the selection or layer that is contiguous with the selection.

Ⓘ Enlarges the selection to include pixels throughout the selection or layer with a similar color.

Ⓙ Chooses a pseudotool that you can use to rotate, resize, or skew (using Command/Ctrl) the selection shape, leaving the content untouched.

Ⓚ Opens a dialog in which you can load a saved selection shape into the current image.

Ⓛ Opens a dialog in which you can save the current selection shape. Saving the current selection shape does not save the content, only the shape.

Warning: Don't confuse inverse (reversing selected and unselected areas) with invert (reversing colors). Both have similar names and similar keyboard shortcuts, but have very different uses.

If you create a particularly complex selection, you will probably want to save it so that if you accidentally deselect it or need it again, you can quickly bring it back. Saved selections appear in the Channels palette.

You can also set a selection to be feathered before it is made using the slider in the Tool Options bar for the Selection tool.

2.8 Filter Menu

The Filter menu collects all the plug-in filters available, including the Extract, Liquify, and Pattern Maker dialogs. You use filters to manipulate the image in a variety of ways. Most filters work as dialogs, asking you to enter information about the changes to be made using the filter and giving you a preview of what the changes will look like.

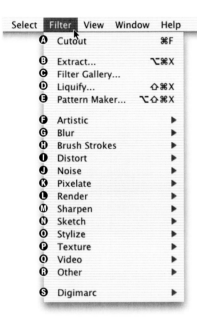

➡ 12.14   Using the Pattern Maker

➡ 13.10   Distorting Images

➡ 14   Filtering Images

➡ 21.8   Extracting Part of an Image

Last filter
⌘ F
Ctrl F

Extract dialog
Option ⌘ X
Alt Ctrl X

Liquify dialog
Shift ⌘ X
Shift Ctrl X

Pattern Maker dialog
Option Shift ⌘ X
Alt Shift Ctrl X

———

As with all menu options, a filter that uses a dialog will have an ellipsis (...).

———

To quickly increase the effect of a filter, use the Last Filter option.

———

To lessen the effect of a filter, choose Edit > Fade immediately after applying the filter.

———

Photoshop allows third-parties to create filters for use in Photoshop. These filters appear in separate menus beneath the built-in filters.

Ⓐ Re-performs the action of the last filter used.

Ⓑ Opens a dialog in which you can extract parts of the image.

Ⓒ Opens a dialog that allows you to apply multiple common filters simultaneously.

Ⓓ Displays a submenu with filters used to create sophisticated smudges in the image.

Ⓔ Displays a submenu with filters used to create tiled background patterns for the image.

Ⓕ Displays a submenu with filters that simulate a variety of drawing, printing, and painting effects.

Ⓖ Displays a submenu that contain filters that blur a layer or a selection in a variety of ways.

Ⓗ Displays a submenu with filters that simulate a variety of paintbrush stroke effects.

Ⓘ Displays a submenu with filters that manipulate the image in a variety of patterns.

Ⓙ Displays a submenu with filters used to add grainy noise, scratches, and dust effects.

Ⓚ Displays a submenu with filters used to add faceted effects.

Ⓛ Displays a submenu with filters used to create special lighting and texture effects.

Ⓜ Displays a submenu with filters used to increase the apparent sharpness of a selection or a layer.

Ⓝ Displays a submenu with filters used to add a variety of effects that simulate sketching.

Ⓞ Displays a submenu with filters used to add different stylized effects to a selection or a layer.

Ⓟ Displays a submenu with filters used to simulate a variety of textured effects.

Ⓠ Displays a submenu with filters for cleaning up images acquired from or being output to a video source.

Ⓡ Displays a submenu with options that do not fit into other categories.

Ⓢ Displays a submenu with third-party Digimarc filters used to add and read watermarks to an image.

2.9   View Menu

The View menu provides control over which windows and palettes are displayed in the Photoshop interface.

Show image in proof colors
⌘ Y
Ctrl Y

Show gamut warning
Shift ⌘ Y
Shift Ctrl Y

Zoom in
⌘ +
Ctrl +

Zoom out
⌘ −
Ctrl −

Fit image on screen
⌘ 0
Ctrl 0

Show image at 100%
Option ⌘ 0
Option Ctrl 0

Show/hide interface elements
⌘ H
Ctrl H

Show/hide target path
Shift ⌘ H
Shift Ctrl H

Switch screen view modes
F

Show/hide grid
⌘ "
Ctrl "

Show/hide guides
⌘ ;
Ctrl ;

Show/hide rulers
⌘ R
Ctrl R

Snapping on/off
Shift ⌘ ;
Shift Ctrl ;

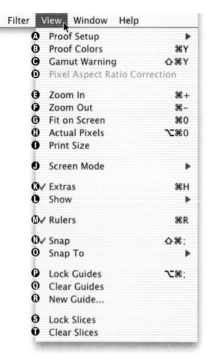

A Displays a submenu with options for simulating how the image will look under different proof color conditions.

B Turns proof colors on/off. Displays the image as it will look (or as close as possible) when printed, using the options set in the Proof Setup submenu.

C Turns gamut highlighting on/off. When on, colors that will not print or display properly based on the Proof Setup submenu are highlighted.

D Allows you to view an image destined for video on the computer monitor while still using the correct video aspect ratio.

E Sets the current magnification of the image in the canvas.

F Changes magnification so that the image fills the screen either horizontally or vertically.

G Shows the image at 100% magnification.

H Shows the image in the size at which it will print.

I Switches between the three screen view modes: Standard, Full Screen With Menu, and Full Screen.

J Shows/hides interface elements as defined in the Show submenu.

K Displays a submenu that you can use to select which elements will be hidden/shown using the Extras option. Select the Photoshop interface elements that you want to show, and then select the Extras option to show and hide them.

L Shows/hides rulers around the edge of the document window.

M Turns snapping on/off. When on, elements snap based on options selected in the Snap To submenu.

N Displays a submenu of snapping options. Options are available if they are currently visible as set in the Show submenu.

O Turns guide locking on/off. Prevents guides from being moved.

P Removes all guides.

Q Opens a dialog in which you can numerically set a new guide.

R Turns slice locking on/off. Prevents slices from being moved.

S Removes all slices from the canvas.

2.10   Window Menu

The Window menu has options for controlling which palettes are currently displayed on the screen. Select different palettes to show and hide them, or use the Workspace submenu to save your favorite layouts and then restore them as needed.

➡ 1.3 The Document Window

➡ 4.1 Organizing Palettes

Ⓐ Displays a submenu that contains options to switch between open documents and organize the document window in the screen.

Ⓑ Displays a submenu with options to save and restore palette locations. Save the layout of your Photoshop workspace, and then quickly switch between layouts for different needs.

Ⓒ Shows/hides the indicated palette or window.

Ⓓ The bottom of the Window menu displays a list of all open document windows.

Status Bar (Windows only) Shows/hides the display of the status bar at the bottom of the Photoshop interface on and off.

Minimize window
`Ctrl` `⌘` `M`

Hide all controls
`Tab`

Hide all controls except Toolbox and tool options bar
`Option` `Tab`
`Shift` `Tab`

Actions palette
`Option` `F9`
`Alt` `F9`

Brushes palette
`F5`

Color palette
`F6`

Info palette
`F8`

Layers palette
`F7`

Unlike previous versions of Photoshop, Photoshop CS lists the palettes in alphabetic order, which makes finding the option you are looking for much easier.

Windows includes an additional option to show and hide the status bar at the bottom of the application window.

CLOUD SISTERS: © MAGGIE TAYLOR; WWW.MAGGIETAYLOR.COM

2.11 Help Menu

➡ 7.3 Setting the Image Size

Photoshop Help

———

Step Backward and Step Forward are similar to the Undo option, but give you much greater control, allowing you to, in effect, undo and redo as many times as desired depending on the number of History states. You set the number of History states in the General Preferences.

The Help menu not only contains an option to open the Photoshop help manual in a web browser, but it also contains several assistants (also often referred to as wizards) to help you with common but complex tasks. You will also find options to obtain additional support for Photoshop.

Ⓐ Opens a web-based version of the Photoshop help manual. You do not need an Internet connection to open this manual.

Ⓑ Opens the dialog that is displayed when you first start Photoshop, allowing you to get instructions and information about the program.

Ⓒ Opens a dialog to help with exporting an image with transparencies.

Ⓓ Opens a dialog that you can use to help find the best way to resize an image with minimal quality loss.

Ⓔ Displays information about the computer, operating system, version of Photoshop, and plug-ins currently in use.

Ⓕ Checks for updates to this version of Photoshop. Requires an Internet connection.

Ⓖ Opens a web browser to the Adobe website registration area, allowing you to register this copy of Photoshop. Requires an Internet connection.

Ⓗ Opens a web browser window to the Adobe Photoshop website. Requires an Internet connection.

Ⓘ Submenus with instructions on how to perform a variety of common Photoshop tasks. Although these instructions are opened in a Web browser, the files are located on your local hard drive so do not require an Internet connection.

Ⓙ Instructions for how to create your own "How To" pages accessible through the Photoshop Help menu. This can be especially useful for creating design documents to maintain in house consistency between projects.

About Photoshop (Windows only) Displays the opening splash screen detailing information about this version of Photoshop. Click the splash screen to close it. OS X places this option in the Photoshop menu.

About Plug-In (Windows only) Displays a submenu that lists all installed plug-ins. Selecting a plug-in displays its information panel. Click the panel to close it. OS X places this option in the Photoshop menu.

The Tools

TO CREATE AND EDIT IMAGES, Photoshop has several dozen tools accessible through the Toolbox. To choose a tool whose icon is visible in the Toolbox, click the tool icon. Your mouse pointer will take on the appearance of the tool icon or a precision icon (depending on how your preferences are set). You can then use the tool to manipulate the image on the canvas.

A small arrowhead in the bottom-right corner of the tool indicates that this is a toolset with other similar tools available for that box. To access the rest of the toolset, click and hold on the arrowhead and select another tool from the pop-out palette. In addition, each toolset has a single-letter keyboard shortcut that chooses the currently selected tool for that toolset. If you forget what a particular tool does or what its keyboard shortcut is, place your mouse cursor over the tool and wait a few seconds. A Tool Tip appears that labels the tool and indicates its shortcut key in parentheses. To cycle through hidden tools in a toolset, press Shift and the shortcut key, or Alt/Option-click the currently visible tool in the Toolbox.

3.1 The Toolbox

Show/hide Toolbox, tool options bar, and open palettes
[Tab]

Show/hide open palettes
[Option] [Tab]

[Alt] [Tab]

Cycle through tools in a toolset
[Shift] plus shortcut key

If you do not see the Toolbox, choose Window > Tools so that a check appears next to Tools in the menu.

Warning: Actions performed with a tool in the canvas are generally applied only to the selected layer.

The Toolbox houses icons that you can click to access all the tools used in Photoshop. To use a tool, click its icon, and then use it in the canvas. Many of the tools are part of a *toolset*, allowing the box to house multiple tools. To select another tool from a toolset, click and hold one of the icons in the Toolbox with a triangle in the bottom-right corner and then choose the desired tool. The following graphic shows the Toolbox in its default configuration with shortcut keys indicated in parentheses. You can also cycle through the tools in a toolset by pressing Shift and that tool's keyboard shortcut.

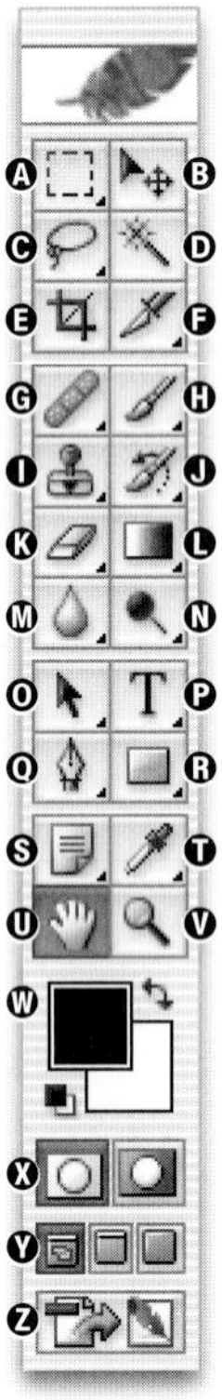

A Marquee toolset (M)

B Move tool (V)

C Lasso toolset (L)

D Magic Wand tool (W)

E Crop tool (C)

F Slice toolset (K)

G Restoration toolset (J)

H Paint toolset (B)

I Stamp toolset (S)

J History Brush toolset (Y)

K Erase toolset (E)

L Fill toolset (G)

M Distortion toolset (R)

N Exposure toolset (O)

O Path toolset (A)

P Type toolset (T)

Q Pen toolset (P)

R Shape toolset (U)

S Annotation toolset (N)

T Eyedropper and Measure toolset (I)

U Hand tool (H)

V Zoom tool (Z)

W Background/foreground color swatches

X Mask modes (Q)

Y View modes (F)

Z Jump To ImageReady

3.2   The Tool Options Bar

Most tools have attributes that specify how the tool behaves when used. You use the tool options bar to set most of these attributes (some attributes can be set in individual palettes), which is initially located at the top of the screen, but can be moved anywhere on the screen. The options available in the bar depend on three criteria: the tool selected, the options selected in the bar, and the action being performed with the tool.

A Tool Preset Picker   Click to choose from a list of tools with preset attributes. The icon represents the currently selected tool.

B Tool Options   Various otions for the currently selected tool will appear in this area. The exact options depend on the tool.

C Palette Toggle   Click this button to show or hide the selected tool's related palette(s). The palettes displayed depend on the tool.

D File Browser Toggle   Click this button to show or hide the File Browser window.

E Palette Well   Drag and drop palettes to dock them into the Palette Well. Click a palette tab to open a palette docked in the well. Click in the canvas or click the tab again to close the palette

Toggle Buttons and the Palette Well

You use the File Browser to quickly find, organize, and manage your images. A permanent button in the tool options bar lets you quickly show and hide this window.

The tool options bar also sometimes has a Palette Toggle button . Clicking this button shows or hides palettes that contain the additional attributes relevant to the tool being used. This button appears only if the selected tool has additional related palettes.

Finally, the tool options bar contains the Palette Well, which is used to dock palettes that are regularly used but do not always need to be displayed.

Click one of the tabs to display a drop-down version of the palette. To dock a palette, simply drag its tab into the well, or choose Dock To Palette Well from the palette's menu.

➠ 4.8   File Browser

➠ 5.1   Preset
        Manager
        Overview

➠ 6.5   Managing
        Images with
        the File
        Browser

Show/hide Toolbox, tool options bar, and open palettes
[Tab]

Cycle through blending modes for the current tool or layer
[Shift] [+] or [Shift] [−]

Using the Tool Preset Picker

The menu bar contains a drop-down menu that you can use to choose from a list of tools with predefined attributes. This list is initially made up of the default tools (the same as in the Toolbox), but over time you can customize the tools for specific needs and use the Tool Preset Picker to save them or load preset tools included with Photoshop.

- To create a new Tool Preset, simply choose the tool in the Toolbox, set the tool options as desired, and then click the New Tool Preset button. The tool is added to the Tool Presets list.

- To save a group of Tool Presets, choose Save Tool Presets… from the Tool Presets menu, enter a name for the new group of Tool Presets (making sure to keep the .tpl extension at the end), and click Save. Until you do this with any new Tool Preset, the new tool will be permanently removed if you reset the Tool Presets.

If you do not see the tool options bar, choose Window > Options so that a check appears next to it in the menu.

If you are unsure what a particular option is in the tool options bar, place the mouse cursor over the option. Within a few seconds a Tool Tip appears with a brief description. If nothing happens, turn Tool Tips on in your preferences (Command/Ctrl-K).

Click the text label next to a field to select the field.

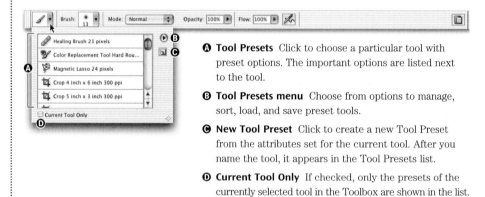

Ⓐ Tool Presets Click to choose a particular tool with preset options. The important options are listed next to the tool.

Ⓑ Tool Presets menu Choose from options to manage, sort, load, and save preset tools.

Ⓒ New Tool Preset Click to create a new Tool Preset from the attributes set for the current tool. After you name the tool, it appears in the Tool Presets list.

Ⓓ Current Tool Only If checked, only the presets of the currently selected tool in the Toolbox are shown in the list.

3.3 Marquee Tools

You use the marquee tools to select regions. To make a simple rectangular or elliptical selection, select the appropriate marquee tool, place the cursor at one corner of the region you want to select, and then click and drag to the opposite corner of the region. As you drag, you will see a flashing outline (often referred to as marching ants) appear around the selected region.

For single row and single column selections, choose the tool and then click in the row or column you want to select. The selection will be 1 pixel wide or high and stretch the length or width of the entire image.

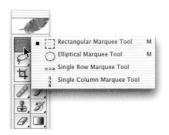

Rectangular Marquee Selects a rectangular region in a layer of the image.

Elliptical Marquee Selects a circular or elliptical region in a layer of the image.

Single Row Marquee Selects a single row of pixels in a layer in the image.

Single Column Marquee Selects a single column of pixels in an image.

Ⓐ Selection Type Choose how the new selection should be treated in relation to the current selection: deselect the current selection and start a new selection, add to the current selection, subtract from the current selection, or intersect with the current selection.

Ⓑ Feather Enter a value (0 to 250) for the amount of fade from the edges of the selection. You must enter this amount *before* making the selection order to affect the selection.

Ⓒ Anti-Aliased If checked, anti-aliasing gives the edges of the selection a smoother appearance with the elliptical marquee.

Ⓓ Style Choose whether the selection is Normal (unconstrained), Fixed Aspect Ratio (forces selection into a square or circle), or Fixed Size (forces selection to be a height and width entered in the fields to the right).

Ⓔ Width Enter the width (0.001 to 999.999) of a selection if using the Fixed Size style.

Ⓕ Swap Values Click to switch the width and height values.

Ⓖ Height Enter the height (0.001 to 999.999) of a selection if using the Fixed Size style.

➡ 9.3 Selecting Rectangular or Elliptical Areas

➡ 12.14 Using the Pattern Maker

Marquee tool
Ⓜ

Cycle marquee tools
Ⓢⓗⓘⓕⓣ Ⓜ (Rectangle and Elliptical Marquees only)

Constrain a new selection to a square or a circle (if no existing selection)
Ⓢⓗⓘⓕⓣ **plus select**

Add to current selection (with existing selection; press Shift again while selecting to constrain proportions)
Ⓢⓗⓘⓕⓣ **plus select**

Subtract from current selection
Ⓞⓟⓣⓘⓞⓝ **plus select**

———

After you make a selection, moving the selection, either with the Move tool or the arrow keys, collapses the selection around the image on the selected layer.

3.4 Move Tool

Move tool
[V]

With the Move tool, Control-click or right-click any part of the image to select from a contextual menu of layers under the cursor.

You always move the selection in the selected layer. Always check your layer before making a move to make sure you have the right one.

Once a selection is made, you can move it about in the image using the Move tool. If there is no selection, you can use the Move tool to move the contents of the currently selected layer.

To move an object, select the layer and then select the region you want to move (if desired). Select the Move tool, place the cursor within the canvas, and click and drag the selection or layer to the new location.

Moving a selection Use the Move tool to change the position of a selected layer or image selection.

Ⓐ Auto Select Layer If checked, click an object in a layer to select that layer.

Ⓑ Show Bounding Box If checked, the rectangular edges of a selected region are shown. If the selection is not rectangular, the bounding box represents a rectangular region of the selection's extreme horizontal and vertical limits. You can use the bounding box to transform the selection (resize, skew, and rotate).

Ⓒ Align Objects You can align two or more linked layers with their top edges, middle edges, bottom edges, left edges, center edges, or right edges.

Ⓓ Distributed Objects Three or more linked layers can have their content distributed between their top, middle, bottom, left, center, or right edges.

3.5 Lasso Tools

The Lasso tools let you make a free-form selection of any shape in the canvas. You can draw the selection by hand or use either the Polygonal Lasso tool or the Magnetic Lasso tool to help you select more precisely.

Lasso Selects regions in the image using free-form straight edges to create a selection with as many sides as desired.

Polygonal Lasso Selects regions in the image using free-form straight edges.

Magnetic Lasso Selects regions in free form but forces the selection to stick to high-contrast boundaries in the image.

➠ 9.4 Creating Free-Form Selections

Lasso tool
⌴ L

Cycle Lasso tools
Shift L

Force selection path into 0°, 45°, or 90° angles
Shift plus polygon select

Add to current selection
Shift plus select

Subtract from current selection
Option plus select

Ⓐ Selection Type Choose how the new selection should be treated in relation to the current selection: deselect the current selection and start a new selection, add to the current selection, subtract from the current selection, or intersect with the current selection.

Ⓑ Feather Fades the edges of the selection by the specified amount. You must enter this amount *before* making the selection in order to affect the selection.

Ⓒ Anti-Aliased When this option is checked, anti-aliasing gives the edges of the selection a smoother appearance.

Ⓓ Width (Magnetic Lasso only) Enter the width in pixels (1 to 256) to be considered around the cursor when making the selection.

Ⓔ EdgeContrast (Magnetic Lasso only) Enter the contrast (as a percentage) to be considered between pixels for determining the selection.

Ⓕ Frequency (Magnetic Lasso only) Enter a number (0 to 100) to set how often anchor points are added to the selection path.

Ⓖ Pen Pressure (Magnetic Lasso only) If checked, a tablet's pen pressure is used to change the width.

3.6 Magic Wand Tool

➡ 12.2 Selecting
Colors with the
Eyedropper

Magic Wand tool
Ⓦ

**Add to current
selection**
[Shift] **plus select**

**Subtract from current
selection**
[Option] **plus select**

The Magic Wand is a selection tool that selects only particular colors in the canvas. You can set it to select only one exact color on one layer in one area of the image, or you can set the tolerance, layers, and contiguous options to select a range of colors throughout the image.

To make a Magic Wand selection, choose the tool, set your options, and then click on (or as close as possible to) a pixel with the color you want to select. Depending on your options, you will see parts of the image selected.

Selecting colors The Magic Wand uses the color of the pixel clicked to select all pixels with that color or similar colors based on the tolerance set. In this example, a tolerance of 50 was used to select part of the eye by clicking the iris.

Ⓐ **Selection Type** Choose how the new selection should be treated in relation to the current selection: deselect the current selection and start a new selection, add to the current selection, subtract from the current selection, or intersect with the current selection.

Ⓑ **Tolerance** Enter a value in the range 0 to 255 (32 is the default) to specify the deviation a color can have to be included in the Magic Wand selection.

Ⓒ **Anti-Aliased** When this option is checked, anti-aliasing gives the edges of the selection a smoother appearance.

Ⓓ **Contiguous** If checked, only pixels touching the selected pixel and within the set tolerance and pixels touching those (and so forth) are included in the selection. Otherwise, the Magic Wand selects all pixels in the image within the tolerance level.

Ⓔ **Use All Layers** If checked, the Magic Wand selects pixels on all layers in the image. Otherwise, the Magic Wand only works within the selected layer.

3.7   Crop Tool

You can change the size of the canvas using the Crop tool to select a region to preserve and then crop to get rid of the remainder.

To crop an image, select the Crop tool, set your attributes, select the region of the canvas to preserve, and press Return/Enter.

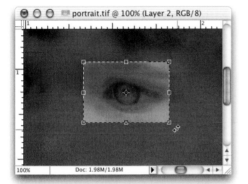

Cropping the image   The selected area is preserved, but the area outside that (shaded) is cropped out of the image when you press Return or double-click. You can also rotate the cropped area by placing the cursor at any corner.

➠ 5.3   Setting Photoshop Preferences

➠ 7.2   Changing the Canvas Size

➠ 7.3   Setting the Image Size

➠ 7.6   Straightening and Cropping Images

Before a crop selection is made, you can set options to specify the final size and resolution to which the cropped region will be resized. This is a quick and easy way to resize the image.

You can retrieve hidden parts of the image by moving the image or by resizing the image.

If you are unsure what a particular option is in the Toolbox or what its shortcut is, place the mouse cursor over the option. Within a few seconds, a Tool Tip appears with a brief description. If nothing happens, turn Tool Tips on in the General preferences.

Ⓐ Width, Height, Resolution   Enter the final dimensions and resolution to which the cropped image should be resized. This is optional. Leave these text boxes blank if you do not want the cropped image resized.

Ⓑ Swap Values   Click to switch the width and height values.

Ⓒ Resolution Units   Choose the units to be used when setting the Resolution of the image.

Ⓓ Front Image   Fills the Width, Height, and Resolution fields with the front-most open image's values.

Ⓔ Clear   Click to clear all values and prevent the image from being resized while cropping.

After you select the cropping region, the tool options bar will change to present you with options to specify what happens to cropped parts of the image and how the cropped region appears while you are working.

UNIVERSAL TASKS   PHOTO AND VIDEO TASKS   PRINT TASKS   WEB TASKS

3.7 Crop Tool *(continued)*

Crop tool

Constrain proportions

Shift plus select

Commits cropping after the selection is made

Return

Cancel cropping after the selection is made

Esc

Ⓐ Crop Treatment Choose Delete from the dropdown to permanently remove cropped regions from the image, or choose Hide to hide those regions.

Ⓑ Shield Region To Be Cropped If this option is checked, the region being cropped will be covered to better differentiate it from the region being preserved.

Ⓒ Shield Color Click to choose the color used to cover the region being cropped.

Ⓓ Shield Opacity Click to select or enter the opacity of the color used to cover the region being cropped.

Ⓔ Perspective If this option is checked, the crop bounding box can be skewed.

Ⓕ Cancel Click to cancel cropping.

Ⓖ Commit Click to crop the image.

3.8   Slice Tools

If you are a web designer, the Slice tools will come in handy for carving up interfaces you designed in Photoshop. You can use the Slice tool to specify particular regions of the canvas that can then be saved separate from one another by choosing File **>** Save For Web....

To create a slice, select the Slice tool, set your attributes, and then select an area of the canvas to be saved independently (often a button or a header graphic). Photoshop draws a grid around the new slice, splitting the entire image into user-specified slices and auto slices. You can add as many slices as you want to a single image.

➡ 29.1   Slicing Your
          Interface

Slice tool
K

Cycle slice tools
Shift K

Constrain proportions
Shift plus select

**Switch between Slice
and Slice Select with
a slice tool selected
(reverts after releasing)**
⌘
Ctrl

Slice   A special selection tool that defines regions of the canvas (slices) to be carved up to create a web interface.

Slice Select   Selects a slice to work with. Double-clicking a slice with this tool opens that slice's Options dialog.

Ⓐ Slice Selection Style   Choose Normal (unconstrained selection), Fixed Aspect Ratio (square selection), or Fixed Size (uses dimensions entered).

Ⓑ Width and Height   If you select Fixed Size, enter the width and height for the slice.

Ⓒ Slices From Guides   Click to convert the canvas guides into slices.

Ⓐ Top   Moves the selected slice above all others.

Ⓑ Move Up   Moves the selected slice up one level.

Ⓒ Move Down   Moves the selected slice down one level.

Ⓓ Bottom   Moves the selected slice below all others.

Ⓔ Slice Options   Click to open the Slice Options dialog in which you can enter information about the selected slice.

Ⓕ Promote to User Slice   Click to turn an auto or layer slice into a user slice.

Ⓖ Divide Slice...   Opens a dialog in which you can numerically divide the selected slice.

Ⓗ Hide Auto Slices   Click to show only user slices.

3.9   Restoration Tools

The Healing Brush tool works a lot like the Stamp tool (see Section 3.11). Select the layer you want to work in and then choose the Healing Brush tool. Press Option (you will notice the cursor change) to select a region of the image with the color you want to replicate into the region being fixed. Then simply brush over the region being repaired.

The Patch tool works as a selection that allows you to copy attributes from one region of the image into another. Select the layer you want to work in, choose the Patch tool, and then select the region you want to repair. Drag the selection to an area with the coloring you want to add to the selection and release. The selected region will be reworked using the new color data.

The Color Replacement tool paints the foreground color over another selected color. Choose a color you want to paint with as the foreground color, select the layer you want to work in, choose the Color Replacement tool, and then begin painting in the layer. The foreground color will paint over any pixels with the color to be replaced (either the background color or a color sampled from the canvas depending on the setting for Sampling).

Healing Brush   A brush that you can use to copy part of the image from one region while preserving the underlying texture, lighting, and shading of the region being brushed.

Patch   A freehand selection tool that you can use to copy one region of the image into another while preserving the underlying texture, lighting, and shading of the original region.

Color Replacement   A brush that lets you paint out one particular color with another color while preserving the underlying texture, lighting, and shading of the region being brushed.

3.9 Restoration Tools *(Continued)*

Restoration tool
[J]

Cycle restoration tools
[Shift] [J]

Switch to Eyedropper with Restoration tool selected (reverts after releasing)
[Option]
[Alt]

Ⓐ Brush Presets Click to set a brush size or select a predefined brush.

Ⓑ Blend Mode Choose from a limited list of blend modes to use with the brush.

Ⓒ Source Choose the source location for healing. You can choose to either sample from the current image or use a preset pattern selected from the drop-down.

Ⓓ Patterns If a pattern is selected, click to choose from a list of preset patterns.

Ⓔ Aligned If this option is checked, every time the Healing Brush tool is applied to an image, the brush will remain relative to the sampling point. If this option is unchecked, every time the Healing Brush tool is stopped and then started again, it begins from the initial sampling point.

Ⓕ Use All Layers If checked, the Healing Brush selects pixels on all layers in the image. Otherwise, the Healing Brush only works within the selected layer.

Ⓐ Selection Type Choose how the new selection should be treated in relation to the current selection: deselect the current selection and start a new selection, add to the current selection, subtract from the current selection, or intersect with the current selection.

Ⓑ Patch Region Choose whether the selected region is to be patched by the region moved to (source) or whether the region moved to is patched by the selection region (destination).

Ⓒ Transparent If checked, the patch will also use transparent pixels in the layer.

Ⓓ Use Pattern Click to apply the selected pattern to the patch selection.

Ⓔ Pattern Choose a pattern to apply to the patch with Use Pattern.

Ⓐ Brush Presets Click to set a brush size, hardness, and other attributes.

Ⓑ Blend Mode Choose from a limited list of blend modes to use with the brush.

Ⓒ Sampling Choose the source for the color being replaced: Continuous (the current color of the pixel in the canvas while painting), Once (the first pixel clicked on in the canvas with the tool), or Background Swatch (the selected background color).

Ⓓ Limits Choose the areas of the image that can be effected by the Color Replacement tool.

Ⓔ Tolerance Use the slider or enter a percentage value (1 to 100) to specify how close a color needs to be to the base color being replaced in order to be replaced. Higher values allow more colors to be replaced.

Ⓕ Anti-Aliased When this option is checked, anti-aliasing gives the edges of the replaced area a smoother appearance.

UNIVERSAL TASKS

PHOTO AND VIDEO TASKS

PRINT TASKS

WEB TASKS

3.10 Paint Tools

Paint tool
B

Cycle paint tools
Shift B

**Switch to Eyedropper
with a Paint tool
selected (reverts
after releasing)**
Option
Alt

———

Press Shift while
drawing to force a
straight line.

———

Warning: Releasing to
stop a stroke is an
action in the History
palette. Consequently,
choosing Edit > Undo
removes only the last
stroke you made.

———

Control/right-click in
the canvas to open a
contextual menu of
the Brush Preset Picker
(see Section 3.2) to
choose from.

———

Hold shift between
clicks while painting,
to draw a straight line
between the end and
beginning of each line.

Photoshop has two primary drawing tools: the Brush and the Pencil. The difference is simply that the edges of the Brush tool are anti-aliased, and the edges of the Pencil tool are not. Other than that, they work much the same.

To use one of the paint tools, select the layer you want to paint on, choose the appropriate brush, set the brush size and other attributes, and then click and drag in the canvas. As you move, a line appears after the cursor, which is referred to as a stroke. Release to stop painting.

Brush Brush that produces soft-edged, paintlike strokes.

Pencil Brush that produces hard-edged strokes.

Ⓐ Brush Presets Click to set the brush size or select a predefined brush.

Ⓑ Blend Mode Choose from a limited list of blend modes to use with the brush.

Ⓒ Paint Opacity Click to select or enter the opacity of the paint.

Ⓓ Paint Flow (Brush only) Click to select or enter the flow of the paint. This option is primarily used by tablets to set how quickly color is laid down for a brush stroke.

Ⓔ Airbrush Mode (Brush only) Click to turn on Airbrush mode that will apply more paint to an area the longer the tool stays over it.

Ⓕ Brushes Palette Click to open or close the Brushes palette.

Ⓐ Auto Erase (Pencil Only) Click if you want the selected background color to draw over the selected foreground color.

3.11   Stamp Tools

The stamp tools are brushlike tools that you use to copy parts of the image or preset patterns into the image.

To use the Clone Stamp tool, select the layer you want to clone in, set your attributes, and Option/Alt-click in the region you want to clone from in the canvas. This is the sample point. Then move the cursor to the region you want to clone to and start painting.

To use the Pattern Stamp tool, select the layer you want to paint in, select the Pattern Stamp tool, select a pattern in the tool options bar, and set your other attributes. Then, simply click and drag to paint the selected pattern into the canvas.

Clone Stamp A special brush you can use to paint one region of the image over another.

Pattern Stamp A special brush you can use to paint preset patterns into the image.

Ⓐ Brush Presets Click to set the brush size or select a predefined brush.

Ⓑ Blend Mode Choose from a limited list of blend modes to use with the brush.

Ⓒ Paint Opacity Click to select or enter the opacity of the paint.

Ⓓ Paint Flow Click to select or enter the flow of the paint. This option is used by tablets to set how quickly color is laid down for a brush stroke.

Ⓔ Airbrush Mode Click to turn on Airbrush mode.

Ⓕ Sample Point Alignment If this option is checked, the brush remains relative to the sampling point every time the clone brush is applied to an image. If this option is unchecked, the clone brush begins from the initial sampling point every time it is stopped and then started again.

Ⓖ Sample From All Active Layers If checked, samples images for cloning from all layers, not just the selected layer.

Ⓗ Brushes Palette Click to open or close the Brushes palette.

Ⓐ Patterns Click to choose from a list of preset patterns to use when stamping.

Ⓑ Impressionist Style Check if you want the pattern to mimic the look of an Impressionist painting.

➡ 13.1   Brush Basics

➡ 13.6   Painting with Patterns

➡ 19.3   Cloning One Area to Another

➡ 21.2   Blending Modes and Opacity

Stamp tool
⑤

Cycle stamp tools
Shift ⑤

Switch to Eyedropper (reverts after releasing)
Option

———

Control/right-click in the canvas to open a contextual menu to use the Brush Preset picker.

3.12   History Brushes

History Brush tool
[Y]

Cycle history brushes
[Shift] [Y]

———

Control/right-click in
the canvas to open a
contextual menu with
the Brush Preset picker.

The history brushes use specific states or snapshots in the image's history as source data to paint over the current image. You can use these brushes to create some interesting painting effects that are less mechanical looking than a filter.

To use the history brushes, first, in the History palette, click in the rectangle next to the History state or snapshot you want to use as the source for the History Brush tool (a History Brush icon will appear next to the source). Select the layer you want to paint into (there must be a corresponding layer in the history source), set your brush options, and then begin to paint.

History Brush A special brush you use to copy a previous version of the image back into the current version.

Art History Brush A special brush you use to copy previous versions of the image using a variety of brush-stroke styles.

ⓐ **Brush Presets** Click to set the brush size or to select a predefined brush.

ⓑ **Blend Mode** Choose from a limited list of blend modes to use with the brush.

ⓒ **Paint Opacity** Click to select or enter the opacity of the paint.

ⓓ **Paint Flow** Click to select or enter the flow of the paint. This option is used by tablets to set how quickly color is laid down for a brush stroke.

ⓔ **Airbrush Mode** Click to turn on Airbrush mode.

ⓕ **Brushes Palette** Click to open or close the Brushes palette.

ⓐ **Brush Stoke Style** Choose from a list of stroke styles to use while painting.

ⓑ **Painting Area** Enter the size of the area to be covered by the brush stroke. The larger the area, the more numerous the strokes.

ⓒ **Painting Tolerance** Click to choose or enter a value limiting the regions to which the paint strokes are applied. The larger tolerance limits paint strokes to areas that contrast from the source color.

3.13 Eraser Tools

There is no creation without destruction, and the eraser tools are the most refined way you have of "destroying" parts of your image.

To use an eraser tool, select the layer you want to erase, choose the desired eraser tool, set the attributes for the eraser, and then click and drag over the region you want to erase.

Eraser Removes pixels or makes pixels transparent on the selected layer of the canvas.

Background Eraser Removes pixels or makes pixels transparent in an image (not necessarily on the Background layer), which is useful for removing an object from a contrasting background.

Magic Eraser Removes pixels or makes pixels transparent on the selected layer for a particular color range.

Ⓐ Brush Presets Click to set the brush size or to select a predefined brush.

Ⓑ Eraser Mode Choose an eraser style: Brush, Pencil, Block (a square block).

Ⓒ Eraser Opacity Click to select or enter the opacity to erase.

Ⓓ Stroke Flow Click to select or enter the flow of the paint. This option is used by tablets to set how quickly color is laid down for a brush stroke.

Ⓔ Airbrush Mode Click to turn on Airbrush mode.

Ⓕ Erase To History Check to erase from the selected History state.

Ⓖ Brushes Palette Click to open or close the Brushes palette.

➡ 13.9 Erasing

Eraser tool
E

Cycle eraser tools
Shift E

The Background Eraser tool ignores a layer's transparency lock.

3.13   Eraser Tools *(Continued)*

ⓐ Erase Limit Mode Choose a limit for the color being erased: Discontinuous erases only the selected color under the brush, Contiguous erases the selected color under the brush and of any connected pixels, and Find Edges erases connected areas but preserves the sharpness and shape of edges.

ⓑ Tolerance Click to set or enter a percentage for the range of similar colors to erase.

ⓒ Protect Foreground Color Click to prevent the selected foreground color from being erased.

ⓓ Color Sampling Modes Choose a method for selecting the color to be erased: Continuous samples colors continuously as you drag, Once erases only the first color selected, and Background Swatch erases only the currently selected background color.

ⓐ Tolerance Enter a value in the range 0 to 255, which specifies the deviation a color can have to be included in the Magic Wand selection.

ⓑ Anti-Aliased When this option is checked, anti-aliasing gives the edges of the erased area a smoother appearance.

ⓒ Contiguous When checked, only pixels touching the selected pixel and within the set tolerance and pixels touching those (and so forth) are included in the selection. Otherwise, the Magic Wand selects all pixels in the image within the tolerance level.

ⓓ Sample From All Active Layers If checked, erases from all visible layers, not just the selected layer.

ⓔ Eraser Opacity Click to select or enter the opacity the eraser erases to in a single stroke.

3.14   Fill Tools

Adding dips and dabs of color is fine, but often you need to add large areas of color quickly to a canvas. Photoshop has two tools to do just that. You use the Gradient tool to add a series of colors that smoothly flow one to the next. You use the Paint Bucket tool to "pour" a solid color over all or part of the image.

To use the Gradient tool, select the layer to add a gradient to, choose the Gradient tool, and set options for the gradient. Then click where you want the gradient to begin and drag to where you want the gradient to end. The regions before and after the points are filled with the beginning and end colors of the gradient.

To use the Paint Bucket tool, select a layer to fill (you can also fill a selection in a layer), select a foreground color, and then choose the Paint Bucket tool. Set the options for the file and then click in the area you want to fill.

➡ 12.7   Applying
          Color Fills

➡ 12.10   Applying
          Gradient
          Color Fills

Fill tool
[G]

Cycle fill tools
[Shift] [G]

———

The farther you drag while adding a gradient, the longer and smoother the graduated area will be.

Gradient Fills the selection or layer with a gradiated color.

Paint Bucket Fills a selection or region in a layer with the selected foreground color.

ⓐ Gradient Presets menu Click to choose a preset gradient. Double-click the gradient image to edit the gradient or create a new gradient.

ⓑ Gradient Style Choose a gradient type: Linear, Radial, Angle, Reflected, or Diamond.

ⓒ Blend Mode Choose a blend mode for the fill to interact with the image.

ⓓ Opacity Click to select or enter the opacity for the fill.

ⓔ Reverse Direction Check to reverse the direction of the gradient colors. The effects of this show up in the Gradient Preset menu.

ⓕ Dither Gradient Check to dither the gradient colors to reduce banding.

ⓖ Transparency Mask Check to use a transparency mask with the gradient.

3.14   Fill Tools *(Continued)*

⇒ 21.2   Blending
Modes and
Opacity

**Switch to Eyedropper
(reverts after releasing)**
[Option]

—

With the Gradient tool,
Control/right-click in
the canvas to open a
contextual menu of
gradient presets.

—

With the Paint Bucket
tool, Control/right-click
in the canvas to open
a contextual menu of
blending modes to use
for the fill.

Ⓐ Fill Type Choose to fill with the selected foreground color or with a pattern.

Ⓑ Patterns If a pattern is selected in the fill type menu, click to choose from a list of preset patterns.

Ⓒ Blend Mode Choose a blend mode for the fill to interact with the image.

Ⓓ Opacity Click to select or enter the opacity for the fill.

Ⓔ Color Tolerance Enter a value in the range 0 to 255, which specifies the deviation a color can
have from the color clicked on in order to be part of the fill.

Ⓕ Anti-Aliased If this option is checked, anti-aliasing gives the edges of the fill a smoother
appearance.

Ⓖ Contiguous If checked, only pixels touching the selected pixel and within the set tolerance
and pixels touching those (and so forth) are included in the fill.

Ⓗ Fill In All Active Layers If checked, the fill affects all visible layers.

TOOLS AND THE MOUSE CURSOR

Every tool that you choose from the Toolbox can use the tool's icon as the mouse
cursor to help you identify which tool is selected. However, these icons are often clunky
when you need to manipulate images precisely. Photoshop lets you choose whether
you want to use the tool icon or a more precise cursor. To set the appearance of the
cursor used for tools, choose Photoshop/Edit > Preferences > Display And Cursors... (see
Section 5.6). Generally, the Brush Size is better for painting and Precision is better for
other tasks. However, while in Brush Size mode, you can use the Caps Lock key to
toggle between the two modes.

3.15　Distortion Tools

The Blur, Sharpen, and Smudge tools are brush tools that allow you to distort the image a little or a lot depending on your needs. The Blur tool does this by blurring the contrast between regions, making them look as if they are out of focus. The Sharpen tool is the Blur tool's inverse, making contrast between areas sharper. The Smudge tool gives you control as if you were running your finger over the image and smearing the colors together.

Blur　A special brush that simulates a loss of focus in the image.

Sharpen　A special brush that sharpens the focus of the image.

Smudge　A special brush that smears the image.

All three tools share the same options except for Smudge, which adds a Finger Painting option.

Ⓐ Brush Presets　Click to set the brush size or to select a predefined brush.

Ⓑ Blend Mode　Choose from a limited list of blend modes to use with the brush.

Ⓒ Stroke Strength　Click to choose or enter a percentage for the strength of the stroke. The higher the percentage, the more pronounced the change.

Ⓓ Use All Visible Layers　If this option is checked, the tool works across all visible layers, not just the selected layer.

Ⓔ Finger Painting　(Smudge Only) If this option is checked, the Smudge tool simulates finger painting, using the selected foreground color.

Ⓕ Brushes Palette　Click to open or close the Brushes palette.

➡ 13.1　Brush Basics

➡ 13.10　Distorting Images

➡ 19.8　Sharpening and Blurring Images.

Distortion tool
Ⓡ

Cycle distortion tools
Shift Ⓡ

Control/right-click in the canvas to open a contextual menu of the Brush Preset Picker (see Section 3.2).

3.16 Exposure Tools

Exposure tool
O

Cycle exposure tools
Shift O

Several tools in Photoshop are meant to mimic actual tools used during the exposure of photographic paper. Dodging is a technique used in the photographic darkroom whereby light is blacked during exposure, often using a black piece of cardboard on a piece of wire, and burning is a technique that uses a hole cut in a piece of black cardboard to allow extra light into certain areas. In Photoshop, you use the Dodge tool to mimic the dodging technique, and you use the Burn tool to mimic the burning technique. You use the Sponge tool to increase color saturation and contrast.

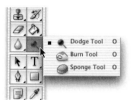

Dodge A special brush you use to lighten the areas of the image.

Burn A special brush you use to darken areas of the image.

Sponge A special brush you use to increase the color saturation and contrast of the image.

The Dodge and Burn tools share the same options.

Ⓐ **Brush Presets** Click to set the brush size or to select a predefined brush.

Ⓑ **Tonal Range** Choose the tonal range in which to burn or dodge: Shadows, Midtones, or Highlights.

Ⓒ **Exposure** Click to choose or enter a percentage for the exposure of the burn or dodge. The higher the percentage, the more pronounced the effect.

Ⓓ **Airbrush Mode** Click to turn on Airbrush mode.

Ⓔ **Brushes Palette** Click to open or close the Brushes palette.

Ⓐ **Brush Presets** Click to set brush size or to select a predefined brush.

Ⓑ **Saturation** Choose Saturate to increase color vibrancy, or choose Desaturate to reduce color to grayscale.

Ⓒ **Stroke Flow** Click to select or enter the flow rate for the brush. The higher the percentage, the more pronounced the effect.

Ⓓ **Airbrush Mode** Click to turn on Airbrush mode.

Ⓔ **Brushes Palette** Click to open or close the Brushes palette.

3.17 Path Selection Tools

You use the path tools in conjunction with the pen tools to manipulate vector paths in the image. To use them, choose a path selection tool and then click a path in the selected layer. The path is highlighted with direction points. Direction points appear as filled circles, selected anchor points appear as filled squares, and unselected anchor points appear as hollow squares.

Path Selection Selects and moves paths.

Direct Selection Selects the entire path or path component and moves points or adjusts Bezier curve handles. This tool has no options.

➡ 16.8 Selecting Paths and Components

Path Selection tool
[A]

Cycle path selection tools
[Shift] [A]

Switch between path selection tools (reverts after releasing)
[⌘]
[Ctrl]

Delete the currently selected path or path component
[D]

———

Alt/Option-click with either tool inside the path and drag to duplicate the path.

Ⓐ **Show Bounding Box** If checked, the rectangular edges of a path are shown. If the path is not rectangular, the bounding box represents a rectangular region of the path's extreme horizontal and vertical limits. You can use the bounding box to transform the path (resize, skew, and rotate).

Ⓑ **Path Interaction** Click to specify how the selected path should interact with other paths in the same layer: Add To Shape Area adds paths at overlap, Subtract From Shape Area masks overlapping paths, Intersect Shape Areas specifies that paths only show at intersections, and Exclude Overlapping Shape Areas specifies that paths only show where they do not intersect.

Ⓒ **Combine Paths** Click to merge the paths in a layer into one path.

Ⓓ **Align Objects** Two or more linked layers can be aligned with their top, middle, bottom, left, center, or right edges.

Ⓔ **Distributed Objects** The content of three or more linked layers can be distributed between their top, middle, bottom, left, center, or right edges.

Ⓕ **Dismiss Target Path** Deselects the selected path.

3.18   Type Tools

➠ 17   Typography

Type tool
T

Cycle type tools
Shift T

———

You can resize a text box using the Type tool to drag the text region's bounding box.

———

If there is too much text to fit in the confines of the text box, a small red plus sign appears in the bottom-right corner of the box.

———

Text boxes can also be resized using the transform pseudo-tool (see 19.11).

You can enter text directly into an image using any font available on the computer. Photoshop can create legible anti-aliased text for print or screen use, but often text is an integral part of the image. It is used as a design element rather than to communicate written information. Photoshop facilitates either use of text.

To use a type tool, select the layer you want the text to appear above (type is automatically added to a new layer), select the desired type tool, set your options, and then click in the canvas where you want your text to begin (left justified), to be centered around (center), or to end (right justified).

In addition, you can create a text box for longer strings of text. Select a type tool and use it just like a selection tool to define the area of the text box. You will see a bounding box. When you enter text in the box, it will not go wider or higher than defined.

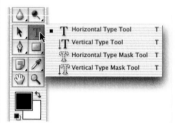

Horizontal Type Type text horizontally across the canvas.

Vertical Type Type text vertically down the canvas.

Horizontal Type Mask Type text horizontally across the canvas to create a mask.

Vertical Type Mask Type text vertically down the canvas to create a mask.

Ⓐ Toggle Text Orientation Click to change the text direction between horizontal and vertical.

Ⓑ Font Choose a font name from the list of fonts available on the computer or click to enter the font name.

Ⓒ Font Style Choose available styles for the selected font or click and enter the style name directly.

Ⓓ Font Size Choose a font size or click to enter the size directly.

Ⓔ Anti-Aliasing Choose an anti-aliasing method for the text: None, Crisp, Sharp, or Smooth.

Ⓕ Text Justification Choose a justification for the text: left, centered, or right.

Ⓖ Font Color Click to open the Color Picker dialog and choose a color for the text.

Ⓗ Warped Text Click to open the Warp Text dialog.

Ⓘ Character & Paragraph Palettes Click to show or hide the Character and Paragraph palettes.

3.19 Pen Tools

Although Photoshop is primarily a bitmap-editing program, it includes several tools for adding and manipulating vector graphics. You use the pen tools to draw vector paths to create elements that can be more easily changed than bitmap elements.

To add a vector path to an image, use the Pen tool to draw anchor points, either one at a time with the Pen tool or freehand with the Freeform Pen tool. Then use the point tools to manipulate the path.

➡ 16   Drawing Paths
         and Shapes

Pen tool
[P]

Cycle pen tools (Pen and Freeform Pen only)
[Shift] [P]

Delete the currently selected path or path component
[Delete]

The Freeform Pen tool in the Tool options bar includes an option to force a free-form path to stick to high-contrast boundaries in the image.

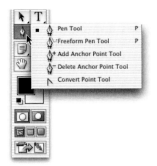

Pen Draws a vector path on a point-by-point basis.

Freeform Pen Draws a freehand vector path.

Add Anchor Point Adds a new anchor point when over an existing vector path. Otherwise, you use this tool to move and reshape existing paths, points, and Bezier curves. This tool has no options.

Delete Anchor Point Removes an existing anchor point. Otherwise, you use this tool to reshape existing paths and Bezier curves. This tool has no options.

Convert Point Reshapes existing paths and Bezier curves. This tool has no options.

This version of the tool options bar shows the options if Shape Layer mode is selected.

Ⓐ Shape Layer Mode Click to draw the vector as a layer mask. If selected, the tool options bar includes style and color options for the fill on the far right.

Ⓑ Paths Mode Click to draw a path (not filled).

Ⓒ Fill Pixels Mode Not available with pen tools. Used with shape tools.

Ⓓ Pen Tools Click to choose the Pen or Freeform Pen tool.

Ⓔ Shape Tools Click to choose a specific shape tool. (See Section 3.20 for more details.)

Ⓕ Tool-Specific Option Click to view further options for the selected pen tool. This option depends on the selected tool.

Ⓖ Auto Add/Delete Automatically adds or deletes a point when overlapping occurs in the path. Only available to the Pen tool.

Ⓗ Mode-Specific Options These options depend on the mode selected.

Ⓘ Path Interaction Click to specify how the selected path should interact with other paths in the same layer.

Ⓙ Lock Click to turn on or off. When on (highlighted), style changes affect the selected path. When off, style changes affect new paths only.

Ⓚ Style Presets Click to select a style preset.

Ⓛ Color Click to select a color to use if no style has been selected.

3.20 Shape Tools

⇒ 16 Drawing Paths
and Shapes

Shape tool
U

Cycle shape tools
Shift U

Like the pen tools, shape tools are used to create vector paths in an image but as specific shapes (rectangles, ellipses, polygons, and so on). The shape tools share the same options as the pen tools, but add one additional mode, Pixel Fill mode, which uses a shape tool to create a bitmap rather than a vector shape.

Rectangle Draws rectangular and square shapes.

Rounded Rectangle Draws rectangular shapes with rounded edges. Enter the radius of rounded edges in the tool options bar.

Ellipse Draws elliptical and circular shapes.

Polygon Draws multisided shapes. Enter the number of sides in the tool options bar.

Line Draws a straight line. Enter the line weight in the tool options bar.

Custom Shape Catchall to draw a variety of predefined shapes. Choose the exact shape in the tool options bar.

- **ⓐ Shape Layer Mode** Click to draw a shape as a layer mask. If this option is selected, the tool options bar includes style and color options for the fill on the far right.
- **ⓑ Paths Mode** Click to draw the shape as a vector path (not filled).
- **ⓒ Fill Pixel Mode** Uses the shape to create a bitmap image rather than a vector image.
- **ⓓ Rectangle Tool** Click to draw rectangular and square shapes.
- **ⓔ Rounded Rectangle Tool** Click to draw rectangular and square shapes with rounded rather than squared corners.
- **ⓕ Ellipse Tool** Click to draw elliptical and circular shapes.
- **ⓖ Polygon Tool** Click to draw multisided shapes.
- **ⓗ Line Tool** Click to draw lines.
- **ⓘ Custom Shape Tool** Click to draw customized shapes.
- **ⓙ Shape Options** Click to set additional options for the selected shape tool. Each shape tool has slightly different options.
- **ⓚ Quick Shape Options** Presents a single option for the selected shape tool (in this example, radius for the rounded rectangle corners).
- **ⓛ Blend Mode** Choose from a limited list of blend modes to use with the brush.
- **ⓜ Paint Opacity** Click to select or enter the opacity of the paint.
- **ⓝ Anti-Aliased** When this option is checked, anti-aliasing gives the edges of the selection a smoother appearance.

3.21 Annotation Tools

If you are working with others on a project, or if you simply want to remind yourself how or why you did something in an image, add a note directly to the canvas. To add a note, select the tool, click the canvas where you want the note to appear, and then enter your text.

To add an audio annotation, select the tool, click the canvas where you want an icon for the note to appear, and use the controls to record your message. Obviously, your computer must be equipped with a microphone. To play the note back, double-click the annotation icon.

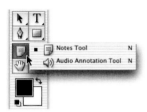

Notes Adds a virtual sticky note to the document.

Audio Annotation Adds a recorded message to the document at a particular spot. Requires a computer with a microphone.

Options for both annotation tools are identical except that the Audio Annotation tool does not include font or size.

ⓐ Author Name Enter the name of the comment's author.

ⓑ Font (Notes tool only) Choose the font in which the note will appear.

ⓒ Font Size (Notes tool only) Choose a relative font size for the note: Smallest, Smaller, Medium, Larger, or Largest.

ⓓ Highlight Color Click to open the Color Picker dialog and select a highlight color for the note.

ⓔ Clear All Click to clear all notes from the current document.

➥ 18.9 Adding Notes

Annotation tool
N

Cycle annotation tools
Shift N

Warning: Sound files can add considerably to the file size, so you might want to use them sparingly.

To delete a single annotation, click the Annotation icon and press Delete.

If your computer does not have a built-in microphone, you will need to plug an external microphone into the computer's "mini" input. If you have one, it will generally have a microphone icon above it.

3.22 Eyedropper and Measure Tools

➡ 12.2 Selecting
Colors
with the
Eyedropper

Eyedropper tool
[I]

**Cycle eyedropper
and measure tools**
[Shift] [I]

**Switch between
Eyedropper and Color
Sampler (reverts after
releasing)**
[Shift]

Selecting the right color is a crucial task in Photoshop. The Eyedropper tool is designed to help you select colors from anywhere on the canvas—in color swatches and even from the Color bar at the bottom of the Color palette. To compare colors, use the Color Sampler tool. This tool lets you select as many as four colors and display their color values in the Info palette.

Eyedropper Selects colors from the canvas, toolbar, Swatches palette, and Color palette.

Color Sampler Select as many as four points in the canvas to display the color value for each point in the Info palette.

Measure Click and drag to measure the distance between two points in the canvas.

Ⓐ Sample Size Method Choose an option to specify how the Eyedropper should select a color. Point Sample selects the color of the clicked pixel, and 3 By 3 Sample and 5 By 5 Sample both average the color of the pixels around the selection point.

Ⓑ Clear (Color Sample only) Clears the selected color samples. Only available with the Color Sampler tool.

Ⓐ Origin Coordinates Displays the X, Y coordinates of the measurement's origin.

Ⓑ Width and Height Displays the distance of the final point from the origin coordinates.

Ⓒ Angle The angle of measurement.

Ⓓ Distances The distances of a maximum of two measurements.

Ⓔ Clear Clears the current measurement lines.

3.23 Hand Tool

Images often fill the screen and go outside the viewable area of the document window, especially if they are large or you have magnified them. Use the Hand tool to move the image within the viewing area.

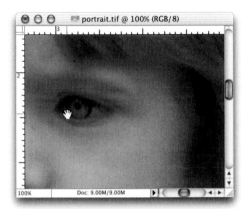

Use the Hand tool to move the canvas within the window. This works like scrolling the window, but is much faster for navigating around different parts of the image, and is especially useful when working in very close on a high-resolution image.

Hand tool
$\boxed{H}$

Switch to Hand tool from any other tool (reverts after releasing)
$\boxed{Spacebar}$

Switch to Zoom In (reverts after releasing)
$\boxed{\mathcal{H}}$
$\boxed{Ctrl}$

Switch to Zoom Out (reverts after releasing)
$\boxed{Shift}$

Ⓐ Scroll All Windows If checked, all open document windows will scroll in unison. This is useful for comparing two images.

Ⓑ Actual Pixels Click to zoom the canvas to 100%.

Ⓒ Fit On Screen Click to maximize the image so that it fills the screen.

Ⓓ Print Size Click to zoom the image to the size it will be when printed.

PHOTOSHOP WORKSPACE

UNIVERSAL TASKS

PHOTO AND VIDEO TASKS

PRINT TASKS

WEB TASKS

3.24 Zoom Tool

➡ 7.1 Canvas Basics

Zoom tool
[Z]

Use the Zoom tool to magnify the image (zoom in) to get a better look at details or pull back (zoom out) to get a bird's eye view of the entire image.

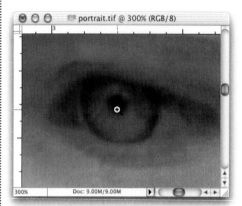

This image is zoomed to 300%.

Ⓐ Zoom Tools Click to select Zoom In or Zoom Out.

Ⓑ Resize Windows To Fit Check to force the window to automatically resize to the size of the canvas.

Ⓒ Ignore Palettes Check to allow resizing to ignore palettes on the screen. Otherwise, the window resizes to the palette edges.

Ⓓ Zoom All Windows If checked, all open document windows will zoom in unison.

Ⓔ Actual Pixels Click to zoom the canvas to 100%.

Ⓕ Fit On Screen Click to maximize the image to fill the screen.

Ⓖ Print Size Click to zoom the image to the size it will be when printed.

3.25   Beyond the Tools

The Toolbox also contains a few other buttons that provide shortcuts to key features. You may use some of these features (such as the Foreground/Background Colors) all the time, and you may never give others a second glance (such as the Jump To ImageReady button).

Adobe Online

The Adobe Photoshop icon at the top of the menu is actually a link to the Adobe website. Click this button to open your default web browser at the Adobe Photoshop web page (`www.adobe.com/products/photoshop`).

 Click to go to the Photoshop area of the Adobe website. On this page you will find marketing information about Photoshop (which, if you already own Photoshop, won't be of much use). You can also download software updates and additions, find out about training and events, report problems, chat with other Photoshop users, and pick up inspiration from the Adobe Gallery.

Foreground/Background Color Swatches

Photoshop allows you to have two selected colors at any time: foreground and background. The foreground color is used by any brush, text, or other tool or option that adds pixels to the canvas. The background color is available for fills, although you can also select other colors. More important, if the image is not using a transparent background (that is, if there is a Background layer), the background color fills areas whenever the canvas is resized or parts of the background are cut or deleted.

To change either color, click its color swatch to open the Color Picker. To change the foreground color, select colors in the Swatches palette, set the color in the Color palette, or use the Eyedropper tool to select a color from the image. To change the background color, use the Eyedropper tool and press Option/Alt while selecting a color from the image.

These are the same colors as shown in the Color palette.

A **Foreground Color Swatch** Click to open the Color Picker and select a new color.

B **Background Color Swatch** Click to open the Color Picker and select a new color.

C **Swap** Click to swap the foreground and background colors.

D **Reset Colors** Click to reset the foreground and background colors to the default black and white.

3.25   Beyond the Tools *(Continued)*

**Swap foreground/
background colors**
 X

**Revert to default
colors**
 D

Cycle mask modes
 Q

**Cycle view modes
(Standard, Full Screen
With Menu Bar, Full
Screen)**
 F

Jump To ImageReady
Shift ⌘ M
Shift Ctrl M

———

To change the Image
Mat color, choose the
color you want as the
foreground color,
choose the Paint Bucket
tool, and option/alt click
outside of the canvas
area in the Image Mat.
The Image Mat will now
be the foreground color.

———

Use the preferences to
set whether the image
is automatically saved,
when switching back
and forth between
ImageReady and
Photoshop.

Quick Mask Mode

Using masks is an easy way to select parts of an image using the brush tools. The Quick Mask mode applies a mask to the entire image, which you can then edit using the standard selection and drawing tools. When you return to Standard mode, the mask is converted into a selection.

A Standard Mode Click to work with the image.

B Quick Mask Mode Click to edit the image mask.

View Mode

Photoshop has three distinctive view modes. You can display the image in a free-floating window that you can move around the screen, or the image can be fixed in the center of the screen with either a gray or a black background.

A Standard Screen Mode Click to display the image in its own window.

B Full Screen Mode With Menu Bar Click if you want the image fixed in a gray field in the center of the screen with a menu bar at the top.

C Full Screen Mode Click if you want the image fixed in a black field with no menu bar available.

Jump To ImageReady

ImageReady is provided with Photoshop to add greater web-editing capabilities. You can easily move images back and forth between ImageReady and Photoshop using the Jump To ImageReady button. On the other side, ImageReady has a button to send the image back to Photoshop when you are finished in ImageReady.

  Click to open the file in ImageReady to edit for the Web. Changes made to the image in one program are immediately imported to the other when you switch back and forth (either using the buttons or by simply using your operating system to move between programs). In addition, while one program is using the file, the document is grayed out in the other program so that there is no confusion over which version you are currently editing.

CHAPTER **4**

PHOTOSHOP WORKSPACE

UNIVERSAL TASKS

PHOTO AND VIDEO TASKS

PRINT TASKS

WEB TASKS

Palettes

ALTHOUGH RECENT VERSIONS OF PHOTOSHOP have shifted attention to the tool options bar in order to access options while editing, the 16 palettes (accessed through the Window menu) still serve as the workhorses of Photoshop CS, providing access to hundreds of options that control brush size to text size and everything in between. In addition to the palettes, the File Browser works as a special window used to open and manage media files on your computer. Although not technically a palette, it is often included with them because it is also accessed through the Window menu.

Every palette is unique and performs specific duties in the interface, yet all palettes share certain qualities. All palettes appear in a special palette window (unless docked in the Palette Well). This window is a miniature version of a regular window but has the elements commonly associated with windows.

4.1   Organizing Palettes

➡ 1.4   Interface
            Objects

To avoid screen clutter, you can arrange and organize the 17 palettes in a variety of ways by docking individual palettes together, docking palette windows together, or docking pallets into a special area called the Palette Well.

Show/hide Toolbox, Toolbox options, and open palettes
[Tab]

Show/hide open palettes
[Shift] [Tab]

Hide currently open palette in the Palette Well
[Esc]

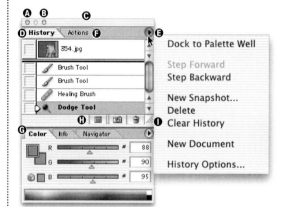

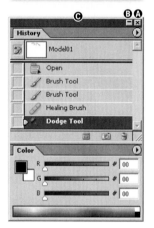

Ⓐ Close Palette Window Click to close this palette window and all its palettes.

Ⓑ Collapse Palette Window Click to toggle between different window sizes for the currently showing palette(s) in the palette window or docked palette windows.

Ⓒ Title bar Click and drag the palette window to position it on the screen. Double-click to collapse the window to just the tabs.

Ⓓ Palette tab Click to display the indicated palette. Double-click to collapse the window to just the tabs. You can also use this tab to move palettes between palette windows and to the Palette Well.

Ⓔ Palette menu Click to access specific options for the palette. The menu button appears in the palette's tab when docked in the Palette Well. Each palette has different options that are also usually provided in the menus at the top of the screen or application.

Ⓕ Docked palettes One or more palettes grouped together into the same palette window.

Ⓖ Docked palette windows One or more palette windows connected together but not in the same group.

Ⓗ Footer controls If available, click to use various buttons and menus depending on the palette.

Ⓘ Resize Palette If available, click to change the size of the palette window.

4.1 Organizing Palettes *(Continued)*

Docking Palettes

Group two or more palettes together in the same palette window by dragging the tab of one palette into the area of another palette window (the entire palette window is highlighted by a thick black border) and release. The palettes now appear in the same palette window and move together as a single unit. To switch between palettes, simply click the tab of the palette you want to view. To ungroup a palette, click and drag its tab out of the palette window and release. The palette is now in its own palette window.

When you move a palette window, it tends to snap around other palette windows on the screen, which makes them easier to accurately position with one another.

You can also add palettes to the Palette Well by selecting Dock To Palette Well in any palette menu.

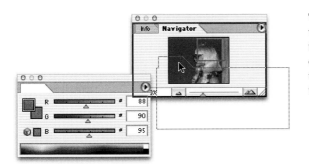

The Color palette is being docked with other palettes. Notice the thick black border around the entire palette window, indicating that the palette is being added to the window.

Docking Palette Windows

Group two or more palette windows on top of each other by dragging the tab of one palette to the top or bottom of another palette window (the area at the bottom or top of the window is highlighted) and release. The palette windows are now stacked on top of each other and not only move together but adjust their positions depending on other palette windows in the same group. You can dock and undock individual palettes as described earlier.

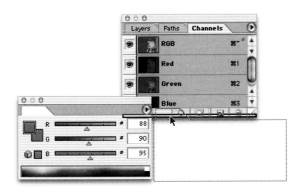

The Color palette window is being docked below another palette window. Notice the thick black border around the bottom of the palette window, indicating that the palette is being docked at the bottom.

4.1 Organizing Palettes (Continued)

The Palette Well is best reserved for palettes that are commonly used but not required for constant reference such as the Color and Styles palettes.

The more tabs you add to the Palette Well, the less space there is to display each tab. The tabs begin to overlap and become increasingly difficult to read.

Docking to the Palette Well

Add palettes to the Palette Well (located on the right side of the tool options bar) by dragging the palette's tab into the area of the Palette Well area and releasing. The tab for the palette now appears as an option in the Palette Well. To view the palette, click the tab. To close the tab, click anywhere outside its area. To remove the palette from the well, simply click and drag its tab out of the Palette Well area. The palette now appears in its own palette window.

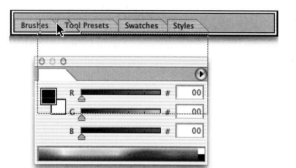

The Color palette is being added to the Palette Well. Notice the thick black border around the Palette Well, indicating that the palette is being added.

Palette Options

Many palettes have a dialog in which you can set specific preferences for the palette. To access the palette's options, choose Palette Options... in the palette's menu.

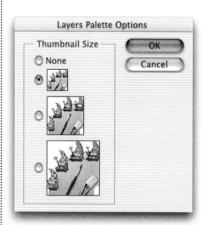

You can set the size of thumbnails displayed in the palette in the Layers Palette Options dialog.

4.2   Customizing Your Workspace

Every designer works to their own drum-beat, and once they have their workspace organized the way they like it, they need to be able to save the setup so that when they have to move palettes around while working, they can quickly return to their customized setup. Once you have your palettes organized and laid out the way you want them, use the workspace.

- To save the current layout, choose Window > Workspace > Save Workspace. Enter a name for the new workspace in the dialog and click OK. The configuration appears at the bottom of the Workspace submenu.

- To reset the palettes to their Photoshop default locations, choose Window > Workspace > Reset Palette Locations.

- To reset the palettes to a previously saved configuration, choose Window > Workspace, and then enter the name of the desired layout configuration.

- To permanently remove a workspace layout, choose Window > Delete Workspace..., choose the workspace configuration from the drop-down menu in the dialog, and then press Delete.

Although every designer has their own preferences for setup, the following sections provide some tips and suggestions for setting up your workspace for different tasks.

4.2 Customizing Your Workspace *(Continued)*

Workspace for Photographers

Photographers will generally be working directly with the total image or refining specific parts of the image to maximize output quality involving color correction and manipulation. For best results, photographers will want to work with the image at 100% magnification, to provide maximum viewing area while keeping only the essential palettes open.

Palettes on the screen: Navigator/Histogram/Color; Info/Swatches; Layers; Channels.

Palettes in the Palette Well: Brushes, Tool Presets, Actions, and History.

Ⓐ The Palette Well contains the Brushes palette, the Tool Presets palette, the Actions palette, and the History palette for quick access.

Ⓑ Since most photographs will need to be enlarged beyond the confines of the screen in order to view them in full detail, the Info palette is invaluable. In addition, photographers will often need to reference the Histogram palette when making image adjustments in order to ensure high-fidelity.

Ⓒ Group the Info and Swatches palettes together in order to be able to quickly choose colors as needed.

Ⓓ The Layers palette is used primarily to add Adjustment layers and masks, so it can be condensed to a relatively small size. If you use vector masks often, you might want to place the Paths palette in this group as well.

Ⓔ Since most photographs are destined for print, it is important to keep an eye on your color channels whether in RGB or CMYK mode. This also allows you to quickly switch between color channels for exact editing. Just Command/Ctrl-click a channel to select it for individual changes.

Ⓕ Work in Full Screen With Menu mode to view the maximum amount of your photographs at 100% magnification.

4.2   Customizing Your Workspace *(Continued)*

Workspace for Print Designers

Whether you are doing illustration or more general graphic design for print or other media, your will be using a lot of layers and working in multiple brush styles. In this setup, the Layers palette is maximized for height with a small space left for History and typography palettes, which you will also be relying on to test various ideas and add text to your design.

Palettes on the Screen: Layers/Layer Comps/Channels; History/Character/Paragraph; Navigator/Info; Layers; Channels.

Palettes in the Palette Well: Brushes; Tool Presets; Paths; Actions; Swatches.

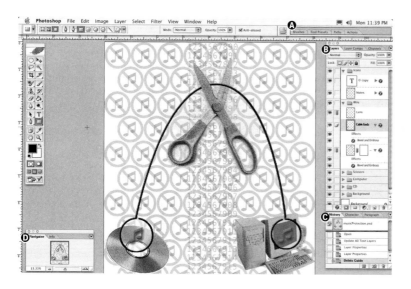

Ⓐ The Palette Well contains the Brushes, Tool Presets, Paths, Actions, and Swatches palettes for quick access.

Ⓑ If you are an illustrator or a graphic designer, you will be using lots of layers, so it is a good idea to open the Layers palette as tall as possible. In addition, you will want to use the Layer Comps palette to try different ideas and be able to quickly move between them. Finally, the Channels palette will be useful to ensure accurate color reproduction.

Ⓒ Although the Layer Comps palette can help you try different ideas, it is good to keep the History palette handy so that you can flip between different history states and test "before" or "after" to see which version works best as well as to take snapshots at different points during development. In addition, the text tool palettes (Character and Paragraph) are handy if you are using type in your design.

Ⓓ Since illustrations are often high-resolution, the Navigator palette should be handy so that you can view a thumbnail of the entire illustration and move quickly from area to area while working. The Info palette should also be available if you need to make measurements with the Measure tool.

4.2   Customizing Your Workspace *(Continued)*

Workspace for Web Designers

Like illustrators, web designers also rely heavily on the Layers palette as well as the Layer Comps palette to create alternate versions of a design based on a single theme. In addition, since text in graphics takes on a greater importance for web designers, in this setup, the typography palettes (Character and Paragraph) are more important.

Palettes on the screen: Layers/Layer Comps/Paths; History/Actions; Character/Paragraph; Info Color.

Palettes in the Palette Well: Brushes; Tool Presets; Swatches; Styles.

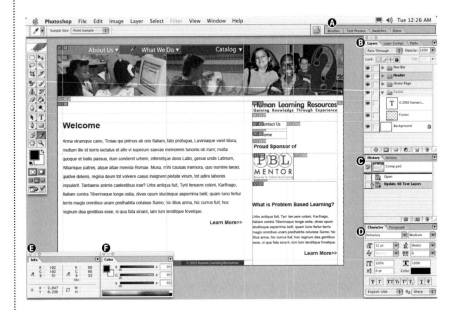

Ⓐ The Palette Well contains the Brushes, Tool Presets, Swatches, and Styles palettes for quick access. Using the Styles palette is a great way to create web buttons quickly.

Ⓑ Web designs often build up numerous layers, so the Layers palette should be available for easy access and reference. The Layer Comps palette will prove invaluable for quickly creating several different versions of a single design using similar elements. Finally, the Paths palette is placed in this group so that you can use it to quickly create buttons or other navigation objects.

Ⓒ The History palette will allow you to try different designs and then quickly revert to other designs. Grouped with this is the Actions palette to allow you to switch over and perform an automated function (for example, colorizing images used in the design).

Ⓓ Web designers often rely on text in graphics to get the exact type they want to use in a web page so you will be using the typography palettes often.

Ⓔ The Info palette will allow you to view different color values and positions of elements in the canvas.

Ⓕ Place the Color palette in close proximity to the Info palette so that you can use both in tandem.

4.3   Actions Palette

The Actions palette stores a series of commands that you can then replay on one image or a batch of images, allowing you to assign keyboard shortcuts to access these actions quickly. The Actions palette has two distinct modes, which you can toggle between using the Actions palette menu:

Record mode   Used to create or play back actions. In the Record mode, you can view all the action sets, actions, and commands.

Button mode   A simplified interface that lets you click a single button to play back an action.

Ⓐ Toggle Action   Click to turn the action or group of actions on or off.

Ⓑ Toggle Dialog   Click to turn the dialog for an action on or off. If on, the dialog is open. If off, the last values in the dialog are used.

Ⓒ Action Set   A collection of actions.

Ⓓ Action   An individual action. Click the action to select it and then click the Play Action button to execute it.

Ⓔ Command   An individual action.

Ⓕ Stop Recording   If an action is being recorded, click this button to stop recording.

Ⓖ Begin Recording   Click to start recording an action. You must have an action selected or use the menu palette to start a new action.

Ⓗ Play Action   Click to play the currently selected action.

Ⓘ Create New Set   Click to add a new action set folder.

Ⓙ Create New Action   Click to start a new action.

Ⓚ Delete Action   Click to delete the currently selected action set, action, or action behavior, or click and drag to this button to delete.

➡ 18.1 Applying Actions

➡ 18.2 Recording Actions

➡ 18.3 Performing Batch Actions

➡ 18.4 Creating Droplets

Show/Hide Actions palette

Option + F9
Alt + F9

The Actions palette menu gives you access to all the action recording options and allows you to save and load action sets in the palette. In addition, you can select whether to use Record mode or Button mode.

4.4   Brushes Palette

➡ 13.1 Brush Basics

Show/Hide Brushes palette
[F][5]

———

The Brushes palette menu lets you edit information about the selected brush, load and save collections of brushes, and set the brush preview size.

———

Option/Alt-click a brush preview to delete the brush.

Brushes are not limited to options such as diameter and softness, but include a multitude of possibilities. A painting tool (Brush, Pencil, History Brush, Stamp, and so on) must be selected for the options in this palette to be active.

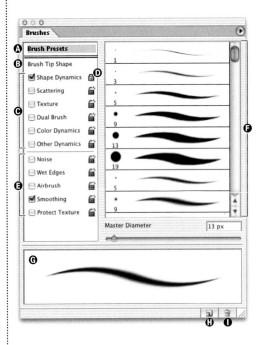

Ⓐ Brush Presets Click to view and choose preset brushes and master diameter in the Brush Settings area.

Ⓑ Brush Tip Shape Click to view and choose the brush tip in the Brush Settings area.

Ⓒ Brush Adjustments Check to adjust the brush shape in accordance with the brush settings. Click the title to view and choose the settings for that adjustment in the Brush Settings area.

Ⓓ Lock Adjustments Click to lock or unlock the particular brush adjustments from being changed when switching between brush presets. If clicked, selecting a new brush preset will preserve the adjustments, preventing them from being replaced by the newly selected brush adjustments.

Ⓔ Brush Options Check to use the option with the brush.

Ⓕ Brush Settings This area displays the Brush Presets, the various options for the brush tip shape, or other brush options.

Ⓖ Brush Preview Displays how the brush appears at flows from 0% to 100%.

Ⓗ Create New Brush Click to add the current brush to the Brush Presets.

Ⓘ Delete Brush Click to delete the selected Brush Preset, or drag a Brush Preset to this button to delete it.

4.5 Channels Palette

The Channels palette displays the color or alpha channels used to create the image. The channels displayed depend on the current Color mode of the image.

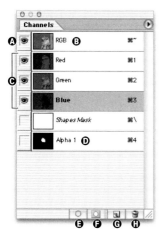

Ⓐ Toggle Visibility Click to show or hide a channel.

Ⓑ Combined Color Channels Controls the color channels.

Ⓒ Color Channels Displays colors used to generate the image. The channels displayed depend on the Color mode of the image.

Ⓓ Alpha Channel The channel used to store a selection as a grayscale image that is useful for storing and viewing layer masks.

Ⓔ Load Channel As Selection Click to convert the current channel into a selection.

Ⓕ Save Selection As Channel Click to convert the current selection in the canvas into an alpha channel.

Ⓖ Add Channel Click to create a new alpha channel.

Ⓗ Delete Channel Click to delete the selected channel.

➡ 8.7 Using Color in Channels

➡ 11.2 Adding Layer Masks

➡ 11.3 Editing Layer Masks

➡ 22.2 Adjusting Tonal Range Using Levels

➡ 22.3 Adjusting Color Levels Using Curves

➡ 22.5 Adjusting Color Balance

Select composite channel

⌘ [~]

[Ctrl] [~]

Select individual color channel

⌘ [1] – [9]
[Ctrl] [1] – [9]

Select layers mask (if one exists)

⌘ [/]
[Ctrl] [/]

———

The Channels palette menu lets you add or delete a variety of channel types.

———

If you need to see more detail in the channel's thumbnail, use the options in the Channels palette to set the size to None, Small, Medium, or Large.

———

To add a spot color channel rather than an alpha channel, Command/Ctrl-click the Add Channel button.

REAL WORLD: JIM YI

Jim Yi's ideas start life as simple pen sketches, his conceptual work being done with just plain ol' ink and paper. He then scans the drawings in at 360 dpi to 600 dpi. "I usually just save files at extremely high dpi and work with the file in CMYK if it's destined for print or RGB if it's meant for the Web. I generally don't give much conscious thought to the midtones, dark, and light; I don't go by histogram... mainly by eye."

But Photoshop is more than just a way to output his images. "I ran different photographs of buildings through a combo of Photoshop's filters like diffuse glow and blurs." He acknowledges that filters often get a bad rap from some Photoshop users, but feels that "filters, whether in-house or third-party, are exceptional shortcuts, and numerous unique effects can be achieved by combining filters."

You can find more of Jim's work at www.skatemafia.com.

4.6   Character Palette

➡ 17.1 Type Basics

➡ 17.3 Formatting
         Characters

Cancel text changes
`Esc`

Commit text changes
`Enter`

The Character palette menu lets you select many of the style character options, including Faux Bold and Faux Italic.

Select a text layer using the Layers palette to make changes that affect all text on the entire layer.

Although the Type tool offers many of the most important options in the tool options bar when it is selected, use the Character palette for more exacting control of the shape and position of characters. Text must be selected for these options to be available.

Ⓐ Font Family Click to choose a font to use for selected text or text to be typed. You can also enter a font name directly in the field. Photoshop tries to match what you type to the closest font in the list.

Ⓑ Font Style Click to choose an available style for this font—generally regular (default), bold, italic, and bold italic although the exact styles vary from font to font. You can also enter a style name directly in the field. Photoshop tries to match what you type to the closest style in the list.

Ⓒ Font Size Click to choose a size for the font in points. You can also enter a numeric value directly into the field (between 0.10 points and 1296 points).

Ⓓ Leading Click to choose the space between lines of text in a paragraph in points. Select Auto if you want Photoshop to determine the optimum leading. You can also enter a numeric value directly into the field (between 0 points and 5000 points).

Ⓔ Kerning Click to choose the space between specific letter pairs in the text of a paragraph. Select Metrics to use the font's built-in kerning. You can also enter a numeric value directly into the field (between –1000 and 1000).

Ⓕ Tracking Click to choose the spacing between selected characters. You can also enter a numeric value directly into the field (between –1000 and 1000).

Ⓖ Vertical Scale Enter a percentage (between 0% and 1000%) to set the height of the letters from their standard height.

Ⓗ Horizontal Scale Enter a percentage (between 0% and 1000%) to set the width of the letters from their standard width.

Ⓘ Baseline Shift Enter a point size (between –1296 and 1296) to shift the selected letter or letters up or down from their natural position, which is especially useful for mathematical notations.

Ⓙ Font Color Click to choose a color for the text.

Ⓚ Faux Styles Click to toggle selected text between Bold and/or Italic.

Ⓛ Caps Style Click to toggle selected text between All Caps or Mini-Caps.

Ⓜ Script Style Click to toggle selected text between Superscript or Subscript.

Ⓝ Line Style Click to toggle selected text between Underline and/or Overline.

Ⓞ Language Click to select the language being used.

Ⓟ Anti-Aliasing Method Click to select an anti-aliasing method to be used for the text layer: None, Sharp, Crisp, Strong, and Smooth.

4.7 Color Palette

Although the Color Picker gives finer control over the exact foreground and background colors being used, the Color palette provides instant access to color-mixing controls, allowing you to make quick changes to colors.

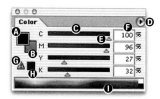

Ⓐ Foreground Color Displays the current foreground color (same as in the Toolbox). Click to select a color to make changes with the color sliders. Double-click to open the Color Picker.

Ⓑ Background Color Displays the current background color (same as in the Toolbox). Click to select a color to make changes with the color sliders. Double-click to open the Color Picker.

Ⓒ Slider Bar Displays the colors currently available to that slider. The color in the slider bar changes dynamically based on the values of the other sliders.

Ⓓ Color Mode Choose the color mode being used from the palette menu: Grayscale, RGB, HSB, CMYK, Lab, and Web.

Ⓔ Color Sliders Click and drag to change the color value.

Ⓕ Color Values Displays the color value. Click to enter the value. The possible value depends on the color mode selected.

Ⓖ Color Warning A caution symbol appears if the color is out of range for CMYK printing. A cube appears if you are working in Web mode and the color is not browser-safe.

Ⓗ Safe Color Click to change a color to a safe color if the selected color is out of range or not a browser-safe color.

Ⓘ Color Ramp Displays a spectrum of colors from which to choose. Click to select a color.

➡ 3.22 Eyedropper and Measure Tools

➡ 12.1 Color, Gradient, and Pattern Basics

➡ 12.3 Selecting Colors with the Color Palette

➡ 12.6 Organizing Color Swatch Presets

Show/Hide Color palette
F 6

You use the Color palette menu to set the Color mode for the sliders (even if it is different from the document's Color mode). Select the Color mode that is being displayed in the color ramp from the palette menu (RGB, CMYK, Grayscale, Current). You can also choose to make the palette web-safe from the palette menu or to copy the color as web-safe.

Click and drag with the Eyedropper tool in the canvas area to display the selected colors in real time in the Color palette.

UNIVERSAL TASKS

PHOTO AND VIDEO TASKS

PRINT TASKS

WEB TASKS

4.8   File Browser

Refresh File View
[F] [5]

Open
[⌘] [O]

[Ctrl] [O]

Edit In ImageReady
[Shift] [⌘] [M]
[Option] [Ctrl] [M]

Close File Browser
[⌘] [W]
[Ctrl] [W]

File Information
[Option] [⌘] [I]
[Shift] [Ctrl] [I]

Select All
[⌘] [A]
[Ctrl] [A]

Select All Flagged
[Shift] [⌘] [A]
[Option] [Ctrl] [A]

Deselct All
[⌘] [D]
[Ctrl] [D]

Flag File
[⌘] ["]
[Ctrl] ["]

**Rotate Image 90°
Clockwise**
[⌘] [ ]]
[Ctrl] [ ]]

**Rotate Image 90°
Counterclockwise**
[⌘] [[ ]
[Ctrl] [[ ]

The File Browser allows you to bypass your operating system's Finder (Mac) or Explorer (Windows) to work with files, especially image files. As its name suggests, the File Browser lets you browse through your hard drive using a common interface (regardless of your operating system) to find, preview, and manipulate image files.

You access the File Browser through the Window menu or by clicking the File Browser button always located to the immediate left of the Palette Well in the tool options bar. The File Browser is not, in fact, a floating palette and cannot be docked with other palettes or in the Palette Well. It is instead a stand-alone window with controls like other windows in your operating system.

Ⓐ File Browser Menus Click any of the menu headings to view a list of menu options specific to the File Browser. This panel also includes a list of favorite files and will display search results.

Ⓑ Folders list Click a folder or a filename to select. Click a triangle/plus to open a folder. Results are displayed in the Thumbnail area.

Ⓒ Folders menu Click to view a list of options for the Folders list.

Ⓓ Preview Click to display the selected image, file icon, or folder icon. Images are displayed as large as possible, depending on the area available.

Ⓔ Metadata Click to display and edit information about the selected image or file.

Ⓕ Keywords Click to display and edit keywords used to identify the selected image or file used when searching.

4.8 File Browser *(Continued)*

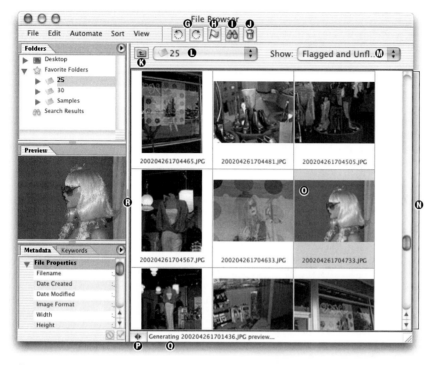

The Folders, Preview, Metadata, and Keywords tabs work much like palettes in the main Photoshop interface. You can click and drag tabs to group them together, and each has its own submenu, accessed using the triangle to the right of the menu group.

To rename a file, select its thumbnail and double-click or press Enter to select only the image name (without selecting the image's extension), type the new name, and press Enter again. With the image name selected, you can also press Tab to move to the next file-name or press Shift-Tab to move to the previous filename.

Select multiple files (Shift-select) to make changes to multiple files simultaneously.

Place the mouse pointer over a thumb-nail image to view a Tool Tip with the image's location, date and time created, and file format.

G Rotate Selected Click to rotate the thumbnail for the selected image 90° clockwise or counter-clockwise. The image itself is not rotated until Photoshop opens it.

H Flag Selected Click to place a marker with the image file. You can then use the Show controls to show only flagged images.

I Search Click to open a Search dialog to find images on your hard drive. Results are displayed in the Folders list.

J Delete Selected Click to place the selected image, file, or folder (and all its contents) in your operating system's trashcan/Recycle Bin.

K Up One Level Click to move up one folder level.

L Select Level Click to view and choose previous folder levels.

M Show Choose whether to show all images (flagged and unflagged), flagged images only, or unflagged images only.

N Thumbnails Click to select. Double-click to open (including folders). Click a name to change it. Control/right-click to access a contextual menu. The selected file or folder will show in the Preview.

O Selected Image The selected image will have a thicker border around it.

P Toggle Expanded View Click to show/hide the left column.

Q System Status Displays current operation being performed or the total number of items displayed in the Thumbnail area.

R Frame borders Click to resize the area available for the browser: Selected Image View, Selected Information View, and Thumbnail area.

UNIVERSAL TASKS
PHOTO AND VIDEO TASKS
PRINT TASKS
WEB TASKS

4.9   Histogram Palette

A *histogram* is a graph showing the number of pixels used in the image for a given color or intensity level. The histogram is used with color correction in the Levels adjustment, but you can also display a histogram of the image to check the distribution of colors throughout an image and to see if there is good tonal distribution.

The previous version of Photoshop placed the histogram into a dialog accessed through the Image menu.

Pixel is short for *picture element*.

The histogram does not allow you to make any changes to the image directly. However, you can use the Levels Adjustment dialog to make tonal changes using a version of the histogram.

Viewing the histogram of an adjustment layer reflects the data for all layers beneath it but not above.

You can also make a selection if you want to view the histogram for a specific area of the image, or you can hold down Option/Alt while choosing the Histogram menu option to include information from spot color and alpha channels.

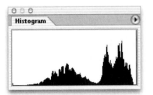

The Histogram palette in compact view shows only the histogram graph. In the palette's menu, choose Expanded View to show the histogram data, or choose All Channels View to show data and individual histograms for each color channel.

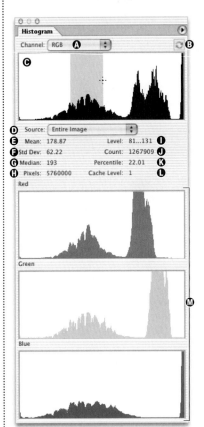

A **Channel Selection** Choose the composite or individual channels to view for the histogram.

B **Refresh Uncached** Click to refresh the histogram for parts of the image that are uncached.

C **Histogram Graph** Displays the number of pixels, or count (see I), for a given intensity level (see H), ranging from 0 on the left to 255 on the right. As you move your mouse over areas of the histogram, values for that position's intensity level are displayed below. Click and select to display values for multiple intensity levels.

D **Source** Choose what part of the image to use for the histogram.

E **Mean** Displays the average intensity value in the selected channel.

F **Standard Deviation** Displays how widely the intensity value varies in the selected channel.

G **Median** Displays the middle value in the range of intensity values.

H **Pixels** Displays the total number of pixels in the selected area or in the image.

I **Level** Displays the intensity level at the mouse cursor's position or selection in the histogram.

J **Count** Displays the number of pixels for the intensity level at the mouse cursor's position or selection in the histogram.

K **Percentile** Displays the total number of pixels at or below the current intensity level at the mouse cursor's position in the histogram as a percentage of the total pixels (see G).

L **Cache Level** Displays the setting for the image cache.

M **Color Channel Histogram Graphs** Displays the histogram for each color channel being used in the image.

4.10   History Palette

The History palette records the actions (called states in the palette) you perform while editing a document and then allows you to move backward and forward through the History State list, basically traveling backward and forward in time. In the History palette menu, you can choose between two distinct working modes that you can set in the History Palette Options dialog:

Linear mode If you move backward in the history and then perform a new action, all previous actions in the history are erased. This is the easiest mode to use since you don't have to keep track of actions you are no longer using in the image; however, all those actions are lost.

Nonlinear mode If you move backward in the history and then perform a new action, all subsequent actions are kept in the history (but ignored), and new actions are added to the bottom of the history. This mode tends to get a bit confusing, but does allow you to preserve actions and go back and perform them again later.

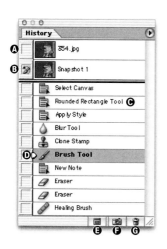

Ⓐ Snapshots Saved states for the image. Click to restore the image to its previous appearance. Click the Create Snap Shot button at the bottom of the palette to add a new snapshot based on the image's current appearance.

Ⓑ History Brush Click in this column to select a state or a snapshot to be used for the history brushes.

Ⓒ History state Every action performed in the canvas is recorded as a History state in this list. Click any state to revert to that point in the image.

Ⓓ Current State Actions prior to this state are displayed in the canvas. Actions after this state are available, but not currently showing in the image.

Ⓔ New Document Click to create a new document from the current History state.

Ⓕ Create Snapshot Click to create a new snapshot from the current History state.

Ⓖ Delete State Click to delete the current History state or drag a state to the button to delete it.

➡ 7.7   Changing Your Mind

➡ 13.7   Painting with History Brushes

Undo/redo last action
⌘ Z
Ctrl Z

Step forward
Shift ⌘ Z
Shift Ctrl Z

Step backward
Option ⌘ Z
Alt Ctrl Z

The History palette menu lets you step forward or backward in the history, create a new snapshot, delete the selected History state, or clear the entire history.

The History palette options let you specify whether a first snapshot is created as soon as the image is started or opened, whether a snapshot is created whenever the image is saved, whether you are using linear or nonlinear history, and whether the New Snapshot dialog opens whenever a snapshot is made.

To duplicate a History state, Option/Alt-click the History state.

Specify the number of History states in the General Preferences panel The default is 20, but adding more states requires more memory and could slow your system.

75

4.11   Info Palette

Info palette options
allow you to set the
First Color Mode,
Second Color Mode,
and Ruler Units.

The Info palette displays information about the color and location of the current pixel that the cursor is over as well as the dimensions of any selections, crops, or slices in the canvas. The palette also displays as many as four color values while you are using the Color Sampler tool.

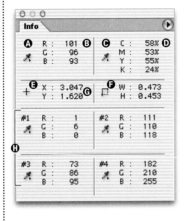

A **First Color Mode** Click to select the color value displayed: Actual, Proof, Grayscale, RGB, Web, HSB, CMYK, Lab, Total Ink, Opacity.

B **First Color Readout** Displays the color values (as selected) for the pixel the cursor is currently over in the image.

C **Second Color Mode** Click to select the color value displayed: Actual, Proof, Grayscale, RGB, Web, HSB, CMYK, Lab, Total Ink, Opacity.

D **Second Color Readout** Displays the color values (as selected) for the pixel the cursor is currently over in the image.

E **Ruler Units** Click to select the units used (pixels, inches, centimeters, millimeters, points, picas, percentages) for the cursor position and selection size.

F **Cursor Position** Displays the X, Y coordinates of the pixels the cursor is currently over in the selected units.

G **Selection Size** Displays the width and height of the currently selected area in the document.

H **Color Sample Values** A maximum of four values can be displayed when using the Color Sampler tool.

4.12   Layer Comps Palette

Layer comps are a new feature in Photoshop CS that let you save multiple iterations of a design called compositions or, more commonly, just comps. Each comp is a variation of the design, either to show different aspects of a design (for example, different pages within a website) or different versions of a design project (for example, multiple versions of a logo to show a client for consideration). Photoshop layer comps allow you to record the visibility, position, and appearance (layer style) for layers in your image and then move between these different versions.

➠ 10.12   Storing Versions with Layer Comps

Layer comps differ from taking snapshots using the History palette because layer comps are saved with the document, whereas snapshots are lost as soon as the image is closed.

If a layer being used in a layer comp is deleted, the layer comp will not be able to fully display, as indicated by a caution icon next to the layer comp.

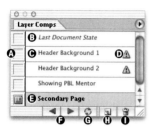

A **Display Comp** Click to display a comp.

B **Last Document State** Click to revert to the last document state before layer comps were applied.

C **Comp name** Double-click to type a new name for the layer comp.

D **Layer Comp Warning** Indicates that the layer comp cannot be fully applied, usually because a layer has been deleted.

E **Currently Displayed Comp** Icon indicates the layer comp currently applied to the canvas.

F **Browse Comps** Click to view the previous or next layer comp in the list.

G **Update Layer Comp** Click to update the currently selected layer comp based on the image's current layout.

H **New Layer Comp** Click to create a new layer comp based on the current layout.

I **Delete Layer Comp** Click to delete the currently selected layer comp.

4.13   Layers Palette

New layer
Shift ⌘ Option N

Shift Ctrl Alt N

Duplicate layer
⌘ Option ↑ ↓ ← →

Ctrl Alt ↑ ↓ ← →

New layer from copied source
⌘ J
Ctrl J

New layer from cut source
Shift ⌘ J
Option Ctrl J

Merge Down/Merge Linked/Merge Group
⌘ E
Ctrl E

Merge Visible
Shift ⌘ E
Shift Ctrl E

Jump to layer above selected layer
Option [ ]
Alt [ ]

Jump to layer below selected layer
Option [ ]
Alt [ ]

Jump to bottom layer
Shift Option [ ]
Shift Alt [ ]

Jump to top layer
Shift Option [ ]
Shift Alt [ ]

You view the composited image in the document window, but the image is composed of one or more layers that you can view as thumbnails in the Layers palette. Layers allow you to independently add objects that can be edited. Each layer can have a separate blending mode, opacity, and fill opacity as well as be moved, shown/hidden, added, and deleted without affecting other layers in the image. You always edit on the *current* layer, which is highlighted and has the Paintbrush icon next to it.

There are four distinct kinds of layers:

Standard   Bitmap image objects that can be edited using most tools.

Text   Vector text that is edited using the text tool.

Adjustment   Adds an adjustment effect to all layers beneath it.

Fill   Adds a color fill to all layers beneath it.

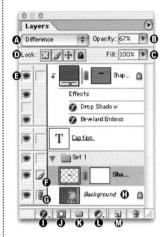

Ⓐ Blending Mode   Click to choose a blending mode for the layer.

Ⓑ Opacity   Click to enter or use the sliders to set the layer's master opacity.

Ⓒ Fill Opacity   Click to enter or use a slider to set the opacity of the layer without affecting the opacity of layer effects.

Ⓓ Locks   Click to lock transparent pixels, image pixels, layer position, or all three in a layer or layer set

Ⓔ Toggle Visibility   Click to show or hide a layer.

Ⓕ Active Layer   Click a layer name to select that layer. The Paintbrush icon is displayed to the left, indicating that the layer is active and ready to be edited. Double-click the layer's title to change it.

Ⓖ Linked Layer   Click to link the layer to the selected layer.

Ⓗ Background Layer   If included, you cannot erase or move the bottom layer.

Ⓘ Add Effect   Click to select a style to add as an effect to the layer.

Ⓙ Add Mask   Click to add a layer mask or a vector mask, depending on the layer type.

Ⓚ New Layer Set   Click to create a new empty layer set.

Ⓛ Add Fill Or Adjustment Layer   Click to select a fill or adjustment layer type to add as a new layer above the currently selected layer.

Ⓜ New Layer   Click to add a new layer immediately above the currently selected layer.

4.13 Layers Palette *(Continued)*

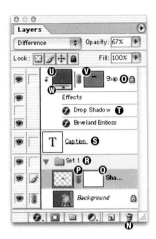

N Delete Layer Click to delete the selected layer, or drag a layer to this button to delete the layer.

O Locked Layer Indicates that the layer has one of the four lock types set.

P Linked Mask Indicates that the mask is linked to the layer.

Q Layer Mask Painting in the layer mask allows you to vary the transparency (rather than the color) of the layer.

R Layer Set A collection of layers that can all be moved, hidden/shown, and deleted as one or worked with individually. Layers in the set are indented underneath.

S Type Layer Indicates that the layer contains text.

T Effects Style applied to the layer. Double-click to change the style.

U Fill Layer Layer filled with a solid color. Click to choose a different color.

V Vector Mask Holds vector elements applied to a fill layer.

W Clipping Layer Indicates that this layer is grouped with the next to create a clipping group.

➡ 10 Layering Images

➡ 11 Masking Layers

➡ 15 Adding Layer Styles

The Layers palette menu lets you add, duplicate, delete, and merge layers as well as open the Effects dialog.

If you need to see more detail in the layer's thumbnail, use the options in the Layers palette to set the size to None, Small, Medium, or Large.

You can edit text layers only with the Type tool.

You can rasterize text layers to turn the text into a bitmap, but then you can no longer edit the text with the Type tool.

UNIVERSAL TASKS

PHOTO AND VIDEO TASKS

PRINT TASKS

WEB TASKS

TURNING: © MAGGIE TAYLOR; WWW.MAGGIETAYLOR.COM

4.14   Navigator Palette

➡ 7.1   Canvas Basics

The Navigator palette options let you control the color of the viewable area's border.

A magnification of 100% displays the image as it will appear on a computer screen.

Double-click the Zoom tool to return directly to 100%.

The Navigator palette works as a remote control for viewing the canvas in the document window. This palette provides a thumbnail view of the entire canvas regardless of magnification, showing you the current viewable area in the canvas as a red rectangle and allowing you to quickly change the location and magnification of the viewable area.

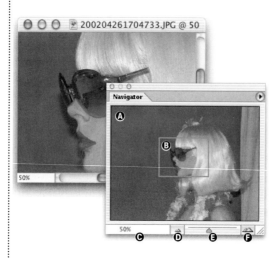

Ⓐ Proxy Preview Area Displays the entire image reduced to fit in the available area of palette.

Ⓑ Viewable Area This box shows the current area displayed in the canvas. Click and drag to change the area shown in the canvas.

Ⓒ Current Magnification Displays the current magnification as a percentage. Click to enter a new magnification for the document directly (0.26% through 1600%).

Ⓓ Zoom Out Click to reduce the document's magnification.

Ⓔ Magnification Slider Click and drag the slider or click the slider line to change the document's magnification.

Ⓕ Zoom In Click to increase the document's magnification.

4.15 Paragraph Palette

You use the Paragraph palette to change the alignment and margins of a single paragraph or an entire text layer.

➠ 17.4 Formatting Paragraphs

Ⓐ Align Text Click to select text alignment (left, center, or right), justified text alignment (left, center, or right), or full justified.

Ⓑ Left Indent Enter a value to set the left margin for the text layer (between 0 points and 1296 points).

Ⓒ Right Indent Enter a value to set the right margin for the text layer (between 0 points and 1296 points).

Ⓓ First-Line Indent Enter a value to set the indention of the first line for the text layer (between −1296 points and 1296 points).

Ⓔ Space Before Paragraph Enter a value to set the top margin for the text layer (between −1296 points and 1296 points).

Ⓕ Space After Paragraph Enter a value to set the bottom margin for the text layer (between −1296 points and 1296 points).

Ⓖ Hyphenate If checked, text in the layer is hyphenated rather than allowing for broken lines.

Cancel text changes
`Esc`

Commit text changes
`Enter`

───

Select a text layer to make changes to the entire layer.

UNIVERSAL TASKS

PHOTO AND VIDEO TASKS

PRINT TASKS

WEB TASKS

STARTRAIN © MICHELLE KWAJAFA; SOULSABYSS.NET

4.16 Paths Palette

The Paths palette menu lets you start, duplicate, and delete paths as well as make the selected path a selection in the canvas, fill or stroke the path, or turn the path into a work or a clipping path.

If you need to see more detail in the channel's thumbnail, use the Channels palette options to set the size to None, Small, Medium, or Large.

The Paths palette records the vector outlines made up of curved and straight line segments using anchor points to determine curvature. You create paths using the pen tools or the shape tools and then manipulate them using the path selection tools.

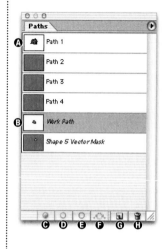

Ⓐ Path Click to select the path.

Ⓑ Work Path A temporary path used to define the path. Double-click it to turn it into a path.

Ⓒ Fill Path Click to fill the selected path with a foreground color.

Ⓓ Stroke Path Click to create a line around the path based on the current brush style.

Ⓔ Turn Path Into Selection Click to load the path into the current layer as a selection.

Ⓕ Turn Selection Into Work Path Click to convert the current selection into a new path.

Ⓖ Add New Path Click to create a new path.

Ⓗ Delete Path Click to delete the selected path.

4.17 Styles Palette

The Styles palette stores collections of effects and blending options as style presets to be applied to a selected layer or a selection in the layer with a single click of the style thumbnail.

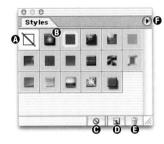

ⓐ Default Style Click to apply the default style that removes other styles (the same as Clear Style).

ⓑ Style Preset Thumbnail Click to apply this style to the selected layer.

ⓒ Clear Style Click to clear all effects and blending options from the selected layer.

ⓓ New Style Click to add the effects and/or blending options of the current layer as a new style to the palette.

ⓔ Delete Style Click and drag a style to this button to delete the style.

ⓕ Style Presets Choose from an extensive list of preset styles to load into the palette.

➡ 5.1 Preset Manager Overview

➡ 15.4 Creating and Applying Style Presets

➡ 15.5 Organizing Style Presets

Use the Styles palette menu to select the size the styles are displayed at as well as to load or save various style groups in the palette.

Just as with color swatches, you can click in the empty area of the Styles palette to add the styles of the currently selected layer as a style preset.

REAL WORLD: SARAH BENISTON

Sarah Beniston likes to collect clippings from magazines and newspapers and then use them to create her own heavily textured illustrations. "The textures I create by scanning various objects/materials to create a rough/odd look. For example, I scan in a picture of marble to create the texture of skin. It depends on the feel of the illustration I am creating."

Commenting on her work, she notes: "I like to keep it simple, both in technique and style. I don't like symmetry or anything that looks perfect. There is always an aspect of my illustrations that has an unfinished/imperfect look because I like to draw quickly, which gives my style an angle."

Her illustrations begin life in Adobe Illustrator, whether they are line or the "finished" product. "To give a 3D look, I create textures in Photoshop, which I then import into Illustrator and make a mask within a boundary."

You can find more of Sarah's work at http://smbeniston.4t.com/.

UNIVERSAL TASKS

PHOTO AND VIDEO TASKS

PRINT TASKS

WEB TASKS

4.18 Swatches Palette

The Swatches palette stores color chips (swatches) for easy access. You can add and save swatches, or you can choose pre-generated swatches for your specific needs from the extensive list in the palette's menu.

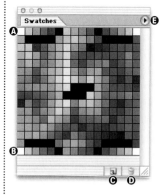

Ⓐ Color Swatch Click a color to select it. Option-click to remove a color from the palette. Hold the mouse over a color to view color information in a Tool Tip.

Ⓑ Empty Swatch Click anywhere in this area to add the current foreground color to the palette as a new swatch.

Ⓒ New Swatch Click to add the current foreground color to the palette.

Ⓓ Delete Swatch Click and drag a swatch to this button to delete the swatch.

Ⓔ Color Swatches Presets Select the colors displayed from the extensive list of color swatch palettes to load into the palette.

You use the Swatches palette menu to select the size the swatches are displayed at as well as to load or save various swatch color palette configurations.

The Swatches palette is a good candidate to place in the Palette Well.

SIGHTS © MICHELLE KWAJAFA; WWW.SOULSABYSS.NET

4.19 Tool Presets Palette

The Tool Presets palette is a list of tools with options already set. Although this palette closely mimics the Toolbox, it has a distinct advantage. The Tool Presets palette allows you to save tools with options preset for specific purposes and then use this palette (or the Tool Presets menu in the tool options bar) to reload the tool with the exact same options set. So, rather than having to make notes on how you got a particular effect out of a particular tool and then reset the options, every time you need it, simply save the tool and then choose it from this palette.

➠ 3.1 The Toolbox

➠ 5.1 Preset
        Manager
        Overview

The Tool Presets palette menu gives you options to create and edit tool presets using the Preset Manager as well as the ability to selectively show and sort tools and load various tool presets.

Ⓐ Presets Click to choose a tool with preset options.

Ⓑ Current Tool If checked, only versions of the currently selected tool in the Toolbox are displayed in the list.

Ⓒ Create Tool Preset Click to add the current tool and options as a tool preset.

Ⓓ Delete Tool Preset Click to delete the currently selected tool preset.

CHAPTER 5

Presets and Preferences

PHOTOSHOP IS A POWERFUL, complex, yet elegant piece of software. Much of the complexity stems from the wide range of tasks this single application is called on to perform by its legion of users, but the elegance flows from its versatility in the face of the myriad demands. You can customize Photoshop in many, many ways to suit your individual needs.

In this chapter, you will learn the basic uses for the Preset Manager and the many preferences that you can set:

- 5.1 **Preset Manager overview**
- 5.2 **Setting keyboard shortcuts**
- 5.3 **Setting Photoshop preferences**
- 5.4 **General preferences**
- 5.5 **File Handling preferences**
- 5.6 **Display & Cursors preferences**
- 5.7 **Transparency & Gamut preferences**
- 5.8 **Units & Rulers preferences**
- 5.9 **Guides, Grid & Slices preferences**
- 5.10 **Plug-Ins & Scratch Disks preferences**
- 5.11 **Memory & Image Cache preferences**
- 5.12 **File Browser preferences**

5.1 Preset Manager Overview

You use the Preset Manager to specify the options that appear in the various preset drop-down menus and palettes available throughout Photoshop. Dealing with the almost infinite number of possibilities available through the program often means limiting the number of choices that you can view at any given moment so that you can see only the options relevant to your current work. To allow this, Photoshop presents you with several lists (pickers) of preset common options such as brushes, color swatches, gradients, styles, patterns, contours, custom shapes, and tools. Although each of these pickers displays different items, they all have similar options, allowing the Preset Manager to deal with them similarly.

To open the Preset Manager dialog, choose Edit > Preset Manager…

Brush presets (while in Preset Manager)
⌘ 1
Ctrl 1

Swatches presets (while in Preset Manager)
⌘ 2
Ctrl 2

Gradients presets (while in Preset Manager)
⌘ 3
Ctrl 3

Styles presets (while in Preset Manager)
⌘ 4
Ctrl 4

Patterns presets (while in Preset Manager)
⌘ 5
Ctrl 5

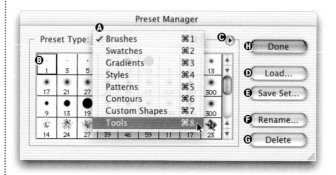

Ⓐ Preset Type Choose from a list to move instantly between preset panels.

Ⓑ Preset A single preset in the list of presets. Click to select. Double-click to rename. Control/right-click to view a contextual menu that contains options to create a new preset, delete this preset, or rename this preset. Shift-click to select multiple presets.

Ⓒ Preset Menu Choose from a list of viewing options, replace or reset the presets, and choose options to load particular preset lists instantly for this preset type.

Ⓓ Click Load…, locate a preset file for the current type, and click Load to append the selected list to the current list.

Ⓔ Select one or more presets, click Save Set…, enter a filename, making sure to preserve the preset's extension, browse to the location where you want to save the preset, and click Save.

Ⓕ Select one or more presets, click Rename…, type a new name for the preset, and click OK. If you select more than one preset, each is displayed in a separate Rename dialog.

Ⓖ Select one or more preset, and then click Delete to remove the preset from the list. You cannot undo this deletion, so be careful.

Ⓗ Click Done when you are ready to return to Photoshop.

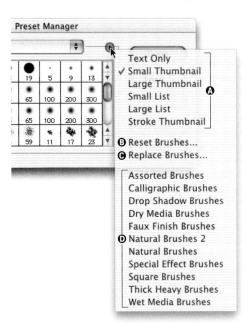

Ⓐ Choose the thumbnail size of the presets.

Ⓑ Choose Reset... and click Append to add the default library to the current list, or click OK to replace the current list.

Ⓒ Choose Replace..., locate a preset file for the current type, and click Load to replace the current list with the selected list.

Ⓓ Choose a preset library name from the bottom of the menu, and then click Append to add the library to the current list, or click OK to replace the current list.

Contours presets (while in Preset Manager)
⌘ 6
Ctrl 6

Custom Shapes presets (while in Preset Manager)
⌘ 7
Ctrl 7

Tool presets (while in Preset Manager)
⌘ 8
Ctrl 8

———

The options for individual Preset Managers are explained in relevant sections throughout this book.

———

You can share preset library files between copies of Photoshop by transferring the file.

———

Each preset library has its own file extension and default folder in the Adobe Photoshop CS/Presets folder.

SETTING PREFERENCES BEFORE YOU BEGIN

If you have plug-ins that are not currently in a recognized plug-ins folder, you can add their folder before Photoshop starts up, allowing you to avoid having to set the folder in the preferences and then having to restart Photoshop for the changes to take effect. Hold down Option-Command/Alt-Ctrl while starting Photoshop to set the location of additional plug-ins. After setting the folder, continue to hold down Option-Command/Alt-Ctrl to set the scratch disks to be used.

5.2 Setting Keyboard Shortcuts

**Open Keyboard
Shortcut dialog**
Shift Option ⌘ K
Shift Alt Ctrl K

Keep in mind that if
you make changes to
the keyboard shortcuts
and override existing
shortcuts, the shortcuts
in this book may not be
accurate.

You can delete extra
shortcuts using the
Delete key without
deleting all the short-
cuts for an option.

Keyboard shortcuts allow you to quickly access software commands, bypassing the often
cumbersome drop-down menus. However, not all commands have keyboard shortcuts,
and often the shortcuts you grow accustomed to are nonexistent or, worse, completely
different in another application. Photoshop CS introduces the ability to customize keyboard shortcuts. To access the Keyboard Shortcut dialog to make changes, choose
Edit > Keyboard Shortcuts...

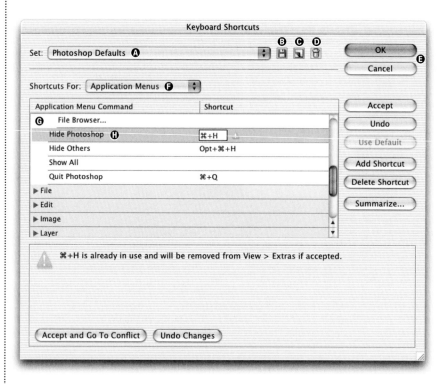

Ⓐ Choose the keyboard shortcut set you want to use. This list will include all saved shortcut sets
in the Adobe Photoshop CS/Presets/Keyboard Shortcuts folder.

Ⓑ Click to save the changes made to the current keyboard shortcut set.

Ⓒ Click to create a new keyboard shortcut set based on the current settings.

Ⓓ Click to delete the currently selected keyboard shortcut set.

Ⓔ Click to accept (OK) or reject (Cancel) the changes. Both buttons close the Keyboard Shortcuts
dialog.

Ⓕ Choose whether to set keyboard shortcuts for application menus, palette menus, or tools. This
will change the list below.

Ⓖ Displays the keyboard shortcuts. Click an option to change its keyboard shortcut.

Ⓗ The selected shortcut option with a new shortcut entered.

5.2   Setting Keyboard Shortcuts *(Continued)*

Keyboard Shortcuts

Set: **Photoshop Defaults**

OK

Cancel

Shortcuts For: **Application Menus**

Application Menu Command	Shortcut
File Browser...	
Hide Photoshop	⌘+H **❶**
Hide Others	Opt+⌘+H
Show All	
Quit Photoshop	⌘+Q
▶ File	
▶ Edit	
▶ Image	
▶ Layer	

Accept **❶**

Undo **Ⓜ**

Use Default **Ⓝ**

Add Shortcut **Ⓞ**

Delete Shortcut **Ⓟ**

Summarize... **Ⓠ**

⚠ ⌘+H is already in use and will be removed from View > Extras if accepted.

❶ Accept and Go To Conflict   **Ⓚ** Undo Changes

It is useful to create and print a web page summary of the keyboard shortcuts as a reference.

Mac users who have gotten used to the standard Command+H keyboard shortcut may notice that Photoshop uses the slightly more difficult-to-press Control+Command+H. This is an obvious choice for changing the keyboard shortcut.

Keyboard shortcut files use the .kys extension.

❶ Indicates that this shortcut is already being used by another option.

❶ Click to accept the change as is (despite the repetition) and immediately view the redundant shortcut to change it.

Ⓚ Click to undo the change, leaving both the change option and the redundant option unchanged.

❶ Click to accept changes made while editing the selected option. This will *not* close the Keyboard Shortcuts dialog.

Ⓜ Click to reject changes made while editing a keyboard shortcut.

Ⓝ Click to use the Photoshop default keyboard shortcut for the selected option.

Ⓞ Click to add an additional keyboard shortcut for the selected option.

Ⓟ Click to delete the keyboard shortcut for the selected option.

Ⓠ Click to create a web page (.htm) showing tables of the current shortcuts.

5.3 Setting Photoshop Preferences

➡ 3.2 The Tool
    Options Bar

**General Preferences
dialog**
⌘ K
Ctrl K

**To delete preferences,
hold down while
starting Photoshop:**
Option Ctrl ⌘
Alt Ctrl Ctrl

**General preferences
(while in Preferences
dialog)**
⌘ 1
Ctrl 1

**File Handling prefer-
ences (while in
Preferences dialog)**
⌘ 2
Ctrl 2

**Display & Cursors
preferences (while in
Preferences dialog)**
⌘ 3
Ctrl 3

**Transparency &
Gamut preferences
(while in Preferences
dialog)**
⌘ 4
Ctrl 4

**Units & Rulers
preferences (while in
Preferences dialog)**
⌘ 5
Ctrl 5

**Guides, Grid & Slices
preferences (while in
Preferences dialog)**
⌘ 6
Ctrl 6

**Plug-Ins & Scratch
Disks preferences
(while in Preferences
dialog)**
⌘ 7
Ctrl 7

**Memory & Image
Cache preferences
(while in Preferences
dialog)**
⌘ 8
Ctrl 8

Before you begin using Photoshop, you will want to customize options for the various features and tools. Except for color settings, which are handled separately, all preference settings are in the same dialog on different panels that you can choose. But you can access each separately from the Preferences submenu in either the Photoshop (OS X) or Edit (Windows) menu. Each panel in the Preferences dialog contains a few or a few dozen options to set preferences pertaining to a specific aspect of Photoshop. These options are presented as a variety of drop-downs, input fields, color selectors, selection boxes, and check boxes.

In addition, each panel contains buttons to navigate between the other panels and to accept or cancel the changes.

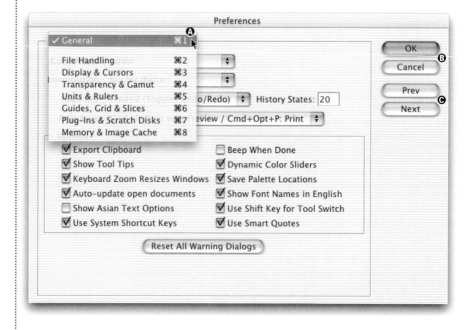

Ⓐ Choose from a list to move instantly between preferences panels, or use the numeric shortcuts (Mac, press Command-1 through 8; Windows, press Ctrl-1 through 8).

Ⓑ Click to accept or reject the changes. Both buttons close the Preferences dialog.

Ⓒ Click to go to the previous or next Preferences panel.

5.4 General Preferences

The General Preferences panel provides a catch-all screen to define several common interface options that do not readily fit into the other categories.

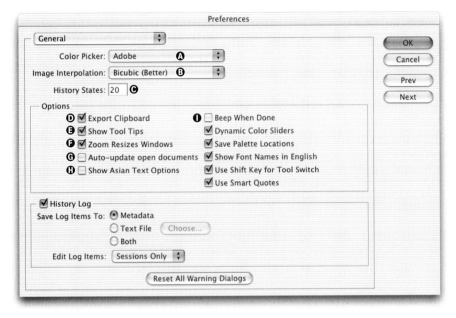

→ 4.7 Color Palette

→ 4.10 History Palette

→ 7.7 Changing Your Mind

→ 7.9 Printing to a Desktop Printer

→ 9.11 Transforming Layer Content

→ 9.12 Moving Selected Content

→ 9.13 Copying or Cutting Selected Content

A Choose whether you want to use Adobe's Color Picker or your operating system's Color Picker.

B Choose the default method by which an image's pixels are resized (interpolated) as a result of resampling or transforming. Bilinear is a medium-quality method. Bicubic is slow but produces higher-quality results. Bicubic Smoother is recommended for enlarging images, and Bicubic Sharp is recommended when reducing image size in order to maintain a high level of detail.

C Enter the maximum number of History states that will be available in the History palette. After this number is exceeded, older History states are removed. A higher number will require more system memory.

D Check if you want the contents of the Clipboard exported to the system Clipboard when switching between applications. This is needed if you want to paste images from Photoshop into other applications.

E Check to display pop-up Tool Tips in the interface.

F Check if you want the document window to resize when you zoom using keyboard shortcuts.

G Check if you want open documents automatically saved when you jump between Photoshop and other applications.

H Check if you want to display Chinese, Japanese, and Korean options in the Character and Paragraph palettes.

I Check if you want Photoshop to "beep" after each command is completed. This is useful if you are performing an action that takes a while to finish, such as applying complex filters.

**Preferences dialog
(Open in General)**
⌘ K
Ctrl K

———

History states require
memory to store and
can quickly become a
memory hog.

Adobe's Color Picker is
more versatile, but you
might already be famil-
iar with your operating
system's Color Picker.

———

If you record the history
log as a part of the files
metadata (information
actually stored in the
image that does not
affect how it appears),
but then need to export
it to a text file, click the
Choose... button next
to the Txt File option to
save all current history
log information with
the text file.

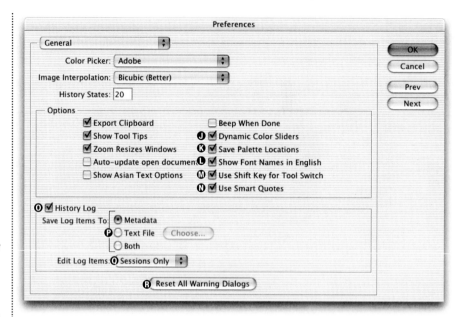

J Check if you want color sliders to display colors in real time, changing as the slider moves.

K Check if you want the palette location saved after you quit and then restored the next time you
open Photoshop. If this option is unchecked, palettes will revert to their default location whenever Photoshop starts.

L Check if you want to display nonroman fonts using their roman names. If this check box is
unchecked, some font names may be illegible.

M Check if you want to require that the Shift key be pressed when you switch between tools in a
group. If this check box is unchecked, pressing the tool's shortcut key switches tools in the
group.

N Check to substitute curly quotes for straight quotes while typing.

O Check to record a textual history of all actions performed on an image. This is useful if you need
to maintain a record of exactly what has been done to the file in Photoshop for your records,
for your client records, or for legal purposes.

P Choose how the history log should be recorded: embedded as metadata in the image file, as a
separate text file, or both. If you choose a text file, you will need to specify the text file's name
and location by clicking the Choose... button.

Q Choose how the history log is recorded: Sessions Only records when the file is opened and
closed; Concise records session data and the text that appears in the History palette; Verbose
includes the Sessions Only and Concise information as well as text that appears on the Actions
palette.

R Click this button to restore all warning dialogs. Most warning dialogs in Photoshop include an
option that prevents them from displaying a second time.

5.5   File Handling Preferences

You use File Handling preferences to specify default information about how an image file should be treated when being saved using the File > Save As… menu option or when being opened as part of a workgroup.

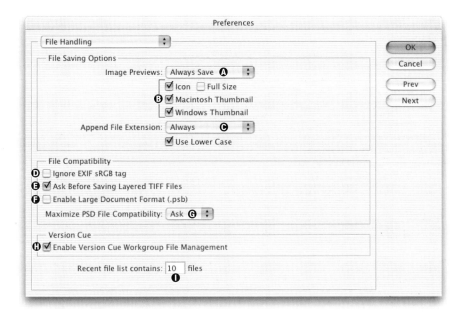

➡ 6.10 Saving
        Images

➡ 18.8 Checking
        Documents
        In and Out

File Handling preferences (while in Preferences dialog)

⌘ 2

Ctrl 2

———

The more preview types you include, the larger the file size.

A Choose when a preview should be saved.

B (Mac only) Check the preview types to be included: Icon (a thumbnail image on the desktop), Full Size (low-resolution PICT used by some applications when importing non-EPS files), Macintosh Thumbnail, or Windows Thumbnail (used by the Open dialogs in those operating systems).

C On the Mac, choose *when* the file extension should be added to the filename, and then check the box if it should be lowercase. In Windows, simply choose whether the extension should be upper or lowercase.

D Check to ignore EXIF sRGB metadata saved in the file about the image's color space.

E Check to display the TIFF Options dialog when saving a TIFF to which layers have been added.

F Check to allow a document of more than 2 GB to be saved in the Large Document Format. This format is not backward compatible with versions of Photoshop before Photoshop CS and will not open in other applications that have not been updated to support this format.

G Choose whether Photoshop should include a flattened composite version of the image with PSD files; the options are Never, Always, and Ask. Doing so increases the file size but provides better compatibility with other applications and future versions of Photoshop.

H Check to turn on Version Cue workgroup functionality. If this option is unchecked, the Version menu options will not be available and will be grayed out in the File menu.

I Enter the number of files to displayed in the File > Open Recent menu option.

5.6 Display & Cursors Preferences

Display & Cursors preferences (while in Preferences dialog)
⌘ 3
Ctrl 3

Cycle cursor style: Standard to Precise Precise to Brush Size Brush Size to Precise
Caps Lock

While you are learning Photoshop, the standard icons (the literal representation of a tool, such as a paintbrush for the Brush tool) help you remember which tool you are currently working with. However, as you become more accustomed to Photoshop, you may find that these cursor icons become more of a distraction than a help. It is often difficult to tell *exactly* where the tool is affecting or over what area. The Display & Cursors preferences give you additional options for cursor display as well as monitor display.

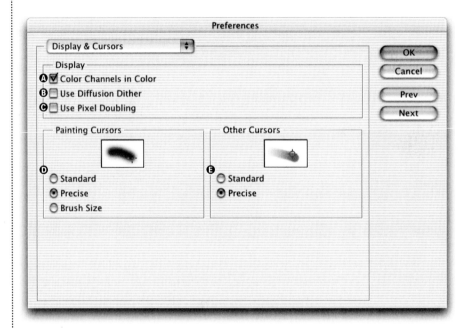

Ⓐ Check to display color channels in color rather than grayscale.

Ⓑ Check to use diffusion dithering for colors that cannot be displayed.

Ⓒ Check to reduce the resolution of objects while they are being moved, which speeds up rendering time. This will temporarily degrade the image, but the change is not permanent.

Ⓓ Choose how to display painting cursors: Standard (tool's icon), Precise (crosshair), or Brush Size (circle indicating the diameter of the brush).

Ⓔ Choose how to display other cursors: Standard (tool's icon) or Precise (crosshair).

 The Standard cursor uses the tool's icon.

 A Precise cursor uses a crosshair with the center point marked.

 A Brush Size cursor shows a circle that is the diameter of the brush being used.

5.7 Transparency & Gamut Preferences

Transparent areas in an image are areas where there are no image pixels or a Background layer. Photoshop represents transparent areas using a checkerboard grid. You can change this pattern to suit your own tastes.

Gamut settings are used when working in RGB or Lab color mode to warn you when particular colors will not print in CMYK.

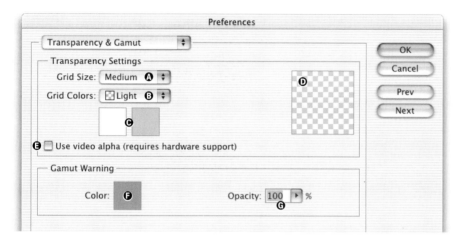

Ⓐ Choose the relative size of the transparency grid.

Ⓑ Choose a color combination for the transparency grid.

Ⓒ Displays the current color combination for the transparency grid. Click to choose other colors for the transparency grid using the Color Picker.

Ⓓ Displays how the transparency grid appears.

Ⓔ Check if you are using a 32-bit video card with chromakeying while editing video to enable alpha channel transparency in the video unless you are editing digital video over FireWire.

Ⓕ Click to choose the color for highlighting colors in the image that are out of the specified color mode's gamut.

Ⓖ Click to enter or select the opacity of the out-of-gamut highlight color.

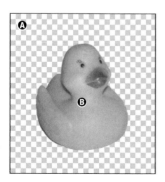

Ⓐ Transparency

Ⓑ Image pixels

➠ 7.5 Using Rulers, Guides, Grids, and Snap

➠ 10.1 Layer Basics

➠ 12.1 Color, Gradient, and Pattern Basics

➠ 12.4 Selecting Colors with the Color Picker

Transparency & Gamut preferences (while in Preferences dialog)
⌘ 4
Ctrl 4

———

Choose View > Gamut Warning to view highlight colors that are out of the gamut range while in RGB or Lab color modes.

5.8 Units & Rulers Preferences

➡ 4.11 Info Palette

➡ 6.1 Image Basics

➡ 17.1 Type Basics

The units used to measure your work depend on your location (whether you use metric or imperial units) and your output medium (screen or print). You can set the default units to use in new documents (which you can easily change while you are working), as well as the resolution of new documents and a few print-specific options.

Units & Rulers preferences (while in Preferences dialog)

⌘ 5

Ctrl 5

———

Double-click a ruler in the document window to open the Units & Rulers preferences panel.

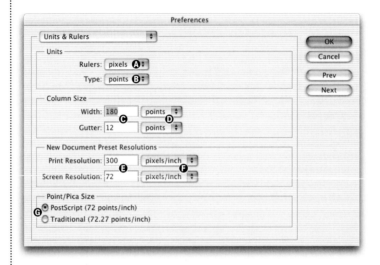

Ⓐ Choose the default measurement unit used in documents.

Ⓑ Choose the default unit used for type (generally points).

Ⓒ Enter the column size and the gutter size, which allows you to define the width of the document in terms of column width. These settings are useful when you import images into a page layout program with set widths for columns and gutters.

Ⓓ Select the units used to measure column size. This is used when exporting images to layout programs such as Quark and InDesign.

Ⓔ Enter the default print and screen resolutions to be used when opening new documents. You will want to use 72 for designs intended for computer or TV display and at least 300 for print.

Ⓕ Select the units used to measure resolution.

Ⓖ Select whether to use the PostScript definition or the Traditional definition to determine the number of points per inch. If you are printing to a PostScript-capable printer, select PostScript.

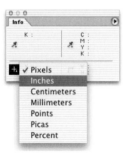

Quickly change the units being used on the Info palette.

98

5.9   Guides, Grid & Slices Preferences

Photoshop provides you with several guideline types to help you precisely place content in the canvas. These lines include the guides, which help you line up objects either horizontally or vertically; grid lines, which help you line up objects at regular intervals; and slice lines, which define areas to be cut in a web interface.

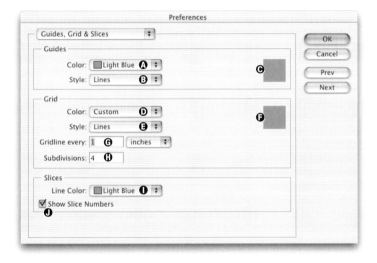

➠ 7.5   Using Rulers, Guides, Grids, and Snap

➠ 12.4 Selecting Colors with the Color Picker

➠ 29.1 Slicing Your Interface

Guides, Grid & Slices preferences (while in Preferences dialog)
⌘ 6
Ctrl 6

―――
If you set a color by clicking one of the color swatches, the color list will show it as a custom color.

Ⓐ Choose the color used to display guide lines.

Ⓑ Choose the style for guide lines (solid lines or dashed lines).

Ⓒ Displays the color being used for the guide lines. Click to choose a different color from the Color Picker dialog.

Ⓓ Choose the color used for the foreground grid.

Ⓔ Choose the style for the foreground grid (Lines, Dashed Lines, or Dots).

Ⓕ Displays the color being used for the grid. Click to choose a different color from the Color Picker dialog.

Ⓖ Enter the distance between each grid line and select the units to be used for the grid.

Ⓗ Enter the interval for bold subdivision grid lines to appear.

Ⓘ Choose the color used to display slice lines.

Ⓙ Check to show slice numbers with slices. Slice numbers appear in the top-left corner of the slice.

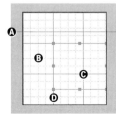

Ⓐ Guide line

Ⓑ Grid lines

Ⓒ Grid line subdivisions

Ⓓ Slice bounding box

5.10   Plug-Ins & Scratch Disks Preferences

➠ 8.1   Image Color
        Basics

➠ 14.1 Filter Basics

**Plug-Ins & Scratch
Disks preferences
(while in Preferences
dialog)**
⌘ 7
Ctrl 7

———

Ideally, the first scratch
disk should not be a
partition on the same
drive as the drive run-
ning Photoshop.

———

The "First" scratch disk is
also commonly referred
to as the "Primary"
scratch disk.

———

Changes you make to
the scratch disks do not
take effect until you
restart Photoshop.

———

Mac OS 9 plug-ins do
not work in Mac OS X.
If you have one, contact
the plug-in maker for
an update.

Photoshop automatically stores the primary plug-ins in the Photoshop application folder.
But in this preferences panel, you can define a second folder that contains Photoshop
plug-ins in another folder on an accessible drive.

In addition, you can set as many as four hard drives to use as scratch disks to store image
information while you are working in Photoshop. These can be either partitions of your
primary hard drive or external hard drives.

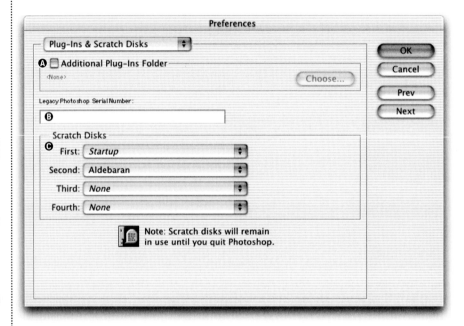

Ⓐ Check if you have a secondary folder of plug-ins (separate from the folder in the Adobe
Photoshop CS folder). Checking this option automatically opens a dialog in which you can
choose the secondary folder. Click the Choose... button to change the folder.

Ⓑ Enter older Photoshop serial numbers to associate with this copy of Photoshop to use with
plug-ins that require an older Photoshop serial number.

Ⓒ Select the first, second, third, and fourth scratch disks used by Photoshop. All available disks
are displayed in the select menus.

5.11 Memory & Image Cache Preferences

Photoshop uses lower-resolution versions of the high-resolution images being worked on to update the screen when you are working on layer or image adjustments. When you view an image at a magnification other than 100%, the displayed image is not recalculated but is based on a smaller cached version already calculated. This approach speeds redrawing, but it means that images are distorted if they are not one of the cached magnifications. To overcome this, you can increase the number of cached versions in the preferences. This will speed magnification changes and make them more accurate, but also requires a lot of memory and hard disk space.

Windows and Mac OS X treat the memory used by Photoshop as a total of the memory available to the computer. The higher the percentage, the more efficiently Photoshop will run, but this efficiency may come at the expense of operation performance in other applications you are running simultaneously.

⇒ 3.24 Zoom Tool

⇒ 4.9 Histogram Palette

⇒ 4.14 Navigation Palette

⇒ 7.4 Changing Your Document View

Memory & Image Cache preferences (while in Preferences dialog)
⌘ 8
Ctrl 8

———

The cache setting also affects the structure of the Save Image Pyramid in TIFF files.

———

If you do not set your memory high enough, you may spend a lot of time waiting. But if you set it too high, you may have trouble running other applications.

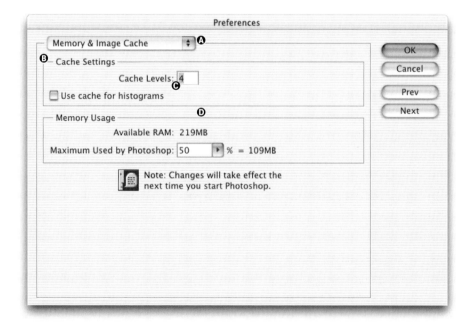

A Enter the number of levels (1 to 8) cached for image data. A higher number improves the quality of image redraw but is slower.

B Check to use sample cached data for histograms. Doing so is faster but less accurate.

C Displays the RAM currently available to Photoshop.

D Enter or select the amount of RAM devoted to Photoshop as a percentage. You will have to quit and restart Photoshop for these changes to take effect.

5.12   File Browser Preferences

➡ 4.8   File Browser

➡ 6.5   Managing
        Images with
        the File
        Browser

**File Browser panel
(while in Preferences
dialog)**
⌘ 9
Ctrl 9

The File Browser allows you to quickly access and organize the files on your hard drive. In order to better control this window, you can use the File Browser preferences to set how images are previewed and metadata is presented.

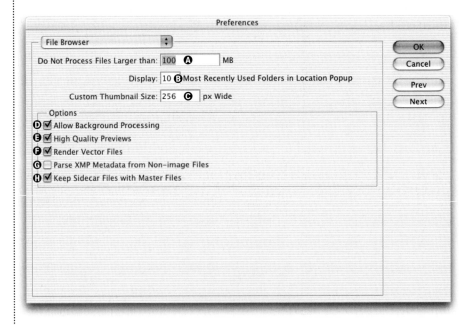

Ⓐ Enter the maximum size for files to display their thumbnails, previews, or metadata. Smaller values will increase the display speed of the File Browser.

Ⓑ Enter the number of folders to be displayed in the Location menu.

Ⓒ Enter the default width to be used for custom thumbnail images accessed by choosing File Managers View > Custom Thumbnail Size.

Ⓓ Check to allow the File Browser to continue processing the previews and metadata while you are doing other tasks. This speeds up File Browser display, but may slow your system slightly.

Ⓔ Check to display previews in highest quality. This will slow down File Browser display and requires more disk space to store.

Ⓕ Check to render vector images when displaying previews. If this option is unchecked, previews that include vector data will not appear in full form.

Ⓖ Check to prepare the metadata for a file even if the file is not an image.

Ⓗ Check if you want files associated with metadata to be moved, copied, deleted, or renamed along with the originating file. This is generally recommended.

UNIVERSAL TASKS

CHAPTER 6

Starting and Saving Images

Working with digital images in Photoshop generally begins with creating a new document, opening an existing image, or bringing an image into Photoshop via scanning or downloading from a digital capture device. You can use the software that came with your digital equipment to scan and download images onto your computer, but you can also open or scan images directly into Photoshop by accessing capture devices and their software through Photoshop's import functions. You can also access and organize files from memory cards, disks, or your computer's hard drive through the File Browser, introduced in Photoshop version 7. Photoshop continues to support an increasing variety of digital file formats compatible with the latest technology and software.

This chapter covers:

6.1 Image Basics

New File dialog

⌘ Ⓝ

Ctrl Ⓝ

Photoshop remembers the parameters you selected the last time you created a new document or uses your Clipboard data for default document dimensions when you create a new document.

You can always change the color mode you select when starting a new image for specific output. Digital devices capture in RGB, and your monitor displays in RGB. Rule of thumb, work in RGB.

Regardless of their intended use, all digital images that you open or create in Photoshop share common characteristics with regard to their digital properties and the manner in which Photoshop will display and store the image data. Although you can also use Photoshop to create vector shapes and PostScript typography, fundamentally Photoshop is a raster or bitmap image-editing program based on pixels. Pixels are dots that carry image data and color information. Raster images are resolution dependent, which means they have a fixed number of pixels. Images are displayed on the screen in percentages of total pixels. Imaging and Photoshop nomenclature with which you might familiarize yourself includes the following:

Document window How or where Photoshop displays your image. You can work in three view modes (Standard Screen Mode, Full Screen Mode with Menu Bar, and Full Screen Mode). Standard view mode displays at the top of the document window the document name, the view percentage of image size, and the color mode.

Image size Is displayed in both pixel dimensions and document size in the Image Size dialog. Pixel dimensions are absolute image size in Photoshop no matter your display or resolution settings.

Document size Print dimensions in Photoshop, taking into account pixel dimensions and resolution. The document size dimensions displayed in the Image Size dialog are the size of your print. You can view these dimensions in several increments, including inches, centimeters, picas, and so on.

Resolution In simplest terms, the area over which the pixels of an image are to be spread when printed. This will generally be displayed as pixels per inch. Increasing image size, resolution, and layers multiplies file size.

Color mode Used by Photoshop and all digital devices to numerically describe colors. Various devices use different color modes to record and reproduce image color. You can use Photoshop to convert between color modes.

Working space The color mode in which you will edit image data in Photoshop. You can change this in your Color Setting preferences.

Color profile A more specific numeric formula for reproducing color, which is generally device dependent. For example, specific digital cameras or scanners have a signature color profile. Specific printer, ink, and paper combinations have different color profiles.

File format The way image information is recorded. Various file formats record data as pixels or vectors and may allow for compression of data or storage of additional file information. File formats can be native to specific software, such as Photoshop's PSD format, or can allow more universal transfer of image data such as the JPEG format.

6.2 File Formats

In Photoshop CS, you can open and save images in a wide variety of file formats. These compatible formats range from the Photoshop native PSD format to more universal file formats such as JPEG, TIFF, EPS, GIF, and PDF. Photoshop continues to expand its support for a variety of software- and product-specific file formats such as Adobe Illustrator native AI files, FilmStrip MOV files associated with QuickTime and Final Cut Pro, and Cineon, ElectricImage, MacPaint, Photo CD, and Wavefront RLA formats.

The following table lists some of the most common formats compatible with Photoshop; those marked with an asterisk (*) can only be opened and must be saved to a different format. To view the complete list of Photoshop compatible formats, choose File > Open As, or, with an image open, browse the Save As drop-down.

Photoshop Image Formats

FORMAT	EXTENSION	USE
Photoshop	.psd	Photoshop's native format
Adobe Illustrator*	.ai	Illustrator's native format; treated as a generic PDF
BMP	.bmp	Common Windows format
CompuServe GIF	.gif	Standard web graphic format
Photoshop EPS	.eps	Common printer format
FilmStrip	.mov	QuickTime movie exported from Adobe Premiere, Final Cut Pro, or Avid
JPEG	.jpg	Standard web format for photographs
Large Document	.psb	PSB allows files to 300,000 pixels and over 2GB in size, must be enabled in preferences
PCX	.pcx	Paintbrush native format
Photoshop PDF	.pdf	Portable Document Format used in Adobe Acrobat
Photo CD*	.pcd	Kodak's native CD file format
Photoshop 2	.psd	Older Photoshop format
Photoshop Raw	.raw	Unlimited pixel dimensions or file size, no layers
PICT File	.pct	Mac graphic format
PICT Resource	.rsr	Mac system graphic format
Pixar	.pxr	3-D animation workstation format
PNG	.png	Up-and-coming web format
Raw	.raw	Mainframe graphic format
Scitex CT	.sct	Common full-color printing format
Targa	.tga	MS-DOS color format
TIFF	.tif	Standard desktop publishing format
Wireless Bitmap	.wbmp	Standard format for wireless devices such as mobile phones
Photoshop DCS 1 and 2	.eps	Common desktop publishing format
Acrobat TouchUp Image*	.pdf	Allows you to open individual images from a PDF document
Generic PDF*	.pdf	PDF file created in other applications
Generic EPS*	.eps	EPS file created in other applications
EPS PICT Preview*	.eps	PICT version of preview image associated with an EPS file
EPS TIFF Preview*	.eps	TIFF version of preview image associated with EPS file

➡ 25.1 File Saving Basics for Print

➡ 25.2 Saving in TIFF Format

➡ 25.3 Saving in EPS Format

➡ 25.4 Saving as Photoshop PDF

——

Avoid repeated saves to "lossy" file formats such as JPEG by archiving files in Photoshop or TIFF format, saving copies as JPEGs. In order to create smaller file sizes, compressed or lossy file formats such as GIF and JPEG throw out bits of image information; most of this information is unnecessary in the given format. However, repeated saves in these formats will cause loss of image quality.

——

If you are creating images for print, use a resolution of at least 244 dpi, with 300 or higher preferred.

——

If you are working with an image and you want to preserve the original, duplicate it immediately after opening (before making changes) so that you do not accidentally save over the original.

6.3   Creating a Blank Document

If you are starting a new project from scratch, you'll need to set certain parameters for the image. In Photoshop, choose File > New... In the New dialog, specify information about the new file and click OK. The canvas for your new image file is created. You can then either begin working on your new image or save the blank image immediately.

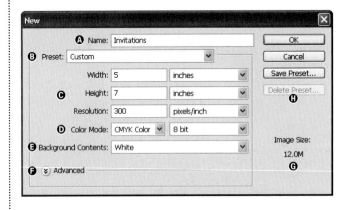

New File dialog
⌘ N
Ctrl N

Photoshop remembers the parameters you selected the last time you created a new document or uses your Clipboard data for default document dimensions when you create a new document.

You can always change the color mode you select when starting a new image for specific output. Digital devices capture in RGB, and your monitor displays in RGB. Rule of thumb, work in RGB.

If you are creating images for print, use a resolution of at least 244 dpi, with 300 or higher preferred.

Ⓐ Enter a name for the new image.

Ⓑ For using predetermined document specifications, choose an image size from the preset menu.

Ⓒ Enter values for image dimensions, resolution, and units of measure.

Ⓓ Choose a color mode.

Ⓔ Choose the color of the Background layer.

Ⓕ For using advanced options, choose color profile and pixel aspect ratio options from the extended dialog.

Ⓖ Displays the calculated file size for the image with the current options.

Ⓗ Choose to save your document settings as presets or select a preset to delete it from the preset drop-down menu.

Duplicating an Image File

Another way to start a new project is to begin with an existing image as the framework. First, open the image you want to use as your starting point (see Section 6.2) and then do one of the following:

■ Choose File > Save As... and save the file in a different location on the hard drive or with a different name in the same location.

■ Choose Image > Duplicate, type a new filename for the duplicate file (if there are layers in the original file, you can also merge them in the new version), and click OK. A new, unsaved version of the image is created.

■ In the History palette, click New Document From Current State 🔲 . A new, unsaved version of the document is created.

6.4   Opening an Existing Image

Photoshop can open a variety of image file formats. The Open or Open As command is the most common way to load files into an application.

1 In Photoshop, choose File > Open… or (in Windows only) choose File > Open As… to open a file in a particular format. (On the Mac, this is handled in the same dialog as opening the file.)

2 Locate the file you want to open using your operating system's Open dialog. To display only certain file formats, select the file format type you want in the drop-down next to Files Of Type or Show. You use the Format dialog (only available in Windows if you selected Open As…) to set the image's format when opened and defaults for the selected files format.

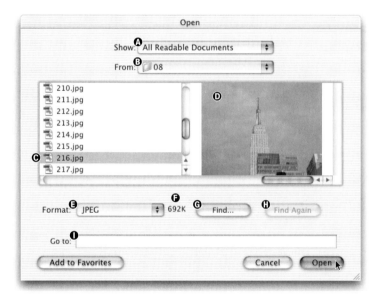

Ⓐ Choose the format of the image you want to find. Select All Readable Documents or All Documents if you are not sure of the format.

Ⓑ (OS X only) Choose from a list of favorite folders to jump to that location on your hard drive.

Ⓒ Use the Mac OS's File Browser to locate the file you want to open. Select the file once and then click Open, or double-click a file to open it.

Ⓓ Thumbnail of the selected file (if available).

Ⓔ Choose the format in which to open the image.

Ⓕ Displays the file size of the image if opened in the selected format.

Ⓖ Click to open a Search dialog to help find files.

Ⓗ Click to repeat the last search using the same parameters to find the next occurrence.

Ⓘ Type the direct path of the file and click Go (which replaces the Open button).

➡ 2.3   File Menu

➡ 18.7 Setting Up
            Workgroups

➡ 18.8 Checking
            Documents
            In and Out of
            Workgroups

➡ 18.10 Using
            Version Cue

Open New File dialog
⌘ O
Ctrl O

**Open As dialog
(Windows only)**
Ctrl O

Open File Browser
Shift ⌘ O
Shift Ctrl O

**Cycle between open
document windows**
Ctrl Tab

———

When opening a document, selecting All Readable Documents from the Files Of Type or Show menu displays non-Photoshop compatible files as grayed out.

———

Some file formats require additional information that you enter through dialogs. For example, PDF, EPS, and Adobe Illustrator files require you to enter information about rasterizing vector images.

———

If you see a Color Profile Mismatch warning and the profile listed for the image is a product name, convert to your working space.

6.4 Opening an Existing Image *(continued)*

Choose File > Open Recent to access a list of the 10 most recently opened files. Select the filename of the image you want to open. The image opens in the frontmost document window.

You set the length of the Open Recent list and specify whether images are saved with a thumbnail in the File Handling Preferences panel (see Section 5.5).

If you open an image that is already open in Photoshop, the image's document window is brought to the front. To open another view of the document, choose Window > Documents > New Window. Changes made in one window are duplicated in the other window.

Not all files that are compatible will be associated with Photoshop; double-clicking the file will not necessarily open it in Photoshop.

You can also, of course, duplicate an image file using your operating system and then open the duplicate to start a new project.

If you are working with an image and you want to preserve the original, duplicate it immediately after opening (before making changes) so that you do not accidentally save over the original.

Ⓐ Use the Windows file browser to locate the file you want to open. Select the file once and then click Open, or double-click a file to open it.

Ⓑ Name of the currently selected file.

Ⓒ Select the image format you are looking for if you know it.

Ⓓ Thumbnail of the selected file (if available).

Ⓔ The selected file's size.

Using Your Operating System

You can also open a Photoshop-compatible image file using the Finder (Mac) or Explorer (Windows) simply by locating a Photoshop file—a PSD or other compatible image file type—and double-clicking it or dragging the file onto the Photoshop application icon or one of its aliases.

Drag a Photoshop-compatible file onto the Photoshop application icon to open the file.

6.5 Managing Images with the File Browser

The File Browser allows you to locate and view previews of multiple images and to rename, sort, group, delete, or move files into separate folders—all without opening the images. It also lets you perform many Photoshop tasks such as adding file information or perform automated tasks, independently of the File menu.

You can now access or toggle on and off the File Browser by clicking a permanent button on the Options bar , or you can choose Window > File Browser or File > Browse. The File Browser window consists of a main window, a palette window, and a toolbar.

Ⓐ The main window displays file thumbnails and folders. Click thumbnails to select, rename, rotate, flag, rank, and sort images. Double-clicking files opens them.

Ⓑ The palette window houses four palettes that you can rearrange or expand by dragging tabs or dividers or by double-clicking tabs to minimize palettes.

Ⓒ The toolbar houses a number of menu items allowing you to automate, sort, and change the view options as well as shortcuts allowing you to flag, rotate, and delete files.

Ⓓ The Folders palette allows you to navigate your computer's file hierarchy to locate and select image folders.

Ⓔ The Preview window allows you to view a selected image in a large-sized preview without opening the image. You can work with very small thumbnails and view large previews.

Ⓕ Keyword and Metadata palettes allow you to view and record file information, add keyword search cues, or search for files using metadata, captions, creation dates, and so on.

➡ 4.8   File Browser

➡ 18.5   Resizing a Folder of Images

Select contiguous files
Shift-click

Select noncontiguous files
Ctrl-click

Refresh File Browser
F5

Rotate Images Clockwise in File Browser
⌘]
Ctrl]

Rotate Images Counter-Clockwise in File Browser
⌘ [
Ctrl [

Flag/Un-Flag Images in File Browser
⌘ '
Ctrl '

———

Images viewed with the File Browser that are located on a CD are treated as Locked files and they will appear with a "lock" icon. You will not be allowed to modify Metadata until the files are moved to your computer and are unlocked.

———

When working with images on a CD, the File Browser will not allow you to create New Folders in the Main Browser window.

Select contiguous files
Shift -click

Select noncontiguous files
Ctrl -click

Rotate Images Clockwise in File Browser
⌘ []
Ctrl []

Rotate Images Counter-Clockwise in File Browser
⌘ []
Ctrl []

Flag/Un-Flag Images in File Browser
⌘ '
Ctrl '

In the File Browser, choose View > Folders to see or hide folders in the main window

In the File Browser, choose View > Unreadable to see or hide other files that may be in folders you are viewing.

You can drag and drop files or folders into the File Browser.

Drag one palette into another to dock the palettes together.

Drag a palette's horizontal divider bar up or down to make the palette larger or smaller.

Drag a palette's vertical divider bar right or left to make the palette larger or smaller.

G Palette options menus on these palettes allow for searching metadata or keywords, adding or editing keywords and selecting palette view options.

H You can create folders within the main window for file organization.

I Selected files are indicated with "active" color. Shift-click to select more than one file. A rotation indicator is also displayed in the example. Files "rotated" in the File Browser are previews only, not actually rotated until files are opened.

J Flagged file and icon. You can quickly flag files (right-click/Control-click and choose Flag) and then view or sort them by choosing Show > Flagged Files.

K Using the Show menu, you can quickly view only flagged or unflagged files or view both flagged and unflagged files in the main window.

L The Location bar allows you to quickly access the last 10 folders opened in the File Browser by default. You can change this number in the File Browser Preferences.

M You can use layout adjustment indicators with a simple click-and-drag of the mouse to customize the File Browser window and palettes.

6.5 Managing Images with the File Browser *(continued)*

Recording File Info or Metadata

Photoshop allows you to view, add, or modify *metadata* information attached to your image files—including author, copyright, descriptive keywords, and date created—using the information standard developed by the Newspaper Association of America (NAA) and the International Press and Telecommunications Council (IPTC) to identify transmitted text and images. You access metadata by choosing File > File Info or through the Metadata palette in the File Browser.

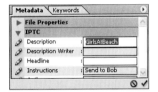

To add file information or edit metadata for a selected image in the File Browser, select the Metadata palette, click the pencil icon at the left of the Info field, and then type in the text box to add or edit information. Click Apply or Cancel, as appropriate, when you're done or to undo your work.

In addition to entering the information directly, you can save file information as an XMP (Extensible Metadata Platform) file, with the .xmp extension, and then load it into other Photoshop files. This is especially helpful if you have a series of files with similar information that you want to be able to quickly attach to them without having to retype it into the panels of each file.

Double-click a palette's tab to minimize it, and click a minimized palette's tab to open it.

Hover the cursor over a thumbnail in the File Browser to display information about the picture.

The first time you use the File Browser to view images in a folder, it must create the thumbnail previews, which takes a few moments. The next time you open the File Browser, the thumbnails are displayed immediately.

When an image is modified, the thumbnail in the File Browser does not reflect the changes unless you press the F5 (refresh) key.

Control-clicking the File Browser toggle button on the Options bar , will bring up the file Browser in Maximized view with palettes hidden.

UNDERSTANDING RESOLUTION

The painter Georges Seurat developed the technique of Pointillism. He placed small points of paint close together to create the illusion of a continuous image. Both printed and computer images use the same concept, either placing dots (printing) or pixels (screen) so close together that they fool the eye into seeing a complete image. Resolution is the measurement of how many units (dots or pixels) are within either a linear inch or a linear centimeter of an image. Higher resolutions (more units per inch or centimeter) produce better-quality images but also a larger file size. In addition, printing presses measure halftone screens using lines per inch (lpi).

6.6   Importing Images

————

Using the PDF Image
import dialog is the
same as opening a PDF
document using the
Acrobat TouchUp
image format.

————

Mac users can import
or open a PICT file, but
importing a PICT file
allows you to control
the size and color
mode, and the image
is anti-aliased.

————

TWAIN is a cross-
platform interface used
to acquire images using
a scanner. You must
install a TWAIN plug-in,
usually provided with
your scanner, before
you can import an
image using Photoshop
and a scanner.

————

Windows Me and Win-
dows XP users can
import scanned docu-
ments using WIA
(Windows Imaging
Acquisition) support.

In most cases, you either start an image from scratch (new) or open an image from another source. However, you can acquire images in Photoshop in a few other ways. Choose File > Import, and then select an import option from the submenu:

Anti-Aliased PICT (Mac) Browse and select a PICT image, and then click Open. In the Anti-Aliased PICT dialog, set the size of the PICT as a constrained proportion or by clearing that option and setting the width and height independently. Then select RGB or Grayscale mode and click OK. The PICT image opens in a new document window embedded in a white background.

PDF Image Browse and select a PDF, and click Open. In the PDF Image Import dialog, select the image you want to import from the PDF and click OK or Import All. Each image opens in a separate document window automatically named with the PDF's filename followed by a four-digit number based on the image order in the PDF.

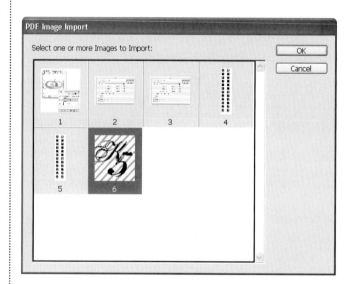

PICT Resources (Mac) Browse and select a file with PICT resources. In the PICT Resource dialog, select the PICT resource to open by using the arrows to browse the resources and then click OK. The resource opens in its own document window.

WIA Support (Windows Me or XP) Choose a destination for the imported images, check Open Acquired Images if desired, and click Start. Select the image or images from the camera and click Get Picture.

Scanning and Downloading Images from a Camera are also considered import functions of Photoshop.

6.7 Placing Vector Images

You can place certain vector file formats (EPS, PDF, and Adobe Illustrator) directly into an open Photoshop document. Follow these steps:

1 Open the Photoshop image into which you want to place a vector image, and choose File > Place...

2 Browse to find the vector file you want, and double-click the file or click it and click Place. The file should have the .eps, .pdf, or .ai extension.

3 If you are placing a PDF file with multiple pages, you will be prompted to select the page you want to place. Select the page and click OK.

4 The vector image is initially placed as a wire frame (a rectangle surrounding a low-resolution version of the image with an *X* through it). Use the mouse or the Option palette controls to transform the wire frame: move, resize, skew, or rotate the image.

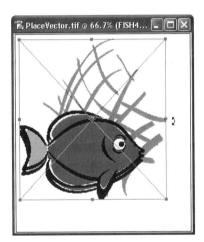 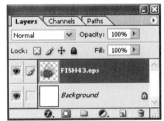

A vector format Illustrator file is being imported. The image can be transformed before it is rasterized into the image.

5 Click the Commit button ✔ or press Enter/Return. The image is rasterized and placed as a new layer on top of other layers in the image. Alternately, click the Cancel button ⊘ or press Esc to cancel the placement.

FILE COMPATIBILITY SOLUTIONS

Although you can open or import a variety of file formats in Photoshop, you have a few options if you find a need for a file format that is not directly compatible with Photoshop. Try opening the image in its native application and see which export file formats are available that might be compatible with Photoshop such as EPS or PDF. You might try Print To File from the native application and then use Acrobat Distiller to create a PDF. A simple yet low-resolution alternative is to select Print Screen, create a new document, and paste.

➡ 16.1 Path Basics

➡ 9.11 Transforming Layer Content

➡ 9.14 Pasting Selected Content

Copying paths from Illustrator and pasting into Photoshop provides you with alternatives to placing a vector image, which can preserve the vector information and path-editing capabilities.

6.8   Importing Images Using a Scanner

Through commands in the File menu, you can access any scanner installed on the computer to scan images directly into Photoshop. The information in this section applies to most scanners. Regardless of who manufactures your scanner, the process of scanning is divided into two general stages: preparing for the scan and scanning the image.

Preparation is critical to achieving a quality scan; you can avoid many hours of work in Photoshop with only a few minutes of prep time, which includes the following tasks:

Clean the scanner glass This sounds really simple, but most users don't do it.

Clean the image being scanned Remove all dust and debris from photos using a soft brush.

Align the picture on the scanner glass Even though Photoshop has an excellent Rotate command that you can use to correct misalignment of an image on the scanner, any time a scanned image is rotated it suffers from mild deterioration that reduces the overall sharpness of the image.

The bottom of the scanner glass might fog sometimes; as a rule, this has little or no effect on the scanned image. Do not attempt to remove the glass unless the manufacturer has provided instructions to do so.

If the picture you are scanning will eventually need to be 256 colors for use on the Web, scan it at the highest available level (24-bit color, or RGB) anyway. This ensures the best color; also, many Photoshop filters won't work on an 8-bit image. Only after the image has been edited should you use Photoshop to convert it to 256 colors.

If you need to enlarge a picture, use your scanner settings whenever possible.

When an image is scanned using Descreen, the result is a softer picture—meaning it loses some of its sharpness. This is a small price to pay for the reduction of those annoying moiré patterns.

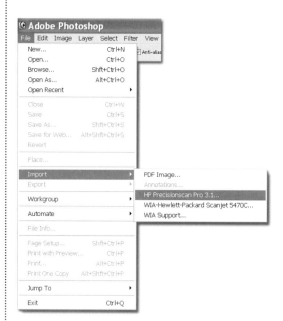

Clicking the Scan button on a scanner launches the scanner's software, not Photoshop. A better way is to start scanning from within Photoshop by choosing File **>** Import, which opens a drop-down. The choices of available input devices are determined by the equipment installed on your computer. Selecting the scanner that you want to use to scan the image launches the scanning software that came with your scanner. (Some older Macs use a plug-in to access the scanner.)

6.8 Importing Images Using a Scanner *(continued)*

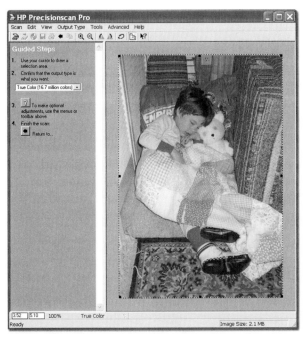

After the scanner interface opens (the HP interface is shown here), preview and define the area to be selected, ensure that the color mode is correct, and then scan.

Scan multiple images into one document, and then use the Crop And Straighten function in the Automate menu to let Photoshop automatically copy each image into its own document and rotate each as necessary.

Using Windows XP or Me, you can control the scanner using the WIA interface. WIA is a generic, "no frills" control interface and therefore not as full-featured as the controls in the software that comes with your scanner.

The best color-quality setting that can be displayed on your computer monitor is 24-bit color. This setting goes by many names: RGB, RGB 24-bit, 16.7 Million Colors, Millions Of Colors, and True Color, to name a few.

Rule of Thumb: Scan at twice your final output resolution.

Most scanning software performs a preview scan at startup. Select the portion of the picture that you want to scan.

You should enlarge an image during scanning for either of two reasons: you want the finished scan larger than the original, or you plan to restore a photo. Increasing the size to 200% makes it is easier to work with the picture. When you are finished, you can resize the image to its original size. Although the picture will suffer some loss of detail when it is resized, you can more than compensate for the loss by using Unsharp Mask filter (choose Filter > Sharpen > Unsharp Mask), which is a sharpening filter.

When you scan a printed image, such as a picture in a magazine, it usually develops a checkered pattern or something that looks like a plaid, a *moiré pattern*, caused by the patterns of tiny dots that are used to print the picture interfering with the scanner's own patterns. To prevent these patterns, select the Descreen function on your scanner software.

6.9 Downloading from a Digital Camera

When you download images from your digital camera using Photoshop, several advantages are available, over downloading all the images to your hard drive directly from the camera. Aside from the obvious image-editing capabilities, many cameras will allow you to use the File Browser to preview, sort, select, and organize your digital captures, add file information (metadata), or perform automated tasks such as batch renaming, without first downloading all the images to your computer.

Each digital camera and associated drivers are unique. You may be able to set up your camera connection so that Photoshop launches automatically when you connect your camera. You may need to choose File > Open from the Photoshop menu or even download images to your hard drive, before the File Browser can recognize the images.

When a digital camera is connected to your computer, in most cases it appears as a mass storage device in any file management dialog. You can use Photoshop's File Open dialog to locate and select the device icon to view pictures from the camera as if they were in any other folder on your hard disk. Remember that for your images to be physically transferred, you must either open them in Photoshop and save them or choose a folder on your hard drive as a destination and copy the files.

INTERPOLATION METHODS

Whenever you resize an image without un-checking the Resample Image option, Photoshop is called upon to analyze image information and add pixels. To this end, Photoshop must employ an "interpolation method" to assign color values to new pixels based on readings of existing adjacent pixels. You can set interpolation preferences and can make a choice in the Image Size dialog when resizing. Photoshop CS offers the choice of two new interpolation methods:

Bicubic Smoother This is recommended when increasing pixel dimensions.

Bicubic Sharper This is recommended when downsizing for the web, email, etc.

6.9   Downloading from a Digital Camera *(continued)*

To open files from a digital camera into Photoshop using the File Browser, follow these steps:

1   Click the File Browser button 🖭 on the Options bar, or choose either Window > File Browser or File > Browse. The first time you open a folder in the File Browser, Photoshop generates thumbnail previews in the main browser window. Preview information is stored in a file in the same folder in which the images are kept; so the next time you open it, the thumbnails appear more quickly in subsequent views.

2   Select individual pictures by clicking them one at a time; select multiple individual pictures by Command/Ctrl-clicking the thumbnails; or select all the pictures in the folder by pressing Command/Ctrl+A.

3   Once pictures are selected, you can place them in another location by clicking the selected thumbnails and dragging them to a location in the Folders palette. You can also load images into Photoshop by dragging them to the Photoshop image window or double-clicking the thumbnail.

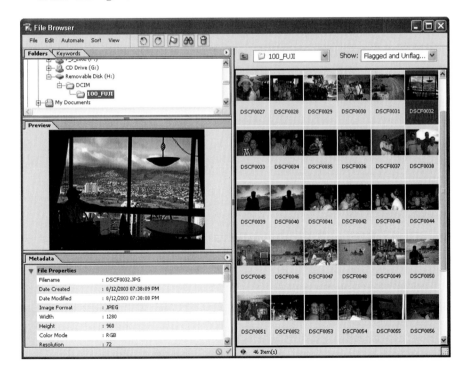

Hover the cursor over a thumbnail in the File Browser to display information about the picture.

The first time you use the File Browser to view images in a folder, it must create the thumbnail previews, which will take a few moments. The next time you open the File Browser, the thumbnails are displayed immediately.

When an image is modified, the thumbnail in the File Browser does not reflect the changes unless you press the F5 (refresh) key.

Create folders in the File Browser main window, and then rename and drag files to new folders to organize.

Using Windows XP or Me, you can import images using the WIA interface to open images in Photoshop.

If your digital camera uses the JPEG file format as its primary method of transferring images, keep in mind that JPEG is a "lossy" file format. If you open and edit JPEG images in Photoshop, it is recommended that you save your work in PSD or TIFF format, saving copies to JPEG as needed.

6.10   Saving Images

**Save the document
(update saved file)**
⌘ S
Ctrl S

Save As dialog
Shift ⌘ S
Shift Ctrl S

**Close the current
window**
⌘ W
Ctrl W

Close all open windows
Option ⌘ W
Alt Ctrl W

Warning: Although you
can work on a file with-
out saving it, you will
lose the image and all
your work if you acci-
dentally close the file
(and this does happen)
or if Photoshop or your
operating system
crashes. It is recom-
mended that you save
the file immediately
upon creating it and
then regularly save
changes. Photoshop
does not have an auto-
save feature.

Save often.

At some time after starting an image (either immediately after creating a new image or after making significant changes to the image), you will need to save the image to a hard drive or other storage medium.

To save an image for the first time, choose File > Save As... Enter information in the Save As dialog and click Save. If you click Cancel at this point, the image will not be saved.

A Choose a location in which to save your file. Photoshop incorporates file management unique to each Windows or Mac OS.

B Enter a filename. You can set preferences for Photoshop to automati-cally add the correct extension for the file format.

C Choose a file format in which to save the image.

D Check to save this file as a copy.

E Check to preserve alpha channels in the saved document. This option is not available for all for-mats or if the document does not contain saved selections.

F Check to preserve layers in the document. This option is not available for all formats.

G Check to save in Proof Setup for printing. This option is available when saving in EPS and PDF.

H Check to embed the document's color profile. This option is not available for all formats (recom-mended, when available, for transferring consistent color between devices).

I Check to preserve annotations added to the document. This option is not available for all formats.

J Check to preserve spot colors if spot channels have been created in the document. This option is not available for all formats.

K Check to include document thumbnails (limited option) or to restrict file extensions to lower-case characters.

Choose File > Save to add the changes made to the image since the last save to the saved file.

If you are finished with an image, you can close its window to clean up your Desktop by choosing File > Close to close the topmost document. To close all open documents, choose File > Close All. You will be prompted to save any documents with unsaved changes.

CHAPTER 7

Working with the Image, Canvas, and View

MOST OF US HAVE at one time chosen File > Print, only to be surprised moments later at what was printed. Photoshop provides us with tools to measure dimensions and angles, resize and rotate images, and crop or add additional area to the image. Photoshop also gives you the option of previewing your print layout and setting a wide range of universal print options as well as those settings specific to your equipment.

7.1   Canvas Basics

New File dialog
⌘ N
Ctrl N

―――

When resizing images
from a digital camera,
clear the Resample
option in the Image Size
dialog to resize without
loss of image quality.

―――

Though today's moni-
tors arguably display at
differing resolution,
Photoshop reads what is
displayed on the screen
as having 72 dpi. To test
this, take a screen cap-
ture or Print Screen.
Creating a new docu-
ment will present the
dimensions of the Clip-
board (your monitor
display size) at 72 dpi.

―――

Monitor display set-
tings are adjusted in
your operating system
controls, not within
Photoshop.

In simplest terms, think of your Photoshop canvas as the area in which you can paint or edit pixel information, much like the canvas that a painter would use for work in oils. You can add additional canvas beyond the existing edges of an image. You can also increase your image size, which will give you a larger canvas. Both of these choices will add pixels to an image and increase the file size.

Measuring the Canvas

The following basic variables used in Photoshop must be understood to effectively control image display, output, storage and measurement:

Image size Is presented in both pixel dimensions and document size in the Image Size dialog.

Pixel dimensions Pixel dimensions reflect absolute image size in Photoshop and will directly effect file (storage) size.

Document size Refers to print dimensions in Photoshop. If the Image Size dialog displays a document size of 4″ square, the resulting printed image will be 4″ square.

Document resolution Refers to how tightly pixels are grouped and affects image print quality. Increasing resolution (while maintaining document size) will increase file size exponentially. An RGB image 4″ by 4″ square at 72 pixels per inch would be roughly 243 KB in size, while growing to 4.12 MB at 300 pixels per inch.

Monitor resolution Affects how your canvas is displayed. You control canvas display size (how big your image appears onscreen) by adjusting pixel size in proportion to monitor display settings by using the Navigator palette, Zoom tool or View menu.

Think of your Photoshop document as having "absolute" dimensions measured only in pixels, with pixels themselves as having no specific size. All other dimensions, or meas-urements, are inter-dependent. For example, when viewed at 100%, a document that is set up 4″ wide at 72 pixels per inch may measure only 3.5″ if you hold a ruler up to your monitor. The image you see depends on your monitor's display settings or screen reso-lution. You could also set the same 288×288 pixel image to print a 1″ square, neither changing any pixel information nor changing the image's appearance on screen.

7.2 Changing the Canvas Size

The canvas is the area in which an image is displayed, and you can set the size of the canvas independently of the image size. For example, if an image is 500 pixels wide, you can size the canvas to 300 pixels, cutting off 200 pixels in the image rather than reducing the image to fit the new size.

The most accurate way to set the size of the canvas is to go to Image > Canvas Size, which opens the Canvas Size dialog. Using this method you can enter exact measurements for the canvas size and then dictate the quadrant in which the size changes are anchored.

Choose Image > Canvas Size… In the Canvas Size dialog, enter the new width and height for the canvas, select an anchor point around which the size changes will be made, and click OK.

The canvas now appears at the new size. If the width and/or height of the new canvas is larger than the original, previously clipped parts of the image are revealed, or the background color set in the Toolbox fills the new area.

Warning: In the Canvas Size dialog, a confirmation dialog warns that parts of the image will be clipped if the size for either width or height is smaller than the original size.

You can change the canvas size directly, using the Canvas Size dialog, or by cropping the trimming or rotating the canvas.

When you rotate the canvas of an image via the Image menu, Photoshop automatically adds canvas to the image.

You can add canvas using the Crop tool. Zoom away from the image to display area around the canvas, drag the Crop tool handles beyond the canvas edges, and commit the crop operation.

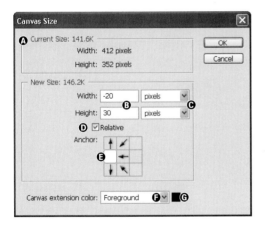

Ⓐ The current dimensions and file size of the canvas.

Ⓑ Enter new dimensions for the canvas. If the Relative option is checked, use +/– units to add or subtract from the current canvas size.

Ⓒ Choose units to be used for setting dimensions.

Ⓓ Check if the amounts entered should be added to/subtracted from the canvas size rather than used to set the absolute size.

Ⓔ Each square represents a quadrant of the canvas. Choose the quadrant around which the canvas will be enlarged or reduced. If quadrants are above and below or to the left and right of the selected quadrant, the changes to the canvas will be equally distributed between them.

Ⓕ Choose a color for the added canvas from the menu.

Ⓖ Canvas extension color is indicated; click on the color square to access the Color Picker dialog.

7.3   Setting the Image Size

———

Increasing image resolution may offer the possibility of better print quality, but may also have an adverse effect on the speed and performance of editing and printing—depending on your equipment.

An image's physical size—its width and height—determine not just its dimensions, but also its file size. Larger physical images require more disk space to record. In addition, image size and image resolution are linked in such a way that an image can be enlarged or reduced without a loss of quality as long as the resolution is similarly increased or decreased. However, the image size and resolution do not have to be set in conjunction. *Interpolation* (or resampling) is the process by which pixels are added or deleted from an image to adjust the dimensions and resolution independently. Doing so causes some degradation of the image quality, but whether the viewer notices that quality loss depends on several factors, including the interpolation method used, the original quality of the image, and (of course) the degree of change.

The image resized by 15%.

SIZE DOES MATTER

The digital size of your image (how much room it takes up on your computer) is measured in bytes—kilobytes (k, KB), megabytes (M, MB), or gigabytes (GB). Images with more pixels packed closer together are capable of printing more detail—or printing at higher resolution, generally providing a higher quality print.

Keep in mind however that file size is directly proportional to the pixel dimensions of your image, and this proportion is exponential in its effect on file size. For example:

- A blank 8.5x11′ image at 100 pixels/inch (ppi) is 2.68M in size when open in Photoshop.

- The same 8.5x11′ image at 200ppi is 10.7M in size when open in Photoshop—or roughly four times larger in file size.

- An 8.5x11′ photo at 300ppi with four additional layers can bring your image to 120.4M

7.3　Setting the Image Size *(continued)*

Resizing an Image

You can resize the entire image (including all layers) using the Image Size dialog. Follow these steps:

1 Open the image to be resized, and choose Image > Image Size… to open the Image Size dialog.

2 Enter a new width, height, and/or resolution for the image. If the image is not being resampled, all three options will change if one is changed. If resampling is on and proportions are constrained, only width and height change in unison. If resampling is on and proportions are not constrained, you can set all three options independently.

3 Click OK. The image is interpolated (if necessary), and the document window now displays the image at its new size and/or resolution. If the interpolation process takes more than a few seconds, you will see a progress bar indicating how long the process will last

➠ 2.5　Image Menu

➠ 6.1　Image Basics

➠ 23.2　Understand-
ing Resolution
and Docu-
ment Size

Crop tool
ⓒ

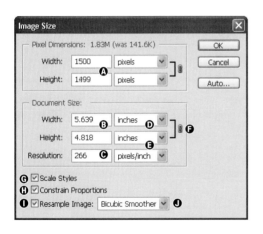

Ⓐ The image dimensions in pixels. You can enter the image dimensions here in pixels or as a percentage of the original size if resampling is checked. See H.

Ⓑ Enter the image dimensions.

Ⓒ Enter the image resolution.

Ⓓ Choose the units for measuring the image's dimensions.

Ⓔ Choose the units for measuring the image's resolution.

Ⓕ Indicates that width and height are locked and cannot be set independently. See H. If resampling is off, this line extends to resolution as well as indicating that all three attributes are set together.

Ⓖ Check if you want Layer Styles and Effects to be scaled or resized in proportion to the increase in image dimensions.

Ⓗ Check if the dimensions and resolution need to be set independently. The lock will be removed from the Resolution field.

Ⓘ Check if the width and height need to be set independently after checking Resample Image. The locks will be removed from the Width and Height fields.

Ⓙ Choose the interpolation method if you are resampling an image.

7.3   Setting the Image Size *(continued)*

You set the default interpolation method used for resampling in the General preferences (see Section 5.4).

Crop tool

Ⓒ

Resizing While Cropping

You can also resize the image when you crop the canvas. Doing so involves using the Crop tool and then setting the image size and resolution that the newly cropped region should fit.

On the left is the image before cropping. On the right is the image after cropping, and the cropped area is resized.

To resize an image while cropping it, follow these steps:

1   Choose the Crop tool ⛏, but *do not* select a crop region yet.

2   In the Options bar, enter a width, height, and resolution that the cropped area should resize to after cropping. Click the Clear button if you do not want to resize, or click Front Image to use the size of the canvas in the frontmost document window. (You can switch back and forth between documents while cropping if you want the image to be resized to the same size as another image.)

3   Select the area of the canvas you want to preserve. You can transform (move, resize, rotate, and skew) the crop selection.

4   Press Enter or click the check mark icon ✔ in the Options bar to crop the image.

The canvas is now cropped to the boundaries of the cropping selection but also resized to the specified dimensions and resolution. However, you may notice some distortion of the image.

7.3 Setting the Image Size (continued)

Using the Resize Image Assistant

If you have difficulty producing high-quality images while manually changing the image size, the Resize Image Assistant is for you. By answering a few simple questions about the results you want from resizing, you can generally get clearer results unless you are well practiced in the art of image resizing. To use the Resize Image Assistant, follow these steps:

1 With the image you want to resize as the active document window, choose Help **>** Resize Image…

2 Choose whether the image is to be used for print or online and click Next.

3 Enter a new width or height for the image. Since these dimensions are linked, changing one changes the other. If you are resizing for print, select the units used. If you are resizing for the screen, click the Preview button to see what the changes will look like (displayed in a copy of the document window that is placed in the top-left corner of the screen). Click Next.

4 If you are resizing for the screen, skip to Step 6. If you are resizing for print, choose a halftone screen to use when your image is printed.

5 Use the slider to set the image quality. If you increase the file size and then increase the "quality," you will actually be decreasing the image quality. The result of the change is displayed. Click Next.

6 Click Finish to resize your image as specified.

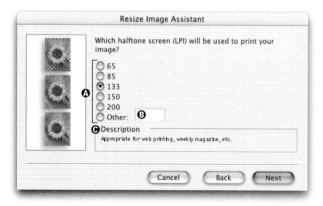

A Choose from the list of common halftone screens. Select a screen based on how your image will be printed. Most newspapers use 85, and glossy corporate reports and art books use 200, because they need sharp images.

B Choose Other and then enter a halftone screen value to the left.

C Displays information about the best use of the selected halftone screen.

Choosing the right halftone screen is vital for getting the best results when printing. Always check with your print shop before specifying this setting.

7.4   Changing Your Document View

➡ 2.9   View Menu

➡ 3.23 Hand Tool

Switch to the Hand tool from any other tool (reverts after releasing)
`Spacebar`

Zoom tool
`Z`

Hand tool
`H`

Zoom in (the window resizes to fit)
`⌘` `+`
`Ctrl` `+`

Zoom out (the window resizes to fit)
`⌘` `−`
`Ctrl` `−`

⸻

Double-click the Zoom tool to instantly zoom to 100%.

⸻

Double-click the Hand tool to instantly change the window size to fit the screen.

You can enlarge or reduce images on the screen without affecting the actual image itself. Changing the apparent size of the image allows you to zoom up or down to see the entire canvas at once or to view smaller details close up.

Zooming In and Out

The Navigator palette displays a thumbnail version of the topmost document, with a rectangular box surrounding the area currently visible in the document window and the current zoom level as a percentage.

To change the zoom level, click the small mountain icon to zoom in, click the large mountain icon to zoom out, or use the slider in between these two icons to zoom up or down. In addition, you can type a percentage directly in the Zoom Level box.

On the left is the image zoomed to 33.33%. On the right is the image zoomed to 100%.

In addition, you can use the Zoom tool to quickly zoom in and out of parts of an image. Follow these steps:

1   Select the Zoom tool 🔍.

2   Set the zoom options in the tool options bar:

- Select zoom in (+) or zoom out (−)

- Check Resize Window To Fit if you want the document window to resize every time the zoom level is changed to show the entire image (or as much of it as the screen will allow). Otherwise, the document window maintains a constant size.

- Check Ignore Palettes if you want the window to resize behind palettes. Otherwise the windows will only resize within the area of the screen not occupied by palettes.

- Click Actual Pixels to display the image at 1:1.

7.4 Changing Your Document View *(continued)*

- Click Fit On Screen to zoom the image to fill the entire screen or the area not occupied by palettes.

- Click Print Size to display the image at the size it would appear if printed.

3 To zoom, move the Zoom tool over the canvas:

- Click a point in the image you want to use as the center of the zooming (either in or out). The image immediately changes apparent size.

- If you are zooming in, click and drag with the Zoom tool in the canvas to select the rectangular area to be magnified. That area will fill the document window.

- Hold down the Alt/Option key to toggle between zooming in and out.

- Press Option/Ctrl and click in the canvas to open a pop-up menu of zoom options.

Moving the Canvas

If the size of the document window is smaller than the size of the total canvas, you will not be able to view parts of the image. You can move the image around within the visible area of the document window in several ways:

- Use the horizontal and vertical scroll bars to move the image up or down and left or right.

- Select the Hand tool 🖑 and click and hold on the canvas. As you move the tool, the image moves within the viewable area of the canvas.

- In the Navigator palette, click and hold within the box showing the current viewable area and move it to the area of the canvas you want to view. As you move the box, the image shifts in real time, allowing you to scan through the entire image.

In the Navigator palette, grab the viewing area and move it around as desired.

→ 3.24 Zoom Tool

→ 4.14 Navigator Palette

Zoom in (the window doesn't resize)
⌘ Option +
Ctrl Alt +

Zoom out (the window doesn't resize)
⌘ Option −
Ctrl Alt −

Fit on the screen
⌘ 0
Ctrl 0

Show actual pixels (100%)
⌘ Option 0
Ctrl Alt 0

———

Since image resolution is independent of the monitor's resolution, an image with a resolution higher than the monitor resolution (generally 72 ppi) displays larger at 100% than its actual size when printed. How much larger depends on the image's resolution.

7.5   Using Rulers, Guides, Grids, and Snap

➡ 1.3   The Docu-
        ment Window

➡ 2.9   View Menu

Show/hide rules
⌘ Ⓡ
Ctrl Ⓡ

Show/hide guides
⌘ ;
Ctrl ;

Show/hide grid
⌘ "
Ctrl "

———

An image size is the measurement of its height and width. When using units such as inches and centimeters (absolute units), the image size is the size at which it is printed. When the units are pixels or points, the image size is based on the resolution of the image.

———

Double-click either of the rulers to open the Units & Rulers preferences.

———

You can show or hide all elements selected in the Show submenu by choosing View > Extras.

Guides and grids allow you to precisely position your content in the canvas by providing lines that float over the image to show either ruler divisions (grid) or custom positions (guides) on the canvas.

Snapping increases precision when placing selections, cropping images, creating slices, and drawing shapes and paths by forcing the cursor and the graphic content to a guide, grid, slice, or the edges of content on a layer.

Showing and Adjusting Rulers

You use rulers to display the size (width and height) of the document, regardless of the image's magnification.

- To show or hide the rulers, choose View > Rulers.

- To adjust the ruler's origin, click and drag the origin box (between the horizontal and vertical ruler in the top-left corner) and drag down to the position where you want the origin of the ruler to appear. To reset the origin to the top-left corner of the canvas, double-click the origin box.

Ⓐ Ruler origin

Ⓑ Horizontal ruler

Ⓒ Vertical ruler

Showing and Setting Guides

Guides appear as either horizontal or vertical lines that you can place anywhere in the canvas.

- To show or hide existing guides, choose View > Show > Guides. If there are no guides in the canvas, this option is not available and will be grayed out.

- To quickly add a guide to the canvas, make sure the rulers are showing, click and drag from either the horizontal or vertical ruler into the canvas, and release on the desired location. As you drag, a gray line will indicate where the guide will be placed. Hold down Shift while dragging to force the guide to stop on ruler tickmarks.

- To add a guide to a precise location, choose View > New Guide, set the options for the guide in the New Guide dialog, and click OK. The guide will appear at the specified position.

7.5 Using Rulers, Guides, Grids, and Snap *(continued)*

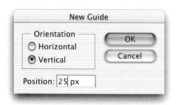

Choose whether the new guide should be horizontal (width) or vertical (height), and enter a value (based on the width and height of the canvas) to set the position of the new guide.

➡ 5.8 Units & Rulers Preferences

➡ 5.9 Guides, Grid & Slices Preferences

Lock/unlock guides
Option ⌘ ⓔ
Alt Ctrl ⓔ

Turn snapping on/off
Shift ⌘ ⓔ
Shift Ctrl ⓔ

Show/hide all elements selected in the Show submenu
Ctrl ⌘ Ⓗ
Alt Ctrl Ⓗ

———

Pressing the Command/Ctrl key while dragging guides or selections with Snap active temporarily toggles Snap off.

———

You can also show all extras by choosing View > Show > All; hide all extras by choosing View > Show > None.

———

You can choose to show or hide additional elements in the Show Extras Options dialog. To open this dialog, choose View > Show > Show Extras Options.

———

To designate individual document elements for the snap function to recognize, choose View > Snap To and select the desired element.

———

Choose View > Snap To and select the specific canvas feature (guides, grid, slices or document bounds) you want the Snap function to react to.

- To lock or unlock the guides, choose View > Lock Guides. When locked, the guides can be added, but not repositioned.

- To move a guide, make sure the guides are not locked, choose the Move tool ▸⊕, and then click and drag on the guide. To change a guide's orientation (horizontal/vertical), hold down the Option/Alt key while dragging it.

- To remove a single guide, make sure the guides are not locked and click and drag the guide out of the canvas.

- To delete all the guides from the canvas, choose View > Clear Guides.

The guides are showing.

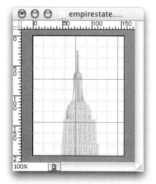

The grid is showing.

Showing and Setting the Grid

Like guides, the grid sets lines above the image in the canvas, but these lines are regularly spaced, based on the rulers, and cannot be moved (though you can set their spacing in the Guides, Grid & Slices preferences). To show or hide the grid, choose View > Show > Grid.

Using Snap

You can choose to have elements being drawn or selections being made to automatically align themselves on guides, grids, slices, or document bounds (edges), if they are being made within 8 pixels of those elements.

- To turn snapping on or off, choose View > Snap.

7.6   Straightening and Cropping Images

Crop tool
Ⓒ

Marquee tool
Ⓜ

———

You can also crop the canvas using the Marquee tool. Choose the Marquee tool, make a selection in the canvas, and then choose Image > Crop. The canvas is now cropped to the size of the selected area. If your selection was not rectangular (for example, a circle), the dimensions of the cropped area are the extremes for the selected area.

———

Using the Image > Canvas Size command, with a setting smaller than the original, will also crop a selected image.

———

The automated Crop and Straighten Photos command also provides you an alternative for cropping and straightening individual images.

Images are often scanned or Photographed slightly skewed, requiring rotation or straightening. Improper framing or composition of an image is also often not quite apparent until you see the image displayed on the screen and oriented properly. These two tasks might be paired simply because they are common Photoshop tasks; they are, however, also commonly paired because the process of rotating an image canvas in Photoshop leaves either an undesirable background fill or angular edges, which are generally immediately trimmed.

Choose File > Automate > Crop and Straighten Photos to access a new feature available in Photoshop CS that is designed to allow you to scan multiple images on a single pass. The automated feature will look for rectangular regions of the image, extract each to its own document, and rotate as necessary.

Rotating the Canvas

With the document to be rotated as the top document, choose Image > Rotate Canvas and select an option from the submenu:

180°, **90° CW** (clockwise), or **90° CCW** (counterclockwise).

Arbitrary Allows you to enter a specific number of degrees in the Rotate Canvas dialog to rotate the canvas clockwise or counterclockwise. Using the Measure tool (Ruler icon located under the Eyedropper tool), you can click and drag a measurement in the image. When you select Arbitray, that measured angle will already be entered for you.

Flip Canvas Horizontally or Vertically

The image is rotated 90° clockwise.

Cropping the Canvas

You use the Crop tool to select a rectangular area of the canvas to preserve while deleting or hiding other areas. Doing so reduces the dimensions of the canvas, as with using the Canvas Size dialog, but gives you direct visual control over what remains.

7.6 Straightening and Cropping Images *(continued)*

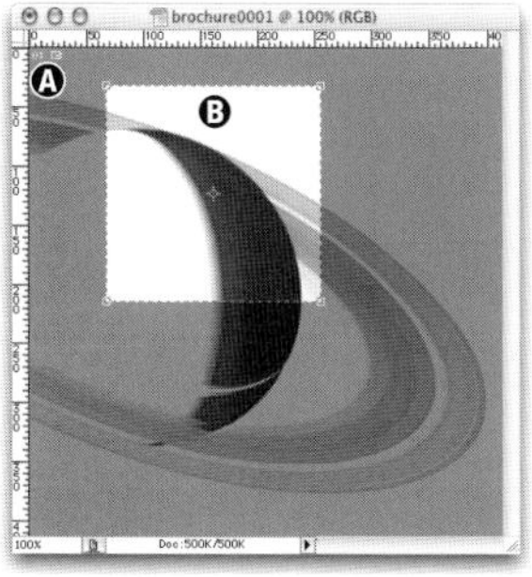

Ⓐ Area will be cropped.

Ⓑ Area will be preserved.

Follow these steps to crop the canvas:

1 Choose the Crop tool, and select the area of the canvas you want to preserve. You can move and resize the crop selection.

2 Set the options bar:

Specify whether cropped parts of the image should be hidden (allowing them to be retrieved later by resizing the canvas) or deleted after cropping.

Checking Perspective in the options bar also allows the crop selection to be rotated and skewed as well as moved and resized.

3 Adjust the crop selection as desired, and press Enter or click the check mark icon in the options bar to crop the image.

The canvas is now cropped to the boundaries of the cropping selection.

Trimming the Canvas

Trimming allows you to quickly crop solid colors or transparent pixels from the edges of the canvas. For example, if you want to remove a solid-colored border from around the image, you can quickly do so using Trim without having to resort to the Crop tool.

Choose the Marquee tool and make a selection in the canvas. Choose Image > Trim… Set the options in the Trim dialog and click OK. The edges of the canvas are cropped based on the options set.

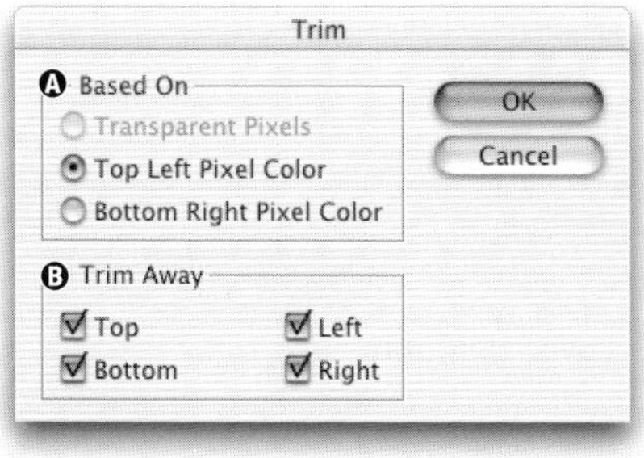

Ⓐ Choose to trim transparent pixels or to use the color of the pixel in the top-left corner or bottom-right corner of the selection. Here, the color of the top-left pixel will be used to trim the image's border.

Ⓑ Check the sides of the canvas to be trimmed.

➠ 9.3 Selecting Rectangular or Elliptical Areas

➠ 9.11 Transforming Layer Content

➠ 9.12 Moving Selected Content

➠ 16.1 Path Basics

Cancel cropping action
Q

Commit cropping action
E

Warning: When pasting between documents, keep in mind the documents' resolutions. Pasting into a document with a lower resolution than the original increases the pasted image; pasting into an image with a higher resolution shrinks the pasted image (see Section 9.14).

You can also use the Crop and Straighten Photos command in the Automate menu to quickly straighten single images or multiple-image scans.

7.7   Changing Your Mind

Undo/redo last action
⌘ Z
Ctrl Z

Step forward in image history
Shift ⌘ Z
Shift Ctrl Z

Step backward in image history
Option ⌘ Z
Alt Ctrl Z

———

In previous versions of Photoshop, Revert was a lot more final than it is now. If you reverted a document, that all changes were lost, and that there was no way to go back. In Photoshop CS, reverting a file is treated as another action in the history and can be undone easily.

———

Warning: Undo and the History palette do not record actions by the Zoom, Hand, and Eyedropper tools.

It happens. You start to make changes to an image, more changes, and still more changes, and you realize that this is not at all what you wanted. Sometimes you only need to get rid of your last change, but sometimes you want to go back several actions or even just start over. You can change your mind in a variety of ways while working on an image in Photoshop.

Undoing/Redoing the Last Change

To instantly get rid of the last change you made in an image, choose Edit > Undo. The last change is listed beside the Undo menu option, letting you know what you will be undoing (for example, Undo Image Size).

If you change your mind and decide to keep the last change, immediately select Edit > Redo (the Redo option replaces Undo in the menu) to reinstate the change.

The Undo and Redo commands have a most important shortcut: Command/Ctrl+Z. This shortcut, when repeated, toggles your last step on and off, allowing you to compare the results of editing actions. Adding another modifier to the shortcut, Command+Option+Z/Ctrl+Alt+Z, allows you to go back several steps in the document history. For example, press and hold down Ctrl+Alt or Command+Option; then each press of the Z key takes away another step. Pressing Command/Ctrl+Z immediately following such a series brings back all the steps in one action.

Reverting to the Last Saved Version

If all else fails, and you want to start over from the point where you were the last time you saved the page, choose File > Revert. This action restores the version of your document currently saved.

7.8 Setting Up the Printed Page

You can print images in Photoshop using any of a number of output devices: everything from inkjet printers to imagesetters. At its simplest, printing requires only one menu selection or keyboard shortcut, yet printing can also be an involved process that requires setting dozens of options to get the exact results.

This section will cover the basics of printing a document using a desktop printer. For advanced printing information, see the "Print Tasks" area of this book.

Obviously, you will need a printer to follow these instructions through completion, but even without a printer, you can view and make changes to all the dialogs.

➡ 8.5 Choosing Color Management Options

➡ 23.1 Print Basics

Page Setup dialog
Shift ⌘ P
Shift Ctrl P

Click and hold the status bar in the document window to display the page preview, which shows the position of the image in the current page setup.

Press Alt/Option and click the status bar to view information about the image.

➟ 23.2 Understand-
ing Resolution
and Docu-
ment Size

**Print With
Preview dialog**
⌘ P
Ctrl P

Setting Up the Page

Before an image is printed, Photoshop needs information about the output medium: the paper size, printer type, and page orientation and whether you want to scale the printed image. To open the Page Setup dialog, choose File **>** Page Setup…, select options, and then click OK to save the changes and close the dialog.

Ⓐ Choose to show and change page attribute settings (shown) or display a summary of the page attributes.

Ⓑ Choose the printer the page is being output to. Doing so displays a list of all currently configured printers, or you can select to format the page for any printer.

Ⓒ Choose the paper size of the page. The items depend on the selected printer.

Ⓓ The current page dimensions.

Ⓔ Choose either portrait or landscape orientation.

Ⓕ Enter a percentage to scale the image. This percentage is in addition to the percentage set in the Print Preview dialog.

Ⓐ Choose the paper size of the page.

Ⓑ Choose the paper-source tray.

Ⓒ Choose either portrait or landscape orientation.

Ⓓ Enter values for the margins of the page.

Ⓔ Click to open a dialog in which you can set the selected printer's properties.

7.8   Setting Up the Printed Page *(continued)*

Previewing the Page before Printing

The term *print preview* is a bit misleading. In the Print Preview dialog, you can do much more than preview the image. You can also adjust the position of the image on the printed page and scale the image up or down. In addition, you can set numerous advanced options for output to printing, which will be discussed in greater detail in the "Print Tasks" area of this book.

To open the Print Preview dialog, choose File > Print With Preview... After adjusting the image size and position as desired, click OK to print the file.

➠ 23.3 Managing
         Color for Print

Print dialog
Option ⌘ P
Alt Ctrl P

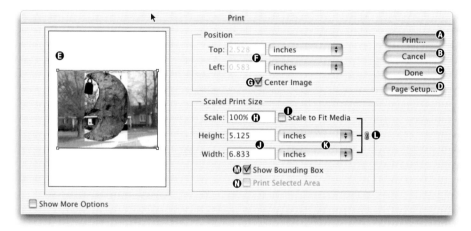

Ⓐ Click to open the Print dialog to print the image using these settings.

Ⓑ Click to return to the image without saving print settings.

Ⓒ Click to save print settings and return to the image.

Ⓓ Click to open the Page Setup... dialog to make adjustments (see the preceding section).

Ⓔ A thumbnail of the image with bounding box. Click and drag edges to resize.

Ⓕ Enter the position of the image from the top-left corner of the page.

Ⓖ Check to automatically center the image on the page.

Ⓗ Enter a value (2.5 to 15000) for the percentage to scale the image for printing. This percentage is in addition to the percentage set in the Page Properties dialog.

Ⓘ Check to force the image to scale to the maximum width or height allowed by the page. This is especially important for printers that make borderless prints.

Ⓙ Enter a value (0.014 to 416.666) for the width or height to scale the image.

Ⓚ Select units to measure the width and height of the image.

Ⓛ Indicates that these values are locked. Changing one value changes the others.

Ⓜ Check to turn on the bounding box in the thumbnail.

Ⓝ Check to print only the selected area. Select an area of the image before selecting Print Preview in order to use this option.

Ⓞ Click to display advanced printing options.

➡ 24 Preparing
Images for
Print

Print one copy

`Option` `Shift` `⌘` `P`
`Alt` `Shift` `Ctrl` `P`

Ⓐ Show More Options

Ⓐ Output

Ⓑ Background... **Ⓔ** Screen... **Ⓖ** ☐ Calibration Bars **Ⓙ** ☐ Caption

Ⓒ Border... Transfer... **Ⓗ** ☐ Registration Marks **Ⓚ** ☐ Labels

Ⓓ Bleed... **Ⓕ** ☐ Interpolation ☐ Corner Crop Marks **Ⓛ** ☐ Emulsion Down

Ⓘ ☐ Center Crop Marks **Ⓜ** ☐ Negative

Ⓝ ☐ Include Vector Data

Encoding: Binary **Ⓞ**

Advanced printing options:

Ⓐ Select Output options (shown) or Color Management options.

Ⓑ Click to select a background color for the page.

Ⓒ Click to set a black border 0 to 10 points (0 to 3.5 mm or 0 to 0.15 inches).

Ⓓ Click to set the amount of overlapping if the image is printing on multiple pages.

Ⓔ Click to set color correction options.

Ⓕ Check to help smooth jagged edges when printing to PostScript Level 3 or later printers.

Ⓖ Check to add color and/or grayscale (depending on the color mode) calibration strips outside the image area.

Ⓗ Check to add marks used to align color separations.

Ⓘ Check to add lines indicating where to trim edges for the final page. This is important when printing files that will be physically trimmed.

Ⓙ Check to add the caption from the File Info dialog to the outside of the image area.

Ⓚ Check to add the image's title and channel names to the outside of the image area.

Ⓛ Check to print to film or photographic paper if the photosensitive layer is facing away from you. If you are unsure which is the emulsion side, examine the developed film under a bright light. The dull side is the emulsion; the shiny side is the base.

Ⓜ Check to print an inverted version of the image for a photonegative. You'll want to do this if you are printing separations directly to film, although in some countries film positives are used.

Ⓝ Check to include the vector data in the image.

Ⓞ Select how the image should be encoded for printing. Binary is generally preferred.

7.9 Printing to a Desktop Printer

Once you set the options, you are ready to print.

■ Selecting Print… in the Print Preview dialog opens the Print dialog. After adjusting the printing options, click Print.

■ To print the image, choose File **>** Print… After adjusting the printing options in the Print dialog, click Print.

■ To quickly print a single copy of the image (bypassing the Print dialog), choose File **>** Print One Copy. The image is sent to the printer you choose in Page Setup.

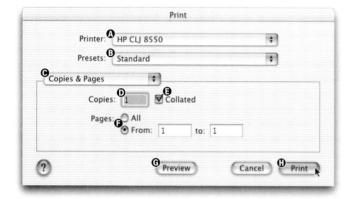

Ⓐ Choose the printer for output. If you do not see the printer you want in the list, choose Edit Printer List… to add a new printer.

Ⓑ Choose either standard options or a custom setting (saved using the Save Custom Settings dialog).

Ⓒ Choose Copies & Pages panel (shown) or Layout Options panel, or select one of the printer-specific Options panels. (Every printer has different options.) You can also choose Summary to display a list of current printing settings or choose Save Custom Settings to custom preset the current settings.

Ⓓ Enter the number of copies to be printed.

Ⓔ Check if you want each copy printed separately. Collating copies in this manner generally takes slightly longer.

Ⓕ Choose whether you want to print all the pages needed to output the image (All) or a specific range (From). If you select From, enter the page numbers for the range in the From and To fields. If you select From, enter the page range you want to print.

Ⓖ Click to preview the image in Adobe Acrobat (if available). This is *not* the same as Print Preview.

Ⓗ Click to send the image to the printer.

➡ 23.1 Print Basics

➡ 23.2 Understanding Resolution and Document Size

➡ 24.1 Preparing to Print

➡ 24.2 Preparing to Print to Inkjet Printers

➡ 25.8 Printing Contact Sheets

➡ 25.9 Printing and Online Services

Page Setup dialog
Shift ⌘ P
Shift Ctrl P

Print With Preview dialog
⌘ P
Ctrl P

———

Most programs (including older versions of Photoshop) use Command/Ctrl-P to open the Print dialog. Photoshop CS defaults to using that keyboard shortcut to print but with a preview dialog screen first. You can change these keyboard shortcuts in the General preferences.

———

Hold down the Alt/Option key in Print Preview to change several buttons. The Print… button becomes Print One Copy, Cancel becomes Reset, allowing you to reset the options, and Done becomes Remember, which saves the options without closing the Print Preview dialog.

7.9 Printing to a Desktop Printer *(continued)*

Print dialog

[Option] [⌘] [P]
[Alt] [Ctrl] [P]

Print one copy

[Option] [Shift] [⌘] [P]
[Alt] [Shift] [Ctrl] [P]

Check with your print
shop to determine
whether it requires pos-
itive emulsion up, neg-
ative emulsion up,
positive emulsion
down, or negative
emulsion down before
setting Emulsion Down
and Negative.

Warning: The image
prints as it appears
when printing is initi-
ated. Hidden layers are
not printed.

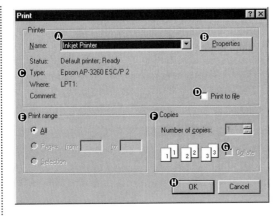

Ⓐ Choose the printer for output.

Ⓑ Click to open the Printer Properties dialog.

Ⓒ Displays the current printer information.

Ⓓ Click to output to a file rather than to a printer.

Ⓔ Choose whether you want to print all the pages needed to output the image (All), a specific range (Pages), or the selected area or the image. If you select Pages, enter the page numbers for the range in the From and To fields.

Ⓕ Enter the number of copies to be printed.

Ⓖ Check if you want each copy printed separately. Collating copies in this manner generally takes slightly longer.

Ⓗ Click to send the image to the printer.

CREATIVE EXERCISE

A great piece to the puzzle of unlocking the power of Photoshop can be found in exercising your own creativity. Many folks put off getting into a Photoshop project, or any creative project for that matter, saying to themselves they just don't have time—so they rarely ever get started. A way to overcome this obstacle is to allow yourself time for smaller creative exercises—short forays into Photoshop if you will. Give yourself 10-30 minutes to open an image or create a blank document:

■ Add some type, run through some filters... try different settings... try the Fade command... try the Fade command with different Blend Modes.

■ Add some Custom Shapes... try out different Styles presets from the Styles palette... Use Layer > Layer Style > Scale Effects to fit the style to your Shape... observe the Layers palette, double-click the effects to see what settings were used.

CHAPTER **8**

PHOTOSHOP WORKSPACE

UNIVERSAL TASKS

PHOTO AND VIDEO TASKS

PRINT TASKS

WEB TASKS

Managing Color and Image Mode

THERE IS A LOT more to consider about color in Photoshop than meets the eye. As you begin working with images, many of your choices regarding image color will simply be perceptual and intuitive—as in choosing or maybe adjusting colors you see on the screen. To work with image color between devices in some predictable manner, Photoshop employs a sophisticated color management system, which works behind the scenes while allowing you to make key choices that affect the final on-screen display or printed color.

Color management may well be the most difficult process for Photoshop users to grasp. This chapter is intended to help you to better understand image color and color management when using Photoshop.

- 8.1   **Image color basics**
- 8.2   **Understanding image modes**
- 8.3   **Editing in 8-bit or 16-bit modes**
- 8.4   **Choosing a color working space**
- 8.5   **Choosing color management options**
- 8.6   **Converting between color profiles and devices**
- 8.7   **Using color in channels**
- 8.8   **Converting between image modes**
- 8.9   **Converting to Bitmap mode**
- 8.10 **Converting to Duotone mode**
- 8.11 **Converting to Indexed Color mode**
- 8.12 **Changing the indexed color table**
- 8.13 **Converting images to gray**

8.1   Image Color Basics

———

CIE Lab color model, sometimes referenced as CIE L*a*b*, is one of several color models produced by the Commission Internationale d'Eclairage. The CIE is a technical, scientific, and cultural non-profit organization concerned with matters related to the science, technology, standardization, and art in the fields of light and lighting.

———

Color is created on the computer or television screen using red, green, and blue light in an *additive* process, in which combining the colors produces lighter colors. Conversely, color is created in print by using inks (most often cyan, magenta, yellow, and black) in a *subtractive* process, in which combining the inks creates darker colors. Obviously, then, if you are designing for print, you cannot see the "true" colors on the screen.

To better understand image color basics, and why you are presented with certain color options in Photoshop, it is perhaps best to look at three topics in simplest terms. First, the system by which digital color is measured and recorded is described using principles of color theory, which define how we see color. Second, though Photoshop is technically more sophisticated (allowing a mix of vector, PostScript, and raster information), it remains primarily a bitmap (or pixel-based) imaging application in terms of how color information is recorded and displayed. Third, Photoshop presents this imaging technology, and applied theory, in an intuitive package for editing images while employing a system of color management that enables you to transfer and control color accurately between devices.

Basic Color Theory

The way we describe and work with color in digital terms with Photoshop is based on how we actually see, and the application of several systems for measuring color. Color perception begins with our eyes capturing electromagnetic wavelengths and our brain's ability to translate this information. The range of colors we can see in full sunlight is our broadest visible spectrum. We see the light of varying wavelengths in this visible spectrum as having different colors. The range of colors we can see depends on the circumstances. We can see a far greater number of colors in direct sunlight, for example, than we can see in low light, on a monitor, or in printed material.

Variations in the range of visible color can be best described by employing color models. A color model provides the system by which color values and their relationships are described, assigning numeric values to measurable differences such as primary colors, lightness, hue, chroma, saturation, and brightness. Photoshop uses four basic color models—RGB (red, green, blue), HSB (hue, saturation, brightness), CMYK (cyan, magenta, yellow, and black), and Lab.

The CIE Lab color model has a fixed, device-independent range of color encompassing the full spectrum of visible colors. For this reason, Photoshop uses Lab color as a reference for color management purposes. Most color models such as CMYK and RGB are device dependent; meaning they have a different "absolute" color range (gamut) depending on the device used for displaying or printing the image. The Lab color model consists of three components: a lightness component, an *a* component for green and red, and a *b* component for blue and yellow.

8.1 Image Color Basics *(continued)*

Bitmap Imaging

Bitmapped or raster images are composed of individual single-colored dots called *pixels,* which are arranged in a grid. The dots are generally so small and so close together that the human eye blends the colors to create the illusion of a continuous tone image. Each pixel is assigned a particular numeric color value, which is dependent on the color mode of the image, much like the chips in a tile mosaic. An image created using this mosaic-style grid is referred to, in computer jargon, as a bitmap. Thus, Photoshop has long been referred to as a bitmap-editing program. Other programs, such as Adobe Illustrator, are referred to as vector-editing programs because images are defined mathematically using vector paths rather than a grid of pixels. Photoshop is actually now a true hybrid application: it allows you to edit and save both vector and pixel data.

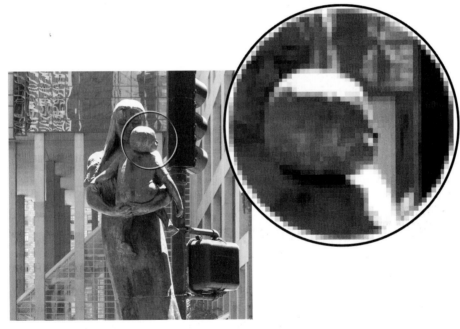

If you magnify the image on the screen, you can see the individual pixels used to create the image.

Color Management

You can look at color management in Photoshop in a couple of ways. Primarily, it is the system by which color from an image or a document is interpreted and converted accurately when an image is moved between devices—for example, from camera, to computer (monitor display), and to print. Second, Photoshop offers many opportunities to actively exercise control over the process of color management and to make choices regarding color, including color working space, image mode, and the assignment of color profiles.

➠ 22.2 Adjusting Tonal Range Using Levels

➠ 22.3 Adjusting Color Levels Using Curves

➠ 23.1 Print Basics

➠ Color Section Color Model Illustration

➠ Color Section Color Management Illustration

Pixel is short for *picture element.*

If you are regularly sharing your files with other Photoshop users, you may want to save and share your color settings so that you are all working with the same options.

The location of the Color Settings preferences depends on the operating system. To find the file, use your operating system Find feature to search for Color Settings. It should be in a folder labeled Adobe Photoshop 7.0 Settings.

8.2   Understanding Image Modes

Don't confuse the general term *bitmap* with the specific Bitmap image mode. The image mode allows only black pixels and white pixels; the general term refers to any image created using tiled pixels.

Some features in Photoshop are not available in all image modes. For example, many filters will not work in CMYK mode. If you must use them, you will need to convert to RGB mode, apply the filter, and then convert back to CMYK mode.

The term *image mode* in Photoshop is synonymous with the color mode of an image. An image mode is similar to a color model in that it determines the method used to store image color information, yet it also defines a specific color space for an image. It is recommended that you edit as much as possible in the original color mode of an image and keep an archive version of the image in its original color mode, since conversion between image modes may cause a loss of color information as the color gamut is shifted. The one exception to color information loss is Lab color, as it has the widest color range of all color modes.

In Photoshop, you can choose from eight color modes, listed here in the order they appear in the menu. Choose Image > Mode to display the following choices:

Bitmap All pixels are recorded as either black or white with no gray values. Images in this mode are called bitmapped 1-bit images because they have a bit depth of 1. Bitmap mode is recommended for output to older PDA or mobile phone devices. Not to be confused with BMP file format.

Grayscale Pixels are recorded in black, white, or as many as 256 shades of gray in between.

When you convert from color to grayscale, every pixel is assigned a brightness value ranging from 0 through 255 to define the grayscale level.

Duotone Uses two (Duotone), three (Tritone), or four (Quadtone) spot colors in combination. You must convert the image to Grayscale mode before converting to Duotone mode. This mode is recommended for printing colorized grayscale images using spot color rather than process color. Save Duotones as Photoshop EPS, Photoshop PDF, or Photoshop DCS 2.0 files.

8.2   Understanding Image Modes *(continued)*

Indexed Color All pixels are forced (indexed) to the closest color value in a color lookup table (CLUT) of as many as 256 possible colors or shades (8-bit). Recommended for web graphics and multimedia presentations in which file size is restricted. Can be saved in a wide variety of file formats, including Photoshop PSD, BMP, GIF, Photoshop EPS, Large Document Format (PSB), PCX, Photoshop PDF, Photoshop Raw, Photoshop 2.0, PICT, PNG, Targa, or TIFF formats.

RGB Pixels are recorded as a combination of red, green, and blue color values, each with a density assigned in the range 0 through 255. Using 3 color channels and 8 bits per channel, RGB offers 16.7 million colors; 16-bit can produce even more colors. RGB mode is the most common, and all Photoshop commands and tools are available in this mode. RGB mode is recommended for multipurpose use and particularly if you are outputting to the computer or television screen or to an RGB printing device.

CMYK Pixels are recorded as a combination of cyan, magenta, yellow, and black (K) color values. CMYK is recommended as a final color mode for images that will be placed in publications or other layout applications. Use CMYK for printing to color printers that clearly specify you send images in CMYK and for creating color separations used in offset printing.

Lab Pixels are recorded by their lightness value and color values on a green–red (the *a* axis) and blue–yellow (the *b* axis) scale. This mode was developed to overcome differences in color between platforms and to provide consistency among printers, monitors, and other output devices. Lab mode is recommended when transferring files between computers running different operating systems. Photoshop uses LAB color as an intermediate color model when converting images.

Multichannel Pixels are recorded using multiple 256-level grayscale channels but without a combined channel. When you convert from other color modes, channels are converted into CMY spot colors. This mode is recommended only for special printing needs. Save in Photoshop DCS 2.0 format.

➧ 12   Working with Colors, Gradients, and Patterns

➧ 12.4 Selecting Colors with the Color Picker

If you delete a channel from an image using RGB, CMYK, or Lab mode, the image mode is automatically converted to Multichannel mode.

Save images using Multichannel mode in Photoshop DCS 2.0 format.

Although image modes are used to *record* colors in an image, color models are also used to *create* or choose colors for use in an image.

8.3 Editing in 8-bit or 16-bit Modes

Editing in 16-bit color has long offered the Photoshop user a much broader range of color to work with. Just as an example, in 16-bit grayscale, you have the advantage of 65,536 shades of gray versus 256 shades of gray in 8-bit grayscale. Some characterize the difference as "professional" versus "recreational" use of Photoshop. With the release of Photoshop CS, Adobe has expanded the editing potential of 16-bit mode to include all tools in the Toolbox (except the Art History Brush tool) and features such as Adjustment Layers and all Tonal Adjustment commands (except Variations).

Although a 16-bit image file will be twice as large as an 8-bit version of the same document, there are marked advantages in expanded tonal range and the ability to do multiple edits without level loss and banding. For years, many professionals have worked around limitations, for the benefits of 16-bit mode, by editing copies of their images in 8-bit to take advantage of features found only in 8-bit.

To take full advantage of editing in 16-bit mode, you must begin with a 16-bit digital capture. An image converted from 8-bit to 16-bit may see some little improvement, but the real advantage is to be found only in 16-bit originals.

To make sure you know you are working with a 16-bit image, Photoshop displays bit information next to the document color mode. Or Choose Image > Mode > 16 Bits/Channel, and be sure 16-bit is checked.

16-bit Color and ImageReady

If you work between Photoshop and ImageReady, be aware that ImageReady converts 16-bit images into 8-bit for editing. Once saved in ImageReady, 16-bit information is lost. However, if you return the image to Photoshop without saving in ImageReady, your 16-bit data will be retained.

Although 16-bit images offer a wider range of color, these greater color distinctions come at a price of nearly twice the file size.

Photoshop now supports 16-bit editing with more tools than it has in the past. For those few filters and tools such as Liquify, the Pattern Maker and the Extract filter it is recommended you duplicate your image and convert the duplicate to 8-bit mode to use these specific tools.

While all filters may be applied to 8-bit images, only the various Blur, Noise, Sharpen, Dust & Scratches, Despeckle, Median, Emboss, Find Edges, Stylize and Solarize filters will work on 16-bit images.

8.4 Choosing a Color Working Space

A working space is equivalent to a default color profile for editing images in Photoshop. Photoshop allows you to choose your own settings for the specific color profile that should be used in a document for a particular image mode. For example, you choose File > New, to create a blank document. You then choose RGB as the color mode, and when the new document opens, it displays sRGB IEC61966-2.1 as its color space. sRGB IEC61966-2.1 is the default RGB color space for Photoshop North American General Purpose Defaults.

Use the Color Settings dialog to set and save your own general color management options or preferences to be used for a new document and documents being opened in the current copy of Photoshop. To open the Color Settings dialog, choose Photoshop > Color Settings… (Mac OS X) or Edit > Color Settings… (Windows).

You can set the color workspace (specify how colors are treated in the document of a certain mode) for the following image modes:

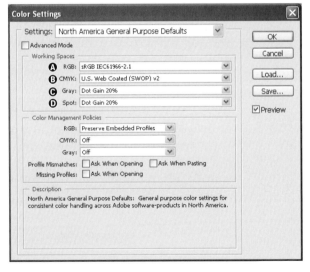

Color Settings dialog
Ctrl Alt K
Shift ⌘ K

———

If you are new to Photoshop and computer-generated color, use the predefined color settings, and leave the advanced options at their defaults.

———

If you are working with a printer or service bureau, always check with them to ensure that the working space profiles you select are compatible with their workflow.

Color settings are especially useful if your image will be used in a variety of output mediums to ensure that colors are consistent when converting between different image modes.

Ⓐ Choose from Adobe RGB (1998), Apple RGB, ColorMatch RGB, and sRGB IEC61966-2.1, or for an extensive list of RGB profiles to embed in images, choose Advanced at the top of the Color Settings dialog. The choice you make will depend on your working needs, but generally Adobe RGB (1998) is best for print work; sRGB IEC61966-2.1 is preferred for web images.

Ⓑ Choose from an extensive list of CMYK profiles. Talk to your print service provider for the setting that works best with their presses.

Ⓒ Choose from a list of Dot Gain percentages or gamma levels to use with grayscale images.

Ⓓ Choose from a list of Dot Gain percentages to use with spot colors.

8.5   Choosing Color Management Options

If you are new to Photoshop and computer-generated color, use the predefined color settings, and leave the advanced options at their defaults.

If you are working with a printer or service bureau, always check with them to ensure that the working space profiles you select are compatible with their workflow.

Color settings are especially useful if your image will be used in a variety of output mediums to ensure that colors are consistent when converting between different image modes.

A working space is a color profile used for newly created or untagged documents for the associated color mode. For example, if you start a new document using the RGB mode, and you have set the RGB working space to sRGB IEC61966-2.1, this working space will be embedded in the new document.

With all the technical labels for color profiles and workflow, it may help to simplify things by remembering two points about color management in Photoshop. First, in simplest terms, color management is just how Photoshop reads the profile and color information of an image, converts that information to its own reference colors (Lab), and then converts to your designated working space. Even if you select the "Color Management Off" setting and turn off all warnings, Photoshop will open images, read their color, and allow you to work using its Adobe (ACE) color engine and passive color management techniques that will emulate the behavior of applications that do not support color management.

Unless directed to use specific color management settings for a desired workflow required by your printer or service bureau, the easiest way to deal with color settings is to use the predefined settings that Photoshop provides as general purpose defaults. These defaults automatically set options for working spaces, color Management Policies, and advanced options. Choose Photoshop **>** Color Settings… (Mac OS X) or Edit **>** Color Settings… (Windows) to open the Color Settings dialog.

Although default setting are recommended for most users, checking the Advanced Mode option at the top of the Color Settings dialog provides a unique learning opportunity along with expanded options. With the option checked, the dialog will extend, providing you with a unique display in the description section at the bottom of the dialog, explaining various option details as you move your cursor over the dialog.

At the very top of the dialog, choose the Settings drop-down, which will offer you the following choices along with your saved presets:

Color Management Off   Does not turn the Photoshop Color Management System off. Emulates the behavior of applications without color management. Does not tag documents with profiles. Not recommended if you work primarily with tagged documents.

ColorSync Workflow   (Mac only) Uses the Mac's ColorSync color management system; recommended if you will be working with a mix of Adobe and non-Adobe applications in your workflow. Not recognized by Windows.

North American General Purpose Defaults   Uses general-purpose color settings for consistent color between Adobe products in the specified region. Japan, Europe, North America.

Emulate Acrobat 4, Photoshop 4, Photoshop 5 Default Spaces   Uses the color-handling behavior of the specified application; recommended if you are transferring the image to machines that use older versions of Photoshop or Acrobat.

8.5   Choosing Color Management Options *(continued)*

European, Japan, or U.S. Prepress Defaults Recommended if you are printing to a press in one of these areas; set for common conditions.

Web Graphic Defaults Sets optimal color settings for creation of web graphics.

Choosing Color Management Policies

Color management policies specify how images being opened in Photoshop will be treated in relation to the default working space profiles you have set. Three policy options are available for each color mode:

Off No working space profiles are embedded in new documents. Working space profiles are turned off for documents being opened unless the embedded profile matches the default working space profile.

Preserve Embedded Profiles The embedded working space profile in the image being opened overrides the default working space profile.

Convert To Working Space The embedded working space profile in the image being opened is replaced by the default working space profile.

Ⓐ Choose one of the three policy settings (RGB, CMYK, Gray) for each color mode.

Ⓑ Check to be alerted when the working space profile embedded in an image being opened is different from the profile that is specified in the working space. This option is recommended; however, you may constantly get warning boxes.

Ⓒ Check to be alerted when the working space profile embedded in an image being pasted is different from the profile of the image into which it is being pasted. This option is recommended.

Ⓓ Check to be alerted when the image opened does not contain a working space profile. This option is recommended. The alert also requires that the color management policy for the corresponding color mode is not set to Off.

The last option areas in the dialog allow you to control how profiles are converted and how image color is displayed on the screen.

Conversion Options Allows you to choose between the Microsoft ICM and the Adobe (ACE) color management engine, choose one of four rendering intents, and choose black point and dither options.

Advanced Controls Allow for desaturating monitor colors and blending, enabling you to visualize color spaces with gamuts greater than that of a given monitor and for controlling the blending behavior of RGB colors. Use these controls with caution as these specific choices will also cause color mismatch between monitor and print.

➡ 6.4   Opening an Existing Image

➡ 23.3 Managing Color for Print

Color Settings dialog
Ctrl Alt K
Shift ⌘ K

The location of the Color Settings preferences depends on the operating system. To find the file, use your operating system Find feature to search for Color Settings. It should be in a folder labeled Adobe Photoshop 7.0 Settings.

If you are regularly sharing your files with other Photoshop users, you may want to save and share your color settings so that you are all working with the same options.

Color is created on the computer or television screen using red, green, and blue light in an *additive* process, in which combining the colors produces lighter colors. Conversely, color is created in print by using inks (most often cyan, magenta, yellow, and black) in a *subtractive* process, in which combining the inks creates darker colors. Obviously, then, if you are designing for print, you cannot see the "true" colors on the screen.

8.6 Converting between Color Profiles and Devices

In the process of working with an image, you might want to change, convert, or even remove the image's current color profile. Change the profile by replacing the image's current profile with a new one selected in the Assign Profile dialog. In this case, the colors will be reinterpreted, which can sometimes lead to a noticeable shift in colors. When you convert one profile to another, colors are recalculated in an attempt to preserve the appearance of the colors as displayed using the current color profile. Although some color shifting might occur, the shift is minimized.

Assigning a Profile

Choose Image > Mode > Assign Profile... to open the Assign Profile dialog, select a profile, and click OK.

Ⓐ Choose to remove all color management profiles from this document.

Ⓑ Choose to use the working space defined for the image's color model (see Section 8.2).

Ⓒ Choose an alternative profile from the drop-down.

Ⓓ Check if you want profile changes shown in the canvas.

COLOR MODES VS. COLOR MODELS

Although many of their names are identical, it is important not to confuse color modes and color models. All documents have a color mode set for them that determines the color gamut available, as well as how colors are output to the monitor or printer. Color models, on the other hand, are used to describe or define colors and allow you to specify particular values used to create colors on the screen and in your image. You can, for example, have a document in CMYK mode and still use the RGB color model to specify color values in the color picker; doing so will not change the color mode of the image, however, this technique will allow you to choose colors that are out of gamut for the document's printable color range.

8.6   Converting between Color Profiles and Devices *(continued)*

Converting a Profile

Choose Image > Mode > Convert To Profile... to open the Convert To Profile dialog, select a profile, and specify how to perform conversion. Click OK to convert the image's profile using the selected options.

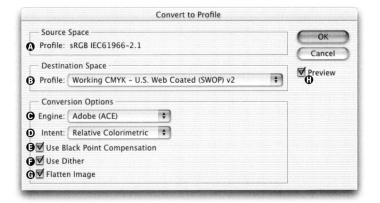

ⓐ Displays the image's current color profile.

ⓑ Choose a new color profile to translate to.

ⓒ Choose the conversion engine you want to use. The exact list depends on your operating system. Adobe (ACE) is recommended.

ⓓ Choose an option for how you want to convert the color. Perceptual is generally preferred.

ⓔ Check to adjust for differences between the black points (the points at which colors are 100% black) in the two profiles. If this option is unchecked, some blacks might turn gray.

ⓕ Check to dither colors with 8-bit/channel images when converting. This setting uses dithering if colors available in one color profile image mode are not available in the image mode of the color to which it's being converted.

ⓖ Check to flatten multiple layers in the image before conversion.

ⓗ Check if you want conversion changes shown in the canvas.

Although you can specify global settings for color management in the Color Settings dialog, each individual document has its own individual profile for controlling how the image should be previewed on the screen and output.

To save the embedded profile in the document file, you must use a file format that supports embedded profiles (Photoshop PSD, PDF, EPS, TIFF) and make sure that the Embed Color Profile option is checked.

If you are given particular ICC profiles to use, they first need to be installed at the system level so Photoshop will recognize them on startup—for example: in Windows 2000 and XP, copy profiles to C:\ WINDOWS\SYSTEM32\ spool\drivers\color. For OSX, copy to Users/ Current User/Library/ ColorSync/Profiles

8.7 Using Color in Channels

Switch to Combined color channel

⌘ ~

Ctrl ~

———

Alpha channels are used to record selections and layer masks as a grayscale image. This allows you to edit selections using any painting tool (see Chapter 13).

———

Spot colors use a special channel to record a single predefined color ink, such as a PANTONE ink.

An image in Photoshop can have as many as 56 channels, and there are three types of channels: color, spot, and alpha. Photoshop uses color channels to store all basic image color information, and color channels are created automatically when you open a document. Each color mode has a signature set of color channels or minimum number of channels. (Grayscale and Index Color modes have one.)

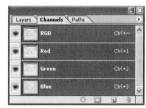  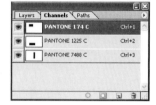

RGB and CMYK images each have a composite channel and a channel for each signature color. Lab color images have composite, Lightness, and two color (a,b) channels. Images using spot colors (such as PANTONE colors) for print separations require individual spot channels for each color used.

Consider color in individual channels of specific color modes to help tackle creative challenges in Photoshop. Many creative options are available to you; here are a few:

RGB Because digital cameras often pick up "noise" in low-light captures, you might try looking at each individual color channel. You will find that one channel will often have more of the visible noise, which you can eliminate by running a blur filter on that individual channel. Sharpening in individual channels can help avoid banding associated with oversharpening.

CMYK Look to individual channels for additional contrast for making difficult selections. When converting to grayscale, look to the individual CMYK channels for detail that might be lost in a standard grayscale conversion. Consider the Channel Mixer set to Monochrome for more control over grayscale conversion.

Lab These channels offer unique options for color adjustments since Lab stores green and red color information together in its a component and blue and yellow color information in its b component. The Lightness channel in Lab color mode also offers you nondestructive sharpening choices and an excellent alternative for grayscale conversion. The Lightness channel is often a superior grayscale image compared with the standard image mode to grayscale conversion.

Spot Channels Allow you specific control in offset printing, when absolute color accuracy is demanded. Spot channels can also be used to designate varnish application for unique design treatments such as gloss and matte coatings.

8.7 Using Color in Channels *(continued)*

Working with the Channels Palette

Color channels are displayed in the Channels palette, where you can edit and add channels for a variety of purposes.

➡ 23.4 Creating Spot Channels for Print

➡ 24.4 Preparing Spot Color and Duotone Images

➡ 24.5 Preparing for Four-Color Printing

➡ 24.6 Creating Color Traps and Knockouts

Switch to a specific color channel
⌘ 1 – 4
Ctrl 1 – 4

Deleting one of the color channels in RGB or CMYK mode automatically converts the image to Multichannel mode.

Duplicating a color channel creates a grayscale version of the channel.

- To **edit** a specific channel, select that channel in the Channels palette, and then use a painting tool to edit the pixels on just that layer. Regardless of the colors selected, you paint in shades of that channel's color.

- To **duplicate** a channel using the Duplicate dialog, select the channel in the Channels palette and then choose Duplicate Channel in the Channels palette menu. In the Duplicate dialog, enter a name for the new channel, and select where to add the channel (in the current document, in another open document, or in a new document). If you select a new document, enter a name for the new document, and then specify whether to invert the channel.

- To **quickly duplicate** a channel, drag the channel's thumbnail to the Create New Channel button The channel is duplicated using the channel's name with the word *copy* added after it.

- To **delete** a channel, select the channel in the Channels palette, and then click the trashcan 🗑 or drag the layer to the trashcan. You can also select Delete Channel from the Channels palette menu.

- To **split** channels into separate documents, choose Split Channels from the Channels palette menu. All the channels in the current document open as new documents.

- To **merge** channels in open, single-layered, flattened grayscale documents into a single RGB, CMYK, Lab, or Multichannel document, open the documents to merge. (This will also work to "unsplit" a split document.) Choose Merge Channels… from the Channels palette menu on any of the open images. In the Merge Channels dialog, choose the image mode for the combined channels, choose the number of channels for the new document, and click OK. In the next dialog, assign the documents to the channels for the color mode selected, and then click OK. The new image is created using the selected options.

8.8   Converting between Image Modes

———

Color modes determine
not only the number of
colors available to the
image (gamut) but also
the number of color
channels available in
the Channels palette
and the file size.

———

Remember, color modes
determine how color is
recorded in the image,
and color models deter-
mine how you define
color for the image.

———

The gamut for RGB and
CMYK modes will also
depend on their color
settings (see Section 8.4).

———

CMYK gamuts are
smaller than other color
gamuts since they con-
sist only of colors that
can be printed using
process-color inks. You
can highlight colors that
are out of gamut in the
image by choosing View
> Gamut Warning.

All images, regardless of the color profiles embedded in them, use a specific color mode to record colors. However, the image mode is not set in stone, and you can quickly move between color modes depending on your needs at any time while working. But be careful. Although you can convert between modes easily, each mode has its own color gamut, and you will likely lose colors and degrade the image quality if you constantly convert back and forth. That said, not all commands and features in Photoshop are available in all image modes. For example, CMYK does not have access to all the filters. In that case, it is best to begin work in RGB mode, make all your edits (being sure not to use color out of the CMYK gamut), and then convert to CMYK when you are satisfied with the image.

1   Choose Image > Mode and select the desired image mode. To convert to Bitmap or Duotone mode, first convert to Grayscale mode and then convert again to Bitmap or Duotone mode (see Section 8.2).

2   A dialog will appear, asking whether you want to flatten or merge layers in the image.

  ■ If you selected Multichannel, Indexed Color, or Bitmap, you must click OK to flatten the image in order to continue. If you click Cancel, the image mode is unchanged.

  ■ If you selected Lab Color, CMYK Color, or RGB Color, you must choose whether you want to merge the layers into a single layer (Merge) or preserve the current layers (Don't Merge) in order to continue. If you click Cancel, the image mode is unchanged.

  ■ If you selected Grayscale, and there is only one layer, you must click OK to discard the image's color information in order to continue. If there are two or more layers, you must choose whether to merge the layers into a single layer (Merge) or preserve the current layers (Don't Merge) in order to continue. If you click Cancel, the image mode is unchanged.

3   If you selected Multichannel, Lab Color, CMYK Color, or RGB Color, the image mode is changed without further interaction. The next four sections explain how to proceed using Bitmap, Grayscale, Duotone, and Indexed Color.

8.9 Converting to Bitmap Mode

Bitmap mode can be accessed only by images currently in Grayscale mode. Follow the instructions in Section 8.6 to convert the image to grayscale, repeat those steps to convert to bitmap, and continue with the following steps:

1 If there are multiple channels in the image, you will be asked to discard the nongrayscale channels.

2 Set the options in the Bitmap dialog and click OK.

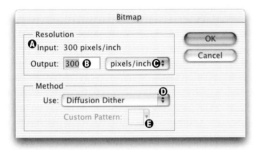

A Displays the current resolution of the image.

B Enter a value (1.000 to 30000.000) for the resolution of the final bitmap image.

C Choose the units used for the output resolution.

D Choose a method for creating the bitmap. If you select Halftone Screen…, you can set the halftone options when you click OK.

E If you select Custom Pattern, choose the pattern from the Pattern Presets drop-down.

3 If you set the method to Halftone Screen… in step 2, set the halftone screen options and click OK.

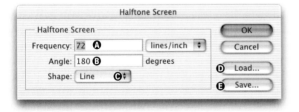

A Enter a value (1.000 to 999.999) for the line frequency (the printing equivalent of resolution) for the bitmap. The drop-down to the right allows you to choose lines per inch or lines per centimeter.

B Enter a value (–180.0000 to 180.0000) for the halftone angle.

C Choose a shape for the halftone screen to be used in the bitmap.

D Click to load Halftone Screen options that have the .ahs extension.

E Click to save the current Halftone Screen options using the .ahs extension.

The image now appears in Bitmap mode.

➡ 8.13 Converting Images to Gray

Bitmap images are not extremely common except in mobile phones and certain PDAs that do not support grayscale or color. The WBMP (short for "wireless bitmap") is a bitmap format.

8.10 Converting to Duotone Mode

➠ 12.4 Selecting Colors with the Color Picker

➠ 12.5 Selecting Custom Spot Colors

➠ 24.3 Preparing to Print to PostScript Printers

To avoid murky colors in your Duotones, place the darkest colors at the top of the Duotone list and the lightest at the bottom. This ensures the best saturation of all colors.

If you want a Duotone to affect only part of an image, convert from Duotone to Multichannel mode (converting the Duotone colors to spot colors). You can then erase colors in the spot channels that you want printed in grayscale.

Photoshop provides several common sample Duotone, Tritone, and Quadtone curves to get you started.

Duotone mode offers you the choice of blending spot colors in one, two, three, or four colors. Typically, a true Duotone is used in design considerations where a single spot color is used along with black typography in a layout; the Duotone is used to provide an interesting photographic treatment without adding additional cost to the two-color print. Duotone mode can be accessed only by images currently in Grayscale mode. To create an image in Duotone mode, choose Image > Mode > Duotone to open the Duotone Options dialog.

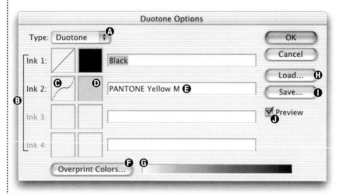

🅐 Choose a tone type: Monotone (one color), Duotone (two colors), Tritone (three colors), or Quadtone (four colors).

🅑 **Inks** Depending on the tone type selected, one to four inks are available to edit.

🅒 **Ink Curve** Displays a thumbnail representation of the application of the ink color at different levels. Click the thumbnail to open the Duotone Curve Editor.

🅓 **Ink Color** Displays the color of the ink used in this tone. Click to open the Custom Color Picker and choose a spot color.

🅔 **Ink Name** Displays the name of the ink. Enter a name for the color if you want to use a name that is different from the Photoshop-assigned name.

🅕 Click to open the Overprint Editor.

🅖 Displays a preview of the tonal range using the selected ink colors.

🅗 Click to load a file of previously saved Duotone options that have the .ado extension.

🅘 Click to save the current options as a Duotone options file that has the .ado extension.

🅙 Check if you want changes made in the Duotone Options dialog previewed in the canvas.

1 In the Duotone Options dialog, choose the tone type you want to use. The number of inks available depend on the tone type selected.

2 Click an ink color to use the Custom Color Picker to choose the spot color you want to use for each ink.

8.10   Converting to Duotone Mode *(continued)*

3   Click the ink curve to adjust the amount of ink being used at different levels (shadow to highlight) for each ink. The curve maps the grayscale value in the original image to a specific ink percentage. If you have Preview checked in the Duotone Options dialog, curve changes are reflected in the canvas. Click OK to return to the Duotone Options dialog when you are satisfied with the curve.

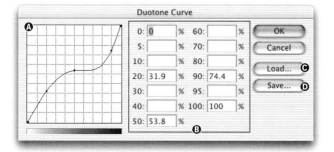

➡ 24.4 Preparing Spot Color and Duotone Images

➡ 25   Saving, Proofing, and Sending to Print

Warning: You will not be able to revert to the original Duotone state (except through the History palette) if you make changes to the image in Multichannel mode. Make all adjustments in the Duotone Curves dialog before converting to Multichannel mode for output.

Choose Duotone mode again while in Duotone mode to reopen the Duotone Options dialog.

To output Duotone images for other applications, save them in EPS or PDF format, unless the image contains spot colors in channels, in which case you should save it as DCS 2.0. Be sure to name the custom colors so that they will be recognized in the other applications.

Ⓐ Ink Curve Displays the amount of ink (vertical) for a particular level in increments of 10. Click any of the vertical lines in the graph to adjust the amount of ink being used at that level. The value is reflected in the level values input fields to the right (see B).

Ⓑ Level Values Displays the value as a percentage for the amount of ink being used at that level. Enter a value (0.0 to 100.00) to change the value directly. The changes are reflected in the ink curve (see A).

Ⓒ Click to load a file of previously saved Duotone Curve options that have the .atf extension.

Ⓓ Click to save the current options as a Duotone Curve options file that has the .atf extension.

4   To view or adjust how overprinted colors display on the screen, click the Overprint Colors… button. Colors are "overprinted" when two or more unscreened inks are printed on top of each other, resulting in new color. Since several variables can affect the resulting color (paper color, order the inks are printed, slight variations in ink colors, and so on), you might need to adjust how the overprinted colors are displayed on the screen to better match how they look when printed, usually based on a preview sample from your printer. This setting does not affect the way overprinted colors are printed. Click OK when you are finished adjusting overprint colors to return to the Duotone Options dialog.

5   Click OK when you are satisfied with the Duotone. The image will now use Duotone mode.

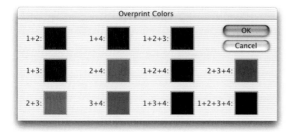

Each square represents how the two or three inks indicated next to it will appear when mixed on the screen (but *not* when printed). Click any square to open the Color Picker and adjust the color manually. Doing so is not generally recommended unless you have calibrated your monitor.

8.11   Converting to Indexed Color Mode

Traditionally, web designers converted images to Indexed Color mode before saving them as GIFs. However, Photoshop's Save For Web dialog lets you save a copy of the image as a GIF without first converting the original image to Indexed Color mode.

Although you can convert an image in Indexed Color mode back to RGB or other color modes, any color lost to indexing cannot be restored.

Indexed Color mode can be accessed only by images currently in RGB, Duotone, Bitmap, or Grayscale mode. Follow the instructions in Section 8.6 to convert the image to Grayscale, Duotone, Bitmap, or RGB mode, and then repeat to convert to Indexed Color mode.

- If you are converting from Grayscale, Duotone, or Bitmap modes, the indexing process is automatic, and no further action is required.

- If you are converting from RGB mode, you will need to specify how the colors should be indexed in the Indexed Color dialog.

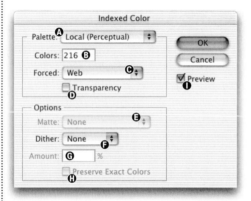

A Choose a color palette to index to: System (Mac or Windows), Web, Uniform, Local (Perceptual, Selective, or Adaptive), Master (Perceptual, Selective, or Adaptive), Custom (allows you to edit the color table), or Previous (to use the last color palette). If the image contains 256 or fewer colors, you can also select Exact to use all the colors in the image. Generally, Perceptual will provide the best image quality.

B Displays the number of colors being used in the palette. For Uniform, Local, or Master palettes, enter a value (3 to 256) to set the number of colors in the palette. Fewer colors decrease file size at the expense of image quality.

C For Exact, Local, and Master palettes, choose which colors should be forced. That is, if a color is close to a particular color value (Black And White, Primaries, or Web Safe Colors), the color is forced into that value. To edit the forced color table, select Custom…

D Check to use 100% transparent areas of the image as a transparent color. If this option is unchecked, transparent areas in the image are filled with the matte color.

E Choose a matte color to be used as the background of the image.

F Choose whether you want colors dithered and the dithering type to be used.

G If dithering is being used, enter a percentage (1 to 100) for the amount of dithering allowed in the image.

H If diffusion dithering is being used, check to preserve the original colors for the dither.

I Check to show a preview of the indexed image in the canvas.

8.12   Changing the Indexed Color Table

Once a color is converted to Indexed Color mode, a color table is generated that contains all the colors in the image. You can view and edit this color table by choosing Image > Mode > Color Table…

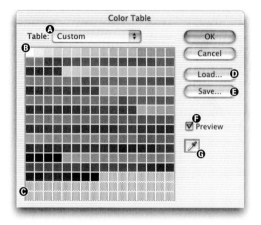

A Select a color table to apply to the image. Custom is the color table generated when converting to Indexed Color mode. Changing the color table might produce some bizarre results.

B **Color squares** Each square represents a color in the image. Click a square to open the Photoshop Color Picker and adjust that color's value. Command/Ctrl-click to delete the color from the table.

C **Blank squares** Represent an unused color square in the possible 256 values in the color table. Click to open the Photoshop Color Picker and add a color in that position.

D Click to load a color table saved with the .act extension.

E Click to save the current color table as a file that has the .act extension.

F Click to preview color table changes in the canvas.

G Click and then select a color square or a color in the canvas to use as the transparent color when saving as a GIF.

Although you can use painting tools to edit in Indexed Color mode, you can only use colors in the indexed color palette and cannot add other colors without editing the color table.

8.13   Converting Images to Gray

As is the case with most tasks in Photoshop, you can convert an image to grayscale in several ways. The differences in the results of these processes are sometimes very subtle, possibly best compared by placing one over the other in a single document and switching its layer visibility on and off. These results will also vary between image types.

This graphic demonstrates three grayscale conversion methods. The top stripe was converted using Lab Color mode's Lightness channel; the center stripe was converted by choosing Image > Mode > Grayscale; and the bottom stripe was converted using a Channel Mixer Adjustment layer.

Using Lab Color Mode

Lab Color mode stores all the grayscale information for an image in the Lightness channel. The results of this process are generally quick and prove to have subtle benefits over switching directly to Grayscale mode:

1   Choose Image > Mode > Lab Color.

2   In the Channels palette, delete the a and b Lab color channels by dragging them to the trashcan icon or choosing Delete from the palette menu. After you delete the first color channel (b), the name of the second (a) changes to Alpha 2. Delete this channel as well.

3   Now choose Image > Mode > Grayscale.

Using the Channel Mixer

Digital capture devices such as cameras and scanners record all image information in three channels: Red, Green, and Blue. Tonal ranges, which you might want for grayscale conversion, can be more prevalent in one of these color channels than in the others. You can use the following method, though more painstaking than others, to better control the conversion:

1   Choose Layer > New Adjustment Layer > Channel Mixer.

2   At the bottom of the Channel Mixer dialog, check the box to indicate you want to work in monochrome.

3   There are three sliders, one for each channel. You will notice that by default the Red channel is set to 100%, with no value in the Blue and Green channels. Play with the sliders to see what information is in the other channels. Rule of thumb is to keep the total range of the three sliders adding up to 100%–110%.

CHAPTER 9

Selecting and Moving Image Content

IN SIMPLEST TERMS, SELECTIONS allow you to single out or isolate pixels from the rest of a document, designating them for some Photoshop process to follow. You can edit, copy and paste, or move selected pixels while protecting the rest of the document from changes. As you select specific content in Photoshop, a marquee or flashing dashed border—often referred to as "marching ants"—will designate the selection edges.

Photoshop allows many options for working with selections. You can select an entire layer or just specific content within a layer. You can save selections, and you can use selections between documents. Just as Photoshop allows you to add, subtract, and transform image information; you can add to, subtract from, and transform selections themselves.

You can make and modify selections in Photoshop with a variety of interchangeable tools and methods. This chapter looks at selection tools and the various ways you can select, move, and copy content in Photoshop:

9.1 Selection Basics

➡ 2.4   Edit Menu

➡ 2.7   Select Menu

➡ 3.3   Marquee
Tools

Lasso tool
Ⓛ

Cycle lasso tools
Ⓢⓗⓘⓕⓣ Ⓛ

Marquee tool
Ⓜ

Cycle marquee tools
Ⓢⓗⓘⓕⓣ Ⓜ

Magic Wand tool
Ⓜ

Move tool
Ⓥ

———

Remember, you can always modify a selection

———

Actions with the selections are recorded in the History palette, so you can choose Edit > Step Backward and Edit > Step Forward.

Selections can be virtually any shape. They can have hard, crisp edges, or they can have soft, feathered edges. You can select with a variety of tools, which can be used independently or in any number of combinations.

Primary selection tools Located in the topmost section of the Photoshop Toolbox; these include the Crop, Marquee, Lasso, and Magic Wand tools. You can use them in any combination and, alternately, create selections in any variety of shapes by adding to or subtracting from them as you work.

Refined selections Using vector tools, such as the Pen tool or shape tools, you can convert vector paths into selections. You can also make selections based on color range. Photoshop offers several more sophisticated tools that allow you to extract objects or erase backgrounds, essentially combining the Select and Delete commands for you.

Masks and channels You can make selections by painting onto masks or channels with any variety of Photoshop brushes and then converting the masks or channels into selections. The Quick Mask option in the Toolbox provides a simple one-click method for converting between selection and mask. All selections saved in Photoshop are stored as alpha channels in the Channels palette.

Each selection tool and selection method offers you specific advantages to be considered or used in combination with your own working style—and given image content. Consider just a few of the options available regarding selection strategies for content in this image, and apply them when considering your own selections:

Ⓐ Currently selected content is designated with a selection border. It can be actively edited, moved, copied, deleted, and so on.

Ⓑ The selection border defines the edges of selected area(s) and is designated by a marquee, or "marching ants." (You can hide these for more accurate editing.)

Ⓒ Nonselected image areas are essentially protected from editing.

Ⓓ You can select sky with the Magic Wand; if you select with Color Range, you can pick up the sky between branches and leaves. In cases in which you need to select the entire background, consider selecting the object rather than the background, or duplicate the layer, and try the Extract filter on the object.

Ⓔ For objects that have smooth curves or little contrast with the background, try using the Pen tool and paths. Look at contrast in each individual channel, more contrast will assist your use of the Magnetic Lasso. Zoom in and add small selections together. You can also easily block in a solid large objects by using a round brush (80%–90% hardness) in Quick Mask mode.

Ⓕ You can select high-contrast edges, such as the lower edge of the truck fender, with the Magnetic Lasso, or you can add/subtract with the Magic Wand at low tolerance settings.

9.1 Selection Basics *(continued)*

After you make a selection, you have several basic options:

Save the selection As in the example, some selections may take time and patience to create; it is always wise to save the selection—even as you go. Save versions of the selection with hard edges before feathering.

Feather selection edges To soften or fade selections, the rule of thumb is to look around at objects in nature. Object edges rarely appear absolutely crisp and sharp. A slight feather almost always looks more realistic—try even a 0.5 pixel feather.

Move selected content Use the Move tool ⊞ to relocate the content within the current layer or between documents. Alt/Opt-Move copies selections.

Copy/cut and paste Use the Clipboard to relocate content within the current document or to another document. Pasting puts the Clipboard on a new layer. Pasting into a selection applies a layer mask in the shape of the selection.

Edit selected content Change the content. Create a new layer, and paint in the selection. Create adjustment layers and masks based on the selection for isolated color correction. Run filters on selected areas or on masks.

Deselecting and reselecting a selection Choose Select > Deselect or click anywhere on the canvas outside the selected area to deselect a selection. To reselect the last selection, choose Select > Reselect. If the last action was to deselect a selection, you can also choose Edit > Undo.

➡ 3.4 Move Tool

➡ 3.5 Lasso Tools

➡ 3.6 Magic Wand Tool

Hide marquee
⌘ H
Ctrl H

Invert selection
Shift ⌘ I
Shift Ctrl I

Deselect
⌘ D

Ctrl D

Reselect lasst selection
Shift ⌘ D
Shift Ctrl D

Always consider your options. Sometimes selecting the opposite of what you want selected is easier.

The Quick Mask option in the Toolbox provides a simple one-click method for converting between selection and mask.

All selections saved in Photoshop are stored as (8-bit) alpha channels in the Channels palette.

ANTI-ALIASING

Several selection and other tools have the option of anti-aliasing pixels. Using anti-aliasing allows Photoshop to soften the edges of images and text, making the edge pixels semi-transparent so that they blend more fluidly into the background color rather than producing a hard edge.

9.2   Selecting a Layer or Its Contents

Select All

Ctrl A

⌘ A

———

A few tools, such as Smudge, include an option that allows you to work with multiple layers simultaneously.

———

If there are no opaque pixels in a selected area (that is, the area is empty), you will not be able to move, copy, cut, or transform the selected area.

———

In this chapter, all the methods for making and working with selections have a common goal: surrounding the area that you want to edit, copy, or move in the fill image. With some selections, close is close enough, but for others, you need to capture the exact pixels as precisely as possible.

A selection isolates pixels in only the currently selected—or active—layer. Therefore, be sure that you first select the specific layer that you want to edit.

When layers contain transparent areas or objects that do not take up the entire layer, you need not reselect their pixels before using selection tools. Photoshop allows you to quickly select a layer's contents at the same time you make the layer itself active for editing.

Selecting a Layer

You can select a layer in the following ways:

In the Layers palette, click the layer's thumbnail or title. The layer is highlighted with a brush icon in the left column to indicate it is active. Here, the Header layer is selected.

Or, with the Move tool selected, Control/right-click in the canvas over the content you want to select. A contextual menu appears listing all the layers with content currently under the mouse cursor. Select the desired layer from the list. You can temporarily toggle to the Move tool from any active tool by pressing the Command/Ctrl key.

This is not to be mistaken for selecting pixels or layer content. If you do not select any specific content in the layer using the techniques shown in the rest of the chapter, your actions or changes are applied to the entire layer.

Selecting a Layer's Content

To select only the opaque pixels of the layer and exclude all transparent pixels, do one of the following:

- Command/Ctrl-click the layer in the Layers palette.
- Control/right-click a layer thumbnail in the Layers palette and choose Layer Transparency from the contextual menu.
- If you Choose Select > All on a layer containing transparent areas, a marquee will appear around the entire canvas. If the content of the layer is moved, the selection marquee snaps to the boundary of the object or pixels on the layer.

9.3　Selecting Rectangular or Elliptical Areas

A common way to make a simple selection is to use the marquee tools, which allow you to select a regular rectangular or elliptical region of the canvas. Making such a selection is often a helpful way to begin a more complex selection or to define the area to begin an edit. For example, if you are creating a rectangular button, select a rectangular area to define the size of the button and then begin to edit the selection.

To use the marquee tools, follow these steps:

1　Select a layer.

2　Choose a marquee tool from the Toolbox:

　　Rectangular Marquee

　　Elliptical Marquee

　　Single Row Marquee

　　Single Column Marquee

3　Set the options in the tool options bar for this selection:

　■ Choose how the new selection should be treated in relation to the current selection: deselect the current selection and start a new selection, add to the current selection, subtract from the current selection, or intersect with the current selection.

　■ If you are using the Rectangular Marquee or Elliptical Marquee tool, enter the amount of feathering for the new selection (0 is no feathering), specify whether you want the selection anti-aliased so that edges are softer, and choose a style for the selection (Normal, Fixed Aspect Ratio, or Fixed Size).

　■ If you select Fixed Aspect Ratio or Fixed Size, enter an aspect ratio or width and height.

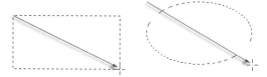

4　Depending on the marquee tool and options selected, do one of the following:

Rectangular or Elliptical Marquee　Click and drag diagonally across the area you want to select.

Single Row, Single Column, or Fixed Size Marquee selections　Click in the image to select, and drag to position the marquee.

5　You can now refine the selection further or edit the selection as explained in the rest of the chapter.

➡ 2.4　Edit Menu

➡ 2.7　Select Menu

➡ 3.3　Marquee Tools

➡ 3.4　Move Tool

➡ 4.11　Info Palette

Marquee tool
[M]

Cycle marquee tools
[Shift] [M]

If there is no existing selection, constrain proportions (square or circle); if there is an existing selection, add to the current selection. (Press Shift again while selecting to constrain proportions.)
[Shift]　plus select

Subtract from the current selection
[Option]　plus select

[Alt]　plus select

Hold down while making a selection to move the marquee
[Spacebar]

Cancel a selection in progress (previous selections are preserved)
[Esc]

If you move a selection, using either the Move tool or the arrow keys, the selection collapses around the content within the selection for the current layer.

As you make your selection, the width, height, and origin point of the selection are displayed in the Info palette.

9.4　Creating Free-Form Selections

Lasso tool
⊡ L

Cycle lasso tools
Shift ⊡ L

Add to the current selection
Shift plus select

Subtract from the current selection
Option plus select

Alt plus select

Cancel a selection in progress (previous selections are preserved)
Enter

Erase the last anchor point of Polygonal or Magnetic Lasso tools
Del

To capture irregular shapes, your primary options are the three free-form lasso tools, or you can use a Quick Mask to "paint" the area to be selected.

Using the Lasso and Polygonal Lasso Tools

The irregular edges of the sunflower as selected with the Lasso tool

The straight edges of the barn roof as captured with the Polygonal Lasso tool

You can use the Lasso and Polygonal Lasso tools to freehand trace the outline of the area you want to select. Follow these steps:

1　Select a layer.

2　Choose the Lasso 🔎 or Polygonal Lasso 📐 tool.

3　Set the options in the tool options bar for the selected tool:

- Choose how the new selection should be treated in relation to the current selection.

- Enter the amount of feathering for the new selection (0 is no feathering).

- Specify whether you want the selection anti-aliased so that edges are softer.

4　Depending on the Lasso tool selected, do one of the following:

Lasso Click and drag around the area you want to select. When you release the mouse button, the selection is automatically closed by a straight line between the starting and stopping points.

Polygonal Lasso Click at points around the area you want to select to create straight sides. To close the selection, click back on the first point. (The Polygonal Lasso icon appears with a circle next to it when you are over the point.) You can also Command/Ctrl-click or double-click to close the selection with a straight line between the starting and stopping points.

9.4 Creating Free-Form Selections *(continued)*

Using the Magnetic Lasso Tool

The Magnetic Lasso tool goes one step further than other lasso tools by reading the image content you are trying to select and automatically sticking to edge contours as you move along with your cursor—so you don't have to work quite as hard to follow exact edges. Photoshop does this by looking at the contrast between areas where you drag your cursor to determine where the edge boundary should be. The results are not always perfect, and you will need to adjust the options for some objects, but this technique can save a lot of time—particularly if you have clear definition between shapes:

1 Select a layer.

2 Choose the Magnetic Lasso tool 🖌.

3 Set the options in the tool options bar for this selection tool:

- Choose how the new selection should be treated in relation to the current selection.

- Enter the amount of feathering for the new selection (0 is no feathering)

- Specify whether you want the selection anti-aliased so that edges are softer.

- Enter the width from the mouse pointer to be considered as part of the path. If the image is high contrast, use a wide line to ensure a solid edge. If there are a lot of small shapes, use a width larger than 10 pixels.

- Enter the percentage of contrast between edges in the image to be considered for the path. Use a high percentage for high-contrast images to ensure a tighter fit.

- Under Frequency, enter a number (1 through 100) for how often anchor points are automatically added along the path. The more points, the tighter the fit, but the more jagged the selection may appear.

- If you are using the Magnetic Lasso tool and a tablet, specify whether you want to allow pen pressure to set the width.

4 Click to set the first anchor point in the selection, and then drag around the edge of the object you are attempting to select. A selection path (a solid line) snaps to the edge of the object as you drag. Your settings for Width, Edge Contrast, and Frequency determine how the tool reads edges and fits your selection.

If you notice that the selection is moving away from the desired edge, try moving more slowly. You can only back up to the last anchor point. Click to manually add anchor points if you are on track, and then continue your selection.

5 To close the magnetic selection, do one of the following:

- Click back on the first point. (The Magnetic Lasso icon appears with a circle next to it when you are over the point.)

➠ 2.7   Select Menu

➠ 3.5   Lasso Tools

➠ 8.7   Using Color in Channels

➠ 11   Masking Layers

➠ 11.1 Mask Basics

You can still make selections in Quick Mask mode to limit the area in which you are making your Quick Mask.

Another way to make a free-form selection is to use the Pen tool to create a path and then turn the path into a selection.

When making precise selections, it is helpful to zoom in to the image as much as possible to see greater detail.

Switch from Magnetic Lasso to Lasso (reverts after release)

Option

Alt

Switch from Magnetic Lasso to Polygonal Lasso (reverts after first click after release)

Option-click

Alt-click

Increase the Magnetic Lasso width by 1 pixel

]

Decrease the Magnetic Lasso width by 1 pixel

[

Toggle Standard and Quick Mask mode

Q

To help make Magnetic Lasso selections, increase the difference between edges in the image by adding a Brightness/Contrast fill layer and increasing contrast.

Double-click the Quick Mask icon in the Toolbox to set Quick Mask options. You can switch between painting masked versus selected areas and change the color and opacity of the overlay.

You may find it useful to make selections without the Feather option preset. Choose Select > Feather... to add situation-specific amounts.

■ Command/Ctrl-click, press Return/Enter, or double-click to close the selection with a magnetic path line directly between the starting and stopping points calculated by Photoshop.

■ Option/Alt-double-click to close the selection with a straight line between the starting and stopping points.

The magnetic selection surrounds the eagle statue.

Using Quick Mask to Make a Selection

Using Quick Mask is a unique alternative to other selection methods that allows you to use painting tools to make quick, rough selections or intricately detailed selections that might otherwise be difficult. Using Quick Mask mode is similar to editing any other mask or channel in Photoshop—painting with black or white to add or remove masked areas—with the added convenience of toggle buttons in the Toolbox, allowing you to switch quickly between mask and selection. Quick Mask appears as a color overlay, which you can manipulate independently of the image itself, allowing you to easily see your selection. Switch to Quick Mask anytime, from any selection, to use Brush tools to edit the selection.

To use Quick Mask to make a selection, follow these steps:

1 Choose the Quick Mask Mode option ▣ on the toolbar. Your foreground and background colors are switched to black and white.

2 Choose any appropriate size and shaped brush to paint areas you want to select. It will appear as though you are painting on a semitransparent layer.

3 After you paint your mask, select the Standard Mode button ▣ in the toolbar to turn the mask into a selection. Click back to Quick Mask mode to turn the current selection back into a mask and continue editing.

The mask is being painted over the image (indicated here by lighter areas). The mask will appear as a semitransparent red or mock-Rubylith by default. Toggle between foreground and background colors (black/white) to alternate between adding and subtracting from the mask.

9.5   Making Color-Based Selections

Photoshop's Magic Wand tool and the Select > Color Range menu option allow you to make selections based on image or pixel color. You can take advantage of large areas of similar color for easy selections, or you can select bits of the same color that are scattered in your image to save time. If the area you want to select contains lots of tonal changes, you might have to play with your settings to get the desired selection.

Using the Magic Wand Tool

You can use the Magic Wand tool to click a single pixel in your image to select that color and similar colors immediately surrounding it or throughout the image. Follow these steps:

1 Select a layer as described in Section 9.2.

2 Choose the Magic Wand tool 🪄 .

3 Set the options in the tool options bar for this selection:

■ Enter the color tolerance (0 through 255) for the selection. This number specifies how similar a color has to be to the color clicked to be included in the selection. The higher the number, the more tolerant the selection.

■ If checked, anti-aliasing is used to give the edges of the selection a smoother appearance.

■ If Contiguous is checked, only pixels touching the selected pixel and within the set tolerance are included in the selection. Otherwise, the Magic Wand tool selects all pixels in the image within the tolerance level.

■ If Use All Layers is checked, the Magic Wand selects pixels on all layers in the image. Otherwise, the Magic Wand tool works only within the selected layer.

4 In the canvas, click a pixel of the color you want to select. You can change the Tolerance setting you have chosen or simply Shift-click to add to your Selection.

A Magic Wand selection with a Tolerance of 25 and Contiguous checked. The selection is stopped by the black line.

A Magic Wand selection with a Tolerance of 150 and Contiguous unchecked. More pixels are selected, and the selection is not stopped by the black line.

➡ 2.7   Select Menu

➡ 3.6   Magic Wand Tool

Magic Wand tool
Ⓦ

Add to the current selection
Ⓢⓗⓘⓕⓣ-click

Consider color information in individual channels or making color adjustments to enhance selection options. You can always duplicate your image, make selections in an extremely altered image, and transfer selections between the images.

9.5 Making Color-Based Selections *(continued)*

➡ 22.9 Using Replace
Color

**Subtract from the
current selection**
Option -click
Alt -click

——

When selecting specific
colors for editing, be
careful not to create
sharp changes in the
color that will look
strange when printed.

Using the Color Range Dialog

You can choose Select > Color Range to make simple color-based selections or to make complex selections reading color subsets and blends:

1 You can first limit the area being considered by making a selection.

2 Choose Select > Color Range to open the Color Range dialog.

3 Click with the Eyedropper on a desired color, and drag the slider in the dialog. Experiment with various settings and combinations:

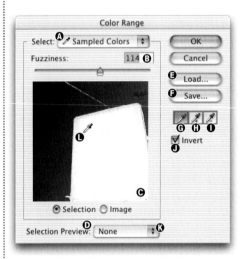

Ⓐ Choose to select colors directly from the image or to select a particular color, luminosity, or out-of-gamut colors.

Ⓑ Click to enter or use the slider to set the level of fuzziness (0 through 200), which is much like color tolerance.

Ⓒ **Preview** Shows the image, the selected area (white indicates a selected area), or a reduced version of the original image.

Ⓓ Choose a preview method for the canvas, showing the selection either as grayscale (shown) or the full image.

Ⓔ Click to load previously saved settings.

Ⓕ Click to save the current settings.

Ⓖ **Eyedropper tool** Click to select a new color. This action deselects other colors currently selected.

Ⓗ **+ Eyedropper tool** Click to select a color to add to the current range (Shift-click).

Ⓘ **– Eyedropper tool** Click to select a color to remove from the current range (Opt/Alt-click).

Ⓙ If checked, the selection is inverted.

Ⓚ Choose a method for previewing the selection in the canvas : None, Grayscale, Black Matte, White Matte, Quick Mask.

Ⓛ Use the Eyedropper tool to select colors in the preview area, in the document windows, or from any color swatch in the interface.

4 When you are satisfied with the preview, click OK.

5 Check what you've got with the next desired command. Undo, make adjustments to the dialog options, and make repeated selections with alternate variables. This is one of those tools that requires experimentation.

9.6 Increasing or Reducing Selection Areas

After making an initial selection, you can add to or subtract from the selection in a variety of ways. The following modifiers appear at the left side of the Options bar when you choose a selection tool from the Toolbox:

Ⓐ New Selection

Ⓑ Add To Selection

Ⓒ Subtract From Selection

Ⓓ Intersect Selections

Using Selection Tools to Add to or Subtract from a Selection

You can use all the selection tools (Marquee, Lasso, and Magic Wand) to add to or subtract from an existing selection. Depending on the tool you are using, the cursor icon will have a plus (+) next to it when adding or a minus (−) when subtracting.

You can add or subtract using the selection tools in two ways:

- Choose a selection tool, and then click the Add To Selection or Subtract From Selection button in the tool options bar. Set other options for the selection tool as desired, and then follow the instructions for selecting with that tool. The new selection is added to or subtracted from the original selection.

- Choose a selection tool, set options in the tool options bar, and then hold down the Option/Alt (subtract) or the Shift (add) key while following the instructions for selecting with the current tool. The new selection is added to or subtracted from the original selection.

The original selection (square) and the new selection.

The new selection has been added to the original selection.

The new selection has been deleted from the original selection.

➡ 2.7 Select Menu

➡ 3.3 Marquee Tools

➡ 3.4 Move Tool

➡ 3.5 Lasso Tools

Move tool
[V]

Invert selection
[Shift][⌘][I]
[Shift][Ctrl][I]

9.6   Increasing or Reducing Selection Areas *(continued)*

➠ 3.6   Magic Wand
         Tool

➠ 9.9   Transforming
         the Selection
         Marquee

➠ 9.11 Transforming
         Layer Content

Deselect
⌘ D
Ctrl D

Reselect last selection
Shift # D
Shift Ctrl D

───

Warning: Don't confuse
inverting the selection
(the Inverse command)
with inverting colors.
The two processes have
similar names and key-
board shortcuts, but
produce very different
results.

Using Selection Tools to Intersect a Selection

Use selection tools to select the common area between an existing selection and a new selection. When you are creating an intersection, the cursor icon will have an X next to it. Follow these steps:

1 Choose a selection tool, click the Intersect button , and set the other options in the tool options bar.

2 Follow the instructions for the tools being used to make a second selection. Make sure that the new selection overlaps the existing selection; if it does not, no pixels will be selected.

The new selection has intersected
the original selection.

Switching Selected and Unselected Areas

Often it is easier to select the area that you do *not* want selected than the area you want selected. For example, it is easier to select a flat, colored background that surrounds a complexly shaped object rather than trying to select the object itself. In these cases, you then need to invert the selection to select the desired area. First make a selection, and then choose Select > Inverse. You can then refine the selection further or edit the selection.

The selection has been inverted.
Notice that the selection marquee
follows the edges of the canvas.

9.7   Modifying Selection Edges

Photoshop gives you numerous options for modifying selection edges, from convenient options for adding and subtracting pixels to softening or feathering selections.

Feathering a Selection

Feathering is the process of softening the edges of a selection, making a gradual fading transition from the boundary of the selection inward. You can set feathering as an option in the tool options bar before making most selections (except with the Magic Wand), but you can also set feathering after making a selection. Follow these steps:

1 Choose Select > Feather…

2 Enter the number of pixels you want to be feathered from the edge of the selection marquee in the Feather Selection dialog. The number you choose depends not only on the amount of fade you want, but also on the size of the actual selection and the resolution of the image.

3 Click OK. The selection is now feathered at the edges.

The content around the center of the image has been selected and feathered.

You can really see the effects of the feathering when the selection is deleted.

➡ 2.7   Select Menu

➡ 3.3   Marquee Tools

Lasso tool
[L]

Cycle lasso tools
[Shift] [L]

Marquee tools
[Shift] [M]

———

Warning: Don't confuse moving the selection marquee with moving the selected content. You can move the marquee using any selection tool, and doing so does not affect the image. You can move the selected content only by using the Move tool.

9.7 Modifying Selection Edges *(continued)*

➡ 3.5 Lasso Tools

Magic wand tool
Ⓦ

Add to the current selection
Shift plus select

To capture an exact area, you must use a variety of methods to make your selection and then further refine and modify the selection. You can continually modify selections at any time while working with them.

Enlarging a Selection Based on Color

To enlarge an existing selection based on similarities in pixel color you can:

Add contiguous pixels Choose Select > Grow to expand the selection to include colors immediately around the image based on the selected area and within the set tolerance in the Magic Wand options.

Add noncontiguous pixels Choose Select > Similar to expand the selection to include colors throughout the image based on the selected area and within the set tolerance in the Magic Wand options.

The original selection to be modified

Grow: The selection grows to include similar pixels in the same area.

Similar: The selection includes similar pixels throughout the image.

Modifying a Selection

The original selection to be modified

A 10-pixel border selected

Smoothed to 20 pixels

9.7 Modifying Selection Edges *(continued)*

Photoshop offers you four basic selection modifiers.

To select a border based on a selection Choose Select > Modify > Border…, enter the size of the desired border, and click OK. The selection is changed to a border of the set thickness around the position of the original border.

To smooth a rough selection Choose Select > Modify > Smooth…, enter the amount of smoothing you want (higher numbers create smoother selections), and click OK. The selection will flatten sharp picks and dips within a jagged selection by the amount you indicated. Smooth is most effective in RGB mode.

To enlarge the size of the selection Choose Select > Modify > Expand…, enter the number of pixels to enlarge the selection, and click OK.

To reduce the size of the selection Choose Select > Modify > Contract…, enter the number of pixels by which to reduce the selection, and click OK.

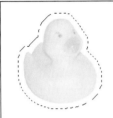

Expanded by 10 pixels   Contracted by 10 pixels

ALPHA CHANNELS AND SELECTIONS

When you save a selection, it is turned into a Mask and saved as an alpha channel in the Channels palette. Having the selection saved as a Mask gives you a lot of power to control and manipulate the selection. The editing of Masks is discussed in detail in Chapter 11.

➡ 3.6 Magic Wand Tool

Subtract from the current selection
[Option] plus select
[Alt] plus select

Cancel a selection in progress (previous selections are preserved)
[Esc]

———

Selection marquees that have been feathered have rounded edges at the corners.

———

To avoid the clipping or rounding of corners associated with expanding and contracting selections, you can switch to Quick Mask and choose Filter > Other > Maximum or Filter > Other > Minimum.

9.8 Moving the Selection Marquee

Move tool
[V]

Invert selection
[Shift][⌘][I]
[Shift][Ctrl][I]

Deselect
[⌘][D]
[Ctrl][D]

Reselect last selection
[Shift][#][D]
[Shift][Ctrl][D]

———

Warning: Don't confuse inverting the selection (the Inverse command) with inverting colors. The two processes have similar names and keyboard shortcuts, but produce very different results.

You can move the selection marquee independently of the actual image content, which allows you to make a selection in one layer or area and then transfer the selection to another layer or area without affecting the content.

The selection is moved, but the content remains in the same place.

- To move the selection marquee **within a layer,** choose any selection tool and select the New Selection button [⊡] in the tool options bar. Now either click and drag anywhere within the selection or use the arrow keys to move the selection.

- To move the selection marquee **to another layer,** simply select the target layer using one of the methods discussed in Section 9.2.

- To move the selection marquee **between open Photoshop documents,** choose any selection tool and select the New Selection button in the tool options bar. Now click anywhere within the selection and drag it from the original document into the target document's canvas. The selection is placed into the currently selected layer of the target document. The selection marquee is still available in the original document as well.

9.9 Transforming the Selection Marquee

You can transform a selection marquee: you can scale it, skew it, distort it, and add perspective to it.

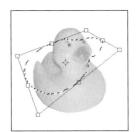

You transform a selection marquee on a bounding box in much the same way that you transform content, but only the selection marquee is affected, not the selected content.

To transform the selection marquee, follow these steps:

1 Choose Select > Transform Selection to display a rectangular bounding box around the entire selection.

2 Make one or more of the following transformations to the marquee:

■ To **move** the entire selection marquee, click and drag within the bounding box except at the exact center.

■ To adjust the **reference point** (which sets the center for transformations), click and drag it to the desired location.

■ To **scale** the selection marquee, click and drag an edge of the bounding box. Click corner points to resize both horizontally and vertically at the same time.

■ To **symmetrically scale** the selection marquee around the reference point, Option/Alt-click and drag an edge or a corner point of the bounding box.

■ To **rotate** the selection marquee around the reference point, click and drag just outside the bounding box.

■ To **skew** the selection marquee, Shift-Command-click/Shift-Ctrl-click and drag an edge of the bounding box.

■ To **distort** the selection marquee, Command/Ctrl-click and drag any of the edges or corner points of the bounding box independently.

■ To **symmetrically distort** the selection marquee around the reference point, Option-Command-click/Alt-Ctrl-click and drag edges or corner points of the bounding box.

■ To add **perspective** to the selection marquee, Control/right-click and select Perspective from the contextual menu. Click and drag on an edge or a corner point to change the selection's perspective.

3 Click the Commit button ✔ in the tool options bar or press Enter/Return to accept the transformations. Click the Cancel button ⃠ or press Esc to cancel transformations and leave the selection unchanged.

➡ 2.7 Select Menu

➡ 3.3 Marquee Tools

➡ 3.4 Move Tool

➡ 3.5 Lasso Tools

➡ 3.6 Magic Wand Tool

➡ 9.9 Transforming the Selection Marquee

➡ 9.11 Transforming Layer Content

Move tool
[V]

Invert selection
[Shift][⌘] [I]
[Shift][Ctrl] [I]

Deselect
[⌘] [D]
[Ctrl] [D]

Reselect last selection
[Shift][#] [D]
[Shift][Ctrl] [D]

9.10   Saving and Loading Selections

Although many of the selections you make will be temporary, you may also find that making precise selections takes considerable effort. Preserving selections to save yourself work in redoing them—should you change your mind or consider another option down the road—might just become part of your routine one day. You can save selections for use between documents; this is particularly helpful in production work or running actions on multiple images.

Saving a Selection

To save a selection, follow these steps:

1   Make a selection.

2   Choose Select **>** Save Selection…

3   Set options in the Save Selection dialog.

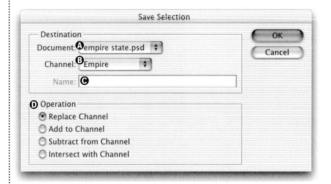

Ⓐ Specify whether you want the selection saved in the current document, an open document duplicated from this document, or a new document.

Ⓑ Select an existing channel to save the selection in, or choose to save the selection in a new channel. If you are creating a new document, New will be the only choice for channel.

Ⓒ If you are creating a new channel for the selection, enter its name.

Ⓓ If you are adding the selection to an existing channel, choose the operation for how the new selection should be placed in the channel.

4   Click OK.

■   If you choose to start a new document, an untitled document is opened with the new channel.

■   If you choose to add the selection to another channel, the selection is now a part of that channel.

■   If you choose to start a new channel for the selection, the channel is added to the document in the Channels palette.

9.10 Saving and Loading Selections *(continued)*

Loading a Selection

To load a selection, follow these steps:

1 Select a layer into which to load the selection. You can also make an initial selection.

2 Set options in the Load Selection dialog.

3 Click OK. The new selection is on the canvas.

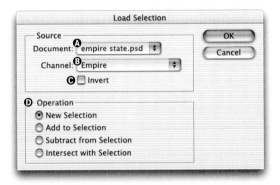

Save a selection as an alpha channel, bypassing the Save Selection dialog, by clicking the Save Selection As Channel button.

Ⓐ Choose the open document you want with the desired selection channel.

Ⓑ Choose the channel from which to load the selection.

Ⓒ Check to invert the selected area.

Ⓓ If you have an existing selection already on the canvas, choose the operation for how the new selection should be treated in relation.

Loading a Selection from the Channels Palette

You can also reload selections directly from the Channels palette.

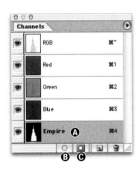

Ⓐ Highlight the alpha channel that contains the selection.

Ⓑ Load the channels as selections.

Ⓒ Save the selection as a channel.

1 In the Channels palette, click the alpha channel that contains the saved selection. The canvas will show the black and white of the alpha channel. White is the selected area.

2 Click the Load Channel As Selection button 	⬭ . The selection will be displayed in the canvas. Select the Combined channel to view the image again.

9.11 Transforming Layer Content

➡ 2.7 Select Menu

Move tool
[V]

———

The Enter key is primarily used in Windows or the Mac to commit a change after it has been made. The Return key also does the same thing on the Mac.

After copying, pasting, extracting, or otherwise isolating an object or image content, you may find yourself wanting to manipulate it—wanting to transform it—to better fit your intentions or its surroundings. Photoshop allows you to transform content by scaling, skewing, distorting, or adding perspective to the selected object or layer.

You can apply transformations using menu commands or by using transformation pseudotools. Accessed via menu command, these pseudotools allow you to intuitively drag control points (C) on a bounding box (A) displayed around the content being manipulated. Several transformations use a movable reference point (B) on which they base their transformation. Click and drag this icon to reposition the reference point. For example, a Rotate command will rotate around this reference point. You can also reposition content while transforming. In all the following examples, the original silhouette at 65% opacity is copied and the duplicate transformed to give you a reference for what was done.

Scale, adjust from corners. Add Shift to constrain.

Skew, sides adjust and remain parallel.

Distort, adjust from sides and corners.

Perspective, adjust from sides and corners.

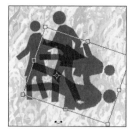

Rotate, with reference point shifted off center.

Flip, horizontal with reference point shifted off center.

9.11 Transforming Layer Content *(continued)*

Using the Free Transform Pseudotool

The most common way to make transformations is to use the Free Transform pseudotool, which allows you to make any of the transformations. Which transformation you make depends on where you click or which keyboard or menu modifiers you choose. To use the Free Transform pseudotool, follow these steps:

1 Select a layer to transform. You can also select specific content on the layer. If no content is selected on the layer, the transformation is applied to the entire layer.

2 Choose Select > Transform Selection to display a rectangular bounding box around the entire selection.

3 Make one or more of the following transformations:

■ To **move** the entire selection, click and drag within the bounding box.

■ To adjust the **reference point** (which sets the center for transformations), click and drag it to the desired location.

■ To **scale** the selection, click and drag an edge of the bounding box. Click corner points to resize both horizontally and vertically at the same time.

■ To **symmetrically scale** the selection around the reference point, Option/Alt-click and drag an edge or a corner point of the bounding box.

■ To **rotate** the selection around the reference point, click and drag just outside (but not touching) the bounding box.

■ To **skew** the selection, Shift-Command-click/Shift-Ctrl-click and drag an edge of the bounding box up or down.

■ To **symmetrically skew** the selection, Option-Command-click/Alt-Ctrl-click and drag an edge of the bounding box up or down.

■ To **distort** the selection, Command/Ctrl-click and drag edges or corner points of the bounding box.

■ To **symmetrically distort** the selection around the reference point, Option-Command-click/Alt-Ctrl-click and drag edges or corner points of the bounding box.

■ To add **perspective** to the selection, Control/right-click and select Perspective from the contextual menu. Click and drag an edge or a corner point to change the selection's perspective.

4 Click the Commit button ✔ in the tool options bar or press Enter/Return to accept the transformations. Click the Cancel button ⊘ or press Esc to cancel transformations and leave the selection unchanged.

➡ 3.4 Move Tool

Free Transform

⌘ T

Ctrl T

———

Add the Option/Alt modifier to the Transform Again command to duplicate content as it is transformed.

———

You can link layers and transform multiple linked layers at the same time, and you can transform the content of an entire layer set as well.

9.11   Transforming Layer Content *(continued)*

Transform Again

[Shift] [⌘] [T]

[Shift] [Ctrl] [T]

Do not confuse trans-
forming the selection
marquee and trans-
forming the selected
content.

Transformed content is
interpolated using the
method currently set in
your preferences

Using Commands and Pseudotools

You can also access each transformation pseudotool independently on the Transform submenu. This allows you to focus on making one kind of transformation without worrying about
whether you have your mouse in the right position or the right keyboard modifier pressed.

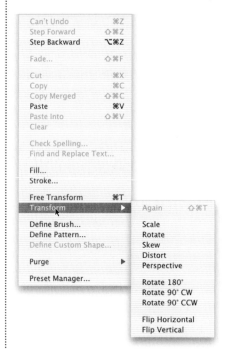

To transform using commands and pseudotools, follow these steps:

1   Select a layer to transform. You can also select specific content on the layer. If no content is selected on the layer, the transformation is applied to the entire layer.

2   Choose Edit > Transform and then one of the options in the submenu. You can select
different pseudotools to work with while making transformations, using either the
Edit > Transform menu or the contextual menu.

Again   Choose to repeat the previous transformation.

Scale   Choose to use the Scale pseudotool. Click and drag an edge of the bounding box
to resize. Click corner points of the bounding box to resize both horizontally and vertically at the same time. Press Option/Alt to scale symmetrically.

Rotate   Choose to use the Rotate pseudotool. Click and drag just outside the edges of
the bounding box to freely rotate the selection.

Skew   Choose to use the Skew pseudotool. Drag an edge of the bounding box up or
down to skew. Press Option/Alt to skew symmetrically.

9.11 **Transforming Layer Content** *(continued)*

Distort Choose to use the Distort pseudotool. Drag edges or corner points of the bounding box. Press Option/Alt to distort symmetrically.

Perspective Choose to use the Perspective pseudotool. Click and drag an edge or a corner point to change the perspective.

Rotate 180°, 90° CW, Or 90° CCW Choose to turn the entire selected region.

Flip Horizontal Or Vertical Choose to reverse the area in the indicated direction.

3   Click the Commit button ☑ in the tool options bar or press Enter/Return to accept the transformations. Click the Cancel button ⊘ or press Esc to cancel transformations and leave the selection unchanged.

Using the Transform Tool Options Bar

Even though they are not real tools (at least they are not in the Toolbox), all transform pseudotools have options in the tool options bar that allow you to make transformations numerically. Follow these steps:

1   Select a layer to transform. You can also select specific content on the layer. If no content is selected on the layer, the transformation is applied to the entire layer.

2   Select a transform pseudotool from the Edit > Transform submenu, or choose Edit > Free Transform.

3   Set the options in the tool options bar.

ⓐ **Reference Point Location** Click one of the open squares to set the relative position of the reference point in relation to the bounding box.

ⓑ **Reference Point Horizontal And Vertical Position** Enter an exact position for the reference point in the canvas.

ⓒ **Use Relative Position For Reference Point** Click if you want the units for horizontal and vertical to show the position of the reference point location relative to its initial location.

ⓓ **Set Horizontal And Vertical Scale** Enter the width and height (as percentages) for the bounding box.

ⓔ **Link Scales** Click if you want the horizontal and vertical values to remain relative to each other.

ⓕ **Set Rotation** Enter a value (–180 through 180) in degrees to specify the angle of the selection.

ⓖ **Set Horizontal And Vertical Skew** Enter values (–180 through 180) in degrees to specify the amount of twist to be applied to the selection.

ⓗ **Cancel Transformation** Click to reject transformation changes.

ⓘ **Commit Transformation** Click to accept transformation changes.

Commit Transformation
[Return]
[Enter]

Cancel Transformation
[Esc]

Particularly in lower-resolution images, multiple transformations or overworking of selections can degrade image content visibly.

You can transform selected content, as opposed to transforming layer information, but keep in mind that transforming content not otherwise isolated will leave a hole in a layer or fill with the background color if you are working on a Background layer.

9.12 Moving Selected Content

➠ 2.7 Select Menu

➠ 3.4 Move Tool

Move tool
[V]

Duplicate content while dragging a selection
[Option]
[Alt]

————

After moving selected content, subtracting from the selection area not only removes those parts of the selection marquee, but it also removes the content.

Moving selected content may sound like a primary function in Photoshop, yet the logistics are most often carried out in a less straightforward way—copying and pasting, extracting or deleting backgrounds, and then moving objects and layers as opposed to moving selected content. Moving selected content between images is both a memory- and a time-saver. Copying while moving (dragging) selected content is an oft-overlooked tool in photo retouching.

Dragging and Dropping Content

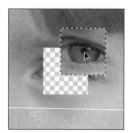

Once an area has been selected, you can use the mouse cursor to drag the selected content anywhere on the document's canvas (or even to a different document) and drop it in a new location. This is not as important on most computers today, but this process is less memory-intensive than copy and paste. The content in the image to the left is being moved across the screen.

To drag and drop content, follow these steps:

1 Select an object or specific content you want to move. If no content is selected on the layer, the entire layer is moved.

2 Choose the Move tool .

3 Do one of the following:

■ To move the content **to another open Photoshop document**, click within the selection and drag it to the canvas of the target document. The content is placed in a new layer immediately above the previously selected layer. This will not remove the content from the originating document. Hold down the Shift key to center pixels in the new layer.

■ To move the content **to another application**, first make sure that the application will accept graphic input. If it does, open a document in that application, switch to Photoshop, click within the selection, and drag it to the document window of the target application.

■ To move the selected content **within the same layer**, simply click within the selection and drag the content to the desired position. You can continue to move the selected content without dropping it until you deselect it or select another layer. The content being moved will leave a hole in the layer, either transparent or filled with background color.

9.12   Moving Selected Content *(continued)*

Dragging and Dropping from Another Application

Photoshop can also receive input from other applications. To drag and drop from another application, do one of the following:

- To move a **bitmap image**, click the image in the application and drag it into the canvas of an open Photoshop document. The content is placed in a new layer immediately above the previously selected layer.

- To move a vector image from Illustrator, select the vector image(s) and drag into an open Photoshop document window. The unrasterized vector image appears on a new layer with a bounding box to which you can apply transformations, or you can specify options in the tool options bar. Click the check mark or press Enter to render the vector image at the image's resolution.

- To move **text**, select the text and click and drag it to an open Photoshop document window. The text is rasterized at the image's resolution. To move as text, you need to copy and paste it into a text layer.

Drag-Copying a Selection

If you are duplicating an object within the same layer, you can simply copy it while dragging to its target location to save time. This is an invaluable way to remove blemishes quickly. Follow these steps:

1 Select the layer with the content to be duplicated, and then select specific content on that layer.

2 Choose the Move tool ![Move tool icon], and then, in the canvas, Option/Alt-click and drag. One of two things will happen:

  - If you selected a layer, the content of the layer is duplicated into a new layer.

  - If you selected content within a layer, the content is duplicated as a selection on the same layer.

3 When you release the Move tool, the duplicated content is set. The original content remains in its initial position.

Press Option/Alt and drag a selection...

...to duplicate it while moving.

➡ 9.9   Transforming the Selection Marquee

➡ 9.11   Transforming Layer Content

➡ 17.2 Adding Text to Images

Switch to the Move tool from most other tools (reverts to original tool when released)

⌘

Ctrl

———

If you are moving selected content between different documents or from another application into Photoshop, remember to take into consideration the resolution of both the source and the destination.

9.13 Copying and Cutting Selected Content

**Copy the selection to
the Clipboard**

⌘ C

Ctrl C

**Copy the flattened
selection (all layers)**

Shift ⌘ C

Shift Ctrl C

**Cut the selection to
the Clipboard**

⌘ X

Ctrl X

**Paste from the
Clipboard centered in
the selection or layer**

⌘ V

Ctrl V

**Paste from the
Clipboard using the
selection as a mask**

Shift ⌘ V

Shift Ctrl V

To paste content
between Photoshop
and another applica-
tion, make sure that
the Export Clipboard
option is checked in the
general preferences.

Whether you copy or cut, you are actually placing information in temporary memory on the Clipboard. Just as in other applications with which you might be familiar, cutting removes selected information, and copying duplicates the selected information—in Photoshop this information can be pixels, vector information, or text. When copying pixels in Photoshop, you can either copy what is on a selected layer or copy all of what you see in a selection (and below it) by copying "merged" pixel information.

Content is moved to the Clipboard whenever you copy or paste a layer or a selected part of a layer, but only one selection at a time, and every time you copy or paste, the previous selection is replaced in the Clipboard. However, you can paste this selection from the Clipboard as many times as desired.

To move selected content to the Clipboard, do one of the following.

- Choose Edit > Copy to move the selected content to the Clipboard but leave the original intact.

- Choose Edit > Cut to move the selected content to the Clipboard and delete the original.

- Choose Edit > Copy Merged to move the selected content on all layers to the Clipboard.

A portion of the image or layer is selected (left). Copying will have no visible effect on the image. Cutting, however, will leave a hole (or fill) in place of the selected content (center). On a Background layer, the fill will be in the color specified as the background color in the Toolbox. When you copy and immediately paste the selection in the same document, it is positioned exactly above where it was. If you choose to cut and paste, the pasted selection will not be aligned (right).

9.14   Pasting Selected Content

Pasting content in Photoshop is generally the second half of a process, as you must first have content in your Clipboard—copied from within a Photoshop document, from another application, or from the operating system as with a screen capture. With content already copied, you have several options. What you paste depends on the resolution of the original.

Pasting in Place

If you are copying and pasting in the same document, without deselecting, your copied content will be pasted in the same position as the original... on a new layer directly above the original content.

As soon as you deselect the area from which you are copying, the information on the Clipboard is document independent and is treated just as if you were working in a new document.

Pasting to Another Document

To paste the content of the Clipboard into a different document, open the document and then do one of the following:

- Choose Edit > Paste. The image in memory is placed in the middle of a new layer, inserted immediately above the active layer in the selected document.

- Make a selection and choose Edit > Paste. The image is placed in a new layer, centered over the selection area.

- Make a selection and choose Edit > Paste Into. The image is placed in a new layer above the active layer, centered in and masked by the selection.

Pasting from Another Application

You are not limited to copying and pasting just within Photoshop. You can also copy images (bitmap and vector) or text in or from other applications and then paste that content into a Photoshop document. Pasting from another document depends more on where and how you copy the content than on the pasting itself.

- Generally, pasting from another application is as described in the previous section. Your resolution depends on the source document and application.

- Pasting text requires you to choose the Type tool $\boxed{T}$, create a text box, or insert your cursor in the document and paste. You can set formatting before or after pasting.

- If you are not getting the results or resolution you need from the copy-and-paste process, explore the (other) application's export formats.

➡ 2.4   Edit Menu

➡ 2.7   Select Menu

➡ 11.2 Adding Layer
        Masks

Copy the selection to the Clipboard
⌘ C
Ctrl C

Copy the flattened selection (all layers)
Shift ⌘ C
Shift Ctrl C

———

To paste content between Photoshop and another application, make sure that the Export Clipboard option is checked in the general preferences.

———

When you start a new document, the size and resolution automatically default to the size and resolution of the current selection in the Clipboard.

———

Undo, History, and large images copied to the Clipboard may cause your computer, or Photoshop, to act sluggishly. To clear the undo, history, or Clipboard from memory choose Edit > Purge, then select the memory location to clear. But be careful—once purged, the information is gone from memory.

9.14   Pasting Selected Content *(continued)*

**Cut the selection to
the Clipboard**
⌘ X
Ctrl X

**Paste from the
Clipboard centered in
the selection or layer**
⌘ V
Ctrl V

**Paste from the
Clipboard using the
selection as a mask**
Shift ⌘ V
Shift Ctrl V

———

Computers sink or swim
based on many factors,
but chief among them
is the computer's mem-
ory. If you fill up your
machine's memory by
copying or cutting large
images, it will begin to
behave sluggishly. To
clear the undo, history,
or Clipboard, choose
Edit > Purge, and then
select the memory loca-
tion to clear. But be
careful—once purged,
the information is gone
from memory.

Pasting a Vector Image from Another Application

Photoshop allows you the option of preserving vector information (paths) you copy from other applications. You can also allow Photoshop to convert or transform the vector data from your Clipboard into pixels or vector shapes. Vector paths from other applications can be edited, filled, stroked, turned into shape presets, and printed from Photoshop with PostScript characteristics intact.

When you paste a vector image selected and copied from another application such as Adobe Illustrator, you are presented with a dialog that gives you three choices:

The art is selected and copied (left) from Adobe Illustrator. The Paste dialog (center) gives you the choices for pasting as Pixels, Path, or Shape Layer. If you select either Path or Shape Layer, you create a work path or a vector mask (right).

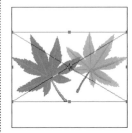

If you paste the vector art as pixels (left), it will be surrounded by a bounding box so that you can scale it as vector information one last time before rasterizing into pixel data. If the vector art is pasted as paths (center), the paths can be resized, stroked, or filled. You can save the path using the Paths palette. If you paste the vector art as a Shape layer (right), the paths take on a fill in the selected foreground color; notice that you also lose all detail in the vector artwork.

Each of the options available in Photoshop for pasting vector artwork has distinct creative or design possibilities, from print considerations to future use and versatility. For example, you can paste a company logo or a vector signature into Photoshop and use it repeatedly as a custom shape. All the color and detail of complex vector artwork can be further stylized with tools available in Photoshop that are not generally available in vector-editing applications.

CHAPTER **10**

PHOTOSHOP WORKSPACE

UNIVERSAL TASKS

PHOTO AND VIDEO TASKS

PRINT TASKS

WEB TASKS

Layering Images

AMONG THE MOST POWERFUL features Photoshop has to offer is the ability to work with layered images. In simplest terms, layers allow you to move images and objects (parts of images) independently just as if you were creating a collage with tangible photos, paper, plastic, or cloth. Layers also allow blending and masking, grouping and aligning, hiding and rearranging, even duplicating and transforming. Most of all, layers allow near-endless possibilities for visual creativity.

- 10.1 **Layer basics**

- 10.2 **The Background layer**

- 10.3 **Creating layers**

- 10.4 **Merging layers**

- 10.5 **Adding Adjustment and Fill layers**

- 10.6 **Creating layer sets**

- 10.7 **Managing layers and layer sets**

- 10.8 **Linking and locking layers and layer sets**

- 10.9 **Deleting layers or layer sets**

- 10.10 **Rasterizing vector layers**

- 10.11 **Aligning and distributing layers**

- 10.12 **Storing versions with Layer Comps**

10.1   Layer Basics

It may help to visualize the properties of layers in Photoshop by thinking of them as sheets of paper or plastic that can be marked, painted, stretched, and stacked upon one another.

In the Layers palette, each layer includes a thumbnail image that displays the content of the layer. To change the layer thumbnail size (or eliminate it entirely), choose Palette Options from the Layers palette menu. In the dialog, choose the desired thumbnail size and click OK.

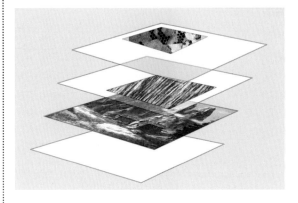

As you create layers, you increase the size of your document. The number of layers you can create is limited only by the ability of your computer to handle the file size. Photoshop can now save files as large as 4 GB and 300,000 pixels by 300,000 pixels.

You can have multiple layers in a single document, and you can edit individual layers without changing the content above or below them. You can directly edit the content of only one layer at a time; yet some tools allow you to edit with pixel information gathered across multiple layers. The purpose of some characteristics of layers, such as masks and Adjustment layers, is to alter the appearance of layers seen through them without permanently altering pixels. All layers have the following characteristics in common:

Layer blending modes Specify how pixels in a selected layer interact with pixels in layers below them.

An image that is 250 pixels by 250 pixels—roughly 183 KB when flat—with 1200 layers takes up approximately 160 MB on disk and 650 MB when open in Photoshop.

Layer opacity Specifies the transparency of all pixels in a selected layer, yet also affects layer styles and blending modes assigned to the layer. Determines the degree to which a layer obscures or reveals what is below it.

Layer fill opacity Specifies the opacity of the interior fill of a layer. Affects only information on a layer, leaving opacity of effects and layer styles intact.

Layer visibility Specifies whether the layer is currently shown or hidden.

Layer styles Specially assigned layer properties such as Drop Shadow or Bevel. Their visibility may be turned on and off, but they are not actual layers. Converting styles to actual layers may affect their appearance.

Layer masks Allow select content on a layer to be hidden or revealed by way of painting in the mask rather than deleting or erasing pixel information.

Clipping groups or clipping masks Allow one layer to be used as a template for clipping or blocking the content of one or more layers above it from view.

10.2 The Background Layer

Generally, when you open an image in Photoshop or create a new Photoshop document, the bottommost layer of the image is designated as the Background layer. In the Layers palette, the Background layer appears as *Background*. This is always the case unless you specify Background Contents Transparent when creating a new document or when you are opening an image that has previously been saved with a transparent background. You can paint or edit the Background layer just as you would any other layer, but Photoshop regards the Background layer as a unique layer in the following ways:

- You cannot move the Background layer above other layers in the document while it is designated as the Background layer.

- The Background layer will not allow any transparency to show through. Thus, if you delete or erase pixel information in the Background layer, it is replaced by the color you designated as your background color in the Toolbox.

- You cannot change the opacity or blending mode of the Background layer.

In the Layers palette, the solid white Background layer is behind (or beneath) the layer with the black graphics.

To convert a Background layer to a regular layer, do *one* of the following:

- Double-click the Background layer in the Layers palette, rename it in the dialog that appears (named Layer 0 by default), and click OK.

- Choose Layer > New > Layer From Background, name the new layer in the dialog that appears (named Layer 0 by default), and click OK.

- To simply duplicate the Background layer, turn off layer visibility on the original. This also keeps an unedited version of the layer handy.

To convert a standard layer to a Background layer, select the layer in the Layers palette and then choose Layer > New > Background From Layer.

➡ 4.13 Layers Palette

Changing the name of a layer to Background will not designate it as a true Background layer.

If you choose Transparent when setting up a new image, no Background layer is added, and instead the transparency shows through.

You can hide the Background layer, allowing the transparency to show through.

10.3   Creating Layers

➡ 4.13 Layers Palette

➡ 9.2   Selecting a
        Layer or Its
        Contents

New layer
Shift ⌘ Option N
Shift Ctrl Alt N

New layer using dialog
Shift ⌘ N
s Shift Ctrl N

New layer using dialog
Option -click the New
Layer icon
Alt -click the New
Layer icon

**New layer below
selected layer/layer set**
⌘ -click the New
Layer icon
Ctrl -click the New
Layer icon

———

To create a layer via
copy, you must select a
layer. However, to cre-
ate a layer via cut, you
must select specific
content on the layer.

———

Although layers give
you a lot of power
when creating images,
they come at the cost of
increased file size; so
use them as needed.

———

After you duplicate a
layer, remember that it
will be over the top of,
and thus obscuring, the
original layer. You will
need to move the
duplicate content or
hide the layer to see
the original.

Creating and working on new transparent layers has many advantages over working on lay-ers with existing imagery. For instance, if you want to paint or fill an area of your image and you do so on a new layer, you can scale back the opacity or blending of what you have painted. You can even turn this layer on and off to compare what you have done with the image below it. This is particularly useful in image restoration or in touch-up work.

To add a new blank layer to your image, simply do one of the following:

■ Click the Create A New Layer button ▣ in the Layers palette to add a new empty layer above the previously active or selected layer. This may well be the preferred method for working quickly.

■ Choose Layer > New > Layer from the main menu or the palette menu. With this method, select options in a dialog, and then click OK. The new layer is again added above the previously active or selected layer.

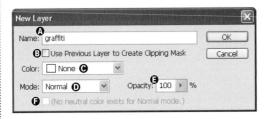

Ⓐ Enter the name for the layer.

Ⓑ Check if you want to automatically group the new layer with the selected layer.

Ⓒ Choose a color for the layer in the palette. This is not a fill color, but rather an organizational aid or color code that does not affect the layer itself.

Ⓓ Choose an initial blending mode for the layer. You can change this later in the Layers palette.

Ⓔ Enter an initial opacity for the layer. You can change this later in the Layers palette.

Ⓕ Depending on the blending mode selected, check this option to fill the new layer with a neutral color relative to the blending mode selected. This option is not available in several of the blending modes. This is an advanced option used for specialized effects or features such as lighting effects, which will not work on layers without pixel information.

10.3　Creating Layers *(continued)*

Duplicating Layers

Duplicating a layer makes an exact copy of the layer (including its position) into a new layer, named by default the originating layer's name plus the word *copy*. You can duplicate layers in several ways, each with a slightly different outcome:

- Click and drag a layer in the Layers palette down to the New Layer button 🔲 at the bottom of the Layers palette and release. The duplicate appears above the layer from which it was duplicated.

- Select a layer and then choose Duplicate Layer from the layer menu, the Layers palette menu, or the layer's contextual menu. Enter information in the Duplicate Layer dialog and click OK. Depending on the options set, the duplicate layer appears above the layer from which it was duplicated.

Remember, when you work on a duplicate a layer, you may not see the effects of actions such as deleting content until you turn off visibility of the duplicate below.

Ⓐ Enter a name for the duplicate layer.

Ⓑ Choose whether the duplicate layer should be added to the current document or another open document or whether a new document should be started for it. If a new document is created, the document will be the same size as the original document from which the layer was duplicated.

Ⓒ If you are placing the layer in a new document, enter a name for the new document.

New Layer from a Selection

When you copy or cut and paste a selection, it is automatically placed in a new layer, but you also have two—more refined—ways to create new layers using duplicated content. First, select content in a layer. Then choose either:

- Layer > New > Layer Via Copy to create a new layer from the selected region and leave the original content intact.

- Layer > New > Layer Via Cut to create a new layer from the selected region and delete the original content.

The new layer appears immediately above the previously selected layer, and the duplicated content appears directly over the top of the original content, obscuring it.

➡ 9.14　Pasting Selected Content

➡ 9.13　Copying or Cutting Selected Content

New layer from copy selection
⌘ J
Ctrl J

New layer from cut selection
Shift ⌘ J
Shift Ctrl J

New layer from copy selection with dialog
⌘ Option J
Ctrl Alt J

New layer from cut selection with dialog
Shift ⌘ Option J
Shift Ctrl Alt J

Duplicate layer
⌘ Option **any arrow key**
Ctrl Alt **any arrow key**

———

Duplicating a layer strengthens any transparencies, blending modes, or other effects.

———

Most folks new to Photoshop will create their first layers quite unintentionally, by copying and pasting or inserting their cursor in an image with the Text tool inadvertently selected. Both these actions create layers.

———

Text layers are a special case, which are added using the Text tool and explained in Chapter 17.

10.4 Merging Layers

➡ 4.13 Layers Palette

➡ 10.10 Rasterizing Vector Layers

Merge Down/Merge Linked/Merge Group
⌘ E
Ctrl E

Merge visible layers
Shift ⌘ E
Shift Ctrl E

Copy visible layers into selected layer
Shift Option ⌘ E
Shift Alt Ctrl E

Copy selected layer into layer below
Option Merge Down (menu option)
Alt Merge Down (menu option)

Copy visible layers into selected layer
Option Merge Visible (menu option)
Alt Merge Visible (menu option)

Copy linked layers into selected layer
Option Merge Linked (menu option)
Alt Merge Linked (menu option)

———

Because text and effects are rasterized when being merged, you can no longer edit them except as painted objects.

———

Though you will see a warning dialog when opting to rasterize text or layer styles, there are distinct advantages for doing so, such as applying duplicate shadows and filters. You can rasterize effects and type layers via commands in the Layer menu.

You can merge two or more separate layers to make one single layer, compositing the content of both. In most cases, the new layer reflects the opacity, blending mode, and styles of the original layers. Appearance of text, layer styles, and Adjustment layers will be rasterized and rendered no longer editable when merged. Thus, the new layer has an opacity of 100%, a normal blending mode, and no styles. You can select Merge options either from the main layer menu or from the palette menu on the Layers palette.

- To **merge a layer into the layer beneath it**, select the top layer and choose the Merge Down command in the Layer menu or the Layers palette menu. The two layers now appear as one, using the bottommost layer's name.

- To **merge all currently visible layers**, select a visible layer, set the visibility of other layers to be merged to show by clicking the Show box so that the Eye icon 👁 shows, and then choose the Merge Visible command in the Layer menu or the Layers palette menu. The layers now appear as one using the topmost layer's name.

- To **merge linked layers**, select a layer, set other layers to be linked by clicking the Link box so that the Link icon 🔗 shows, and then choose the Merge Linked command in the Layer menu or the Layers palette menu. The layers now appear as one using the selected layer's name.

- To **merge layers in a clipping mask**, select the bottom layer in the group, and then choose the Merge Group command in the Layer menu or the Layers palette menu. The layers now appear as one using the bottom layer's name.

- To **merge all layers** ("flatten" the image), choose the Flatten Image command in the Layer menu or the Layers palette menu. The layers now appear as one in the Background layer. If there are hidden layers, you will be asked to confirm that these layers should be deleted.

- Use **Copy Merged** if the merging of layers has resulted in an unwanted shift in appearance of layer blends. Choose All > Copy Merged. This is often effective when multiple layers with different blending modes are stacked.

10.5   Adding Adjustment and Fill Layers

Fill and Adjustment layers are a special class of layer used to change the appearance of layers beneath them. Fill layers create a layer with a solid color, pattern, or gradient filling the entire layer. Adjustment layers allow you to add a single layer that adjusts images only on the layers beneath it. (Refer to the color section "Adjustments" to see how the various adjustments affect the image.)

Adjustment layers are arguably among the most important Photoshop tools. You can use them to make unlimited nondestructive edits or changes to image adjustments. Furthermore, with the use of their respective layer masks, you can selectively apply image adjustments to portions of an image or apply several adjustments. Color Fill layers also afford the user many advantages in combination with layer blending modes. There are 14 types of Fill and Adjustment layers, and each is discussed individually throughout the book. However, you add each type in the same way:

1   Select the layer you want the Fill or Adjustment layer to be placed above. If a selection is active when you add the Fill or Adjustment layer, it is used as a layer mask.

2   Choose Layer > New Fill Layer or Layer > New Adjustment Layer.

Fill and Adjustment layers are also conveniently available though the Create New Fill Or Adjustment Layer button . You can easily edit Adjustment and Fill layers. Double-click the corresponding layer thumbnail to open the original dialog to readjust or reselect settings.

3   Depending on the Fill or Adjustment layer selected, you'll see a dialog in which you can specify options about the new layer. Set the options (you should see the changes affect the image in real time), and then click OK.

4   The new layer appears above the previously selected layer with a layer thumbnail and a layer mask. To change the options for the layer, double-click the layer thumbnail to reopen the dialog.

All Adjustment and Fill layers always include a layer mask that you can use to control the application of the layer.

A fill thumbnail displays the color, gradient, or pattern in that layer.

FILL AND ADJUSTMENT TYPES

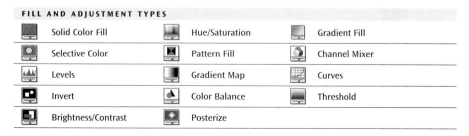

Solid Color Fill	Hue/Saturation	Gradient Fill
Selective Color	Pattern Fill	Channel Mixer
Levels	Gradient Map	Curves
Invert	Color Balance	Threshold
Brightness/Contrast	Posterize	

UNIVERSAL TASKS

PHOTO AND VIDEO TASKS

PRINT TASKS

WEB TASKS

10.6   Creating Layer Sets

➡ 4.13 Layers Palette

➡ 10.8 Linking and
        Locking Lay-
        ers and
        Layer Sets

**Set selected layer set's
blending mode to Pass
Through**

[Shift] [Option] [P]

[Shift] [Alt] [P]

**Create new layer set
below the current
layer/layer set**

[⌘]-click the New Layer
Set icon

[Ctrl]-click the New
Layer Set icon

**Create a new layer set
using dialog**

[Option]-click the New
Layer Set icon

[Alt]-click the New
Layer Set icon

———

To move a layer into a
set, click and drag the
layer onto the layer set
folder. The layer is
placed at the bottom of
the group.

———

You can also move a
layer directly into a
position in the group by
dragging it between
two layers in a group.

———

To move a layer out of
a set, drag and drop it
on the set's folder, or
simply drag it out of
the set to the desired
position.

———

If you select a layer set
and then add new lay-
ers, they are automati-
cally placed in the
selected layer set.

Photoshop now allows you to work with an almost unlimited number of layers in a document. To aid in keeping numerous layers organized and manageable, you can group them
and work with layer sets. Layer sets are simply folders created in the Layers palette,
which allow you to manipulate layers or groups of layers individually or in sets. You can
create and nest layer sets up to five levels deep (sets of sets). You can set opacity and
blending modes for sets of layers and for individual layers.

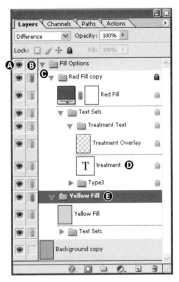

Ⓐ Click to show or hide all layers in the set.

Ⓑ Click to link all layers in the set.

Ⓒ Click to expand or contract the layer set view.

Ⓓ Nested layer sets 3 and 4 levels deep.

Ⓔ Layer not included in a set.

To **create an empty layer set,** click the New Set button at the bottom of the Layers
palette, or from the Photoshop menu choose Layer > New > Layer Set. You can also
choose New Layer Set from the Layers palette menu. The new layer set appears immediately above the previously active or selected layer.

To **create a layer set from linked layers or linked layer sets** [ ] with one linked layer or
layer set selected, choose New Layer Set From Linked… from the layer menu or the Layers palette menu. The new layer set appears with the linked layers inside it immediately
above the previously selected layer.

Ⓐ Enter the name for the layer set.

Ⓑ Choose a color for the layer set in the
palette. This color does not affect the
layer set itself, but allows you to color-
code sets depending on use.

Ⓒ Choose an initial blending mode for the layer set. This options determines how layers in the set
affect layers outside the set. Modes set for individual layers affect only other layers in the same
set. You can change the blending mode later in the Layers palette.

Ⓓ Enter an initial opacity for the layer. You can change the opacity later in the Layers palette

10.7 Managing Layers and Layer Sets

Once you create layers or layer sets, you can manage them in a variety of ways to help you better organize them for particular uses.

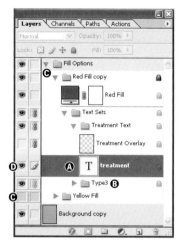

A The currently selected (active) layer.

B Click a layer thumbnail or name to activate it. Double-click the name to change or edit the label. Right-click to open the Layer Properties dialog and color code.

C Layer visibility off.

D Layer visibility on.

You can assign each layer and layer a unique name and a color code. To change these properties, select the layer or layer set, click its thumbnail, and choose Layer Properties... (or Layer Set Properties...) in the Layers palette menu. In the following dialog, enter the name and color and click OK.

Activating Layers

You can edit only the selected, active layer. The active layer or layer set is highlighted in the Layers palette. To activate a layer, do one of the following:

- Click the layer thumbnail or name in the Layers palette.

- Control/right-click content in the layer, and select the layer name from the context menu.

- Click the layer set folder or name. You cannot paint or edit in active layer sets (you have to select individual layers within it), but you can move active layer sets as if they were linked.

➡ 4.13 Layers Palette

Move the selected layer backward/forward one level
⌘
Ctrl [or]

Select the layer below/above current layer
Option [or]
Alt [or]

———

You set a layer set's properties and visibility in much the same way that you set a layer's properties (see Section 9.4).

➡ 9.2 Selecting a
Layer or Its
Contents

**Move the selected
layer to the back/
front (or back/front
of layer set)**
[Shift][Option] [[] or []]
[Shift][Alt] [[] or []]

**Select the back/front
layer**
[Shift][Option] [[] or []]
[Shift][Alt] [[] or []]

**Jump to the topmost
layer under the cursor**
[⌘][Ctrl][Option]-click in
canvas
[Alt] right-click in
canvas

You can change the
layer name directly in
the palette by double-
clicking the layer name,
typing the new name,
and pressing Enter.

Changing Layer Stacking Order

The order in which layers appear on top of each other dramatically affects the image itself. You can view the order of the layers in the Layers palette. The most common way to arrange layers or layer sets is to click and drag the layer or layer set in the palette up or down and release at the desired position. As you drag, a thick black bar appears between layers, indicating where the layer will be placed when dropped.

In addition, you can select a layer or layer set and then choose one of the options from the Layer > Arrange submenu:

Bring To Front Places the layer on top.

Bring Forward Moves the layer up one level.

Send Backward Moves the layer down one level.

Send To Back Places the layer beneath all other layers except the Background layer.

Showing or Hiding

You can selectively hide or show layers, layer sets, and layer effects at any time while you are working. The Eye icon 👁 appears next to layers that are currently visible, and clicking this icon toggles the visibility on or off for that layer or all the layers in a layer set. In addition, you can show and hide layers by doing one of the following:

- Option/Alt-click the Eye icon 👁 to hide all other layers. Option/Alt-click the icon 👁 again to show all other layers.

- Drag through the eye column to quickly change the visibility of multiple layers and layer sets.

Duplicating Layer Sets

Like duplicating a layer, duplicating a layer set creates an exact copy of the layers in a set immediately above and in the same position as the originating set.

- Click and drag a layer set from the palette to the New Layer Set button 📁 and release. The duplicate set appears above the layer set from which it was duplicated.

- Select a layer set and then choose Duplicate Layer Set… from the layer menu, the Layers palette menu, or the layer's contextual menu. Enter information in the Duplicate Layer dialog and click OK. Depending on the options set, the duplicate layer appears above the layer from which it was duplicated.

10.8   Linking and Locking Layers and Layer Sets

Linking

Linking lets you adjust the positions of different layers simultaneously. If two layers are linked and you move one, the linked layer moves by that same amount. To link layers, follow these steps:

1   Select the first layer that will be linked to others.

2   Click the link box ![] next to each layer you want linked to the first layer.

3   You can now move, align, create sets, lock, merge, or delete these layers as one unit.

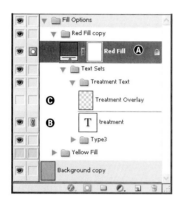

Ⓐ   An active layer has had its transparent pixels and positions locked.

Ⓑ   The layer linked to the active layer.

Ⓒ   The layer *not* linked to the active layer.

Locking

To prevent a layer or layer set from being moved and/or edited, you can lock it. First select the layer or layer set, and then click one of the lock icons in the Layers palette.

- ▪   ![] Click to lock transparent pixels in the layer. You can edit only regions of the layer that currently contain content. This lock is only available to draw layers.

- ▪   ![] Click to lock image pixels in the layer. Prevents image on the layer from being edited, but it can still be moved as a layer. This lock is only available to draw layers.

- ▪   ![] Click to lock the layer's position.

- ▪   ![] Click to enact all available locks for the selected layer.

- ▪   To lock the selected layer and all layers linked to it, choose Layer **>** Lock All Linked Layers… or choose Lock All Linked Layers… from the Layers palette menu. In the dialog, check the link types(s) you want to enact, and click OK.

- ▪   To lock a selected layer set, choose Layer **>** Lock All Layers In Set… or choose Lock All Layers In Set… from the Layers palette menu. In the dialog, check the link types(s) you want to enact, and click OK.

After you apply any of the locks to a layer, a lock icon ![] appears on the far right side of the layer in the Layers palette. The specific lock icon is highlighted in the lock buttons.

➠   4.13 Layers Palette

When layers are linked, all linked layers activate when any of the linked layers is selected (not just the originally linked layer).

Unless you always want two layers to move together, it is best to unlink layers when you are finished moving them. Otherwise, you might move both layers when you only mean to move one of them.

To unlock a layer or a layer set, select the layer or layer set and click the highlighted lock.

10.9 Deleting Layers or Layer Sets

➡ 4.13 Layers Palette

If you are not sure whether you will need a layer again, you might simply want to hide the layer rather than deleting it.

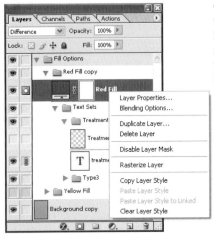

Often you will find that you no longer need the content of an entire layer in the image, and since extra layers add to the file size even if they are not visible, it is a good idea to delete them. Right-click the layer title (not the thumbnail) to view the menu that includes the Delete Layer option.

Deleting Layers

There are about as many ways to delete a layer from your canvas as there are ways to create them, but all the deletion methods begin with the same action. First select the layer to be deleted, and then do one of the following:

- To **quickly delete** a layer, click and drag the layer to the trashcan icon 🗑 at the bottom of the Layers palette and release.

- To **delete the layer and all layers linked to it**, choose Layer > Delete > Linked Layers. Click Yes to confirm the deletion.

- To **delete all hidden layers** in the document, choose Layer > Delete > Hidden Layers. Click Yes to confirm the deletion. This removes all layers that do not have the Eye icon 👁 next to them in the Layers palette.

- To **delete the selected layer**, click the trashcan icon 🗑 at the bottom of the Layers palette and then click Yes to confirm the deletion.

- To **delete the selected layer**, Control/right-click the layer's name or click the Layers palette menu and choose Delete Layer. Click Yes to confirm the deletion.

- To **delete the selected layer**, choose Layer > Delete > Layer. Click Yes to confirm the deletion.

10.9 Deleting Layers or Layer Sets *(continued)*

Deleting Layer Sets

To quickly delete a layer set and all layers in it, click and drag the layer set to the trashcan icon 🗑 at the bottom of the Layers palette and release.

You can also choose whether to delete the set but keep the layers inside it. First, open the Delete Layer Set dialog:

- Select the layer set to be deleted in the Layers palette and click the trashcan icon 🗑 in the Layers palette.

- Control/right-click the layer set's name and choose Delete Layer Set.

- Click the Layers palette menu and choose Delete Layer Set.

Then, in the dialog, click one of these:

- Set Only to remove the set but retain the layers inside.

- Set And Contents to remove the set and all the layers it contains.

You can also delete masks or effects by dragging their thumbnail or icon to the trashcan icon.

EDITING ON ALL LAYERS

Most tools allow you to edit on only a single layer at a time, but a few tools allow you to use all the layers while editing for various purposes.

Magic Wand Selects colors from any visible layer rather than just from the active layer.

Clone Stamp Samples image data from all layers for cloning rather than just from the active layer.

Magic Eraser Selects the color for deletion from any visible layer but still deletes only from the active layer.

Paint Bucket The fill area is limited by all visible layers, but the fill is applied only to the active layer.

Blur, Sharpen, Smudge Copies edited areas of visible layers into the active layer. The original layers remain unaffected.

10.10   Rasterizing Vector Layers

➡ 4.13 Layers Palette

———

Warning: Once you ras-
terize a text or other
vector layer, you can
edit only pixels rather
than type, paths, or
shapes. You can always
undo the change using
the history, but once the
image is saved and
closed, the rasterization
is fixed and cannot be
undone.

———

Rasterizing a vector
layer fixes that layer's
resolution to be the
image's resolution.

You cannot use filters and tools used to paint in layers in vector layers such as type, shape, and vector masks. However, you can convert vector layers to pixel-based layers by rasterizing them.

■ To **rasterize a single layer**, select the layer with the vector information on it that you want to rasterize. Choose Layer > Rasterize > Layer. You can also choose to rasterize specific vector content in the layer (Type, Shape, Fill Content, or Vector Mask) or to rasterize this layer and any layers linked to it.

■ To **rasterize all layers** in the document, choose Layer > Rasterize > All Layers. This will rasterize not only the vector layers but text and vector masks as well.

It is generally practical to rasterize a duplicate of your Type or Vector layer.

UNDERSTANDING FILE SIZE

The file size indicates how much disk space is required to store the data used to create the image on a hard drive or other storage media. How much memory an image takes is based on several factors:

Image Size The larger the dimensions of the image, the more data that has to be recorded.

Resolution The more information packed into the area of an image, the more information that has to be recorded.

Color Mode Different modes require different amounts of data to be recorded.

Layers The more layers added to an image, the more data required.

Bits/Channel The more bits used to record a single channel, the more data is required.

Metadata Any other information recorded with the image (author name, workgroups, keywords, and so on) will add slightly to the file size.

10.11 Aligning and Distributing Layers

Aligning the content of layers with the content of other layers allows you to more precisely place layers in relation to each other. Alignment and distribution work only with the active pixels in the layers.

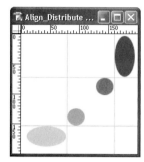 

The original lineup. Each of the four layers has a shape on it. Because layer 4 (the dark gray oval in the top-right corner) is selected, all alignments are based on that layer. The guidelines have been retained to help you see the changes.

Aligning Layers

To align layers, follow these steps:

1   Link [icon] two or more layers that you want to align. Select the layer to which you want the other layers to align.

2   Choose the Move tool [icon], and select the alignment buttons from the tool options bar; or with any tool, choose Layers > Align Linked and then an alignment option, or click one of the alignment buttons in the tool options bar. The entire contents of the linked layers align as defined using the selected layer as the base. So, for example, if you are aligning to the top, all layers will be aligned to the top of the selected layer.

Alignment Options

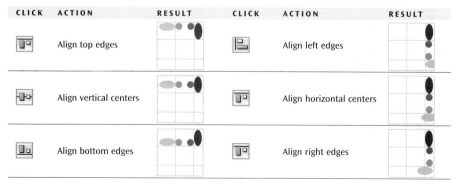

———

Distributing layers may not always produce the desired results. Often you will have to manu-ally space objects to get them to appear visually distributed the way you want them.

———

Remember that only the opaque pixels on the layer are aligned or distributed. If the alignment or distribu-tion is not working as expected, you might have pixels that are not showing up for some reason. (For example, they are the same color as the content behind them.)

Distributing Layers

To distribute layers, follow these steps:

1 Link 🔗 three or more layers that you want to align. Select the layer to which you want the other layers to align.

2 Choose the Move tool ⊹ and select the distribution buttons from the tool options bar; or with any tool choose Layers > Distribute Linked and then an alignment option, or click one of the distribution buttons in the tool options bar. The entire contents of the linked layers are distributed as defined using the selected layer as the base.

Distribution Options

CLICK	ACTION	RESULT	CLICK	ACTION	RESULT
	Distribute top edges			Distribute left edges	
	Distribute vertical			Distribute horizontal	
	Distribute bottom			Distribute right edges	

10.12 Storing Versions with Layer Comps

Layer Comps were introduced to Photoshop as a tool for saving and displaying multiple versions of a layout or states of the Layers palette, to be more specific. Designers often say they are showing comps, meaning that they are showing examples (samples or variations) of work. Layer Comps are thus meant to fit into this workflow of artists and designers who work with multiple variations of design projects. By saving Layer Comps, you can simply open the Layer Comps palette, select previously saved Layer Comps, and cycle through variations of a design or layout without having to create individual documents or turn on and off numerous layers and layer sets.

Using Layer Comps, you can take snapshots of the Layers palette, recording three key layer elements; visibility of layers, the position of layers in the document, and the appearance of layers regarding layer styles and blends.

A The Apply Layer Comp icon ⬛ and associated row of optional Layer Comp choices. Click in any of the boxes next to a Layer Comp to apply that "state" to the document.

B Highlighting indicates a selected Layer Comp. Shift-click selects more than one, and Command/Ctrl-click selects multiple noncontiguous comps, allowing you to cycle through only specifically selected comps.

C Clicking the triangular button expands the Layer Comp title field to include any notes you entered. Simply double-click in the bar to edit data or rename the Layer Comp.

D As in other Photoshop palettes, you have easy access to common commands by way of buttons (left to right). Cycle through Layer Comps by clicking the triangles forward or back. You can click the Update Layer Comp button 🔄 at any time during editing or when layers have been altered. Similar to the New Layer button on the Layers palette, clicking the New Layer Comp button opens the Layer Comp dialog, and of course the trash icon 🗑 will delete a selected Layer Comp.

E The Layer Comp palette menu gives you access to the choices in D in a more formal context: New Layer Comp, Delete, Update, Apply, Restore.

The Layer Comp Options dialog allows you to apply a name to the comp and select parameters for recording information regarding visibility, appearance, and location. You can also log comments in the Comment field.

New Layer Comp without dialog
Alt -click the New Layer Comp button
Option -click the New Layer Comp button

Open Layer Comp Options dialog
Double-click Layer Comp

Rename inline
Double-click Layer Comp name

Select/Deselect multiple contiguous Layer Comps
Shift -click Layer Comps

Select/Deselect multiple discontiguous Layer Comps
⌘ -click Layer Comps
Ctrl -click Layer Comps

___

In some instances, a caution icon will appear on the comp slots. You can click the caution icon to view a message that explains the warning. Choosing Clear to remove the alert icon will allow the remaining layers to stay unchanged. Right-click or Ctrl-click the caution icon to view a popup menu that lets you choose to clear warnings.

CHAPTER 11

Masking Layers

IN SIMPLEST TERMS, MASKS in Photoshop allow you to hide portions of a layer (or layer set) nondestructively—that is, without permanently deleting or erasing the pixels in the layer. There are basically two types of masks in Photoshop:

Layer masks are pixel-based masks that can be edited with all of Photoshop's painting tools and techniques—brushes, fills, gradients, selections, and so on. Layer masks are associated, or linked, with a particular layer or layer set.

Vector masks are, as the name implies, vector based and utilized for their crisp edges, Post-Script printing qualities, and resolution independence (scalability). They are created and edited with all of Photoshop's vector tools—as paths and vector shapes.

- 11.1 **Mask basics**
- 11.2 **Adding layer masks**
- 11.3 **Editing layer masks**
- 11.4 **Hiding, applying, or removing layer masks**
- 11.5 **Turning masks into selections**
- 11.6 **Adding vector masks**
- 11.7 **Editing vector masks**
- 11.8 **Applying or removing vector masks**
- 11.9 **Saving vector masks as clipping paths**

11.1   Mask Basics

Masks are primarily used to block portions of a layer or a layer set to view content in layers below them. The content remains, but is hidden behind the mask. Unlike selections, masks *appear* only to protect pixels or image information from being edited. Masks actually allow editing across areas they hide. For example, running a blur filter on a masked layer blurs the entire layer—the mask can then be altered to either reveal or hide more of the blurred area.

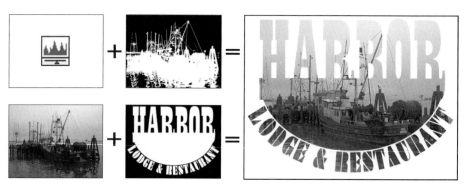

Top: A Levels adjustment layer with its associated layer mask is used to lighten the dark area of the boats without lightening the fog further. Bottom: A vector mask, created with type converted to paths and edited, is applied to the image of the harbor. Right: The effects of both masks are combined in the image.

When editing masks, your foreground and background colors are restricted to black and white. You can edit masks in the image window, directly observing the result without a mask overlay, or you can select the temporary channel in the Channels palette and edit in a mask overlay.

Selected layer masks appear as temporary channels in the Layers palette and can be saved like selections as alpha channels. Vector masks appear in the same way in the Paths palette and can be saved there. This gives both types of masks alternatives for use in your workflow. In either case, they appear in italics and are temporary until saved.

Ⓐ Mask selected Indicated by the Mask icon 🔲.

Ⓑ Layer thumbnail Click to select the layer for editing. The above icon 🔲 will switch to 🖌.

Ⓒ Mask links Indicates masks and content are to be moved jointly. Click to toggle the mask's link to the layer content.

Ⓓ Layer mask thumbnail Click to select the mask for editing. Right-click to access the option to enable/disable the mask. A disabled mask is indicated by a red X. Double-click to open the Layer Mask Options dialog.

Ⓔ Vector mask thumbnail Always appears to the right of a layer mask thumbnail. If no layer mask is attached to the layer, the vector mask thumbnail moves to the left. Click once to select the layer; click again to select the vector mask. Clicking a third or fourth time on the vector mask thumbnail toggles the path visibility.

11.2 Adding Layer Masks

To create a layer mask you must first have a layer that is not a Background layer. When added to a layer, the layer mask works essentially like an alpha channel with regard to viewing and editing the mask. Remember, an alpha channel is a saved selection, and without the marquee or marching ants, a selection is invisible. With this in mind, consider that you can edit, alter, or add a layer mask with three view options:

- You can simply click the Add Layer Mask button to create a new mask. The layer mask will be active; just paint in the image window. (Your Toolbox swatches are limited to white and black.) The effect of the mask is revealed by what you see happen to the image, with the mask itself essentially invisible except for the thumbnail in the Layers palette.

- You can view the mask as an overlay to aid your editing in some situations. Shift-Option/Alt-click the layer mask's thumbnail in the Layers palette.

- You can also view and edit the mask itself, as a grayscale image, by turning off the visibility of all channels in the Channels palette except the layer mask.

Turning a Selection into a Layer Mask

A valuable option for creating a layer mask is to begin with an existing selection as the base for the masked area. Select the layer to which you want to add a layer mask; it cannot already contain a layer mask. Create or load a selection, and then do one of the following:

- To quickly add a layer mask, click the Add A Mask button at the bottom of the Layers palette. This adds a layer mask using the selection to mask the layer, with non-selected areas masked.

- To show the layer content within the selection, choose Layer > Add Layer Mask > Reveal Selection. The mask covers nonselected content in the layer.

- To show only the layer content outside your selection, choose Layer > Add Layer Mask > Hide Selection. The mask hides the content in the selection.

➡ 2.6 Layer Menu

➡ 4.13 Layers Palette

➡ 9.2 Selecting a Layer or Its Contents

➡ 9.4 Creating Free-Form Selections

Show/hide layer mask as a bitmap
Option click layer mask thumbnail

Alt click layer mask thumbnail

———

Masks and selections have much in common. It is often said that masks protect an image from being edited. This is because a selection is in essence a type of mask. A layer mask itself does not protect pixels until converted into a selection.

———

If you select a layer mask in the Layers palette, it also displays as a temporary alpha channel in the Channels palette.

———

Quick Mask mode, accessible from the Toolbox, allows you to use Mask-editing techniques as shown in this chapter, yet is independent of any layer and is actually a selection tool despite its name.

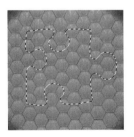

The original selection. Notice that the layer has a shadow and a bevel applied.

The selection is turned into a layer mask using Reveal Selection.

The selection is turned into a layer mask using Hide Selection.

11.2 Adding Layer Masks *(continued)*

➡ 9.10 Saving and
Loading
Selections

➡ 10.1 Layer Basics

➡ 10.5 Adding
Adjustment
and Fill Layers

**Show/hide layer mask
overlay**
⬚Shift ⬚Option -click
layer mask thumbnail

⬚Shift ⬚Alt -click layer
mask thumbnail

———

Layer masks are also
accessible in the Chan-
nels palette. They
appear there as tempo-
rary alpha channels
while their associated
layer is active in the
Layers palette. Their
names appear in italics
until saved as alpha
channels.

———

Unlike other alpha
channels, the layer
mask channel can only
be turned on or off for
the associated layer or
layer set with which it is
connected.

Creating a Blank Layer Mask

You can choose to add a completely empty (white) or completely filled (black) mask that
you can then edit as desired. This essentially allows you to then hide or reveal content by
painting the opposite color in the mask. First select the layer to which you want to add a
layer mask. Note: The layer cannot already contain a layer mask.

Do one of the following:

- Click the Add A Mask button  at the bottom of the Layers palette. You can also
  drag the layer to the Add A Mask button. Click again to add a vector mask.

- To add an empty layer mask (regardless of current selections), choose Layer **>** Add
  Layer Mask **>** Reveal All. The mask will not cover any of the layer.

- To add a filled layer mask (regardless of current selections), choose Layer **>** Add
  Layer Mask **>** Hide All. The mask will cover all the content in the layer.

When the mask is created, it is selected and ready for editing. In
this example, a star-shaped brush was used to indicate painting in
the mask. Painting with white in the Hide layer reveals the layer;
painting with black in the Reveal layer further masks, or hides,
layer content.

Setting the Layer Mask Options

To open the Layer Mask Display Options dialog, double-click the layer mask's thumbnail
or Control/right-click the thumbnail and choose Layer Mask Options…. In the dialog, set
the properties for the mask overlay and click OK.

Click the swatch to choose a color for the layer
mask; in the Opacity field, enter the opacity for
the layer mask as a percentage, which can be
viewed as an overlay by Shift-Option/Alt-clicking
the layer mask's thumbnail 🔳.

11.2　Adding Layer Masks *(continued)*

Turning a Layer's Content into a Layer Mask

If used in combination, methods for creating selections and masks can be nearly as varied as you can imagine. Each method for selecting, editing, or painting is best suited for a particular task, image content, or working style. Whether masks are similar to selections or selections are actually masks, layer content is the next best thing to a saved selection.

- Simply Command/Control-click a layer to select it. Click the Add A Mask button ▣, and you've got a mask.

- To create a mask from a particular layer's content in another selected layer, drag that layer's thumbnail to the Add Layer Mask button ▣ at the bottom of the Layers palette and release. You can even use the selected layer to create a mask of itself.

- To create an inverted mask from a layer's content in another selected layer, Option/Alt-drag the thumbnail of the layer mask to be copied to the Add A Mask button ▣ at the bottom of the Layers palette and release.

In this example (observing the Layers palette) the topmost layer, with visibility off and a prepared edge treatment, acts as a template to create the frame effect as a mask on subsequent layers. A similar project could begin by creating hand-torn paper edges and scanning the shape for the mask. Turn on and off the layers to print them individually, using the document and original layer as a template. The saved template can also be used in a recorded Action to automate the process.

To add a mask to a selected layer, based on the content of another layer, simply click the layer thumbnail with the content you want to use as a mask, and drag it to the Add A Mask icon.

➡ 10.8　Linking and Locking Layers and Layer Sets

➡ 13　Painting in Images

➡ 16　Drawing Paths and Shapes

Generally you want to set the layer mask color to contrast with the image and not be the same color as other highlight colors, such as the Gamut highlight.

Color selection defaults to grayscale when the layer mask is active.

11.3   Editing Layer Masks

Duplicating an entire
layer also duplicates
that layer's masks.

To view the layer mask
as a grayscale mask,
hiding the image
underneath, Option/
Alt-click the layer mask
thumbnail. Repeat to
return to normal view-
ing mode.

To view the mask over-
lay in the canvas, Shift-
Option-click/Shift-Alt-
click the layer mask's
thumbnail. This is espe-
cially useful when mov-
ing the layer mask.

After you add a layer mask to a layer, you can add to it or subtract from it, move it, or copy and paste it—most of Photoshop's resources are available for editing the mask. You can make selections and use fills, gradients, filters, and custom brushes. Your only limitations might lie in the type of image you are working with; even then, with a little imagination, the possibilities are as endless as your supply of images.

 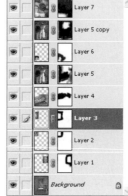

You have by now probably repeatedly read the words "paint in the mask." This example illustrates a quick collage of images—nine images. No cutting. No pasting. No selections. The individual layers were simply dragged onto the Background layer from their respective document. The layer mask thumbnails indicate (in black) the areas that were painted to make the blends. All the layers except layer 5 are at 100% opacity in the Normal blend mode; layer 5 is set to Overlay.

Adding to or Subtracting from a Layer Mask

You can use any tool you would normally use to edit or paint in the canvas to edit or delete the layer mask. As you edit the mask, you hide or reveal layer content, and it can appear as though you are painting with textures and blends. To edit a layer mask, follow these steps:

1   Click the layer mask thumbnail in the Layers palette to make it active (indicated by a black box around the thumbnail). All edits will now be applied to the layer mask.

2   Optional: To view the layer mask as a colored layer, still showing the image underneath, Shift-Option-click/Shift-Alt-click the layer mask thumbnail. You see the exact color in which the layer mask appears in the layer mask options.

3   Choose any editing or painting tool. Since the layer mask works as a grayscale channel, you can paint only with black, white, or gray.

  ■ To **add to the mask**, hiding the image on the layer, paint in black.

  ■ To **erase from the mask**, revealing the image on the layer, paint in white.

  ■ To **make the mask transparent**, partially revealing the image, paint in shades of gray. Any colored swatch you select will present you with a shade of gray when editing layer masks. However, the black and white swatches in the Toolbox, along with the Brush Opacity control in the Options bar, will also give you control over transparency.

Remember, you also have layer blend modes, advanced blending, and layer opacity controls.

11.3   Editing Layer Masks *(continued)*

Moving a Mask within the Layer

You can link a layer mask so that it moves with the content of the layer, keeping the mask in the same relative position, or you can unlink a layer mask so that it moves independently. You can then change the content being masked.

1   Choose the Move tool ![move tool icon].

2   To move the layer content and the layer mask independently, click the link icon ![link icon] between them so that it is not showing.

3   Click the layer mask thumbnail to select it, and then move the layer mask within the canvas.

Copying a Mask to Another Layer

A mask can be copied to another layer by following these steps:

1   Select the layer to which you want to copy the layer mask. This layer must not currently contain a layer mask.

2   Do one of the following:

■   To **duplicate** the mask, drag the thumbnail of the mask to be copied to the Add A Mask button ![mask button] at the bottom of the Layers palette.

■   To **invert the mask while duplicating**, Option/Alt-drag the thumbnail of the layer mask to be copied to the Add A Mask button ![mask button] at the bottom of the Layers palette.

Apply a Gradient to a Layer Mask

Gradients applied to layer masks give you the option of smooth transitions between images or layers. Click the layer mask thumbnail in the Layers palette ![thumbnail icon] to make it active, and then do one of the following:

■   Choose the Gradient tool ![gradient tool icon] in the Toolbox and set your gradient options.

■   Click and drag in the image. If you want to reset the gradient, just click and drag again.

➡ 9.4   Creating Free-Form Selections

➡ 9.10 Saving and Loading Selections

➡ 10.1 Layer Basics

➡ 10.5 Adding Adjustment and Fill Layers

➡ 10.8 Linking and Locking Layers and Layer Sets

➡ 12.8 Creating and Editing Gradients

➡ 13   Painting in Images

➡ 16   Drawing Paths and Shapes

To invert a layer mask, reversing the masked and unmasked regions, select the layer mask by clicking the layer mask's thumbnail and choosing Image > Adjustments > Invert.

While painting in layer masks, you can quickly toggle foreground and background colors by pressing the X key and using the bracket keys ([]) to increase or decrease your brush size.

11.4 Hiding, Applying, or Removing Layer Masks

➠ 2.6 Layer Menu

➠ 4.13 Layers Palette

Enable/disable layer mask
[Shift]-**click layer mask thumbnail**

You can undo the application or deletion of a layer mask.

Although masks add only a little to the overall file size, at times you will want to either apply the mask permanently to the layer or remove it altogether. First select the layer mask, and then do one of the following:

- To **temporarily hide** a layer mask, choose Layer > Disable Layer Mask, or Control/right-click the layer mask thumbnail and select Disable Layer Mask, or Shift-click the layer mask thumbnail. A red X appears over the layer mask thumbnail, and you can see how the layer would look without the mask without deleting the mask. Repeat (selecting Enable Layer Mask instead) to show the mask.

A red X appears next to the layer mask when it is disabled.

- To **permanently apply** the layer mask to the layer, choose Layer > Remove Layer Mask > Apply, or Control/right-click the layer mask thumbnail and select Apply Layer Mask. The layer mask is discarded, but its effects remain. This option is available only if the layer is rasterized, so it cannot be applied to type.

- To **delete** the layer mask, choose Layer > Remove Layer Mask > Discard, or Control/right-click the layer mask thumbnail and select Discard Layer Mask. The layer mask is discarded along with its effects.

- To **remove** the layer mask, click the trashcan icon 🗑 , or click and drag the layer mask thumbnail to the trashcan icon. Click Apply to remove the layer mask while keeping the changes, click Discard to remove the layer mask and changes, or click Cancel to keep the layer mask.

11.5 Turning Masks into Selections

You can quickly turn masks into selections, and, in fact, this is a great way to create complex selections based on the layer's content. There are, however, a few differences in the options available between converting layer masks and vector masks. You can convert either type of mask into a selection by simply Command/Control-clicking the respective mask thumbnail  in the Layers palette.

Converting a Layer Mask into a Selection

For options in converting the layer mask into a selection, Control/right-click the layer mask thumbnail, and do one of the following:

- To turn the mask into a selection, choose Set Selection To Layer Mask.

- To combine the layer mask with the current selection, choose Add Layer Mask To Selection.

- To remove part of a currently active selection using a layer mask, choose Subtract Layer Mask From Selection. If none of the pixels in the selection are more than 50% opacity, a dialog will appear warning you.

- To overlap the currently active selection with a selection based on a layer mask, choose Intersect Layer Mask With Selection.

Converting a Vector Mask into a Selection

Since a vector mask is based on paths, your options are different from those for the layer mask. Other than Command/Control-clicking the mask thumbnail in the Layers palette, selection conversion options are available to you via the Paths palette.

In the Paths palette, select the vector mask path (in italics), if it is not already highlighted.

In the Paths palette options drop-down, choose Make Selection to open the Make Selection dialog. Here you can set feather, anti-aliasing, and options for how the new selection should interact with any active selection.

Clicking the button at the bottom of the palette converts the path to a selection (directly, without options). The Paths palette options also allow you to stroke and fill the selected path or save the temporary vector mask as a path.

➡ 2.6   Layer Menu

➡ 4.13   Layers Palette

➡ 4.16   Paths Palette

➡ 9   Selecting and Moving Image Content

➡ 16.1   Path Basics

Use layer mask as selection

⌘-click layer mask thumbnail

Ctrl-click layer mask thumbnail

⌘-click vector mask thumbnail

Ctrl-click vector mask thumbnail

11.6   Adding Vector Masks

Keep in mind that Photoshop allows you to create hybrid images with both raster and vector elements. Resizing may affect the quality of the image itself (pixels), but the vector lines and shapes will remain distortion free when enlarged.

PostScript is the code or language that communicates type to a printer, allowing it to look crisp and clean, even when the image behind it doesn't look very clear.

Vector elements saved as clipping paths allow the vector mask to knock out background color when the image is placed in a layout application.

Vector masks work much like layer masks in that they can be used to hide portions of a layer from view. However, vector masks are generally added to images for several characteristics that set them apart from layer masks. These characteristics include the following:

- Distinctively crisp or well-defined edges and the capability of creating elegant curves that can be edited and adjustable angles.

- Resolution independence due to their mathematical definition rather than pixel-based definition in the document.

- Ability to be saved with the image file, allowing PostScript printing technology to transfer the crisp edges into print. Vector information can also transfer transparency information to layout applications via saved clipping paths.

Just as with layer masks, adding a vector mask to an image is quite simple. Select a layer that already has a layer mask and click the Add A Mask button [◉] at the bottom of the Layers palette, or do one of the following:

- To add an empty vector mask, choose Layer > Add Vector Mask > Reveal All. The mask will not cover any of the layer.

- To add a filled vector mask, choose Layer > Add Vector Mask > Hide All. The mask will cover all the content in the layer.

The key to making vector masks useful is in learning to use Photoshop's vector-editing tools and vector-shape tools. Once you create a vector mask as described previously, you edit or draws primarily with the Pen tool [✎] and vector tool variables accessible in the Options bar.

Turning a Path into a Vector Mask

You can turn any path into a vector mask. Follow these steps:

1 Select the layer to which you want to add a vector mask, and create your path or select a path from the Paths palette.

2 Do one of the following. The area outside the vector will be masked; you can then edit the mask as desired.

    - To quickly add a vector mask to a layer that already has a layer mask, click the Add A Mask button [◉] at the bottom of the Layers palette.

    - To add a vector mask regardless of whether the layer has a layer mask, choose Layer > Add Vector Mask > Current Path.

11.6   Adding Vector Masks *(continued)*

Turning a Shape into a Vector Mask

Photoshop's custom shape presets provide several options for exploring vector masks. You can even import vector paths from other applications and save them into the presets. To add a vector mask to a layer based on a shape or a custom shape, follow these steps:

1 Select the layer to which you want to add a vector mask.

2 Select the Custom Shape tool ![icon] from the Toolbox, and choose a shape preset from the Custom Shape picker drop-down menu in the Options bar. All shape tools work the same.

3 In the Options bar, select the Paths ![icon] option. This will let you draw a shape and its paths with no fill.

4 Click and drag in your image to apply the shape. Holding down the Shift key constrains the proportions of the shape as you draw. You might want to explore the modifiers on the Options bar that will allow you to add ![icon], subtract ![icon], exclude ![icon], or intersect ![icon] multiple shapes.

5 Do one of the following. The area outside the vector will be masked; you can then edit the mask as desired.

- To quickly add a vector mask to a layer that already has a layer mask, click the Add A Mask button ![icon] at the bottom of the Layers palette. If the layer doesn't have a mask already, click it twice.

- Choose Layer > Add Vector Mask > Current Path.

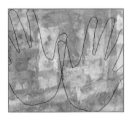 

Left: The original vector shape on a layer that has the opacity set to 50%. Right: The vector shape has been turned into a vector mask, and the layer opacity has been increased to 100%. An easy way to get a feel for vector editing it to use Photoshop's many ready-made vector-shape presets.

By applying a preset shape to a vector mask or using the shape to create the vector mask, you can access the (Path) Direct Selection tool ![icon] from the Toolbox and explore editing the shape. This can give you a feel for how vector shapes are drawn.

The original vector shapes (paths) from the previous illustrations have been altered in this example. You can clearly see all the anchor points used in the creation of the original shape.

16.9 Editing Paths and Path Components

21.1 Compositing Basics

25.2 Saving in TIFF Format

25.3 Saving in EPS Format

25.4 Saving as Photoshop PDF

Any selection in the canvas can also be turned into a path which, in turn, can then be turned into a vector mask. With the selection active in the canvas, Control/right-click the Make Work Path From Selection button.

———

When a vector mask is selected in the Layers palette, it also shows up as a temporary path in the Paths palette.

PHOTOSHOP WORKSPACE

UNIVERSAL TASKS

PHOTO AND VIDEO TASKS

PRINT TASKS

WEB TASKS

11.7   Editing Vector Masks

➟ 3.17 Path Selection
        Tools

➟ 3.19 Pen Tools

➟ 3.20 Shape Tools

Pen tool
P

Cycle pen tools
Shift P

_____

Choose the Move tool to move the content and vector mask together or turn linking off between them, and then move the content independently of the vector mask.

_____

When you place your mouse over a vector thumbnail, after a few seconds the vector mask will be outlined in the canvas until you move off the thumbnail. When you click to select the vector mask, the outline will persist in the canvas.

Once a vector mask is added to a layer, you can edit the mask further using any of the options for editing an existing path. Before editing a path, set your options as shown in the follow these steps to ensure that the tools will function as intended:

1 Select the Paths option, this will let you draw paths with no fill.

2 Choose the modifier on the Options bar that reflects what you want to do in relation to existing paths. Select to add 🔲 ; subtract 🔲, exclude 🔲, or intersect 🔲 new paths with existing paths.

To edit a vector mask, you can use the Pen tool 🖋 to draw or add new paths to the mask. You can use any of the various shape tools to add to the mask. You can also copy and paste whole paths or path segments from other paths—or from other applications—and paste them into the mask.

Editing Path Anchor Points in a Vector Mask

While the layer containing the vector mask is active in the layers palette, the Direct Selection tool 🔼 (accessible in the Toolbox) allows you to click and select any path segment or anchor point in the vector mask for editing.

ICON	TOOL
🔼	Direct Selection. Allows you to select anchor points or segments for editing.
🖋⁺	Add Anchor Point. Click a path segment to add anchor points. Click and drag to add and edit a curve simultaneously.
🖋	Subtract Anchor Point. Click an anchor point to delete it.
🔺	Convert Point. Click or click and drag an anchor point to convert a curve to an angle or an angle to a curve.

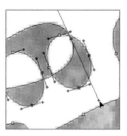

When you click a path in the vector mask, the anchor points of the path become visible. Shift-clicking can select multiple anchor points. Simply click any segment, anchor, or adjustment handle and drag to edit the mask.

11.7 Editing Vector Masks *(continued)*

Adding Paths to a Vector Mask

The primary vector drawing tool for adding paths is the Pen tool . Photoshop also has a Freeform Pen tool accessible in the Toolbox with a Magnetic Pen option available via the Options bar.

1 Select either of these tools and set the options described in the previous paragraph.

2 In the Layers palette, click the layer mask thumbnail.

3 In the image window, click or click and drag, observing the developing path.

In some cases you might find it easier to edit in the mask with the mask disabled so that the fill of the layer does not get in the way of editing. Right-click for the option.

Moving a Vector Mask within the Layer

You can move a vector mask independently of the layer's content using the Path Component Selection tool. This process differs slightly from using the Move tool, which can be used either to move the content and vector mask together or to move the content independently of the vector mask by unlinking them.

1 Choose the Path Selection tool or the Direct Selection tool.

2 Do one of the following to select the vector mask:

- In the Layers palette, click the layer thumbnail (not the vector mask thumbnail) with the vector mask you want to move.

- In the canvas, click the vector mask's path.

You can now reposition the vector mask's path in the canvas by dragging it to a new location and releasing.

Left: The path is being created using the Ellipse tool. Center: The path is being repositioned using the Select tool. Right: The path is moved, masking a different part of the layer.

➡ 4.16 Paths Palette

➡ 16.7 Drawing with Pen Tools

➡ 16.8 Selecting Paths and Path Components

Path Selection tool
[A]

Cycle path selection tools
[Shift] [A]

———

Duplicating an entire layer also duplicates that layer's masks.

———

You can easily reapply vector masks because their paths can be saved independently of the layer in the Paths palette or as custom shape presets.

11.7   Editing Vector Masks *(continued)*

Shape tool
〔U〕

Cycle shape tools
〔Shift〕〔U〕

———

Clicking the layer's thumbnail selects the layer content and the vector mask, but not the layer mask.

———

Clicking the vector mask's thumbnail once selects the layer the mask is on, but not the mask itself. Once a layer is selected, click the vector mask thumbnail again to select the mask.

Copying a Vector Mask to Another Layer

You can duplicate a vector mask from one layer to another layer that does not have a vector mask. Follow these steps:

1 Select the layer you want to copy the layer vector mask to (the target layer). This layer must not currently contain a vector mask.

2 Do one of the following:

- To **duplicate the vector mask**, drag the thumbnail of the mask to be copied to the Add A Mask button 〔▣〕 at the bottom of the Layers palette.

- To **invert the mask while duplicating**, Option/Alt-drag the thumbnail of the layer mask to be copied to the Add A Mask button 〔▣〕 at the bottom of the Layers palette.

The vector mask will now appear in the target layer.

MASKS AND EFFECTS

You will notice that the effects applied to a layer are not hidden by masks. Instead, the effects conform to the mask as if it were a transparent area in the layer. Options in the Blending Options panel of the Layer Styles dialog allow you to set both vector and layer masks so that they will also mask effects in the layer (see Sections 15.2 and 15.7).

11.8　Applying or Removing Vector Masks

Although masks add only a little to the overall file size, at times you will want to either apply the mask permanently to the layer or remove it altogether. First select the layer mask, and then do one of the following:

- To **temporarily hide** a vector mask, choose Layer > Disable Vector Mask, or Control/right-click the layer mask thumbnail and select Disable Layer Mask, or Shift-click the vector mask thumbnail. A red *X* appears over the vector mask thumbnail, and you see what the layer would look like without the mask without deleting the mask. Repeat (selecting Enable Vector Mask instead) to show the mask.

A red *X* will appear in the vector mask when it is disabled.

- To **apply** the vector mask to the layer, choose Layer > Rasterize > Vector Mask, or Control/right-click the layer mask thumbnail and select Rasterize Vector Mask. The vector mask is discarded, but its effects are rasterized into the layer mask.

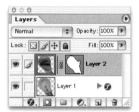 

Left: The original vector mask. Right: The vector mask has been rasterized and placed in the layer mask.

- To **delete** the vector mask from the layer, choose Layer > Delete Vector Mask > Apply, or Control/right-click the vector mask thumbnail and select Delete Vector Mask, or click and drag the vector mask thumbnail to the trashcan icon 🗑. The vector mask is discarded along with its effects.

➡ 2.6　Layer Menu

➡ 4.13　Layers Palette

You can convert the temporary vector mask in the Paths palette into a permanent path. Click the Paths drop-down and select Save Path.

Once a vector mask is rasterized, you cannot revert it to its original vector shape. You can, however, convert it into a selection, convert the selection into a path, and then convert the path into a vector mask. However, this vector shape will never be precisely the same as the original.

11.9 Saving Vector Masks as Clipping Paths

Photoshop lets you export specialized vector masks called clipping paths with images that are destined for placement in page-layout applications. Clipping paths take advantage of both the mask and its vector qualities. The mask itself allows you to transfer transparency or a knockout of the background. The vector characteristics allow you to take advantage of PostScript translation of the clean vector edges into print.

In page-layout applications, the knockout, or transparency, allows the application to apply a text wrap, which reads the clipping path, using it as a guide to allow text to run up to the specified distance from the vector mask. In this example, the leaf was selected with the Pen tool in Photoshop, and the path or vector mask was then saved as a clipping path. The image was saved as a TIFF for placement in the layout application.

USING ALPHA CHANNELS WITH LAYER MASKS

An alpha channel is a special channel used to record a selection as a grayscale. A layer mask will also appear as a temporary alpha channel in the Channels palette when the layer it is on is selected. However, the temporary alpha channel can also be saved as a permanent alpha channel and then loaded into other documents. In addition, when the layer mask is loaded, it can also be edited using painting tools.

11.9 Saving Vector Masks as Clipping Paths *(continued)*

Saving a Vector Mask as a Clipping Path

To save a vector mask as a clipping path, select the vector mask layer and then open the Paths palette. You will see the vector mask active in the Paths palette. Now follow these steps:

1 In the Paths palette, choose Save Path from the drop-down palette menu. Name the path in the dialog that opens.

2 From the drop-down palette menu once again, choose Clipping Path....

3 In the Clipping Path dialog, choose your path from the Path drop-down. Adobe recommends saving with the Flatness field blank the first time, which will use the printer's defaults. If you experience any errors, you can come back and set the values at 1–3 for normal resolutions and 8–10 for high resolution. Your printer or service bureau may give you a value for their purposes.

- If you are going to print to a non-PostScript printer, save the file as a TIFF.

- If you are printing to a PostScript printer, save the file in EPS, DCS, or PDF format.

- If you are placing your own file into InDesign CS for page-layout purposes, you may choose to work with layers preserved. However, if you are sending your files to anyone else for placement, clear the Layers check box in the Save As dialog.

CHAPTER **12**

PHOTOSHOP WORKSPACE

UNIVERSAL TASKS

PHOTO AND VIDEO TASKS

PRINT TASKS

WEB TASKS

Working with Colors, Gradients, and Patterns

WHEN WORKING IN PHOTOSHOP, you always have two colors actively selected and displayed in the Toolbox. By default, these colors are black and white, and they are designated as your foreground and background colors. They influence more than just what you want to paint; they also affect how areas are filled when you delete content, add canvas, or apply certain filters. This chapter presents several methods for selecting and organizing chosen colors.

Photoshop gives you several options for applying color to your image beyond the standard brushes and painting tools. You can also apply color as fills and specialized Fill layers—which work much like Adjustment layers—with their masks and blending options. Once you create patterns and gradients, you can manage and apply them in much the same way you work with a solid color.

In this chapter, you will learn how to choose colors, create gradients and patterns, and then fill areas of the canvas. You will also learn how to create and manage sets of colors, gradients, and patterns.

12.1   Color, Gradient, and Pattern Basics

Though they may seem quite different in concept, patterns, gradients, and solid colors are in several ways interrelated. All three design elements, or tools, have their own unique application method that can be accessed via their respective icons in the Toolbox or the Options bar; however, you can apply each as a specialized fill layer via the layer menu or the Layers palette.

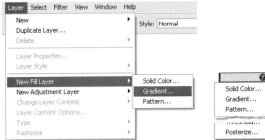

Once you define a color swatch, gradient, or pattern, you can manage it and access it from within Photoshop's Preset Manager (choose Edit > Preset Manager > Preset Type). Simply choose an item from the drop-down to navigate to your preselected (preset) color swatches, gradients, or patterns.

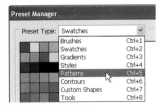

You can enter colors in any of the four color models regardless of the color mode of the image.

The foreground color will always be the color you paint; the background color will be the color of your canvas.

The CMYK model is generally used for high-quality print work. The HSB and RGB models and hexadecimal color values are generally used for web and television work, although they can be used when printing to RGB printers. Use the Lab model when you are striving for consistency between different computer platforms.

Color You can make color choices with the Eyedropper tool, the Color palette, the Swatches palette, or the Color Picker. Simply select the Eyedropper in the Toolbox and click a pixel in a document window to sample that color and display it as your foreground color in the Toolbox. You can make more sophisticated color choices using the Color Picker or the Color palette. You can choose colors from one of several color models—HSB, Lab, RGB, and CMYK—use hexadecimal (web) color values or choose spot colors from the Custom Colors dialog.

Gradients You choose gradients from predefined samples using the Presets Manager and Options menu or build them using the Gradient Editor. Understanding the Color Picker is helpful as it is your alternative to the Eyedropper for adding and editing color stops to a gradient.

Patterns You can define patterns using any selection of pixels made in Photoshop—simply make a selection and choose Edit > Define Pattern and click OK in the dialog which appears—to add your selection to the pattern presets. Making patterns that are effective fills, however, can take a bit more finesse. The Photoshop Pattern Maker is available from the Filter menu, which you use to quickly generate pattern effects.

12.2 Selecting Colors with the Eyedropper

The Eyedropper is an integral tool used throughout Photoshop for color selection. It can be used both on its own as it appears in the Toolbox  and as a part of several more sophisticated color-based processes such as using the Color Picker and the color palette and making color range selections and various color adjustments.

You use the Eyedropper to select or sample the color of pixels displayed in any open image or dialog. You can use it to select color from individual pixels, or through the Options menu, you can set it to average information from several pixels.

To use the Eyedropper, follow these steps:

1 Choose the Eyedropper tool  from the Toolbox.

2 Choose your intended sample size in the Options bar.

3 Select a color by doing one of the following:

- Click a pixel in the canvas of any open document; the document does not have to be in the front.

- Click and drag over the canvas of any open document. The color of the pixel the cursor is currently over is previewed with its color value in the Color palette. Release to select the current color.

- Click any visible color square or color swatch.

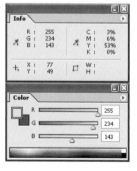

A color is selected from the canvas with the eyedropper. Notice that the Info palette and the Color palette on the right both display the selected color's values.

The Swatches Palette You can use this to select and store sampled colors.

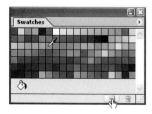

After clicking in an image to sample a color, you can move your cursor over the Swatches palette. The cursor changes to the Eyedropper, allowing you to select a new swatch. If you move your cursor over an empty space in the Swatches palette, the Paint Bucket appears, allowing you to click and save a swatch of the newly sampled color. You can also click the New Swatch button at the bottom of the Swatches palette to create a swatch of the sampled color.

Temporarily switch to the Eyedropper tool to sample a new color, while using any selected shape tool or painting tool.
Option Alt

Toggle foreground and background swatches.
X

(with Eyedropper) Switch selection of foreground or background as color (reverts after release)
Option
Alt

You can choose the foreground or background color square in the Color palette; however, If the color square is already selected, do not click again unless you want to open the Color Picker.

While using any selected shape tool or painting with the Pencil, Brush, or Paint Bucket tool, you can temporarily switch to the Eyedropper tool to sample a new color.

12.3   Selecting Colors with the Color Palette

(with Eyedropper)
Switch selection of foreground or background as color (reverts after release)
[Option]
[Alt]

———

As you move the cursor over an image, the color value of the pixel the cursor is currently over is displayed in the Info palette.

———

Although you can select the color model to use for the sliders in the Color palette from the palette's menu, using the same model as the color mode of the image is recommended.

———

You can change the colors displayed in the color ramp by selecting a different color model in the palette's menu. You can choose RGB Spectrum, CMYK Spectrum, Grayscale Ramp, or Current Colors (the colors in the current image).

By default, you'll find black selected as your foreground color and white as your background color; these colors are displayed in the Toolbox as well as in the Color palette. If you look at the Color palette, you will find you can select either the foreground or the background color by clicking the Swatch icon. (Clicking a selected Swatch icon displays the Color Picker.)

You can adjust your selected color using any of several color models available in the palette menu. You can input numeric color values for precise color control or visually adjust color by using the sliders to adjust the values associated with the color model you chose.

HSB Enter values for hue (0 through 360), saturation (0 through 100), and brightness (0 through 100).

RGB Enter values (0 through 255) for the amount of red, green, and blue in the color.

Lab Enter values for luminance (0 through 100); "a" axis (–128 through 127), which represents the green-to-red value; and "b" axis (–128 though 127), which represents the blue-to-yellow value.

CMYK Enter values (0 through 100) as percentages of the amount of cyan, magenta, yellow, and black in the color.

Hex (web) Enter a value (#000000 through #FFFFFF) for the color.

Grayscale Enter a value (0 through 100) for the percentage of black to use.

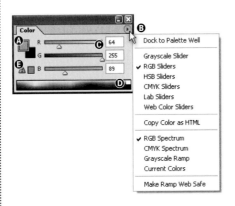

Ⓐ **Selected Color** In this case, the foreground color swatch indicates it is selected for editing. Clicking the swatch again displays the Color Picker.

Ⓑ **Color Palette Menu** Allows you to select one of several color models from the drop-down. You can select color models for both the main palette window and for the color ramp separately.

Ⓒ **Color Sliders and Values** Displays the current color values using the selected color model. Slide the triangle underneath to change the color value, or enter the color value directly in the text field. Any changes are immediately reflected in the selected color square.

Ⓓ **Color Ramp** The color ramp represents the spectrum of the color model selected via the palette menu. Move your cursor over the color ramp in the Color palette (the cursor will automatically switch to the Eyedropper 🖊), and then click a color. You can also set the color ramp to grayscale and "current colors" via the palette menu; the current colors setting allows for adjustment of saturation or lightness based on a selected color value.

Ⓔ **Gamut or Web-safe Warning** A triangle with an exclamation mark ⚠ indicates that the selected color is out of the print gamut and cannot be printed. A cube 🔲 indicates that the selected color is not browser-safe and may not display properly on all computer monitors. Click the color swatch underneath to convert the color to a similar color that is in gamut or Web-safe.

12.4 Selecting Colors with the Color Picker

Although the Color palette provides basic controls for quickly choosing and adjusting colors, Photoshop places its advanced color selection options into the Color Picker. The Color Picker provides an intuitive interface for selecting colors, while allowing you to monitor several color models at once for color accuracy. The Color Picker also provides access to the most common spot color systems and color books via the Custom Colors button and dialog.

You'll find color squares at various locations in the Photoshop interface—the two most prominent being the foreground and background squares—but they also often appear in the tool options bar and in dialogs (although color squares may be more rectangular than square). These squares generally define the color to be used by specific tools or commands. You change them using the Color Picker:

1   Click a color square in the Photoshop interface to open the Color Picker.

2   Select a color by clicking in the color field, adjusting a slider, or entering numeric values directly into one of the text fields.

3   Click OK when you are finished. The color appears in the selected color square and is ready for use.

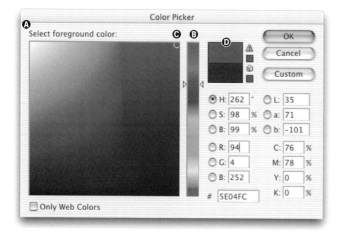

A Indicates the type of color square currently being selected. In this example, the foreground color is being selected.

B **Color Slider** Displays the values available for the selected color value (see I). Move the triangles on either side up or down to change the value. For example, if you select S (for Saturation in HSB), the slider displays all the saturation levels for the current hue and brightness settings. If you select G (for Green in RGB), the slider displays all the greens.

C **Color Field** Displays all the colors available based on the color currently selected in the Color slider. Click any color in this area to select it. The circle indicates the currently selected color.

D **New Color** Displays the color selected in the Color field.

➡ 3.22 Eyedropper and Measure Tools

➡ 4.7 Color Palette

➡ 4.11 Info Palette

➡ 4.18 Swatches Palette

When you are working in Bitmap or Indexed Color mode, you can choose only colors that are currently in the image's color table.

While you are using the Color Picker, you can also click any color square, swatch, or image to choose a color using the Color Picker.

You can use your operating system's Color Picker instead of the Photoshop Color Picker by changing the preference in the General preferences (see Section 5.4).

When you are working
in Bitmap or Indexed
Color mode, you can
choose only colors that
are currently in the
image's color table.

While you are using
the Color Picker, you
can also click any
color square, swatch,
or image to choose a
color using the Color
Picker.

You can use your oper-
ating system's Color
Picker instead of the
Photoshop Color Picker
by changing the prefer-
ence in the General
preferences (see
Section 5.4).

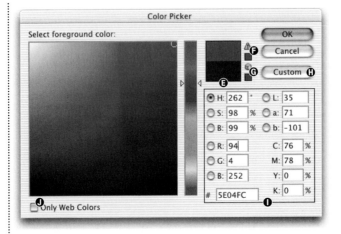

E **Current Color** Displays the color being replaced. Click to reset to this color.

F **Gamut Warning** Indicates that the selected color is out of the print and NTSC television gamut and cannot be printed or be displayed on televisions used in North America. Click the color swatch underneath to convert the color to a similar color that is in gamut.

G **Web Safe Warning** Indicates that the color is not web safe and might not display properly on all computer monitors. Click the color swatch underneath to convert the color to a similar color that is web safe.

H Click to open the Custom Color dialog, in which you can select PANTONE and other special colors.

I **Color Values** Displays the numeric values of the selected color in HSB, RGB, Lab and CMYK color models and hexadecimal values. You can enter the numeric values for the color directly, or you can choose a radio button next to a color value if you want the Color slider (see B) and Color field (see C) to display using that value type.

J Check to only display web-safe colors in the Color slider and Color field.

12.5   Selecting Custom Spot Colors

If you are using spot colors instead of process colors for printing, you can select from a wide range of spot color systems or color books in the Custom Colors dialog. Follow these steps:

1 In the Color Picker, click the Custom button to open the Custom Colors dialog.

2 Select the spot color catalog from which you want to choose colors, select the color range in the slider, and then select the exact spot color to use.

3 Click OK when you are finished. The color now appears in the color square you selected. If you are actually using this as a spot color for printing, add an additional channel for this color.

➭ 8.7   Using Color in Channels

➭ 8.10 Converting to Duotone Mode

(in Preset Manager) Jump to swatches
⌘ ②
Ctrl ②

With the Custom Colors dialog open, start typing the name of a particular spot color in the selected catalog, and Photoshop will attempt to find it.

Spot colors are still used as process colors (except in Duotone) unless you add them to specific spot color channels.

Spot colors are especially useful when creating a Duotone.

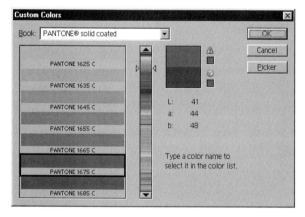

A Spot Color Books Select the spot color system or book you want to use. The most common of these are the PANTONE color books, but check with your printer or service bureau to see what ink colors are available.

B Color Range Displays a compressed list of the colors. Click a color to select that range for it and display in the color display. You can also drag the triangles on either side up and down or use the arrows at the top and bottom to move through the list.

C Color Display Displays a list of colors based on the color range selected. Click a color to select it or use the Up and Down arrow keys to scroll through the list.

D New Color Displays the color currently selected in the Color field.

E Current Color Displays the color being replaced. Click to reset to this color.

F Gamut Warning Indicates that the selected color is out of the print gamut and cannot be printed. Click the color swatch underneath to convert the color to a similar color that is in gamut.

G Web Safe Warning Indicates that the color is not web safe and might not display properly on all computer monitors. Click the color swatch underneath to convert the color to a similar color that is web safe.

H Displays the Lab color values for the selected spot color.

I Click to open the Color Picker. The selected spot color is converted to a process color value.

12.6   Organizing Color Swatch Presets

➧ 4.7   Color Palette

➧ 4.18 Swatches
       Palette

Saving color swatches is
great for storing color
palettes used in partic-
ular projects.

A good place to save
your swatches is the
Color Swatches folder in
the Photoshop folder.

Storing frequently used colors in saved color swatch presets is a handy way to have quick access to specific sets of colors. For example, if you are a web designer, you might want to save all the web-safe colors used for a given project in one place. If you are working on a print project, you might want to store your client's corporate or project-specific PANTONE colors in a set. You can make changes to swatch presets (saved swatches) in the Swatches palette itself or in the Swatches Preset Manager, which can be accessed via the Edit menu or the Swatches palette menu.

Editing Presets

The color swatch list is made up of color swatches, the small squares in the Swatches palette. Each swatch has a name, and you can easily add or delete swatches from the list.

- To **delete a color swatch**, Option/Alt-click the swatch in the Swatches palette or in the Swatches Preset Manager (the mouse cursor turns into a pair of scissors). You can also click and drag the swatch to the trash can button 🗑 or, in the Swatches Preset Manager, click one or more colors (Shift-click, Ctrl-click to select multiple swatches) and press Delete. The color is removed, and all other colors in the palette shift to fill its space.

- To **add the currently selected color** (foreground or background) to the Swatches palette, click anywhere in the blank area of the palette or choose New Swatch from the palette menu. Enter a name for the new swatch in the New Color Swatch Name dialog and click OK. The new color is added at the bottom of the list.

- To **change a swatch's name**, double-click the swatch in the Swatches palette, enter the new name in the Color Swatch Name dialog, and click OK. You can also select the swatch in the Swatches Preset Manager, click the Rename… button, enter a new name in the Color Swatch Name dialog, and click OK.

- To **change a swatch's position** in the list, click and drag the swatch in the Swatches Preset Manager to the desired location.

Saving Presets

After you create and edit personalized color swatches, you can easily save them for future use. To save your color swatches as a Preset list, do one of the following:

- Choose Save Swatches from the Swatches palette menu.

- In the Swatches Preset Manager, select the colors you want to save as a Preset list, and then click the Save Set… button. Enter a name for the new swatch list, making sure to preserve the .aco extension, browse to the folder in which you want to save the swatch list, and click Save.

12.6 Organizing Color Swatch Presets *(continued)*

Loading Presets

You can add to (or completely replace) the color swatches in the Swatches palette by choosing to reset, load, or replace swatches with saved preset lists from the Swatches palette menu.

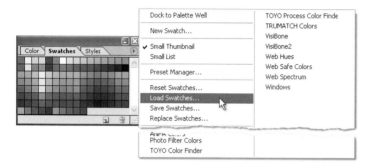

- To **reset the swatches** to factory fresh, choose Reset Swatches… from the Swatches palette menu or the Swatches Preset Manager menu. Choose whether you want to append the default colors to the current list (at the bottom) or to replace the current list.

- To **load a list of swatches**, choose Load… from the Swatches palette menu or click the Load… button in the Swatches Preset Manager. Browse to locate the swatch file that has the .aco extension, and double-click the file. The colors are appended to the bottom of the current list.

- To **quickly load a new list** of swatches, choose from the list at the bottom of the Swatches palette menu or the Swatches Preset Manager menu. Choose whether you want to append the new list to the current list (at the bottom) or to replace the current list.

- To **replace the current swatches** with a new list, choose Replace Swatches… from the Swatches palette menu or the Swatches Preset Manager menu. Browse to locate the swatch file that has the .aco extension, and double-click the file.

 5.1 Preset Manager Overview

(in Preset Manager) Jump to swatches
⌘ 2
Ctrl 2

———

Hold the mouse cursor over a color in the Swatches palette to view the color name in a Tool Tip.

Although Adobe offers a wide assortment of color swatches, the Visibone 2 swatches are highly recommended for web designers.

12.7   Applying Color Fills

➡ 3.14 Fill Tools

➡ 10.1 Layer Basics

Fill selected pixels or entire layer using foreground color
`Option` + `Del`
`Alt` + `Del`

Fill selected pixels or entire layer using background color
`⌘` + `Del`
`Ctrl` + `Del`

―――

Solid color fills applied with blend modes can be used effectively to enhance colors: for example, try Hue and Saturation with color fills.

―――

You can also apply patterns to an entire layer using the Pattern Overlay effect.

You can apply color to the canvas in a variety of ways, but often you need to fill large areas or even the entire canvas with a solid color. You can do this with the Fill command, the Paint Bucket tool, or a Solid Color Fill layer.

The selection to be filled   After using the Fill command

Using the Fill Command

You can use the Fill command to fill an entire layer or a selection within a layer without worrying about the content in that layer. To use the Fill command, follow these steps:

1 Pick the color you want to fill with. (The color can be in either the foreground or background square.)

2 Select the layer you want to fill. You can also make a selection to fill.

3 Choose Edit > Fill to open the Fill dialog, set the options, and then click OK. The layer or selection is now filled.

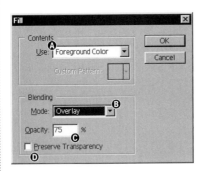

Ⓐ Choose the source for the fill. You can choose the foreground color, the background color, black, 50% gray, or white.

Ⓑ Choose a blending mode to use with the fill. Since you are editing a layer, you can choose Behind and Clear in addition to the standard blending modes.

Ⓒ Enter a value (1 through 100) to specify the opacity of the fill as a percentage.

Ⓓ Check to preserve the transparency of pixels in the layer when the fill pixels are applied. This will change the colors without affecting the opacity of pixels in the image.

12.7   Applying Color Fills (continued)

Using the Paint Bucket Tool

The Paint Bucket tool will also fill the layer, but will confine the area of the fill based on the content in the selected layer. Follow these steps:

1   Pick the color you want to fill with as the foreground color.

2   Select the layer you want to fill. You can also make a selection to confine the area of the fill.

3   Select the Paint Bucket tool and set the options in the tool options bar:

- Make sure the Fill menu is set to Foreground.

- Choose a blending mode to use with the fill. Since you are editing a layer, you can choose Behind and Clear in addition to the standard blending modes.

- Set the opacity for the fill.

- Set the tolerance for the fill. The higher the number, the larger the area that is filled.

- Check whether you want the fill to be anti-aliased, contiguous (only pixels touching each other), and/or using all layers.

4   Click with the Paint Bucket on the spot where you want the fill to begin. The area of the fill is limited by the first color click, the tolerance value, any selection, whether the fill is contiguous, and whether the fill is using all layers.

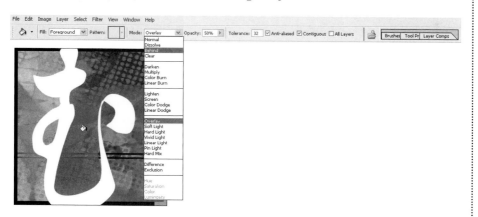

After using the Paint Bucket tool to fill. The blending mode is set to Overlay, opacity is set to 50%, and tolerance is set to 100%.

⇒ 11.1 Mask Basics

⇒ 13   Painting in
            Images

Fill only visible pixels in layer using fore-ground color

Option Shift Del
Alt Shift Bksp

Remember, the selection you use with a fill can be feathered to soften the edges of the fill.

Since the Fill command is only available using the Edit menu, you have to be in Standard or Full Screen mode with the menu bar open to access it.

12.7 Applying Color Fills *(continued)*

➡ 15.12 Applying the
Overlay
Effects

**Fill only visible pixels
in layer using back-
ground color**
⌘ Shift Del
Ctrl Shift Bksp

―――

If you fill an image in
CMYK mode using the
Black option in the Fill
dialog, all channels are
filled with 100% black,
which may cause prob-
lems with your printer.
Instead, choose black
for the foreground
color, and then fill
using the foreground
color.

―――

Hold down the Shift key
while using the fill
bucket to fill only visi-
ble pixels in the
selected layer.

Adding a Solid Color Fill Layer

Another versatile way to add a fill to the canvas is to use a Fill layer, which allows you to fill with a single color on a separate editable layer with a built-in mask. Filling on a separate layer allows you more blending and opacity options while the layer mask allows for adjustment of the fill area. To add a fill layer, follow these steps:

1 Select the layer above which you want to insert a Solid Color Fill layer. You can also make an addition selection in that layer. The selection will be used as a layer mask in the Fill layer.

2 To insert the Solid Color Fill layer, do one of the following:

■ Choose Layer > New Fill Layer > Solid Color… Set options in the New Layer dialog and click OK.

■ Choose Solid Color… from the Adjustments menu  at the bottom of the Layers palette.

3 Choose the color to be used in the Fill layer, and click OK.

After adding a Solid Color (gray) Fill layer, layer blending mode set to exclusion. Note the Fill Layer icon ■ in the layer's palette and the associated layer mask. Double-clicking the icon displays the Color Picker, allowing you to change colors. A rectangular selection was used to generate fill in the layer mask.

12.8 Creating and Editing Gradients

Photoshop provides dozens of preset gradients. The easiest way to access them is to select the Gradient tool from the Toolbox and then choose from the Options bar. Clicking the menu selector ▾ gives you access to selected presets. More than likely you will want to create or edit your own gradient. Simply click the gradient preview in the Options bar to access the Gradient Editor. The Gradient Editor allows you to create new gradients, edit and rename gradients, and save gradient sets. To edit or create a gradient, follow these steps:

1 Click the gradient preview to open the Gradient Editor.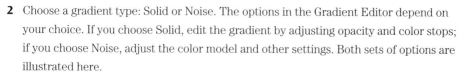

2 Choose a gradient type: Solid or Noise. The options in the Gradient Editor depend on your choice. If you choose Solid, edit the gradient by adjusting opacity and color stops; if you choose Noise, adjust the color model and other settings. Both sets of options are illustrated here.

3 Click OK when you're done. The new gradient appears in the gradient preview window and in the Gradient Presets drop-down.

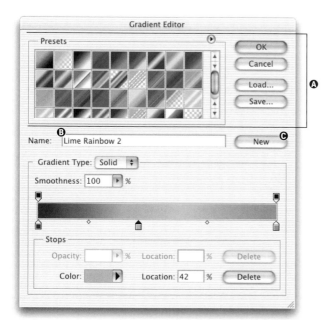

A Presets This area works the same as the Gradients Preset Manager (see Section 12.7). Click one of the gradient presets to load it into the editor below.

B Displays the name of the current gradient. Although you cannot change the name here, you can enter a new name to create a new gradient.

C Click to record the gradient using the name (see B) in the Presets list. This does not permanently save the gradient in the Presets list.

➡ 1.4   Interface
          Objects

Fill tools

 G

Warning: This gradient is not permanently saved until you save the list of gradients in which it is stored.

The gradient pattern and drop-down are accessible with the Gradient tool selected.

Cycle Fill tools
`Shift` `G`

———

Gradients cannot be added to images in Bitmap or Indexed Color modes.

———

You can control the color and the opacity of a gradient at any point, allowing you to create opacity gradients.

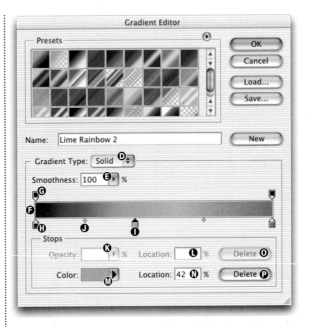

D Select either Solid or Noise for the gradient type. Solid is the more traditional gradient in which you set color points along the line. Noise allows you to adjust overall color values for the gradient, but randomizes the color points.

E Use the drop-down slider or enter a value (0 through 100) for the smoothness of the gradient.

F **Gradient Line** Displays the current appearance of the gradient. Click anywhere immediately above the gradient line to add an opacity stop. Click anywhere immediately below the gradient line to add a color stop.

G **Opacity Stop** Defines the opacity (see K) at a location (see L) in the gradient line. Click to select and change the values. Click and drag to move along the line or up to remove the stop.

H **Color Stop** Defines the color (see M) at a location (see N) in the gradient line. Click to select and change the values, or click anywhere immediately above the gradient line to add an addition point.

I **Selected Stop** The currently selected stop (opacity or color) has a black triangle rather than white. Click and drag to move, or press Delete to remove the selected stop.

J **Midpoint** Defines the midpoint location between two colors. Click and drag to move, or enter the location below.

K Enter a percentage value (0 through 100) for the selected opacity stop (see G).

L Enter a percentage value (0 through 100) for the location of the selected opacity stop (see G).

M Click to choose a color using the Color Picker for the selected color stop (see H). You can also choose one of the color options from the drop-down. In addition, you can click in the gradient line, in any open image, in any color swatch, or in any color square to select that color using the Eyedropper tool, which appears automatically.

N Enter a percentage value (0 through 100) for the location of the selected color stop (see H).

O Click to delete the selected opacity stop.

P Click to delete the selected color stop.

12.9 Organizing Gradient Presets

You can add, delete, rename, and reorder gradients in the Gradients Preset Manager. In addition, you can save and load stored libraries of gradients as needed. Gradients can be accessed via the Gradient Editor or through the Gradients Preset Manager.

Editing the Gradients Preset List

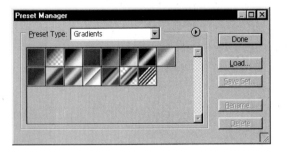

You can open the Gradients Preset Manager from the Gradient Picker's drop-down menu. You can remove, rename, or move the gradients in the drop-down.

➡ 3.14 Fill Tools

(Preset Manager) Jump to gradients
⌘ 3
Ctrl 3

——

If you create a gradient, as shown in Section 12.5, save it as a preset; otherwise it will be lost if you replace the gradients in the list.

- To **delete a gradient preset**, Option/Alt-click the thumbnail in the Gradients drop-down, the Gradient Editor, or the Gradients Preset Manager. The gradient is removed, and all other gradients in the drop-down shift to fill its space.

- To **change a gradient's name**, click the gradient in the Gradients drop-down, select Rename Gradient... in the drop-down's menu, enter the new name, and click OK. You can also select the gradient in the Gradients Preset Manager. Click the Rename...button, enter a new name, and click OK.

- To **change a gradient's position** in the list, click and drag the gradient in the Gradients Preset Manager to the desired location.

WHEN IS A COLOR OUT OF PRINT GAMUT?

Gamut refers to the range of colors that a particular color model can display. When you select a color using one of the color models other than CMYK, it is possible to create a color that cannot be printed. Selecting a color that is out of gamut means that there is no ink combination that can be used to create the color. If the image is being used for the screen only, this is not a problem, but, obviously, if you are printing using CMYK, you will want to select a different color.

12.9   Organizing Gradient Presets *(continued)*

⇒ 5.1   Preset Man-
            ager Overview

Fill tools
[G]

Cycle Fill tools
[Shift] [G]

——

It is a good idea to save
all the gradients you
use in a project as a single gradients file that
you can then quickly
load as needed.

Loading Presets

You can load lists of default gradient presets or lists that you created.

- To **reset** the gradients in the Gradients drop-down, choose Reset Gradients… from the Gradient Picker's drop-down menu, the Gradient Editor's menu, or the Gradients Preset Manager's menu. Specify whether you want to append the default gradients to the current list (at the bottom) or to replace the current list.

- To **load** a list of gradients, choose Load… from the Gradient Picker's drop-down menu or click the Load… button in the Gradients Preset Manager or Gradient Editor. Browse to locate the gradient file that has the .grd extension, and double-click the file. The gradients are appended to the bottom of the current list.

- To **quickly load** a new list of gradients, choose from the list at the bottom of the Gradient Picker's drop-down menu or the Gradients Preset Manager's menu. Specify whether you want to append the new list to the current list (at the bottom) or to replace the current list.

- To **replace** the current gradients with a new list, choose Replace Gradients… from the Gradients drop-down, the Gradient Editor, or the Gradients Preset Manager's menu. Browse to locate the gradient file that has the .grd extension, and double-click the file.

Saving Presets

To save a list of gradients, do one of the following:

- Choose Save Gradients from the menu in the Gradients drop-down. Enter a name for the new gradients list, making sure to preserve the .grd extension, browse to the folder in which you want to save the swatch list, and click Save.

- In the Gradients Preset Manager or the Gradient Editor, select the gradient thumbnails you want to save as a list (click the first color and then Shift-click additional colors), and then click the Save… button. Enter a name for the new swatch list, making sure to preserve the .grd extension, browse to the folder in which you want to save the swatch list, and click Save.

12.10 Applying Gradient Color Fills

Gradients are added to the canvas either across an entire layer, within a selection, or as part of a fill layer. Whenever you apply a gradient, you can select from five gradient styles.

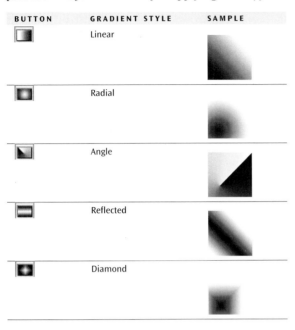

BUTTON	GRADIENT STYLE	SAMPLE
	Linear	
	Radial	
	Angle	
	Reflected	
	Diamond	

Using the Gradient Tool

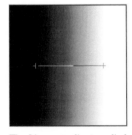
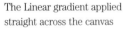

The Linear gradient applied straight across the canvas

The Linear gradient applied at an angle

1 Select the layer to which you want to add a gradient. You can also make a selection to confine the area of the fill. You might want to create a new layer to add the gradient to; otherwise, images on the current layer will be replaced by the gradient.

2 Select the Gradient tool 🔲 and set the options in the tool options bar:

■ Choose a gradient from the Gradient drop-down or double-click the gradient thumbnail to open the Gradient Editor. The first two gradients in the list are based on the currently selected foreground and background colors.

➡ 3.14 Fill Tools

➡ 10.5 Adding Adjustment and Fill Layers

➡ 12.9 Organizing Gradient Presets

Fill tools
Ⓖ

12.10   Applying Gradient Color Fills *(continued)*

➡ 15.9   Applying the
       Glow Effects

➡ 15.12 Applying
       the Overlay
       Effects

Cycle Fill tools
Shift G

- Choose a blending mode to use when applying the gradient. Since you are editing a layer, you can choose Behind and Clear in addition to the standard blending modes.

- Choose a gradient style: Linear, Radial, Angle, Reflected, or Diamond.

- Set the opacity for the gradient when applied.

- Check whether you want to reverse the gradient direction, dither the gradient, and use gradient transparency settings.

3   Click with the Gradient tool at the point where you want the first color to set the stop location of the first color in the gradient, and then drag and release to set the stop location of the last color in the gradient. The gradient is applied based on the style selected.

Adding a Gradient Fill Layer

A Fill layer has been added with the center shape selected. The gradient is from black to transparent using the Angle style set to a 90° angle.

1   Select the layer above which you want to insert a Gradient Fill layer. You can also make an additional selection in that layer. The selection will be used as a layer mask in the Gradient Fill layer.

2   To insert the Gradient Fill layer, either choose Layer > New Fill Layer > Gradient…, or choose Gradient… from the Adjustments menu 🖌 at the bottom of the Layers palette.

3   In the Gradient Fill dialog, choose the gradient to use and set other options. You can also adjust the gradient's position by clicking it and the canvas and dragging.

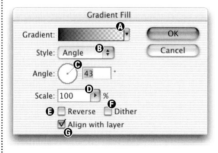

Ⓐ Select a gradient from the Gradient drop-down, or double-click the gradient thumbnail to open the Gradient Editor.

Ⓑ Select a gradient style.

Ⓒ Use the angle wheel or enter an angle value (–360 through 360) for the gradient.

Ⓓ Use the drop-down slider or enter a percentage value (10 through 150) for the gradient's scale.

Ⓔ Check to reverse the direction of the gradient.

Ⓕ Check to dither the gradient.

Ⓖ Check to align the fill with the layer rather than with the selected area.

12.11 Creating Patterns

You create patterns using rectangular selections in the canvas. This selection is then used to define the pattern and added to the pattern presets for use. Follow these steps:

1 Using the Rectangular Marquee tool [⬚], select an area in the canvas from which you want to create a pattern. This selection will be used to create the pattern sampling from all visible layers.

2 Choose Edit > Define Pattern…

3 Enter a name for the new pattern and click OK. The new pattern appears in the Patterns Preset drop-down and the Patterns Preset Manager.

The selection in the canvas to be used to define a pattern

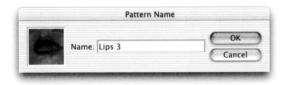

The Pattern Name dialog. A thumbnail of the new pattern appears next to the name.

The pattern applied to the canvas using a Fill layer

➡ 2.4 Edit Menu

➡ 2.7 Select Menu

➡ 3.3 Marquee Tools

➡ 9.3 Selecting Rectangular or Elliptical Areas

➡ 12.14 Using the Pattern Maker

➡ 28.7 Creating Seamless Backgrounds

You can make more complex and abstract patterns using the Pattern Maker filter (see Section 12.14).

You can create complex seamless patterns using the Offset filter on several layered objects.

Warning: A pattern is not permanently saved until you save the list of presets in which it is stored. If you replace the current list before saving, the pattern will be lost.

You cannot use feathering to create a pattern.

You can import or copy a shape created in a vector image into the canvas to create more precise geometric patterns.

12.12   Organizing Pattern Presets

5.1   Preset Man-
      ager Overview

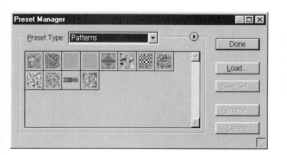

You can add patterns to and remove patterns from the presets either through a Pattern drop-down or using the Patterns Preset Manager. In addition, you can rename or save patterns as a set.

Editing the Patterns Preset List

You can use the Pattern drop-down or Patterns Preset Manager to remove, rename, or move particular presets.

- To **delete a pattern preset**, Option/Alt-click the thumbnail in the Pattern drop-down or the Patterns Preset Manager. The pattern is removed, and all other patterns in the drop-down shift to fill its space

- To **change a pattern's name**, click the pattern in the Pattern drop-down, choose Rename Pattern... from the menu, enter the new name, and click OK. You can also select a pattern in the Patterns Preset Manager, click the Rename... button, enter a new name, and click OK.

- To **change a pattern's position** in the list, click and drag the pattern in the Patterns Preset Manager to the desired location.

Loading Presets

You can change the presets listed in the Pattern drop-down by loading new lists to append to or replace the existing list. The easiest place to do this is in the Patterns Preset Manager, but you can also directly edit the patterns that show up in the Pattern Presets drop-down accessible throughout the Photoshop interface.

- To **reset** the patterns in the Pattern drop-down to their defaults, choose Reset Patterns... from the Patterns palette or the Patterns Preset Manager. Choose whether you want to append the default patterns to the current list (at the bottom) or to replace the current list.

- To **load** a list of patterns, choose Load... from the Patterns palette menu or click the Load... button in the Patterns Preset Manager. Browse to locate the pattern file that has the .pat extension, and double-click the file. The pattern is appended to the bottom of the current list.

12.12   Organizing Pattern Presets *(continued)*

- To **quickly load** a new list of patterns, choose from the list at the bottom of the Patterns palette or the Patterns Preset Manager. Choose whether you want to append the new list to the current list (at the bottom) or to replace the current list.

- To **replace** the current patterns with a new list, choose Replace Patterns… from the Pattern drop-down or the Patterns Preset Manager. Browse to locate the pattern file that has the .pat extension, and double-click the file.

(Preset Manager) Jump to patterns

⌘ 5

Ctrl 5

Saving Presets

To save a list of preset patterns, do one of the following:

- Choose Save Patterns from the menu in the Pattern drop-down. Enter a name for the new pattern list, making sure to preserve the .pat extension, browse to the folder in which you want to save the swatch list, and click OK.

- In the Patterns Preset Manager, select the pattern thumbnails you want to save as a list (click the first pattern, Shift-click additional patterns), and then click the Save Set… button. Enter a name for the new pattern list, making sure to preserve the .pat extension, browse to the folder in which you want to save the pattern list, and click OK.

WHAT ARE WEB-SAFE COLORS?

Web-safe colors are the 216 color values that display more or less consistently across both the Mac and Windows operating systems. Although web-safe colors are rapidly becoming a moot point, since most monitors can display thousands or more colors, many web designers still stick with them.

It's actually not that hard to remember all 216 safe colors, not by name of course, but either on the RGB or hexadecimal scales. Both scales use a list of three separate values. The first value tells the computer how much red to mix in the color, the second is green, and the third is blue. To be browser safe, for RGB you can use 0, 51, 102, 153, 204, or 255. For hexadecimal you can use 00, 33, 66, 99, CC, and FF, in any combination in the three slots. So 153 0 102 is the same as 990066 and produces a reddish purple.

12.13   Applying Patterns

You can also apply patterns to an entire layer using the Pattern Overlay effect.

You can apply a pattern to an entire layer, to a selection in a layer, or as part of a Pattern Fill layer.

Using the Paint Bucket Tool

The Paint Bucket tool will also fill the layer, but will confine the area of the fill based on the content in the selected layer.

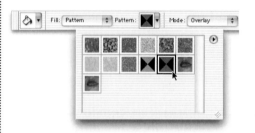
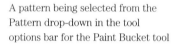

A pattern being selected from the Pattern drop-down in the tool options bar for the Paint Bucket tool

The diamond pattern applied to the image with 75% opacity

1 Pick the color you want to fill with as the foreground color.

2 Select the layer you want to fill. You can also make a selection to confine the area of the fill.

3 Select the Paint Bucket tool 🪣 and set the options in the tool options bar:

   ■ Make sure the Fill menu is set to Pattern.

   ■ Choose a blending mode to use with the fill. Since you are editing a layer, you can choose Behind and Clear in addition to the standard blending modes.

   ■ Set the opacity for the fill.

   ■ Set the tolerance for the fill. The higher the number, the larger the area filled.

   ■ Check whether you want the fill to be anti-aliased, contiguous (only pixels touching each other), and/or using all layers.

4 Click with the Paint Bucket tool on the spot where you want the fill to begin. The area of the fill is limited by the first color click, the tolerance value, any selection, whether the fill is contiguous, and whether the fill is using all layers.

12.13 Applying Patterns (continued)

Adding a Pattern Fill Layer

Using a Pattern Fill layer is the most flexible way to apply a pattern to an image since it allows you to edit and mask the pattern without affecting the other layers in the image.

➤ 15.12 Applying the
      Overlay
      Effects

➤ 15.13 Applying the
      Stroke Effect

You can transform scaling patterns using the default interpolation method.

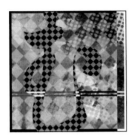

A Pattern Fill layer has been added. The selection is used as a layer mask.

1 To insert the Pattern Fill layer, either choose Layer > New Fill Layer > Pattern…, or choose Pattern… from the Adjustments menu [◑,] at the bottom of the Layers palette.

2 In the Pattern Fill dialog, choose the pattern to use and set other options. You can also adjust the pattern's position by clicking it and the canvas and dragging.

3 Click OK to place the pattern layer.

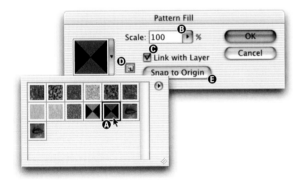

A Choose a pattern from the Pattern drop-down.

B Use the slider or enter a percentage value (1 through 1000) to scale the pattern.

C Check to link the pattern with the layer. When this option is checked, the pattern moves with the layer.

D Click to add the current pattern to the Pattern Presets list.

E Click if you want the top-left corner of the pattern to align with the origin (usually the top-left corner of the image unless it has been shifted).

12.14   Using the Pattern Maker

➡ 3.3   Marquee
        Tools

➡ 3.23 Hand Tool

➡ 3.24 Zoom Tool

The Pattern Maker can only be used with 8-bit images in RGB Color, CMYK Color, Lab Color, and Grayscale image modes.

Simply tiled patterns are created using the Edit > Define Pattern command, but for more organic patterns, you might want to use Photoshop's Pattern Maker, which can be accessed through the Filter Menu. The Pattern Maker works by randomly rearranging the pixels in a selected region of the image. The tiles can be as small as 1 pixel or as large as the image from which they are being generated. This feature is especially useful for generating seamless backgrounds for web pages, but has a variety of other design uses as well.

 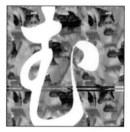

The original image with a selected area

A tile created from that selection

The tiled pattern applied to the image

To create a pattern using the Pattern Maker, follow these steps.

1   In the original image, make a rectangular selection. You can reshape this selection in the Pattern Maker dialog.

2   Choose Filter > Pattern Maker.

3   In the Pattern Maker dialog, adjust the selection as desired, or choose Use Clipboard As Sample to use a selection from another image. Set the pattern options as desired, and then click Generate. The new tile is displayed in the tile history, and the tiled pattern is displayed in the pattern preview. To generate a different pattern, click Generate Again. All the patterns you generate are recorded in the tile history.

4   Once you have a tile you want to apply to the entire layer, display the tile in the tile history, and click OK.

12.14 Using the Pattern Maker *(continued)*

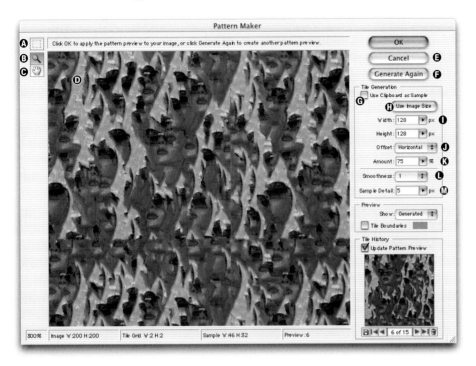

➠ 9.3 Selecting Rec-
   tangular or
   Elliptical
   Areas

➠ 9.13 Copying or
   Cutting
   Selected
   Content

If the transparency in
the selected layer is
locked, the Pattern
Maker will not allow
the pattern to tile into
transparent pixels.

Ⓐ Rectangular Marquee Tool Used to make a selection in the pattern preview to use as the source to generate the pattern.

Ⓑ Zoom Tool Used to zoom into the pattern preview.

Ⓒ Hand Tool Used to move the pattern in the pattern preview.

Ⓓ Pattern Preview Displays what the pattern in the tile preview will look like when tiled.

Ⓔ Press Option/Alt and then click to reset the dialog to its state when you originally opened it.

Ⓕ Click to generate a new pattern based on the options set in G–M.

Ⓖ Check to use the image stored in the Clipboard to generate the pattern rather then the selection.

Ⓗ Click to set the width and height to the width and height of the image.

Ⓘ Use the slider or enter a pixel value for the width and height of the pattern. These values must be at least 1, but cannot exceed the width or height of the image.

Ⓙ Choose an offset for the pattern tiles. This can help prevent the pattern from looking too regular.

Ⓚ Use the slider or enter a percentage value (0 through 99) for the selected offset.

Ⓛ Choose a value (1 through 3) for how smooth the transition between tiles should appear.

Ⓜ Use the slider or enter a pixel value (3 through 21) to set the size of details in the pattern. Larger values take longer to generate.

PHOTOSHOP WORKSPACE

UNIVERSAL TASKS

PHOTO AND VIDEO TASKS

PRINT TASKS

WEB TASKS

➡ 9.14   Pasting
        Selected
        Content

➡ 12.11 Creating
        Patterns

Increase the smooth-
ness value to produce
better tiling images.

You cannot create a
pattern from a nonrec-
tangular selection. If
you open the Pattern
Maker dialog with a
nonrectangular selec-
tion active, the Pattern
Maker selects the
extreme width and
height of the selection
as the rectangular
selection.

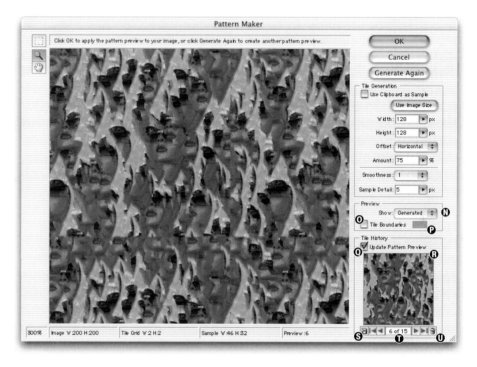

N Choose whether the preview displays the original image or the current pattern tile sample.

O Check to show colored boundaries between tiles in the preview.

P Click to use the Color Picker to set the boundary line color.

Q Check to show the tiles in the tile history in the pattern preview.

R **Tile Preview** Every time you click the Generate Again button, the tile is added to the history and
    previewed here.

S Click to save the tile displayed in the tile preview as a Pattern Preset.

T Click controls to move forward or backward in the tile history. The tile is displayed in the Tile
    Preview.

U Click to delete the tile displayed in the Tile Preview.

CHAPTER 13

Painting in Images

THE SIGNIFICANCE OF PAINTING in Photoshop is twofold. First, because many Photoshop's features rely on painting or brush application for much of their power, ease of application, and control. Second, but not necessarily less important, because of advancements in the sophistication or power of Photoshop's brush controls. Adobe completely revamped the painting tools in the previous version of Photoshop, revising how brushes are selected and created. In this version, our exploration of brushes is aided by locking panels in the Brushes palette to limit settings when changing among brush presets—and for the first time, brushes work in 16-bit mode.

Although you can now build, manage, and fine-tune brushes to produce an outstanding array of sophisticated effects, you can still use all Photoshop tools that require brush application or brush control with great results, using simple brushes chosen from the presets. This chapter introduces you to painting, the controls of the Brushes palette, and a bit more:

13.1   Brush Basics

Restoration tool
[J]

Paint Brush tools
[B]

Stamp tool
[S]

History Brush tool
[Y]

———

Jitter refers to varia-
tions in the brush
stroke to simulate the
random oscillations
that might occur while
painting with a physical
brush.

———

The term paint is used
throughout this chapter
either as a noun mean-
ing any color or pattern
that is applied with a
brush or as a verb refer-
ring to the action of
painting.

Photoshop includes 16 individual tools that use the brush options to paint colors or a pattern onto the canvas; this chapter refers to these tools collectively as the painting tools. Most of these tools allow you to use Brush Presets to quickly select a brush style and then adjust the exact nature of the brush in the Brushes palette. As a response to popular demand, basic adjustments of both brush diameter and hardness are again readily available through the Brush Preset picker on the menu bar.

Painting Tools

	BRUSH NAME	SEE ALSO
	Brush	13.5 Painting with a Brush or Pencil
	Pencil	13.5 Painting with a Brush or Pencil
	Pattern Stamp	13.6 Painting with Patterns
	Art History Brush	13.7 Painting with the History Brushes
	Eraser	13.9 Erasing
	Background Eraser	13.9 Erasing
	Smudge	13.10 Distorting Images
	Clone Stamp	19.3 Cloning One Area to Another
	Healing Brush	19.4 Repairing from Sampled Pixels
	History Brush	19.6 Repairing Images Using a Previous State
	Color Replacement tool	19.7 Replacing a Color
	Blur	19.8 Sharpening and Blurring Images
	Sharpen	19.8 Sharpening and Blurring Images
	Dodge	19.12 Dodging and Burning Images
	Burn	19.12 Dodging and Burning Images
	Sponge	19.13 Using the Sponge Tool

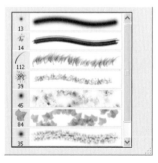

A brush tip defines the basic settings for a brush; including the shape, size, angle, roundness, hardness, and spacing for the general nature of how the brush's stroke will appear. Photoshop also provides you with a variety of other options allowing you to adjust the exact way in which the brush tip is applied to create a stroke; these options include settings for how colors are used by the brush along with other variables such as scatter and opacity. You can view brush tips in the Brush Preset Picker; they are shown to the left in "stroke thumbnail" view.

13.1 Brush Basics *(continued)*

Brush Settings and Brush Dynamics

Dynamic controls allow you to influence how color and effects are applied, and change, across the length of a brush stroke. These controls are either variables set in the Brushes palette options for Jitter or are influenced in the process of drawing with a digital tablet and stylus.

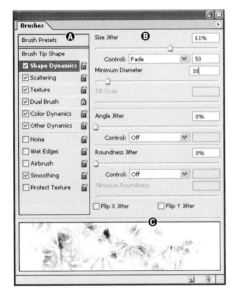

A Variable settings You can turn on and off each of the variables in this column by clicking the associated check box. You can also lock them to keep the settings from changing as you cycle Brush Presets. Selecting each of the six variable choices in the top grouping give you a specific submenu of controls and settings, as will selecting brush tip shape.

B Submenu Settings specific to the dynamics controls for shape, scatter, texture, dual brush, color dynamics, and the "other dynamics" category control opacity and flow jitter.

C Stroke Preview window Allows you to monitor or preview changes in settings as you adjust variables. The preview is in grayscale. Many of your color variables will be influenced by your foreground and background color selections, so this preview may not be entirely accurate—when white is replaced with a color, for instance.

➥ 3.15 Distortion Tools

➥ 3.16 Exposure Tools

➥ 4.4 Brushes Palette

Eraser tool
[E]

Distortion tool
[R]

Exposure tool
[O]

———

Since Photoshop 7, the Airbrush tool was replaced with Airbrush mode, in which you can use a variety of brush types as if they were airbrushes (see Section 3.2).

———

When you apply a stroke to the canvas using one of the painting tools, the cursor you see depends on the option you selected for the Display & Cursors Preferences (see Section 5.6).

You can control several brush options dynamically while painting in the canvas. Three of these options require a pen-and-tablet device, which you must purchase separately. The dynamic control pull-down menu options are:

Fade Reduces the value of the option to 0 over the entered number of steps. This creates an illusion of the brush fading over the course of a stroke.

Pen Pressure (Requires tablet) Uses the pressure you apply to a tablet to vary the value for the option between its minimum and maximum.

Pen Tilt (Requires tablet, but not available with all tablets) Uses the angle of the pen on the tablet to vary the value for the option between its minimum and maximum.

Stylus Wheel (Requires tablet) Allows you to use the pen's wheel (if it has one) to change the values of the option between its minimum and maximum.

Initial Direction (Angle Jitter only) Sets the jitter angle based on the direction in which the stroke starts.

Direction (Angle Jitter only) Sets the jitter angle value based on the current direction of the stroke.

13.2   Selecting and Adjusting Brushes

Before brush selection options become available in Photoshop, you must first actively select one of the brush-sensitive tools in the Toolbox.

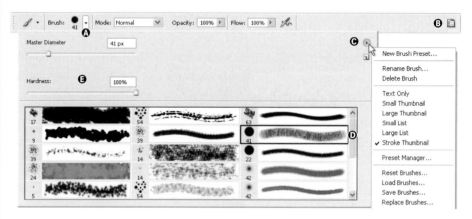

Ⓐ Brush Preset Picker   Displays current brush size. Click to open .

Ⓑ Brushes Palette   Click to toggle the Brushes palette.

Ⓒ Preset Picker menu   Allows for the saving and loading of brushes and presets along with choices for viewing the brush preset thumbnails.

Ⓓ Brush Presets thumbnails   The selected brush preset is highlighted, as presented in the Stroke Thumbnail view.

Ⓔ Master Diameter/Hardness   Sliders allowing control of the size of your brush and the edge feather or softness of the brush.

Perhaps the easiest way to begin painting is to select a brush from the Brush Preset Picker, which is available on the options menu. You can also select brushes via the Brushes palette. To choose a brush Preset, follow these steps:

1 Choose a painting tool in the Toolbox. (The Healing Brush, Background Eraser, and the new Color Replacement tool allow only standard round settings.)

2 Choose a brush Preset either in the Brush drop-down in the tool options bar or in the Brush Presets panel in the Brushes palette. Each preset has a default value for its diameter that is displayed beneath the brush thumbnail.

3 Adjust the diameter of the brush using the slider or by entering a value (1 through 2500) in the Master Diameter field. (The diameter is equivalent to brush size, even if you select a square brush.)

You can now adjust the brush further in the Brushes palette or begin to paint with the selected brush in the canvas.

13.2 Selecting and Adjusting Brushes *(continued)*

Adjusting Brush Settings

Choose one of the painting tools (except the Healing Brush or Background Eraser) and set the brush options in the Brushes palette. As you make changes to the options, a simulated stroke appears at the bottom of the palette.

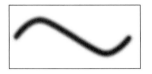  

You use Brush Tip Shape to set the basic shape of the brush when it is applied to the canvas as a stroke. Left to right: spacing is set to 25%, 75%, and 150%.

➠ 3.2 The Tool
Options Bar

You can also select Brush Presets from the Tool Presets drop-down in the tool options bar or in the Tool Presets palette (see Section 4.19).

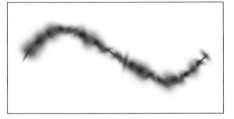

Shape Dynamics Check to add options to the brush that "jitter" (randomize) the size, angle, and roundness of the brush stroke.

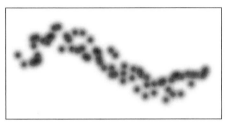

Scattering Check to add options that simulate the scattering of paint as it is applied to the canvas.

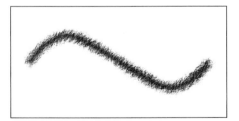

Texture Check to add options that simulate a texture for the canvas as brush strokes are being applied.

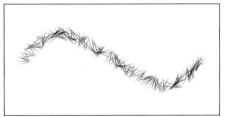

Dual Brush Check to add a second brush shape to mask the first brush, creating more organic brush strokes from their overlap.

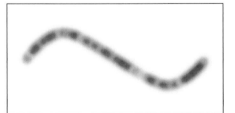

Color Dynamics Check to add options to change the color used by the brush as the stroke is applied.

Other Dynamics/Opacity Check to vary the opacity of the stroke.

Decrease brush size (with a brush tool selected)

Increase brush size (with a brush tool selected)

⬚

————

Brush options not available for a particular painting tool are grayed out in the Brushes palette. For example, Wet Edges is not available for the Pencil tool.

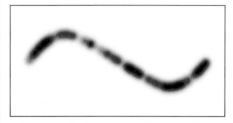

Other Dynamics/Flow Jitter Check to allow the flow value to jitter between its maximum and minimum values.

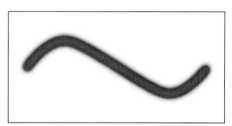

Noise Adds random static to the brush edges.

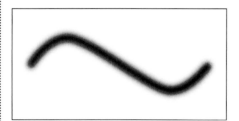

Wet Edges Simulates painting with wet paint; edges are darker than the stroke.

Airbrush mode A painting stroke in Airbrush mode will build up paint wherever the brush lingers in the canvas.

You can now save this brush as a new brush preset or begin using it in the canvas with the selected brush.

In the following table, an asterisk (*) indicates that the setting can be controlled dynamically (see Section 13.1).

Brush Settings

SETTING	VALUE RANGE	DESCRIPTION
TIP SHAPE		
Brush Presets		Select the initial brush shape from the list of presets.
Diameter	1 to 2500px	Circular width and height of the brush tip in pixels.
Angle	−180° to 180°	Simulated angle that the brush is applied.
Roundness	1 to 100%	Shape of the brush from 1 (elliptical) to 100 (circular).
Hardness	0 to 100%	Area of the brush tip with maximum application of paint.
Spacing	1 to 1000%	Interval between brush strokes.

Continues

Brush Settings *(continued)*

SETTING	VALUE RANGE	DESCRIPTION
SHAPE DYNAMICS		
Size Jitter*	0 to 100%	Random variation in the diameter of the brush as you are painting.
Minimum Diameter*	1 to 100%	Smallest diameter the brush can have as a percentage of the maximum diameter.
Tilt Scale*	1 to 100%	Scale factor applied to the brush when the Size Jitter control is set to Pen Tilt.
Angle Jitter*	0 to 100%	Random variation in the angle of the brush as you are painting.
Roundness Jitter*	0 to 100%	Random variation in the roundness of the brush as you are painting.
Minimum Roundness*	1 to 100	Smallest roundness the brush can have as a percentage of the maximum roundness.
SCATTERING		
Scatter*	0 to 1000%	Simulated scattering of daubs of paint while painting.
Both Axes		Check to use symmetrical scattering.
Count*	1 to 16	Number of paint daubs used in the scatter.
Count Jitter*	0 to 100%	Random variation in the count as you are painting.
TEXTURE		
Pattern		Pattern to be used as a texture (see Section 12.12).
Scale	1 to 1000%	Size of the pattern used to create the texture. If you use a value other than 100%, Photoshop resizes the pattern using the default interpolation method (see Section 5.4).
Texture Each Tip		Check to add texture to each tip in the brush rather than a single stroke.
Blending Mode		Mode used between the brush and the texture (see Section 21.2).
Depth	0 to 100%	Simulated depth of the texture. Higher values create more contrast between "high" and "low" areas of the texture.
Minimum Depth	0 to 100%	Restrains the variation between lowest and highest values.
Depth Jitter	0 to 100%	Random variation in the depth as you are painting.
DUAL BRUSH		
Blending Mode		Select the blending mode used between the two brushes (see Section 21.2).
Brush Presets		Select the second brush shape.
Diameter	1 to 2500px	Circular width and height of the second brush stroke in pixels.
Use Sample Size		Click to reset the brush diameter to its default.
Spacing	1 to 1000%	Interval between brush strokes for the second brush.
Scatter	0 to 1000%	Simulated scattering of daubs of paint for the second brush while painting.
Both Axes		Check to use symmetrical scattering for the second brush.
Count	1 to 16	Number of paint daubs used in the scatter for the second brush.

Continues

Decrease brush hardness (with a brush tool selected)

[Shift] [[ ]

Increase brush hardness (with a brush tool selected)

[Shift] [ ]]

For instructions on using the Healing Brush, see Section 19.4.

PHOTOSHOP WORKSPACE

UNIVERSAL TASKS

PHOTO AND VIDEO TASKS

PRINT TASKS

WEB TASKS

Each of the painting tools will have their own options. When you switch from one painting tool to another, the options in the Brushes palette remember the previous settings used with the given tool. You may revert to default settings by selecting "Reset Tool" in the Tool Preset picker's drop-down menu.

There are numerous online sources for Photoshop brushes. A simple web search with "photoshop brushes" as the search parameters will tap you into a wealth of information; ranging from free brush downloads to brush trading resources, and tutorials.

Brush Settings *(continued)*

SETTING	VALUE RANGE	DESCRIPTION
COLOR DYNAMICS		
Foreground/Background Jitter*		0 to 100% Random fluctuation between the foreground and background color (including colors in between) while painting. Values above 50 favor the background color.
Hue Jitter	0 to 100%	Random variation in paint color hue while painting.
Saturation Jitter	0 to 100%	Random variation in paint color saturation while painting.
Brightness Jitter	0 to 100%	Random variation in paint color brightness while painting.
Purity	−100 to 100%	Shift in the color toward or away from the neutral value (0%).
OTHER DYNAMICS		
Opacity Jitter*	0 to 100%	Random variation in paint opacity (set in the tool options bar) while painting.
Flow Jitter*	0 to 100%	Random variation in paint flow (set in the tool options bar) while painting.
OTHER OPTIONS		
Noise		Applies random noise to the brush stroke.
Wet Edges		Simulates a wet brush while painting with opaque edges and a transparent center.
Airbrush		Check to use Airbrush mode with this brush (see Section 13.1).
Smoothing		Check to have strokes smoothed from the actual mouse path used. This may slow painting.
Protect Texture		Check to apply the same texture for all brushes used while editing the image. This allows you to keep a consistent simulated texture for the canvas.

PAINTING BEHIND CONTENT

One of the blending modes that is available with painting tools (but not with individual layers) is the Paint Behind mode. In this mode, you can paint in the transparent areas of the layer, but mask solid pixels and blend semitransparent pixels. The upshot is that it will look as if you are painting behind the content already on the layer.

13.3 Creating and Saving Brushes

You can create a new brush from any selected content, scan, texture or image, or you can adjust the options for an existing brush tip, then save the changes as a new brush. This second option is particularly valuable as a learning tool, given the complexity of many presets, yet it does not allow you to alter the primary shape of the brush.

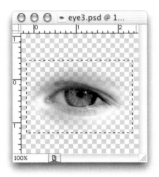

In this case, the edges around the eye, or selection, are already transparent. When you make selections for creating brushes, you may choose to take an interim step, copying content to a new layer, which will allow you to soften or add texture to your brush edges, turn off other layers and to adjust contrast or density for your brush.

The brush tip defines the overall shape of the brush. Browsing through the Brush Presets, you will quickly see that brushes can be practically any shape you want. They can also be nearly any size, with limits at 2500 pixels square. To create a new brush with a customized brush tip, follow these steps:

1 Choose any selection tool and set your Feathering.

2 Select the part of the image you want to turn into a brush. The selection can be a maximum of 2500 pixels by 2500 pixels.

3 Select the Brush tool from the Toolbox and then adjust the brush options in the Brushes palette (see Sections 13.1 and 13.2). These options will be used as the default settings for your new brush.

4 Choose Edit > Define Brush Preset. This will sample from all visible layers in the selection to create a grayscale image that is then used as a brush tip. White areas will be empty, and darker areas will be filled when used as a brush.

5 Enter a name for the new brush in the New Brush dialog and click OK.

The new brush will appear in the Brush Presets list, ready for painting in the canvas.

Saving Brushes

Changing a brush's options does not change the original brush preset's options permanently; the next time you select that brush preset, it returns to the default options set for it. To save the current options as a new brush, choose New Brush Preset… from the Brushes palette menu or the Brushes drop-down, or click the New Brush button at the bottom of the Brushes palette or in the Brushes drop-down. Enter a name for the new brush in the New Brush dialog, and click OK. The new brush appears in the Brush Presets list.

When learning to create brushes, it may be helpfull to use the Clear Brush Controls option in the Brushes palette menu before choosing to define a brush preset. This will allow you to create Brush presets for Brush Tip Shapes separate from more complex variations you can also save as either Brush or Tool presets.

If you create a new brush, the brush has not been permanently saved until you save it as part of a Brush Presets list (see Section 13.4).

13.4   Organizing Brush Presets

➡ 3.2   The Tool
            Options Bar

➡ 4.4   Brushes
            Palette

It is a good idea to save lists of customized brushes you are using on a project so that you can quickly load them again when you need them.

You may find as you create and save more brushes that you can find them faster by bay name rather than by the stroke preview. This is particularly true if you have several brushes that look similar yet are different in size.

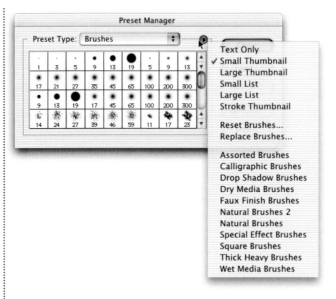

Both the Brush drop-down in the tool options bar and the Brushes palette have a list of Brush Presets. In addition, as with all presets, you can organize Brush Presets in the Preset Manager (choose Edit > Preset Manager…). To organize Brush Presets in the Brushes palette, the Brush Presets panel must be displayed.

Editing Presets

Photoshop comes with dozens of Brush Presets, but it is unlikely that you will use all of them. To spend less time scrolling through long lists of brushes, edit the list.

- To **delete a brush preset**, Option/Alt-click the brush (the mouse cursor turns into a pair of scissors) in the Brushes palette, Brushes drop-down, or Brushes Preset Manager. In the Brushes palette, you can also drag the brush to the trashcan 🗑 or select a brush, click the trashcan icon, and click OK to confirm deletion.

- To **delete multiple Brush Presets** at the same time in the Brushes Preset Manager, Shift-click one or more brushes and click Delete. The brushes are removed, and all other brushes in the palette shift to fill its space.

- To **change a brush's name**, double-click the brush in the Brushes palette or Brushes Preset Manager, enter the new name in the Brush Name dialog, and click OK. You can also select the brush in the Brushes Preset Manager and click Rename… to open the dialog.

- To **change a brush's position** in the list, click and drag the brush in the Brushes Preset Manager to the desired location.

13.4 Organizing Brush Presets *(continued)*

Saving Presets

After you create and edit a personalized brush list, you can easily save the list for later use. To save your list of Brush Presets, do one of the following:

- Choose Save Brushes… from the Brushes palette menu or Brushes drop-down.

- In the Brushes Preset Manager, select the brushes you want to save as a list (click the first brush and then Shift-click additional brushes), and then click the Save Set… button.

Enter a name for the new brush list, making sure to preserve the .abr extension, browse to the folder in which you want to save the brush list, and click Save.

Loading Presets

You can load additional brushes into the Brush Presets list. Photoshop comes with several lists, but you can also load your own saved lists or even trade brushes with other Photoshop users. To load a Brush Presets list, use one of the following commands or options from the Brushes palette menu, Brushes drop-down, or Brushes Preset Manager menu:

- To **reset the brushes** to factory fresh, choose Reset Brushes…

- To **load a list of brushes**, choose Load… or click the Load… button.

- To **replace the current brushes** with a new list, choose Replace Brushes….

When loading or replacing, browse to locate a brush file that has the .abr extension, and double-click the file. When resetting or doing a quick load, you can choose whether you want to append the default brushes to the current list (at the bottom) or to replace the current list.

USING PAINTING TOOL PRESETS

You can use the Tool Presets with virtually any tool in the Tool Box, but they are especially useful with painting tools. Brush Presets only save the brush options, which can then be used with any of the painting tools except for the Healing Brush and Background Eraser. The Tool Presets allow you to associate a brush tip and options settings with a particular painting tool and save that combination as a preset. See Section 4.19 for more details on Tool Presets.

➡ 5.1 Preset Manager Overview

Jump to brushes (in Preset Manager)

⌘ 1

Ctrl 1

The Photoshop folder contains a Brushes folder, which is a good place to save your brush lists.

Hold the mouse cursor over a brush in the Brushes palette or Brush drop-down to view the brush name in a Tool Tip.

13.5 Painting with a Brush or Pencil

➡ 3.10 Paint Tools

➡ 12.2 Selecting Colors with the Eyedropper

➡ 12.3 Selecting Colors with the Color Palette

➡ 12.4 Selecting Colors with the Color Picker

➡ Color Section Blending Modes

Paint a straight line
[Shift]-click

Switch from brush to Eyedropper tool (reverts after release)
[Option]
[Alt]

Cycle blending modes in tool options bar (with painting tool)
[Shift] [+] **or** [Shift] [−]

Cycle Brush Presets (with painting tool)
[or]
Choose Opacity (example 7 = 70%)
[0] **to** [9]

———

The Pencil tool creates hard-edged freehand lines in a bitmap mode which does not allow anti-aliasing or softening of the edges.

———

In the Clear blending mode, you can remove rather than add paint to the canvas (much like an eraser), leaving behind transparent pixels. Brushes in Clear mode do not work on the Background layer.

The most common way to apply colors to the canvas is by using the basic Brush tool or the Pencil tool. Since the same brush tips are available to both Pencil and Brush tools, there is little difference between their use; however, the Brush produces soft anti-aliased edges while the pencil produces hard jagged edges. This means that a few of the edge-based brush options (Airbrush, Wet Edges, Dual Brush, and Flow Jitter) are not available to the Pencil. To paint using the Brush or Pencil, follow these steps:

Two brush strokes and the same brush tips used for a pencil stroke. The pencil stroke shows jagged edges while the brush stroke is anti-aliased. Don't be entirely mislead. Despite the jagged appearance, the pencil has its purposes particularly in straight lines and pixel-by-pixel editing.

1 Select the layer in which you want to paint. Additionally, you can limit the area in the canvas to be painted by making a selection (see Chapter 9).

2 Choose the Brush tool 🖌 or Pencil tool ✏ from the Toolbox.

3 Set your brush options:

  ■ Select a foreground color. You will paint with this color.

  ■ Choose a brush type and set the brush master diameter from the Brushes pull-down or Brush Presets panel in the Brushes palette.

  ■ In the tool options bar, choose a blending mode and set the opacity and flow rate for the color being applied to the canvas.

  ■ If you want to utilize a Brush tool with airbrush-like build-up effects, applying gradual tones to an image, click the Airbrush icon 🖌 in the options bar or turn on the Airbrush option in the Brushes palette.

  ■ Adjust the brush settings in the Brushes palette (see Section 13.2).

4 Place the mouse cursor in the canvas where you want to begin your stroke and click and drag to paint a stroke. Repeat this step as many times as desired.

13.6   Painting with Patterns

Although it is one of the stamp tools, the Pattern Stamp really works as a paintbrush for applying patterns (instead of colors). To paint using the Pattern Stamp, follow these steps:

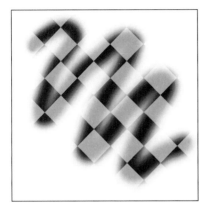 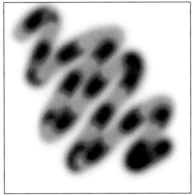

Painting with a pattern: left, with Impressionistic unchecked, and right, with Impressionistic checked.

1   Select the layer in which you want to paint. Additionally, you can limit the area in the canvas to be painted by making a selection.

2   Choose the Pattern Stamp tool ![icon] from the Toolbox.

3   Set your brush options:

■ Select a pattern to paint with in the tool options bar. In addition, specify whether you want the pattern aligned with the top-right corner of the canvas and whether you want to paint in Impressionistic (blurred) mode.

■ Choose a brush type and set the brush's diameter from the Brushes pull-down or Brush Presets panel in the Brushes palette.

■ In the tool options bar, choose a blending mode and set the opacity and flow rate for the color being applied to the canvas.

■ If you want to utilize a Brush tool with airbrush-like build-up effects, applying gradual tones to an image, click the Airbrush icon in the options bar or turn on the Airbrush option in the Brushes palette.

■ Adjust the brush settings in the Brushes palette.

4   Place the mouse cursor in the canvas where you want to begin your stroke and click and drag to paint a stroke. Repeat this step as many times as desired.

Stamp tool
[S]

Cycle stamp tools
[Shift] [S]

Paint a straight line
[Shift]-click

Cycle blending modes in tool options bar (with painting tool)
[Shift] [+] or [Shift] [−]

Cycle Brush Presets (with painting tool)
[or]
Choose Opacity (example 7 = 70%)
[0] to [9]

─────

If you are using Airbrush mode, the longer you keep the brush in an area, the more paint builds up.

13.7 Painting with History Brushes

History Brush tool
[Y]

Cycle History Brush tools
[Shift] [Y]

Paint a straight line
[Shift]-click

Cycle blending modes in tool options bar (with Painting tool)
[Shift] [+] or [Shift] [−]

Cycle Brush Presets (with painting tool)
[or]
Choose Opacity (example 7 = 70%)
[0] to [9]

———

To help guide you while painting, make a copy of the layer you are painting in and set its opacity to a low value (such as 25%). Then, fill the original layer with a color and begin painting.

———

If you are using Airbrush mode, the longer you keep the brush in an area, the more paint builds up.

Two quite different options are available in Photoshop's two history brushes. One, the History brush is a serious tool (of course, with its creative value)—the other, the Art History brush, is whimsical, allowing you to paint Impressionistic, highly stylized works in the canvas based on previous History states or snapshots.

Working with either of these brushes requires you to first familiarize yourself with the History palette and to have created History snapshots in an image. As an example, open an image and run a filter—create a snapshot, run another filter, paint—create another snapshot. To paint with the History brushes, follow these steps:

1 Select one of the two history brushes in the toolbox. Choose a tip or brush preset and set your variables.

2 Select the History state or snapshot you want to use as the source for your painting by clicking in the left column in the History palette. A brush icon appears next to the History state or snapshot you will be painting with.

3 Select the layer in which you want to paint. The only catch is this layer must have existed in the History state or snapshot you selected in step 2.

4 Set your brush options in the tool options bar—this will require some time to experiment: Choose a blending mode and set the opacity and flow rate for the paint being applied to the canvas.

   ■ In the case of the Art History brush, choose the painting style you want from the Style pull-down menu—Dab, Curl, Tight, Long, and so on. This controls the shape of the stroke being used to repaint the layer. Set the area to be covered by the strokes—the larger the value, the more strokes added.

   ■ Set the tolerance, which will limit the color of pixels that strokes are applied to by defining how different the color can be from the first pixel clicked when starting the stroke. Higher values restrict the area in which you can paint.

5 Place your cursor in the canvas where you want to begin your stroke and click and drag to paint a stroke. Repeat these steps and adjust variables as desired.

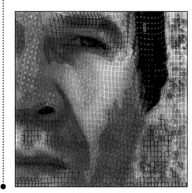

You can paint an image with the History Brush using color and texture from various history snapshots. Select a history state in which to paint, then click the button ☐ next to a history state with which you want to paint. The actively selected "painting" state is designated with the ✎ brush icon.

13.8　Painting with Shapes

Photoshop's custom shapes presets, available through the Preset Manager and options bar while the shape tools are selected, offer a wide variety of shapes to paint with. Chapter 16 describes how to draw paths and shape layers of your own design using the shape tools. Although these are vector tools, you can also use them to paint rasterized shapes with Fill pixels selected or use them as a basis for creating brushes.

➡ 3.20 Shape Tools

➡ 13.3 Creating and Saving Brushes

➡ 16.4 Setting Shape Tool Options

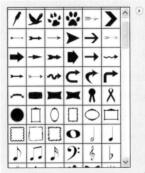

Using Fill Pixels, you can paint shapes directly into layers. In this example, musical notation symbols from the custom shapes presets were painted into the image in varying sizes and colors.

1　Choose a shape tool and click the Fill Pixels button [▢] in the tool options bar.

2　Select a layer in the Layers palette. Additionally, you can limit the area in the canvas to be painted by making a selection.

3　In the tool options bar, set the appropriate shape tool's options, blending mode, and opacity, and check Anti-Aliased to smooth the edges of the shape.

4　Click and drag to draw the shape. Release the mouse button when the shape is the desired size.

Shape tool
[U]

Cycle shape tools
[Shift] [U]

Force proportion while drawing
[Shift]

Skew and distort shape while drawing
[Option]
[Alt]

Cycle blending modes in tool options bar (with painting tool)
[Shift] [+] or [Shift] [−]

**Cycle Brush Presets (with painting tool)
[or]
Choose Opacity (example 7 = 70%)**
[0] to [9]

PAINTING TOOL CURSORS AND BRUSH TIPS

When you apply a stroke to the canvas using one of the painting tools, the cursor you see depends on the option you selected for the Display & Cursor Preferences (see Section 5.6). Your best option is to view the Brush Size. This not only displays the brush at the size at which it will create a stroke, but also shows an outline of the exact brush tip, allowing you to preview how the stroke will appear.

13.9   Erasing

➡ 3.2   The Tool
Options Bar

Eraser tool
E

Cycle eraser tools
Shift E

The Background layer
will not erase to trans-
parent. Instead, erasing
on the Background
layer erases to the
selected background
color.

Another way to erase is
to use the Brush, Pen-
cil, or Paint Bucket
tools in the Clear blend-
ing mode. Rather than
applying paint, the
Clear mode removes
paint from the canvas,
leaving behind trans-
parent pixels. Brushes
in Clear mode do not
work on the Back-
ground layer.

Destruction is always a part of creation. One of the most common ways to delete content in Photoshop is to simply make a selection and press the Delete (Mac) or Backspace (Windows) key. However, you can also remove content using the brush strokes using the Eraser tool. In addition, Photoshop provides two sophisticated eraser tools that allow you to selectively erase a background or a particular color range in an image.

Using the Eraser tool in an image removes paint with the brush rather than adding it

Use the Background Eraser to erase areas of similar but inconsistent color on the can-vas—in this case, the fore-ground figure.

The light-gray plastic tarp is erased with the Magic Eraser.

Using the Eraser

The Eraser tool simply removes any pixels that get in its way. It uses a brush, a pencil, or a block to paint away unwanted parts of an image.

1   Select the layer from which you want to erase content. Additionally, you can limit the area in the canvas to be erased by making a selection.

2   Choose the Eraser tool ◢ from the Toolbox.

3   Set your eraser options in the tool options bar:

■ Choose the Eraser mode from the Mode pull-down: Brush (brush with soft edges), Pencil (brush with hard edges), or Block (rectangle with hard edges).

■ If you are using Brush or Pencil mode, choose a brush type, set the brush master diameter from the Brushes pull-down, and set the opacity to specify the strength of the erasure (100% completely erases pixels).

■ If you are using Brush mode, set the flow rate. If you want to use the eraser as an Airbrush, choose that option in either the tool options bar ⸚ or the Brushes palette.

■ If you want to erase the layer back to a previous History state or snapshot, select the History state or snapshot you want to use as the source by clicking in the left col-umn in the History palette. A History Brush icon ⸚ appears next to the History state or snapshot. If the selected state or snapshot has an analogous layer in the current image, you can then check the Erase To History option and continue.

13.9 Erasing *(continued)*

4 Place the mouse cursor in the canvas where you want to begin erasing and click and drag. The content along the stroke will be removed either completely (if opacity is 100%) or partially, and the area will now be fully or partially transparent. Repeat this step as many times as desired.

Erasing the Background

You use the Background Eraser to remove part of an image while leaving other parts unaffected, by specifying a base color to be erased and then a tolerance of similar colors that can be erased. The tool samples the color at the center of the brush and uses that as the base color to determine whether other colors should be erased as the brush is moved across the canvas. One important difference between the Background Eraser and other painting tools is that it does not use the Brushes palette, instead using a simplified brush picker that allows only circular and elliptical brushes.

1 Select the layer from which you want to erase content. Additionally, you can limit the area in the canvas to be erased by making a selection.

2 Choose the Background Eraser tool from the Toolbox.

3 Set the eraser options in the tool options bar:

■ Use the brush picker to specify the diameter, hardness, spacing, angle, roundness, and dynamic controls.

■ Set the erasure limits: Discontiguous (anywhere on canvas), Contiguous (must be in touch with the first pixel erased), Find Edges (must be a high-contrast boundary).

■ Set the tolerance, which will limit the pixels that are erased based on their difference from the sampled base color. Higher values restrict the area you can erase.

■ Check Protect Foreground Color to protect the selected foreground color from being erased.

■ Set the color sampling method for use to determine the base color to be erased: Once to sample the first pixel erased as the base color; Continuous to resample every pixel as the base color; Background Swatch to use the selected background color as the base color.

4 Place the mouse cursor in the canvas where you want to begin erasing and click and drag. The content along the stroke will be removed. The color at the center of the brush will be used as the sampled base color if you choose the Once or Continuous sampling method. Repeat this step as many times as desired.

➡ 3.13 Eraser Tools

Remove content in selection

⌨ Del

———

Another way to extract complex shapes such as smoke and hair from a background is to use the Extract command (see Section 21.8).

———

Using the Magic Eraser in Continuous method can slow down your machine.

13.9   Erasing *(continued)*

➡ 21.8 Extracting
Part of an
Image

Switch to Eraser from Erase To History (reverts after release)

Option

Alt

Don't forget that the Eraser tool in Brush mode can have all the same brush options as any brush, allowing you to do things such as erase with noise or erase with a texture.

A nondestructive way to "erase" parts of an image without actually removing the content is to use masks (see Chapter 11).

The Background eraser overrides the transparent lock set for any layers.

Using the Background and Magic erasers can produce some gritty weathered effects.

Erasing a Color with the Magic Eraser

If you need to quickly erase a color from the image, the Magic Eraser is the tool for you. By simply clicking a pixel, you can remove all pixels of that or similar colors. To use the Magic Eraser, follow these steps:

1 Select the layer from which you want to erase content. You can limit the area in the canvas to be erased by making a selection. The Magic Eraser is one of the few tools that also allows you to work in all layers simultaneously.

2 Choose the Magic Eraser tool ![icon] from the Toolbox.

3 Set the Magic Eraser options in the tool options bar:

■ Set the tolerance, which will limit the pixels that are erased based on their difference from the base color. Higher values restrict the area you can erase.

■ Check Anti-Aliasing to produce smoother edges in the erasure.

■ Check Contiguous if you want erased pixels to be in touch with the first pixel erased.

■ Check Use All Layers to sample the base color from any visible layer.

■ Set the opacity in the tool options bar to specify the strength of the erasure; 100% completely erases pixels.

4 Place the mouse cursor in the canvas over the color you want to erase and click. The color at the center of the cursor will be used as the sampled base color, and all colors within tolerance of this color will be erased. Repeat this step as many times as desired.

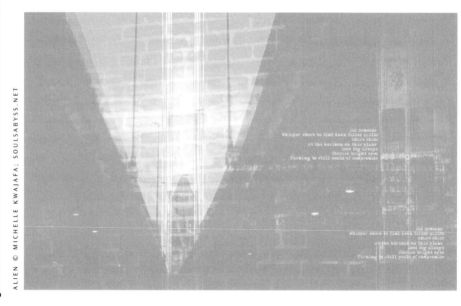

ALIEN © MICHELLE KWAJAFA; SOULSABYSS.NET

13.10 Distorting Images

Two Photoshop tools allow you to distort images or existing pixels by dragging controlled brush strokes across the canvas: the Smudge tool and the Liquify filter. The Smudge tool picks up the color of the pixels where the brush stroke starts (and from other layers, if selected), allowing you to push the pixels in the direction of the stroke. The Smudge tool allows you to work directly in the image window with a variety of brushes. The Liquify tool, on the other hand, must be used within its own dialog, with its own brush controls. The Liquify tool has continued to evolve over the last several versions of Photoshop and is once again enhanced with new masking capability, added brush controls, and new working or backdrop-view modes.

Smudging the Image

You can use the Smudge tool to perform minor distortions and "touch-up" of images to change the shape of features and objects. The Smudge tool is particularly effective for cleaning up or blending edges. To use the Smudge tool, follow these steps:

1 In the Toolbox, select the Smudge tool.

2 Beyond the standard brush options, there are two further Smudge tool options: Use All Layers and Finger Painting.

   ■ Use All Layers smears the pixels on all visible layers. If it is not selected, the Smudge tool smears only the active layer.

   ■ Finger Painting forces the tool to use the foreground color to create each brush stroke. If this check box is cleared, the Smudge tool uses the color information under the brush pointer at the beginning of each stroke.

3 Click and Drag the Smudge tool as desired in the image.

This image illustrates three uses of the Smudge tool: Across the word smudge, you'll notice a couple of brush strokes pulled randomly to illustrate default tool settings. One option for controlled use of the Smudge tool can be found in creating a path, choosing a brush, and stroking the path via the Paths palette. This can be seen used on the doll's ear. Another practical use for the tool is demonstrated here for use in "cleaning," or smoothing, selection edges (observed across the top of the doll's forehead). Make a selection of an object with rough edges, smooth the selection, and contract the selection slightly, depending on image resolution; add a slight (0.5 pixel) feather and invert the selection. Select a large brush and smudge toward the object edge (see arrows); the rough edges will disappear.

➡ 3.15 Distortion Tools

Forward Warp tool (in Liquify dialog)
W

Turbulence tool (in Liquify dialog)
A

Twirl Clockwise tool (in Liquify dialog)
R

13.10   Distorting Images *(continued)*

Pucker tool (in Liquify dialog)

P

Bloat tool (in Liquify dialog)

B

Shift Pixels tool (in Liquify dialog)

S

Liquifying the Image

The tools accessed in the Liquify dialog have great value in serious image editing and can provide great fun for more whimsical distortions. The distortion of the Liquify tool is more sophisticated than that of the Smudge tool and can be used for serious pixel movement with less blur in the image—allowing for a smooth waist or thigh-reduction as might be needed in fashion photography. But you can also have great fun with the pulling and pushing of pixels. Have some fun and explore the interface; this is the only way to learn. Try using bigger brushes than you might normally employ, while making changes in smaller increments or shorter strokes.

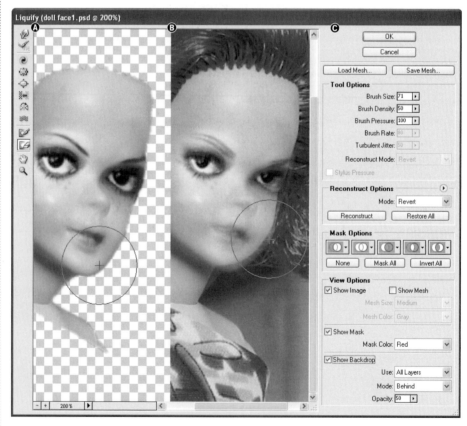

Ⓐ **Liquify tools**   You'll find the tools in four groupings.

Ⓑ **Preview Image**   Two of several variables for working with the image/dialog preview are shown. On the left, working on the Object layer in isolation at full opacity. On the right, the image with backdrop (behind-mode) and all layers visible. The area being distorted is viewed at 50% opacity under the brush.

Ⓒ **Variable Controls**   Tool Options, Reconstruct Options, Mask Options, and View Options.

13.10   Distorting Images *(continued)*

Liquify Tools

	TOOL NAME
	Forward Warp. Push pixels forward with various brush controls.
	Reconstruct. Paint in controlled undo of effects.
	Twirl Clockwise. Opt/Alt for opposite spin. Rotates pixels.
	Pucker. Moves pixels toward center of brush coverage.
	Bloat. Pushes pixels out from center of brush coverage
	Push Left. Moves pixels left from the edge of brush coverage. Opt/Alt opposite.
	Mirror. Copies pixels from beyond edge into coverage area. Opt/Alt opposite.
	Turbulence. Smoothly scrambles pixels. As for fire or waves.
	Freeze Mask. Protect areas with painted "freeze"; add to selections.
	Thaw Mask. Release areas for editing. Undo masks or selected areas.
	Hand. Common canvas navigation.
	Zoom. Common canvas navigation.

Reflection tool (in Liquify dialog)

 M

Reconstruct tool (in Liquify dialog)

E

Freeze Mask tool (in Liquify dialog)

 F

All the effects and options of the Liquify filter are applied within its own self-contained dialog, except for the Edit **>** Fade command available after you accept a Liquify session. The operation of the filter is as follows:

1   Choose a layer you want to manipulate. Make selections first if you like.

2   From the main menu, choose Filter **>** Liquify.

3   Select a tool from the left side of the dialog.

4   Click and drag in the preview or click the image and hold down the mouse button. Experiment with defaults. Your immediate options are:

■   The topmost tool, Forward Warp, or other distortion tools—click and drag in the preview. ⌘/Ctrl+Z will undo your last stroke.

■   Adjust your selection or mask areas with the Freeze and Thaw tools.

■   Try the Reconstruct tool as an alternate to the undo command.

13.10 Distorting Images *(continued)*

Thaw Mask tool (in Liquify dialog)

Zoom tool (in Liquify dialog)

Hand tool (in Liquify dialog)

You can save and load a distortion mesh to apply transformations to other images.

Getting a feel for the defaults will give you a base for comparing variables in the controls in the right panel. The brush size of the tools determines how much of the image is affected; however, some of the tools read the pixels under the edge of the brush or from beyond the brush to copy or move into the brush coverage area.

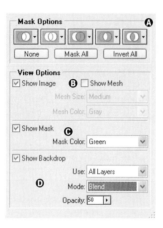

Ⓐ Mask Options   Work in conjunction with selections, transparency, or layer mask in the original image window and selected layer, as well as alpha channels saved in the document. Mask Options are (left to right) to replace the mask, add to the mask, subtract from the mask, intersect with the mask, or invert the mask. There are also buttons to turn on, turn off, or invert the masks, which can yet be adjusted with the Freeze/Thaw tools.

Ⓑ View Options   Variables include Show/Hide image, which will allow you to see the distortion mesh alone. You can view the distortion mesh as an overlay. A distortion mesh can be saved and loaded to apply transformations to other images.

Ⓒ Show Mask   You can choose to turn on and off mask visibility and select mask overlay colors from the drop-down.

Ⓓ Show Backdrop   Options allow you to see a representation of the image original and distortion together for added control. The Use drop-down allows you access to all your document layers. The modes are options to show the backdrop blended in front of or behind the distortion preview. The visibility of the backdrop is an important addition to the Liquify tool, yet also takes a bit of getting used to. Turn the features on and off as you work to find a comfortable method of your own. Have fun.

CHAPTER 14

Filtering Images

FILTERS ALLOW YOU TO apply special effects to your image. These effects can be used individually and in combination, both as part of creative exploration and as part of technical processes. Filters are in essence plug-in modules, which are small software programs that manipulate pixels in some way. Filter plug-in modules are installed in folders on your system for Photoshop to read on startup, and you access them through Photoshop's Filter menu. Adobe provides a variety of filters, which come with Photoshop, and a wide variety of third-party plug-in filters are available separately.

This chapter introduces you to filters and the Filter Gallery, a new function that includes the old Gallery Effects filters in a new interface, allowing this set of filters to be applied in combination. Along with a basic introduction to the Filter interface functions, this chapter invites you to explore your own creativity and online resources for filter use and additional plug-ins.

See the "Filters" section of the color insert for a complete set of examples of all Photoshop filters.

- 14.1 **Filter basics**
- 14.2 **Applying filters**
- 14.3 **Applying multiple filters with the Filter Gallery**
- 14.4 **Adding a motion or depth-of-field effect**
- 14.5 **Finding online filter resources**

14.1 Filter Basics

Move to next input field

Tab

Because filters irrevocably change the content of a layer (although you can undo or use the History palette to go back), you might want to duplicate the layer before applying the filter and then hide the duplicated layer.

Several options in the Filter menu (Pattern Maker, Liquify, and Extract) do not work like other filters and are presented in relevant chapters throughout the book.

Most filters shipped with Photoshop use similar input boxes, and the Gallery Effects filters share the Filter Gallery dialog. Although they do not always use the same settings, most of the input boxes used are self-explanatory and simply require you to experiment with specific settings or adjust sliders to achieve the effects you want. If you are stuck on exactly what a particular input option is for, you can refer to the following list for a brief description of each.

Photoshop Filter Settings

SETTING	DESCRIPTION
Amount	Sets how strongly the filter should be applied.
Angle	Sets the angle at which or to which the effect is applied.
Background Level	Adjusts shadow contrast.
Balance, Direction Balance	Sets the direction of simulated strokes. Lower values set all strokes from left to right. Higher values set all strokes from right to left. Medium values mix stroke directions.
Brightness	Sets the color brightness. Larger values increase the brightness of colors in the image.
Brush Size	Sets the simulated thickness of the brush used for a stroke.
Cell Size	Sets the maximum length of a facet.
Chalk Area	Sets the amount of chalk (white) to use. Higher numbers add more white.
Charcoal Area	Sets the amount of charcoal (gray) to use. Lower numbers add more gray.
Contrast	Sets the contrast between highlights and shadows.
Dark Intensity, Darkness	Increases the amount of shading.
Definition	Increases highlight and shadow contrast.
Density	Sets the number of dots in a given area of the canvas.
Detail, Brush Detail, Stroke Detail	Sets the number of pixels used from the original image to create effect.
Distance	Sets how far to apply the filter effect from pixels in the image.
Distortion	Sets the size of distorted areas.
Edge	Select Lower to trace outlines of colors below the specified level. Select Upper to trace outlines of colors above the specified level.
Edge Brightness	Increases the brightness of edges. Higher numbers are brighter.
Edge Fidelity	Sets the detail used for object edges. Higher values produce more abstract results.
Edge Intensity	Increases contrast at object edges.
Edge Simplicity	Sets the abstraction used for object edges. Higher values produce more Cubist results.
Edge Thickness	Sets the amount of the edge to be used in the effect.
Edge Width	Sets the width of the outer edge of objects affected.
Fiber Length	Sets the size of the simulated fiber in the paper.
Foreground Level	Adjusts highlight contrast.
Glow Brightness	Adjusts the contrast between highlights and shadows.
Glow Color	Click a color square to open the Color Picker and select a color to use.
Glow Size	Sets the amount of glow. Positive values invert the image while applying the glow.

continues

14.1 Filter Basics *(continued)*

Photoshop Filter Settings *(continued)*

SETTING	DESCRIPTION
Grain, Graininess	Sets the amount of staticlike noise used in a given area of the canvas for the effect.
Height	Sets the displacement of the effect to simulate height.
Highlight Area, Highlight Strength	Increases the brightness of highlights.
Image Balance	Sets the cutoff level between black and white pixels.
Intensity	Increases contrast, strength of the effect or amount of the color or tone. The intensity setting (when increased) favors the designated value, as in Light Intensity (black, white, shadow, or dark).
Level	Sets the RGB color levels (0 through 255) to use in the effect.
Light/Dark Balance	Sets the cutoff level between dark and light pixels.
Magnitude	Sets the frequency of ripples.
No. Levels	Sets the number of posterization levels.
Paper Brightness	Sets the brightness of background areas that show through the effect.
Pencil Width	Sets the width of the simulated brush.
Posterization	Sets the number of posterization levels (see Section 22.15).
Radius	Enter how far the filter searches for differences among pixels.
Ridges	Sets the number of wave crests.
Ripple Size	Sets the height of a ripple crest.
Shadow Intensity	Decreases brightness of shadows.
Sharpness	Increases the contrast between edges.
Smoothness	Smooths transitions between shadows and highlights.
Softness	Softens the tone of an image.
Spray Radius	Sets the amount of spattering in the image.
Strength	Sets the contrast between strokes.
Stroke Length	Sets the length of a simulated stroke.
Stroke Pressure	Sets the simulated pressure used in a stroke. Higher values create darker strokes.
Stroke Size	Sets the simulated size of the palette knife.
Texture	Sets the roughness of object edges.
Texture Coverage	Controls the amount of texture visible at object edges.
Threshold	Sets the cutoff point for pixels to be used with the filter.

➠ 13.10 Distorting Images

➠ 21.2 Blending Modes and Opacity

➠ 22.15 Setting Posterize and Threshold Levels

➠ Color Section Filters

Several filters use the selected foreground and background colors. If you are getting unexpected colors, undo and reset the color choices.

A few filters, such as the Emboss filter, give you an unexpected gray that can be mistaken for an ineffective outcome. All that is needed is a Fade command set to Hard Light to complete the process.

If you need to enlarge an image beyond the point where you notice degradation of image quality, you might achieve pleasing results using filters to slightly rearrange or blend the pixellation caused by enlarging.

Filters are an area of Photoshop's tools that are possibly best learned by taking some time to explore and play around. The new Filter Gallery invites you to try using filters in combination within its interface; you might keep this in mind when exploring filters in general. For added control over the effect, try them in combination, try them on selected areas, and try scaling them back using the Edit > Fade command after you run the filter.

The Fade command is available via the Edit menu immediately after running a filter or a command. This command allows you to scale the opacity and blend modes.

14.2   Applying Filters

**Reapply last filter
using same settings**
⌘ F
Ctrl F

**Reapply last filter
using dialog**
⌘ Option F
Ctrl Alt F

The most recent filter
actually applied
appears as the top
option in the Filters
menu. If you start to
use a filter, but cancel
before the effect is
applied, that filter will
not show up as the
most recent filter.

You can fade the effect
by choosing Edit >
Fade and then setting
the fade opacity and
blending mode.

Sketch filters use the
foreground and back-
ground colors to create
their effects.

Be sure to deselect the
Preserve Transparency
option in the Layers
palette if you want to
apply the Blur filter to
the edges of a layer.

Despite their great image-editing power, filters are relatively easy to apply:

1 Select the layer to which you want to apply the filter. You can also make a specific
   selection on that layer to confine the effects of the filter.

2 Choose one of several options available from the Filter menu. Any filter that is followed by an ellipsis (…) opens the filter's dialog; all other filters are applied immediately and you are finished.

3 Set the options for the filter. Every filter has unique settings, but you set most options
   using an input box with a slider, drop-downs, or radio buttons. For more details about
   the various filter settings, see Section 14.1.

4 Click OK. The filter may take a moment to be applied, depending on your system.

Don't be concerned when the Filter Gallery opens after selecting an individual filter. More
than half of Photoshop's filters are now bundled in the Filter Gallery, which opens even if
they are selected for use individually.

Before and after choosing Filter > Other > Maximum.

Ⓐ **Image Preview**   Most filter dialogs include a preview of how the image will look at 100% magnification after the filter is applied. You can increase the
magnification by clicking the Plus ⊞ or Minus ⊟
button. You can also click and drag in the preview
to move the visible area.

Ⓑ Check to show the effects of the filter in the canvas. This option is not available for all filters.

Ⓒ **Input Options**   You set most filter options using
an input field and/or a slider. You can also set
options using drop-downs, radio buttons, and
check boxes. The options will be the same for individual filters operating in the Filter Gallery, with a
bigger preview.

14.2   Applying Filters *(continued)*

Texturizing Filters

Texturizing filters have the unique property of working in conjunction with the options settings of several other basic filters, an option separate from the filter-combining function of the Filter Gallery. The filters that work with the Texturizer functionality added include Underpainting, Conté Crayon, Glass, and Rough Pastel. These filters allow you to select a texture style from a list of presets or load another texture (image) as a texture. If available, you will see the Texturizer controls at the bottom of the respective filter's dialog. You can also choose Filter > Texture > Texturizer.

Ⓐ Choose the texture type. You can also choose to load a saved texture, which can be any Photoshop native file (.psd).

Ⓑ Use the slider or enter a percentage value (50 through 200) for the scale of the texture, leaving the original image unchanged. Since textures are bitmapped, the default interpolation method is used to resize it.

Ⓒ Use the slider or enter a value (0 through 50) for the contrast between raised and lowered areas of the texture. The higher the contrast, the more the original image is obscured.

Ⓓ Choose a direction for the simulated lighting applied to the texture.

Ⓔ Check to invert the texture. (Raised areas become lower areas.)

The canvas texture applied to a preselected area with the Texturizer filter.

➠ 20.5   De-interlacing Video Stills

➠ 21.2   Blending Modes and Opacity

➠ 22.15 Setting Posterize and Threshold Levels

➠   Color Section Filters

Fade filter (after filter is applied)
⌘ Shift F
Ctrl Shift F

Move to next input field
Tab

Unsharp Mask has a far more prominent effect on the screen version of an image than on the printed version. It is best to print the image to check the settings.

If you want to apply the Blur filter to the edge of a layer's content, make sure the Preserve Transparency option is turned off in the Layers palette.

You can also selectively blur or sharpen areas of the image using the Blur and Sharpen tools.

Before the Drop Shadow effect was added to Photoshop, drop shadows were created by duplicating the layer, filling it with black, moving it behind the original version, and adding a Gaussian Blur.

14.3 Applying Multiple Filters with the Filter Gallery

➡ 13.7 Painting with History Brushes

➡ 21.2 Blending Modes and Opacity

Move to next input field

[Tab]

———

Expand your options or effect by choosing Edit > Fade after you run the filter.

———

Although much of the function of filters is easily put into the category of "fun things to try," filters also have a serious side to their existence, from simple sharpening with the Unsharp Mask filter to using Blur to get rid of moiré patterns in scanned images. There are many subtle uses for Photoshop's filters in serious imaging.

———

A Blur and a saved history snapshot allow you to paint away dust and scratches with the History brush.

———

Running the High Pass filter on a duplicate layer set to Hard Light or Soft Light can be used for unique image sharpening.

The Filter Gallery allows you to apply filters in a cumulative succession or in repetition from one dialog interface with a large preview window. Creative artists have long used the effects of filters most successfully when applied in combinations. Although this tool may not replace practiced techniques for combining filters, fades, and layer blends, the Filter Gallery does provide a unique opportunity to experiment and combine this core set of Photoshop filters. The Filter Gallery does not use all filters and plug-ins loaded on your system; it works only for the classic set of Gallery Effects plug-in filters, which make up a bit more than half of Photoshop's filters.

Ⓐ Large preview window.

Ⓑ Thumbnail representations of filter characteristics. To allow larger previews, toggle this panel closed.

Ⓒ Use the ⊗ button to minimize thumbnail previews. Clicking OK applies the Filter stack. Holding down Option/Alt key toggles Cancel to reset the dialog options.

Ⓓ All the filter choices available via thumbnail view are available from this drop-down.

Ⓔ Filter-specific options display in this section.

Ⓕ The Filter stack is displayed in this window. The filter selected for variable input is clearly highlighted. Filters are applied in the order they are selected, or you can rearrange their order by dragging them as you would layers. The effects of each filter may be significantly different in a different position. Use the 👁 button to temporarily disable the effect.

Ⓖ Use the 🖫 button to create or add a new filter for the stack sequence. Highlight a filter in the sequence and click the trashcan 🗑 to delete.

Ⓗ Clicking the thumbnails switches the selected filter in the stack to the newly selected filter

Ⓘ Allows you to adjust the magnification of the preview.

Ⓙ Filters are grouped by category and can be expanded as needed.

14.4   Adding a Motion or Depth-of-Field Effect

Blur effects may arguably be the workhorses of the basic Photoshop filter set. Designers use them in many subtle techniques that range from removing unwanted noise from images to smoothing transitions in displacement maps.

Just as in traditional photography, a blur can be used in Photoshop to focus the viewer's attention. Both motion blurs and depth-of-field blurs are characteristic of traditional photography techniques and lens limitations. When used purposefully, they can enhance an image.

In this image, a simple horizontal motion blur was used on a duplicate layer. The blur is masked to the original image to focus attention on one of three faces.

The Lens Blur filter is a new tool in the Photoshop arsenal. In its advanced dialog, you can incorporate depth maps and control subtle light characteristics called specular highlights. You can use a selection or a depth map to tell the filter what is to be in focus. To access the dialog, choose Filter > Blur > Lens Blur.

➡ 2.8   Filter Menu

➡ 9.4   Creating Free-Form Selections

➡ 9.10 Saving and Loading Selections

➡ 10.3 Creating Layers

➡ 11.1 Mask Basics

➡ 11.2 Adding Layer Masks

Marquee tool
Ⓜ

Zoom tool
Ⓩ

———

You may notice specular highlight adjustments only with bright sources present in your blur. With the brightness threshold adjusted correctly, and a suitably bright specular highlight, you can expect to notice the effects of the iris shape. This is by far the most subtle of blur effects. You'll find it apparent when bright points, such as background light sources, are included in a lens blur with a slightly lowered brightness threshold.

NOT WHAT YOU EXPECT

- One website includes the Plastic Wrap filter in its list of "useless filters," while another site describes the subtle use of the Plastic Wrap filter in a text effect. The Plastic Wrap filter can be used to add unique highlights to give a "wet" or "watery" effect when the filter is run and a Fade command, set to Hard Light, is used following the filter.

- Another filter that made the aforementioned "useless" list was the Emboss filter. When it is used alone, it might be useless. With the Fade command set to Hard Light or Soft Light, this filter was used with rather dramatic effects in a "chrome text" tutorial.

14.4   Adding a Motion or Depth-of-Field Effect

(continued)

Hand tool

H

The Unsharp Mask filter gives more exacting control over how edges in the image are sharpened. It is especially useful when you need to correct blurring problems associated with photographing, scanning, resampling, and printing.

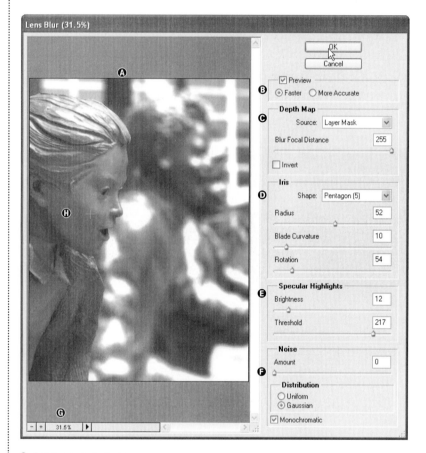

Ⓐ Large preview window.

Ⓑ Preview and quality setting for faster or accurate performance.

Ⓒ A *depth map* is a channel in which white areas are treated to appear behind black areas. From the drop-down, you can select an alpha channel, a layer mask, or a transparency. You can set Blur Focal Distance in relation to pixel values 1–255; if set to 100, 1 and 255 blur while portions of the image or mask with tonal values of 100 are unaffected.

Ⓓ The iris shape function mimics the shaping of specular highlights in relation to lens aperture—a very subtle effect. You can set the lens shape and adjust the amount of blur using radius and blade curvature sliders.

Ⓔ Drag the sliders to set brightness and cutoff values for specular highlights.

Ⓕ Film grain and noise are removed by blur effects; you can add noise to counter this.

Ⓖ Specify preview zoom settings.

Ⓗ With a depth map selected, your can click in the image to select the Blur Focal Distance.

14.5 Finding Online Filter Resources

A simple search of the Web for "Photoshop filters" yields hundreds of thousands of results. Browsing through the first few pages of those listing, you will quickly find a wealth of information on filters—or plug-ins as they are commonly known. Online resources can be categorized into three primary groups for discussion.

Filter Use Tutorials Add the name of any Photoshop filter and the word *tutorial* to your web search, and you will find a wealth of information. Sometimes seeing what other people are doing will give you just the nudge of inspiration you need.

Plug-in Downloads A variety of plug-in downloads are available, both for sale and for free. Folks have been trading Photoshop plug-ins for many years; you'll have to watch for compatibility with your operating system.

Creating Filters If you are inclined to write code, you can even create your own filters. A search will undoubtedly give you some background.

You can explore all three categories via the official Adobe website or Expert Center. Click the Photoshop CS icon [ ] at the top of the Toolbox. Browse for tutorials, plug-in downloads, or software development kits (SDKs) to learn about creating your own filters.

➥ 5.10 Plug-Ins & Scratch Disks Preferences

Windows 98 plug-ins continue to work on Windows, as long as they're compatible with some of the minor operating system changes that come with running on Windows 2000 or XP.

Mac OS 9 plug-ins are not supported by Photoshop CS; they're not OS X compatible. However, plug-ins written for Photoshop 7 on OS X will continue to work.

REMOVING IMAGE NOISE

Digital cameras often create or capture unwanted random noise or specks in images taken in low light. You might want to look into the following options:

- In the Channels palette, turn on and off individual channels to observe which one might have more noise. Run a slight blur on that channel alone.

- You can achieve remarkable nondestructive noise reduction and sharpening without filters or plug-ins. Use a digital camera on a tripod to take four *identical* shots. Combine them into a single Photoshop document with four layers (including the Background). Set the opacity of Layers 1, 2, and 3 to 75%, 50%, and 25% respectively. Try it. The results can be amazing.

➡ Color Section
   Filters

_____

Remember that for Photoshop 7, the mechanism required to use those old OS 9–only plug-ins was to start Photoshop 7 in classic mode. Photoshop CS no longer runs in OS 9 or classic mode at all.

_____

Every time you start Photoshop, it loads all the available filters. You might want to remove some filters and store them in another folder to speed up your Photoshop startup. To do this, simply drag filter files from the designated plug-in folder (most likely Photoshop/Plug-Ins/Filter) and place them in a folder not used for plug-ins. You might want to call this folder something like Plug-Ins (Disabled).

Installing Plug-ins

Photoshop allows you to add a variety of plug-in files 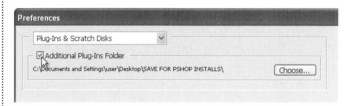 to the interface by adding them to the Photoshop/Plug-Ins folder . You will find plug-ins that let you add formats in which images can be opened or saved, that will let you scan or import, and that will let you create displacement maps or textures.

Installing new filters is as easy as dragging or copying the filter file into the Plug-Ins folder within the Photoshop folder on your machine and then restarting Photoshop. You can also save all your plug-ins to a folder of your own, and then choose Edit > Preferences > Plug-Ins & Scratch Disks. Check the Additional Plug-Ins Folder check box, and browse to select the location of your filters.

Once installed, your filters will appear at the bottom of the Filter menu

Finding More Filters

Adobe provides dozens of filters with Photoshop, but third parties are making hundreds more. These third parties range from individual programmers to large corporations such as Procreate, which makes the popular KPT filter set (`www.procreate.com`), Alien Skin Software, which makes the popular Eye Candy and Splat! series (`www.alienskin.com/`) and Nik Multimedia, makers of popular Photographers' tools: Nik Color Efex, Sharpener and Dfine (`www.nikmultimedia.com`). For more details on downloading free and low-cost filters, check out the Adobe website (`www.adobe.com/products/plugins/photoshop/`) or Plugins.com (`www.plugins.com/photoshop/`). You can also make your own plug-ins by downloading the Photoshop CS Scripting plug-in (`www.adobe.com/support/downloads/`).

CHAPTER 15

Adding Layer Styles

YOU CAN USE PHOTOSHOP'S layer styles to apply special effects such as drop shadows, bevels, and glow effects to a layer to change its appearance. In addition to simply applying effects, you can also control a variety of blending options for how the effects and layers interact. Perhaps more important, you can remove or hide these effects as easily as you apply them, even save the complex combination of variables you create as Layer Style presets. Each of these elements, effects, blending options, and Style Presets is accessible via the Layer Styles dialog.

15.1　Style Basics

➠　2.6　Layer Menu

➠　Color Section
　　　Effects

————

Effects are vector-based, which accounts for their versatility but also means that they cannot be painted on until they are rasterized.

————

Styles, with their effects and blending options, are always applied to a single layer at a time. However, they may be copied and pasted to linked layers via the Layer menu.

Whether you want to apply a single drop shadow to a layer or a complex set of effects to a text layer, Photoshop offers you the controls and setup in a single (master) Layer Style dialog. Layer styles are composed of two components that are applied to individual layers:

Blending options　Allow you to exercise exact control over how effects and the layer to which they are linked interact with one another and with other layers. For example, you can control the opacity of the content on a layer without affecting the styles applied to the layer.

Effects　You can assign and adjust shadows, glows, bevels, overlays, and strokes for a particular layer to change its appearance. These effects are applied as Layer Styles and are designated with an f icon 🅕 in the Layers palette. Each effect applied to a layer is assigned a line item below the layer, allowing effects to be turned on and off individually.

You can apply Layer Styles individually by choosing Layer > Layer Style, or you can apply them via numerous Style Presets that are included with Photoshop. Style Presets provide a unique opportunity for you to see how effects are built and used in complex combinations. Keep in mind that presets are built to a scale that may not be "fit" your image; for a more custom effect choose Layer > Layer Style > Scale Effect.

This illustration is used as a base throughout this chapter to present examples of Layer Styles. The illustration is designed to help you visualize how styles might effect different types of content; such as text (top-right quadrant), cutout elements (top-left quadrant), and solid shapes or buttons (bottom-right quadrant). In the examples throughout this chapter (and in the Color Section), Layer Styles and Effects will be applied to two different layers in the image: The square in the bottom right quadrant will have Layer Styles applied individually, allowing you to compare application of effects on a shape alone. The other elements of the example will have received an overall application of the same style or effect, yet applied to them as an overall layer.

In this example for instance, the radial highlight is centered once on the "button" (bottom-right square) and also in the center of the four quadrants, where it appears more-diffused as applied across the entire image or several objects.

15.1 Style Basics *(continued)*

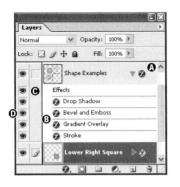

Ⓐ Style in layer Click the triangle to show or hide a list of effects applied to this layer.

Ⓑ Effects Each line item represents an individual effect applied to the layer.

Ⓒ All effects in the layer are currently visible. Click to show or hide all effects in the layer.

Ⓓ This effect is currently visible. Click to show or hide only this effect in the layer.

➡ 4.17 Styles Palette

Deleting a layer also deletes all its effects.

It's easy to confuse styles and effects. Just remember that a group of effects is referred to as a *style*.

Setting Global Lighting

Several effects, such as shadows and beveling, use a simulated light source to create the effect. This lighting source is composed of two variables:

Angle Sets the position of the light source in a 360° circle around the content.

Altitude Sets the height above the content for the light source.

To keep a consistent light source for all effects, which is important for preserving realistic images, you can set a global lighting source for the image. This option, when checked, applies the same lighting source or direction to subsequent effects. Choose Layer **>** Layer Style **>** Global Light..., complete the dialog, and click OK.

Ⓐ Enter a value (from –360 through 360) for the angle of the simulated light source.

Ⓑ Enter a value (from 0 through 90) for the altitude of the simulated light source.

Ⓒ Click around the edge to set the light angle. Click within the circle to set the altitude.

Ⓓ Check to preview the changes to styles that are using global lighting in the canvas.

In the example on the left, Global Light was unchecked, allowing for the incongruously opposed drop shadows. In the example on the right, Global Light was employed and the shadows adjusted in unison.

15.1 Style Basics *(continued)*

➡ Color Section
   Blending
   Modes

➡ Color Section
   Effects

___

Several effects, such as shadows, only use the global light settings angle and ignore the altitude.

Creating Contours

Several layer effects—bevels, glow effects—use a contour to help shape the effect. You choose contours from a drop-down of contour presets that shows a thumbnail 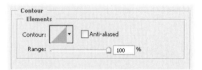 representing a side view of the contour. You can edit contours by simply double-clicking the contour thumbnail to open the Contour Editor dialog and adjusting the points of the contour.

In the Layer Effects dialog, double-click the thumbnail next to the Contour drop-down (center of dialog) to open the Contour Editor.

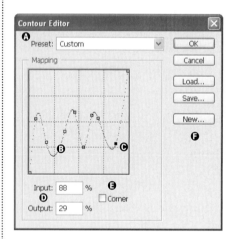

Ⓐ Choose a preset contour shape. Editing a preset resets the name to Custom.

Ⓑ **Contour curve** Click a point on the line to select it and move it up and down or left and right to adjust the graph.

Ⓒ **Selected point** Selected points are solid black squares. You can move them directly in the graph, or you can enter values below.

Ⓓ Enter numeric values to set the input levels for x and y coordinates of the selected point in the graph.

Ⓔ Check to use the selected point as a corner, rather than as a curved, point.

Ⓕ Standard Photoshop options are available for applying, resetting, loading, and saving settings. Click New... to add the current contour to the contour presets.

In each of these three examples, the Style Preset Dented Thin Aluminum was applied. Left: The preset Bevel uses the 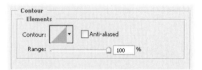 gloss contour shape. Center: The preset Bevel's gloss contour was changed using this shape 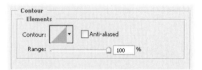 from the drop-down in the Layer Style dialog. Right: The preset Bevel's gloss contour was edited to this shape 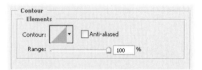 using the Contour Editor.

15.2 Applying Effects and Styles

You can begin applying effects with Layer menu choices, or you can assign presets via the Styles palette. However they are applied, a most important aspect of styles, effects, or their presets is being able to custom tailor them to a specific layer and situation.

You can control all aspects of Layer Styles, from advanced layer blending and individual effect settings to applying Style Presets, via the Layer Style dialog. Basic access and function of the Layer Style dialog are presented here, with further sections in this chapter detailing how to set the options for each specific effect.

➡ 2.6   Layer Menu

➡ 4.13 Layers Palette

➡ 4.17 Styles Palette

Effects are vector-based, which accounts for their versatility but also means that they cannot be painted on until they are rasterized.

Deleting a layer also deletes all its effects.

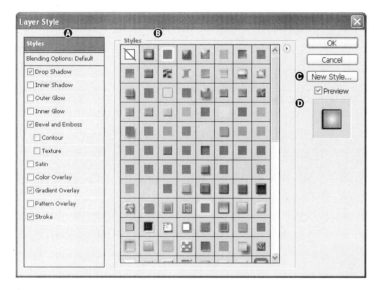

Ⓐ Select from this column to choose major dialog options: Styles (access presets); Blending Options (access advanced layer blending options); Individual Effects (access-specific controls for effects from Drop Shadows through Stroke). Each choice changes the context of the options in (B).

Ⓑ In this case, Style Preset thumbnails are displayed. Click the palette options selector ▶ to change the thumbnail view to lists of names and to access more presets. This portion of the dialog changes to reflect the choices in (A).

Ⓒ Click to save your options as a new Style Preset.

Ⓓ Click to preview your options in the image canvas. The thumbnail representation of the combined effects associated with the current layer remains displayed here regardless of the check.

➡ 9.2 Selecting a
Layer or Its
Contents

➡ Color Section
Blending
Modes

➡ Color Section
Effects

It's easy to confuse
styles and effects. Just
remember that a group
of effects is referred to
as a style.

Several effects, such as
shadows, only use the
global light settings
angle and ignore the
altitude.

Accessing the Layer Style Dialog

The Layer Style dialog opens each time you choose an individual effect such as Bevel, Glow, or Drop Shadow. This dialog also opens when you access advanced layer blending options for a layer in the Layers palette.

- Select the layer to which you want to apply one or more styles, and then do one of the following to open the Layer Style dialog:

- Choose a specific layer style to apply from the menu at the bottom of the Layers palette 🔘 or by choosing Layer > Layer Style. The Layer Style dialog opens to that style, applying its default options to the layer.

- Double-click the layer's thumbnail or title. The Layer Style dialog opens to Blending Options. Click other styles to access their options.

- Double-click an existing effect associated with the layer. The Layer Style dialog opens to the selected effect.

- Control/right-click an existing effect in the layer, and choose a layer effect from the contextual menu.

Click the check box next to the effects you want to apply to the layer, and then click the title of each effect to set the options for that style. (Clicking the title also applies the style.) The options for each style are described in Sections 15.8 through 15.13.

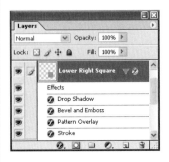

Click OK after you set effects. The effects appear as a list below the layer.

15.3 Duplicating or Removing Styles

As with all things Photoshop, you can apply Layer Styles or effects in several ways. You can drag and drop existing styles from one layer to another or copy and paste them via the Layers menu. You can always turn layer style visibility on and off via the Layers Palette icon 👁. You might, however, want to discard styles altogether. Following are several options for doing so.

Copying and Pasting Styles

You can copy and paste the effects of one layer as a style to one or more layers. To copy a single effect from one layer to another, click the effect, drag it underneath the target layer, and drop it.

To copy all the effects from one layer to another, you can either drag the effects line underneath the layer or follow these steps:

1 Select the layer from which you want to copy styles.

2 Choose Copy Layer Style from the style's contextual menu (Control/right-click the layer or any of the styles in the layer), or choose Layer > Layer Style.

3 The Layer Style is now in memory. To paste it into a layer, select the target layer and then do one of the following:

■ To paste the style into the layer, choose Paste Layer Style from the style's contextual menu (Control/right-click the layer or any of the effects in the target layer), or choose Layer > Layer Style.

■ To paste the style to all layers linked to the selected layer, choose Paste Layer Style To Linked from the style's contextual menu (Control/right-click the layer or any of the effects in the target layer), or choose Layer > Layer Style.

The styles display below the layer, overwriting any existing styles of the same type already associated with the layer.

Removing Styles

Once you apply an effect to a layer, it remains until you remove it, either individually or as part of the layer style.

■ To clear a single style, open the Layer Style dialog, clear the Style check box, and click OK. If you want to reinstate the style later, simply open the Layer Style dialog again, and check the style. The previous options are reapplied.

■ To clear all styles in a layer, select the layer, choose Layer > Layer Style > Clear Layer Style or Control/right-click a style in the Layers palette, and choose Clear Layer Style. Alternatively, you can click the Clear Styles button ⊘ at the bottom of the Styles palette.

■ To clear styles via the Layers palette, click and drag the individual effect or the entire effects set to the trashcan icon.

➡ 2.6 Layer Menu

➡ 4.13 Layers Palette

➡ Color Section
   Blending
   Modes

➡ Color Section
   Effects

You can also apply styles to a background image, but, obviously, styles such as the Drop Shadow, which appear outside the content, will not appear.

ImageReady allows you to add effects to layers, but handles this through the Layer Effects palette rather than a dialog (see Section 26.4).

The contour and texture effects that are indented under the Bevel And Emboss effect are applied only to the area affected by the Bevel And Emboss effect and not to the entire layer.

When copied, Layer Styles are placed in their own memory location independent of the location used to store content copied by choosing Edit > Copy. The effect stays in memory until another effect is copied.

15.4 Creating and Applying Style Presets

Style Presets are a saved copy of a particular set of effects and/or blending options. All currently loaded Style Presets are displayed in the Styles palette. You can also access your currently loaded Style Presets via the Layer Style dialog.

Ⓐ Styles palette menu Access options for saving and loading presets and changing display options—Thumbnail, Text, List, and so on.

Ⓑ Style Preset thumbnails Click once to apply the style to the selected layer; double-click to rename the style.

Ⓒ Clear Styles Click to remove the style from the selected layer.

Ⓓ Add Style Click to add a new style to the palette based on the style in the selected layer.

Ⓔ Delete Style Drag a style to this icon to delete it from the Styles palette. Deleting a style does not affect the saved version of the style group.

Creating a Style Preset

Open the Layer Style dialog and create your style as described in Section 15.1. To turn this style into a Style Preset, click the New Style... button, complete the New Style dialog, and click OK. The Layer Style dialog remains open, but the new Style Preset is inserted at the bottom of the Styles palette.

In addition, you can create Style Presets directly from styles already applied to layers. To turn a layer's styles into a Style Preset, first select the layer and then do one of the following:

- Click any blank spot in the Styles palette.
- Click the Create New Style button ⬛ in the Styles palette.
- Choose New Style... from the Styles palette menu or contextual menu (Control/right-click any style).

Regardless of which method you use, complete the New Style Preset dialog, and then click OK. The new style appears at the bottom of the Styles palette.

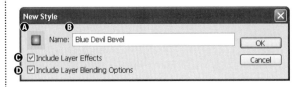

Ⓐ Displays a thumbnail preview of the style.

Ⓑ Enter a name for the style.

Ⓒ Check to include the layer effects in the new style.

Ⓓ Check to include the advanced layer blending options in the new style.

15.4 Creating and Applying Style Presets *(continued)*

Applying a Style Preset

To apply a Style Preset to a layer, do one of the following:

- Select the layer in the Layers palette, and then click the style you want to apply in the Styles palette. The styles appear below the layer in the Layers palette, overwriting any existing styles of the same type that were already associated with the layer.

- Drag a Style Preset from the Styles palette and drop it onto the layer in the canvas to which you want to apply it. This method requires you be accurate with cursor positioning. The styles appear below the layer in the Layers palette, overwriting any existing styles of the same type that were already associated with the layer.

Learning from Presets

Style Presets can provide a unique insight into how Photoshop's effects and blends interact. Keeping in mind that the preset may not have been built to the scale or resolution of your image, choosing Layer > Layer Style > Scale Effects allows you to fit the effects. Click the various effect settings and blend settings in the Layer Style dialog—click the name of the options with a ✔ next to them—to see which settings and blends were used to provide a combination you find interesting.

Left: The preset style Mercury was applied. The effect looks washed out across the layer at the preset scale. Right: The style has been scaled to 30% on the greater image and 50% on the lower right "button"—looking more like the style name implied.

The Layer Style dialog's displayed list of effects shows that there has been a change from default Blending Options, as Custom is now displayed at the top of the list. Clicking the Blending Options heading displays the blend settings. Likewise, clicking any of the effects displaying a ✔ next to them displays the options used for that effect.

You can observe the complexities developed for this style both by the sheer number of effects applied to the layer and by their individual settings. This single preset used the six contour settings shown, a different one in each of six effects: Shadow, Inner Shadow, Inner Glow, Bevel Emboss, Contour, and Satin.

➡ 2.6 Layer Menu

➡ 4.17 Styles Palette

➡ 5.1 Preset Manager Overview

➡ Color Section Blending Modes

➡ Color Section Effects

You can change the size of the Style Preset thumbnail displayed in the Styles palette by selecting a size option at the top of the Styles palette menu.

Use presets as a base, and then make adjustments and variations.

The Styles palette is a good candidate for docking in the Palette Well. You can then quickly access it without cluttering your desktop.

ImageReady also has a Styles palette that allows you to add styles to a layer, and it also includes the ability to store rollover states as a part of the Style Preset.

You can keep applying Style Presets to the same layer to try different looks.

15.5   Organizing Style Presets

➥ 2.4   Edit Menu

➥ 4.17 Styles Palette

Style Preset lists are generally saved in the Adobe Photoshop/Presets/Styles folder.

To rename a style, double-click its thumbnail in the Styles palette or click the Rename… button in the Style Preset Manager.

You can apply Style Presets using the Styles palette, the Layer Style dialog, or the Preset Manager. Each choice provides workflow and preset management options, but the Style Preset Manager also allows you to select multiple styles to be managed simultaneously. You use this dialog to sort and manage your Style Presets and set characteristics of the palette. To open the Preset Manager, do one of the following:

- Choose Edit **>** Preset Manager, and then choose Styles from the Preset Type menu.

- Choose Preset Manager… from the Styles palette menu. This action opens the Preset Manager directly in the Style panel.

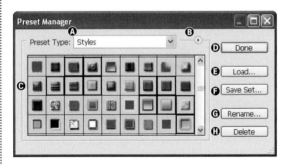

Ⓐ Choose a preset type to open its panel.

Ⓑ **Style Preset menu** Choose options to change the style's thumbnail appearance, reset styles in the list, or replace styles in the list.

Ⓒ **Style Preset thumbnails** Click to select one style, double-click to change the name, Shift-click or Command/Control-click to select multiple styles.

Ⓓ Click when finished with the Style Preset Manager.

Ⓔ Click to load preset lists.

Ⓕ Select one or more styles, and click to save them as a new Style Preset list.

Ⓖ Select one or more styles, and click to rename them.

Ⓗ Select one or more styles, and click to delete them.

Saving Style Presets

You can save a group of styles to be loaded later by doing one of the following:

- Choose Save Styles… in the Styles palette menu, and enter a name for the Style Preset, making sure to preserve the .asl suffix. Browse to the location on your hard drive where you want to save the Style Preset list, and click OK.

- Open the Style Preset Manager, select the styles in the list you want to save as a separate Style Preset by Shift-clicking the styles, click Save Set…, and enter a name for the Style Preset, making sure to preserve the .asl suffix. Browse to the location on your hard drive where you want to save the Style Preset list, and click OK.

15.5 Organizing Style Presets (continued)

Loading Style Presets

You can load a group of saved presets by either appending a new list to the end of the current list of presets or by replacing the current list with the new list. Both the Styles palette and the Style Preset dialog contain options to load styles, and you can perform the actions from either place. To load a group of Style Presets, do one of the following.

- To **reset** the styles in the Styles palette to the original list, choose Reset Styles… from the Styles palette menu or the Style Preset Manager menu. Click Append to add the original list to the current list, or click Replace to remove the current list and replace it with the original list.

- To **load** a style list to the current list, choose Load Styles… from the Styles palette menu or click Load… in the Style Preset Manager, browse to the location of the Style Preset list on your hard drive, and double-click it. The new list is placed below the current list.

- To **replace** the current style list with a new list, choose Replace Styles… from the Styles palette menu or the Style Preset Manager menu, browse to the location of the Style Preset list on your hard drive, and double-click it. The new list replaces the current list.

- To quickly **add** a preset list, choose a style list name from the bottom of the Styles palette menu or the Style Preset Manger menu. Click Append to add the new list to the current list, or click Replace to remove the current list and replace it with the new list.

Managing Presets within the Layer Style Dialog

You can conveniently access and manage Layer Style presets without leaving the Layer Style dialog. With the Layer Style dialog open:

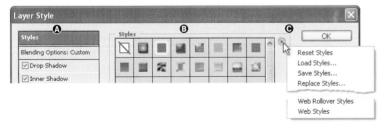

Ⓐ Choose Styles.

Ⓑ Click thumbnails to apply styles, Control/right-click thumbnails to access a contextual menu.

Ⓒ Click to access a drop-down for preset management and set selection options.

➠ 5.1   Preset Manager Overview

➠ Color Section Blending Modes

➠ Color Section Effects

You can select multiple styles in the Preset Manager to save a set, rename a set, or delete a set.

15.6 Working with Effects

Once you apply an effect to a layer, either as a single effect or as part of a group of effects in a style, you can work with the individual effects to show or hide them, to scale them, or to convert them into rasterized layers.

Hiding Effects

You can temporarily hide an effect, just like hiding a layer, so that its impact does not show up in the image.

- To hide a single effect, click the eye icon ![eye] next to the effect in the Layers palette. Click again to show the effect.

- To hide all the effects in a particular layer, click the eye icon ![eye] next to the Effects line for the layer in the Layers palette. All the effects for that layer are hidden. Click again to show the effects.

- To hide all the effects in a document, choose Layer > Layer Styles or Control/right-click any of the styles in the Layers palette and choose Hide All Effects. Repeat and select Show All Effects to show the effects.

Scaling Effects

You can scale the effects of a Layer Style to fit them to the situation.

To scale effects in a layer, select the layer for which you want to scale the effects, choose Layer > Layer Styles > Scale Effects…, enter the amount by which to scale the effects in the numeric field or use the slider to adjust the effects, and click OK. Enter a percentage in the Scale field (1 through 1000) by which to scale the effects. Check Preview to see your adjustments in the canvas.

The illustration on the left shows the Chromed Satin preset applied without adjustment. The illustration on the right shows the same preset effect after having been scaled to 24% for the overall layer and to 69% for the lower-right square.

Converting Effects to Layers

Styles are actually vector information that Photoshop uses to create special effects. Although you can easily change and reshape vector images, you cannot manipulate them with painting tools. To rasterize the effects into individual layers so that you can paint and edit them with other Photoshop tools, do the following.

15.6 Working with Effects *(continued)*

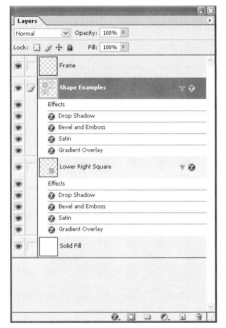

Before conversion, the effects appear below the associated layer.

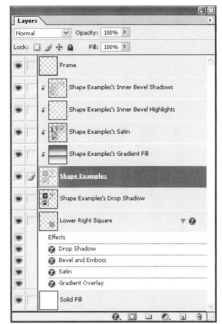

After conversion, several of the effects are layers grouped to the original layer that contained the effects, but the drop shadow is a layer beneath it.

1 Select the layer that contains the effects you want to convert to layers.

2 Choose Layer > Layer Style > Create Layers.

3 An alert may appear if some of the effects cannot be rendered as layers. If you do not want to see this alert again, check the Don't Show Again box in the bottom-left corner of the alert. Click OK to continue.

The effects now appear as layers grouped with the original layer or new layers above or below the original layer.

➡ 2.6 Layer Menu

➡ 4.13 Layers Palette

➡ 21.7 Compositing with Clipping Masks

➡ Color Section Blending Modes

➡ Color Section Effects

———

Scaling effects provides a quick alternative to making multiple adjust-ments in the Layer Style dialog, particularly when working with pre-sets which have been designed to be most effective at a specific resolution or object scale.

———

If you are dissatisfied with the results of ras-terizing your effects, you can choose Edit > Undo or use the History palette to return to the state before the changes were made, thus retaining the effects.

———

You can reset alert mes-sages to display in the General preferences.

15.7 Applying Advanced Blending Options

The power of the blending sliders is understated here. You can use these for complex image compositing and blends. Option/Alt-click the triangles and drag them to soften blends.

The Layers palette includes options to set the blending mode, opacity, and fill opacity for an individual layer. The Layer Style dialog includes these options, but adds the ability to set the color channels used for the layer, create layer knockouts, specify how effects blend with the layer and other layers, and set blending in particular color channels.

Follow the instructions in Section 15.2 to open the Layer Style dialog, and then fill out the options for blending.

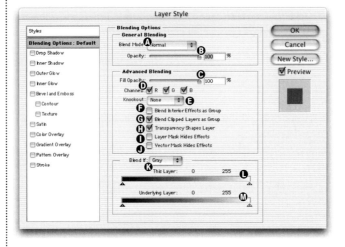

Ⓐ Click to select the blending mode for the layer. You can also change the blending mode in the Layers palette.

Ⓑ Enter a value (0 through 100) for the layer opacity. You can also change this opacity in the Layers palette.

Ⓒ Enter a value (0 through 100) for the opacity of image pixels. You can also change the fill opacity in the Layers palette.

Ⓓ Check to select the color channels being used in the layer (Red, Green, or Blue). This option affects only the selected layer.

Ⓔ Choose a Knockout style. Selecting this option makes the layer transparent, showing the content of layers beneath: None, Shallow (shows the content of the layer beneath), or Deep (punches through to the background layer or transparency).

Ⓕ Check if you want glow, satin, and interior effects blended with their associated layer before blending with the rest of the document.

Ⓖ Check to blend any clipped layers or clipping masks as grouped objects before blending them with the rest of the document.

Ⓗ Check if you want the transparency of the layer to set the edges of the shape and the effects.

Ⓘ Check if you want the layer mask to hide the effects rather than reshaping them.

Ⓙ Check if you want the vector mask to hide effects rather than reshaping them.

Ⓚ Choose a color channel for which to set an individualized blending mode.

Ⓛ Set the blending range for the particular color channel in the selected layer by sliding the triangles at either end to limit the spectrum.

Ⓜ Set the blending range for the particular color channel for the layer underneath the selected layer by sliding the triangles at either end to limit the spectrum.

15.8 Applying the Shadow Effects

You use shadows to add the illusion of depth and three-dimensionality to content in the canvas. Follow the instructions in Section 15.2 to open the Layer Style dialog, and then fill out the options for the Shadow effects.

Drop Shadow

Inner Shadow

Combined with distance, choke, and size adjustments

➡ Color Section Blending Modes

➡ Color Section Effects

With either the Drop Shadow or Inner Shadow panels open, you can drag the shadow directly on the canvas to position it. However, doing so also changes the global lighting settings.

To prevent shadows from being affected by the global light setting or to allow experimentation with multiple light-source effects, create layers out of the Shadow effect.

Ⓐ Click to choose the blending mode (see Section 15.1).

Ⓑ Drop-shadow color Click to open the Color Picker and select the color for the shadow.

Ⓒ Enter a value (0 through 100) for the opacity of the drop shadow.

Ⓓ Enter a value (−360 through 360) for the angle of the simulated light source of the shadow. You can also use the dial to change the angle.

Ⓔ Check to use global lighting with the shadow.

Ⓕ Enter a value (0 through 30000) for the distance the shadow will be offset from the source. Zero places the shadow directly beneath the source.

Ⓖ Spread (Drop Shadow) or Choke (Inner Shadow) Enter a value (0 through 100) for the size of the layer mask creating the shadow. For both Spread and Choke, the larger the number, the harder the edge on the drop shadow.

Ⓗ Enter a value (0 through 250), in pixels, for the size of the shadow.

Ⓘ Select a contour style for the shadow. Double-click the contour thumbnail to open the Contour Editor. The linear contour is the standard for most shadows.

Ⓙ Check to use anti-aliasing with the shadow, which can improve its smoothness.

Ⓚ Enter a value (0 through 100) for the stochastic noise to be applied to the shadow. This has the effect of dithering the shadow, making it appear less smooth.

Ⓛ (Drop Shadow only) Check to prevent the drop shadow from showing through transparent fill pixels when the fill opacity is less than 100%.

15.9   Applying the Glow Effects

A glow is a simulated lighting effect that creates the appearance of a colored light behind or inside the object. You can apply the glow outside the content of the layer (Outer Glow) or inside the content (Inner Glow) and either around the edges or emanating from the center of the layer's content. Follow the instructions in Section 15.2 to open the Layer Style dialog, and then fill out the options for the glow effects.

Outer Glow

Inner Glow Added

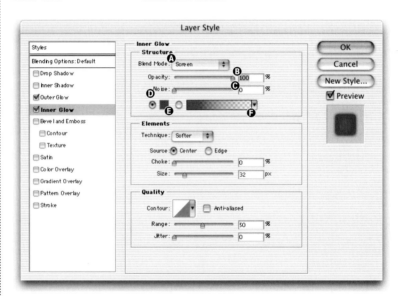

Ⓐ   Chose a blending mode for the glow style. (See the color section "Blending Modes.")

Ⓑ   Enter a value (0 through 100) for the opacity of the glow.

Ⓒ   Enter a value (0 through 100) for the stochastic noise to be applied to the glow. Selecting this option has the effect of dithering the glow, making it appear less smooth.

Ⓓ   Choose to use a solid color or a gradient for the glow.

Ⓔ   Click to open the Color Picker and select the solid color for the glow.

Ⓕ   Click to select a gradient preset to use for the glow. Double-click the gradient to open the Gradient Editor.

15.9 Applying the Glow Effects *(continued)*

➠ 12.9 Organizing
     Gradient
     Presets

➠ 12.10 Applying
      Gradient
      Color Fills

➠ Color Section
     Blending
     Modes

➠ Color Section
     Effects

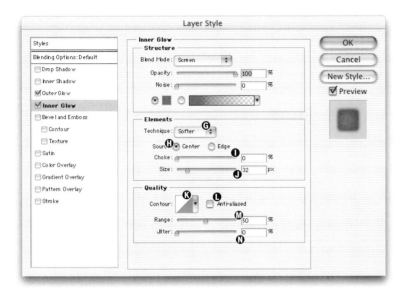

G Choose Softer if you want the color or gradient to fade to transparent gradually, or choose Precise if you want the color or gradient to fill the entire area of the glow.

H **(Inner Glow only)** Choose whether the glow should start at the outer edge of the source or the center.

I **Spread (Outer Glow) or Choke (Inner Glow)** Enter a value (0 through 100) for the size of the layer mask creating the shadow. For both Spread and Choke, the larger the number, the harder the edge on the drop shadow.

J Enter a value (0 through 25) for the size of the glow.

K Select a contour style for the glow. Double-click the contour thumbnail to open the Contour Editor. The linear contour is the standard for most glows.

L Check to use anti-aliasing with the glow, which can improve its smoothness.

M Enter a value (1 through 100) to control which parts of the glow are used in the contour.

N Enter a value (0 through 100) to add noise for the glow's color and transparency.

STYLES AND TEXT

Although you cannot double-click the Text Layer icon to open the Layer Style dialog (double-clicking a text layer's icon selects the text), you can apply styles to text that can be edited just as easily as you can apply them to any other layer type. However, effects can sometimes obscure the text if they are not applied judiciously.

15.10   Applying the Bevel and Emboss Effects

➠ 12.2 Selecting Colors with the Eyedropper

➠ 12.3 Selecting Colors with the Color Palette

➠ 12.4 Selecting Colors with the Color Picker

The contour and texture effects that are indented under the bevel and emboss effects are not applied to the entire layer.

Beveling and embossing, like shadowing, are other ways to add a 3-D appearance to your content, but these effects create the illusion that the content is raised off the surface rather than simply floating above it. Both effects—which are mutually exclusive—work much the same, highlighting half the object while placing the other half in a shadow. Bevels create a hard edge around the content, and embossing creates a soft edge around the content. Follow the instructions in Section 15.2 to open the Layer Style dialog, and then fill out the options for the Bevel or the Emboss effect.

Left to right: Outer Bevel (hard chisel); Inner Bevel (smooth), Emboss (chisel hard, image color inverted); and Pillow Emboss (smooth)

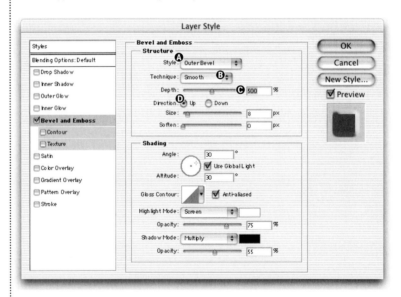

Ⓐ Choose a shading style: Outer Bevel, Inner Bevel, Emboss, Pillow Emboss, Stroke Emboss.

Ⓑ Choose an edge technique to use for the shading: Smooth, Chisel Hard, or Chisel Soft.

Ⓒ Enter a value (1 through 1000) for the depth of the shading. Selecting this option has the affect of increasing the contrast between the highlight and the shadow.

Ⓓ Choose a direction for the bevel or emboss. Selecting this option has the affect of reversing the lighting angle.

15.10 Applying the Bevel and Emboss Effects

(continued)

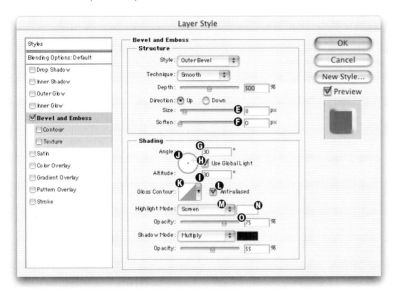

➠ 12.8 Creating and Editing Gradients

➠ 12.9 Organizing Gradient Presets

➠ 12.11 Creating Patterns

The contour and texture effects described here are apparent only if a bevel or an emboss effect is applied to the layer.

ⓔ Enter a value (0 through 250) for the size of the shading.

ⓕ Enter a value (0 through 16) for the softness of the shading edges. The larger the number, the softer the edges.

ⓖ Enter a value (–180 through 180) for the angle of the simulated lighting source used for the shading.

ⓗ Check to use global lighting (see Section 15.1) for the bevel or emboss.

ⓘ Enter a value (0 through 90) for the altitude of the simulated lighting source used for the shading.

ⓙ Click to set the angle or altitude of the simulated lighting source (see G and I).

ⓚ Select a contour style for the shading. Double-click the contour thumbnail to open the Contour Editor.

ⓛ Check to use anti-aliasing with the contour shading. Using anti-aliasing can improve the smoothness of the shading.

ⓜ Choose a blending mode to be used with the highlight, the shadow, the bevel, or the emboss. (See "Blending Modes" in the color section.)

ⓝ Click to open the Color Picker and choose the highlight or shadow of the bevel or emboss.

ⓞ Enter a value (0 through 100) for the opacity to be used for the highlight or shadow of the bevel or emboss.

Bevel and Emboss with Contour

This differs from the Gloss Contour setting in the Bevel And Emboss Shading options, which affects only the apparent reflection (glossiness) of the bevel and not its actual shape. Contour changes the shadows in the effect to create different shaped edges. Once you set the Bevel or Emboss effect as described, check and click the Contour option, and then set the options.

15.10   Applying the Bevel and Emboss Effects

(continued)

The key to getting a good bevel is to choose the right gloss contour. Play around with different contours until you find one that works, or create your own.

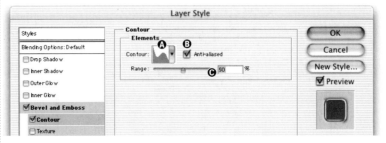

Ⓐ Select a contour style for the shading. Double-click the thumbnail to open the Contour Editor.

Ⓑ Check to use anti-aliasing with the contour shading. Using anti-aliasing can improve the smoothness of the contour.

Ⓒ Enter a value (0 through 100) to control the range used in the contour. The higher the number, the sharper the edge of the contour.

Left: This contour shape was added to the basic bevel shape.

Right: Texture effect was applied using the Satin texture preset.

Bevel and Emboss with Texture

Texture allows you to apply a preset pattern to the effect's edges. Once you set the Bevel or Emboss effect as described, check and click the Texture option, and then set the options.

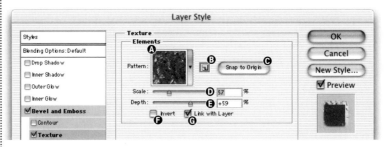

Ⓐ Choose a texture from the list of presets to apply to the shading.

Ⓑ Click to add the currently selected texture to the list of presets.

Ⓒ Click if you want the texture to snap to the top-left corner of the layer or document.

Ⓓ Enter a value (1 through 1000) to set the scale of the texture pattern.

Ⓔ Enter a value (–1000 to 1000) to set the strength (depth) of the texture pattern. A negative number inverts the texture.

Ⓕ Check to invert the texture pattern.

Ⓖ Check if you want the texture linked to the layer. If this check box is cleared, the pattern will not move when you move the layer.

15.11   Applying the Satin Effect

A Satin effect creates two solid-color copies of the content. When you space out these copies, you will see only the two copies where they do *not* overlap. Applying the Satin effect can create some interesting effects beyond beveling, as if the content were made from cloth. Follow the instructions in Section 15.2 to open the Layer Style dialog, select the Satin effect on the left of the dialog, and then fill out the options for the Satin effect.

➠ Color Section Effects

➠ Color Section Blending Modes

The Satin effect applied using the Double-Ring contour

The Satin effect works best with complex content that has multiple sides.

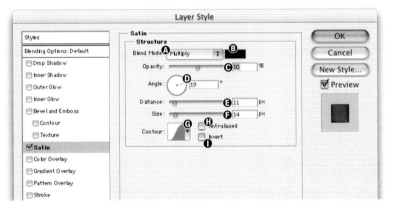

Ⓐ Click to choose the blending mode for satin shading (see "Blending Modes" in the color section).

Ⓑ **Satin color** Click to open the Color Picker and select the color for the satin shading.

Ⓒ Enter a value (0 through 100) for the opacity of the satin shading.

Ⓓ Enter a value (–360 through 360) for the angle of the simulated light source of the satin shading. You can also use the dial to change the angle.

Ⓔ Enter a value (1 through 250) for the distance the satin shading copies will be offset from the edges of the source.

Ⓕ Enter a value (0 through 250), in pixels, for the size of the satin shading. The larger the number, the softer the edges of the shading.

Ⓖ Select a contour style for the satin effects. Double-click the contour thumbnail to open the Contour Editor.

Ⓗ Check to use anti-aliasing with the satin shading's contour, which can improve the smoothness of the contour.

Ⓘ Check to invert the satin shading.

UNIVERSAL TASKS

PHOTO AND VIDEO TASKS

PRINT TASKS

WEB TASKS

15.12 Applying the Overlay Effects

Using overlays is a quick way to add a solid color, a gradient, or a pattern over a layer. Using overlays is preferable in many cases to adding a fill layer, since you can apply an overlay to a single layer rather than to all layers below the fill layer. Follow the instructions in Section 15.2 to open the Layer Style dialog, select one of the Overlay effects, and then fill out the options for that effect.

The original

The Color overlay

The Gradient overlay, with the Soft Stripes preset

The Pattern overlay, using the Gravel preset from the Rock Patterns set

Color Overlay

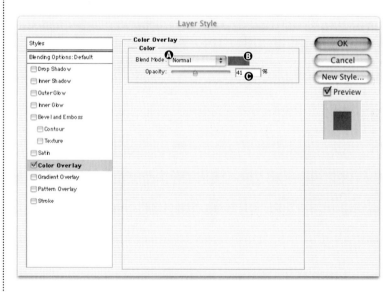

A Click to choose the blending mode for a color overlay (see Section 15.1).

B **Overlay color** Click to open the Color Picker and select the color for the overlay.

C Enter a value (0 through 100) for the opacity of the Color overlay.

Color overlay demonstrated in grayscale may not seem to have much value, yet the results of a color overlay are actually often a much better choice—and much easier—than a fill of a selection, particularly at lower resolution.

15.12   Applying the Overlay Effects *(continued)*

Gradient Overlay

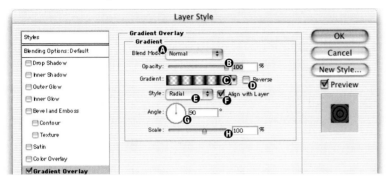

A Click to choose the blending mode for the Color overlay (see Section 15.1).

B Enter a value (0 through 100) for the opacity of the Color overlay.

C Click to select a Gradient preset to use for the glow. Double-click the gradient to open the Gradient Editor.

D Check to reverse the gradient direction.

E Choose a gradient style: Linear, Radial, Angle, Reflected, or Diamond.

F Check to center the gradient with the content of the layer. If this check box is cleared, the gradient aligns with the center of the canvas.

G Enter a value (–360 through 360) for the angle of the gradient.

H Enter a value (10 through 150) for the scale of the gradient.

Pattern Overlay

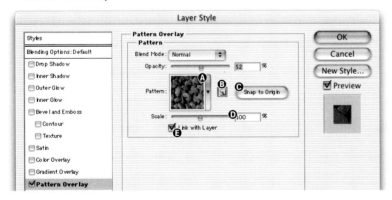

A Choose a pattern from the list of presets to be used for the overlay.

B Click to add the currently selected pattern to the list of presets.

C Click if you want the pattern to snap to the top-left corner of the layer or document.

D Enter a value (1 through 1000) for the scale of the pattern.

E Check if you want the pattern linked to the layer. If this check box is cleared, the pattern will not move when you move the layer.

The overlay effects are an easy way to add solid color, pattern, and gradient fills to the content of a layer and are often a versatile option for the methods presented in Chapter 12.

PHOTOSHOP WORKSPACE

UNIVERSAL TASKS

PHOTO AND VIDEO TASKS

PRINT TASKS

WEB TASKS

15.13   Applying the Stroke Effect

———

Although you can rig
the Outer Glow effect to
do the same thing, the
Stroke effect adds the
ability to apply a gradi-
ent or a pattern to the
border.

———

The Stroke effect tends
to round off even hard
edges of shapes.

A stroke is a solid line around the contours of an object that creates a border.

The original

With a 3-pixel stroke applied

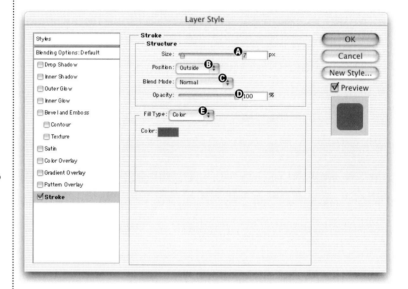

Ⓐ Enter a value (1 through 250) for the size of the stroke in pixels.

Ⓑ Choose where the stroke should be placed: outside the source, inside the source, or centered on
   the source's edge.

Ⓒ Click to choose the blending mode for the stroke (see Section 15.1).

Ⓓ Enter a value (0 through 100) for the opacity of the satin shading.

Ⓔ Choose a fill type to use for the stroke: Color, Gradient, or Pattern. Each fill type will have controls identical to those in the corresponding overlay styles (described in the preceding section).

CHAPTER 16

Drawing Paths and Shapes

PHOTOSHOP INCLUDES AN ADVANCED selection of vector-editing tools that make it a unique hybrid imaging application that allows you to work with vector paths and shapes in a variety of ways, in what are essentially raster images. You can create images with resolution-independent components—with the crisp, sharp-edge definition associated with vectors and PostScript printing—or you can use the Pen tool to simply make smooth, curved selections. The vector shape features also allow you to quickly apply complex saved or preset shapes as editable vector masks—to which you can apply all of Photoshop's styles, such as bevels or drop shadows.

This chapter shows you how to use the pen and shape tools to draw paths and how to create custom vector masks and shapes.

16.1 Path Basics

Curves in vector graphics are often referred to as Bezier curves.

The direction handles are a common way to control Bezier curves in most vector-editing software. If you are familiar with Macromedia FreeHand or Adobe Illustrator, you'll find that the concept is much the same as in those products.

Vector tools in Photoshop can be divided into two basic categories—paths and shapes. *Paths* are the base component for vector drawing and constructing shapes. *Shapes*, especially custom shapes, are much like brush presets—ready to use—click in your image and drag. Photoshop handles vector shapes a bit differently from other vector-editing applications such as Adobe Illustrator. Instead of working with paths having stroke and fill properties, Photoshop handles paths independent of layers, fills, and strokes. Photoshop's shape tools use editable vector masks rather than common fills.

Vector tools are a fundamental part of a designer's digital arsenal. The nature of vector graphics is that they are resolution independent and infinitely scalable—making them ideal for use in logos, which might be very small on a business card and huge on a billboard or the side of a jet. Another key asset of vector graphics is they have clean, crisp edges in print. Like typography, vectors carry PostScript characteristics for print devices. The PostScript and vector characteristics of paths and shapes are, however, dependent on how you save them in your final document. Just like fonts, vectors must be preserved in layers or embedded in .psd, .tif, .eps, or .pdf files.

Vector Options for Pen and Shape Tools

ICON	EFFECT
	A new Shape layer is created. Vector Mask on a Color Fill layer.
	Creates paths independent of any layer.
	Creates a pixel fill (or rasterized version) of the path or shape.

Vector Shape Tools

ICON	TOOL
	Rectangle. Click and drag arbitrary rectangles, or use the Options bar to specify numeric values for fixed sizes.
	Rounded Rectangle. Click and drag arbitrary rectangles, with the Options bar setting for Corner Radius.
	Ellipse. Click and drag arbitrary ellipses or use the Options bar to specify numeric values for fixed sizes.
	Polygon. Set Polygon options for the number of sides and the corner radius. Use to make polygons and star shapes.
	Line. Creates straight lines and arrows.
	ShapeCustom. Choose from a variety of Shape presets, or define a custom shape such as a logo or a signature.

16.1   Path Basics *(continued)*

Pen/Path Editing Tools

ICON	TOOL
�	Path Selection. Selects an entire path in order to move, copy, and so on.
▸	Direct Selection. Selects anchor points or segments for editing.
✐	Pen. The cornerstone of vector drawing tools. Used to draw straight lines with a series of mouse-clicks or to create Bezier curves with a click-and-drag technique.
✐	Freeform Pen. A specially simplified click-and-draw vector tool.
✐	Magnetic Pen. Select from the Options bar with the Freeform Pen tool selected in the Toolbox. The Magnetic Pen tool follows the cursor and reads the edge contrast in the image within a set distance of the cursor.
✐+	Add Anchor Point. Click a path segment to add anchor points.
✐−	Subtract Anchor Point. Click an anchor point to delete it.
⌐	Convert Point. Click or click and drag an anchor point to convert a curve to an angle or to convert an angle to a curve.

Anatomy of a Path

A path can contain multiple path components, which in turn are made up of two elements: anchor points and path segments.

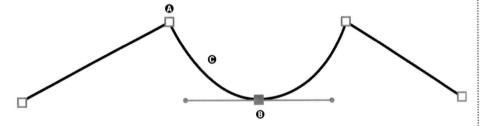

A path component (often referred to simply as a path if there is only one component) is a series of connected path segments making up a vector graphic. This image is a single path component.

Ⓐ **Anchor point**   Defines a corner or a curve in the path. Unselected anchor points appear as empty squares.

Ⓑ **Selected anchor point**   Point ready to be edited. Selected points are filled squares.

Ⓒ **Path segment**   The lines between anchor points that make up the path component.

———

Like the Pen and Freeform Pen tools, the shape tools can be used to create paths and Shape layers. However, you can also use the shape tools to quickly draw rasterized shapes (in Fill Pixels mode) directly into a layer.

———

Using Bezier curves and paths is an excellent way to create selections for smooth curves of necks, arms, and legs.

16.1   Path Basics *(continued)*

Photoshop allows you to create and save Clipping Paths which can be used to knock out the background of flattened images when they are placed in page layout applications. Creating a path outline around an object is the first step in the process. Once you save the Path, you can select the Clipping Path option in the Paths palette menu.

Anchor Point Types

Three types of anchor points determine whether a path segment is straight or curved and how the segments intersect—as a corner, as a curve, or as both.

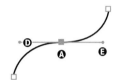

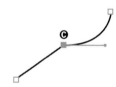

Ⓐ Curve point   A point where the path segments on both sides are curved and the curve on one side flows into (and affects) the curve on the other side.

Ⓑ Corner point   A point where the path segments on both sides are straight.

Ⓒ Dual point   A point where the path segment on one side does not affect the path segment on the other when reshaped. This allows you to have a straight segment on one side and a curved segment on the other or two noncontinuous curved segments.

Ⓓ Direction handle   Used to change the curvature of path segments connected to a curve or dual anchor point. Dragging the direction point toward the anchor point decreases the size of the curvature. Dragging the direction point around the anchor point changes the curve's angle.

Ⓔ Handlebar   Indicates the direction and size of the curve as set by the direction handle.

DRAWING VERSUS PAINTING

Computer graphics come in two basic flavors: bitmap and vector. With bitmap graphics (not to be confused with Photoshop's bitmap mode), images are created by placing small dots of color (pixels) spaced closely together to fool the eye into seeing a continuous image. Vector images, on the other hand, create geometric shapes that are defined mathematically rather than mapping out each point. To distinguish between these two methods of creating images, editing bitmap images is referred to as painting, and editing vector images is referred to as drawing.

Painting is a more versatile way to create a variety of image types, allowing you to apply colors gradually over an area with irregular transitions. However, painted images are locked into their size and resolution, which can only be changed by sacrificing image quality.

Drawing creates more exact images that are resolution independent, allowing you to resize the image without worrying about distortion. However, drawn images have a regularity that makes them impractical for images such as photographs.

16.2   Setting Pen Tool Options

Regardless of the mode you are working in (Shape layer or Path), setting any of the universal vector-tool options is identical. For the Pen tool, however, you can also set options for previewing path segments as you draw them, and you can specify the Auto Add/Delete function. Auto Add/Delete gives you editing choices as you work by displaying alternate tools when you hover the cursor over an anchor or a path segment—allowing you to add or delete anchor points.

To begin using the Pen tool, select it in the Toolbox, and then set its options in the tool options bar. You can then follow the instructions for drawing vector paths (Section 16.5) or for drawing Shape layers (see Section 16.6).

- Check Rubber Band to preview the path segment between the last anchor point and the next anchor point as you draw it. If this option is cleared, the path segment does not appear until you add the next anchor point.

- Check Auto Add/Delete if you want to be able to add new anchor points to an existing path while working. If this option is checked, clicking an existing segment adds a new anchor point to the segment, splitting it into two new segments. If this option is cleared, clicking an existing segment creates a new anchor point over the segment. This is useful if you want to be able to edit the path on the fly, but might get in the way if you need to create tight paths where anchor points are close together.

Universal Photoshop Vector-Tool Options

ICON	NAME	DESCRIPTION
	Shape	Vector mask on a Color Fill layer.
	Path	Paths independent of any layer.
	Pixel Fill	Rasterized version of the shape.
	Add	The new path component is added to the path.
	Subtract	The new path component is subtracted from existing path components.
	Intersect	Path components are created from the intersection of the new path component and existing path components.
	Exclude Overlapping	Paths are created by removing the overlapping areas of the new path component and existing path components.

➡ 3.19 Pen Tools

➡ 16.5 Preparing to Draw Vector Paths

➡ 16.6 Preparing to Draw Shape Layers

Pen tool
P

Cycle pen tools (Pen and Freeform Pen only)
Shift P

The Pen tool is great for creating precise vector paths, especially if you require straight lines.

As you work with the Pen tool, you might find it valuable to try the following modifiers. The Command/Ctrl key will toggle you to the Direct Selection tool, allowing you to edit the Bezier handles or move your anchor points, as you create them. The Command+Option/Ctrl +Alt keys will toggle the Convert Point tool. These tools or modifiers may save you from having to undo as often.

16.3 Setting Freeform Pen and Magnetic Pen Tool Options

Pen tool
[P]

Cycle pen tools (Pen and Freeform Pen only)
[Shift] [P]

The Freeform Pen tool is great for creating vector paths of oddly shaped objects; however, it takes a steady and practiced hand to get the shapes just right.

The Magnetic Pen tool allows you to create paths based on bitmap images. In many ways this is superior to using the Magnetic Lasso tool, since vectors can be used for selections and much more.

If you need to draw objects with more flowing lines, rather than straight or regularly curved lines, the Freeform Pen might provide the options you need. In addition, the Freeform Pen tool includes the Magnetic option, which allows you to closely trace the edges in an image to create a path (much like the Magnetic Lasso tool).

Both the path and shape modes use the same options as the Freeform Pen tool. Magnetic is actually an option of the Freeform Pen tool, not a stand-alone tool itself, but it acts as its own unique tool.

To begin using the Freeform Pen tool, select it in the Toolbox, and then set its options in the tool options bar. You can then follow the instructions for drawing vector paths (see Section 16.5) or for drawing Shape layers (see Section 16.6).

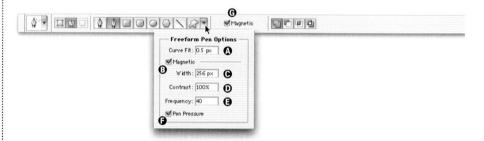

Ⓐ Enter a value (0.5 through 10) to set the error tolerance for fitting curves. A higher value smooths the path you draw; a lower value keeps the path closer to the way you draw it.

Ⓑ Check to use the Magnetic Pen tool (similar to the Magnetic Lasso tool), which creates a path by following the sharp contrast contours of the image in the selected layer.

Ⓒ (With Magnetic only) Enter a value (1 through 256) for the width from the mouse pointer to be considered part of the path. If the image is high contrast, use a wide line to ensure a solid edge. If there are a lot of small shapes, use a larger width.

Ⓓ (With Magnetic only) Enter a value (1 through 100) for the percentage of contrast between edges in the image to be considered for the path. Use a high percentage for high-contrast images to ensure a tighter fit.

Ⓔ (With Magnetic only) Enter a value (5 through 40) for how often anchor points are automatically added along the path. The more points, the tighter the fit but the more jagged the selection may look.

Ⓕ (With Magnetic only) If you are using a tablet, check this if you want to allow pen pressure to set the width value.

Ⓖ Check to turn the Magnetic option on. This option is redundant to the one in the tool's drop-down options panel.

16.4　Setting Shape Tool Options

Each shape tool has different option settings that you must consider when drawing the shape.

To begin using a shape tool, select the desired shape in the Toolbox, and then set its options in the tool options bar. You can then follow the instructions for drawing vector paths (see Section 16.5) or for drawing Shape layers (see Section 16.6).

Rectangle and Rounded Rectangle Tool Options

The settings for the Rectangle and Rounded Rectangle tools are almost identical, except for the ability to set the corner radius for rounded rectangles.

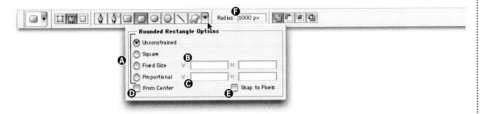

- **Ⓐ** Choose a shape constraint: Unconstrained (freeform rectangle), Square, Fixed Size, or Proportional.
- **Ⓑ** If you chose Fixed Size, enter a value (1 through 30000) in pixels for the width and height of the rectangle.
- **Ⓒ** If you chose Proportional, enter a value (1 through 1000) for the width and height proportions.
- **Ⓓ** Check to draw the shape from the center rather than from the top-left corner.
- **Ⓔ** Check to snap the edges of the shape to the pixel's edges in the image.
- **Ⓕ** (Rounded Rectangle only) Enter a value (0 through 1000) for the corner radius of the rounded rectangle. A value of 0 produces square corners.

Ellipse Tool Options

You use the Ellipse tool to draw circles and elliptical shapes, either in freeform or with precision by setting the exact or relative dimensions of the shape.

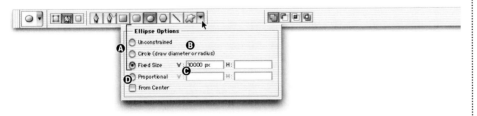

- **Ⓐ** Choose a shape constraint: Unconstrained (freeform ellipse), Circle, Fixed Size, or Proportional.
- **Ⓑ** If you choose Fixed Size, enter a value (1 through 30000) in pixels for the width and height of the ellipse.
- **Ⓒ** If you choose Proportional, enter a value (1 through 1000) for the width and height proportions.
- **Ⓓ** Check to draw the shape from the center rather than from the top-left corner.

➠ 3.2　The Tool Options Bar

➠ 3.17　Path Selection Tools

➠ 3.20　Shape Tools

➠ 4.16　Paths Palette

➠ 5.1　Preset Manager Overview

Shape tool
[U]

Cycle shape tools
[Shift] [U]

———

You can add shapes to the canvas as vector paths or shape layers as discussed in this chapter, and you can also add them as painted shapes as shown in Section 13.8.

———

Custom shapes are managed in the Preset Manager (see Section 5.1).

➠ 13.8 Painting with
          Shapes

➠ 16.5 Preparing to
          Draw Vector
          Paths

You can also edit
the arrowheads after
they have been drawn
using the path and
direct selection tools
(see Sections 16.8
and 16.9).

Polygon Tool Options

You use the Polygon tool to draw multisided shapes with anywhere from 3 to 100 sides. In addition, you can turn these shapes into star patterns in which the interior of the path segments indent.

Ⓐ Enter a value (1 through 15000) for the radius of the polygon.

Ⓑ Check to round off the corners.

Ⓒ Check to indent the polygon sides to create a star shape.

Ⓓ (With Star only) Enter a value (1 through 99) to set the percentage that the sides are indented.

Ⓔ (With Star only) Check to round off the indentions.

Ⓕ Enter a value (3 through 100) to set the number of sides for the polygon.

Line Tool Options

Not only can you quickly draw a line, often referred to as a "rule" in printing, but you can also add arrowheads to each end of a line and adjust the arrowhead shape.

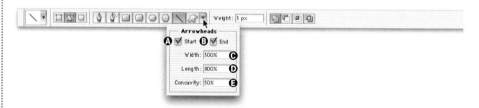

Ⓐ Check if you want an arrowhead at the start of the line.

Ⓑ Check if you want an arrowhead at the end of the line.

Ⓒ Enter a value (10 through 1000) for the width of the arrowheads relative to the weight of the line.

Ⓓ Enter a value (10 through 5000) for the length of the arrowheads relative to the weight of the line.

Ⓔ Enter a value (from –50 through 50) for the concavity of the back of the arrowheads.

   Top, Concavity 50%; bottom, Concavity –50%

16.4 Setting Shape Tool Options *(continued)*

Custom Shape Tool Options

Custom shapes are unique among the Shape tools because you can access and organize them in the Preset Manager dialog like brushes. A variety of shapes are available in several preset custom shape libraries, ranging from animals to cartoon talk bubbles. You can also copy or import vector art work such as logos, signatures, and clip art from a variety of sources and add these shapes to your own custom shapes presets:

You can add paths to the Custom Shape menu by selecting the path to be added and then, clicking the Add to Shape area button 🔲 in the options menu and choosing Edit > Define Custom Shape... Enter a name for the new shape in the dialog , and click OK. The new shape appears in the Shapes drop-down with the Custom Shape tool.

Select a shape and set options as you would for rectangles or elipses:

1 From the Shape drop-down, click a preset shape thumbnail to select a shape. Click the arrow at the top right to access the Preset Shapes menu, or open the Preset Manager dialog to load other preset shape groups or save the current set.

2 From the Custom Shape Options drop-down, choose a constraint: Unconstrained (freeform shape), Defined Proportions (uses the proportions set when the shape was created), Defined Size (uses the size set when the shape was defined), or Fixed Size.

2 If you chose Fixed Size, enter a value (1 through 30000) in pixels for the width and height of the shape.

3 Check to draw the shape from the center rather than from the top-left corner.

➡ 16.6 Preparing to Draw Shape Layers

➡ Color Section Blending Modes

———

Although ImageReady does not include either of the path drawing tools, it does include several of the shape tools, which can be used to add draw layers or painted shapes.

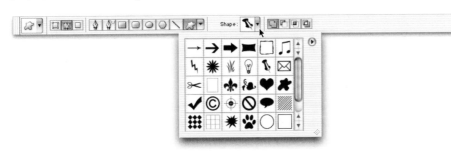

Drawing with a Selected Shape Tool

To use any of the shape tools, follow the steps from section 12.4 to set basic options. If you selected the Pixel Fill or Paths options, you must also select a layer on which you want to work. Whichever options you selected, simply click and drag in your image to draw or apply the shape. Holding the Shift key constrains your proportions. If you selected the Fixed Size option, simply click in the image. As you hold down the mouse button drawing your shape, hold down the spacebar on the keyboard while dragging to reposition the shape as you draw. Release the mouse button when the shape is the desired size.

16.5   Preparing to Draw Vector Paths

Pen tool
[P]

Cycle pen tools
[Shift] [P]

Shape tools
[U]

Cycle shape tools
[Shift] [U]

Vector paths are added to the Paths palette and can be used for a variety of purposes when drawing and painting in the canvas. However, they do not, by themselves, add to the image.

You use the Pen tool to create path components by plotting anchor points in the canvas that can be either straight (corner points) or curved (curved points). (You can also use the shape tools to draw vector paths, as described shortly.) To prepare to draw a vector path, follow these steps:

1 Choose the Pen tool [✒], Freeform Pen tool [✒], or one of the shape tools in the Toolbox; if you want to use the Magnetic Pen tool, choose the Freeform Pen tool and check Magnetic in the tool options bar. You can also select any of these tools and then switch between them in the tool options bar (see Section 3.2).

2 Click the Paths button [▦] in the tool options bar, and select a path in the Paths palette:

  ■ To add a path component to a new path, click the Create New Path button [▣] at the bottom of the palette.

  ■ To add a path component to the work path, either select the work path or, if there is no work path, deselect all paths by Shift-clicking the currently selected path. (When you start to draw, the Work path is automatically added.)

  ■ To add path components to an existing path, select that path.

3 Set the options for your tool in the tool options bar, and choose the overlap mode for the new path component:

ICON	NAME	DESCRIPTION
[▣]	Add	The new path component is added to the path.
[▣]	Subtract	The new path component is subtracted from existing path components.
[▣]	Intersect	Path components are created from the intersection of the new path component and existing path components.
[▣]	Exclude Overlapping	Paths are created by removing the overlapping areas of the new path component and existing path components.

16.6   Preparing to Draw Shape Layers

Using Shape layers is an easy way to add a vector mask with a Fill layer to your image. This allows you to quickly add shaped designs of solid color or styles. Although this uses paths to create shapes, this tool is used to add vector shapes directly to the selected layer in the Layers palette, rather than to the Paths palette. However, the path will show up as a work path in the Paths palette when the layer is selected. When you are adding shapes to a Shape layer, you are in fact adding path components to the layer's vector mask, which is a work path for that layer.

Drawing a Shape layer with a pen tool is similar to drawing vector paths and using the shape tools to draw. To prepare to draw a Shape layer, follow these steps:

1 Choose the Pen tool ⟨⟩ , Freeform Pen tool ⟨⟩ , or one of the shape tools; to use the Magnetic Pen, choose the Freeform Pen tool and check Magnetic in the Options bar.

2 Click Shape Layers ⟨⟩ in the tool options bar, and select a layer in the Layers palette:

- To create a new Shape layer, click the layer you want the Shape layer to appear above. Make sure that Create New Shape Layer ⟨⟩ is selected in the Options bar.

- To add additional shapes to an existing Shape layer's vector mask, select that layer; then, in the tool options bar, choose the overlap mode for the new component:

ICON	NAME	DESCRIPTION
⟨⟩	New	A new Shape layer is created automatically.
⟨⟩	Add	The new shape path component is added to the vector mask of the selected layer.
⟨⟩	Subtract	The new shape path component is subtracted from the vector mask of the selected layer.
⟨⟩	Intersect	The vector mask is created from the intersection of the new shape path component and existing path components in the mask.
⟨⟩	ExcludeOverlapping	The vector mask is created by removing the overlapping areas of the new shape path component and existing masks path components.

3 Set the options for your tool in the tool options bar, then do one of the following:

- If you are adding to an existing vector mask and want to apply a new style to the layer or change that layer's style or color, click the Link button ⟨⟩ so that the button is highlighted (darker). Otherwise, style and color changes made in the tool options bar are applied only to new Shape layers.

- Choose a style for the Fill layer. If you do not want to apply a style, choose Default Style (none) with the red slash.

- Click the color swatch and choose a color for the Fill layer. If a style is used, it covers the color of the Fill layer.

Shape tool
⟨U⟩

Cycle shape tools
⟨Shift⟩ ⟨U⟩

Pen tool
⟨P⟩

Cycle pen tools
⟨Shift⟩ ⟨P⟩

16.7 Drawing with Pen Tools

➡ 3.17 Path Selection Tools

Path Selection tool
[A]

Cycle Path Selection tools
[Shift] [A]

Pen tool
[P]

You can move a shape to adjust its location on the canvas while it is being drawn, by temporarily holding down the spacebar as you drag to draw the shape.

Whether you are drawing a vector path or a Shape layer, the process of drawing with the pen tools is much the same in Photoshop as in any other vector-editing application. Working with the Pen tool can take some practice, yet can be most rewarding once you get the feel for it. After you draw the path, you can always edit it further or use it to create fills, strokes, selections, or vector masks as explained in the rest of this chapter.

Using the Pen Tool

To use the Pen tool, first follow the steps in either Section 16.5 or 16.6. Next, click in the canvas to place your first anchor point; then place the next anchor point by doing one of the following:

Corner point: Click to create the next anchor point. Release the mouse immediately after clicking to make it a corner anchor point. This creates a straight path segment between the current anchor point and the previous anchor point.

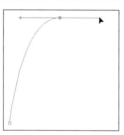

Curved point Click and drag away from the anchor point to add a curved anchor point using Bezier curves. This creates a curved path segment between the current anchor point and the previous anchor point. Direction handles appear as you drag, allowing you to control the shape and direction of the curve as you move the handlebars. When you are satisfied with the curve, release the mouse button. You can edit the curve of the last anchor point added by clicking it and adjusting the handlebars.

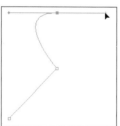

Dual point Option/Alt-click when placing an anchor point to add a dual anchor point. The next segment you create by clicking will be curved independent of the previous segment. This allows you to have a straight-line segment on one side and a curved-line segment on the other or two curved-line segments that can be independently shaped.

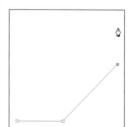

45° straight line Shift-click to add the next anchor point at 45° increments from the previous anchor point.

16.7 Drawing with Pen Tools *(continued)*

If you are using the Pen tool to draw a Shape layer, the style or color you selected in step 3 automatically begins to fill the area defined by the path as you add anchor points. If you are not adding to an existing vector mask, a new Fill layer appears in the Layers palette with a vector mask.

Create as many anchor points as necessary. When you are finished drawing your path, do one of the following:

- To leave the path open, Command/Ctrl-click the canvas or choose any tool. Any fills added to the path will assume a straight-line closure between the first and final anchor points.

- To close the path, click the first anchor point. When your mouse pointer is positioned over the first anchor point, the cursor will show the Pen tool icon with a circle next to it. You can still click and drag to make the final path segment curved.

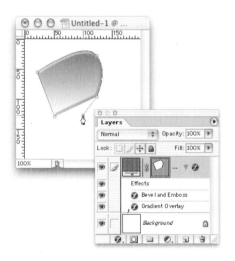

The Pen tool is creating a Shape layer with a style applied.

Using the Freeform Pen Tool

If you are using the Freeform Pen tool *without* the Magnetic option, first follow the steps in either Section 16.5 or 16.6. Then click in the canvas and draw your path without releasing the mouse button. When you are finished drawing your path, do one of the following:

- To leave the path open, release the mouse button. Any fills added to the path will assume a straight-line closure between the first and final anchor points.

- To close the path, click the first anchor point. When your mouse pointer is positioned over the first anchor point, the cursor will show the Freeform Pen tool icon with a circle next to it.

➡ 3.19 Pen Tools

Cycle Pen tools (Pen and Freeform Pen only)
[Shift] [P]

Shape tool
[U]

Cycle Shape tools
[Shift] [U]

Switch from Pen or Freeform Pen to Direct Selection tool (reverts after releasing)
[⌘]
[Ctrl]

———

To create an S curve between two anchor points, use the Add Anchor Point tool to click on the path and drag perpendicular to the path segment.

➡ 4.16 Paths Palette

Switch from Pen or Freeform Pen to Convert Point tool while over an anchor point other than the first or last (reverts after releasing)

Option

Alt

Delete currently selected path or path component

Del

Move path while drawing

Spacebar

Constrain shape proportions while drawing

Shift

———

Use the Paths palette to choose > New Path each time you want to draw a new separate path segment. Only the path segments on the actively selected path in the Paths palette will be visible for editing (unless they are filled or part of a Shape Vector Mask).

———

The more anchor points you include, the larger the file size.

- To close the path with a straight line from the current position to the first anchor point, press Command/Ctrl and release the mouse pointer.

You can use the Freeform Pen tool to draw a variety of shapes.

A freeform path drawn with a style applied.

Using the Magnetic Pen Tool

To use the Freeform Pen tool *with* the Magnetic option, first follow the steps in either Section 16.5 or 16.6. Then, click in the canvas to set the first anchor point in the path. Drag around the edge of the object for which you are attempting to draw a vector path.

A path (a solid line) snaps to the edge of the object as you drag. The settings for Width, Edge Contrast, and Frequency determine the fit of the path. If you notice the path moving away from the object's edge, move back to the point where it started to deviate, click to manually add an anchor point, and then continue your selection.

When you are finished tracing the path, do one of the following:

- To close the path, click the original anchor point. When you place the mouse cursor over the original anchor point, the cursor will change to a Pen icon with a circle next to it.

- To close the path with a magnetic path line drawn between the starting and stopping points (as calculated by Photoshop), Command/Ctrl-click, press Return/Enter, or double-click.

- To close the selection with a straight line directly between the starting and stopping points, Option/Alt-double-click.

The Magnetic Pen tool is being used to trace the outline of the puppy.

16.8 Selecting Paths and Path Components

After you draw a path or Shape layer using any of the drawing tools, it appears in the Paths palette where you can select and edit it.

Selecting Paths

The Paths palette contains three types of paths: paths (also referred to as saved paths), the work path (of which there is only one at a time), and vector mask paths. Work paths and vector mask paths are temporary paths, and their names are always italicized.

- To **select** a path, click the path name in the Paths palette. The selected path is highlighted.

- To **deselect** a path, Shift-click the path name in the Paths palette, press Esc, or click in the empty area beneath all the paths in the Paths palette.

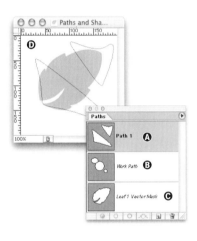

Ⓐ Path Click to select the path. Shift-click to deselect the path. Both shapes in this path are individual path components.

Ⓑ Work Path Click to select the path. Shift-click to deselect the path. Double-click or drag it to the Create A New Path button 🔲 at the bottom of the Paths layer to turn the path into a saved path. The work path is a temporary path used to record paths' components until they are saved.

Ⓒ Vector Mask Path Click to select the path. Shift-click to deselect the path. Double-click or drag it to the Create A New Path button 🔲 to save as a path. A vector mask is a temporary path that appears only if the layer it is in is selected. The name of the layer is part of the path's name.

Ⓓ Selected path Selected paths are highlighted in the Paths palette and appear as an outline in the canvas.

Selecting Path Components

After you select a path in the Paths palette, you can select an individual path component within the path or a path segment within a component. To select paths, choose the Path Selection tool 🔼 , select the path in the Paths palette or the layer with the vector mask in the Layers palette, and then do one of the following:

- To select a path component in the canvas, click anywhere within the path component in the canvas. The anchor points for that path component will appear, letting you know it was selected. If there are multiple path components in the path, only the path component under the mouse pointer is selected.

- To select multiple path components, click and drag over one or more components. All path components within the selection marquee (even if only partially) are selected.

- To add path components to the selection, Shift-click the desired path components.

➡ 3.17 Path Selection Tools

➡ 3.19 Pen Tools

➡ 4.16 Paths Palette

Switch from the Path Selection tool to the Direct Selection tool (reverts after releasing)
⌘
Ctrl

Once selected, paths and path components can be transformed (scaled, rotated, skewed, distorted) just as you would transform layer content, except that the menu option is Transform Path instead of just Transform (see Section 9.11).

16.9   Editing Paths and Path Components

➠   10.11 Aligning and
Distributing
Layers

Switch from the
Path Selection tool
to the Direct Selection
tool (reverts after
releasing)

⌘

Ctrl

———

Once selected, paths
and path components
can be transformed
(scaled, rotated,
skewed, distorted)
as you would transform
layer content, except
the menu option is
Transform Path
instead of Transform
(see Section 9.11).

After you draw a path or Shape layer using any of the drawing tools, it appears in the Paths palette where you can select and edit it.

Changing a Path Component's Overlap Mode

When drawing paths, you specify how the new path component interacts with the path and other components already on the path. You can change the overlap mode of an existing path component using the icons on the tool options bar.

1   Using the Path Selection tool , select one or more path components in the canvas.

2   In the tool options bar, select one of the overlap modes:

ICON	NAME
🗗	Add
🗗	Subtract
▣	Intersect
🗗	Exclude Overlapping

Adjusting Paths and Path Components

You can move path components as a group by selecting the path they are on, or you can move them individually by selecting one or more path components. In addition, you can align path components, you can combine them into a single path component, and you can delete a single path component or an entire path.

■   To move a path, select it in the Paths palette, choose the Move tool ⊹, and then click and drag within the canvas, moving the path to the desired location.

■   To move path components, select one or more path components in the canvas, choose the Path Selection tool ▶ or the Move tool ⊹, and then click and drag within any of the selected path components, moving them about on the canvas to the desired location.

■   To combine path components, select two or more path components in the canvas (they must be in the same path), and use the Path Selection tool ▶. Click the Combine button in the tool options bar. The selected path components merge (based on their overlap mode) into a single path component.

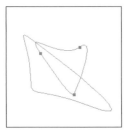 

16.9   Editing Paths and Path Components *(continued)*

- To align and distribute path components, use the Path Selection tool �N, and select two or more path components to align or three or more path components to distribute. Click one of the alignment or distribution options in the tool options bar.

- To delete a path, select the path in the Paths palette and click the trashcan icon 🗑, drag the path to the trashcan icon, or choose Delete Path from the Paths palette menu.

- To delete a path component, select the path component and press Delete. If this is the last path component in a vector mask, you will be asked whether you want to delete the entire layer, delete only the mask and retain the layer's content, or delete only the contents of the layer and retain the vector mask.

Transform Path and Free Transform Path

All Transform commands and pseudotools are available for altering paths and shapes by following these steps:

1 Select a path or shape to transform.

2 Choose Edit > Free Transform Path or Edit > Transform Path and then one of the options in the submenu. You can interchange submenu options while making transformations, by choosing Edit > Transform or by using the contextual menu.

Again Repeats the previous transformation.

Scale Uses the Scale pseudotool. Click and drag an edge of the bounding box to resize. Click corner points of the bounding box to resize both horizontally and vertically at the same time. Press Option/Alt to scale symmetrically.

Rotate Uses the Rotate pseudotool. Click and drag just outside the edges of the bounding box to freely rotate the selection.

Skew Uses the Skew pseudotool. Drag an edge of the bounding box up or down to skew. Press Option/Alt to skew symmetrically.

Distort Uses the Distort pseudotool. Drag edges or corner points of the bounding box. Press Option/Alt to distort symmetrically.

Perspective Uses the Perspective pseudotool. Click and drag an edge or a corner point to change the perspective.

Rotate 180°, 90° CW, or 90° CCW Turns the entire selected region.

Flip Horizontal Or Vertical Reverses the area in the indicated direction.

3 Click the Commit button ✔ or the Cancel button ⊘ .

➡ 16.10 Editing Path Segments

——

If you are moving a curved segment, hold down the Shift key to constrain the movements to 45° multiples.

——

Hold down Option/Alt and move the path component to duplicate it in the mask.

16.10 Editing Path Segments

➡ 3.17 Path Selec-
tion Tools

➡ 3.19 Pen Tools

**Switch from the
Path Selection tool to
the Direct Selection
tool (reverts after
releasing)**

⌘

Ctrl

———

You can click and drag
in the image with the
Direct Path Selection
tool to select multiple
path segments or
anchor points.

———

Remember that styles
can be applied and
changed for the Fill
layer.

To change the shape of a path component, you must edit the path segments or the anchor points used to define the path segments. First, you select the anchor point or path segment to be edited, and then you can adjust or reshape the segments as desired.

Selecting Anchor Points and Path Segments

First, choose the Direct Path Selection tool ▶, and then do one of the following:

- To select an anchor point, click it to display the point's direction handles. Shift-click additional anchor points to include them in the selection.

- To select a path segment, click it.

- To select multiple path segments, click outside the path component and drag over the path. All anchor points within the selection marquee are selected, even those between path components. You can also Shift-click each anchor point individually.

- To select all anchor points within a path component, Option/Alt-click within the path component. To add path components to the selection, Shift-Option-click/Shift-Alt-click within other path components in the same path.

Moving and Deleting Path Segments

First choose the Direct Path Selection tool ▶, and then do one of the following:

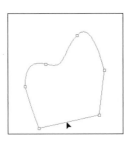

- To move a straight path segment, click and drag the path segment to the desired position. You can also select multiple path segments, even those between path components, and move them together.

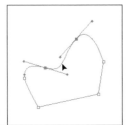

- To move a curved path segment, select the path segment by clicking the anchor points on either side, and then move the segment as desired. The curve does not change shape as it moves, but the segments on either side of it change shape to adjust.

16.10 Editing Path Segments *(continued)*

■ To delete a segment, select the path segment and press Delete/Backspace. The segment is removed, leaving a blank space between the two anchor points. Pressing Delete/Backspace again deletes the entire path component.

➠ 4.16 Paths Palette

If you have the Pen tool selected and have the Auto Add/Delete option checked in the tool options bar, any time you place the Pen tool over a line segment of a selected path component, it will automatically switch to the Add Anchor Point tool. Likewise, when you are over an anchor point, the Pen tool will switch to the Delete Anchor Point tool.

Adding and Deleting Anchor Points

You can add or delete anchor points from a path component to change the shape of the component or to simplify the shape.

■ To add an anchor point to a path segment, choose the Add Anchor Point tool , and click the position in the path segment where you want to add the new anchor point. You can click and move to immediately adjust the curvature of the path segments around the new anchor point.

Hold down Option/Alt and move the path component with the Move tool to duplicate it in the mask.

■ To delete an anchor point without erasing the line segment, choose the Delete Anchor Point tool, click the path component to select it, and then click the anchor point you want to remove. If you want to reshape the curve while removing the anchor point, click the anchor point and then drag the path.

■ To convert a curve into a corner point, choose the Point tool, click the path component to select it, and click a curved anchor point. This will now be a corner anchor point.

■ To convert a corner into a curved point, choose the Point tool, click the path component to select it, click a corner anchor point, and drag out to adjust the curve using the direction handle. This will now be a curved anchor point.

■ To create a corner point with curves, choose the Point tool, click the path component to select it, and then click and adjust the direction points on one side of a curved anchor point. You can now adjust the curves on either side of the anchor point independently.

16.11 Reshaping Curves

➟ 3.17 Path Selection Tools

➟ 4.16 Paths Palette

Switch from the Direct Selection tool to the Path Selection tool (reverts after releasing)

⌘

Ctrl

The Add Anchor, Delete Anchor, and Convert Point tools will be the Direct Selection tool until they are over a path segment or an anchor point.

You create curves initially by clicking and dragging while adding an anchor point with the Pen tool, by using the Freeform Pen tool to draw curved shapes, or by using part of a predefined custom shape. After you add a curve to a path, you can reshape the curve in a variety of ways to get the desired affect.

To reshape a curve, first choose the Direct Path Selection tool, and then do one of the following:

- Click a curved path segment and move the cursor. As you move the cursor, the curve changes its shape, adjusting both anchor points.
- Click a curved path segment and adjust the direction handles of the anchor points on either side. This allows you to adjust the curvature of both anchor points independently.
- Click an anchor point connected to a curved path segment, and use the direction handles to reshape the curves in segments on both sides of the anchor point.

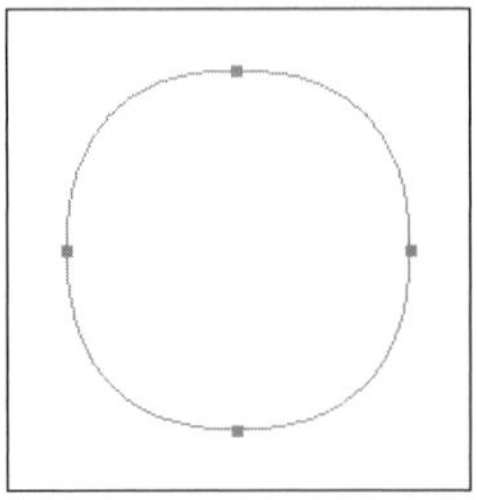

The original curve

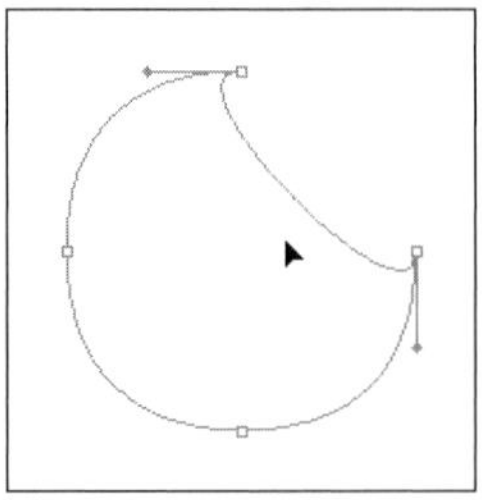

Moving the path segment directly adjusts the entire curve, but leaves curves on either side unchanged.

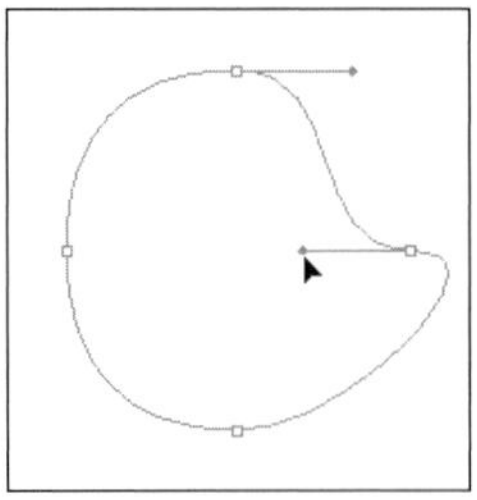

Selecting the curve and then adjusting the direction handles allows you to change the curvature at the anchor points for curves on both sides.

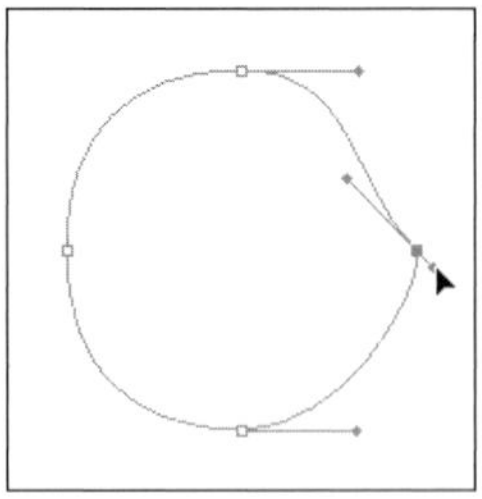

Selecting a single anchor point allows you to reshape curves on both sides of that anchor point.

16.12   Managing Paths

You manage paths using the Paths palette. You can create new blank paths, convert temporary paths into saved paths, duplicate paths and path components, and set options for the paths.

Creating a New Path

In the Paths palette, do one of the following:

- To create a new path in the Paths palette, click the New Path button ⬛ .

- To create a new path using the New Path dialog, choose New Path from the Paths palette menu, or Option/Alt-click the New Path button ⬛ . Enter the name for the new path and click OK.

- To convert a vector mask path or work path into a path, double-click its name. In the dialog, enter a new name for the path. The new path appears in the palette. Changes to this path do not affect the vector mask path.

Duplicating a Path or Path Component

To duplicate a path component, choose the Path Selection tool �▶ from the Toolbox, and Option/Alt-click inside the path component and drag. The original path remains, but the duplicate moves with the mouse.

To duplicate a path, drag the path to the New Path button ⬛ at the bottom of the Paths palette.

To duplicate a path using the Duplicate Paths dialog, select the path in the Paths palette, choose Duplicate Path… from the Paths palette menu, enter a name for the new path, and click OK.

Setting Path Options

To rename a path, double-click the path name in the Paths palette, type the new name, and press Enter/Return.

To change the stacking order of a path, click and drag the path up or down within the Paths palette until a heavy black line appears in the location where you want the path, and then release the mouse button. You cannot move vector mask paths or the work path.

➡ 3.17 Path Selection Tools

➡ 4.16 Paths Palette

If you need to see more detail in the channel's thumbnail, use the Channel palette options to set the size to Medium or Large.

If you have a hard time seeing the paths in the Paths palette, set the thumbnail size by choosing Palette Options… in the Paths palette menu and then choosing a new size.

16.13 Converting between Paths and Selections

Turn path into selection

⌘-click path thumbnail

Ctrl-click path thumbnail

———

Although you can convert from selections to paths and back again, there will always be some distortion in the process even with the tolerance set low, and you will never get exactly the same selection or path when converting back and forth.

Paths and selections are easily interchangeable. Consequently, you can use the Pen tool to define an area and then quickly change it into a selection or take a selection and convert it into a vector path, turning a bitmap image into a resolution-independent vector image.

Converting a Path into a Selection

To convert a path into a selection, follow these steps:

1 Select the path in the Paths palette.

2 Do one of the following:

■ To convert the path directly to a selection, click the Load Path As Selection button ⬚ at the bottom of the Paths palette.

■ To convert the path to a selection using the Make Selection dialog, Option/Alt-click the Load Path As Selection button ⬚ at the bottom of the Paths palette, or choose Make Selection in the Paths palette menu.

3 If you chose to convert using the Make Selection dialog, specify the selection options and then click OK.

Ⓐ Enter a value (0 through 250) for the Feather Radius to set the softness of the edges of the selection.

Ⓑ Check to use anti-aliasing to smooth the edges of the selection. If checked, set Feather Radius to 0.

Ⓒ Choose how the selection should be added to existing selections in the layer. If there are no other selections in the layer, only New Selection is available.

Converting a Selection into a Path

To convert a selection into a path, follow these steps:

1 Make a selection in the canvas (see Chapter 9).

2 Do one of the following:

■ To convert the selection directly into a path, click the Create new path button ▣ at the bottom of the Paths palette.

■ To convert the selection to a path using the New Path or Make Work Path dialogs, Option/Alt-click the Create New Path button ▣, or choose Make Work Path from the Paths palette menu.

3 If you chose to convert using the Make Work Path dialog, enter a value (0.5 through 10) for the tolerance used to create the path. A higher tolerance smooths the edges of the selection when making the path.

The new work path appears at the bottom of the Paths palette, replacing the previous work path.

16.14 Stroking and Filling Paths

You can also use paths to add bitmap elements to a layer. A *stroke* is line that follows the path outline; a fill simply fills the area of the path with a particular color or pattern. You can use paths to precision-guide brush strokes, particularly useful for smudging and dragging fine lines. You can perform both stroke and fill actions with the click of single palette button, or you can use a special dialog to set options.

➡ 3.17 Path Selection Tools

➡ 4.16 Paths Palette

If the Stroke Path option is grayed out or does not appear to function, try saving the path first and make sure you are not on a Shape layer.

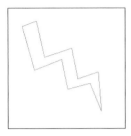

The original path

The path has been stroked with a solid black line and simulated pressure.

The path has been filled with a stone pattern.

To use a path to add a stroke or a fill to a layer, select the path or path component you want to use, select the layer you will be working in, and then do one of the following.

- To fill the path with the foreground color, click the Fill Path button ⬤ at the bottom of the Paths palette.

- To stroke a path using existing settings in the Stroke Path dialog and the current foreground/background colors as applicable, first select the tool or brush tip you want to use, and and then simply click the Stroke Path button ◯ at the bottom of the Paths palette.

WHAT ARE BEZIER CURVES?

Vector lines that use handlebars to modify their shape are referred to as Bezier curves, named after the programmer Pierre Bézier, who developed them for use in computer-aided design (CAD) programs. For more details about the mathematics behind the design, visit www.moshplant.com/direct-or/bezier/.

PHOTOSHOP WORKSPACE

UNIVERSAL TASKS

PHOTO AND VIDEO TASKS

PRINT TASKS

WEB TASKS

16.14   Stroking and Filling Paths

➡ Color Section
    Blending
    Modes

_____

The stroke and the fill are rasterized (that is, painted) rather than vector, so you edit them with painting tools.

- To fill a path using the Fill Path dialog, choose Fill Path... from the Paths palette menu. Specify your options in the dialog and click OK. The filled area now appears on the selected layer.

- To stroke a path using the Stroke Path dialog, first select the tool or brush tip you want to use along with foreground and background colors as applicable, and then choose Stroke Path... from the Paths palette. Specify your options in the dialog and click OK. The stroked area now appears on the selected layer.

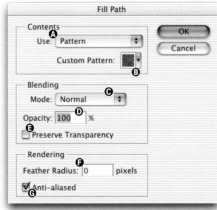

Ⓐ Choose the color to be used: Foreground Color, Background Color, Pattern, History (using the selected History state), Black, 50% Gray, or White.

Ⓑ If you selected Pattern (see A), choose the pattern to be used for the stroke.

Ⓒ Choose a blending mode to be used with the fill.

Ⓓ Enter a value (1 through 100) for the opacity of the layer.

Ⓔ Check to keep the current transparency of the selected layer.

Ⓕ Enter a value (0 through 250) for the Feather Radius to set the softness of the edges of the selection.

Ⓖ Check to use anti-aliasing to smooth the edges of the selection. If checked, set Feather Radius to 0.

Choose a tool type from the Tool drop-down to be used when creating the stroke. The current settings for that tool are used to create the stroke with the current foreground color. Check the Simulate Pressure check box to vary the width of the stroke.

CHAPTER **17**

PHOTOSHOP WORKSPACE

UNIVERSAL TASKS

PHOTO AND VIDEO TASKS

PRINT TASKS

WEB TASKS

Typography

WHAT YOU SAY IS not always as important as how you say it. With the written word, *text* refers to the actual words (what you are saying), and *typography* refers to the way in which those words are presented (how you are saying it). There is no such thing as text without typography, and the term *type* is generally used to refer to formatted text. Even if you use the plainest, simplest fonts, you are still speaking through the presentation of the text. With that said of formal typography, you might also keep in mind that type can also be used simply as a creative design element within artistic images in which the meaning of the text may be more subtle and obscured.

In this chapter, you will learn how to add and edit text to an image and how to use the tools in Photoshop to turn plain text into formatted type.

- 17.1 **Type basics**
- 17.2 **Adding text to images**
- 17.3 **Formatting characters**
- 17.4 **Formatting paragraphs**
- 17.5 **Editing type**
- 17.6 **Warping type**
- 17.7 **Converting type to other formats**
- 17.8 **Spell-checking and searching text**
- 17.9 **Creating text on a path**

17.1 Type Basics

➡ 3.18 Type Tools

Type tool
⊞ T

Cycle type tools
⊞ Shift ⊞ T

———

The fonts that Photoshop has at its disposal depend on the fonts installed on your computer. If you need to add a font to Photoshop, first add it to the fonts of your operating system and then restart Photoshop.

———

When Photoshop starts up, it loads all currently available fonts on your system. If you have a lot of fonts, startup can take a while. Programs such as Extensis Suitcase (www.extensis.com/fontman/) can help you manage your fonts more efficiently.

———

If you know the name of the font you want to use, you can type it directly in the Font Name field. As you type, Photoshop tries to match the font name.

Type is structured, and an individual character can be broken down and described by component parts to better understand how letters are displayed and interact with one another. Although you can simply pour text into a Photoshop image, giving no thought to the typography, this rarely leads to pleasing results. This chapter doesn't try to provide a complete introduction to the topic of text and type, but you need to know a few terms to better format your text in Photoshop to communicate effectively.

A *font* or, in Photoshop, *font family* is a complete set of characters in a particular design, usually including uppercase and lowercase letter, numerals, punctuation, and perhaps some symbols.

Many fonts also contain several *styles*—variations that make the text **bolder**, lighter, or *italic* or in other ways change the form of characters. These styles are actually independent versions of the font that the font maker created.

In word-processing programs, you can usually boldface or italicize any font regardless of whether that style was created for the font; such on-the-fly changes are called "faux styles." The Character palette provides Faux Bold or Faux Italic styles for fonts without available styles, but these options are not recommended, as they will not be transferred to PostScript print processing.

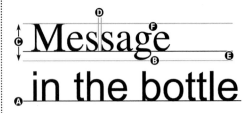

Ⓐ Baseline The imaginary line connecting the lowest point of all capital letters.

Ⓑ Descender The part of a letter that extends below the baseline.

Ⓒ Type size The distance from the highest point of the capital letters to the lowest point of letters that have descenders.

Ⓓ Tracking/kerning Adjustments to the amount of space between letters. Tracking refers to the general change in spacing on both sides of one or more letters. Kerning refers to the adjustment of space between two specific letters. For example, if two letters in your text are too crowded, you can increase the kerning. If letters are generally too far apart, decrease the tracking.

Ⓔ Leading The distance from one baseline to the next.

Ⓕ Serif A small ornamentation on a character. Fonts without serifs, such as in the second line here, are called *sans serif.*

17.1 Type Basics *(continued)*

Type Size

Type size is the measure from the top of the ascenders to the bottom of the descenders. For the most part, fonts are measured in *points* (abbreviated pt), and that is the default for Photoshop. You can enter font values in several other measurement systems (enter the value and then the unit abbreviation), and Photoshop translates this measurement into point size. The alternative units are centimeters (cm), inches (in), millimeters (mm), picas (pica), and pixels (px).

Easy Typographic Options

Although the rest of this chapter introduces the technical aspects of typography along with Photoshop's sophisticated controls, you also have easy access to type tool controls via the Options bar. Simply select the Type tool T from the Toolbox, insert your cursor in an image, and type on the keyboard. Click the Commit button ✔ to commit the edit.

Reinsert the cursor in the type to select a character, or double-click the Type layer thumbnail in the Layers palette to select all the type in a layer. With the type selected, you can change the font, font size, justification, color, and so on in the Options bar.

Selected text will be highlighted with a "reversed color" as in the *p* character. Choose View > Extras to hide or toggle the selection highlighting on and off to aid in choosing colors or previewing fonts, without the distraction of the reverse color. You can also easily cycle font choices as they are displayed visually in the image by inserting your cursor in the font family selector in the Options bar and using the keyboard arrow keys.

Choose Edit > Free Transform to resize type that has been committed. You can visually stretch type or pull handles of the transform pseudotools to resize type, rather than entering numerical values for font size in the type dialog or options bar. When type has been transformed to desired proportions, click the Commit button ✔ to commit the transformation.

➡ 4.6   Character Palette

Toggle Extras (highlighting)
⌘ Ⓗ

―――

Using Faux Italic does not truly italicize your type. Instead, it simply slants the text, making it oblique. This is OK for some purposes, but tends to reduce readability.

―――

Photoshop measures type size in points, using the PostScript value in which one point is equal to 1/72 of an inch in a 72 ppi image (ppi is an abbreviation for pixels per inch). You can switch between using the PostScript and the traditional point size definition in the Units & Rulers section of the Preferences dialog.

➠ 4.15 Paragraph
     Palette

➠ 9.11 Transforming
     Layer Content

Ctrl H

Free Transform
⌘ T

Ctrl T

――――

Which anti-aliasing method you choose depends on the font and type size you are using.

――――

Type designers use the term *font* to refer to the set of characters in a specific size and the term *font face* or just *face* to refer to the collection of all sizes; to a designer, Helvetica is a face and Helvetica 12 is a font. We'll use the Photoshop definition: Helvetica is a font or font family.

――――

Resolution is especially important if you are creating graphics to be displayed on television or the Web. Anti-aliasing generally creates a much more professional and readable text, especially at text sizes over 12pt.

――――

Anti-aliasing may increase the number of colors in your web graphics and limit your ability to reduce file sizes.

――――

Alignment

Alignment defines how text is positioned horizontally within a line of a paragraph if there is surplus space in the line. You can align text in the following ways:

Ragged (Left, Center, or Right) The alignment of the visual reference is defined left, center, or right—with a ragged edge on the outside edge(s) as in the paragraphs on this page.

Justified (Left, Right, Centered, Full) Extra spaces are placed in the lines so that both the left and right sides of the paragraph are flush (justified). Justification can, however, create some unattractive large spaces within lines. The Left, Right, Centered, and Full options determine how the final line of text in the justified paragraph is treated.

Anti-Aliasing

To produce crisp edges in print, type is generally represented by mathematically defined lines and curves using PostScript information. As type is rasterized for bitmap graphics or viewing onscreen, edges may appear rough or jagged without anti-aliasing, which smoothes the edges of letters by adding semitransparent pixels at their edges. Photoshop allows you to choose from the following five anti-aliasing options:

The original letter with no anti-aliasing

None: No anti-aliasing is used. Letterform edges appear jagged.

Sharp: Produces darker heavy type with slight anti-aliasing. Best for large sans serif fonts.

Crisp: Produces lighter type with slight anti-aliasing. Best for small sans serif fonts.

Strong: Produces heavy type with heavy anti-aliasing. Best for small serif fonts.

Smooth: Produces lighter type with heavy anti-aliasing. Best for large serif fonts.

17.2 Adding Text to Images

By and large, you add text to a Photoshop image using the Type tool—of course you could draw or paint text into the image—which creates vector-based text on an independent layer called a Type layer. You can add text as a Type layer using two modes:

Paragraph Adjusts the flow of letters over the entire Text layer. If a Type layer is in Paragraph mode, you can resize the text box. See Section 17.5 for a diagram of the text box.

Point Adjusts the flow of each line independently of other lines in the Text layer by placing a carriage return at the end of each line. If a Type layer is in Point mode, you cannot resize the text box.

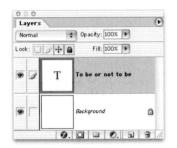

The Type layer is added to the Layers palette automatically. It uses a *T* for the thumbnail and uses the first few words in the text as the layer title.

To add type that you can edit to an image, follow these steps.

1 Choose the Type tool **T** or the Vertical Type tool **IT** from the Toolbox, and then in the Layers palette select the layer above which you want the new text to appear.

2 Set the options for the tool in the tool options bar. You can set additional options for the type in the Character and Paragraph palettes.

   ■ Click the Orientation button in the tool options bar to switch between horizontal and vertical, which is the same as switching between the Type and Vertical Type tools. Clicking this button changes the text orientation for the entire Type layer.

   ■ Choose a font from the Font list.

   ■ If available, choose a style for the font.

   ■ Enter a point value (0.08 through 1085.69) for the font size. You can also directly select from a list of font sizes ranging from 6pt to 72pt.

   ■ Choose an anti-aliasing level for the text (see Section 17.1). You can also select the anti-aliasing level by choosing Layers > Type.

   ■ Choose justification: left, center, or right. Additional justifications are available in the Paragraph palette.

   ■ Click the color square to set the color of the text.

   ■ If you want to warp the text, click the Create Warped Text button and use the Warped Text dialog.

➡ 3.18 Type Tools

➡ 4.6 Character Palette

➡ 4.15 Paragraph Palette

➡ 9.11 Transforming Layer Content

Type tool
T

———

While you are typing text in a Type layer, you can change any option in the tool options bar or the Character and Paragraph palettes. Changes affect only text typed after the changes are made, if you have not first selected text (see Section 17.5).

———

After you click in the canvas with the Type tool, you cannot start or edit another Type layer until you either commit or cancel the current Type layer.

———

With vertical type, individual letters still maintain a horizontal orientation, but the letters are stacked on top of each other. To actually turn the text horizontally, you use the Rotate Text option in the Character palette or the transform pseudotool (see Section 9.11).

PHOTOSHOP WORKSPACE

UNIVERSAL TASKS

PHOTO AND VIDEO TASKS

PRINT TASKS

WEB TASKS

Cycle type tools
[Shift] [T]

You can change the name of the selected layer by choosing Layer Properties in the Layers palette menu and entering a new name. This name remains with the Type layer regardless of changes made to the layer.

Warning: You cannot use the keyboard shortcuts to access tools while you are typing in a Type layer.

3 To begin typing, place the mouse cursor over the canvas in the top-left corner of where you want to begin, and do one of the following. Regardless of which method you choose, a new Type layer is inserted immediately above the selected layer.

- Click and begin typing (Point mode). You can type across the entire width of the canvas and beyond, but text that runs off the canvas will not be visible unless you resize the canvas.

- Click and drag to insert a text box, which defines the maximum width and height that the text can occupy in the canvas, and then begin typing (Paragraph mode). A line break is inserted between words that exceed the width of the text box, and text that exceeds the height of the box is not visible until you resize the text box. To resize the text box, click one of the four sides or corners and drag.

4 If you want, you can also copy and paste text from other sources (either inside or outside Photoshop). Copy the text from the original source, and then choose Edit **>** Paste.

5 When you are finished typing, do one of the following;

- To **commit** the text changes, click the Commit button ✔ . You can also commit the changes by choosing another tool, layer, channel, or path in the Toolbox or a palette.

- To **cancel** the text changes, press Esc or click the Cancel button ⃠ . If this Type layer is new, the layer is also deleted.

Converting between Text Editing Modes

To convert between Paragraph and Point modes, select the Type layer to convert, and then choose Layer **>** Type **>** Convert To Paragraph Text or Convert To Point Text depending on the current mode. This gives you the freedom to switch modes if you decide you need the advantages of one over the other.

CREATING A TYPE MASK

You can also type to create quick masks (see Section 9.4) using the Horizontal Type Mask and Vertical Type Mask tools. Select one of the tools and follow the directions for creating a Text layer. However, rather than creating a Type layer, the text you type is used to create a selection in the active layer.

17.3 Formatting Characters

The Character palette provides additional options for formatting individual characters in the text. In addition to setting the font, font style, type size, and anti-aliasing (see Section 17.1), you can set the following options (and others that are self-evident from their names):

➠ 4.6 Character Palette

➠ 12.4 Selecting Colors with the Color Picker

If the font you are using does not have a bold or an italic style, you can use Faux Bold or Faux Italic. Keep in mind, however, that these are not typographically correct and will not look nearly as good as a true bold or italic version of the font.

Ⓐ Leading   Leading controls the vertical spacing between two lines of text in a paragraph. If you set this value to Auto, Photoshop calculates leading based on the current type size. If you override this setting, using a leading value larger than the current font size adds space between lines; using a smaller leading value squeezes lines together. Leading is applied only to selected lines of text in a paragraph.

Ⓑ Tracking and Kerning   Both tracking and kerning control the space between letters in text. You can use tracking when one or more letters of text are selected, and you can apply kerning only when the insertion point is between two characters (no selection) to change the space between those two individual letters.

Ⓒ Vertical and Horizontal Scaling   You can stretch characters either horizontally or vertically from their natural state. Values below 100% compress the horizontal or vertical scale of the characters. Values above 100% stretch the horizontal or vertical scale of the characters.

Ⓓ Baseline Shift   Allows you to adjust the position of the text up or down from the baseline without changing the type size.

Ⓔ Color   Click the color square to select the color for the text using the Color Picker.

Typography is not only a technology but is in itself a natural resource or staple, like cotton or timber or radio; and, like any staple, it shapes not only private sense ratios but also patterns of communal interdependence.
Marshall McLuhan

Typography is not only a technology but

is in itself a natural resource or staple,

like cotton or timber or radio; and, like

any staple, it shapes not only private

sense ratios but also patterns of

communal interdependence.

Marshall McLuhan

Leading: left Auto, right 20pt. (Font size is set to 10pt.)

To be or not to be

To be or not to be

To be or not to be

Tracking: top 0, middle –75, bottom 75

Horizontal Scale: left 100%, center 50%, right 150%

Vertical Scale: left 100%, center 50%, right 150%

Typography

Base Line Shift: The *T* is using 8pt. The final *Y* is using –8pt.

Faux Bold	SuperScript^2
Faux Italic	Subscript$_2$
ALL CAPS	<u>Underline</u>
SMALL CAPS	~~Strikthrough~~

Other character styles

In addition to many of the character options also accessible in the main palette, the Character palette menu gives you access to the following options:

Rotate Character With the Type layer using the horizontal orientation, choose this option to turn the letters so that the text is sideways rather than stacked (or vice versa).

Change Text Orientation Choose to change the text orientation for the Type layer between horizontal and vertical. Selecting this option is the same as clicking the Orientation button ⬚ in the tool options bar.

Ligatures, Discretionary Ligatures, or Old Style Choose if you need to use ligatures and old-style typographic numerals available in some font sets.

Fractional Widths Choose to allow the Type layer to use a fraction of a pixel width for type spacing. This option is generally preferable for print images. Turning it off, though, might improve readability for images used for the television or computer screens.

System Layout Choose to preview the selected text using your operating system's default text-handling method, which is useful when you are designing user interfaces.

No Break Choose to prevent words from breaking at the ends of lines for the selected words in the Type layer.

Reset Characters Resets the text appearance to default character values.

17.4 Formatting Paragraphs

You use the Paragraph palette to set formatting options for paragraphs of text. Besides alignment (see Section 17.1), you can set the following options for selected paragraphs:

Ⓐ Left and Right Margin Indent Set how far in the edges of the paragraph should be from the default state.

Ⓑ Indent First Line This indent affects only the first line of a paragraph and is a standard way to indicate a new paragraph.

Ⓒ Space Before and After Paragraph Lets you add space before and after a paragraph of text. Extra space is another way to indicate paragraph breaks.

Ⓓ Hyphenation To make text flow more smoothly from line to line in a paragraph, you can hyphenate words at line breaks, indicating that the word continues on the next line. This works best with justified text.

> She drew her foot as far down the chimney as she could, and waited till she heard a little animal (she couldn't guess of what sort it was) scratch-Ⓔ ing and scrambling about in the chimney close above her: then, saying to herself 'This is Bill,' she gave one sharp kick, and waited to see what would happen next.
>
> ——————————Ⓓ——————————
>
> Ⓐ The first thing she heard was a general chorus of 'There goes Bill!' then the Rabbit's voice along—'Catch him, you by the hedge!' then silence, and then another confusion of voices—'Hold up his Ⓑ head--Brandy now—Don't choke him—How was it, old fellow? What happened to you? Tell us all about it!'
>
> Ⓒ Last came a little feeble, squeaking voice, ('That's Bill,' thought Alice,) 'Well, I hardly know—No more, thank ye; I'm better now—but I'm a deal too flustered to tell you—all I know is, something comes at me like a Jack-in-the-box, and up I goes like a sky-rocket!'

Ⓐ The paragraph's left margin is indented 8pt.

Ⓑ The paragraph's right margin is indented 16pt. Since this text is left justified, though, the margin sets the maximum indent.

Ⓒ The paragraph's first line is indented 16pt.

Ⓓ Four points of space is added above and below each paragraph.

Ⓔ Text is hyphenated.

17.4   Formatting Paragraphs *(continued)*

➡ 4.15 Paragraph
    Palette

Type tool
⊤

Cycle type tools
Shift ⊤

———

Although the effect of scaling the text is similar to that of changing the horizontal and vertical scale, they are not the same, and one does not change the values of the other.

In addition to the many paragraph styles, the Paragraph palette menu also gives you access to the following options:

Roman Hanging Punctuation   Choose if you want punctuation marks, such as quotes, that fall at the beginning or the end of a line of text displayed outside the text box.

> "We must burn the house down!" said the Rabbit's voice; and Alice called out as loud as she could, "If you do. I'll set Dinah at you!"

Roman Hanging Punctuation: the opening quotation mark is outside the text margin.

Advanced Justification and Hyphenation   Choose to open dialogs in which you exactly control the justification and hyphenation used in the Type layer. Unless you are well practiced in the art of typography, leave these options at their default values.

Adobe Single-Line Composer and Adobe Every-Line Composer   Choose to set how word breaks in a paragraph should be evaluated in order to minimize hyphenation. The Every-Line Composer is a little slower but generally produces far superior results.

Reset Paragraph   Resets the paragraph appearance to default paragraph values.

MISSING FONTS

If you attempt to load an image that uses fonts that are not installed on your computer, Photoshop alerts you that one or more fonts are missing in an Alert dialog that lists all the missing fonts. If you click OK, Photoshop replaces the missing fonts, and Type layers with substituted fonts include a Warning icon in the layer's thumbnail.

17.5 Editing Type

After you add type to an image, you can edit or add to that type in a variety of ways. Because the text is vector, rather than bitmap, you have great flexibility for formatting and editing the text and controlling the typographic appearance. In addition, text is resolution independent and can be transformed and resized without loss of image quality. However, you cannot paint on Type layers or apply filters to them until they are rasterized. After a Type layer is rasterized, however, you can no longer edit it using the Type tool, and it is subject to the same constraints as all other bitmap components in your image.

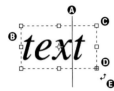

Ⓐ Insertion cursor Indicates where added text is inserted.

Ⓑ Text box A special bounding box that indicates the area in which text using Paragraph mode is displayed.

Ⓒ Resize handles Click and drag any of these squares to resize the text box area and change the layout of the text.

Ⓓ Additional text A plus sign in the bottom-right corner resize handle indicates that additional text in the text box is not being displayed. Resize the text box to display the hidden text.

Ⓔ Limited transform The text box has a limited number of transform functions: resize and rotate. Press Shift to rotate in 45° increments.

Selecting and Changing Type

You can directly edit text—a single character, word, or paragraph—by selecting the text to edit in the canvas and then using the tool options bar, the Character palette, or the Paragraph palette. To select and change type in an existing Type layer, follow these steps:

1 Choose the Type tool [T] or the Vertical Type tool [IT] from the Toolbox, and then select the Type layer you want to edit in the Layers palette. Which tool you choose does not actually matter since the Type layer's orientation determines the orientation you are editing.

2 To select text to change, do one of the following:

- To place the insertion point at a particular place in the text, click in the canvas where you want to add new text and begin typing or paste text that is in memory.

- To select specific text in the Type layer, click in the text and drag across and down.

- To select a single word, double-click the word.

- To select an entire line of text, triple-click in the line.

- To select an entire paragraph, quadruple-click in the paragraph.

- To select all the text in the Type layer, quintuple-click in the Type layer or double-click the Type layer's thumbnail in the Layers palette.

➡ 9.11 Transforming Layer Content

➡ 9.13 Copying or Cutting Selected Content

➡ 9.14 Pasting Selected Content

➡ 10 Layering Images

Type tool
[T]

Cycle type tools
[Shift] [T]

Cut selection in layer
[⌘] [X]

[Ctrl] [X]

To resize the text box while editing text, click one of the four sides or corners and drag. Even though they look much alike, this technique is different from transforming the layer box, which stretches and can distort the text, rather than simply increasing the display area for the text in the canvas.

Many menu commands are not available as you add or edit a Type layer. For example, you need to either cancel or commit the text changes you are making before you can save the document.

Changes, such as paragraph alignment, affect only the paragraph that contains the insertion point.

Copy selection in layer
⌘ C

Ctrl C

Paste contents of Clipboard into selected layer
⌘ V

Ctrl V

———

When you edit a Type layer, its name changes to reflect the new text it contains unless you renamed the Type layer using the Layer Properties dialog.

———

You cannot use any brush-based tools in a Type layer without first rasterizing the layer. If you do this, you can no longer edit the text with the Text tool. You might want to duplicate the Type layer and hide it so that you have a backup copy to edit if changes to the text are required.

———

You can create a blank layer above a Type layer to paint on. Create a clipping mask by Option/Alt-clicking the divider between the layers; then you can use brushes or paint tools on the Masked layer.

3 To change the selected text, do one of the following:

■ Set the options for the selected text or paragraph independent of other text in the layer by using the tool options bar.

■ Set options in the Character palette for the selected characters.

■ Set options in the Paragraph palette for the paragraph that contains the cursor or the selection.

■ You can also press Delete or simply start typing to remove selected text.

4 When you finish editing the type, you can commit the text changes by clicking the Commit button or by choosing another tool, layer, channel, or path. Cancel changes by pressing Esc or clicking the Cancel button .

Changing the Type Layer

You can also change all the text in a Type layer by simply selecting that layer in the Layers palette. With any tool selected, choose the Type layer you want to edit in the Layers palette. You can also choose the Type tool if you want to change options using the tool options bar. Then, to make changes to the text, do one of the following:

■ If the Type tool is selected, you can set the options for the selected Type layer's characters or paragraph using the tool options bar.

■ Set options in the Character palette for all the text in the Type layer.

■ Set options in the Paragraph palette for all the paragraphs in the Type layer.

Text as a Layer

Although they are created differently from other types of layers, Type layers are still layers, and you can edit and manipulate them in most of the usual ways:

Moving and transforming You can move Type layers using the Move tool , and you can transform (rotate, scale, or skew) them using the transform pseudotools. Although scaling the text has an effect similar to the effect that results from changing the horizontal and vertical scale, they are not the same, and one does not change the values of the other.

Opacity and blending modes You can change the opacity and blending mode of Type layers freely at any time (see Section 10.1).

Effects and styles You can apply all effects and preset styles to Type layers (see Chapter 15).

Clipping mask You can use Text layers as a part of a clipping mask of a layer or layers above by Option/Alt-clicking between the layers in the Layers palette.

Masks You can apply layer and vector masks to Type layers (see Chapter 11).

17.6 Warping Type

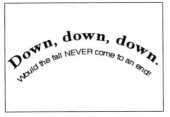

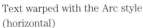

Text warped with the Arc style (horizontal)

Text warped with the Arc style (vertical)

➡ 3.18 Type Tools

You can click and drag to move the Type layer while working in the Warp Text dialog.

As you make changes to warped text in the dialog, it is previewed in the canvas. However, this can be slow depending on the image size.

The Type layer thumbnail in the Layers palette changes to the warped text thumbnail.

When you first add text to a Type layer, the text baseline follows a straight horizontal line. You can use the Warp Text dialog to set a shape for the text to follow, distorting the shapes of the text in interesting ways. To distort the shape of your text, follow these steps:

1 Choose the Type layer you want to warp in the Layers palette.

2 Choose Layer > Type > Warp Text, or, with one of the text tools selected, click the Warp Text button 🔲 .

3 Set the warp style, warp orientation, amount of bend, and horizontal and vertical distortion in the Warp Text dialog.

4 After you distort the text, click OK. You will notice that the thumbnail for the Type layer changes to the warped text thumbnail.

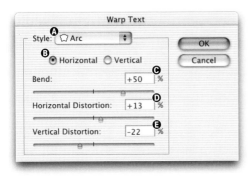

Ⓐ Choose a warp style from the drop-down. Each style has a small thumbnail next to it that indicates its general shape.

Ⓑ Choose whether to warp the text horizontally or vertically.

Ⓒ Use the slider or enter a percentage value (–100 through 100) for the maximum bend in the warped text.

Ⓓ Use the slider or enter a percentage value (–100 through 100) for the maximum horizontal distortion for the warped text. This affects the perspective, with positive numbers causing the left side of the text to appear farther away.

Ⓔ Use the sliders or enter percentage values (–100 through 100) for the maximum horizontal and vertical distortion for the warped text. This affects the perspective, with positive numbers causing the top of the text to appear farther away.

343

17.7   Converting Type to Other Formats

———

When Type layers are converted, they preserve the layer name based on the last text they contained.

———

Warning: When you convert from Paragraph to Point mode, all text that is not visible within the text box is deleted. Make sure that all text is visible before converting.

Because type is in vector format in Photoshop, you can convert it to other formats, including a path and a vector mask, or you can rasterize the text. To convert the Type layer, first select the layer you want to convert in the Layers palette, and then do one of the following:

- To **turn the text into a work path** based on the Type layer, choose Layer > Type > Create Workpath. This technique uses the letterforms to create a working path in the Paths palette, but does not delete the original Type layer.

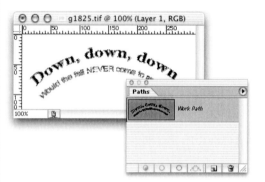

The text is now also a work path.

- To **convert the text to a vector mask,** choose Layer > Type > Convert To Shape. This technique uses the letterforms to create a vector mask with a fill layer using the color or style of the original text. The original Type layer is deleted.

- To **rasterize the text,** choose Layer > Rasterize > Type *or* Layer. This converts the layer into a Bitmap layer, which you can then edit using brushes (see Chapter 13), using filters (see Chapter 14), or importing into video applications (see Chapter 20). Remember, though, that once you rasterize the text, you cannot edit it with the Type tool, as the original Type layer is converted to a normal layer.

- To **paint with text,** select some type. You might want to turn off visibility in other layers. Choose Edit > Define Brush Preset.

A simple single word has been used as a defined Brush Preset, then painted in the image using Dual Brush, Color Dynamics, and Scattering settings available in the Brushes palette.

17.8　Spell-Checking and Searching Text

Photoshop users waited a long time for the introduction of spell-checking and find-and-replace features. Although the spell-checker is extremely basic, it saves time over having to copy and paste your text into a word processor. To spell-check a single Type layer or all Type layers in your document, follow these steps:

1　Select the Type layer you want to check in the Layers palette. If you want to check the spelling of all layers in the document, you do not have to select any particular layer.

2　Choose Edit **>** Check Spelling…

3　Use the Check Spelling dialog to scan your document for misspelled words. Click Done when you are finished.

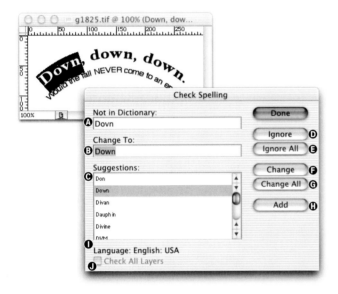

Ⓐ　Displays suspect words that were not found in the dictionary.

Ⓑ　Displays the most likely correct spelling for the suspect word. Click and type an alternate word.

Ⓒ　Displays a list of other possible correct spellings. Click to select one of these suggestion.

Ⓓ　Click to ignore this instance of the word.

Ⓔ　Click to ignore this particular word throughout the document during this spell-checking session.

Ⓕ　Click to use the Change To word (see B) in place of the suspect word (see A) for this one instance.

Ⓖ　Click to use the Change To word (see B) in place of the suspect word (see A) for this and all instances throughout this document.

Ⓗ　Add the suspect word (see A) to the Photoshop dictionary.

Ⓘ　Displays the current dictionary being used to spell-check the document.

Ⓙ　Check to spell-check all Type layers in the document.

17.8   Spell-Checking and Searching Text *(continued)*

➠ 2.4   Edit Menu

The spell-checker always starts checking from the beginning of the text in a layer.

Photoshop also allows you to search the text in your document and replace words. To do so, follow these steps:

1   Select the Type layer you want to search in the Layers palette. If you want to search all layers in the document, you do not have to select any particular layer.

2   Choose Edit > Find And Replace Text…

3   Use the Find And Replace Text dialog to scan your document looking for words and replacing as necessary. As you search, the words found are highlighted in the canvas. Click Done when you are finished searching.

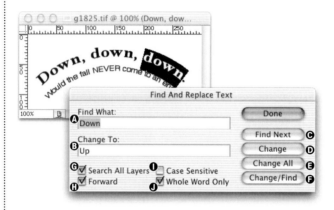

Ⓐ   Enter the text you want to find.

Ⓑ   Enter the replacement text.

Ⓒ   Click to begin the search or to continue to the next instance of the find text without replacing.

Ⓓ   Click to replace the found text with the revised text.

Ⓔ   Click to replace all occurrences of the found text in the Type layer or document with the revised text.

Ⓕ   Click to replace the found text with the revised text and then continue to the next occurrence of the find text.

Ⓖ   Check to Search all layers.

Ⓗ   Check to search forward (left to right/up to down) in the text.

Ⓘ   Check to find only text that is the same case as the find text.

Ⓙ   Check to find only the entire text, disregarding matches that are embedded in other words.

17.9 Creating Text on a Path

Photoshop CS introduces text on a path, a feature that has long been solely in the domain of vector applications such as Adobe Illustrator. To use this feature in Photoshop, you must first create a path on which to apply the type. The primary vector drawing tool for adding paths is the Pen tool ; however, the most common application of the option is probably in applying text to an ellipse.

1. Select any vector drawing or shape tool such as the Ellipse tool. In the Options bar, select the Paths button. This will let you draw a shape and its paths with no fill. Click and drag in the image to create a shape or a path.

2. Choose the Type tool **T** from the Toolbox, and move your cursor over a desired path. Click when you see the cursor change to the Text On Path icon. Enter your desired text; you can always change the font.

3. Choose the Path Selection tool or the Direct Selection tool, and position it near the type until the cursor changes to the Move Text On Path icon. Click and drag to adjust the type position

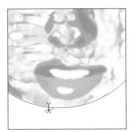

Click and drag to create a path. Move the Type tool **T** over the path until it becomes the Text On Path icon. Click the path, insert type, and edit the text as needed. Click the Commit button to apply.

Choose a Path Selection tool. When positioned near the text, it becomes the Path icon, allowing you to position text. Click the Commit button to apply. You can position text on paths or inside paths. You can transform text on paths to resize it independently or as part of grouped layers. Using transform pseudotools to resize type will not rasterize the type layer.

Free Transform
⌘ T

Ctrl T

Commit Transformation
Return

Enter

Cancel Transformation
Esc

———

Use the Direct Selection tool to edit or alter the shape of any path, even after text has been placed.

———

Add text to a filled shape or a more complex path by using the Direct Selection tool to select a path segment you want the text to follow. Copy and paste the path segment and apply the text to the duplicate.

CHAPTER 18

Automation and Workgroups

AUTOMATION AND WORKGROUPS ARE two complex processes that Photoshop has incorporated to help simplify your imaging production workflow. Through the use of task automation, Photoshop gives you the ability to program or record repetitive, even complex, imaging tasks to increase your productivity and decrease the potential for errors. The ability to effectively manage files and workflow, whether you are working alone or as part of a group, is a valuable asset that Adobe has once again expanded for this most recent release of Photoshop.

Photoshop CS provides for an expanded role of the File Browser in task automation, allowing access to the Automation menu directly from within the File Browser window. Photoshop still includes three general categories of automation tools: actions, batch actions, and droplets. You can use these tools for tasks as simple as changing a group of files from one format to the other or as complex as processing multiple images into a PDF presentation.

When more than one person is working on a document or when a project involves multiple parts with many people working on it, setting up a workgroup becomes necessary. To this end, Photoshop already supported WebDAV, which allows users to collaboratively edit and manage files on remote web servers. In this release, Photoshop has expanded workflow management capabilities with Adobe Version Cue, a new feature that allows for integration between the major Adobe applications released in the Creative Suite of products. Version Cue is designed to streamline the process of creating file versions, locating files, managing files and file histories, and backing up or restoring entire projects.

- 18.1 **Applying actions**
- 18.2 **Recording actions**
- 18.3 **Performing batch actions**
- 18.4 **Creating droplets**
- 18.5 **Resizing a folder of images**
- 18.6 **Creating PDF presentations**
- 18.7 **Setting up workgroups**
- 18.8 **Checking documents in and out of workgroups**
- 18.9 **Adding notes**
- 18.10 **Using Version Cue**

18.1 Applying Actions

➡ 4.3 Actions
        Palette

**Choose multiple dis-
contiguous actions**
[Shift] click
[Alt][Ctrl][Tab][Ins]
[Option][Num Lock]

**Choose multiple con-
tiguous actions**
[⌘] click
[Alt][Ctrl][Tab][Ins]
[Option][Num Lock]

[Ctrl]-click action

———

You can play actions
only if the conditions
are right for the com-
mands being executed.
For example, you can-
not use the Cut com-
mand if there is no
selection. If an action
attempts to perform a
command that is not
available, you will be
alerted.

———

Actions created in Pho-
toshop CS might not run
on previous versions of
Photoshop if they use
features available only
in Photoshop CS.

———

Many sources are avail-
able via the Internet.
What you can use in
Photoshop CS might be
limited due to the
operating system.

———

For advanced computer
users, Photoshop
allows you to write
scripts using Visual
Basic, AppleScript,
or JavaScript. See the
documentation in your
Photoshop CS/Scripting
Guide folder for further
information.

Actions are simply a recorded sequence of commands and tool operations that you can apply to an image or a batch (group) of images. For example, if you have a series of images you want to process in a particular style, you can record an action as you go through the steps on one image—in order to do this all automatically on subsequent images. You can record most commands and processes as part of an action and then apply them as desired; however, you will need to do some planning to automate some tasks smoothly.

Once actions are recorded, you can apply them via the File menu and the File Browser. Initially, you record and apply actions using the Actions palette, which you can view and use in two modes: Button and Edit. You can toggle between these two palette modes by selecting the Button Mode option in the Actions palette menu.

To play back an action, select the layer you want to apply the action to using the Layers palette, make any additional selection, and then do one of the following:

In **Button mode,** click the button for the action, or press the associated keyboard short-cut, which, if there is one, is listed on the right side of the button.

In **Edit mode,** click the action or a step in the action, and then choose Play in the palette menu or click the Play button ▶ . If you choose a step in the action, the playback begins from there and continues through the subsequent steps to the end of the action.

Photoshop applies all the commands in the action in sequence to the selected layer. Some actions can take a long time to complete, depending on the size of the image, how complex the action is, the power of the computer, and the available system resources.

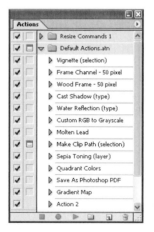

Left: the Actions palette in Button mode. Click any button to execute that action. Function key shortcuts are displayed to the right of the action name (for example, Cut is F2). Right: the palette in Edit mode (Button mode turned off). Click any action to select it, and then click the Play button or choose Play to execute that action.

18.2 Recording Actions

Although Photoshop comes equipped with dozens of actions, you can record, edit, save, and load your own actions and sets of actions. To record a new action, follow these steps:

1 In the Actions palette, turn off Button Mode in the Actions palette menu, and then click the New Action button  or select New Action... in the palette menu.

2 Enter details about the action in the New Action dialog and click Record. The Record button ⬤ turns red as long as the action is being recorded.

3 Do one or more of the following:

■ Perform the actions you want to record. Most operations you perform while recording (tools, menu commands, dialogs, palette settings, and so on) are added to the action in the Actions palette as you perform them. However, several operations and commands cannot be recorded; these include setting preferences and applying paint strokes. Likewise zoom tools, windows, and view commands cannot be recorded.

■ Choose Insert Command... from the Actions palette menu, choose a menu command, and click OK. The command is performed as a part of the action.

■ Choose Insert Stop... from the Actions palette menu, enter a message, specify whether you want to include a Continue button with the stop message, and click OK. The action stops at this point and waits for the user, who can either click Stop or, if you checked the Continue option, continue.

■ Select a path in the Paths palette, and then choose Insert Path from the Actions palette menu. The selected path is added to the image as part of the action.

4 To stop recording, do any of the following:

■ Click the Stop button ⬛ .

■ Choose Stop Recording from the palette menu.

■ Press the Escape key.

New Action dialog

Ⓐ Enter a name for the action.

Ⓑ Choose the action set to which the action should be added. This action is not saved with the action set until the action set is resaved.

Ⓒ Choose a function key and modifier keys to activate the action. You can choose only keyboard shortcuts not currently being used by other actions.

Ⓓ Choose a color code for the action's background in the Button mode of the Actions palette.

➠ 4.3 Actions Palette

Cut selection (with Commands.atn loaded)
[F2]

Copy selection (with Commands.atn loaded)
[F3]

Paste (with Commands.atn loaded)
[F4]

Show Color palette (with Commands.atn loaded)
[F6]

The preset actions provided with Photoshop are in the Presets/Photoshop Actions folder in the Photoshop application folder on your hard drive.

One extremely useful action preset is the Commands list (Commands.atn). It includes actions for the most common menu commands, adding function key shortcuts.

It is best to plan the actions you are going to record before actually recording them. This saves a lot of editing and rerecording time.

Keep in mind that you can edit actions, and can use them to initiate other action sequences.

Editing Actions and Action Sets

Show Layers palette (with Commands.atn loaded)

[F7]

Show Info palette (with Commands.atn loaded)

[F8]

Show Actions palette (with Commands.atn loaded)

[F9]

Show Navigator palette (with Commands.atn loaded)

[F10]

———

You can cause one action to play another by recording the Play command for another action.

———

If the action being recorded will be applied to files of different sizes, change the ruler units to percent so that commands will be proportional to the file sizes.

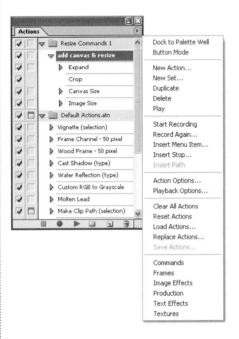

The commands used to record, edit, load, and save actions are located in the Actions palette menu.

To **delete** actions or action sets from the Actions palette, choose the action or action set in the Actions palette and click the trashcan icon [trash], or choose Delete from the palette menu and click OK in the dialog to confirm deletion. In addition, you can drag the action or action set directly to the trashcan icon to delete instantly. The action or action set is removed from the palette but can be reloaded if it was saved.

After you record an action, you can edit it in several ways. First, turn Button mode off using the command in the palette menu; then do one or more of the following:

- To **rerecord** an action, in the Actions palette, select the action and then choose Record Again... If the action uses a tool, use the tool differently and then press Return/Enter to record the changes. If the action is a dialog, set the options and click OK to record the changes.

- To **add** to an existing action, in the Actions palette, select the action and then click the Record button [●]. Perform the actions to be added, and then click the Stop button [■].

- To **create a new action set**, in the Actions palette, click the New Set button [□] or choose New Set... from the palette menu. Enter a name for the new action set, and click OK. The new action set appears in the Actions palette menu. You can then group actions into a single folder, making it easier to save them as a set.

- To **duplicate** an action or an action set, in the Actions palette, select the action or action set and then choose Duplicate. You can also Option/Alt drag the action to another location on the Actions palette or drag the action to the New Actions button [⬒].

18.2 Recording Actions *(continued)*

- To set **playback options** for an action, in the Actions palette, select the action or action set and then choose Playback Options… In the Playback Options dialog, choose the speed at which you want the actions played: choose Accelerated for best performance, choose Step By Step for slower playback, or choose Pause and enter the number of seconds to delay. You can also pause the action after any audio annotations in the action to ensure that it plays all the way through. Generally, you want to use the Accelerated option, but if you are debugging an action, you will want to slow it down to help you detect errors.

- To change the **action options** or to **set options**, in the Actions palette, select the action or action set and then choose Action Options… in the palette menu. Change the options in the Action Options or Set Options dialog and click OK.

Loading and Saving Action Presets

You can save actions as independent files and then load them into Photoshop as needed. This is especially helpful if you set up specific actions for a project that you want to save for later use or to send to another Photoshop user.

- To **load** a list of preset actions, choose Load Actions… from the Actions palette menu, choose a file that has the .atn extension, and click OK. The actions are added to the bottom of the list in the Actions palette.

- To **quickly load** a list of preset actions, choose one of the action filenames from the bottom of the Actions palette menu. You can add a list of actions to the quick load list by saving the actions file in the Presets/Photoshop Actions folder in the Photoshop application folder. If Photoshop is running, you will need to restart before the file appears in the Actions palette menu.

- To **replace** the current list of actions, choose Replace Actions from the Actions palette menu. Choose a file that has the .atn extension, and click OK. The current list of actions is cleared and replaced with the selected list.

- To **reset** actions to the default list of preset actions, choose Reset from the Actions palette menu. Specify whether you want the action set to be added to the bottom of the current list (Append) or to completely replace the current list (OK).

- To **save** the current action set, with Button mode turned off, choose one of the action filenames from the bottom of the Actions palette menu. Enter a name for the new action file, making sure to preserve the .atn extension, choose a folder on your hard drive to save in, and click Save.

- To **clear** all actions and action sets in the Actions palette, choose Clear All Actions from the Actions palette menu, and click OK in the dialog to confirm that you want to delete all the actions. The Actions palette will now be empty.

Open Image Size dialog (with Commands.atn loaded)
`F11`

Revert to saved version (with Commands.atn loaded)
`F12`

You can create an undo for actions. When recording a new action, first record Create A New Snapshot. With this as the first step, you can revert to the previous image state by clicking the most recent snapshot when you run the action.

If the action includes the Save As command, do not change the filename; if you enter a new filename, Photoshop uses that exact filename every time the action is played. As a workaround, copy the files to a new folder, and save the reconfigured files as the same name. This way you don't lose your source medium.

18.3   Performing Batch Actions

➠ 4.3   Actions
        Palette

It is recommended that Suppress Color Profile Warnings be checked to turn off display of color policy messages, which can stop batch processing. You can also do this via the Edit menu under Color Settings.

You can speed up batch procedures by reducing the number of saved history states and turning off the Automatically Create First Snapshot option in the History palette.

You can also use a Create Snapshot command as the first step of an action, which will create an undo or toggle action option for you to use after the action runs.

An action can be applied to a single image or to an entire folder of images.

In addition to applying a recorded sequence of commands, you can apply several options to files for after they are processed. You can leave the files open, close them with the changes saved to the original files, or save modified versions of the files to a new location (leaving the originals unchanged).

To apply an action to a batch of files, you can choose File > Automate > Batch from the main menu or work from within the File Browser and use the Automate menu. Set the options in the Batch dialog and click OK to begin the batch action. You will see the files quickly open, actions applied, and then the file close again, until all files are processed.

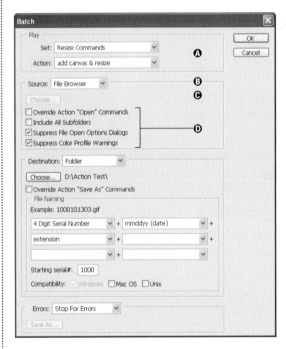

Ⓐ First choose a currently loaded set of actions, and then choose an action to be performed from the drop-down. Load sets of actions via the Actions palette to make them accessible here.

Ⓑ Choose the source for the images to be batch processed: from a selected folder, imported from a selected source, using the currently open files, or using the File Browser. The File Browser offers unique advantages for sorting, selecting, or rotating images to be processed.

Ⓒ If you selected folder as the source, choose or locate the folder. The selected folder's path is displayed to the right.

Ⓓ Check the options appropriate for your situation. You can choose to override File Open commands written into an action; however, deselect this option if your files are already open or if there are specific files to be opened to perform the action. You can include all folders within chosen folders. Choosing to suppress File Open options has been added particularly for processing camera raw files (default or last-used settings will be used).

18.3 Performing Batch Actions *(continued)*

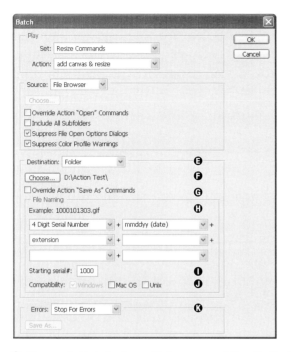

➧ 6.5 Managing Images with the File Browser

Creating a new action and recording a batch command provides a way to perform multiple actions from a single action.

If you have a digital camera or a scanner with a document feeder, you can also import and process multiple images with a single action.

You might benefit from taking your time and writing notes as you create more complex actions.

You can record actions that play other actions, and you can program menu commands and stops that allow you to make custom or individualized edits within an action sequence.

E Choose what is to be done with the processed files: Destination: None leaves the files open without saving changes; Save And Close saves the files in their current location, overwriting the original files; Folder saves the processed files in another location.

F If you are using a folder as the destination, choose the folder in which to save the processed files. The selected folder's path is displayed to the right. Although you can save the files back into the original folder and even replace the original files, it is recommended that you save the processed files in a new folder so you can keep the originals.

G If you are using a folder as the destination, check to prevent the Save As command from being executed. This prevents the process from being interrupted by the Save As dialog.

H Choose from the drop-downs how the files should be named. An example of how the new filename will be structured appears at the top. You can choose to add a combination of alphanumeric prefixes/suffixes date and existing filename combinations.

I This new feature lets you choose a starting serial number, allowing you to continue or add to a previous sequence of numbered files.

J Specify other operating systems with which you want to force the filename to be compatible.

K Choose how errors should be processed: you can either stop to deal with them or log them to a text file. You can set the location for the text field by clicking the Save As... button.

18.4 Creating Droplets

➠ 4.3 Actions
Palette

➠ 29.3 Optimizing
Images

ImageReady can also create droplets for optimizing web images (see Section 29.3).

You can drag multiple images or entire folders of images over the droplet to open the images one by one and perform the action.

You can specify that droplets save images automatically in a specific folder on your hard drive, which preserves the original version of the image.

A close relative of batch processing is the droplet. A *droplet* is a mini-application that can apply an action to an image or a folder of images when you simply drag the image or the folder over the droplet's icon. You don't even have to open Photoshop to use a droplet.

The procedure and options for creating a droplet in Photoshop are almost identical to those previously discussed for batch processing. To create a droplet, choose File > Automate > Create Droplet and enter the options for the droplet.

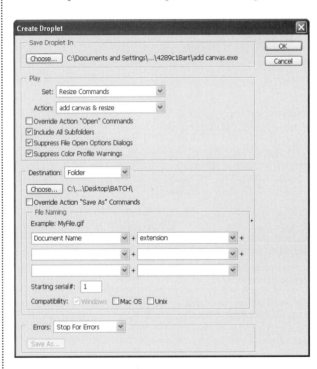

Choose a location in which to save the droplet. The current location is displayed to the right. When selecting the location, place it where you can easily drag the image file(s) or folder to it, probably the Desktop. Other options in this dialog are identical to those in the Batch dialog, which was discussed in the previous section.

ADD CANVAS
DROPLET

MY WEB PAGE

After you create the droplet, simply drag and drop a compatible image file, multiple selected image files, or an entire folder of image files onto the droplet icon to process them.

18.5 Resizing a Folder of Images

Chances are, one day you will find yourself face to face with the repetitive task of resizing a folder full of images—one of the more common tasks for which you might find some automated help welcome. All you need to do is think things through and then record an action as you go through the procedure on a single image.

Make a Plan, a New Action Set, and a New Action

For more complex actions, you can benefit from writing down a plan of attack or taking notes as you run through the process you have in mind on a trial image. For the purposes of this example, the plan is simply to resize a folder of images for print, making a second set of JPEGs at web resolution while we are at it.

Begin by opening the Actions palette:

1 To keep from mixing your own set of actions in with defaults, click the New Action Set button [ ] at the bottom of the palette and create a new action set.

2 To create a new action, simply click the New Action Button [ ] , name it, and assign it to the set you have chosen.

3 By default, the new action is in Record mode, assuming you are ready to begin. If necessary, you can use the Stop Action button [ ] any time to pause recording and then click the Record Action button [ ] when you are ready to resume.

Record a Runthrough on a Duplicate Image

Continue by opening a sample image on which to record the action. Choose one of the images in the folder you want to process:

1 Choose Image > Duplicate and close the original.

2 Click the Record Action button [ ] if you have paused recording.

3 Choose Image > Image Size from the main menu. For the purposes of preserving pixel data as is, clear the Resample Image selection. This will adjust the resolution in correlation with the document size you enter. Enter a value for your desired document size. You will more than likely need to set one dimension and then crop the image for the second dimension. Click OK.

5 Chose Image > Canvas Size. In the dialog, enter the value for your second dimension— which will be smaller. This will prompt a warning, but will also crop the image to center.

6 Click the Stop playing/recording button [ ] when you are finished adding any additional steps you might want to add to the images.

7 Close the duplicated image you have used to write the Action—do not save it to the folder of images you wish to process with your new Action. Your Action and the folder of images are ready to use and process.

18.5 Resizing a Folder of Images *(continued)*

Add Options and Save As Commands

It is quite simple at this point to record an optional couple of steps to duplicate the image and resize copies for Web or e-mail use.

1 Choose Image > Duplicate

2 Choose Image > Image Size from the main menu. For the purposes of electronic transfer, you will want to decrease file size—choosing the Resample Image option will allow you to enter 72dpi as a target resolution.

3 Choose File > Save As. For electronic transfer, JPEG at high quality is selected in the example.

4 Choose File > Close... for the JPEG duplicate.

At this point the image is resized, and you can exercise options for saving the document. This is particularly important when working with valuable originals and originals in lossy or compressed file formats. Save a copy in a suitable file format.

1 Choose File > Save As for the original. For the example, TIFF was selected as a file format suitable for archiving digital images.

2 Choose File > Close from the main menu.

3 Click the Stop Action button ▣ to finish recording.

Take Advantage of the File Browser

You can now launch actions directly from the File Browser's menu. Use the File Browser to sort your images, assign rotations, and select specific groups of images. In the example, a group of the portrait-oriented pictures is selected for processing. Rather than running an action on a whole folder and then reorienting images or writing a separate action for landscape and portrait oriented images; you can assign rotation in the File Browser independent of an action. Rotation assigned in the File Browser takes effect when the file is opened next.

18.6   Creating PDF Presentations

The PDF Presentation command available from the File menu or the File Browser allows you to create multipage PDF documents or slideshow presentations. PDF options also let you set security and exercise choices such as embedding fonts and vector information. The Presentation function lets you select features such as transitions, timing, and looping play.

The PDF Presentation dialog offers several options for adding files to a presentation or a multipage layout:

- Select and organize files in the File Browser.

- Add files that are open in the Photoshop workspace.

- Browse for files via the Common File Locator dialog.

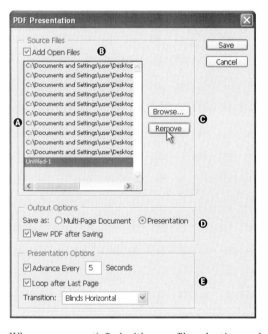

Ⓐ All selected source files are listed. If you begin by selecting files in the File Browser, they will appear in the window when you select PDF Presentation from the menu. Simply click and drag files to rearrange their presentation order.

Ⓑ Check to add files you have open in the Photoshop workspace.

Ⓒ Choose Browse to select additional files, or choose Remove to delete selected files from the presentation or multipage layout.

Ⓓ Choose between Multi-Page Document or Presentation. Check to view PDF immediately.

Ⓔ Select presentation options such as transition effects (available via the drop-down). Check to select timing and presentation loop options.

When you are satisfied with your file selection and options, click Save. You will be presented with a PDF Options dialog in which you can choose to include font and vector information, make file compression choices, and select security options such as password protection.

➡ 4.3   Actions Palette

➡ 4.8   File Browser

➡ 6.5   Managing Images with the File Browser

➡ 25.4 Saving as Photoshop PDF

Including vector data preserves any vector graphics such as shapes and type for PostScript output.

Embedded fonts are displayed and printed properly even on computers that do not have the fonts installed. Faux bold style type and warped type cannot be embedded.

Embedding fonts and vector information slightly increases file size.

You can choose to select Outline Text if embedding fonts results in a file that is too large, if you plan to open the file in an application that cannot read PDF files with embedded fonts, or if a font seems to present problems. This option will not preclude you from reopening the file and editing the type in Photoshop.

If both Embed Fonts and Use Outlines For Text are deselected, your PDF may be displayed with font substitutions.

18.7   Setting Up Workgroups

➡ 5.5   File Handling
         Preferences

―――

Adobe GoLive also
uses workgroups to
manage files.

If you are working in a collaborative environment and others in your organization regularly view or edit your Photoshop files, you will need to manage your files to avoid confusion. Photoshop's Workgroup commands, based on the WebDAV server technology, let you share files with other users while ensuring that two people do not edit files at the same time and that changes made by one person are not overwritten by those of another person. You can use the Workgroup commands to place files on a special central computer (called a *server*) that allows you and others in your group to download files, lock them from being changed while you are working, and then upload the file for others to view or change. Think of this as a library from which you can check documents in and out.

When using workgroups, there are two versions of the image file:

Local This version resides on your hard drive and is the version you actually edit. When you open a file from the Workgroup server, you actually download the most recent version from the server to your computer.

Server This version is available to all users in the workgroup on the WebDAV server. When you save the file, you upload your local version to the server.

Before you begin using workgroups, you need to make sure that the functionality is enabled in the File Handling Preferences panel. Check the Enable Workgroup Functionality option and set the other workgroup options. This opens the File > Workgroup submenu and the Workgroup drop-down (located in the document window in the Mac operating system or in the application window in Windows).

Before using the Workgroup commands in Photoshop, you need to connect to a WebDAV server. The WebDAV server software comes with Photoshop CS. Follow the instructions provided to install it on the computer being used as the server, which must be connected to the Internet. However, if you are not technically inclined, ask your system administrator to install the software for you.

When the WebDAV server software is installed, you need to connect your computer, which also has to be connected to the Internet and to the server. To do this, you will need to know the URL for the WebDAV server.

18.7 Setting Up Workgroups *(continued)*

To **set the server or servers** you want to use, choose File > Workgroup > Workgroup Servers. In the Workgroup Servers dialog, specify the folder on your computer where you want to store shared files, and then choose the WebDAV server or servers you want to use. (This is where the global version of the files is stored.) Click Done when you are finished.

If you are having trouble connecting to your WebDAV server, your computer or the WebDAV server might be behind a firewall that is interfering with communication. Check with your system administrator or take a look at the documentation that came with your firewall software to set options that permit communication.

Some servers require you to log on only once, the first time you use a Workgroup command. However, some servers require you to log on for every Workgroup command you issue.

A Click to choose the folder on your hard drive in which you want workgroup files from newly added WebDAV servers saved. This is where your local version of the files will be saved; the currently selected folder is displayed to the left. You can also select a Workgroup server and then change its folder location.

B Open the local Workgroup folder using Explorer (Windows) or the Finder (Mac).

C Displays a list of connected WebDAV servers. Click to select.

D Click to set up a new WebDAV server. Enter a nickname and a URL or IP address for the server in the dialog and click OK. You must be connected to the Internet to add a WebDAV server; Photoshop will verify that you can access the server.

E Select a Workgroup server, and then click to edit the nickname and the URL for the server.

F Select a Workgroup server, and then click to remove the server from the list.

To **log on to a server**, select any of the commands from the File > Workgroup submenu or the Workgroup drop-down 🖳 in the document window (Mac) or application window (Windows), and choose the server from the dialog. Depending on how the server is configured, you will be asked to enter a username/ID and password, which you should get from your system administrator.

To **log off all servers**, choose File > Workgroup > Logoff All Servers. This disconnects you from all servers you have logged on to.

18.8 Checking Documents In and Out of Workgroups

If you open a managed file without checking it out, other workgroup users can still check the file out and make changes, potentially leading to confusion.

After you set up a Workgroup server to be used with Photoshop, you can open (download) files from the server or save (upload) files to the server. In addition, while opening a file, you can check it out to prevent other users in your group from editing the image while you are working on it. Then, when saving the file, you can check it back in, freeing the file to be edited by other members of your group.

■ To **add** a new managed file to the server, open the file and choose Save As... from the File > Workgroup submenu or from the Workgroup drop-down. Enter options for which server and how you want the file saved and click Save. The file is now on the server and available to the workgroup.

■ To **open** a managed file, choose File > Workgroup > Open... Choose the server, folder, and file you want to open, and click Open to open the file *without* checking it out from the server or click Check Out to open and check out the file.

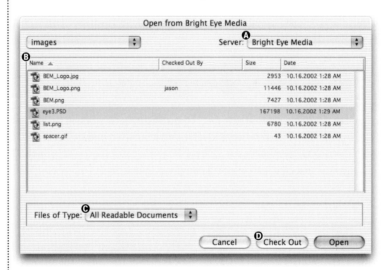

Ⓐ Choose a server from the list. You can then locate the exact folder in which you want to save the file on the server.

Ⓑ Choose a file to download. You can click the column heads to sort files based on that criteria.

Ⓒ Choose a file format.

Ⓓ Choose to immediately check out the file after saving.

18.8   Checking Documents In and Out
of Workgroups *(continued)*

➡ 6.10 Saving Images

To save the changes to the server version, choose Save from the File > Workgroup submenu or from the Workgroup drop-down. The server version of the file is updated based on your local version.

When adding a file to a WebDAV server, make sure that you include a file extension if the file will be downloaded to a Windows computer.

To check out the open file, choose Check Out from the File > Workgroup submenu or from the Workgroup drop-down. The file must have been saved on a WebDAV server. You might want to verify the file before checking it out.

To verify that a local file can be checked out, open the file and choose Verify State from the File > Workgroup submenu or from the Workgroup drop-down.

To check in the file while saving changes, choose Check In from the File > Workgroup submenu or from the Workgroup drop-down. The server version of the file is updated based on your local version and unlocked.

To check in the file without saving changes, choose Cancel Check Out from the File > Workgroup submenu or from the Workgroup drop-down. The file is unlocked on the server but not updated.

To revert the checked-out local version of a file to the version on the server, choose Revert from the File > Workgroup submenu or from the Workgroup drop-down. All unsaved changes made to the local version will be lost.

To update the local version of a file (if it has not been checked out) from the version on the Workgroup server, open the file and choose Update from the File > Workgroup submenu or from the Workgroup drop-down. All unsaved changes made to the local version will be lost.

LEARNING MORE ABOUT WEBDAV

Although Adobe supports the WebDAV technology in many of its products, WebDAV is not owned by Adobe. Instead, it is an open standard being developed by the IETF (Internet Engineering Task Force) WebDAV Working Group and can be included with any software that wants to support it. To find out more about the WebDAV standard, check out the WebDAV Resources website (www.webdav.org).

18.9　Adding Notes

➡ 3.21 Annotation
Tools

Notes/Audio Annotation tool
[N]

Cycle note tools
[Shift] [N]

───

To show or hide note icons for the image, choose View > Show > Annotations.

───

Warning: Sound files can add considerably to the file size, so you might want to use them sparingly.

───

To remove all annotations from an image, click the Clear All button in the tool options bar.

───

To delete a single annotation, click the Annotation icon and then click Delete.

Often while working on an image, especially one you might be sharing with others who will be working on it, you need to add notes to the canvas itself. Notes do not affect the final output of the image.

Ⓐ　Click and drag the Note icon to select and move it to a new location on the canvas. Double-click to show/hide the associated note. (The note might be anywhere on the canvas.) Place the mouse pointer over the note and wait for a Tool Tip displaying the note author's name.

Ⓑ　Displays the note's author. Click and drag to move the note.

Ⓒ　Click to hide the note.

Ⓓ　Enter note comments.

Ⓔ　Click and drag to resize the note.

Ⓕ　Click and drag the Audio Annotation icon to move it to a new location on the canvas. Double-click to play the audio note. (Be sure your volume is sufficient.) Place the mouse pointer over the note and wait for a Tool Tip displaying the note author's name.

Text Notes

Text notes work a lot like the sticky notes available with most operating systems. There are two parts to a note: the Note icon (a button representing the note) and the note itself that can be moved independently of the icon. To add a text note, do the following:

1　Choose the Notes tool [▤] and set the options for the note's author, font appearance, and background color.

2　Click the canvas in the location where you want the note to appear. The Note icon will appear there, and a space appears underneath where you can type the note.

3　Enter your note comments. You can then hide the note and continue working or add other notes.

Audio Notes

Audio annotations allow you to record your voice to create a note. Of course, you need a microphone hooked up to your computer, and you need the proper audio software installed for your operating system. To add an audio note, do the following:

1　Choose the Audio Annotation tool [◀»] and set the note's author and icon color.

2　Click the canvas in the location where you want the note's icon.

3　In the Audio Annotations dialog, click Start… to begin recording your message. Speak clearly and evenly into the microphone. Click Stop when you are finished recording.

4　To play back the note, double-click the Audio Annotation icon.

18.10   Using Version Cue

Adobe Version Cue is a new feature of the Adobe Creative Suite (CS) designed to assist you in areas of productivity and workflow whether you are working alone or with others. Version Cue is designed to allow you seamless integration of file versioning, security, and file management between all applications in the Adobe CS tailored to your workflow.

Personal or Group Workflow

If you are working alone, Version Cue is designed to do the following:

- Streamline the process of creating file versions and maintaining a file history
- Assist in locating and managing files by allowing you to browse file thumbnails, search file information, search version comments, and back-up or restore entire projects

If you are working with others in a collaborative environment, Version Cue is designed to provide the previous workflow improvements along with the following:

- Instant project sharing with file management safety and security

Workspace Administration

Version Cue Workspace Administration allows you to take care of the following advanced tasks:

- Duplicating, exporting, backing up, and restoring projects
- Viewing information about projects in the workspace
- Importing files to the workspace using FTP or WebDAV
- Deleting file versions and removing file locks
- Creating project users and defining their project privileges
- Restricting access to a specific projects

Enabling Version Cue

If you purchased Photoshop CS separately and don't own the Creative Suite of products, you must be granted network access to an existing Version Cue Workspace. Before accessing a Version Cue Workspace, you must do the following:

- Enable Version Cue at the system level via Control Panel or System preferences
- Enable Version Cue workgroup file management in your Photoshop preferences.
  Choose Edit > Preferences > File Handling > ✔ Version Cue

```
┌─ Version Cue ──────────────────────────────────────────────────┐
│ ☑ Enable Version Cue Workgroup File Management                  │
└────────────────────────────────────────────────────────────────┘
```

➡ 2.3   File Menu

➡ 2.4   Edit Menu

➡ 5.3   Setting Photoshop Preferences

➡ 5.5   File Handling Preferences

You can view the complete Version Cue documentation as a PDF or print it by opening the VersionCueHelp.pdf file located on your Creative Suite CD or your Photoshop CS CD.

Version Cue must be installed and turned on at the system level, then may be enabled and accessed by individual users through Photoshop preferences and other Creative Suite applications individually.

Color Section

Additive Color (Red + Green + Blue = White) Projected red, green, and blue light wavelengths combine to produce nearly all the colors we can see. This is the basis for what is called *additive color*. One hundred percent of red, green, and blue light adds to create white, similar to the way all light wavelengths in sunlight are seen as white light. When you see magenta on the computer screen, red and blue light sources are combined to produce magenta.

Subtractive Color ([Red + Green + Blue] – Green = Magenta) More specifically, our vision is affected by which light wavelengths are being absorbed by varying inks or pigments. This is the basis for what is called *subtractive color*. Cyan ink absorbs red light; magenta ink absorbs green light; yellow ink absorbs blue light. One hundred percent of cyan, magenta, and yellow combine to absorb all light, and we see black. What we see as magenta in print is actually a pigment that absorbs green light wavelengths, allowing our eyes to see only the reflected red and blue light from a full-spectrum white light source.

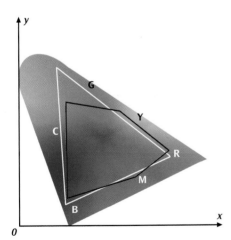

This illustration depicting gamut shows the relationships between the visible spectrum or Lab color space (the larger shaded area) and the possible range available with each of the RGB and CMYK color models. See Chapters 8 and 23 for further information on the effects and characteristics of color.

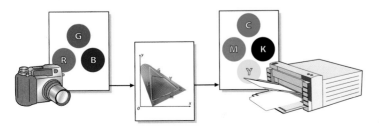

A digital capture device such as a scanner or a camera records color information using an equipment-specific formula. Your color management system translates the color information from the original capture to reference color, working space, or output device specifications.

Fills and Adjustments

You use fills to add a solid color, a gradient, or a pattern to a layer, either directly or as part of a Fill layer. You use adjustments to control the colors and tones in an image and to correct imperfections or create interesting effects. The following images show some of the possibilities for each. The Fill or Adjustment layer's icon is shown in the top-left corner.

Original image

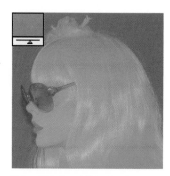

Color Fill A red fill color has been applied with 50% opacity.

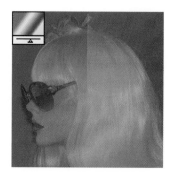

Gradient Fill An angle gradient has been applied with 50% opacity.

Pattern Fill Pattern scaled to 13% and 50% opacity.

Levels Input levels have been adjusted to heighten contrast.

Curves The curve has been S-curved to solarize the image.

Color Balance Red and yellow have been added to midtones, turning gray areas beige.

Brightness/Contrast Brightness and contrast increased to create sharp areas of black and white, while preserving midtone grays.

Hue/Saturation The saturation in the hair has been reduced to give the model white hair.

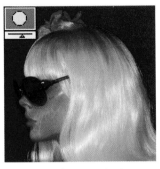

Selective Color CMYK colors have been adjusted in the neutral range to colorize the image.

Gradient The image's color table has been replaced by a gradient color table.

Replace Color The model's face has been turned wicked-witch green. Replace Color is only applied using the Adjustments menu.

Invert The image's brightness values have been reversed.

Photo Filter A colored filter effect is applied to simulate a filter placed over the camera's lens.

Shadow Shadows in the image have been reduced. Shadow is only applied using the Adjustments menu.

Channel Mixer Color channels have been mixed in the mono-chrome to evenly adjust the contrast.

Threshold A threshold level of 137 has been set.

Posterize A posterization level of 6 has been set.

Blending Modes

Throughout Photoshop, you use blending modes to specify how colors should be combined between layers, effects, or certain editing and painting tools. The color of each pixel in a layer is combined independently of other colors on the layer. You can specify blending modes in three primary places:

In the Layers palette When working with a layer, you can set the blending mode to specify how the colors of the active layer are combined with layers beneath it. You can also adjust layer blending in the Blending options of the Layer Style dialog.

In the Layer Style dialog With some effects, you set the blending mode for the specific effect, to specify how the colors of the effect are combined with the associated layer and layers beneath it.

In the tool options bar With certain editing and painting tools, you set the blending mode to specify how colors applied by the tool are combined with the active layer. However, most tools use only a subset of the blending modes listed here. For example, the Healing Brush has only eight modes.

When combining colors, you must consider three color types:

Blend Either the color of the pixel on the layer or effect with the mode being set or the color used to edit or paint the image.

Base The color of the pixel in the underlying layer or layers being affected by the blend color.

Result The color created by combining the blend and base colors using the specified blending mode.

The order of the blending modes here reflects their order in blending mode menus.

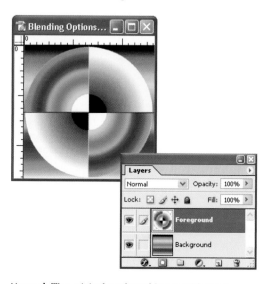

Normal The original unaltered image with two layers. The Foreground layer (currently in Normal blending mode) is the circle with color and grayscale gradients. The Background layer is a linear color gradient. Normal is called Threshold when you are working in Bitmap or Indexed Color mode.

Dissolve Creates a random grainy effect based on the blend colors' opacity or the brush pressure.

Behind (Not available as a layer mode) Used to edit or paint in the transparent areas of the layer. This mode works only if the transparent lock is off.

Clear (Not available as a layer mode) Used to edit or paint only the transparency of pixels. Set the target transparency in the tool options bar. This mode works only if the transparent lock is off.

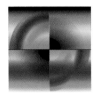 **Darken** If the blend color is darker than the base color, the blend color is used as the result color; otherwise, the base color is preserved.

 Multiply Multiplies the color value of the blend color by the base color, producing a darker color.

 Color Burn The base color is darkened by increasing its contrast based on the blend color contrast. Blending with white produces no change.

 Linear Burn The base color is darkened by decreasing its brightness based on the blend color brightness. Blending white produces no change.

 Lighten If the blend color is lighter than the base color, the blend color is used; otherwise, the base color is preserved.

 Screen Multiplies the inverse color value of the blend and base colors, producing a lighter result color.

 Color Dodge The base color is lightened by decreasing its contrast based on the blend color contrast. Blending with black produces no change.

 **Linear Dodge** The base color is lightened by increasing its brightness based on the blend color brightness. Blending with black produces no change.

 **Overlay** Darker blend colors darken the base color, and lighter blend colors lighten base colors, but luminosity is preserved. Black and white base colors remain unchanged, so details are preserved.

 **Soft Light** The base color is darkened or lightened depending on the grayscale level of the blend color. If the blend color is darker than 50% gray, the base color is darkened. If the blend color is lighter than 50% gray, the base color is lightened. This produces an effect similar to shining a dim spotlight on the image.

 Hard Light The base color is multiplied or screened depending on the grayscale level of the blend color. If the blend color is darker than 50% gray, the base color is multiplied (darkened). If the blend color is lighter than 50% gray, the base color is screened (lightened). This produces an effect similar to shining a bright spotlight on the image.

Continues

Blending Modes *(Continued)*

Vivid Light The contrast of the base color is increased or decreased based on the grayscale level of the blend color. If the blend color is darker than 50% gray, the base color is darkened by increasing contrast. If the blend color is lighter than 50% gray, the base color is lightened by decreasing contrast. This produces an effect of bright sunlight.

Linear Light The brightness of the base color is increased or decreased based on the grayscale level of the blend color. If the blend color is darker than 50% gray, the base color is darkened by decreasing brightness. If the blend color is lighter than 50% gray, the base color is lightened by increasing brightness. This produces an effect similar to soft light but less diffuse.

Pin Light Colors are replaced based on the grayscale level of the blend color. If the blend color is darker than 50% gray, base colors darker than the blend color are replaced by the blend color. If the blend color is lighter than 50% gray, base colors lighter than the blend color are replaced by the blend color. This produces an effect similar to shining a bright but sharp light.

Hard Mix This newest addition to the blending modes is a posterizing, contrast enhancement. The fill opacity of the top layer governs how strongly it posterizes, and the color being blended in governs the center point for the contrast enhancement.

Difference The blend and base color values are subtracted from each other to produce the result color. White inverts the base color, and black produces no change.

Exclusion Similar to the Difference mode, but produces result colors that are of lower contrast.

Hue Uses the luminance and saturation of the base color and the hue of the blend color to produce the result color.

Saturation Uses the luminance and hue of the base color and the saturation of the blend color to produce the result color.

Color Uses the luminance of the base color and the hue and saturation of the blend color to produce the result color.

Luminosity Uses the hue and saturation of the base color and the luminance of the blend color to produce the result color.

Effects

You add effects to layers using the Layer Style dialog, discussed in Chapter 10. In these examples, the label indicates the predominant effect.

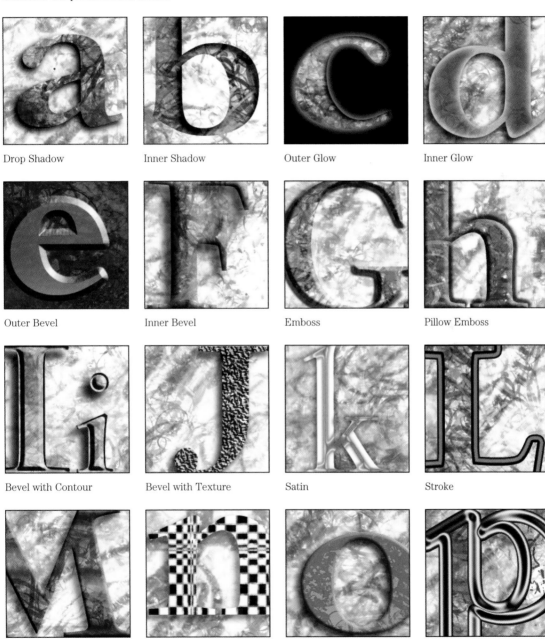

Drop Shadow	Inner Shadow	Outer Glow	Inner Glow
Outer Bevel	Inner Bevel	Emboss	Pillow Emboss
Bevel with Contour	Bevel with Texture	Satin	Stroke
Gradient Overlay	Pattern Overlay	Color Overlay	Chrome—Fat, Preset

Filters

You add filters to layers using the Filter menu, discussed in Chapter 14.

The original image. Several filters use the foreground and background colors set in the Toolbox when applying their effect. A dark-brown foreground color and a light-tan background color were used in the following examples.

Artistic > Colored Pencil (uses the background color for the pencil stroke)

Artistic > Cutout

Artistic > Dry Brush

Artistic > Film Grain

Artistic > Fresco

Artistic > Neon Glow (foreground, background, and a glow color)

Artistic > Paint Daubs

Artistic > Palette Knife

Artistic > Plastic Wrap

Artistic > Poster Edges

Artistic > Rough Pastels

Artistic > Smudge Stick

Artistic > Sponge

Artistic > Underpainting

Artistic > Watercolor

Blur > Blur Average (new; requires a selection)

Blur > Blur

Blur > Blur More

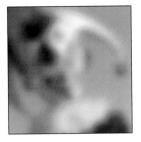

Blur > Gaussian Blur

Blur > Lens Blur (new; using a mask as a depth map)

Blur > Motion Blur

Blur > Radial Blur (Spin)

Blur > Radial Blur (Zoom)

Blur > Smart Blur (Normal)

Blur > Smart Blur (Edge Only)

Blur > Smart Blur (Overlay Edge)

Brush Strokes > Accented Edges

Brush Strokes > Angled Strokes

Continues

Filters *(Continued)*

Brush Strokes **>** Crosshatch

Brush Strokes **>** Dark Strokes

Brush Strokes **>** Ink Outlines

Brush Strokes **>** Spatter

Brush Strokes **>** Sprayed Strokes

Brush Strokes **>** Sumi-e

Distort **>** Diffuse Glow (uses the background color for the glow)

Distort **>** Displace (requires a second image as a displacement map)

Distort **>** Glass

Distort **>** Ocean Ripple

Distort **>** Pinch

Distort **>** Polar Coordinates

Distort **>** Ripple

Distort **>** Shear

Distort **>** Spherize

Distort **>** Twirl

Distort > Wave

Distort > ZigZag (Around Center)

Distort > ZigZag (Out From Center)

Distort > ZigZag (Pond Ripples)

Noise > Add Noise

Noise > Despeckle

Noise > Dust & Scratches

Noise > Median

Other > Custom

Other > High Pass (fade to Hard Light or Soft Light blending mode)

Other > HSB/HSL (Input: HSB, Output: RGB)

Other > Maximum

Other > Minimum

Other > Offset

Pixelate > Color Halftone

Pixelate > Crystallize

Continues

Filters *(Continued)*

Pixelate > Facet

Pixelate > Fragment

Pixelate > Mezzotint (Long Lines)

Pixelate > Mosaic

Pixelate > Pointillize (uses background color)

Render > 3D Transform

Render > Clouds (fade to Overlay blending mode)

Render > Difference Clouds (uses background and foreground colors)

Render > Fibers (uses background and foreground colors; fade to Soft Light)

Render > Lens Flare

Render > Lighting Effects (Crossing Down)

Sharpen > Sharpen

Sharpen > Sharpen Edges

Sharpen > Sharpen More

Sharpen > Unsharp Mask

Sketch > Bas Relief

(All Sketch filters use background and foreground colors.)

Sketch > Chalk & Charcoal

Sketch > Charcoal

Sketch > Chrome (Overlay blending mode)

Sketch > Conté Crayon

Sketch > Graphic Pen

Sketch > Halftone Pattern (Dot)

Sketch > Halftone Pattern (Line)

Sketch > Note Paper

Sketch > Photocopy

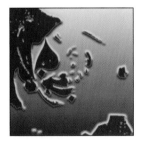

Sketch > Plaster

Sketch > Reticulation

Sketch > Stamp

Sketch > Torn Edges

Sketch > Water Paper

Stylize > Diffuse (Anisotropic)

Stylize > Emboss (fade to Hard Light or Soft Light blending mode)

Continues

Filters *(Continued)*

Stylize **>** Extrude (Blocks)

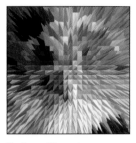

Stylize **>** Extrude (Pyramid)

Stylize **>** Find Edges

Stylize **>** Glowing Edges

Stylize **>** Solarize

Stylize **>** Tiles (Inverse Image)

Stylize **>** Trace Contour

Stylize **>** Wind (Wind)

Stylize **>** Wind (Blast)

Stylize **>** Wind (Stagger)

Texture **>** Craquelure

Texture **>** Grain (Stippled)

Texture **>** Mosaic Tiles

Texture **>** Patchwork

Texture **>** Stained Glass (uses foreground color for the border)

Texture **>** Texturizer

Gallery

▲ **The Great Migration**
© Teodoru Badiu;
www.apocryph.net

Badiu uses masks (see Section 11.3) to blend and erase the image. He then uses the Stamp and Healing Brush tools to fill in areas before adding the background and the textures.

▲ **Feel the Silence**
© Teodoru Badiu;
www.apocryph.net

Badiu works with adjustment layers (see Section 10.5), blending modes (see Section 21.2), and hue and saturation controls (see Section 22.7) to bring all the elements from different photos together, creating a composition that looks as natural as possible despite its multifaceted origin.

Continues

Gallery *(Continued)*

◀ **Awake**
© Teodoru Badiu;
www.apocryph.net

Despite the shadowy nature of his work, Badiu avoids layer effects such as drop shadows, bevels, or glows to create his effects. Instead, he works in the alpha channels (see Section 9.1), using the blur (see Section 14.2) and render filters, and with layers and selections together with blending modes and transform tools (see Section 9.11), to create much deeper and more realistic shadows.

▼ **Nightwatch**
© Teodoru Badiu;
www.apocryph.net

To begin his images, Badiu imports all the pictures and the textures and starts to knock out the parts he needs for compositing, using the Pen tool (see Section 16.1), alpha channels, Color Range (see Section 9.5), or Magnetic Lasso (see Section 9.4), depending on the complexity of the shape he needs to knock out.

◀ **Untitled**
© Ian Rogers;
`www.greynotgrey.com`

Rogers is a new media artist and designer living in Montréal, Québec. Although trained as a painter and nondigital multimedia artist, he has worked extensively with manipulated photography and digital graphics. He is strongly influenced by Dadaism and approaches the kind of digital images he creates in much the same way he would approach collage.

▲ **Untitled**
© Ian Rogers;
`www.greynotgrey.com`

Rogers places images in a new Photoshop file and begins by changing layer settings to see how the images relate to one another. Once he has achieved effects he likes, he removes unnecessary elements to reinforce the composition and adds elements on new layers that will emphasize the harmonic relationships between the imagery. His work relies primarily on simple layer adjustments (see Section 10.1), duplicated layers, standard tools and filters, and extensive masking (see Section 11.1).

Continues

Gallery *(Continued)*

▲ **Untitled**
© Ian Rogers;
`www.greynotgrey.com`

Rogers always carries a digital camera and takes shots with dynamic elements in mind. He processes all the photos by adjusting layers for color balance (see Section 22.5) and Lab colors to remove digital noise, as well as hue/saturation to correct any color imbalances (see Section 22.7). When planning a new image, he first selects three or four photos that are striking compositionally and would work well together, looking for continuation of form in line and contrast.

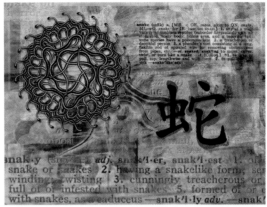

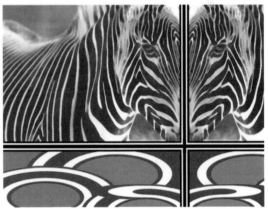

◄▲ **Collaborative Sequence from 2002:
first 5 of 10 images (left to right)**
© Ian Rogers and Walt Dietrich

More and more artists are exploring collaborative
work, through a wide variety of arrangements such as
Photoshop Tennis, muraling, and the Exquisite
Corpse project. This series of images is part of a Photoshop Tennis match between Ian Rogers and Walt
Dietrich. Rogers's focus is on the growing online digital arts medium as an interconnected evolution upon
traditional arts. At present, his central interests are
historicity within evolving contexts and new media as
a development upon fine art. He is a forum moderator
for the online design community at twelvestone.com.

Continues

Gallery *(Continued)*

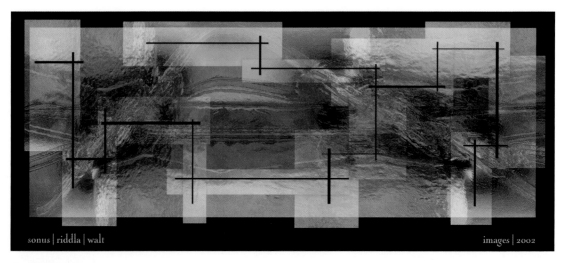

sonus | riddla | walt   images | 2002

▲ **Abstract: 2t**
© Walt Dietrich;
waltdietrich.com

Dietrich is one of the most active participants in the world of collaborative digital art, "competing" in Photo-shop Tennis in many forums and exchanging art and ideas in many more. His work relies on, among many methods, digital photography, layer collage, and blending modes, including his favorite mode, Difference; this preference most likely relates to his experience with raku-fired ceramics, in which the results have a somewhat unpredictable nature.

This abstract, for example, was created as part of a running online variation of the Photoshop Tennis theme. It developed from a single image of a strand of barbed wire, using various combinations of layers (see Section 10.1), blending modes (see Section 21.2), and layer transformations (see Section 9.11).

◄ **Waterplay: 2**
© Walt Dietrich;
waltdietrich.com

This image was created as an early volley in a year-long Photoshop Tennis match with Michelle Kwajafa. It is a combination of two primary photographs that fit well together, one by Kwajafa and the second by Dietrich—the two youths were present together only in the final image. Additional layers of water were blended and masked over the image.

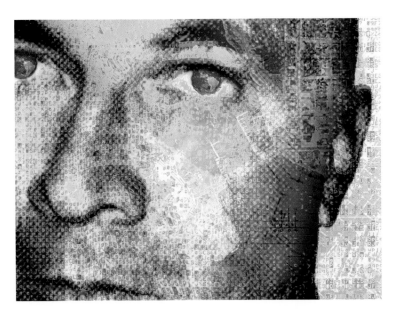

◀ **FARAWAYEYES**
© Walt Dietrich;
waltdietrich.com

Dietrich often explores textures, here building upon a self-portrait with layers and masks of an aerial photo and the Alien Skin SPLAT! patchwork ASCII filter (see Section 14.5), all of which were slightly distorted to facial contours using displacement maps.

◀ **Bugvariant**
© Walt Dietrich;
waltdietrich.com

The body and wings of the butterfly shape are a collage of bugs—a variant of a bug kaleidoscope—which was given added relief using the Displace filter and set against a stylized portion of a building.

Continues

Gallery *(Continued)*

This image was created as return volley in another collaboration between Dietrich and Kwajafa. Dietrich expanded on a freeware dingbat, re-creating the shape using the Pen tool and Photoshop paths (see Section 16.7), transforming and editing variations of the shape, adding layers of code as a backdrop, and masking in layers of abstract color.

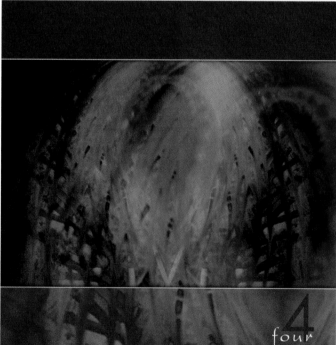

This image uses the Smudge tool (see Section 13.10) in repetition, stroking paths on various layers in several blending modes. Again, Difference mode is prevalent as Dietrich's personal favorite, with Screen mode adding apparent depth and light to the layers.

◀ **The Philosopher's Daughter**
© Maggie Taylor;
www.maggietaylor.com

Taylor collects various kinds of small objects and old tintype photographs from flea markets and eBay. She then scans the objects and photographs directly on her flatbed scanner (see Section 6.8) to produce sharply contrasting images.

▲ **Optimist's Dress**
© Maggie Taylor;
www.maggietaylor.com

▲ **Optimist's Suit**
© Maggie Taylor;
www.maggietaylor.com

Although Taylor temporarily uses the drop-shadow effect (see Section 15.8), she quickly converts it to bitmap format and then directly manipulates the shadow to create a more realistic shadow (see Section 10.10).

Continues

Gallery *(Continued)*

◀ **Dreamer**
© Maggie Taylor;
www.maggietaylor.com

After scanning, Taylor begins piecing things together and tries different objects on different backgrounds, moving the layers around (see Section 9.12) until something interesting appears.

◀ **Stray Thoughts**
© Maggie Taylor;
www.maggietaylor.com

Taylor uses blending modes to create some of the effects, but avoids Exclusion or Difference, relying instead on the Multiply, Overlay, and occasionally Luminosity modes (see Section 21.2). To create the natural-looking smoothness in her images, though, Taylor has to spend time working with the Paintbrush (see Section 13.1) and Eraser (see Section 13.9) to smooth the seam between elements on different layers.

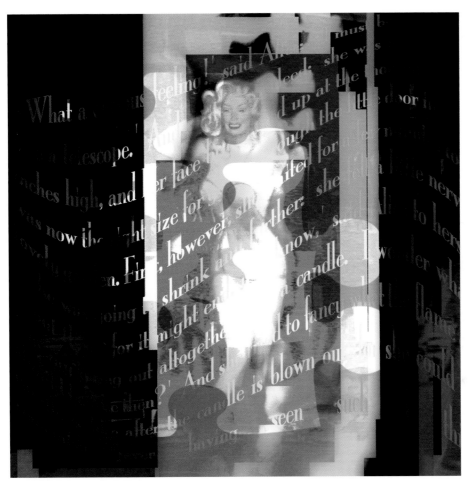

▲ **Alice**
© Jason Cranford Teague;
`www.webbedenvironments.com`

Most of Teague's images start life as digital photographs. One of his favorite techniques is to layer an image over the top of itself, make dramatic changes to the copy, and then using a layer or a vector mask (see Sections 11.2 and 11.6) to partially reveal the original image.

Continues

Gallery *(Continued)*

◀ **Argentina**
Michelle Kwajafa;
www.soulsabyss.net

When it comes to Photoshop, Kwajafa likes to think of herself as an artist first and a designer second. She tries to make provocative, interesting imagery that—if she could afford it—she would print on giant canvasses.

▲ **Curtain**
© Michelle Kwajafa;
www.soulsabyss.net

◀ **Filmrose**
© Michelle Kwajafa;
www.soulsabyss.net

◀ **Bmorecode**
© Michelle Kwajafa;
www.soulsabyss.net

Often, the trends in
web design are added
to images as an after-
thought; text, for
example, is actually
something Kwajafa
uses sparingly, to
avoid imposing a
meaning on the
viewer.

Continues

Gallery *(Continued)*

◀ **Young**
© Michelle Kwajafa;
www.soulsabyss.net

◀ **Salmonella**
© Philip Baca;
www.pixeldelic.org

Continues

Gallery *(Continued)*

◀ **Confession**
© Philip Baca;
www.pixeldelic.org

Baca loves the
Liquify filter. All
his images shown
here are a combina-
tion of Liquify (see
Section 13.10) and a
few other simple
techniques. Lots of
Liquify, plus layers
of paint daubs, dry
brush, blur (see Sec-
tion 14.3), and hue
and saturation tweaks
(see Section 22.7)
usually make up
the core.

▲ **Rats**
© Philip Baca;
www.pixeldelic.org

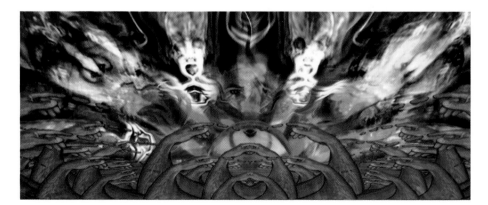

▲ **Here Comes the Set**
© Philip Baca;
www.pixeldelic.org

Baca's influences come from all over. Some of his favorites are master artists everyone knows, such as Salvador Dali and Pablo Picasso, but he also turns to Mark Ryden, Rick Griffin, Robert Crumb, Robert Williams, and Alex Grey.

Continues

Gallery *(Continued)*

◀ **Coma White**
© Philip Baca;
www.pixeldelic.org

◀ **Run**
© Philip Baca;
www.pixeldelic.org

Other big influences on Baca's
work are psychedelic poster art
from the '60s, sleepless nights,
and music from the Butthole
Surfers or The Crystal Method.
In fact, many of his images' titles
come from specific songs he was
listening to while creating them.

PHOTO AND VIDEO TASKS

CHAPTER **19**

PHOTOSHOP WORKSPACE

UNIVERSAL TASKS

PHOTO AND VIDEO TASKS

PRINT TASKS

WEB TASKS

Working with Digital Photos

ALTHOUGH PHOTOSHOP HAS ALWAYS been about photography, for much of its life the primary way to get photographs into Photoshop was to scan hard copies created by film-based cameras. Although film cameras are still immensely popular, especially among professional photographers, digital cameras are becoming increasingly more powerful and more popular. Regardless of which method (scanner or digital camera) you use to capture your photos for import into Photoshop, several tools and techniques are at your disposal for fixing defects and enhancing the quality of your photographs. For the most part, these tools mimic or replace tools that you might find in any darkroom full of chemicals and enlargers. These days many photographers forgo the rigors of the red light for the bright glow of the computer screen.

This chapter shows you how to do the following:

- 19.1 **Digital photo basics**

- 19.2 **Working with camera raw photos**

- 19.3 **Cloning one area to another**

- 19.4 **Repairing from sampled pixels**

- 19.5 **Repairing selected areas**

- 19.6 **Repairing using a previous History state**

- 19.7 **Replacing a color**

- 19.8 **Sharpening and blurring images**

- 19.9 **Creating panoramic views**

- 19.10 **Adding lighting effects**

- 19.11 **Transforming images in 3-D**

- 19.12 **Dodging and burning images**

- 19.13 **Adjusting saturation with the Sponge tool**

19.1 Digital Photo Basics

Stamp tool
[S]

Cycle stamp tools
[Shift] [S]

Healing Brush tool
[J]

Cycle restoration tools
[Shift] [J]

————

Many prosumer-level digital cameras record images using the JPEG file format, but most high-end digital cameras can also take images using the camera raw format.

————

The PNG-24 file format is similar to the PNG-8 file format, but because it uses 24 bit rather than 8 bit, it is better suited for complex images such as photographs. However, PNG-24 produces larger file sizes.

Whether you are scanning in a film-based photograph or downloading an image directly from a digital camera, all images that are edited in Photoshop are translated into pixels: a mosaic of small colored tiles that visually merge to create a continuous image. Although you can use any file format with photographs, four primary formats are commonly used for various purposes:

Camera Raw (.crw) Camera raw files are a native file format for some digital cameras that use minimal compression to record the image. Although this produces the highest-quality images, these files tend to be very large. Although Photoshop cannot save files in this format, it can open them using a special plug-in that ships with Photoshop CS. Once the file is open in Photoshop, you will need to save the image in a different format for permanent storage.

TIFF (Tagged Image File Format) (.tif or .tif) The TIFF file format is traditionally used for printing images. TIFF allows some limited file-size compression without loss of image quality and is supported by all image-editing and layout software.

JPEG (Joint Photographic Experts Group) (.jpg or .jpeg) The JPEG file format (pronounced jay-peg) can be used for print; however, it is the most common format used to present photographs on the screen (including for websites). The JPEG format lets you set varying levels of compression based on the desired image quality, from low quality (0%) to high quality (100%). At 100% there is no noticeable image quality loss (although there is also almost no file size compression) while the closer you get to 0% the more you will notice square artifacts in the image.

PNG-24 (Portable Network Graphics/24 Bit) (.png) Although not as common as JPEG, the PNG-24 file format is also supported by many web browsers for display of photographs.

Improving Your Image Quality

To improve the quality of an image, follow these steps:

1 Clean up the image:

■ If you are opening a camera raw file, use the Camera Raw dialog to make initial corrections using the Image Adjustment controls.

■ If the image has been scanned and contains any defects (scratches, creases, stains, and so on), apply the Despeckle filter (Filter > Noise > Despeckle) and then use the Restoration, Stamp, Distortion, and other tools to repair the damage before making other changes.

■ If the image is captured from video, use the De-interlacing filter to clean up the field lines.

19.1 Digital Photo Basics *(continued)*

2 Use the Histogram palette to check the tonal range quality of your image.

3 Use adjustment commands and/or layers to correct unwanted color casts, saturation problems, and hue shifts. If you want to make visual changes to color, consider using the Variations dialog.

4 Adjust the tonal range of your image using the Levels or Curves adjustments.

5 Use the Unsharp Mask filter or the Sharpen tool to bring out the contrast at the edges of images to return some details to the image.

USING THE BLUR TOOL WHEN CREATING COMPOSITE IMAGES

The Blur tool is a subtle tool that Photoshop users often ignore because the effects are not of the scale or magnitude of filters such as Liquify; yet this tool is one of the most important for creating composite images. When adding new elements to images as layers, at times the edges of these layers are hard and give the appearance of being pasted in rather than part of the original image. Applying the Blur tool to the edges of these layers or even to objects that have already been flattened helps to blend them into the images in a more seamless fashion.

To produce a slight blurring on the edges of new elements, it is important to use the lowest-possible setting that will produce a visible result when applied. The larger the image, the greater the amount of the blur setting necessary. Another consideration when using the Blur tool on large images is that large brush sizes take a lot of processor power to apply; therefore, be patient and apply the blurring to edges using a small brush. Applying a blur to the edge and then applying a second application with a slightly larger brush size to the same area achieves some of the best effects. As the Blur tool is applied the second time, the area nearest the edge receives additional blurring, which achieves a graduated blurring toward the edge of the new object.

History Brush tool
[Y]

Cycle history brushes
[Shift] [Y]

Distortion tool
[R]

Cycle distortion tools
[Shift] [R]

If you try to make tonal adjustments before repairing the image, you run the risk of making defects in the image more pronounced.

If you are working on a photograph that is destined for the Web, remember that it will need to be resized to 72dpi.

19.2   Working with Camera Raw Photos

Open a file
⌘ O
Ctrl O

——

Do not confuse the camera raw format (.crw) with the Photoshop Raw format (.raw), which is used to transfer images between applications and operating systems.

Camera raw images are captured directly from the camera's sensor without any filters or adjustments made by the camera itself. Although many cameras can automatically enhance the image, this often leads to some loss of information. The camera raw file does apply some lossless compression, much like the TIFF format, but does no other processing on the image, instead leaving that to you when you initially open the file in Photoshop. To open and edit a camera raw file, follow these steps:

1 Choose File **>** Open and then browse to the camera raw file, which has a .crw extension. Although different camera manufacturers use different camera raw formats, Photoshop's Camera Raw plug-in can open a variety of formats.

2 In the Camera Raw dialog, adjust the image. As you make changes, they will show up in the work area.

3 After you finish making adjustments, click OK. The image is placed into a new document window ready for additional editing. You will need to save the image in a different file format since Photoshop cannot save files in camera raw format.

PERSEUS AND MEDUSA ("MYTH IN A BOX" SERIES):
© TEODORU BADIU; WWW.APOCRYPH.NET

19.2　Working with Camera Raw Photos *(continued)*

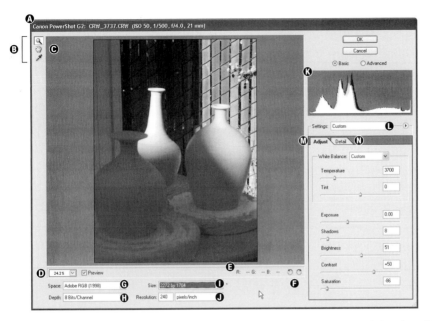

➡ 7.3　Setting the Image Size

➡ 8.4　Choosing a Color Working Space

➡ 22.1 Adjustment Basics

As with most dialogs, hold down the Option/Alt key to use the Cancel button as a Reset button to restore initial settings.

Ⓐ Image Information The header displays basic information about the image being viewed, including the camera used, filename, and f-stop.

Ⓑ Tools The dialog includes basic Zoom, Hand, and Eyedropper tools.

Ⓒ Work Area Disaplys a preview of the image reflecting any adjustments made.

Ⓓ Magnification and Preview Click to change magnification. Click the preview check box to toggle between showing a preview based on adjustments and showing the original image in the work area.

Ⓔ RGB Values Displays the RGB value of the current pixel the mouse pointer is over.

Ⓕ Rotate Image Click to rotate the image clockwise or counterclockwise.

Ⓖ Color Space Choose the color space that should be used with the image.

Ⓗ Bit Depth Choose how many bits are used per pixel in each color channel.

Ⓘ Image Dimensions Choose the image dimensions.

Ⓙ Image Resolution Enter the resolution for the image. For print, a minimum of 240 pixels/inch is recommended although 300 is preferred.

Ⓚ Histogram Displays the red, green, and blue histograms of the image. Wherever these histograms overlap appears as white.

Ⓛ Presets Choose from several predefined adjustment settings for a variety of purposes.

Ⓜ Image Adjustments Adjustthe image's white balance (temperature and tint) or use a preset. You can also adjust the exposure, shadows, brightness, contrast, and saturation. For more information about adjustments, see Chapter 22.

Ⓝ Image Details View information about the image, including the current settings and any meta data included in the file.

PHOTOSHOP WORKSPACE

UNIVERSAL TASKS

PHOTO AND VIDEO TASKS

PRINT TASKS

WEB TASKS

19.3   Cloning One Area to Another

➡ 3.11 Stamp Tools

➡ 13.1 Brush Basics

Stamp tool
[S]

Cycle stamp tools
[Shift] [S]

Sample Selection
[Option]
[Alt]
[Ctrl]

Although the Clone tool is useful for some heavy-duty cleanup, the newer Healing Brush and Patch tools are better suited for more subtle image corrections.

Before you try to clone out every little speck in your image with the Clone tool, try using the Despeckle filter first (Filter > Noise > Despeckle). This filter can often fix widespread problems in an image with only a little loss of image quality.

Avoid cloning the same part of the image over and over, as this can create a distinctive and obvious pattern.

Defects become greatly magnified and obvious when any form of sharpening or adjustment is applied to the image, so it is a good idea to perform repairs first.

The Clone Stamp tool, or simply the Clone tool, is a special brush that lets you copy the content of one area of the image into another area. This literally allows you to paint between different parts of the image, between different layers, and even between different images. Although you can use this technique to create interesting effects, it has been the primary choice for photographers wanting to repair rips, stains, scratches, or other gross defects in an image as well as remove entire objects. The Clone Stamp requires that you first select the region of the image you want to clone from (sampling point) and then begin painting in the region you want to clone into (target).

The Clone Stamp is one of the most effective tools at your disposal for radically altering an image, allowing you to not only repair small defects, but to also realistically remove objects and people, even when against textured backgrounds. In this example, the little old man's head is replaced by leaves, making him into the invisible man.

To use the Clone tool 🖎, follow these steps:

1   Choose the Clone Stamp tool from the toolbar and set the tool's options. The Clone tool has all the standard brush settings, including Airbrush mode, plus two other options:

   ■ Check Aligned if you want the relationship between the sampling point and the point where the cloning to remain fixed. For example, if the sampling point is initially set one inch above and to the left of the Clone tool brush, it will always retain that relative position with the brush until a new source is selected. If unchecked, the sample point always starts at the position clicked and then moves relative to the brush during painting. When the stroke is finished, the source point snaps back and starts from that location again for the next stroke.

   ■ If the source image has layers, checking Use All Layers in the tool options bar copies pixels from all visible layers in that image. When the Use All Layers check box is cleared, the Clone tool samples only from the active layer.

19.3 Cloning One Area to Another *(continued)*

2 Set the sampling point by positioning the cursor on the part of the image to be copied and hold down the Option/Alt key while clicking the point. The selected point is the point the cursor is over when the mouse button is pressed, not the point the cursor is on when the mouse is released. Generally, you want to choose the center of an area that you want to clone into the target area. You can repeat this as many times as you want to get the correct sampling point.

3 Position the cursor at the point where the copied pixels are to be painted, and click and drag the mouse. As you move, a crosshair appears in the sample area showing you what you are copying into the target region. Generally, you want to use short strokes with alignment turned on so that you do not inadvertently copy part of the image that has already been copied, creating noticeable patterns.

 As you brush away the object, a crosshair also appears, showing you where you are sampling pixels from.

4 You can change the tool options and the sample point at any time while working, allowing you to combine pixels from a variety of sources in the image. Keep in mind the following points while working:

■ When the area being used for source pixels is small, use short strokes to keep the sampling point inside the area of source pixels. Remember, each time the mouse button is released, the source point snaps back to its starting point.

■ When cloning large areas of natural material (clouds, trees, rocks, and so on), use medium strokes with alignment on to prevent the development of visual patterns. Avoid the temptation to create a single long brush stroke, which creates a long duplicate of another part of the image.

■ When copying a large area that you want to clone exactly (for example, a person in one part of the image into another), use a large brush and turn alignment on so that the mouse stays in the same relative position while you are copying, even if you release while painting.

■ Although the Normal blending mode allows you to clone parts of the image exactly, you can play around with other blending modes to get some interesting compositing effects.

➧ 13.2 Selecting and Adjusting Brushes

➧ 21.2 Blending Modes and Opacity

Switch to Move tool

——

Choose a soft brush to prevent hard edges that make the cloned areas stick out.

——

To use the Clone tool between two images, both must be in the same color mode.

——

When replacing missing areas of an image with the Clone tool, first make a rough selection around the area to prevent applying cloned pixels outside the desired area.

——

When using the Clone tool to retouch a photograph, use a lower opacity setting to blend the cloned pixels more uniformly.

——

When using the Clone tool to remove a defect or an object in a photograph, don't sample too close to the defect or object. If you work too close, part of the defect or object might actually find its way into the cloned pixels.

19.4   Repairing from Sampled Pixels

Healing Brush tool
[J]

Cycle restoration tools
[Shift] [J]

Set source point
[Option] click

Because the Healing Brush must process both source and target pixels, you cannot apply it to a transparent layer.

When repairing with pixels from the image, select a small area to produce the best result.

If you are using a pressure-sensitive tablet, you can use the Pen Pressure option at the bottom of the Brush Settings dialog to vary the size of the Healing Brush by the amount of pressure applied during a pen stroke. The Stylus Wheel option varies the brush size based on the position of the pen thumbwheel (not a mouse thumbwheel).

The Healing Brush tool is a special brush that can be used to repair imperfections in an image using sampled pixels from another part of an image.Unlike the Clone Stamp, however, the Healing Brush matches the texture, lighting, and shading of the sampled pixels to the source pixels. As a result, pixels painted by the Healing Brush blend better with the surrounding image, preserving details while removing defects, scratches, rips, and discolorations.

The Healing Brush is used to seamlessly remove a nasty crease in the photograph by using another area of the image with similar texture and coloring.

When the Healing Brush samples the pixels, it analyzes the texture, color, and luminosity of the source pixels. When you then paint, the Healing Brush merges the texture from the sample area into the color and luminosity of the destination area. The Healing Brush reads an area around the brush that is between 10 and 12 pixels, so you'll obtain the best results using a hard-edged brush.

To use the Healing Brush, follow these steps:

1 Select the Healing Brush 🖌 from the Toolbox and set the options in the tool options bar:

   ■ Choose a source: Sampled uses only pixels from the image while Pattern allows you to apply a pattern, selected in the drop-down to the right. Generally, Sampled is your best bet, but Pattern can be useful for cleaning up an area that has a regular pattern that you are trying to re-create.

   ■ Check Aligned if you want the relationship between the sampling point and the point where the cloning begins to remain fixed. If Aligned is cleared, the sample point always starts at the position clicked and then moves relative to the brush while painting. When the stroke is finished, the source point snaps back and start from that location again for the next stroke.

   ■ If the source image has layers, checking Use All Layers in the tool options bar copies pixels from all visible layers in that image. When the Use All Layers check box is cleared, the Clone tool samples only from the active layer.

19.4 Repairing from Sampled Pixels *(continued)*

2 Option/Alt-click the area of the photo that contains pixels that match the area of the photo to be replaced. (The cursor briefly becomes a target when you select the sampling point.)

3 Click and apply the Healing Brush tool to the area to be retouched. Don't be alarmed if it looks as if you are actually cloning from the sampling point while you are brushing. To heal an area, Photoshop combs the source and target pixels, which cannot be done in real time. After you release the mouse button, you will notice a lag of several seconds (the time depends on the length of the stroke and the file resolution) until you see the final results. Repeat this step for as many strokes as you need.

4 You can change the tool options and the sample point at any time while working, allowing you to combine pixels from a variety of sources in the image. Keep in mind the following points while working:

■ Use the Fade command (Edit **>** Fade Healing Brush) to soften the effect of the last stroke, much like reducing its opacity.

■ Although the Normal blending mode is best for repair work, you can play around with using other blending modes to get some interesting compositing effects.

➡ 13.2 Selecting and Adjusting Brushes

➡ 21.2 Blending Modes and Opacity

Alt click

Fade
Shift ⌘ F
Alt Ctrl F

—

Avoid applying the Healing Brush tightly up against strong contrasting edges in an image. When Photoshop applies the blending algorithms, the darker pixels blur, creating a smudged appearance.

19.5 Repairing Selected Areas

➡ 3.9 Restoration Tools

➡ 9.1 Selection Basics

Healing Brush tool

J

You can also make an initial selection using any selection method discussed in Chapter 9 and then use that as the selection for the Patch tool.

Although the pattern patch may not seem terribly useful for photo editing, it can actually come in handy if you need to repair an area with a regular pattern. You can create your own patterns using the instructions in Section 12.11.

Like the Healing tool, the Patch tool can be used to repair damage to an image by. However, unlike the Healing tool, which works like a brush, the Patch tool works like a selection tool. You can copy one section of the image into another, which lets you quickly apply the pattern from one area into another, matching the texture, lighting, and shading of the sampled pixels to the source pixels.

Even though the Patch tool is an excellent tool for removing wrinkles and other facial imperfections, it also is the tool of choice when you need to easily and quickly remove objects such as power lines, flying birds, and other unwanted items from skies. Although you can achieve the same effect using the Clone tool, using the Patch tool is much faster.

In this example, the Patch tool has been used on the original image (left) to remove the wrinkles around the eye, creating a more youthful look (right). Who needs plastic surgery when you have Photoshop?

To use the Patch tool, follow these steps:

1 Select the Patch tool ⊘ in the Toolbox.

2 In the tool options bar, choose how the selection you will be making should be applied to any existing selection in the image (New, Add, Subtract, Interesct), and select the patching mode you want to use:

Source mode Choose this option to repair the selected area. This is the mode of choice when the selected area contains mottled but similar toned areas.

Destination mode Choose this option to use the selected area to repair other areas of the image. When the area being repaired needs to match a pattern or lines in the image, use this mode.

Transparent Check to apply the patch as a semitransparent area, allowing the image underneath the patch to blend equally. If Transparent is cleared, the patch is used as a solid pattern covering the image underneath it.

19.5 Repairing Selected Areas *(continued)*

3 Using the Patch tool, make a free-form selection around the area in the image you want to patch (Source mode) or the area you want to use to repair other areas (Destination mode). To make changes to the selection, do one of the following:

- Hold down Shift and make a selection in the image to add to the existing selection.

- Hold down Option/Alt and make a selection in the image to subtract from the existing selection.

- Hold down Option/Alt-Shift and make a selection in the image to select an area that intersects with the existing selection.

4 With the selection made, do one of the following:

- If you are using Source mode, click and drag the patch selection area to an area with the texture and color you want to copy. As you move the patch selection, you will notice that the original area mirrors the content of where you are dragging. When you are over the area you want to use, release the mouse button. After a few seconds, the selected region will change based on the area to which you dragged it.

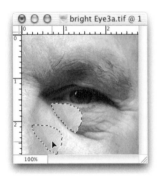

The patch selection is being dragged to an area that contains the texture to be applied to the selected area.

- If you are using Destination mode, click and drag the selection to the area you want to repair. As you drag, it will appear as if you are dragging the selected content, but the original content will remain unchanged. When you are over the area you want to repair, release the mouse button. After a few seconds, the area will change based on the patch selection.

- If you want to patch the selected area based on an existing preset pattern, choose the pattern in the tool options bar, and click the Use Pattern button. After a few seconds, the pattern will be applied to the patch selection.

➡ 12.11 Creating Patterns

Cycle restoration tools
Shift J

When using either the Healing Brush or the Patch tool, be careful not to place new source pixels too close to areas with dark or defined edges. Photoshop will include these darker pixels in the blending calculations, and they will appear as a darker blur.

19.6 Repairing Using a Previous History State

History Brush tool
[Y]

Cycle history brushes
[Shift] [Y]

You cannot use the History Brush tool between History states or snapshots with different image dimensions or image color modes.

Applying the History Brush tool with reduced opacity is a good way to partially and selectively reduce a filter effect such as sharpening.

The History palette uses a lot of memory. If your system resources are becoming low, you can clear the History states either by selecting Clear History from the History palette menu or by choosing Edit > Purge > History.

For critical work you can use a selection to restrict the application of the History Brush tool to a specific area and prevent it from being applied to other areas.

The History Brush tool works much like the Clone tool, but allows you to copy portions of an image from previous history states and apply an effect globally to an image and then retouch the image, compositing from previous versions. The History Brush tool works in conjunction with the History palette where you can select a previous history state or snapshot to copy from.

Here, the original photograph (left) had several artistic ink filters applied to the entire image (center). Then, the History Brush was used to restore the model's face (right), creating an abstract pattern around the model.

To use the History Brush tool, follow these steps:

1 Select the History Brush 🖌 in the Toolbox.

2 In the History palette, click the left column of the state or snapshot to use as the source for the History Brush tool.

3 Set the tool's options. Since the History Brush is a brush tool, it has all the parameters associated with brushes. Of importance when using the History Brush to restore a portion of an image is the Opacity setting. When it is set at less than 100%, the amount of the previous state that is restored is proportional to the Opacity setting.

Click in the History Brush column next to the History state or snapshot from which you want to copy.

4 Paint the areas that need to have effects removed with the History Brush tool. Like the Clone tool, the History Brush has a variable opacity, which allows the partial removal of effects or tonal corrections.

19.7　Replacing a Color

Although you can use the Color Replacement tool to replace any color in the image with another color using a brush, it is obvious that this tool is primarily intended as a way to quickly get rid of red-eye. Not only is the tool tailor-made for the purpose, but it's a dead giveaway when you realize that its icon includes an eye with a red pupil.

Before the eye pupil is recolored (left), there is a noticeable red tone that looks gray in black-and-white images. After using the Color Replace brush with black (right), the pupil looks natural, but the brush leaves the twinkle in the eye.

This tool works much like the Replace Color adjustment to change one color in an image to another while leaving surrounding colors alone (adjusting them slightly to prevent color casting). The Color Replacement tool allows you to be more selective about where colors are replaced (brushed into particular areas). To use the Color Replacement tool, follow these steps:

1　Choose a foreground color to as the base color to replace other colors in the image.

2　Choose the Color Replacement tool ![icon] from the Toolbox.

3　In the tool options bar, set the parameters for the brush:

- Choose from a limited list of image modes. If you are replacing the color, you will want to stick with the Color Image mode that will replace only the color, leaving luminosity alone.

- Choose how the target color should be sampled, either continuously sampling while painting, using the first pixel clicked, or using the background color. Generally, you'll want to use Once for replacing particular colors.

- Choose how to limit the area the Paintbrush can affect, either anywhere in the image (discontiguous), only in areas touching the first pixel clicked (contiguous), or stop at hard-color transitions (find edges).

- Set how close a color in the image has to be to the target color to be replaced by the base color. The lower the percentage, the closer the color has to be to the target color.

- Check if you want to use anti-aliasing while painting. This is generally recommended since it will create smoother results.

4　In the canvas, click a pixel with the color you want to replace and paint over the areas with the color. You will see the base (foreground) color replace the target color.

Restoration tool
[J]

Cycle restoration tools
[Shift] [J]

Switch to Eyedropper tool
[Option]
[Alt]

19.8 Sharpening and Blurring Images

➠ 3.15 Distortion Tools

➠ 13.2 Selecting and Adjusting Brushes

Distortion tool

———

Photoshop also provides filters to blur and sharpen images. You use the filters to apply the effect to the entire image; you use the Blur and Sharpen tools to apply the effect selectively without the need to create complex selections.

———

The Blur tool can make part of an image that is in focus into one that is out of focus. The Sharpen tool cannot make an out-of-focus photograph into one that is in focus.

———

Avoid using large brush sizes combined with long brush strokes when using the Blur tool. Because the blur action is processor intensive, the effect will lag behind the brush stroke.

Both the Blur and Sharpen tools are used to simulate changing the apparent focus of an image, allowing you to create a variety of effects to emphasize certain areas of the image over others. You can apply Blur to make the image look out of focus and to make background objects look farther away by increasing the apparent depth of field. Sharpen, on the other hand, gives the appearance of increasing the focus in the image, adding detail by increasing contrast.

Overuse of either tool can cause unwanted effects. Overblurring an image can eliminate all representation, leaving an abstract image. Oversharpening an image can cause unwanted artifacts in which the contrast causes sharp colorcasts.

The original image (left) is slightly blurry and probably needs some sharpening. The second image (right) is split in two with the left side overly blurred, rendering it almost unrecognizable, and then overly sharpened on the right side, which not only sharpens details in the photograph, but also makes cracks, dust, and other unwanted noise far more obvious.

To apply either the Blur or Sharpen tool to an image, follow these steps:

1 In the Toolbox, select the Blur tool 🔵 or the Sharpen tool 🔺.

2 Set the options for the tool in the tool options bar.

- Choose a brush size and edge hardness. The softer the edge, the better the effect will blend. However, if you are trying to keep a definite border to an area, you will want to use a hard edge on the brush.

- Choose the Blending mode to blur or sharpen. Although the list is limited, using a Blending mode other than Normal can create some interesting effects, especially with lighten and darken, which can create a glowlike effect.

382

19.8 Sharpening and Blurring Images *(continued)*

- Choose a strength at which the brush should be applied. A weaker brush (lower percentage) fades the effect, allowing for more subtle application.

- Choose whether to blur or sharpen only the active layer or all visible layers. With Use All Layers checked, the tool affects the pixels on all visible layers.

3 Paint the areas that need to be blurred or sharpened. You can increase the apparent effect of blurring or sharpening by repeatedly applying to the same area.

The Blur tool is used to blur the gentleman's face, giving it a more abstract artistic look as if it were drawn with pastels.

➡ 14.2 Applying
    Filters

Cycle distortion tools
Shift R

It is difficult to get uniform blurring over a large area with the Blur tool. If you need to apply blurring to a large area, don't use the Blur tool. Instead, make a loose selection of the area, feather the selection, and apply the Gaussian Blur filter.

Avoid "scrubbing" a portion of an area with the Sharpen tool, because this causes repetitive applications of sharpening to be applied to the area and results in some pixels becoming white (also called blowouts).

DOWNLOADING ACTIONS AND OTHER RESOURCES FROM ADOBE STUDIO EXCHANGE

Although dozens of websites allow you to download Photoshop actions, brushes, custom shapes, and other Photoshop plug-ins, one of the best collections is provided by Adobe itself at the Adobe Studio Exchange website, part of the larger Adobe Studio website (`http://share.studio.adobe.com`). This site is stuffed with the best (mostly free!) resources you will find for Photoshop, including thousands of actions for creating frames and borders, patterns, text effects, and textures.

What really sets this site apart from other Photoshop resource sites, though, is that you can "shop" for downloads, add them to your basket, and then download everything at once. You will need an Adobe ID to use it, but this is free of charge.

19.9   Creating Panoramic Views

Photomerge Select tool
[A]

Photomerge Rotate tool
[R]

Photomerge Set Vanishing Point tool
[V]

Photomerge Zoom tool
[Z]

Most cameras have a limited field of view (width) that is actually much less than human vision. Photoshop allows you to create panoramic images that better reflect a true human view by "stitching" two or more photographs together using Photomerge. Naturally, the images should be connected and the edges overlapping somewhat, but Photoshop can then take these images and match them to create the wide shot.

To create a panoramic image, follow these steps:

1   Choose File **>** Automate **>** Photomerge.

2   In the Photomerge Source dialog, choose two or more files that you want stitched together. You can choose to open files one at a time, open a folder of images, or use the images already open in Photoshop. When you are finished, click OK.

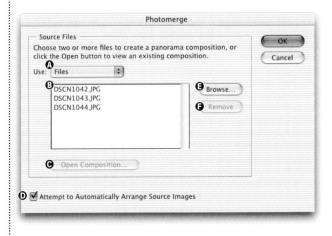

Ⓐ File Source   Choose whether to browse for individual images, browse for a folder of images, or use the currently open images.

Ⓑ Selected Files   Lists the files currently queued for merger.

Ⓒ Open an Existing Composition   Click to open a file that you have already used Photomerge to create in order to further edit it.

Ⓓ Automatic Image Arrangement   Check if you want Photoshop to initially arrange the images as a panoramic view. This generally works well and saves a lot of time.

Ⓔ Browse to add images   Click to select additional images for merger. While browsing, you can add multiple files by Command/Ctrl-clicking files.

Ⓕ Remove Image   Click to remove the selected image from the list.

3   In the Photomerge dialog, drag images from the lightbox and adjust them in the work area to fine-tune the stitching with the controls. When you're set, click OK.

19.9 Creating Panoramic Views *(continued)*

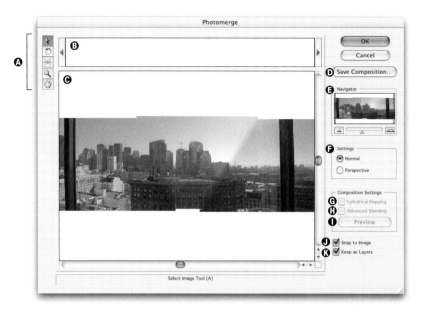

Photomerge Move tool
[H]
___

If you use the Keep As Layers option, each image is placed on a separate layer. Although they will overlay each other, Photoshop will not actually merge the images.

ⓐ **Photomerge Tools** In addition to the Select, Zoom, and Move tools, Photomerge includes tools to rotate images and set the vanishing point if you are using Perspective mode.

ⓑ **Lightbox** Holds images that have not been placed into the work area for merging.

ⓒ **Work Area** Drag images from the lightbox into this area and then arrange them to create your panorama. Photoshop automatically tries to fit overlapping images together.

ⓓ **Save composition for later editing** Click to save the current composition as a single file that can be later be retrieved and edited.

ⓔ **Image Navigator** Displays a view of the entire work area with controls similar to the Navigator palette to zoom in and out of the work area.

ⓕ **Panorama mode settings** Choose whether you want to create a normal (straight across) or perspective (simulated 3-D) panorama.

ⓖ **Cylindirical Mapping** Check to reduce distortion while using Perspective mode.

ⓗ **Advanced Blending** Check to reduce colorcast between the edges of merged images often caused by exposure differences.

ⓘ **Preview compositions settings** Click to see the effect of the composition settings on the image. Click again to return to Edit mode.

ⓙ **Snap To Image** Check if you want Photoshop to automatically merge images placed into the work area.

ⓚ **Keep As Layers** Check if you want Photoshop to create the new Photomerge file by placing each of the images on a separate layer.

4. The new panoramic image will be placed into a new document window, ready to be edited. Don't forget to save.

19.10   Adding Lighting Effects

➡ 12.4 Selecting Colors with the Color Picker

Rendering lighting effects can soak up a lot of memory. If you use this effect often and your computer has less than 256MB of memory, you might want to think about adding more memory.

To duplicate a light source, Option-drag (Mac) or Alt-drag (Windows) it to the new location.

You use the Lighting Effects filter to add simulated light sources that appear to shine on the flat surface of your image. You can place as many as 16 independent light sources, and you can control the circumference, direction, focal distance, focus, intensity, and color of each separately. To add lighting effects, follow these steps:

1 Select the layer to which you want to apply the filter. You can also make a specific selection on that layer to confine the effects of the filter.

2 Choose Filter > Render > Lighting Effects.

3 Add lights to the work area and adjust the circumference, distance, and/or direction of the light as well as the intensity, focus (for spotlights), and color of the light. In addition, adjust the properties of the simulated surface to which the light is being applied.

4 When you are satisfied, click OK to render the lighting effect onto the selected layer in the canvas.

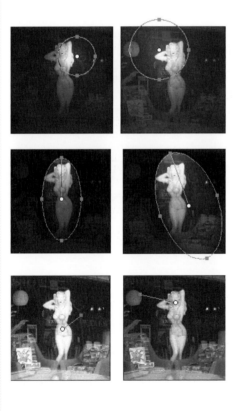

Omni lights have a circular circumference that can be resized, but they do not have direction or distance.

Spotlights have an elliptical circumference, distance, and direction that can be reshaped, resized, and redirected.

Directional lights have a direction and distance, that can be redirected and resized, but they do not have circumference.

19.10 Adding Lighting Effects *(continued)*

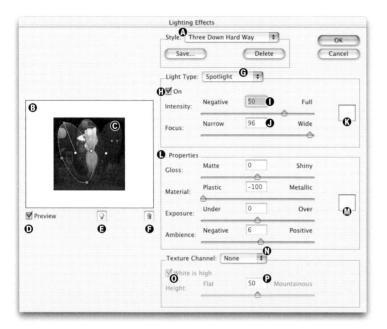

➥ 14.1 Filter Basics

➥ Color Section
   Filters

Every time you start Photoshop, it loads all the available filters. You might want to remove some filters and store them in another folder to speed up your Photoshop startup. To do this, simply drag filter files from the designated plug-in folder (most likely Photoshop/Plug-Ins/Filter) and place them in a folder not used for plug-ins. You might want to call this folder something like Plug-Ins (Disabled).

Ⓐ **Preset Styles** Select from an extensive list of preset lighting effects. You can also save the current settings to this list or delete the current settings from the list.

Ⓑ **Work Area** Thumbnail preview of effect; manipulate lights here.

Ⓒ **Selected Light** Round dots indicate light focal points. Click to select the light and make changes; drag to move. Currently selected light shows its circumference, direction, and distance (depending on light type); click a square gray anchor point to adjust these.

Ⓓ Check to preview the lighting effects in the work area. This will *not* preview in the canvas.

Ⓔ **Add Light** Click and drag into the work area to add a new light source.

Ⓕ **Delete Light** Click and drag a light from the work area to this icon to delete.

Ⓖ Choose the light type for the currently selected light in the work area.

Ⓗ Check to turn the selected light on and off.

Ⓘ Use the slider or enter a value (–99 through 100) for the intensity of the selected light. Negative values use the complementary color for the light.

Ⓙ (Spotlight only) Use the slider or enter a value (–99 through 100) for the focus of the selected light if it is a spotlight. Negative values use the complementary color for the light.

Ⓚ Click and use the Color Picker to choose the color for the selected light.

Ⓛ Use sliders or enter values (–99 through 100) for Gloss (how reflective), Material (simulated surface substance), Exposure (amount of light added), or Ambience (amount of ambient light).

Ⓜ Click and use the Color Picker to choose the color for the ambient light in the image.

Ⓝ Choose a color channel (Red, Green, Blue) to use to create a texture in the image.

Ⓞ Check to use lighter color as the high areas in the texture.

Ⓟ Use slider or enter value (0-100) to define texture relief. Lower numbers produce flatter texture.

19.11 Transforming Images in 3-D

Marquee tool

Ⓜ

If there is not enough information to create the full shape while you are rotating, Photoshop places a simple grayscale shade on empty areas.

Although it will never rival the software used to create *Toy Story*, Photoshop's 3-D rendering tool lets you select an area of the image and then resize or rotate the object as if it were a 3-D- object.

1 Select the layer to which you want to apply the filter. You can also make a specific selection on that layer to confine the effects of the filter.

2 Choose Filter **>** Render **>** 3-D Transform.

3 Draw shapes in the work area using the 3-D shape tools. The 3-D Transform dialog works as its own mini-interface, complete with its own toolbar on the left. Add 2-D path-based shapes to define the shapes you will then be manipulating in three dimensions.

4 After you create the desired shape, manipulate it in 3-D using the Pan and Rotate tools and the Field Of View or Dolly settings. This creates a copy of the content in the area within the path for you to manipulate.

5 When you are happy with the changes, click OK to render the 3-D shape onto the selected layer in the canvas.

The 2-D globe has been spun in 3-D.

19.11 Transforming Images in 3-D *(continued)*

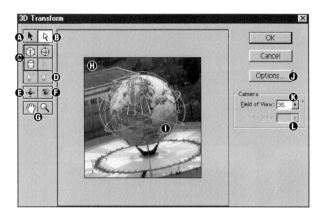

➠ Color Section
Filters

Zoom tool
[Z]

Hand tool
[H]

If the wireframe turns red as you are adjusting it, it cannot be rendered.

Ⓐ Selection tool Choose to select and move individual wireframes. Select a wireframe and press Delete/Backspace to remove it.

Ⓑ Direct Selection tool Choose to move an individual wireframe or to change its shape by clicking and adjusting anchor points.

Ⓒ 3-D shape tools Choose between a cube, a sphere, and cylinder shapes, and then draw the shapes as wireframes in the work area.

Ⓓ Point tools (Require Cylinder shape in the work area) Similar to path tools, these tools allow you to convert an anchor point between curved and corner, add an anchor point, or subtract an anchor point from the sides of a cylinder wireframe.

Ⓔ Pan tool Drag wireframes to move their contents.

Ⓕ Rotate tool Drag around the wireframes to rotate their contents.

Ⓖ Hand and Zoom tools Drag in the work area to move the viewable area of the canvas or magnify areas of the image.

Ⓗ Work area Previews the image in grayscale. Draw and manipulate your 3-D wireframes here.

Ⓘ Wireframe A globe wireframe is currently selected in the work area. Drag the outer edge with the Selection tool to move it; drag the handlebars with the Direct Selection tool to resize it. Use the Pan tool, Rotate tool, Field Of View setting, or Dolly setting to manipulate the area of the image selected by the wireframe in 3-D.

Ⓙ Click to open an options dialog in which you can set the resolution of rendered objects, the level of anti-aliasing used, and whether you want the original image displayed in the work area while you are manipulating the 3-D object.

Ⓚ Use the slider or enter a degree value (0 through 130) for the field of view. Larger values reduce the size of the 3-D object.

Ⓛ Use the slider or enter a value (0 through 99) for the dolly (closeness) to the 3-D object. Larger values reduce the size of the object.

19.12   Dodging and Burning Images

➡ 3.16 Exposure
        Tools

➡ 13.1 Brush Basics

Exposure tool

☐

———

When working on shadows and highlights, remember that the purpose is not to remove them but to recover detail in them. A photo with no shadows or highlights lacks detail and is uninteresting.

———

When applying either of the tools, select a brush large enough to cover the entire area you are working on rather than apply multiple brush strokes with a smaller brush size, which tends to give it an uneven appearance.

When working with photographs, areas of the image are often either to dark or too light when compared with the rest of the image. If you have ever worked in a dark room developing photographs, you have no doubt used the technique of holding a circle of dark cardboard over an area you want to lighten (dodging) or holding a piece of dark cardboard with a circle cut out over the area you want to darken (burning). Not only will this help improve the overall tonal balance of the image, but it also helps to restore detail in these areas by balancing the contrast. Photoshop has virtual versions of these brushlike tools.

When a photograph is taken with varying degrees of light falling on it (left), some areas end up in shadow, and other parts are washed out as shown. Using the Dodge tool, you can lighten the darker areas (right: man's head). Next, you can darken the washed-out areas slightly to finish the job (right: man's shirt). The effects are slightly exaggerated so that you can better see what is going on.

To use the Dodge or Burn tool, follow these steps:

1 In the Toolbox, select either the Dodge tool 🔍 or the Burn tool 👌.

2 Beyond the normal brush tool options, the tool options bar includes tool-specific options that require adjustment:

■ Choose the range: Shadows (darker pixels), Midtones (middle range pixels), or Highlights (lighter pixels).

■ Set the exposure for the tool: typically, you set the exposure to a low value and then use the Airbrush mode to gradually build up an area so that it does not become overexposed or underexposed.

■ Choose Airbrush mode: you can choose whether you want to use the tool in Airbrush mode to gradually build up the effect.

19.12 Dodging and Burning Images *(continued)*

3 Drag the brush over the part of the image you want to adjust.

The effects of the Dodge and Burn tools are subtle and additive. Apply the tool several times at low values (less than 10%) rather than once at a large setting.

➡ 13.2 Selecting and Adjusting Brushes

➡ 13.3 Creating and Saving Brushes

The Dodge and Burn tools can only recover detail in an image; they cannot create it. If applying the Burn tool (set to Highlight) to a bright white area of an image doesn't produce any details, it is a blowout, and the Burn tool will only shade the white portions into gray. Likewise, if the detail isn't in the shadows, you can't recover it using the Dodge tool.

THE CAPTURE OF PEGASUS ("MYTH IN A BOX" SERIES); © TEODORU BADIU; WWW.APOCRYPH.NET

19.13 Adjusting Saturation with the Sponge Tool

Exposure tool
⊙

Cycle exposure tools
Shift ⊙

When using the Sponge tool in Saturate mode, use small values such as 10% to 20% to make colors more vivid. This is especially true if you are working on an image that will be printed. Oversaturated areas tend to lose detail because all the color saturation values become too high.

An effective way to focus the viewer's attention on a particular subject in a color photograph is to partially desaturate everything but the subject. This technique is quite popular with advertisers. For example, a model holds the product (in full color) while everything else in the photo is in grayscale.

The Sponge tool changes the color saturation of the pixels over which it is dragged. On color images, the saturation of the color is increased, and the colors appear more vivid when the Sponge tool is set to Saturate mode. When applied to the same image in Desaturate mode, the colors appear faded. If the Sponge tool is used at 100% with Desaturate, all the color is removed, and the affected areas appear to be grayscale. If applied to a grayscale image, the Sponge tool increases or decreases contrast. To use the Sponge tool, follow these steps:

1 In the Toolbox, select the Sponge tool 🔘.

2 In the tool options bar, aside from the typical brush options such as size, set the following options:

■ Choose the mode: Saturate (increase color) or Desaturate (decrease color).

■ Choose the Flow setting: For weak effects, use a low percentage value; for strong effects, enter a higher value. Generally, use a low flow setting and the Airbrush mode to gradually build up the color change to avoid stark colorcasts.

■ Choose Airbrush mode: you can choose whether you want to use the tool in Airbrush mode to gradually build up the color effect.

3 Drag over the part of the image you want to modify.

CHAPTER 20

Working with Digital Video

ALTHOUGH PRIMARILY THOUGHT OF as a program for creating print and web designs, Photoshop is also an indispensable tool for working with video imagery. Whether you are creating backdrops to blue screen into a scene, complex titles, or preparing stills from your latest cinematic masterpiece, Photoshop CS can meet your needs.

- 20.1 **Digital video basics**
- 20.2 **Starting a new image for video**
- 20.3 **Viewing for video**
- 20.4 **Saving and exporting images for video**
- 20.5 **De-interlacing video stills**

20.1   Digital Video Basics

➟ 2.9   View Menu

➟ 8.2   Understand-
ing Image
Modes

**Open Color Settings
dialog**
[Shift] [⌘] [K]
[Ctrl] [Alt] [K]

———

Many video applica-
tions such as Adobe
Premiere do not sup-
port 16 bit per channel
images, so scale back to
8 bit.

Photoshop CS offers several new features targeted toward video filmmakers, including the ability to work with nonsquare pixels, to create documents for the most common video formats, including guides for action and title-safe areas, and to export layers to individual files for import into video applications.

Video Formats

Just as there are multiple image file formats, there are myriad video formats. However, unlike computer files, which video format you use depends on the world for which you are producing your footage:

NTSC (National Television Standards Committee) runs at 29.97 frames per second (fps). Countries that use NTSC include Bahamas, Canada, Costa Rica, Greenland, Jamaica, Japan, South Korea, Mexico, Netherlands, Philippines, Puerto Rico, Taiwan, the USA.

PAL (Phase Alternating Line) runs at 25 fps. Countries that use PAL include Australia, Austria, Belgium, Canary Islands, China, Denmark, Finland, Germany, Ghana, Gibraltar, Greece (also SECAM), Iceland, India, Indonesia, Ireland, Israel, Italy, Kuwait, Luxembourg (also SECAM), New Zealand, Norway, Portugal, Saudi Arabia (also SECAM), South Africa, Spain, Swaziland, Thailand, Turkey, United Kingdom, Yugoslavia.

SECAM (Systeme Electronique Couleur Avec Memoire) runs at 25 fps. Although not as widely supported in Photoshop, you can follow the instructions for PAL to get the correct results. SECAM countries include Czech Republic, Egypt, France, Greece (also PAL), Haiti, Iran, Iraq, Libya, Luxembourg (also PAL), Monaco (also PAL), Poland, Romania, Russia and other former Soviet Republics, Saudi Arabia (also PAL), Slovakia, Viet Nam.

HDTV (High Definition Television) is the new digital standard in North America.

Photoshop is video format neutral, meaning that it can work on an image going to or coming from any of these formats, but you will need to specify the correct dimensions for your file when starting a new document and set the appropriate color settings.

Square or Nonsquare Pixels

Although both computer designs and video designs are presented on relatively flat screens, computer screens use square pixels and video monitors use rectangular pixels (sometimes called nonsquare pixels). If you design using standard resolution for a computer screen, the image will be distorted, looking squeezed on the video monitor.

Fortunately Photoshop CS introduces a new feature that allows you to view the image in an aspect ratio corrected for video, allowing you to work in the correct resolution for video without noticeable distortion. Still, it is vital to remember that when designing in Photoshop, what you see on the computer screen is not always what you will see when working in a video application.

20.1 Digital Video Basics *(continued)*

An image using square pixels on a computer monitor

The image viewed on a video monitor if not corrected for square pixel aspect ratio

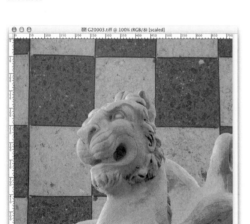

The image viewed on a computer monitor with the correct pixel aspect ratio. This looks as close as the computer can get to what the final version will look like on a video monitor.

➤ 8.4 Choosing a Color Working Space

➤ 12.4 Selecting Colors with the Color Picker

Remember that video operates at 72 dpi on the RGB color palette. However, if you are doing "pan and scan" techniques with still images, your images' resolution should be 300 dpi.

You will probably want to save the color settings in the default Settings folder in the Photoshop folder.

Setting Your Color Workspace for Video

Like web projects, video projects use the RGB color model to define how colors are recorded and presented on the screen. Before starting any graphic work in Photoshop that will end up in video, first configure your color settings so that they match the color gamut used by video on NTSC and PAL. To customize your color workspace for video, follow these steps:

1 Choose Color Settings from either the Photoshop (OS X) or Edit (Windows) menu.

2 In the Color Settings dialog, click the Advanced Mode check box.

3 In the Working Spaces RGB drop-down, select SMPTE-C if you are [...] of D65. Select PAL/SECAM for PAL or SECAM projects; the CRT gamma is 2.8.

4 Click OK.

20.2   Starting a New Image for Video

Open a new document
⌘ Ⓝ
Ctrl Ⓝ

———

When adding an image to a nonsquare image intended for video, Photoshop automatically converts and scales the image to the appropriate pixel aspect ratio.

———

When NTSC television was introduced, the decision was made to emulate the Academy Format format, but round off the proportions to whole numbers, 4:3 or 1.33:1.

———

If you're designing for DVD productions with software such as DVD Studio Pro, base your canvas size for NTSC DV format (720×534) or the PAL DV format (768×576).

Before starting a new image for video, you must consider a variety of image aspect ratios associated with different video stocks and hardware/software applications. Before you begin designing graphics for your video project, be sure to talk with the editor about the video format that will be used. Find out specifically what the image aspect ratio is in terms of pixel dimensions.

1   When starting your video image, first answer the following questions:

■ Which video format are you working in: NTSC, PAL/SECAM, or HDTV?

■ Do you want to design with square pixels? If so, your image will be squashed when displayed on a video monitor unless you manually scale it, which is not recommended.

■ If you are using NTSC, are you using DV (4:3 aspect ratio) or D1 (0.9:1 aspect ratio)?

2   Choose File > New, and based on your answers to the questions from step 1, choose one of the video presets and click OK.

Canvas Sizes by Format

VIDEO FORMAT	ASPECT RATIO	SQUARE PIXELS	RECTANGULAR PIXELS
NTSC DV	0.9	720¥534	720¥480
NTSC DV Widescreen	1.2	864¥480	720¥480
NTSC D1	0.9	720✕540	720¥486
NTSC D1 Square Pix	Square	720x540	720¥486
PAL D1/DV	1.066	768¥576	720¥576
PAL D1/DV Square Pix	Square	768x576	720¥576
PAL D1/DV Widescreen	1.42	1024¥576	720¥576
HDTV (720)	Square	1280¥720	N/A
HDTV (1080)	Square	1920¥1080	N/A

In the table, if the format is in rectangular pixels, "square pixels" refers to canvas size without aspect ratio correction.

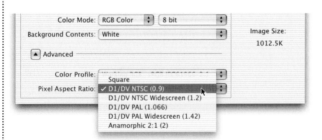

When starting a video project in Photoshop, you can, in the New dialog, choose a preset canvas size and then adjust the pixel aspect ratio as desired in the advanced controls. Generally, though, you will want to keep the pixel aspect ratio at its default.

3   You can begin editing your image in the canvas using any standard Photoshop techniques. Notice that the window also includes guides to show where it will be safe to include key content; the outer guides mark the action-safe area, and the inner guides mark the title-safe area.

20.3 Viewing for Video

Since images destined for video will use different size pixels than the standard computer monitor, it is extremely helpful while working to be able to simulate the way the image will look in its final environment by simulating the pixel aspect ratio. Photoshop CS allows you to not only quickly turn on this simulation, but also to specify which aspect ratio should be used:

To view the image as it will appear on a video monitor, choose View > Pixel Aspect Ratio Correction. You will see the canvas change size accordingly and the message [Scaled] will appear in the title bar of the document window when the correction is turned on.

To change the pixel aspect ration being simulated in the image, choose Image > Pixel Aspect Ratio, and select the aspect ratio for the video format you want to view. Choose Anamorphic for Widescreen DVD formats.

To create your own customized aspect ratio, choose Image > Pixel Aspect Ratio > Custom Pixel Aspect Ratio… In the Custom Aspect Ratio dialog, enter a name and the factor to use for the aspect ratio (0.1000 to 10.00). The higher the number, the wider the pixels.

➡ 7.4 Changing Your Document View

➡ 7.5 Using Rulers, Guides, Grids, and Snap

Toggle gamut warning
[Shift] [⌘] [Y]
[Shift] [Ctrl] [Y]

———

Even though you have title-safe and action-safe zones on the graphic image, you can leave design elements in the clipped-out areas. Some television monitors clip out very little on the edges, so it's a good idea to have some graphical filler for those monitors.

RASTERIZING FOR VIDEO

If you are using Type layers, layer effects, or other vector-based content in your image, you will need to rasterize the image before you can import it into some video applications. This is especially the case with Final Cut Pro and DVD Studio Pro, which do not include any vector tools for images.

After you rasterize a layer, you cannot edit it except with the painting tools. It's recommended that you save a copy of your document before you rasterize it, in case you need to re-edit the file later (see Section 6.10).

For more details on how to rasterize your image, see Section 10.10.

20.4 Saving and Exporting Images for Video

ImageReady offers a more advanced wizard for exporting layers (choose File > Export > Layers As Files…) that is similar to the version in Photoshop that also allows you to specify the format for each layer.

Once an image destined for video has been created, there are a few further steps you will need to take before you are ready to save it to be imported into your video editing software. If you are outputting for NTSC format, you need to first correct any out-of-gamut colors. Then use the check list on this page to make sure that all of your i's are dotted and t's crossed before following the instructions for saving your image presented in Section 6.10, or the instructions for outputting individual layers explained in this section.

Correcting Color in NTSC

The NTSC Colors filter is a last step to take before saving your NTSC Photoshop file to be imported into your video application. Its function is to safeguard the color gamut and prevent colors from bleeding across the television screen. Employing the NTSC Colors filter will have minimal effect on your image, since you should not have any out-of-gamut colors. Nonetheless, you can never be too safe when working with colors that are going to be broadcast.

When your design work is complete, choose Filter > Video > NTSC Colors before you save your project. You are then ready to bring your Photoshop file into your video application. You must be in RGB mode for this to work.

Saving Video Images

Although the process for saving your image for use in video is little different from saving your image for use in any other medium as explained in Section 6.10, you have some special considerations:

- Be sure that the layers you want to use are visible, in the desired order, and each with its own unique name. Deleting any layers you do not plan to use in your video application is also recommended.

- If you created your design using square pixels and it is destined for a nonsquare video format, you will need to resize your image. To do so, choose Image > Image Size… and then enter the rectangular pixel dimensions for the image based on the aspect ratio you are using, as shown in the table in Section 20.2. For example, if you started your image as an NTSC D1 Square Pix, resize it from 720×540 to 720×486.

- You can save your file in a variety of formats, including JPEG, but to ensure that layers are preserved, save in either the Photoshop native format (.psd) or the TIFF format with layers preserved.

20.4 Saving and Exporting Images for Video *(continued)*

Exporting Layers

Although most of today's video-editing software such as Adobe Premiere and Apple Final Cut Pro allow you to directly import a Photoshop file and use each layer independently, it is sometimes useful to create each layer as its own file and then import the layers into your video-editing software separately. Photoshop CS introduces a new wizard that allows you to quickly and easily export each layer as an independent file.

To export each layer as its own file, follow these steps:

1 Flatten any layers used for compositing (such as clipping groups), and rasterize any vector components.

2 Choose File > Scripts > Export Layers To Files.

3 In the Export Layers To Files dialog, set the output options and then click Run.

➡ 10.10 Rasterizing Vector Layers

➡ 20.2 Starting a New Image for Video

If your video application requires that you scale your graphic files to match the native video format, rasterize your image only *after* you've scaled it down to its proper aspect ratio.

Export Layers To Files

Destination:
Ⓐ ~/Movies   [Browse...]   [Run]

File Name Prefix:
Ⓑ Background for Movie   [Cancel]

Ⓒ ☑ Visible Layers Only

File Type:
Ⓓ ○ JPEG   ● PSD   ○ TIFF
   ○ PDF   ○ Targa ○ BMP
Ⓔ ☑ Include ICC Profile
Ⓕ PSD Options:
   ☑ Maximize Compatibility

Please specify the format and location for saving each layer as a file.

Ⓐ Enter a path, or browse to define where the new files should be saved.

Ⓑ Enter the prefix to be used in front of each layer's filename.

Ⓒ Check if you want to export only layers that are currently visible. If this check box is cleared, all layers will be exported.

Ⓓ Choose the file format in which you want the layers output.

Ⓔ Check if you want the ICC (International Color Consortium) metadata included with each file.

Ⓕ Check to ensure maximum compatibility with other software, including previous versions of Photoshop. This may disable some advanced features that are only available in Photoshop CS.

Photoshop will automatically create a new file for each layer and save it based on the options you set, using the layer name for the filename. This may take a few seconds or a few minutes depending on the image size and the number of layers.

PHOTOSHOP WORKSPACE

UNIVERSAL TASKS

PHOTO AND VIDEO TASKS

PRINT TASKS

WEB TASKS

20.5   De-interlacing Video Stills

Not all NTSC video stills have artifacts. This is the case when the two fields' video content is exactly the same. Nonetheless, it's still a good idea to use the De-Interlace filter to make sure that you have only one video field in your image.

Remember that you should always calibrate your colors for the medium in which your design work is going to be finished. For example, if you are taking video stills that will end up on a web-based project, don't use the color settings specific to video projects, but those specific to your web project.

NTSC video works by producing two fields in one image frame at every given moment. This function is called *interlacing* and was invented as a way to squeeze the television signal down to be read quickly enough by the television monitor. The speed of video technology has since come of age in this regard, but interlaced video is still the standard for the NTSC video format.

This technology, however, does pose a slight problem for designers who are working with graphic assets taken from NTSC video. If you are working in Photoshop with video stills exported from a nonlinear editor, you will sometimes notice a motion artifact in the still image, which often looks like broken lines on areas of motion. (This is because video applications read pixels in a different way than Photoshop reads them.) The only way to cut out one of the two motion fields in Photoshop is to use the De-Interlace function.

To de-interlace a video still, open or import a video still image, choose Filter > Video > De-Interlace…, and set the options in the De-Interlace dialog. When you are finished, click OK. You will notice that the motion artifacts have disappeared, leaving you with a more resolute image.

Choose which field you want to eliminate. In terms of how the action plays out linearly, the even field is the "first" field, and the odd field is the "second." Then choose to replace the field you intend to eliminate either by duplicating the chosen field or by interpolating from the chosen field. Technically, choosing Duplication maintains your colors more efficiently because it simply copies the pixels of the selected scan. Choosing Interpolation fills in the colors based on the selected image. However, in practice, you will rarely notice a difference in the two methods.

The video image before being de-interlaced (left) and after (right)

CHAPTER **21**

PHOTOSHOP WORKSPACE

UNIVERSAL TASKS

PHOTO AND VIDEO TASKS

PRINT TASKS

WEB TASKS

Image Compositing

UNLESS YOU ARE SIMPLY retouching photos, you will most likely want to combine photos using Photoshop to create a collage of images. Composition is the process by which images from different sources are combined and interact with one another to create new images. The most obvious way to combine images is through copying and pasting (see Sections 9.13 and 9.14), which allows you to overlap images of different sizes or with transparent pixels. However, Photoshop offers several more advanced methods for compositing images that go far beyond simple collage.

- 21.1 **Compositing basics**
- 21.2 **Blending modes and opacity**
- 21.3 **Creating knockouts**
- 21.4 **Conditional blending**
- 21.5 **Applying one image to another**
- 21.6 **Combining images through Calculations**
- 21.7 **Compositing with clipping masks**
- 21.8 **Extracting part of an image**

21.1   Compositing Basics

___

Opacity controls exist in a variety of locations within the Photoshop, but opacity is primarily set in a layer-by-layer basis using the controls in the Layers palette.

Compositing is the act of bringing two or more images together—layering them one on top of the other—to create a single new image. Basically, you are stacking images and then adjusting the dimensions, opacity, and pixel blending of these layered images in order to expose the content of images underneath. Chapter 10 discusses at length how to layer images on top of each other, and this is the beginning of compositing. Now it is time to further explore how to allow images on different layers to visually interact with each other by adjusting the images' following properties:

Opacity   Opacity makes an entire layer more transparent. Think of lowering the opacity as turning the image from a photographic print, which you cannot see through, into an overhead projector transparency, which retains the color and shape of the image, but allows you to see any other images that lie beneath. By stacking images and adjusting the opacity of higher-level layers so that they become more transparent, you can see all or parts of the images in layers underneath.

Blending   Like opacity, blending allows you to see through higher layers into the lower layers, but rather than simply making the layer translucent, blending allows you to specify exactly how the pixels in the higher layer interact with the pixels in layers beneath it and can be applied on a layer-by-layer basis in the Layers palette, as part of a layer effect, or using the Apply and Calculations commands as well as using brush tools. The 25 blending modes (including Normal) are all explained with examples in the Color Section of this book.

Masking   You can use one layer to hide parts of the layers above or below it using masking. Masking does not erase those hidden parts of the layer, but simply hides them from view, allowing you to easily change the parts being hidden. Chapter 11 explores three important mask types (quick, layer, and vector), but there are also knockout and clipping masks, which allow much greater versatility.

BLENDING MODES WITH BRUSHES: BEHIND AND CLEAR

Although most blending modes can be applied directly to a layer, there are two blending modes that are specific to the brush tools: Behind and Clear. Behind allows you to paint behind existing pixels in the image, but leaves completely transparent areas alone. Clear allows you to paint to change the transparency of pixels (rather than their color), allowing you to use the selected foreground color to set the pixel opacity based on its relative grayscale value. For more details, see the Blending Modes section in the Color Section.

21.2   Blending Modes and Opacity

Layers not only allow you to build up overlapping images, but also allow you to set how those layers interact. The primary way to set how layers interact in the Layers palette is to use blending modes and opacity.

Setting the Blending Mode

The original layered image. A drop-shadow effect has been added to Layer 2.

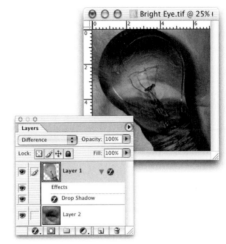

Layer 2's blending mode has been set to Difference, creating an inverted look in the area of the lightbulb image.

The blending mode assigned to a layer determines how that layer affects the pixels of layers underneath it. For a description of each blending mode, see the "Blending Modes" section in the Color Section.

To quickly change the blending mode, select a single layer or layer set, and then choose one of the blending modes from the blending mode pop-up menu in the Layers palette.

When you first create a layer set, its blending mode is set to Pass Through by default, which preserves the blending modes of the individual layers within the set. If you set a blending mode other than Pass Through for a layer set, the layers are composited (with the modes being applied only to other layers in the set) and then treated as a single layer in the image using the layer set's blending mode.

➥ 4.13 Layers Palette

➥ 10.1 Layer Basics

Normal blending mode
Shift Option N
Shift Alt N

Dissolve blending mode
Shift Option I
Shift Alt I

Multiply blending mode
Shift Option M
Shift Alt M

Screen blending mode
Shift Option S
Shift Alt S

Overlay blending mode
Shift Option O
Shift Alt O

Soft Light blending mode
Shift Option F
Shift Alt F

Hard Light blending mode
Shift Option H
Shift Alt H

Color Dodge blending mode
Shift Option D
Shift Alt D

Darken blending mode
Shift Option K
Shift Alt K

———

Two blending modes, Behind and Clear, are available only when you are using brush tools, so they do not appear in the Layers palette.

➡ 10.5 Adding
      Adjustments
      and Fill
      Layers

➡ Color Section
      Blending
      Modes

Lighten blending mode
[Shift][Option][G]
[Shift][Alt][G]

Difference blending mode
[Shift][Option][E]
[Shift][Alt][E]

Exclusion blending mode
[Shift][Option][X]
[Shift][Alt][X]

Hue blending mode
[Shift][Option][U]
[Shift][Alt][U]

Saturation blending mode
[Shift][Option][T]
[Shift][Alt][T]

Color blending mode
[Shift][Option][C]
[Shift][Alt][C]

Luminosity blending mode
[Shift][Option][Y]
[Shift][Alt][Y]

You can also change a layer's blending mode and opacity as part of the advanced Blending Options available in the Layer Styles dialog.

You cannot change the blending mode and opacity in the Background layer or locked layers.

You cannot change blending mode and opacity selectively in a layer. Settings affect the entire layer evenly.

Setting the Opacity

A layer's opacity is a percentage value that defines the transparency of image pixels. If the opacity is less than 100%, the pixels are translucent, and images from layers underneath show through.

To change the opacity of the pixels in a layer, select the layer or layer set and then in the Layers palette enter a new opacity, or use the Opacity slider to set the percentage. If you are using the Opacity slider, you can view the change to the layer in real time as you slide it back and forth.

If you set the opacity for a layer set, this setting is used as the base opacity for the layers in the set. Setting the opacity of a layer within the set then is not cumulative, but rather the percentage scale is compressed.

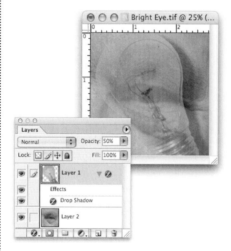

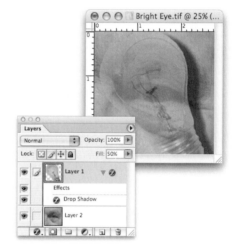

Layer 2's opacity has been set to 50%. Notice that the shadow being created by the drop-shadow effect is also faded by 50%.

Layer 2's fill opacity has been set to 50%. Notice that the shadow remains at the original strength.

Setting the Fill Opacity

The fill opacity allows you to set the opacity of pixels that have been painted or of shapes drawn into the layer. Unlike opacity, which affects all the content of the layer—including layer styles and blending modes applied to the layer—the fill opacity affects only pixels that you have placed on the layer using drawing, painting, or vector tools.

To change the fill opacity of the pixels in a layer, choose the layer and then in the Layers palette enter a new fill opacity, or use the Fill Opacity slider to set the percentage. If you are using the Fill Opacity slider, you can view the change to the layer in real time as you slide it back and forth.

21.3 Creating Knockouts

Knockouts allow you to use the content of a layer as a mask to "punch through" to the layers directly beneath the set (shallow) or to the Background or Transparency layer (deep). This works much like using layers as part of a clipping mask but gives you much greater flexibility.

To use a layer's content as a knockout, follow these steps:

1 Select the layer to be used as the Knockout layer. Follow these guidelines when deciding which layer to select:

■ To use a layer to punch through all other layers beneath it to the Background or Transparency layer, you can select any layer as the Knockout layer.

■ To punch through one or more layers to another layer or layers in the image, create a layer set with the layer being used as the knockout at the top of the set and the layers to be knocked through beneath it in the same set. Make sure this layer set's Blending option is set to Pass Through in the Layers palette. Place the layer or layers you want knocked through directly underneath the set.

2 Open the Blending Options panel in the Layer Style dialog (choose Layer > Layer Style > Blending Options…).

3 Set a blending mode or lower the fill opacity for the layer. This allows you to control the strength of the knockout.

4 Choose an option from the Knockout drop-down: None, Shallow, or Deep.

5 You can preview the effect of the knockout and try different blending modes and opacities before clicking OK to commit the changes.

➡ 9.2 Selecting a Layer or Its Contents

➡ 10.6 Creating Layer Sets

➡ 15.2 Applying Effects and Styles

➡ 15.7 Applying Advanced Blending Options

➡ Color Section Blending Modes

If the Knockout layer is not part of a layer set or a clipping mask, both Shallow and Deep punch through to the Background layer or the Transparency layer.

None No knockout used. In this example, the Text layer and the Starburst layer are in a common set, with the photograph below the set.

Shallow Punches through all layers in the layer set to layers directly beneath the layer set. Here, the Text layer uses a shallow knockout to punch through the Starburst layer, so the photograph shows through. Notice that the drop-shadow effect is still apparent.

Deep Punches through all layers directly beneath the Knockout layer to reveal the Background layer (if being used) or Transparency layer. In this example, the Text layer uses a deep knockout to show through to the black Background layer.

21.4 Conditional Blending

You use the blending mode to specify how the pixels in one layer interact with the pixels in the layers beneath it. However, this setting is applied indiscriminately over the entire layer. You can also blend pixels over certain color value ranges in the different color channels using the Blend If options in the Advanced Blending options in the Blending Options panel. These controls allow you to set the color values at which pixels are blended together or to set a smoother partial blend between layers.

To conditionally blend pixels over a particular layer, follow these steps:

1 Select the layer to which you want to apply selective blending.

2 Open the Blending Options panel in the Layer Style dialog (choose Layer **>** Layer Style **>** Blending Options…).

3 Set the Blend If options by choosing a color channel (or choose gray to affect all channels), and then use the sliders to change the black and white blending values for the channel in the selected layer (This Layer) or layers below the selected layer (Underlying Layers).

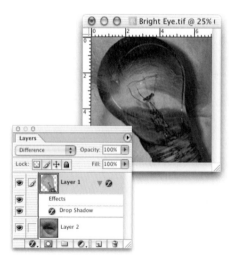

The original image with the image of a lightbulb using the Difference blending mode.

EXPORTING ALPHA CHANNELS TO VIDEO

You can set up the parts of the graphic or title you want to be solid, transparent, or translucent by adjusting the alpha channels and then import the image as a .psd into programs like Apple Final Cut Pro or Adobe Premiere. These programs will reproduce the transparency and opacity settings you applied in Photoshop. Even better, they are not static, and you can change them using controls in the video software.

21.4 Conditional Blending *(continued)*

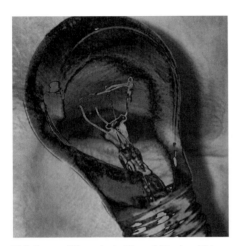

➡ 15.7 Applying
Advanced
Blending
Options

➡ Color Section
Blending
Modes

Conditional blending can often lead to sharp colorcast, in which parts of the image suddenly change color with no transition. To overcome this problem, use partial blending to smooth out these abrupt transitions.

This Layer (The selected layer) Pixels within the range will be blended with pixels in layers underneath. Fill pixels with values outside this range in the selected layer will be made 100% transparent. However, pixels that are created as a part of an effect (such as a drop shadow) will be unaffected by this change.

Underlying Layers (All layers below the selected layer) Pixels within the range will be blended with pixels in the selected layer. Pixels outside this range in the layers below the selected layer will be 100% opaque in place of pixels in the selected layer, including pixels created as a part of an effect.

4   You can also split the White and/or Black blending values to create areas of partially blended pixels. To define a range of partially blended pixels, Option/Alt-click one side of a blending value slider, and move it left or right (depending on the side clicked). The range of pixels between the two halves of the slider will blend smoothly to help eliminate colorcasts in the transitions.

Ⓐ Blend If Choose the color channel to which you want to apply the blending options. Choose Gray to apply the blending options to all channels.

Ⓑ Black blending value Use the slider to choose the lower values (0 through 255) for the brightness range at which pixels should be blended. Option/Alt-click the slider to set a partial blending range to smooth transitions.

Ⓒ Current blending value Displays the value set by the sliders below.

Ⓓ White blending value Use the slider to choose the upper values (0 through 255) for the brightness range at which pixels should be blended. Option/Alt-click the slider to set a partial blending range to smooth transitions.

Ⓔ Partial blending range The slider has been split, and the colors in the range between the two halves will gradually blend to create a smooth transition.

Ⓕ Current Partial Blending Values Displays the value limits that pixels will be partially blended between.

21.5 Applying One Image to Another

If the two images being applied to each other use different color modes (see Section 8.3)—for example, one is RGB and the other CMYK—you can apply a single channel only between the images and not between the images and the composite channel.

Although you can achieve a similar effect by simply copying a layer from one image to another and then setting the blending mode, the Apply Image dialog allows you greater versatility and subtlety by providing channel controls and masking.

You can blend a layer or a color channel of any two open images using the Apply Image dialog. This allows you to select a specific layer (or merged layers) and a specific color channel (or the composite channel) using a particular blending mode. To apply one open image to another open image, follow these steps:

1 Open two images: one to be used as the target image to be changed and the other as the source image to apply to the target. Both images must have the same dimensions in pixels but can be different color modes.

2 With the target image active, select the layer to which you want to apply changes.

3 Choose Image > Apply Image…

4 Set your options in the dialog and click OK. The source image will be applied to the selected layer in the target image.

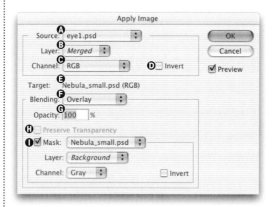

A Choose the source image. All images that are currently open and have the same dimensions in pixels as the target image will be displayed in this list.

B Choose the layer from the source image to apply to the layer you selected in step 2. Choose Merged to use the entire image.

C Choose the channel from the source image to apply to the channels for the target image. Choose Composite (RGB, CMYK, etc…) to apply the image to all channels.

D Check to invert the source image when applying.

E Displays the filename and information for the target image.

F Choose a blending mode to use when applying the source image.

G Enter a percentage value for the opacity, which sets the strength of the composite effect.

H Check if you want the composite image applied only to opaque pixels.

I Check to use an open image with the same dimensions in pixels as a mask in the composite. You then choose the image to use, the layer in that image, and the channel in that image and specify whether the mask should be inverted.

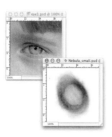
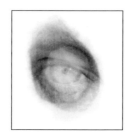

Left: The eye1.psd image will be used as the source, and Nebula_small.psd will be the destination. Right: The results of using the Apply Image dialog.

21.6 Combining Images through Calculations

The Calculations dialog allows you to combine images from two different channels, either in a single image or from two different open images and then output these combined images as an alpha channel, a selection, or a grayscale version of the composited image layers.

To combine two images using the Calculations dialog, follow these steps:

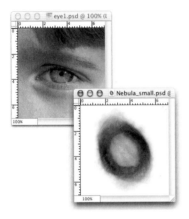
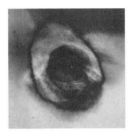

Use the Calculations dialog to create a new document with an alpha channel (grayscale image) based on the calculations made between the two images.

1 Open two images. Both must be the same dimensions in pixels.

2 Choose Image **>** Calculations…

3 Set your options in the dialog and click OK.

➡ 7.3 Setting the Image Size

➡ 8.7 Using Color in Channels

Calculations cannot be made using the composited channel.

WHAT IS AN ALPHA CHANNEL?

An *alpha channel* is like an onionskin over the image—a layer of information that records the transparency and composite mode of each pixel in the image allowing you greater control over transparency than simple opacity changes allow. Normally an image will display the color channels that make up the full image. The alpha channel is a graphic map of the opacity values of the clip across its surface. However, you can view alpha channels in the Channels palette.

In the Channels palette, the image you see in the thumbnail is a grayscale depiction of transparency. Solid areas are seen as pure white, while completely transparent areas are completely black. Parts of the image where you've applied intermediate degrees of transparency appear as gray areas.

21.6 Combining Images through Calculations

(continued)

➡ 22.17 Other Adjustments: Brightness, Desaturation, and Inversion

Calculations can help you make complex selections based on the content of the color channel. This is also useful if you want to create random-looking selections to edit, adding a more natural look to your image.

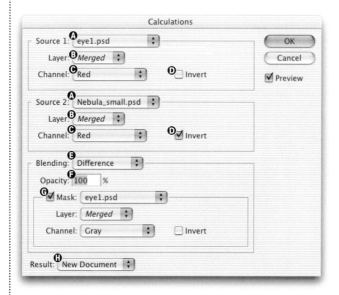

A Choose the two source images. All images that are currently open and have the same dimensions in pixels will be displayed in this list. You can choose the same image for both, allowing you to use the image itself to make complex selections or alpha masks.

B Choose the layer to use for the calculation in the source images. These layers will be evaluated based on the color channel and blending mode. Choose Merged to use the entire image.

C Choose the channel from the source image to use for the calculations. Choose Gray to get the same effect as converting the image to a grayscale image.

D Check to invert the channel performing the calculation.

E Choose a blending mode to use when calculating the source images.

F Enter a percentage value for the opacity, which sets the strength of the calculation effect.

G Check to use an open image with the same dimensions in pixels as a mask in the composite. You then choose the image to use, the layer in that image, and the channel in that image and specify whether the mask should be inverted.

H Choose how the calculations should be output: to a new document with a grayscale version of the composited layers, to a new alpha channel that will appear in the Channels palette, or to a selection.

21.7 Compositing with Clipping Masks

Clipping masks allow you to use one layer (called the base layer) to mask the content of one or more layers above it. Unlike layer and vector masks, which allow you to mask the content of a single layer with an alpha channel or a vector path, clipping masks use the shape and transparency of an existing layer to mask multiple layers.

⇒ 4.13 Layers Palette

Add layer to clipping mask
⌘ G
Ctrl G

The original unclipped images

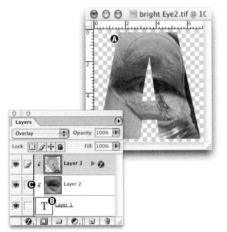

Ⓐ Clipped Layers 2 and 3 are clipped by Layer 1 underneath.

Ⓑ Clip arrow Indicates that the layer is being clipped by the layer beneath it. If there are multiple arrows, each layer is being clipped by the bottom layer after the last clip arrow.

Ⓒ Base layer The bottom layer to which the above layers are grouped for masking. An underline indicates that this is the base layer.

Adding Layers to a Clipping Mask Group

Unlike layer and vector masks, which are set up within individual layers, clipping masks are created between different adjacent layers; the lower layer (the Base layer) is used to clip layers above. That is not to say that the base layer will mask *all* layers above it, but only those that have been added to the clipping "group." You can add layers to this group by choosing the commands in the Layers menu or by clicking in the Layers palette.

⟶ 11 Masking
Layers

**Release layer from
clipping mask**
Shift ⌘ G
Shift Ctrl G

———

In Photoshop 7,
making a clipping
mask was referred
to as "grouping."

To clip one layer with the layer beneath using the Layers palette, press Option/Alt, point to the divider between the two layers, and click. You will notice that, when you are right over the layer divider line, the cursor changes to two interlocking circles. The top layer will now be clipped by the bottom (base) layer. Repeat this process for any layer immediately above a clipping group to add that layer to the group.

Layer 3 is being added to the clipping mask group by Option/Alt-clicking the divider line between it and Layer 2, which is already being clipped. Notice that the cursor has changed to two interlocking circles.

To clip one layer with the layer beneath using the Layers menu, select the layer in the Layers palette and choose Layer > Create Clipping Mask.

To add multiple layers simultaneously, select one of the layers to be clipped, link the other layers to be clipped by clicking the link column 🔗 in the Layers palette, and choose Layer > Create Clipping Mask From Linked.

Releasing Layers from a Clipping Mask Group

To release a layer and all the layers above it from the clipping mask group using the Layers palette, press Option/Alt, point to the divider between the two layers, and click. You will notice that, when you are right over the layer divider line, the cursor changes to two interlocking circles. Repeat for as many layers as desired.

To release a layer and all layers above it from the clipping group mask using the Layers menu, select the layer and choose Layer > Release From Clipping Mask. If you perform this action on the base layer, all clipped layers are released.

21.8 Extracting Part of an Image

You can separate parts of an image from other parts of an image in many ways. You can make a selection to delete unwanted parts of the image, you can use the Eraser tool, you can erase the background, or you can erase selected colors.

However, none of these methods is particularly good for erasing an object that has fine details at its edges. For example, if you are trying to separate a cat from a complex background, you will find that the fine details of the cat's fur will be lost. If this is the case, you will want to resort to the Extract dialog, which gives you greater control over how the edges of objects form their backgrounds. To use the Extract dialog, open your image and follow these steps:

1. Choose the layer in the image from which you want to extract an object.

2. Choose Filter > Extract...

3. Choose the Edge Highlight tool, and set the tool options and extraction options. Then trace the outline of the object you want to extract, making sure to surround the entire object. If the object has fuzzy edges (such as fur or hair), make sure that the entire transition between the solid object and its edges is within the highlight. You can also use the Eraser tool to remove parts of the highlight.

4. Choose the Fill tool, and click within the area bound by the highlight area. This will protect the area from being erased. However, if the highlight was not closed, the entire image will be filled. Areas outside the highlights will be erased.

5. Click the Preview button. If you are not satisfied with the results, do one of the following:

   ■ In the Preview controls, choose Extracted from the drop-down, check Show Highlight and Show Fill, and then edit the highlighted area by repeating steps 3 and 4.

   ■ Use the Clean Up and Edge Touchup tools to erase parts of the image directly.

6. When you are satisfied with the extraction, click OK.

Left: the original image; right: the extracted cat. Notice that the fine fur details at the edge have been preserved.

→ 9.2 Selecting a Layer or Its Contents

Extract dialog
Option ⌘ X
Alt Ctrl X

Edge Highlighter tool (in Extract dialog)
B

Fill tool (in Extract dialog)
G

Eraser tool (in Extract dialog)
E

Eyedropper tool (in Extract dialog)
I

It is usually a good idea to duplicate the layer you are working in with the Extract dialog so that you have a backup in case you change your mind later.

PHOTOSHOP WORKSPACE

UNIVERSAL TASKS

PHOTO AND VIDEO TASKS

PRINT TASKS

WEB TASKS

Edge Touchup tool (in Extract dialog)
[T]

Zoom tool (in Extract dialog)
[Z]

Hand tool (in Extract dialog)
[H]

Cleanup tool (in Extract dialog)
[C]

———

The Extract dialog is also a great way to create torn/eroded edge effects around objects. Use the Highlight tool, but keep the smoothness low. When extracted, you will get nicely eroded objects.

———

Using the Smart Highlighting option works much like the Magnetic selection (see Section 9.4), allowing you to easily create highlights around well-defined edges in an image.

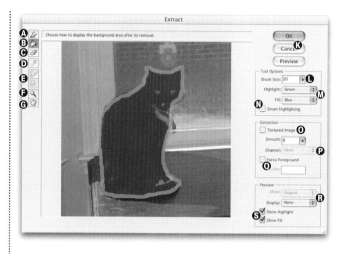

Ⓐ Edge Highlighter tool Use to select the edge of the object you want to extract. Use the Tool options to set the brush size or use Smart Highlighting (see M, O, and P).

Ⓑ Fill tool Use to fill an area of the image to protect it from extraction.

Ⓒ Eraser tool Use to erase areas created by the Edge Highlighter tool (see A).

Ⓓ Eyedropper tool Use to select a force foreground color in the preview area (see R).

Ⓔ Cleanup tool Use in preview mode to erase areas or hold down Option to un-erase extracted areas. You can choose the brush size (see M) or press 0 to 9 to set the erase opacity.

Ⓕ Edge Touchup tool Use in preview mode to erase stray pixels at the edge of the extraction or hold down Command/Ctrl to move the highlight edge. You can choose the brush size (see M) or press 0 to 9 to set the erase opacity.

Ⓖ Zoom and Hand tools Used to zoom in the preview area and to move the image in the preview area.

Ⓗ Preview area Displays the image either in its original state or after the extraction has been applied (see S).

Ⓘ Highlight selection The edge of the selection. Pixels in this area will be deleted only if they differ from the pixels in the fill selection (see K) area or forced foreground color (see R).

Ⓙ Fill selection Area of the image that will be preserved. The rest of the image will be erased.

Ⓚ Click to preview the extraction in the preview area (see I). You can control the preview using the Preview options (see O).

Ⓛ Use the slider or enter a value (1 through 999) for the brush size to use for selecting edges.

Ⓜ Choose colors to use for the highlight selection (see J) and fill selection (see K).

Ⓝ Check whether you want to use Smart Highlighting for the edges.

Ⓞ Use the slider or enter a value (0 through 100) for the smoothness used when eliminating artifacts produced in the extraction. Higher values produce smoother results, but may not retain the fine details of edges.

Ⓟ Choose an alpha channel to use for the selection. Black areas are used as the highlight selection, and white areas are treated as a fill selection.

Ⓠ Check to set a foreground color that will be extracted in the highlight area. You can then use the Eyedropper or click the color square beneath to select the forced foreground color to be used.

Ⓡ Choose whether you want to view the original or extracted version of the image in the preview area (see I) and what kind of matte to use for transparent areas created by the extraction.

Ⓢ Check to show highlight and/or fill areas in the preview area (see I, J, and K).

CHAPTER **22**

PHOTOSHOP WORKSPACE

UNIVERSAL TASKS

PHOTO AND VIDEO TASKS

PRINT TASKS

WEB TASKS

Making Image Adjustments

ADJUSTMENTS ARE USED TO change the tones and colors in an image to correct imbalances, to fix blemishes, and sometimes simply for effect. By editing the image using adjustments, you can minutely refine color to produce better print results, colorize an image, or create wild special effects.

To these ends, you can adjust not only "color," but brightness, contrast, hue, and saturation. You can selectively replace colors, desaturate colors, invert colors, and equalize color luminance. And that's just the beginning. It's easy to be overwhelmed with all the options. The key, therefore, is to know what you want to change, color-wise, in the image before starting and to know how to get the desired results.

22.1 Adjustment Basics

———

Always keep the Histogram palette visible while making adjustments, even if you need to move dialogs around to see it, so that you can compare the current histogram with the adjusted histogram.

———

Remember that you can view the Histogram palette in three configurations, allowing you to preview a histogram not only for the combined color channels, but for each channel individually as well.

———

All adjustment commands are applied directly to the layer selected in the Layers palette. You can confine the area that the adjustment affects by selecting an area in that layer.

———

Adjustments are methods you can use to correct or alter the visual qualities of an image. Although you have many tools at your disposal for changing the visual appearance of the image (such as image modes), methods are specifically designed to give you exacting control over the luminosity, color, and contrast in the image. For photography, these controls are a necessity, allowing you to correct inadequacies in the original image.

You can apply adjustments to a layer in two distinct ways depending on whether you want to permanently change the contents of a single layer or create a new layer that can be used to dynamically change the layers beneath it:

Adjustment commands Applying an adjustment to a layer using a command (Image **>** Adjustments) affects all the pixels on a single layer or within a selected area of the layer, but the changes are permanent.

Adjustment layer Adjustment layers offer greater flexibility than using commands. You can hide and delete an Adjustment layer, removing the effects of the adjustment. In addition, you can apply layer masks to mask portions of the adjustment. However, the Adjustment layer applies the adjustment to all layers beneath it or beneath its selected area.

This chapter references three image properties: shadows, midtones, and highlights. Although these concepts are straightforward, illustrating them is important.

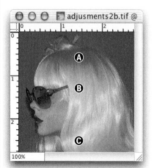

Ⓐ Shadows The darkest regions of an image.

Ⓑ Midtones Colors in the 50% gray luminosity range.

Ⓒ Highlights The brightest colors in the image.

Adjustments and the Histogram Palette

One of your most powerful tools for getting the best results out of adjustments is the Histogram palette, which graphs the relative pixels in an image in the y axis based on their luminosity from 0 (black) on the left to 255 (white) on the right. Therefore, darker images will show a histogram shifted to the left while lighter images will shift to the right.

While you are making adjustments to an image, the Histogram palette will show two graphs: the current histogram in light gray and the adjusted histogram (based on changes being made) in black. Once the adjustment changes are committed, though, the Histogram palette displays only the changes.

22.2 Adjusting Tonal Range Using Levels

The Levels dialog presents you with a histogram of the image's pixels, displaying the number of light to dark pixels. You can adjust the image's brightness and contrast by adjusting the shadows, midtones, and highlight levels to set pixels before a certain level to be black, to set pixels after a certain level to be white, and to adjust the midtones' intensity.

1 Select the layer you want to apply level changes to, or select the layer you want to insert a Levels Adjustment layer above. You can also select a part of the layer if you want the the adjustments to apply only to the selection.

2 To start adjusting levels, do one of the following:

- Choose Image > Adjustments > Levels…

- Choose Levels… from the Create New Fill Or Adjustment Layer menu 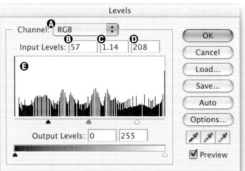 at the bottom of the Layers palette.

3 Set the level options in the Levels dialog.

4 Click OK to apply the changes to the layer or the Adjustment layer.

Ⓐ **View levels in color channel** Choose the color channel for which you want to set the levels. The channels that appear in this drop-down depend on the current color mode. Generally, you want to edit the combined color channels.

Ⓑ **Shadow input** Enter a value (0 through 253) for the shadow input level. Increasing the value darkens the shadows in the image. The shadow input slider will adjust accordingly (see F).

Ⓒ **Midtone input** Enter a value (9.99 through 0.10) for the midtone input level. A value higher than 1 lightens the image's midtones. A value lower than 1 darkens the image's midtones. The midtone input slider adjusts accordingly (see G).

Ⓓ **Highlight input** Enter a value (2 through 255) for the highlight input level. The highlight input slider adjusts accordingly (see H).

Ⓔ **Input histogram** This graph displays the relative number of pixels for a particular luminance from dark to light. The higher the peak, the more pixels have that particular luminance in the image. More pixels to the left of the shadow slider will result in more pronounced and darker shadows. More pixels to the right of the highlights slider will result in more vibrant and brighter highlights.

➡ 2.5   Image Menu

➡ 4.9   Histogram Palette

➡ 8.1   Image Color Basics

➡ 9.1   Selection Basics

Change Cancel button to Reset (while in dialog)
Option
Alt

Levels dialog
⌘ L
Ctrl L

To automatically adjust the image levels based on the options set in the Auto Color Correction Options dialog, choose Image > Adjustments > Auto Levels. The image immediately changes if any adjustments are needed. This is the same as clicking the Auto button in the Levels dialog and using Enhance Per Channel Contrast.

Although there are no hard and fast rules for making perfect adjustments with photographs, images with an even distribution of pixels, centered in the midtones as shown in the histogram, generally provide the most attractive images.

→ 10.5 Adding
Adjustment
and Fill
Layers

→ 22.4 Setting the
Auto Color
Correction
Options

→ Color Section
Fills and
Adjustments

Auto Levels
`Shift` `⌘` `L`
`Shift` `Ctrl` `L`

**(Levels dialog) Switch
to combined channel**
`⌘` `~`
`Ctrl` `~`

**(Levels dialog) Switch
to a specific color
channel**
`⌘` `1` `4`
`Ctrl` `1` `4`

———

You can select multiple
channels, but not nec-
essarily all of them,
in the Channels palette
to edit only those
channels.

———

Reversing the positions
of the two output sliders
inverts the image.

———

You can adjust the
levels set by a Levels
Adjustment layer by
double-clicking its
thumbnail icon in
the Layers palette.

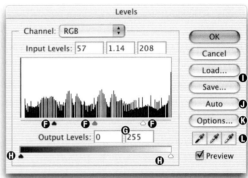

F **Shadow/Midtone/Highlight sliders**   Use these sliders to adjust the shadow input value (see B), adjust the midtone input (see C), or highlight the input value manually (see D). As you use either the shadow or highlight slider, the midtone slider adjusts the relative position of the midtones in the histogram, but not the midtone input level.

G **Black/White outputs**   Enter a value for black (0 through 255) or white (255 through 0) to set the output level. For black, the higher the value, the lighter the image up to 255, which turns the image white (see K). For white, the lower the value, the darker the image down to 0, which turns the image black (see L).

H **Black/White sliders**   Use these sliders to manually set the black or white output (see G).

I **Load/Save Levels**   Click to save the current Levels settings or load saved Levels settings. Levels settings have .alv as their extension.

J **Auto Color Correction**   Click to use the Auto Color Correction Options dialog to adjust the levels (same as the Auto Levels command).

K **Auto Adjustment Options**   Click to open the Auto Color Correction Options dialog.

L **Set Black, Gray, or White Point tools**   Click one of these eyedropper tools and then select a pixel in the canvas, or double-click the tool's icon and select a color using the Color Picker. The selected color is used to "clip" the other colors in the image. Clipping uses the selected color as either the darkest (black point), midtone (gray point), or lightest (white point) color in the image and adjusts all other colors in the image accordingly.

BALANCING COLOR CHANNELS

Adding color to one channel means adding or subtracting color from another. For example, when you add blue to the blue channel, that means removing yellow from the yellow channel. However, this can lead to unattractive color casts. (The colors change abruptly rather than blending smoothly.) When you adjust an individual channel, consider making changes in other channels to offset color casts.

22.3 Adjusting Color Levels Using Curves

You can also use the Curves dialog to adjust an image's levels. Instead of a histogram, the Curves dialog uses a line graph that can be adjusted at any point along the Input/Output axis. This gives you much greater control over the image's tones and even lets you produce some surprising effects through sharp color changes. For example, by creating a double-crested curve, you can solarize the image, inverting some colors while leaving others alone. To adjust the image using the Curves dialog, follow these steps:

1 Select the layer you want to apply level changes to using Curves, or select the layer you want to insert a Curves Adjustment layer above. You can also select a part of the layer if you want the adjustments to apply only to the selection.

2 To start adjusting curves, do one of the following:

- Choose Image > Adjustments > Curves…

- Choose Curves… from the Create New Fill Or Adjustment Layer menu ▮ at the bottom of the Layers palette.

3 Set the level options in the Curves dialog.

4 Click OK to apply the changes to the layer or Adjustment layer.

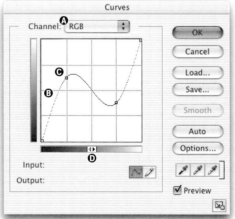

Ⓐ View levels in color channel Choose the color channel for which you want to set the levels. The channels that appear in this drop-down depend on the current color mode. Generally, you want to edit the combined color channels.

Ⓑ Curve graph Plots the color input versus output. Highlight colors are in the top-right corner, and shadow colors are in the bottom-left corner. Option/Alt-click in the graph to change the grid size.

Ⓒ Anchor point With the Curve tool selected, click to select and then drag in the graph to manually adjust its input (see E) or output (see F) values. The selected anchor point is a solid black square. Press Delete to remove a selected anchor point.

Ⓓ Value toggle Click to toggle input and output values between numeric and percentage.

➡ 2.5   Image Menu

➡ 4.9   Histogram Palette

➡ 8.1   Image Color Basics

Change Cancel button to Reset (while in dialog)
[Option]
[Alt]

Curves dialog
[⌘] [M]
[Ctrl] [M]

―――

If you are using an Adjustment layer with a selection, the selection is turned into a layer mask, limiting the area affected by the adjustment.

―――

If the Preview option is on while you're making adjustments using a dialog, but you don't notice the changes in the canvas, it could be that Photoshop is still calculating the adjustment. While Photoshop is thinking, a line blinks under the Preview check box.

(Curves dialog) Switch to combined channel

⌘ ~

Ctrl ~

(Curves dialog) Switch to color channel

⌘ 1 4

Ctrl 1 4

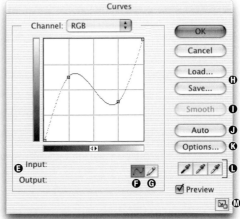

E **Selected point's Input/Ouput values** Displays the input value of the cursor's location or selected anchor point. With an anchor point selected, enter a value for the anchor point's input value. The possible values cannot be higher or lower than the values of adjacent anchor points, but will vary from 0 through 255 (numeric) or from 1 through 100 (percent). For Input, the higher the value (the farther left in the graph), the darker the image. For Output, the higher the value (the farther up in the graph), the lighter the image.

F **Curve tool** Click to select and adjust anchor points in the curve graph.

G **Freeform tool** Click to draw freeform curves in the curve graph.

H **Load/Save Curves** Click to load saved Curves settings or save the current settings. Curves settings have .acv as their extension.

I **Smooth Curve** With the Freeform tool selected, click to smooth the line into a continuous curve.

J **Auto Levels** Click to use the Auto Color Correction Options dialog to adjust the levels (same as the Auto Levels command).

K **Auto Adjustment Options** Click to open the Auto Color Correction Options dialog (see Section 22.4).

L **Set Black, Gray, or White Point tools** Click one of these eyedropper tools and then select a pixel in the canvas, or double-click the tool's icon and select a color using the Color Picker. The selected color is used to "clip" other colors in the image. Clipping uses the selected color as either the darkest (black point), midtone (gray point), or lightest (white point) color in the image and adjusts all other colors in the image accordingly.

M **Resize Curves Dialog** Click to enlarge/reduce the size of the Curves dialog while working.

22.4   Setting the Auto Color Correction Options

You can change the settings for automatic color correction using the Options button in the Levels or Curves dialog to open the Auto Color Correction Options dialog. In this dialog, you can adjust the tonal range of an image, specify clipping percentages, and assign color values for shadows, midtones, and highlights. You can apply these settings once as part of the Levels or Curves dialog, or you can save the settings as the default and apply them again using the Levels, Curves, Auto Levels, Auto Curves, or Auto Colors commands. To adjust the auto color correction options, follow these steps:

1   In the Levels dialog or the Curves dialog, click the Options... button.

2   Set the options you want. If the Preview option is checked in the Levels or Curves dialog, the changes display in the canvas as you make them. Click OK when you are finished.

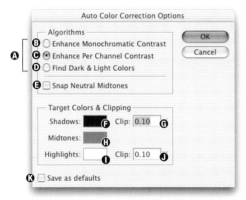

Ⓐ   Choose an algorithm option to specify whether you will adjust the levels, contrast, or color of the image.

Ⓑ   Click to set Auto Levels, to preserve the colors while increasing the contrast between shadows and highlights evenly across color channels.

Ⓒ   Click to set Auto Levels to change colors by increasing the contrast between shadows and highlights on a per channel basis.

Ⓓ   Click to set Auto Levels to average the lightest and darkest pixels in the image and uses this average to maximize contrast while minimizing the color change.

Ⓔ   Check to force color values close to a neutral color value in the image to true neutral values.

Ⓕ   Click to select a color for the image's shadows. This has the effect of colorizing the darkest areas of the image with this color. The default is black.

Ⓖ   Enter a value (0.00 through 9.99) to specify the percentage of colors that should be ignored when determining the darkest colors. In other words, if you set 1%, the first 1% of the darkest colors in the image are ignored when identifying the darkest colors.

Ⓗ   Click to select a color for the image midtones. This has the effect of colorizing the neutral areas of the image with this color. The default is 50% gray.

Ⓘ   Click to select a color for the image highlights. This has the effect of colorizing the lightest areas of the image with this color. The default is white.

Ⓙ   Enter a value (0.00 to 9.99) to specify the percentage of colors that should be ignored when determining the lightest colors in the image. In other words, if you set 1%, the first 1% of the lightest colors in the image are ignored when identifying the lightest colors.

Ⓚ   Check to save these settings for use as the defaults when using the Auto... buttons in the Levels or Curves dialog or when using the Auto Levels, Auto Contrast, or Auto Colors commands.

➡ 2.5   Image Menu

➡ 4.9   Histogram Palette

➡ 8.1   Image Color Basics

➡ 9.1   Selection Basics

➡ 10.5   Adding Adjustment and Fill Layers

➡ 22.2   Adjusting Tonal Range Using Levels

➡ 22.3   Adjusting Color Levels Using Curves

➡   Color Section Fills and Adjustments

Change Cancel button to Reset (while in dialog)

Option

Alt

If you are new to color correction, it is best to stick with the default values until you become more familiar with how changing the auto options will affect your image.

Generally a range of 0.5% to 1.0% is recommended for clipping to preserve pure white or pure black areas of the image.

22.5   Adjusting Color Balance

Change Cancel Button to Reset (while in dialog)
Option
Alt

Color Balance dialog
⌘ B
Ctrl B

Auto Color
Shift ⌘ B
Shift Ctrl B

———

To automatically adjust the image colors based on the options set in the Auto Color Correc- tion Options dialog, choose Image > Adjust- ments > Auto Colors. The image immediately changes if any adjust- ments are needed. This is the same as clicking the Auto button in the Levels or Curves dialog and using Find Dark & Light Colors.

———

Unless you are going for a specific color effect, you will proba- bly only need to adjust the color balance slightly to correct color problems in the image.

Just as you can adjust an old-fashioned TV set, you can directly control the color balance of an image by mixing the relative amounts of the colors being used in the image. To adjust the color balance of an image, follow these steps:

1   Select the layer to which you want to apply color changes, or select the layer you want to insert a Color Balance Adjustment layer above. You can also select a part of the layer if you want the adjustments to apply only to the selection.

2   To start adjusting curves, do one of the following:

■ Choose Image > Adjustments > Color Balance…

■ Choose Color Balance… from the Create New Fill Or Adjustment Layer menu at the bottom of the Layers palette or in the Layer > New Adjustment Layer submenu.

3   Set the color options in the Color Balance dialog.

4   Click OK when you're done.

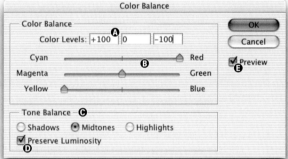

Ⓐ   Enter values (–100 through 100) for the Cyan/Red, Magenta/Green, and Yellow/Blue color levels. A negative value adjusts the colors in the image toward the first color in the pair. A positive value adjusts colors toward the second value in the pair (see B).

Ⓑ   Use the sliders to manually adjust color level values between the two color extremes (see A).

Ⓒ   Choose whether you want the changes to the color levels to affect the shadows, midtones, or highlights in the image.

Ⓓ   Check to prevent color changes from affecting the luminosity of individual pixels. This tends to increase the contrast and preserve image details.

Ⓔ   Check to show a live preview of color balance changes on the canvas.

22.6 Adjusting Brightness and Contrast

To control the tonal range of the entire image, use the Brightness and Contrast controls. Follow these steps:

1 Select the layer to which you want to apply brightness and contrast changes, or select the layer you want to insert a Brightness/Contrast Adjustment layer above. You can also select a part of the layer if you want the adjustments to apply only to the selection.

2 To start adjusting the brightness and contrast, do one of the following:

- Choose Image > Adjustments > Brightness/Contrast…

- Choose Brightness/Contrast… from the Create New Fill Or Adjustment Layer menu 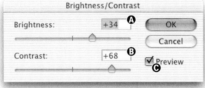 at the bottom of the Layers palette or in the Layer > New Adjustment Layer submenu.

3 Set the Brightness and Contrast options in the Brightness/Contrast dialog.

4 Click OK to apply the changes to the layer or the Adjustment layer.

Ⓐ Enter a value (–100 through 100) or use the slider to change the image's brightness. Values above 0 brighten the image, and values below 0 darken it.

Ⓑ Enter a value (–100 through 100) or use the slider to change the image's contrast. Values above 0 increase the image's contrast toward stark black and white, and values below 0 reduce the image's contrast toward a neutral gray.

Ⓒ Check to show a live preview of brightness and contrast changes on the canvas.

Change Cancel button to Reset (while in dialog)
Option
Alt

Auto Contrast
Option Shift ⌘ L
Alt Shift Ctrl L

———

To automatically adjust the image contrast based on the options set in the Auto Color Correction Options dialog, choose Image > Adjustments > Auto Contrast. The image immediately changes if any adjustments are needed. This is the same as clicking the Auto button in the Levels or Curves dialog and using Enhance Monochromatic Contrast.

———

Adjusting brightness and contrast is not generally recommended for high-quality print output because it may result in the loss of detail in the image.

22.7 Adjusting Hue, Saturation, and Lightness

➡ 2.5 Image Menu

➡ 4.9 Histogram Palette

Change Cancel button to Reset (while in dialog)
[Option]
[Alt]

Hue/Saturation dialog
[⌘] [U]
[Ctrl] [U]

Desaturate Colors
[Shift][⌘] [U]
[Shift][Ctrl] [U]

Switch to Master color range
[⌘] [~]
[Ctrl] [~]

———

Adjusting hue, saturation, and lightness allows you to do some deep fine-tuning with color that is less constricted than using levels or tools. This is especially true if you need to carefully adjust individual color channels.

You can adjust the hue (color value), saturation (amount of gray), and lightness (amount of black and white) of an image in the Hue/Saturation dialog. Using this dialog is a coarser way to correct color than using levels or curves, but you can nevertheless produce some interesting effects. For example, you can desaturate and lighten the color of an image for a faded look or increase the saturation for an over-the-top but colorful effect. To adjust the hue, saturation, and color, follow these steps:

1 Select the layer to which you want to apply hue and saturation changes, or select the layer you want to insert a Hue/Saturation Adjustment layer above. You can also select a part of the layer if you want the adjustments to apply only to the selection.

2 To start adjusting curves, do one of the following:

■ Choose Image > Adjustments > Hue/Saturation…

■ Choose Hue/Saturation… from the Create New Fill Or Adjustment Layer menu ◐ at the bottom of the Layers palette or in the Layer > New Adjustment Layer submenu.

3 Set the color options in the Color Balance dialog.

4 Click OK to apply the changes to the layer or the Adjustment layer.

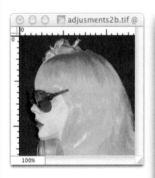
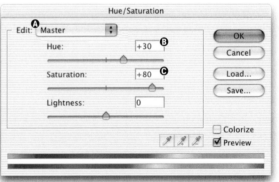

Ⓐ Choose Master to adjust all colors, or choose from the list of preset color ranges to edit.

Ⓑ Enter a value (–180 through 180) or use the slider to set the color's hue based on a standard color wheel. If you are making changes to a particular color range, hue changes are reflected in the Color Adjustment bar at the bottom of the dialog.

Ⓒ Enter a value (–100 through 100) or use the slider to set the saturation of colors. The higher the value, the more saturated the colors appear. A value of –100 changes all colors to grayscale. If you are changing a particular color range, saturation changes are reflected in the Color Reference bar at the bottom of the dialog.

22.7 Adjusting Hue, Saturation, and Lightness *(continued)*

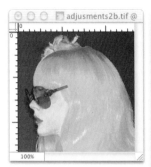 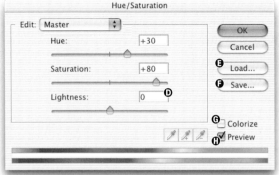

➠ 8.1 Image Color Basics

➠ 9.1 Selection Basics

Switch to Red color range
⌘ 1
Ctrl 1

Switch to Yellow color range
⌘ 2
Ctrl 2

Switch to Green color range
⌘ 3
Ctrl 3

To colorize an image, the image must be in RGB color mode.

D Enter a value (−100 through 100) or use the slider to set the lightness of colors. The higher the value, the lighter the colors appear. A value of −100 turns the image black. If you are changing a particular color range, lightness changes are reflected in the Color Reference bar at the bottom of the dialog.

E Click to load saved hue and saturation setting files that use the .ahu extension.

F Click to save the current level settings as a file using the .ahu extension.

G Check to colorize the image using the color created by the selected hue, saturation, and lightness. This option is available only for the master color range (see A).

H Check to show a live preview of color balance changes on the canvas.

Adjusting in a Color Range

You can also adjust the hue, saturation, and lightness of a selected color range, without affecting other colors in the image. Follow these steps:

1. In the Hue/Saturation dialog, choose the color range, and then use the range editing options to refine the exact color range to edit.

2. Enter hue, saturation, and lightness values for the color range. These changes are reflected in the Color Adjustment bar.

3. You can repeat steps 1 and 2 as necessary to refine the color range adjustment.

22.7　Adjusting Hue, Saturation, and Lightness *(continued)*

➡ 10.5 Adding
　　　Adjustment
　　　and Fill
　　　Layers

➡ Color Section
　　　Fills and
　　　Adjustments

Switch to Cyan color range
⌘ 4
Ctrl 4

Switch to Blue color range
⌘ 5
Ctrl 5

Switch to Magenta color range
⌘ 6
Ctrl 6

───

Another way to desaturate the image is to turn it to black and white and set the saturation to –100.

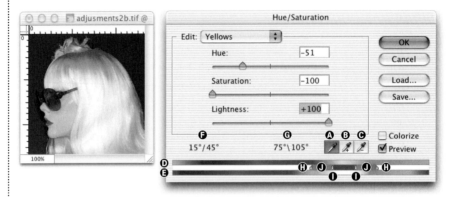

ⓐ Select Color　Click and then select a color in the canvas to choose the color range to edit. Shift-click to add colors to the selection, or Option/Alt-click to subtract colors. The changes are reflected in the color range extremes (see H).

ⓑ Add Color To Selection　Click and then select a color in the canvas to add colors to the color range being edited. The changes are reflected in the color range extremes (see H).

ⓒ Subtract Color From Selection　Click and then select a color in the canvas to remove colors from the color range being edited. The changes are reflected in the color range extremes (see H).

ⓓ Color Reference Bar　Displays the natural full-color spectrum for reference with the Color Adjustment bar.

ⓔ Color Adjustment Bar　Displays the current color spectrum for the selected color range. This spectrum depends on the hue, saturation, and lightness values.

ⓕ Left Color Value Extremes　Displays the color values for the leftmost color range extreme and color fall-off point (see H and I).

ⓖ Right Color Value Extremes　Displays the color values for the rightmost color range extreme and color fall-off point (see H and I).

ⓗ Color Range Extremes　Click and drag to define the color extremes of the color range (see F and G).

ⓘ Color Fall-Off Points　Click and drag to define the point at which the color begins to blend with surrounding colors (see F and G).

ⓙ Color Fall-Off Ranges　The area between the range extreme and fall-off point defines the range of colors to blend with surrounding colors in the image. Click and drag this area to adjust the fall-off range without changing the relative positions of the range extreme and fall-off point.

22.8 Matching Color Palettes between Images

A color palette (or table) is the list of colors being used in a particular image. The Match Color command allows you to apply the color palette of one image or layer to another image or layer within an image to achieve visual consistency. This is especially useful when trying to match the appearance of two photographs for side-by-side presentation. For example, if the skin tones in the two photographs are radically different, you can use Match Color to equalize them. However, you can also use Match Colors superior controls to adjust the luminance and color components within a single image to reduce color casting. To apply Color Match to an image, follow these steps:

1 If you want to apply the color palette of one image to another, open both images in Photoshop. The image you will be applying color matching to is the *target* image, and the other image is the *source* image. Keep inn mind, though, that a single image can serve as both target and source.

2 Choose the layer in the target image to which you want to apply the adjustments. If you want to limit the area considered for color matching, select an area within the canvas of the source and/or target images. Limiting the area in the source image limits the area from which colors are matched. Limiting the area in the target image limits the area where colors are applied.

3 With the target image active, choose Image > Adjustments > Match Color…

4 Set the color options in the Match Color dialog.

■ If you are matching colors between two different images, set the source image to be the other image and then choose a layer within the source.

■ If you are matching colors between two layers in a single image, set the source image to be the same as the target image, and then choose the desired layer to be applied.

■ If you want to use Match Color's advanced luminance and color intensity controls within a single layer, set the source image to be the same as the target image, and then choose the layer to be the same as the target layer.

5 After you make your adjustments, click OK to apply the changes to the layer or the Adjustment layer.

➡ 2.5 Image Menu

➡ 4.9 Histogram Palette

➡ 8.1 Image Color Basics

Change Cancel button to Reset (while in dialog)
Option
Alt

The Replace Color command is one of the few adjustments without a corresponding Adjustment layer.

Match Color will try to prevent color cast and color clipping; however, these unwanted artifacts can still occur, so watch your image carefully while making adjustments.

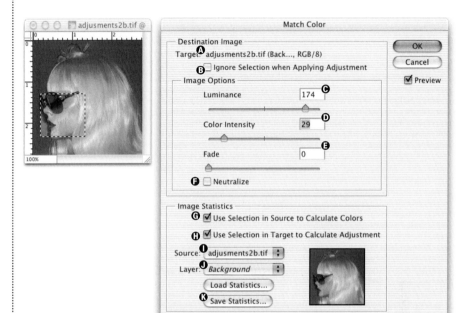

Ⓐ Displays the filename and statistics of the target image color matching is being applied to.

Ⓑ Check to ignore the selected area in the target image and apply adjustments over the entire layer.

Ⓒ Enter a value (1 through 200) or use the slider to set how the source image color's brightness (luminance) is applied to the target image. A value of 100 uses the same luminance as the source colors; lower values are darker, and higher values lighter.

Ⓓ Enter a value (1 through 200) or use the slider to set how the source image color's saturation (color intensity) is applied to the target image. A value of 100 uses the same color intensity as the source colors; lower values are desaturated, and higher values saturated.

Ⓔ Enter a value (0 through 100) or use the slider to set how intensely the changes are applied. A value of 100 uses full intensity, while higher values diminish the strength of the adjustments.

Ⓕ Check to eliminate color casts (sharp changes in color) in the image.

Ⓖ Check to use the selection made in the source image for color matching. If unchecked, the entire source image is used.

Ⓗ Check to use the selection made in the source image for luminance and color intensity adjustments. If unchecked, the entire source image is used.

Ⓘ Choose the source image from the drop-down list of currently open files.

Ⓙ Choose the layer to use from the source image. Choose Merged to use the entire image.

Ⓚ Click to load saved color match statistics files or save the current statistics using the .sta extension.

22.9 Using Replace Color

The Replace Color command works a lot like the Color Range dialog for selecting colors, but you can immediately replace the selected color with a new color.

1 Select the layer in which you want to replace the colors. You can also select a part of the layer if you want the adjustments to apply only to the selection.

2 Choose Image > Adjustments > Replace Color…

3 Set the color options in the Replace Color dialog. First, select the color or range of colors to be replaced, and then use the Hue, Saturation, and Lightness controls to define the replacement color.

4 After you make your adjustments, click OK to apply the changes to the layer or the Adjustment layer.

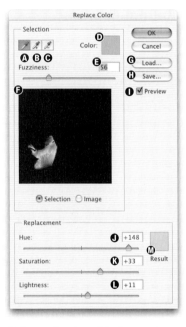

Ⓐ Select Color Click the Eyedropper tool and then select a color in the canvas or image preview (see B) to choose the color to replace. Shift-click to add colors to the selection, or Option/Alt-click to subtract colors.

Ⓑ Add Color To Selection Click and then select a color in the canvas or image preview (see B) to add colors to the color range being replaced.

Ⓒ Subtract Color From Selection Click and then select a color in the canvas or image preview (see B) to remove colors from the color range being replaced.

Ⓓ Base Color for Replacement Displays the currently selected color being replaced. Click to open the Color Picker to select the color directly.

Ⓔ Color Fuzziness Range Enter a value (0 through 200) or use the slider to set the fuzziness to use when selecting colors to change. The higher the value, the more colors similar to the selected color or colors are included in the change.

Ⓕ Image Preview Displays a color preview of the original image or the selected colors to be replaced. In Selection mode, white shows selected regions of the image.

Ⓖ Load Settings Click to load saved replacement color setting files that use the .axt extension..

Ⓗ Save Settings Click to save the current replacement color settings as a file using the .axt extension.

Ⓘ New color's hue Enter a value (–180 through 180) or use the slider to set the replacement color's hue.

Ⓙ New color saturation Enter a value (–100 through 100) or use the slider to set the replacement color's saturation.

Ⓛ New color lightness Enter a value (–100 through 100) or use the slider to set the replacement color's lightness.

Ⓜ Replacement color Displays a sample swatch of the color used to replace the base color. Click to open the Color Picker to select the color directly.

➡ 2.5   Image Menu

➡ 4.9   Histogram Palette

➡ 8.1   Image Color Basics

➡ 9.1   Selection Basics

➡ 10.5 Adding Adjustment and Fill Layers

➡ Color Section Fills and Adjustments

Change Cancel button to Reset (while in dialog)
⌥ Option
Alt

The Replace Color command is one of the few adjustments without a corresponding Adjustment layer.

22.10   Adjusting Selective Colors

Change Cancel button to Reset (while in dialog)

Option

Alt

————

The Selective Color feature is generally only used for high-end printing jobs in which the amount of ink used to create a primary color needs to be adjusted without affecting the CMYK values in the rest of the image.

————

Even if you are using RGB mode, you can still adjust the colors using CMYK colors to correct the image.

You can use Selective Color to increase and decrease the amount of process colors (cyan, magenta, yellow, and black) needed to print the primary colors (red, green, blue, black, neutral, and white) of an image. To adjust colors selectively in an image, follow these steps:

1 Select the layer to which you want to apply color changes, or select the layer above if you want the adjustments to apply only to the selection.

2 To start replacing selective colors, do one of the following:

   ■ Choose Image > Adjustments > Selective Color…

   ■ Choose Selective Color… from the Create New Fill Or Adjustment Layer menu at the bottom of the Layers palette or in the Layer > New Adjustment Layer submenu.

3 Set the color options in the Selective Color Options dialog.

4 Click OK to apply the changes to the layer or the Adjustment layer.

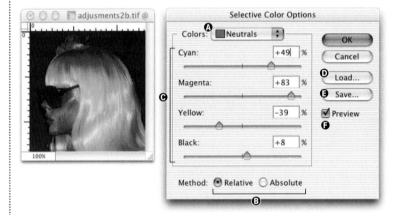

Ⓐ Select the color you want to selectively modify from the list.

Ⓑ Choose whether the values entered should be treated as a percentage relative to the current amount of cyan, magenta, yellow, or black used in the selected color or as an absolute amount of that color added to the selected color. For example, if there is currently a 10% value for cyan in the selected color, increasing it by 20% relatively changes the value to 12%. The same change made absolutely changes the value to 30%.

Ⓒ Enter values (–100 through 100) or use the sliders to set the percentage to increase or decrease the cyan, magenta, yellow, or black mix for the selected color.

Ⓓ Click to load saved selective color setting files that use the .asv extension.

Ⓔ Click to save the current selective color settings as a file using the .asv extension.

Ⓕ Check to show a live preview of color replacement changes on the canvas.

22.11 Colorizing Images with Photo Filter

Photo Filters allow you to simulate placing a colored filter over a camera lens when shooting to adjust either for color balance or color temperature or to simply colorize the image:

1 Select the layer to which you want to apply color changes, or select the layer above which you want to insert a Photos Filter layer. You can also select a part of the layer if you want adjustments to apply only to the selection.

2 To start replacing selective colors, do one of the following:

   ■ Choose Image > Adjustments > Photo Filter…

   ■ Choose Photo Filter… from the Create New Fill Or Adjustment Layer menu [icon] at the bottom of the Layers palette or in the Layer > New Adjustment Layer submenu.

3 In the Photo Filter dialog, choose the filter or color to use, set filter density, and specify if you want to preserve the original luminosity in the image. The filters are:

   Warming Filter (85) and (81) Tunes the white balance in the image, making it yellower (warmer) to adjust for bluish high-color temperature in the ambient light. A value of 85 will have a stronger effect than 81.

   Cooling Filter (80) and (82) Tunes the white balance in the image, making it bluer (cooler) to adjust for yellowish low-color temperatures in the ambient light. A value of 80 will have a stronger effect than 82.

   Colors Sets the color from a predefined list.

   Underwater Sets a turquoise color to simulate underwater conditions.

4 Click OK to apply the changes to the layer or the Adjustment layer.

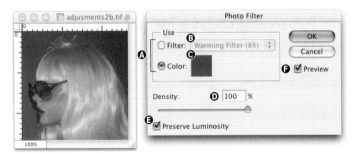

Ⓐ Click to select whether to use a simulated camera filter or a color.

Ⓑ If using a filter, choose the simulated filter type you want to apply. This list includes most standard filters used with camera lenses.

Ⓒ Displays the color used for the filter. Click to use the Color Picker to choose a color.

Ⓓ Enter a value (1 through 100) or use the slider to set the percentage for the strength the filter should be applied.

Ⓔ Click to prevent highlights from being colorized, thus darkening the image.

Ⓕ Check to show a live preview of color replacement changes on the canvas.

➡ 2.5 Image Menu

➡ 4.9 Histogram Palette

➡ 8.1 Image Color Basics

➡ 9.1 Selection Basics

➡ 10.5 Adding Adjustment and Fill Layers

➡ Color Section Fills and Adjustments

Change Cancel button to Reset (while in dialog)

[Option]
[Alt]

22.12　Quickly Correcting Shadows and Highlights

➡ 2.5　Image Menu

➡ 4.9　Histogram Palette

➡ 8.1　Image Color Basics

Change Cancel button to Reset (while in dialog)

Option

Alt

———

If you see only Amount controls for Shadows and Highlights when first opening the Shadow/Highlight dialog, check Show More Options.

Images that are under or over exposed can be difficult to effectively correct. Working in levels can help correct overall tonal problems, but the one-size-fits-all approach that levels applies to the image may dull the image. The Shadows/Highlights adjustment provides exacting controls for controlling the tones in highlights and shadows of an image separately, allowing you to bring back detail in areas without sacrificing image quality. To adjust highlights and shadows in an image, follow these steps:

1　Select the layer in which you want to replace the colors. You can also select a part of the layer if you want the adjustments to apply only to the selection.

2　Choose Image > Adjustments > Shadow/Highlight…

3　Set the color options in the Replace Color dialog. First, select the color or range of colors to be replaced, and then use the Hue, Saturation, and Lightness controls to define the replacement color.

4　After you make your adjustments, click OK to apply the changes to the layer or the Adjustment layer.

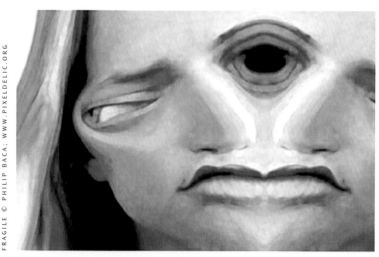

FRAGILE © PHILIP BACA.: WWW.PIXELDELIC.ORG

22.12 Quickly Correcting Shadows and Highlights *(continued)*

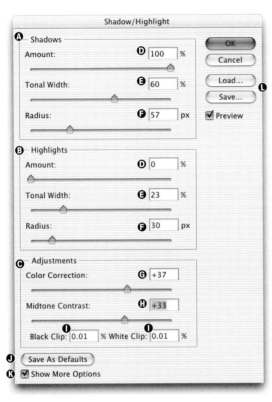

Ⓐ Controls for setting how shadows (darker areas) are adjusted in the image.

Ⓑ Controls for setting how highlights (lighter areas) are adjusted in the image.

Ⓒ Controls for fine-tuning colors within the image to adjust for shadow and highlight adjustments being made. These controls affect only areas of the image where the show or highlight controls have made adjustments.

Ⓓ Enter a value (0 through 100) or use the slider to set the intensity of shadows or highlights. Higher values create darker shadows or brighter highlights.

Ⓔ Enter a value (0 through 100) or use the slider to set how dark or bright a color needs to be to be adjusted. Higher values increase the lightness value a color must have to be adjusted.

➡ 9.1 Selection Basics

➡ 10.5 Adding Adjustment and Fill Layers

➡ Color Section Fills and Adjustments

It is easy to "overcook the stew" when using adjustment controls, so watch your image carefully for signs of noise and other artifacts, especially at the edges of objects where sharp transitions can lead to unwanted color casts and clipping.

Ⓕ Enter a value (0 through2500) for how far pixels will consider other pixels when calculating values. A higher radius will consider more pixels in the image.

Ⓖ Enter a value (−100 through 100) or use the slider to set the saturation in areas adjusted by the shadow and highlight controls. Values below 0 desaturate the image, and values above 0 increase saturation. This control is replaced by Brightness in grayscale images.

Ⓗ Enter a value (−100 through 100) or use the slider to set the contrast of midtone (gray) pixels in areas adjusted by the shadow and highlight controls. Values below 0 decrease contrast, and values above 0 increase contrast.

Ⓘ Enter values (0.00 through 50.00) to reduce dramatic changes between shadows and highlights while making adjustments. Higher values reduce color casts, but may also reduce detail in the image. Generally a value under 1 produces best results.

Ⓙ Click to use the current settings as the default values when applying shadow and highlight adjustments.

Ⓚ Check to show advanced options for shadow and highlight adjustments (shown here). If unchecked, you will be able to adjust the amounts (see D) only in shadows and highlights and nothing else.

Ⓛ Click to load saved shadow/highlight setting or save the current settings as a file using the .shh extension.

22.13 Mixing Channels

You use the Channel Mixer dialog to modify a single color channel using a mix of the other color channels in the image. With some practice, you can correct color more precisely this way than using the other adjustment methods, or you can create high-quality black-and-white or colorized images. To mix channels, follow these steps:

1 Select the layer to which you want to apply channel mixing, or select the layer you want to insert a Channel Mixer Adjustment layer above. You can also select a part of the layer if you want the adjustments to apply only to the selection.

2 To start mixing channels, do one of the following:

- Choose Image > Adjustments > Channel Mixer…

- Choose Channel Mixer… from the Create New Fill Or Adjustment Layer menu at the bottom of the Layers palette or in the Layer > New Adjustment Layer submenu.

3 Set the color options in the Channel Mixer dialog.

4 Click OK to apply the changes to the layer or the Adjustment layer.

Change Cancel button to Reset (while in dialog)

`Option`

`Alt`

When you click the Monochrome option, you can precisely control the amount of detail and contrast when converting an image to black and white. You can then turn Monochrome off and modify each channel separately to produce a sharp, hand-tinted effect.

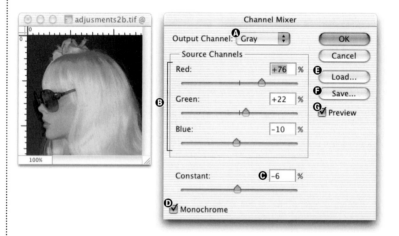

Ⓐ Choose the output channel where one or more source channels will be blended. The options in the Output Channel drop-down depend on the image's color mode.

Ⓑ Enter values (–200 through 200) as a percentage to increase or decrease the source channel color in the selected output channel. Negative values invert the source channel before blending it with the output channel. The Source Channels options depend on the image's color mode.

Ⓒ Enter a value (–200 through 200) as a percentage to add either a black or a white channel. This results in positive values, increasing the amount of the selected color in the blend, and negative values, increasing the amount of the blend's inverse color.

Ⓓ Click to apply the settings to all output channels, creating a monochrome image.

Ⓔ Click to load saved channel mixer setting files that have the .cha extension.

Ⓕ Click to save the current channel mixer settings as a file using the .cha extension.

Ⓖ Check to show a live preview of channel mixing changes on the canvas.

22.14 Mapping a Gradient to the Image Colors

You can completely replace an image's color table with a graduated color table. This can produce sublime tint effects or stark high-color effects, depending on the gradient you select. To map a gradient to the image colors, follow these steps:

1 Select the layer to which you want to apply gradient map changes, or select the layer you want to insert a Gradient Map Adjustment layer above. You can also select a part of the layer if you want the adjustments to apply only to the selection.

2 To start adjusting curves, do one of the following:

■ Choose Image **>** Adjustments **>** Gradient Map...

■ Choose Gradient Map... from the Create New Fill Or Adjustment Layer menu at the bottom of the Layers palette or in the Layer **>** New Adjustment Layer submenu.

3 Set the gradient options in the Gradient Map dialog.

4 Click OK to apply the changes to the layer or Adjustment layer.

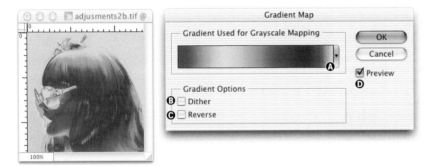

Ⓐ Select a gradient you want to use from the drop-down menu, or double-click the gradient pattern to open the Gradient Editor and create your own gradient.

Ⓑ Check to use a dithered gradient rather than a smooth gradient. This will have the effect of adding noise to the image on low-resolution monitors. If your monitor supports thousands or more colors, you will not notice any change.

Ⓒ Check to reverse the direction of the gradient.

Ⓓ Check to show a live preview of gradient changes on the canvas.

➠ 2.5   Image Menu

➠ 4.9   Histogram Palette

➠ 8.1   Image Color Basics

➠ 9.1   Selection Basics

➠ 10.5 Adding Adjustment and Fill Layers

➠ 12.8 Creating and Editing Gradients

➠ 12.9 Organizing Gradient Presets

➠ Color Section Fills and Adjustments

Change Cancel button to Reset (while in dialog)

[Option]

[Alt]

Although you can map a black-to-white gradient to desaturate the image, mapping a gradient is really best reserved for special effects.

22.15 Setting Posterize and Threshold Levels

Change Cancel button to Reset (while in dialog)

Option

Alt

Although it may not seem to be a helpful effect, Threshold is useful for identifying the darkest and lightest areas in your image.

You can also select a part of the layer if you want the adjustments to apply only to the selection.

Using Posterize, you can convert the image so that it uses large areas of flat color, drastically reducing the tonal values. You can specify the number of colors (levels) available to each color channel. For example, if you set the level to 3, the image is composed of nine colors, three on each channel. Similarly, you can use Threshold to set a level above which all lighter pixels are converted to white and all darker pixels are converted to black. This produces a stark black-and-white image with no grayscales.

To posterize or add a threshold to an image, follow these steps:

1 Select the layer to which you want to apply the poster or threshold changes, or select the layer you want to insert a Posterize or Threshold Adjustment layer above. You can also select a part of the layer if you want the adjustments to apply only to the selection.

2 Do one of the following:

■ Choose Image > Adjustments > Posterize… or Threshold…

■ Choose Posterize… or Threshold… from the Create New Fill Or Adjustment Layer menu ![icon] at the bottom of the Layers palette.

3 Set the number of levels in the dialog.

4 Click OK to apply the changes to the layer or the Adjustment layer.

 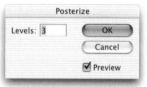

Enter a value (2 through 255) for the tonal level. The higher the value, the less posterized your image looks. Check the Preview option to show a live preview of posterized changes on the canvas.

 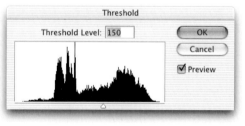

Enter a value (1 through 255) for the threshold level, or use the slider underneath the histogram to set the value manually.

22.16 Using Color Variations

You can use the Variations dialog to quickly change the color balance, contrast, and saturation in a single, highly visual interface. Rather than using precise numeric input and abstract sliders, you can view a thumbnail preview of how the change you are about to make will affect the image. This tends to work if you are more intuitive in your color correction and less worried about precision. To make color variations in the image, follow these steps:

1 Select the layer in which you want to adjust the colors using color variations. You can also select a part of the layer if you want the adjustments to apply only to the selection.

2 Choose Image > Adjustments > Variations…

3 Set the tonal range to adjust (Shadows, Midtones, Highlights, or Saturation), set the coarseness level, and then begin adding colors or lightening or darkening the image.

4 After you make your adjustments, click OK to apply the changes to the layer or the Adjustment layer.

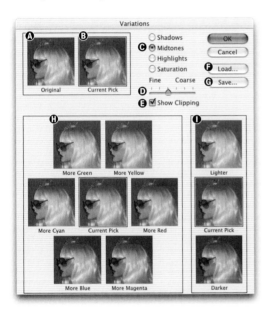

A Displays the original image. Click to revert to this version.

B Displays the image based on the current settings.

C Choose whether to apply color variations to the image's shadows, midtones, highlights, or saturation.

D Use the slider to set how much color is applied using the variations. Fine applies only a little color at a time, and Coarse applies the maximum amount of color.

E Check to highlight areas in the preview that will be clipped by the color adjustment. Clipped areas are converted to pure black or white and may cause unwanted color shifts. Clipping does not occur when you are working with midtones.

F Click to load saved variation settings files.

G Click to save the current variation settings as a file.

H Each "More" preview thumbnail displays how adding that color will affect the image. Click one of the color previews to add more of that color to the image. You can repeat this as many times as desired for as many colors as desired. Each click updates the preview thumbnails to display the current options. The amount of color added with any single click depends on the coarseness setting (see D).

I Displays a thumbnail preview of how lightening or darkening will affect the image. Click the preview as many times as desired to lighten or darken the image. Each click updates the thumbnails to display the current options. The amount of color added with any single click depends on the coarseness setting (see D).

➡ 2.5   Image Menu

➡ 4.9   Histogram Palette

➡ 8.1   Image Color Basics

➡ 9.1   Selection Basics

➡ 10.5 Adding Adjustment and Fill Layers

➡ Color Section Fills and Adjustments

Change Cancel button to Reset (while in dialog)
Option
Alt

——

Variations do not work with images in Indexed Color mode.

——

Clicking a color preview diagonally across from the last color added will have the effect of canceling that color change. For example, if you click blue and then click yellow, the blue color addition is essentially undone.

22.17 Other Adjustments: Brightness, Desaturation, and Inversion

Invert image colors
⌘ I
Ctrl I

———

Desaturating is the same as setting the saturation to –100 in the Hue/Saturation dialog.

———

Although an inverted image looks a lot like a film negative, you can't use the Invert command to create an exact color negative of the image because a true color negative also contains an orange mask.

———

As you can do with other actions in Photoshop, you can fade the effects of an adjustment immediately after the action. Fading dilutes and blends the effect of the adjustment. To fade the adjustment, choose Edit > Fade *name*...

Equalizing Image Brightness

The Equalize command evens out the distribution of brightness values in an image to create a smoother range and often has the effect of improving overall image quality. Here is our model example image after equalization. You can use Equalize to quickly correct scanned images that appear darker than the original.

To equalize the brightness in the image, select the layer you want equalized (you can also select part of that layer), choose Image > Adjustments > Equalize. If you select part of the layer, specify whether you want to equalize only the selected area or the entire area based on the selection, and then click OK.

Desaturating the Image

Desaturation removes all color information from the selected layer, changing it to grayscale, without changing the image's color mode. This is the same as setting the saturation to –100 in the Hue/Saturation dialog. To desaturate the selected layer, choose Image > Adjustments > Desaturate.

Inverting the Image

The Invert command inverts the color values for each pixel. The effect looks something like a photographic negative of the image and can produce some stark images. Here is the model image after inversion.

- To invert the selected layer, choose Image > Adjustments > Invert.

- To add an Inversion Adjustment layer, select the layer above which you want the Adjustment layer to be added, and choose Invert from the menu 🖤, at the bottom of the Layers palette. All layers below this Adjustment layer are inverted.

PRINT TASKS

CHAPTER 23

Designing for Print

WHETHER YOUR INTERESTS ARE printing to your home printer or fine art print making, obtaining state-of-the-art photographic prints or sending an ad to a magazine production department, the basic principles regarding print work are much the same.

This chapter focuses on the basic issues of size and color, as they relate specifically to Photoshop and print output.

- 23.1 **Print basics**
- 23.2 **Understanding resolution and document size**
- 23.3 **Managing color for print**
- 23.4 **Creating spot channels for print**

23.1   Print Basics

One way to avoid font problems with a service bureau is to convert text to Paths before saving the version of your file being sent for print. However, this will prevent you from editing the text directly.

When considering work destined for print, it helps to have a basic understanding of how we see color and how color is printed. It also helps to have enough familiarity with print technology to be able to ask questions and make informed choices regarding your print project. A key consideration for printing with a print house versus printing to your desktop printer is that someone else is going to be receiving and handling your files. If at all possible, select a printer before beginning a print project. Simply asking what is needed for best results may help you greatly.

Monitor vs. Print Output

Our eyes physically see everything as a combination of red, green, and blue light wavelengths. Red, green, and blue lights (as from your monitor) and colored inks (in print) mix to form the color we see in two distinctly different ways:

Additive Color
Red + Green + Blue = White

Projected red, green, and blue light wavelengths combine (add) to produce nearly all the colors we can see. This is the basis for what is called additive color; 100% of red, green, and blue light will add to create white. This is similar to the way that all light wavelengths in sunlight are seen as white light. When we see magenta displayed on the computer screen, we see light from red and blue light sources combined to produce magenta.

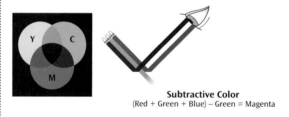

Subtractive Color
(Red + Green + Blue) – Green = Magenta

More specifically, our vision is affected by which light wavelengths are being absorbed by varying inks or pigments. This is the basis for what is called subtractive color. Cyan ink absorbs red light. Magenta ink absorbs green light. Yellow ink absorbs blue light. When 100% of cyan, magenta, and yellow combine to absorb all light, we see black. What we see as magenta in print is actually a pigment that absorbs green light wavelengths, allowing our eyes to see only the reflected red and blue light from a full-spectrum white light source.

A further consideration with regard to color reproduction and the two basic types of color must be given to variables in technology. Variables and color ranges with regard to specific equipment are measured as differences in gamut.

23.1 Print Basics *(continued)*

Print Technologies

When deciding what type of print output to use for a Photoshop image and considering who you will have do your work, several considerations determine what type of printing or printer is best. The primary considerations for your job are likely the quantity to be printed and cost. In general, when you are printing a large number of copies (more than 1000), offset printing is the output of choice because it is the most cost effective. The correlation between the quality you demand and the associated cost is also certainly a factor. Significant advances in digital printing technology over the past several years make it increasingly affordable for artists and photographers to print smaller quantities, and larger prints, at more reasonable prices.

Offset printing This is a process in which a printing plate makes an inked impression on a rubber-blanketed cylinder, which in turn transfers the impression to the paper. This process requires an individual plate for each color to be printed, and each color must be run separately. Although technology has improved to allow digital files to be transferred directly to plate, this process often requires a service bureau to produce film for the production of plates. Creating separations, film, and plates and running ink individually generally makes this process cost prohibitive for small quantities of prints.

Color inkjet printers The printers most in use today, these can produce excellent color for print jobs in small quantities. As a rule, inkjet printers are too slow and the cost per copy is too high for production work. The standard color inkjet printer uses four inks, and the photo printer uses either six or seven inks. The difference between their output is in subtle color enhancement.

Laser printers Often found in businesses today, these are available for printing in black and white or color. A color laser can produce small print runs that require color but are not large enough to justify the cost of using offset. Commercial models can handle large-format prints. Color laser printers can almost always handle PostScript information and can produce accurate color in small to medium production runs. Restrictions are with cost and time.

Dye-sublimation printers These printers (known as "dye-sub" printers) produce vivid and accurate color, but their cost per page is high.

Photographic digital prints These are becoming more common and widely available. The equipment available ranges from more generic photo-processing units to larger high-quality Chromira photographic printers. This technology generally uses photographic paper exposed with red, green, and blue lasers and then processed with traditional chemicals.

Giclée or fine art prints These have grown in acceptance developing from Iris inkjet printing. Years of development and testing of archival inks and papers along with large-format print technology allow for high-quality 4- to 12-color prints at large sizes.

➡ 23.2 Understanding Resolution and Document Size

➡ 23.3 Managing Color for Print

➡ 24.1 Preparing to Print

———

The term *giclée,* to distinguish "fine art prints" from other commercial processes, was coined by Jack Duganne in 1991 from the French word for spray—*gicler*—in reference to the inkjet process.

23.2 Understanding Resolution and Document Size

➥ 7.3 Setting the Image Size

You can always check the print size of an image by choosing Image > Image Size and noting the document size in the dialog. This displays the actual print size. If width is indicated at 3 inches, your document will be 3 inches wide, whether at 72 or 300 dpi regardless of the resolution value displayed.

Choosing View > Actual Pixels will give you an accurate view of image detail regardless of your monitor's display settings.

Choosing View > Print Size will not always give an accurate representation of output size, as it is dependent on monitor settings. However, if you understand your monitor display, choosing View > Print Size may give you a close representation of what to expect in print.

You can often get excellent output from a desktop photo printer (inkjet or dye-sub) using a Photoshop image at a resolution of 120–150 dpi. Make a few test prints on your own printer to see where the balance of print speed and quality is optimal.

For quick reference, you can configure your Photoshop status bar to display document dimensions.

Document size and image resolution are multifaceted concepts that should be understood when designing for print. These elements are of concern with regard to the physical dimensions of your document in final output, as well as the scale of detail when viewing your images onscreen. These elements will also impact file size and require consideration with regard to transferring your images to your printer or service bureau.

Document size refers to print dimensions in Photoshop. Since Photoshop images are made up of pixels, the correlation between pixel dimensions (how many pixels) and resolution (how far the pixels are spread out in print) determines print dimensions. The document size dimensions displayed in the Image Size dialog will be the actual size of your print as long as you do not select the Fit To Page option in your printer setup. The following are also document size considerations to keep in mind:

Setting up your document for a bleed Bleed is the print term for running to the edge of the paper, and if you want a document to bleed, you will need to add to your document dimensions (generally 1/4″ to 3/8″ for each edge that bleeds). Printers do not generally print to the edge of paper. The image is printed beyond the edge, and the paper is trimmed to size. Bleeding involves additional cost for larger paper and trimming.

Safe area and trim size These areas are dimensions given for the edges of your image or design. Particularly when designing ads for placement in publications, you may be given dimensions for actual page size, a smaller trim size, and another dimension as a safe area. When multipage documents are bound, they are generally trimmed after stapling, and the trim may make artwork or design elements too close to the edge appear crooked or poorly placed. If you are given these dimensions, keep critical design elements such as lines parallel with edges or critical typographic elements inside the safe area.

23.2 Understanding Resolution and Document Size *(continued)*

Resolution

When printing to your own printer, consult the documentation specific to your product for optimum image resolution. When setting the resolution for prepress or commercial printing, consult the service bureau or printer that you will be using. They will advise you as to what resolution they are expecting. Each printing process and piece of equipment is unique.

Pixel dimensions The basis of image size in Photoshop. A pixel also stores basic color information. Display size of an image on the screen is determined by the pixel dimensions of the image in relation to the size and settings of the monitor.

Monitor resolution The number of pixels or dots displayed per unit of measure on the monitor, typically measured in dots per inch (dpi). Optimum monitor resolution settings depend on the size of the monitor plus its pixel settings or personal preference.

20"

640x480/1024x768

15"

640x480/832x624

Any given image may appear to be larger or smaller on various monitors, due to individual monitor display settings and personal preferences.

Image resolution The number of pixels per unit of printed length of an image, generally measured in pixels per inch (ppi). Image resolution and pixel dimensions are mutually dependent. The amount of information or detail possible in an image depends on the pixel dimensions; this information in print clarity or quality depends on resolution.

Print resolution This is, in fact, a complex issue. If you do not have input from the printer, the rule-of-thumb choice for reasonable-quality prints using commercial or offset printing is 300 dpi at a 100% output size. This standard 300 dpi recommendation is based on another old rule regarding dpi optimized at twice the line-screen resolution. Typical recommended line screen for quality black-and-white print has long been 133–150 lines. Many designers also use 266 dpi as their base resolution for print.

Photoshop treats what is displayed on the screen as having 72 dpi. To test this, choose Print Screen > File > New. The dimensions of the Clipboard or screen capture will be your monitor setting size at 72 dpi.

Professional and amateurs frequently use the terms *ppi* (pixels per inch) and *dpi* (dots per inch) interchangeably. Although this is incorrect, it isn't a problem since they usually know what they are talking about. To be absolutely accurate, be aware that scanners, digital cameras, and computer monitors are measured in ppi, and printers are measured in dpi.

Unless specifically instructed to do so by your service bureau or printer, do not increase the resolution of a photographic image to more than 300 dpi.

When changing the size of an image, always try to do so without resampling. If you need to resample an image, avoid increasing the size because adding pixels tends to make the image appear soft and ever so slightly out of focus.

Inkjet printers produce a microscopic spray of ink, not actual dots.

Changing the output size of an image by changing its resolution is called *interpolation*.

23.3   Managing Color for Print

Toggle gamut warning
⌘ Shift Y
Ctrl Shift Y

———

An exclamation point appears in the Info palette to the right of CMYK values that are out of gamut any time the pointer is moved over them.

———

You can easily correct problem areas using Adjustment layers and their associated layer masks.

———

When working in RGB, save your original and convert a copy to CMYK. When you know where your image will be printed and what the printer expects, you can convert to the specific color profile they request.

———

Spot colors are an option if a design or client requires typography in colors that would prove difficult in the four-color process.

Controlling how colors are interpreted, converted, and reproduced accurately between devices is generally known as color management. Photoshop's default color engine or the Adobe (ACE) Color Management Module, performing complex tasks in the background, allows even beginners to work with and print images without having to give color management much thought. However, a basic understanding of it helps you exercise some control over color in the print process. This is particularly true with regard to correcting for colors that don't convert well between devices.

Even if you turn off color management (Edit > Color Settings > Settings > Color Management Off), Photoshop always employs its default color management system in the background. By selecting Advanced Mode in the Color Settings dialog, you can exercise a variety of conversion options and controls for how Photoshop reads and converts image color data or load specific color profiles for output as recommended by your printer.

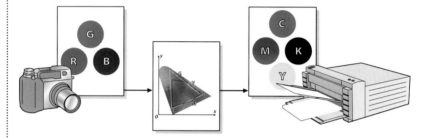

A digital capture device records color information using an equipment-specific formula. A color management system translates that information to reference color, working space, or output device specifications.

In simplest terms, a color management system needs to do three things:

- Interpret the color space of the image by reading an assigned device profile or by assigning color numbers.

- Utilize a color reference or basis for absolute color. Photoshop currently employs Lab color as its reference.

- Convert color data so the destination device can best handle the information. Specific color profiles for destination device/ink/paper combinations will allow more accurate conversion of color data.

Gamut and Gamut Warnings

Every device has a different range of color, which is called its *gamut*. The challenge is that the gamut of color models for print is smaller than that of any RGB display. The gamut of each printing process, device, or ink and paper combination is also slightly different. Since the human eye sees a wider range of color than possible in either CMYK or RGB color models, we can detect subtle differences between display and print.

23.3 Managing Color for Print *(continued)*

The Color Section shows the relationships between the visible spectrum or Lab color space and the possible range available with each of the RGB and CMYK color models. If you follow the lines between the RGB and CMYK markers, you will see areas where each model is limited in relation to the other.

Photoshop does an excellent job of bringing colors into gamut when you convert to CMYK. Even if a color is out of gamut, you won't necessarily get a bad print. You might, however, want to identify areas in your image that are out of gamut and adjust the color manually. To display all out-of-gamut colors in an RGB image, choose View > Gamut Warning.

Intuitive Color Management Choices

Color management can be a technical process of calculations or decisions made by complex systems to control color accuracy. In simplest terms, color management also encompasses all choices you make regarding color when working in Photoshop. Many color management choices are simply intuitive.

- When opening an image, you can choose to convert images to your own working space preference, work with the previously embedded or assigned profile of an image, or allow Photoshop to run in default mode by selecting Don't Color Manage.

- When starting a new image, you choose a color mode and a color profile. Although there are several options, RGB Color and Adobe RGB (1998) are default settings with a wide gamut. Though not the most common choice, you can also choose to begin work directly in CMYK if your image is destined only for placement in print or publication.

- You can also choose to select spot colors or colors from specific swatch libraries as you work if you need absolute color uniformity. These types of colors have values for printing independent of conversion color models and gamut.

Photoshop uses the Lab color model as its reference for color management. You may also find that the Lab color model provides useful options for you as well. Correcting colors in Lab color mode offers unique alternatives to RGB and CMYK in that it allows working with green and red together in one channel and blue and yellow together in another channel.

➡ 8.10 Converting to Duotone Mode

➡ 10.5 Adding Adjustment and Fill Layers

➡ 19.8 Sharpening and Blurring Images

➡ 24.5 Preparing for Four-Color Printing

In a traditional print workflow, you print a hard copy to view color shifts. A calibrated workflow allows Photoshop to display not only CMYK, but also show you representations of various equipment profiles in a soft proof.

Try sharpening or levels adjustments on the Lab color mode's Luminance channel to avoid problematic halos that often result from unsharp mask filtering on RGB or CMYK images.

Colors that can be problems when printed include oranges, purples, greens, reproduction of proprietary spot colors (such as PANTONE) in CMYK, light screen tints, and grays.

23.4   Creating Spot Channels for Print

——

You can create spot color channels in most color modes; however you can save them only in Grayscale, CMYK, and Multichannel color mode formats.

——

Spot color channels are saved or exported using Photoshop DCS 2.0 EPS as the traditional file format. You can also use Photoshop PDF for exporting the spot colors to other applications for separated output.

——

Colors to watch for that have issues when printed in CMYK include orange, purple, green, light screen tints, grays, and reproduction of proprietary spot colors (such as PANTONE colors).

Spot channels are necessary to create additional plates or separations for spot colors to be printed from Photoshop documents in common commercial or offset printing. Spot colors are custom premixed ink colors, such as PANTONE (PMS) colors, which may be selected to avoid problems associated with registration and color accuracy. Spot channels and their separations are independent of any other colors being printed using the primary (CMYK) plates in offset printing and can also be used to apply coatings such as varnish.

Creating a Spot Color Channel from a Selection

To create a spot color channel from a selection, follow these steps:

1 Create or load a selection for the spot color channel.

2 Choose New Spot Channel from the Channels palette menu to open the New Spot Channel dialog.

3 Click the Color box to select a color. Colors most commonly used will be from the PANTONE Solid Coated swatch book. The name of the selected ink will appear in the Name field of the New Spot Channel dialog and should exactly match the name used in other software if it is to separate properly.

4 The Solidity option is for visual display only and will not affect the density of the final separation. As with the Duotone mode Overprint Colors option, this is intended to manually simulate the visual interaction of the combined spot inks when viewed or printed as a composite.

23.4 Creating Spot Channels for Print *(continued)*

Creating a Spot Color Channel from an Alpha Channel

To convert a spot color channel from an existing alpha channel, follow these steps:

1 Double-click the alpha channel thumbnail in the Channels palette, or select the alpha channel and choose Channel Options from the Channels palette menu. Note that a channel with a grayscale percentage will separate as a tint of the spot color.

2 Click the Spot Color radio button, and select the appropriate Color and Solidity options as described in the preceding section.

Remember that this method will eliminate the alpha channel, which you might otherwise want to preserve. Unlike a standard alpha channel—which is often a "negative" image of white on black—a spot color channel is often a "positive" image of black on white. If the results of converting to a spot color channel are opposite than expected, simply invert the spot channel.

➡ 9.2 Selecting a Layer or Its Contents

➡ 10.5 Adding Adjustment and Fill Layers

➡ 24.6 Creating Color Traps and Knockouts

You can choose Save As > TIFF to save spot channels, but this can cause problems for many printers and pre-press operators.

By default, spot color channel data is set to overprint. Thus, you may get unwanted results where spot colors overlap if you do not create knockouts and traps.

The alpha channel was originally defined by Apple without any specific purpose in mind. Photoshop was one of the first applications to use the alpha channels and has been instrumental in establishing the alpha channel as a space for saving selections in the form of masks as well as spot color channels.

When moving images to other applications for print, always verify that the spot color name used in Photoshop and in illustration and page-layout software is exactly the same.

SPOT COLORS VS. DUOTONES

Spot color channels are commonly confused with Duotone mode, which also provides users with the option to output separations in spot color ink mixes. In Duotone mode, the separate Duotone ink plates are all generated from the same original Grayscale mode source data and are varied via special Duotone transfer curves. As their name suggests, spot color channels do not have the same limitations as Duotone mode and were a later addition to the Photoshop toolset by Adobe to address a different prepress need. (Photoshop 4 or earlier requires a third-party plug-in to designate spot color and save EPS DCS 2.0 files.) A Duotone mode file that is converted to Multichannel mode allows for the separate editing of the Duotone color plates—although it is not possible to return the file to Duotone mode once any editing has taken place.

CHAPTER 24

Preparing Images for Print

IF YOU HAVE BEEN working on individual images and plan to print only small quantities, maybe to your own home or office printer, your work is nearly done. This chapter includes topics that discuss considerations for printing to your desktop printer.

If you are considering working with a commercial printer on a project, you will have several more considerations. Designing and completing the creative work on an image or print project is most often only the first step in the larger process of getting a project printed. Converting your images to the color profile designated by your printer or to CMYK may also be just another small step in preparing your file, which might yet require being set up for bleeds, trapping, knockouts, separations, or processing to film. These considerations are also discussed in this chapter.

- 24.1 **Preparing to print**
- 24.2 **Preparing to print to inkjet printers**
- 24.3 **Preparing to print to PostScript printers**
- 24.4 **Preparing spot color and Duotone images**
- 24.5 **Preparing for four-color printing**
- 24.6 **Creating color traps and knockouts**

24.1   Preparing to Print

➡ 7.8   Setting Up the
        Printed Page

➡ 8.2   Understand-
        ing Image
        Modes

Color Settings dialog
[Shift] [⌘] [K]
[Shift] [Ctrl] [K]

Page Setup
[Shift] [⌘] [P]
[Shift] [Ctrl] [P]

———

When possible, work
at the image size and
resolution in which
the final image will
be printed.

———

Many printers and
service bureaus accept
full-color images as
JPEG files with low com-
pression (high quality)
because the degrada-
tion caused by the file
format is not visually
noticeable.

———

All work done to pre-
pare a project for a
commercial printer is
called prepress

Before you can prepare an image for print, you must decide which form of output you are going to use for the job. The earlier you make print considerations in the design process, the better off you will be.

If an image will be printed in large quantities, offset printing is probably the best choice. Preparing an image for offset printing is not complicated, but it does involve more preparation than would be necessary for a desktop printer.

It is important to make sure that the image is in the correct color space and color mode for the type of printing and equipment. Regardless of the type of printing, to ensure accurate reproduction you need to set up Photoshop for the specific printer. To do all this, you use the Color Settings dialog (choose Edit > Color Settings in Windows; choose Photoshop > Color Settings in Mac OS X).

Working with Your Printer/Service Bureau

When selecting a printer or a service bureau, the first step is to shop around. Find a provider that has experience with the platform (Macintosh or Windows), formats, applications, and workflow that you use, and you'll save yourself time and effort. The lowest bidder or the service bureau that "everyone else" uses may not be a good fit with your requirements and methods and might end up costing you more than you thought you could save! Once you are satisfied with a printer or service bureau, stay with them and establish a working relationship. Doing so will pay great dividends in the long run—especially when you find yourself in a jam under a deadline.

Before submitting a job to a service bureau or a printer, you need to ask the following questions:

What file formats are acceptable? Although most printers can read and use Photoshop files, many times they want the files in either TIFF or even EPS format. Also check to see which platform (Windows or Mac) they prefer. Most shops can use either one, but some are platform-specific, and if they are not comfortable with the one you use, the job can suffer. If your printer or service bureau leaves you the choice of image formats, it is generally best to save images for print in either TIFF, or EPS format. Most shops agree that these image formats preserve both the color and the sharpness of your pictures the best. Avoid using file formats such as GIF or low-resolution (72 dpi) JPEG because the compression they use can introduce color shifts and blurring.

On what media are jobs accepted? Many shops accept files online through an FTP site. Photoshop files can be quite large. If a shop accepts files on media, ask about any restrictions. For example, if you bring your job on a Jaz disk, you might discover that they cannot read the files. The most popular media for transporting images are CD-R and CD-RW discs.

24.1   Preparing to Print *(continued)*

Can pictures from digital cameras be used? Many printers and service bureaus now accept JPEG files, as they are the typical format used by digital cameras. However, if your camera is set to RAW format, you will need to first convert your files. Also ask how your images will be handled or if there is a processing fee. You may need to first resize images, changing their resolution for print.

What resolutions should be used? Your printer knows exactly the resolutions to use for the type of printing, so be sure to ask about the resolution requirements. Most printers and service bureaus will give you a handout that contains detailed instructions about the type of image and resolution they expect. Without direction from the printer, either scan or resize your images using a resolution of 300 dpi at the final dimensions you intend to use them. Doing this results in the best color and edge definition. If your image isn't the correct size or resolution, open it in Photoshop and resize it. This can result in loss of detail unless Resample Image is unchecked, as described in Section 7.3.

Do you need to send the fonts with the job? If you use any fonts from sources other than those found in a PostScript printer, you need to gather copies of them, archive them using a zipping or stuffing program, and send them with your layout file. If you don't know how to do this, go through your document carefully and make a list of any fonts used. Send that list to the printer or service bureau.

IMPOSITION AND BACKUP

The term *imposition* describes how pages and objects on pages are arranged so that, when the sheets are printed and folded, the pages will be in the correct order.

The term *backup* refers to printing on the back side of the sheet that has already been printed on one side. For example, if you create a brochure, it is normally turned over from right to left (as turning the page of a book).

When sending a multipage document to print, you need to ensure that the back side reads correctly—not upside down when it is folded.

➧ 8.6   Converting between Color Profiles and Devices

➧ 23.1   Print Basics

Print
Option ⌘ P
Alt Ctrl P

Print With Preview
⌘ P
Ctrl P

A service bureau in simplest terms is a printing company or facility that provides film output (negatives) or high-end scanning for your job, which you will take to another print shop of your choosing.

By default, all visible layers and channels are printed. To print an individual layer, make it the only visible layer before choosing the Print command.

When sending images to a printer as a TIFF file, make sure you have flattened the image before saving. This reduces the size of the resulting file and prints faster.

To print only part of an image, select that part with the Rectangular Marquee. In the Print With Preview dialog, select Print Selected Area.

24.2   Preparing to Print to Inkjet Printers

[Shift] [⌘] [P]
[Shift] [Ctrl] [P]

Print
[Option] [⌘] [P]
[Alt] [Ctrl] [P]

———

Using higher resolu-
tions available with
inkjet printers (that is,
2880 dpi) doesn't usu-
ally noticeably improve
the output, but it takes
longer and can use
twice as much ink. For
best results for your
workflow, check the
documentation for your
particular printer. It
also pays to run test-
prints at different
settings.

———

Pigment-based inks
cannot produce colors
as vivid as dye-based
inks, but they have
greater archival proper-
ties. If you are printing
for your personal use,
dye-based inks will give
you more vivid colors,
and, even after several
years, you can print
another copy.

———

If you use normal
paper, print at a low
resolution, such as 360
dpi. If you use special
coated paper, such as
inkjet paper or glossy
film, print at a high
resolution.

When setting the resolution of the file to print on an inkjet printer, be careful not to set the resolution too high, which is tempting with a printer that is advertised to produce extremely high resolutions. For an inkjet printer running at a setting of 720×720 dpi, the maximum resolution of a photographic image should be 240 dpi. Anything higher is auto-matically resampled down by the printer's software. The newer photo printers often offer imaging at 1440/2880 dpi, even though manufacturers recommend that the files be a max-imum of 360 dpi for optimum quality output. In practice, the visual difference between printed output of images at the two resolutions is almost indistinguishable. For continu-ous-tone digital imaging (dye-sub printers), the necessary resolution is relative to the printer's resolution; follow the manufacturer's recommendation.

With regard to color and most InkJet printers, although they do use CMYK inks (CcMmYK for photo printers), most inkjet printers from major manufacturers (such as Hewlett Packard, Epson, Canon, and Lexmark) require that the image be in RGB mode and not CMYK mode. The print drivers supplied with these printers cannot interpret CMYK image data and will produce unpredictable and generally unacceptable results.

The kinds of built-in color management that some printers provide can interfere with the color management of Photoshop. The two color-management systems are trying to cor-rect for each other, which sometimes produces unacceptable results. One way to get the best possible color is to use the following procedure:

1 Before opening the image, change two settings in the Color Settings dialog (choose Edit > Color Settings in Windows and Mac OS 9; choose Photoshop > Color Settings in Mac OS X):

■ In the Working Spaces section, choose RGB: Adobe RGB (1998).

■ In the Color Management Policies section, choose RGB: Convert To Working RGB.

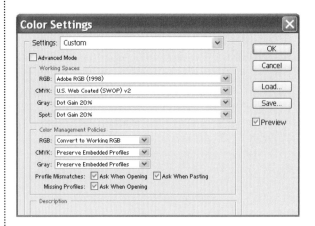

24.2   Preparing to Print to Inkjet Printers *(continued)*

2   Open the image. If an Embedded Profile Mismatch warning appears, select Convert Document's Colors To The Working Space and click OK.

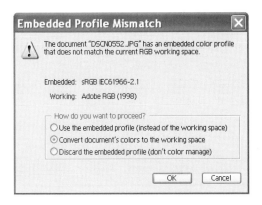

Print With Preview
⌘ P
Ctrl P

If you are scanning images for a project you know will be printed in CMYK, check your scanner specifications—you may save yourself work, and image quality, by scanning in CMYK.

3   With the image selected, choose File > Print With Preview and, in the Print dialog, do the following:

■   Check Show More Options and select Color Management from the drop-down.

■   Under Source Space, select Document; in the Print Space section, select Printer Color Management from the Profile drop-down.

Always check the printer's Properties dialog before printing to make sure that the correct medium is selected.

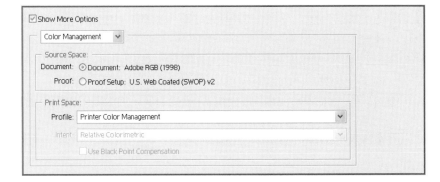

Avoid using ink refill kits with your inkjet printer cartridges. The colors may not be as vivid, and, in most cases, doing so voids the printer warranty.

4   Click the Page Setup button to open the printer's Properties dialog, and change the color adjustment properties to ICC Profile (this is usually accessed by clicking an Advanced button). After you set up the printer, return to the Print dialog and print the image.

24.3　Preparing to Print to PostScript Printers

Save As
Shift ⌘ S
Shift Ctrl S

Page Setup
Shift ⌘ S
Shift Ctrl S

Print
Option ~ C M P
Alt C t r l P

Print With Preview
⌘ P
Ctrl P

————

Most desktop color inkjet printers are non-PostScript printers, including Hewlett Packard LaserJet, Canon Bubble Jet, and Epson Stylus.

————

When printing to file for a RIP at a service bureau or printer, check to see which version of the RIP software driver they want you to use.

Many laser printers (black-and-white and color) now support PostScript. If the printer is local, all you need do to print the documents is adjust the settings that are unique to PostScript. If the target printer is a raster-image processor (RIP) at a service bureau, you need to create a PostScript file that can be sent to the output device. To do so, select the printer and then select the Print To File option. If the printer or RIP that is used by the service bureau or printer is not installed on your system, download it from the Internet and install it.

Before printing, ensure that the image is at the correct resolution. For grayscale halftones, the traditional rule of thumb is that the dpi (equivalent to ppi, or pixels per inch) should be twice the lpi (lines per inch). For a typical 300 dpi laser printer, which prints only up to 53 lpi, 100 dpi grayscale scans are adequate.

To print to a PostScript-capable printer, follow these steps:

1　To print to a color printer that is PostScript Level 2 or higher, it may be necessary to first convert the image to the appropriate color mode for your output device. For example, the setting that is most often used with color laser printers is CMYK.

2　Choose File **>** Page Setup and, in the Page Setup dialog, do the following:

■ Click the Printer button; in the Printer dialog, choose the correct color printer from the drop-down. The driver for the printer must be installed on your system for its name to appear in this menu. Click OK.

■ Select either Landscape or Portrait in the Orientation section. Click OK.

3　Choose File **>** Print With Preview; in the Print dialog, do the following:

■ Choose Document as your Source Space in most cases.

■ In the Print Space section, choose Printer Color Management. This option sends all the file's color information along with the Source Space profile to the printer. In this way the printer, rather than Photoshop, controls the color-conversion process.

■ From the Intent drop-down, choose Relative Colorimetric.

24.4 Preparing Spot Color and Duotone Images

The choices you have regarding preparation of spot colors and Duotones can be taken in two directions. If the use of spot colors or Duotones is simply for achieving a distinctive color or appearance, converting the document to CMYK will allow it to be printed in four-color process.

However, if your use of spot colors or Duotones is intended for their more traditional purposes, such as creating separations for offset printing or for use in another application for layout and separation, you must first ensure that your spot colors are isolated into specific spot channels. Spot color channels also require you to consider halftone screens and overprinting of other inks. It is generally recommended that you knock out the parts of the image that lie underneath the spot colors manually if the printing application does not do so automatically. When knocking out portions of images, ask your printer if trapping is required to compensate for possible misalignment.

Preparing Halftone Screens

When preparing spot colors and Duotones for printing, both the order in which the inks are printed and the screen angles visually affect the final output. You control the screen angles in the Halftone Screens dialog. The following procedure shows how this feature is used:

1   Choose File > Print With Preview > Output > Screen to open the Halftone Screens dialog.

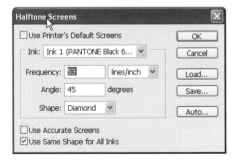

2   Click the Auto… button, which causes Photoshop to apply the optimal screen angles and frequencies for the type of image being printed.

3   When printing to a PostScript Level 2 (or higher) printer or to an imagesetter equipped with an Emerald Controller, select the Use Accurate Screens option in the Auto Screens dialog.

For solid spot colors (100%), halftone screens are not required. But when printing tinted spot colors that overlap, ensure that each halftone screen has a different angle to prevent moiré patterns.

You can place a PSD file containing spot colors directly in InDesign CS without special preparation.

To export a Duotone to a page-layout application, save the image in EPS or PDF format. If the image contains spot channels, convert it to Multichannel mode, and then save it in DCS 2.0 format.

You can convert a spot color channel into either the RGB or the CMYK color equivalents by selecting Merge Spot Channel from the Channel palette drop-down, which is a quick way to create comps for preview or approval. It isn't necessary to merge spot colors before printing them to a color printer.

24.5   Preparing for Four-Color Printing

➠ 7.8   Setting Up the
            Printed Page

➠ 8.2   Understand-
            ing Image
            Modes

➠ 8.4   Choosing a
            Color Working
            Space

The Adobe Color Picker supports various color models. Ensure that you select the same color model that is used by the service bureau or printer.

If your work requires creating accurate color for prepress work, consider investing in a system that will create color profiles. Several excellent systems cost less than $50.00 and will calibrate all the parts of your system and produce an accurate ICC profile that can be used by the service bureau or printer to ensure that the color you see on your screen matches what the four-color press produces.

When an image is converted between various color modes, some small image-color information is always lost. Converting from RGB or CMYK to Lab or from Lab back to RGB or CMYK does not cause an identifiable loss of color information. Photoshop uses Lab as a color reference in color management.

When printing using colored ink on paper, the CMYK (cyan, magenta, yellow, and black) process colors for four-color offset printing are used, and generally the PMS (Pantone Matching System) is used for spot ink color designation. The following sections present some guidelines for using CMYK effectively.

Using the CMYK Working Space

A working space is a predefined setting meant to represent a color profile that produces the most accurate color for several specific output conditions. You can begin an image in the working space of the final output. One of the most commonly used profiles is the U.S. Prepress Defaults setting, which uses a CMYK working space designed to create accurate colors under the standard Specifications Web Offset Publications (SWOP) press conditions. When working with a service bureau or printer, you may be asked to use one of Photoshop's preset working spaces, which you can find by choosing Edit > Color Settings, or you can ask the printer or service bureau for specific ICC (International Color Consortium) profiles for their equipment.

Convert to CMYK or Convert to Profile

People often work with more multipurpose goals. If your image is in RGB color space, do any and all image editing in RGB mode before converting the image to CMYK. Although CMYK is a standard color model for prepress work, the exact range of colors that can be reproduced vary between your equipment and the equipment used to create film separations; even the stock (paper or other media used for printing) has a dramatic effect on the accuracy of color reproduction. This range of color difference is documented in ICC profiles. Your service bureau or printer may be able to provide you with ICC profiles to install on your computer, which will be read by Photoshop with your currently installed printer settings, which are available in the drop-down in the Color Settings dialog or in the Convert To Profile dialog. Choose Image > Mode > Convert To Profile.

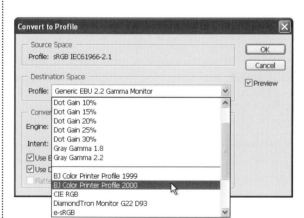

Once you have an ICC profile, it needs to be installed at the system level on your computer so that Photoshop will recognize it upon startup. For indows 2000 and XP, copy to the profile C:\WINDOWS\system32\spool\drivers\color. For Mac OS X, copy the profile to Users/Current User/Library/ColorSync/Profiles.

24.5 Preparing for Four-Color Printing *(continued)*

Verifying Bleed Settings

Bleed is the term for any printing that extends to the edge of the paper. It is impossible for most offset printers to print to the very edge of the paper so, by using a bleed, they can print the job on oversized paper and then trim the paper to the correct size, resulting in the final printed piece appearing to go to the very edge of the paper. Your printer will tell you what they prefer, but in most cases ensure that the edge of your document is at least 0.25' beyond trim size in all dimensions.

If you intend for your image to bleed, you will need to allow for this when you originally create the file by setting the dimensions of the file to the bleed size, not the trim size. Your printer may also ask that you include trim marks in your document as guides.

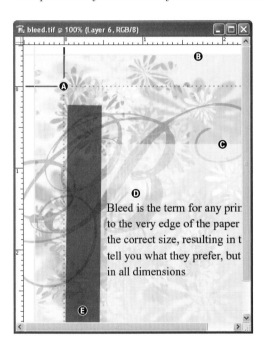

Ⓐ Crop marks and trim line (dotted representation).

Ⓑ Indicates extent of bleed (in this case, 0.3750' beyond trim).

Ⓒ Indicates safe area, far enough in from trim for important objects or text.

Ⓓ Text within safe area and background element. If an object is to be cut off, position it so it looks intentional.

Ⓔ The dark rectangle is positioned at a slight angle to demonstrate what can happen if objects are placed too close to a trim edge; anything out of parallel is exaggerated.

Make sure that any photographs or backgrounds that you want to bleed extend to the perimeter of the document, past the guidelines. Also make sure that any important text or objects are well within the trim or *safe area* to avoid their being cut inadvertently. You can easily use ruler guides to lay out your document edge-references.

If you discover that you need to add a bleed to a slightly under-sized original image, you can use the Resize command or increase the size of the canvas by choosing Image > Canvas Size. Using the Clone tool or copied image content as necessary, you can extend a small edge around the image to accommodate the bleed specified by your printer or service bureau.

➡ 8.6 Converting between Color Profiles and Devices

➡ 8.7 Using Color in Channels

➡ 23.1 Print Basics

➡ 25.2 Saving in TIFF Format

Ensure that your Photoshop file is the exact dimensions you want printed. If the file used a default size but your document is larger or smaller, resize your page accordingly before sending it to the printer.

When choosing a paper stock for a print job, consult with your printer. Many decorative papers cannot be used for offset printing for a variety of reasons.

Although the traditional rule of thumb is that the dpi should be twice the lpi, most printers agree that 265 dpi is more than adequate and that anything more results in larger file sizes and longer RIP time with little to no improvement in the final output.

Logos and line art will produce superior results when originally generated as vector files, especially if trapping is involved.

If you have line art that was scanned at a resolution lower than 1200 dpi, save it as a grayscale image.

24.6   Creating Color Traps and Knockouts

_____

Traditionally, *traps* are also known as "spreads" or "chokes"; this was originally a graphic reproduction term originating with the photographic preparation of film sep-arations.

_____

Always check with your printer or service bureau as to how much misregistration can be expected. Since trap-ping isn't always neces-sary, apply it only if your printer says that it is necessary. Many serv-ice bureaus add the trap themselves, and a trap added by Photo-shop will interfere with this. Your service bureau will provide the values to enter in the Trap dialog.

_____

As a general rule, don't create traps for color photographs.

_____

Always keep an original untrapped version of your image file, in the event you want to edit the image later.

Commercial printers using traditional offset or lithographic methods must run each ink color on their presses individually after individual plates are prepared for each color. Align-ment of these plates is critical for producing high-quality printed results. Any misalign-ment in the plates will produce noticeable flaws in the printed work. The use of trapping can help you avoid gaps in ink coverage, with little or no color, indicating misregistration.

Trapping consists of what are known as chokes and spreads. A *choke* traps a light background to a dark foreground as in the left side of the illustration. A *spread* is used to trap a light foreground to a dark background as in the right side of the illustration. A solid color overlapping both light and dark areas will require both types of traps.

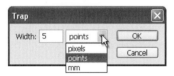

To create a trap, choose Image > Trap and, in the Trap dialog, enter the trapping value provided by your printer or service bureau. It is wise to talk to your printer or service bureau before trapping a document. Since a flattened file will result from Photoshop's Trap command, it is suggested you use a duplicate of your file. The command is applied to the current active channel(s).

By default, spot color channels in Photoshop are designated to overprint other inks. By design, you can use this overlapping of inks or colors to your advantage. Unwanted color blending, resulting from overprinting, can be disastrous. You can apply knockouts, delet-ing information from the color channels below spot channels, to avoid this type of problem. To create a knockout, follow these steps:

1 Drag the spot color channel to the Load Channel As Selection icon [icon] in the Channels palette.

2 Select the appropriate color information channel or another spot channel, and fill the selection with pure white to remove any data in the area underlying the spot color channel.

Notice in the second illustration that the left side has a knockout in the SPOT 5 channel. The SPOT 4 color (the letter M) is then overprinted on the right and printed alone on the left. Knockouts are generally more common than overprints, so it is critical to master this simple task. Because creating a knockout removes pixel data from the color information channels and other spot channel data, it is recommended that this operation be performed in a duplicate document so that the original data is intact.

CHAPTER 25

Saving, Proofing, and Sending to Print

WHEN A PHOTOSHOP PROJECT is destined for professional printing or publication, it is generally necessary to perform a few final tasks after design completion. The previous chapter discussed preparing files for print. This chapter discusses saving your work; both as good file management and as specific to the requirements of the folks who will be printing your work or handling your files.

Looking at accurate proofs, before final printed output, is also an import part of the printing process. Proofing allows you to better preview the limitations that printing will have with your image and also allows you to share expectations with print professionals. The proof process should eliminate some unwelcome surprises or wasted time and money.

Photoshop also provides you with automated tasks to create contact sheets, or Picture Packages, with which you can easily create an assortment of picture presentations or page layouts.

25.1　File-Saving Basics for Print

➠ 6.10 Saving Images

Save
⌘ S
Ctrl S

———

Photoshop's Faux Bold and Faux Italic font settings cannot be embedded into PostScript files.

With regard to professional print output and Photoshop files, it is important to keep in mind good file management and communication.

Archive copies of your work. Preserve all your editable layers, effects, masks, styles, and text in Photoshop native PSDs or layered TIFFs. Next, prepare and convert duplicates of your files or images, saving these copies to the specifications provided by whoever will be receiving your files.

Always ask. Be sure you understand each specific situation. Always communicate with the folks who will be getting your files and printing your job. Technology is always changing; you may learn something new. The key is to ask at least the basic questions regarding any specifications or preferences they have for receiving files or images. For example: What resolution values do they expect? Do they have color profiles for you to use for their output devices? Do they want fonts or outlined text? Will they take care of any trapping needs? How should you send the files?

Always include fonts and vectors with your files. Missing fonts are the most common holdup at service bureaus. It is a good rule to always supply printers, service bureaus, or publishers who will be handling your files every font used in the job—before they ask. For PostScript Type 1 fonts, submit both the printer and screen font (Mac) or PFB and PFM files (PC). As you archive files for clients, particularly if you use unique or stylish display fonts, it is a good habit to organize and save copies of the fonts with your files. If text has been converted to paths, the printer will not require these fonts; however, you will need to check the appropriate places in Save As dialogs to include vector data.

Consider how you will need to transfer your files. The mode of delivery, such as using a CD or DVD delivered by the postal service, may require you to think in advance regarding both packaging and file-size limitations—generally about 650 MB. Sending or transferring files electronically is generally preferred, though e-mail or FTP may require you to consider Internet connection speed and file size more closely.

Although there are many graphic file formats, only three types are predominantly used for transfer between platforms and applications for print purposes: Tagged Image File Format (TIFF), Encapsulated PostScript (EPS), and Portable Document Format (PDF). To save in any of these formats for print, open your archive file, or create a duplicate to work with. (It is important to keep all text and shape layers intact; do not "flatten" your file.) Choose File > Save As and consider the following options:

25.1   File-Saving Basics for Print *(continued)*

⟹ 24.3 Preparing to Print to PostScript Printers

Save As

⌘ Shift S

Ctrl Shift S

If you included spot colors in your document, you need to save to either TIFF or the specialized EPS format called Photoshop DCS 2.0.

Ⓐ Choose where you will save the document. Consider using a new folder in which to gather all files you are sending to print, with their fonts, instructions, source images and so on.

Ⓑ Type the name of the file. If you usually save files by client name or job, you may now need to save by your name or company name in order for the printer to recognize the file.

Ⓒ Specify one of the above formats in the drop-down.

Ⓓ Check to preserve your original for archival purposes.

Ⓔ Clear to remove all unnecessary channels from your print file.

Ⓕ Clear to allow Photoshop to write the PostScript and vector information from the layers to the "flat" print file.

Ⓖ Clear unless you have agreed to communicate with those printing or placing your file by using annotations.

Ⓗ Check if you want spot colors included in TIFF or Photoshop DCS 2.0 EPS files; clear if your intent is to print in four colors. (Your spot color will be converted to process color.)

Ⓘ If you have not yet converted your image to CMYK or to a color profile provided by your printer, you can use this option to save the document in compliance with your proof setting (View **>** Proof Setup).

Ⓙ Check to include your ICC Profile, or the next computer to open your file will need to reassign color values to your document.

Ⓚ Include file extensions when transferring files that will be opened on other computers; this is most important across platforms, specifically Mac to PC.

25.2   Saving in TIFF Format

_____

When saving TIFF files for applications other than Photoshop, don't include selections stored in alpha channels since that will prevent most applications from opening the files.

_____

Most paint, image-editing, and page-layout applications can read TIFF files.

_____

Some older applications do not support TIFF files with either ZIP or JPEG compression. To ensure compatibility with these older applications, save using either LZW or no compression.

The Tagged Image File Format (TIFF) may just be the workhorse of print files. It is the perfect choice for any non-PostScript print need and is also a very versatile alternate format to the Photoshop PSD for most archival purposes. TIFF supports CMYK, RGB, Grayscale, Lab, Indexed, and Bitmap color modes with both lossless and compressed options. Long regarded as a "flat" file format and used extensively in publishing, Photoshop allows you to save both layers and alpha channels in files as large as 4 GB.

Most applications that can handle TIFFs don't yet support files of more than 2 GB, don't read Photoshop's layers, and tend to respond better to files without alpha channels—it is wise to delete any unnecessary information. Choose File > Save or File > Save As, and then choose TIFF from the Format drop-down. Click Save to open the TIFF Options dialog:

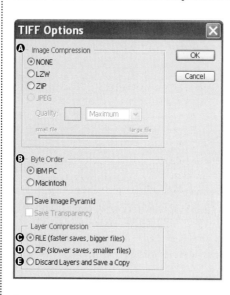

Ⓐ Choose a compression option. LZW is a lossless standard that reduces file size by an average of 50%. ZIP provides a higher compression, but some older applications might not be able to read the TIFF file. JPEG is a lossy compression that provides the maximum file-size compression but, like Zip, might be incompatible with older applications.

Ⓑ Choose the byte order. Since most applications today can read files saved in either order, change this option only if you know the file will be opened on the opposite platform from the one you are using.

Ⓒ Check to preserve multiresolution information; useful only when saving an image for an application that supports it.

Ⓓ Check to reserve an additional alpha channel to preserve transparency information. If the file being saved doesn't have transparency, this option is not available.

Ⓔ Select the method for compressing data in the layers. Choose Discard Layers And Save A Copy to save the image as a flattened copy.

25.3 Saving in EPS Format

Encapsulated PostScript (EPS) format is widely used for its ability to contain both vector and bitmap graphics. EPS files can be read by most PostScript-aware illustration and page-layout applications and by PostScript printers. This format supports Lab, CMYK, RGB, Indexed Color, Duotone, Grayscale, and Bitmap color modes.

Though EPS does not support alpha channels, it has the ability to contain clipping paths for use in publishing. To take full advantage of the PostScript capabilities of this format, *do not flatten your file before saving.* To save a Photoshop file in Photoshop EPS format, choose File > Save or File > Save As, and then choose Photoshop EPS from the Format drop-down. After selecting any options in the dialog, click Save to open the EPS Options dialog:

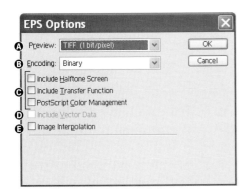

A Choose the color depth of the preview to be used by other applications to view and place the file.

B Choose how information is stored and sent to the PostScript printer. ASCII takes the most space but can be used by any Post-Script device. Binary is more compact and is the default setting. If Binary doesn't work, switch to ASCII. If JPEG is selected, it produces the smallest files but can only be used to print to either a Level 2 or a Level 3 PostScript printer.

C Choose Halftone Screen, Include Transfer, and PostScript Color Management (PCM) only if advised by your printer or service bureau. PCM converts file data to the printer's color space; don't select this option if the image will be opened in a color-managed document. PCM is not for the average user and is usually avoided, although for some very specific workflows there may be a small advantage.

D Saves any vector graphics (such as shapes and type) in the file. Even though the vector data in EPS files is available to other applications; it is rasterized if you reopen the file in Photoshop. To preserve vector data as vector data when the image is opened, it must be saved in PSD format.

E Applies anti-aliasing to improve the appearance of a low-resolution image when it is printed. If the image is high-resolution raster, using this option will soften it.

Transparent Whites is an EPS option (not shown) only available for bitmap (1-bit black-and-white) images. If selected, the white areas of the image will be transparent when the image is placed page layout applications.

Post-Script Color Management (PCM) for CMYK images is available only on PostScript Level 3 printers. If you are using a Level 2 printer, you must convert the image to Lab mode before saving in EPS format. (Only use PCM if your service provider requires it.)

➡ 6.10 Saving Images

➡ 25.1 File-Saving
         Basics for
         Print

Photoshop DCS 2.0 format is a version of the standard EPS format that allows you to save color separations of CMYK images or to export images that contain spot channels. Choosing File > Save As > Photoshop DCS 2.0 > Save opens a DCS 2.0 Format dialog that allows you to save individual documents for each color separation.

To use the JPEG preview option with EPS files in Mac OS requires that QuickTime be installed.

Even though Photoshop can embed vector data from paths, shapes, and type layers for other applications in the Photoshop EPS format, Photoshop will not reopen these EPS files without rasterizing them.

When saving an EPS file for placement in another application, be sure the application supports the level of preview bitmap. For example, Adobe FrameMaker can print a file with a color bitmap preview, but when this file is displayed, it appears as a gray box.

25.4   Saving as Photoshop PDF

As an option for creating a PDF from Photoshop or any application, you can create a PostScript file by choosing Print > Print To File and then using Adobe Acrobat Distiller to convert this print file (.ps) into a PDF.

You can use the Save As command to save RGB, Indexed Color, CMYK, Grayscale, Bitmap, Lab Color, and Duotone images in Photoshop PDF format.

Portable Document Format (PDF) is another versatile file format allowing for image transfer both across platforms and multiple applications while including bitmap, vector, and PostScript information. Among the many reasons to consider PDF as an option for your Photoshop images or print files is that PDF can store 16-bits-per-channel images, to contain navigation features such as electronic links, and now allows you to save multiple-page documents out of Photoshop.

Saving to PDF also allows for image compression of smaller file sizes and ease of electronic transfer, making PDF an excellent format for sending proofs for review or files to print via FTP or e-mail. Almost anyone can view or print PDF Files with the free Acrobat Reader download. To take full advantage of the PostScript capabilities of this format, *do not flatten your file before saving.* To save a Photoshop file in PDF format, choose File > Save or File > Save As, and then choose Photoshop PDF from the Format drop-down. After selecting any options in the dialog, choose Save to open the PDF Options dialog:

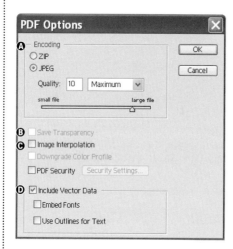

Ⓐ Choose the type of compression applied.

Ⓑ Check to preserve transparency when the file is opened in another application.

Ⓒ Check to apply anti-aliasing to improve the printed appearance of a low-resolution image.

Ⓓ Only available if the image includes vector data (shapes and type). If selected, Include Vector Data preserves any vector graphics as resolution-independent objects, which results in smoother output when the PDF is printed. If vector data is included, you can select two additional options: Embed Fonts or Use Outlines For Text. Your printer may ask you for text outlines.

25.4   Saving as Photoshop PDF *(continued)*

Multi-Page PDF

With Photoshop CS, you can now save multiple-page documents that contain Photoshop images without having to exit Photoshop. You can elect to create your Multi-Page PDF using saved files that are closed, using documents that are currently open within Photoshop, or selecting files from the File Browser.

Simply choose File > Automate > PDF Presentation from the main menu to open the PDF Presentation dialog:

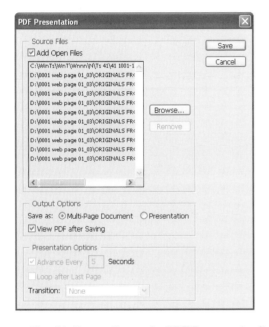

- To add all open files to the PDF Presentation list, check Add Open Files.

- Click Browse to access the standard Open dialog to identify other files to add.

- To remove files from the list, click a filename in the Presentation List window and click Remove.

- Check Multi-Page Document in the Output Options section.

- Checking View The PDF After Saving opens the PDF in a viewer such as Acrobat Reader after it is saved.

- Click Save to open the PDF Options dialog shown earlier.

You might save time by opening the File Browser before creating your multi-page PDF. Organize and select a group of files in the main File Browser window, and then from the File Browser menu, choose Automate > PDF Presentation. Your selected files will appear already listed in the PDF Presentation dialog.

➡ 25.1   File-Saving Basics for Print

Selecting Use Outlines For Text in the PDF Options dialog saves text as paths rather than fonts. Selecting this option results in a smaller PDF file, but the quality of the displayed fonts can suffer, especially if the image contains display fonts. Text saved as outlines cannot be searched or selected in a PDF viewer. You can still edit the text if you reopen the file in Photoshop.

A scaling option in the Page Setup dialog box is available when printing to PostScript printers such as AdobePS and LaserWriter. This scaling affects the size of all page marks, such as crop marks and captions. When you scale in Photoshop using the Print With Preview command, only the size of the printed image (and not the size of page marks) is affected.

25.5   Creating Color Proofs

➡ 8.2   Understand-
       ing Image
       Modes

➡ 8.4   Choosing a
       Color Working
       Space

Toggle Proof Colors on and off
⌘ Y
Ctrl Y

————

The color accuracy of the soft-color proof depends on the calibration and profiling of the monitor and the profile chosen for the proof setup.

————

The print professionals you choose may have several types of proofs for you to look at, depending on the accuracy you demand and are willing to pay for. This part of the proof process can include digital preproofing with dye-sublimation or inkjet printers or more specialized PANTONE proofing, match prints, or bluelines.

Proofing is an integral part of the overall printing process. When you proof a document, you preview what it will look like in final production. You can print several proofs in-house to double-check your work and what you intend for a design and then use an accurate printed proof as a "mock-up" to show your print professional a representation of what you want.

Soft Proofing in Photoshop

Colors displayed on an RGB monitor have a different color space and gamut than any CMYK printing process can completely reproduce. With Photoshop's color management, you can create "soft proofs"—setups that allow the monitor to mimic what an image will look like when printed. Using soft proofs to aid in color adjustment, you can make the job look as good as possible within the limitations of your selected printing process.

To display a soft proof for an image, simply choose View > Proof Colors. You may also find it beneficial to view both the working image and soft proof side by side. To do so, choose Window > Arrange > New Window (select from open documents)—then with the new window active, choose View > Proof Colors. This will give you a proof that displays your adjustments as you work on the original.

To display a soft proof for an image and a specific color model, particular device, or print process, you must first choose View > Proof Setup > Custom, and select a proof profile from the submenu:

Custom   This opens the Proof Setup dialog used to define the color display device as well as other information necessary to get an accurate soft proof. Choosing Custom creates a soft proof using the color profiles of specific devices and paper and ink combinations. This option is recommended.

Working CMYK or Individual Color Plates   Selecting any of the working settings causes the active image to display a soft proof of the selected CMYK working space or individual working plate without the need to convert the color mode of the image. The title bar of the image displays the color mode of the image and the currently selected working space. For example, an RGB image with Working CMYK selected will display (RGB/CMYK).

RGB working spaces   Macintosh RGB, Windows RGB or Monitor RGB (only available when viewing an RGB image) allow you to see what the image would look like when viewed in either of the alternate RGB color spaces.

Simulate   (only available when viewing CMYK images) Simulate Paper White previews the shade of white of the print medium defined in the document's profile; Simulate Ink Black previews the actual dynamic range defined by a document's profile. These options are only available for viewing images that contain paper white and black ink information and can only be used for soft proofing, not for printing.

25.5   Creating Color Proofs *(continued)*

Using the Proof Setup Dialog

By default when Proof Colors is selected, Photoshop simulates the conversion from the document's current work space to Working CMYK. To change this setting to a specific color model or profile requires changing settings in the Proof Setup dialog box, accessed by choosing View > Proof Setup > Custom:

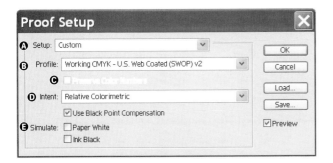

Ⓐ Used to recall previously saved proof setups. If no setups have been saved, the only choice is Custom.

Ⓑ Used to specify the proofing space that is to be simulated. You can choose any profile on the list, but if you choose an input device (scanner or digital camera), most of the other options will be grayed out.

Ⓒ When enabled, causes the image to appear as it will look if it is sent to the selected output device without actually converting the image color space. This feature is only available when the image is in the same color mode as the selected profile. When this option is selected, the Intent menu becomes grayed out because no conversion is required.

Ⓓ Select the rendering intent to be used in the conversion from the image color space to the soft proof color space.

Ⓔ Paper White and Ink Black control the rendering of the image proofing color space to the monitor being used. When both are turned off, the rendering maps paper white to monitor white and ink black to monitor black. When Ink Black is enabled, the black seen on the monitor is the actual black that will appear on the output (within limitations of the monitor settings). Enabling the White Paper check box causes Absolute Colorimetric rendering to be used when rendering the proof color space to the monitor. Black Ink becomes checked and grayed out. In most cases, enabling Paper White produces the most accurate soft proofs.

To quickly turn color proofing on and off, choose View > Proof Colors to turn the soft-proof display on and off. When soft proofing is being displayed, the name of the selected proof profile appears next to the color mode in the document's title bar, and a check mark appears next to the Proof Colors command in the View menu.

➥ 8.5   Choosing Color Management

➥ 8.6   Converting between Color Profiles and Devices

➥ 23.3 Managing Color for Print

Color proofs are a convenient way to see how an image will appear on different RGB monitors. For example, when working on an image in Windows, choosing Macintosh RGB displays the image on the screen as it would appear on a Mac, which is typically brighter because Mac OS and Windows use different gamma settings.

25.6   Creating Picture Packages

➠ 23.1 Print Basics

When applying labels, be aware that Photoshop tends to write the text over the photo regardless of the position selected.

The Picture Package automation allows you to arrange either an individual image or multiple images in a variety of sizes for print on one page. To make or arrange these layouts, the file need not be open. Photoshop allows you to select the automation from either the File Browser Automation menu or the main File menu. Choose File > Automate > Picture Package, and set the options in the Picture Package dialog.

Ⓐ Select images to include by choosing File or Folder and navigating the Browse feature to locate files; by choosing Frontmost Document to begin with your most recently active open image in Photoshop; or by using selected images from the File Browser. Click any image thumbnail in the Layout area to replace it with another image.

Ⓑ Choose predefined page sizes and layouts from the drop-downs. You can customize, modify, and save your own presets by clicking the Edit Layout button at the bottom of the dialog.

Ⓒ Choose an output resolution and color mode. If printing to your home printer, you might give the default setting a try, changing the setting as necessary for quality later.

25.6 Creating Picture Packages *(continued)*

➡ 25.7 Editing Picture Package Layouts

To select alternate images once the first image has been presented in a layout, simply click any image thumbnail to open the Select an Image File dialog that you can use to navigate to any other image file to replace the one selected.

D Check to flatten layers, which creates a smaller document filesize. Making a layered Picture Package provides you with an editable template for laying in other images, turning layers on and off, and so on.

E Choose or enter label information to be printed with your Picture Package. You can include metadata or file info such as copyright information, filename, or caption from the drop-down. If you choose Custom Text, you can type that text in the Custom Text field.

F Arrange the font, font size, color, and so forth. Professional photographers often use Picture Package "proofs" with text or copyright restrictions printed across the image. Positioning the text, especially its orientation horizontally or vertically, might require adjustment.

G Opens the Picture Package Edit Layout dialog in which you can customize and save your layouts.

25.7   Editing Picture Package Layouts

When applying labels, be aware that Photoshop tends to write the text over the photo regardless of the position selected.

You can easily set up your own template for printing multiple-image layouts by first creating a blank document at your desired paper size... then using ruler guides, layers or masks position "blanks" or placeholders for future layouts.

You can easily modify Picture Package layouts to your own personal specifications and save them for later use. First choose Automate > Picture Package from the main File menu or from the File Browser menu. Click Edit Layout to open the Picture Package Edit Layout dialog.

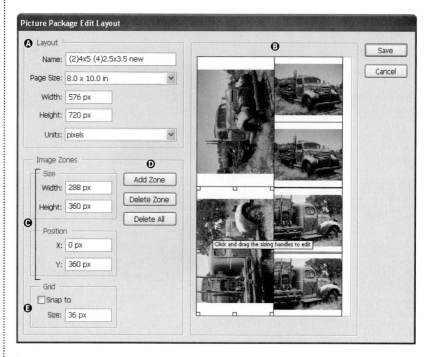

Ⓐ   Enter a name for your layout, and choose or change the page size.

Ⓑ   Click a pane to select that image placeholder "zone." Once selected, a zone displays sizing handles, a move cursor, or rotate handles. Resizing image zones is automatically constrained to the original proportions, and images are automatically rotated to maximize the layout.

Ⓒ   Enter values to set the size and position of the selected image zone.

Ⓓ   Click to add, delete, or clear all image placeholder zones from the layout.

Ⓔ   Check the box and set a grid size value to aid in arranging your layout.

Click Save when your layout is complete to return to the main Picture Package dialog.

Multi-Image Layout Options

You can use a new or saved Picture Package layout (with layers intact) as a simple template for other images. Drag a layer from another image onto your Picture Package and Option/Alt-click in the Layers palette between the newly placed layer and the existing layers to "clip" or mask your new layer to the existing layout. Simply choose Edit > Transform (Ctrl+T) to resize and fit the "clipped" layer.

25.8　Printing Contact Sheets

A *contact sheet* is a page containing thumbnail representations of image files. It provides a visual index of images. By displaying a series of thumbnail previews on a single page, you can easily preview contact sheets and catalog groups of images. You can automatically create and place thumbnails on a page by choosing File > Automate > Contact Sheet II, setting your options, and clicking OK when you're satisfied.

To speed up your work, you can preview, organize, and select a group of files within the File Browser first and then choose Automate > Contact Sheet II from the menu in the File Browser window to have those files preselected for the contact sheet.

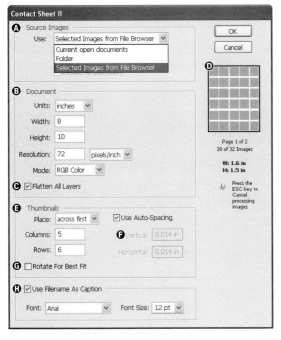

Ⓐ Choose a source for your images from the drop-down. Click Browse to choose a folder of images.

Ⓑ Set the page size, resolution, and color mode for the final contact sheet document.

Ⓒ Check to flatten layers, which creates a smaller document file size.

Ⓓ The right side of the dialog displays a preview and lists the number of pages, images per page, width, and height.

Ⓔ Arrange image thumbnails, placing them across first or down first and choosing the number of rows and columns.

Ⓕ Check to have images spaced automatically.

Ⓖ Check to have images automatically rotated to maximize image size and paper usage.

Ⓗ If this option is checked, you can specify font and font size for the caption.

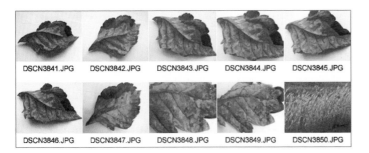

➠ 23.1　Print Basics

➠ 25.6　Creating Picture Packages

➠ 25.7　Editing Picture Package Layouts

To convert the custom proof setup into the default proof setup for documents, close all document windows and then choose View > Proof Setup > Custom.

Photoshop will begin to place all the thumbnails into however many document pages it will take to fit in all that were selected. If a folder contains a lot of images, creating all the contact sheets could take a long time. Contact sheets can be saved, printed, or both.

When selecting a folder to use for Contact Sheet II, be careful of folders containing lots of images. The program will continue to generate the contact sheets until all the files in the folder have been positioned.

Because there is the potential for Contact Sheet II to create a large number of contact sheets, ensure that all open files and other applications that could consume system resources are closed.

25.9   Printing and Online Services

———

Commercial printing services offer most reasonable prices for 4″ by 6″ prints. Typical digital cameras are not designed to capture images at this aspect ratio. Ask your printing service how their equipment handles the aspect ratio difference, you may want to crop and save your images before sending them to processing.

———

The newest wave of film processing equipment uses photographic paper, exposed with red, green and blue lasers and processed with traditional photo chemicals. This type of processing becoming standard even for 35mm Photo processors.

———

Photographic prints of your digital files can be ordered online for as little as $0.45 for a 4″ by 6″ print. Upload digital files and receive prints in the mail.

Photoshop offers a unique workflow option for uploading files and accessing remote service providers for online sharing, printing and imaging services via the Online Services menu command—without leaving the Photoshop workspace. The Online Services Wizard lets you take advantage of selecting all currently open files or pre-selecting files in the File Browser. You can organize, edit or otherwise prepare images for printing, then select this option following these steps:

1 Choose File > Online Services from the main menu... or choose Automate > Online Services from the File Browser menu.

- Your computer will automatically connect to the Internet.
- Your computer will access and download a list of online services.
- The Online Services Wizard dialog will open

2 Select a provider and service from the list presented in the dialog.

3 Choose > Next... at this point Photoshop must have access to the Internet and permission to transfer files. If you experience any error in connection you may need to check your firewall settings or System Internet Options safety settings.

The Online Services Wizard dialog will present several sets of options. First, choose from service options as shown here. Once your computer and the Online Services Wizard are connected to the Internet and ready to transfer information and files, you will be prompted to logon or sign-up with your selected service. When you have entered your personal registration info or password, Choose > Next... the dialog will present you a final set of options for selecting files to upload.

Follow the options specific to the service you have chosen. Once your images are uploaded, you will be connected to the web page of your chosen service provider. Upon returning to the Photoshop workspace and the Online Services Wizard dialog, Choose > Finish... Photoshop will disconnect from the service.

WEB TASKS

CHAPTER 26

Working With ImageReady

IMAGEREADY IS A SEPARATE, stand-alone program used to create and output images destined for the Web. ImageReady works much like Photoshop, and once you learn one of these programs, mastering the other will not take long. ImageReady and Photoshop include the same menus and most of the same menu options, the same tools, and the same palettes that can be docked to each other.

However, there are differences. Unlike Photoshop, which is designed to create images for a variety of mediums, ImageReady is designed to create, optimize, and output graphics for theWeb. To that end, ImageReady has a more limited toolset (in the Toolbox), adds a menu (Slices), and adds several palettes tailored for web designers. Some of the differences are the natural consequences of ImageReady being devoted to creating web graphics. Other interface differences, however, are less explicable and may take some getting used to.

This chapter outlines the differences between Photoshop and ImageReady and discusses how to use these two programs with Adobe's other flagship web product, GoLive.

Version 8.0
Color palette created...

Jon Clauson, Alan Erickson, Troy Gaul, Tim Gogolin, Julie Kmoch, John Ojanen, Lori Slater, Jon Steinmetz, Tim Wright, Jesse Zibble, Tom Attix, David Dobish, Michael Lewis, Jackie Lincoln-Owyang, Domnita Petri, Jeff Tranberry, Jeff Van de Walker, Bettina Zengel, Sandy Alves, Grace Kim, John Nack, Sau Tam, Ken Dunne

Copyright © 1998-2003 Adobe Systems Incorporated. All rights reserved. Adobe, the Adobe logo and ImageReady are either registered trademarks or trademarks of Adobe Systems Incorporated in the United States and/or other countries.

Jason Cranford Teague
webbedENVIRONMENTS
1045002898440295 2965

Adobe ImageReady CS

- 26.1 **ImageReady document windows**

- 26.2 **ImageReady menus**

- 26.3 **ImageReady tools**

- 26.4 **ImageReady palettes**

- 26.5 **ImageReady preferences**

- 26.6 **ImageReady with Photoshop, GoLive, and other applications**

26.1 ImageReady Document Windows

Minimize window
Ctrl ⌘ M

Close window
⌘ W
Ctrl W

Close all open windows
Option ⌘ W
Shift Ctrl W

Show/hide everything but the document windows
Tab

Show/hide all palettes
Shift Tab

Cycle through open document windows
Ctrl Tab
Alt Tab

To open multiple document windows open and juggle them, choose Window > Documents.

ImageReady maintains the same basic concept for the document window used in Photoshop: it's the place you edit the image. However, ImageReady adds and changes several features of the Photoshop window to make it more conducive to web design.

- You can preview a document using a variety of optimization settings. You access the views through the four tabs along the top of the document window.

- The information displayed at the bottom of the document window includes more options for optimizing the image for the Web.

- Rulers display only in pixels.

- The document window contextual menu also includes the layer unification commands, preview options, and Jump To options.

Ⓐ Title bar Not only displays the name of the file being viewed, but also the magnification and the optimization view.

Ⓑ Optimization view tabs The preview tabs allow you to switch between the four optimization view types.

Ⓒ Magnification Displays the current image magnification, but unlike Photoshop, this is a drop-down that allows you to choose the magnification.

Ⓓ Optimization information Both drop-downs allow you to select from a list of optimization information to display, including original/optimized file sizes, information about the optimization options set, the image dimensions, watermark strength, number of undos/redos, file-size savings due to optimization, and estimated download time based on Internet connection speed.

Ⓔ Right-click/Control-click in the document window to access options to select layers, unify layers in animations and rollovers, preview options, and send the image to other applications for editing.

26.2   ImageReady Menus

Although the ImageReady menu bar looks almost identical to its Photoshop counterpart—except for the Slices menu—there are some significant differences under the hood. For the most part, these differences are limited to either options not available in ImageReady or options that were not available in Photoshop. However, in several cases, options in Photoshop have been moved, renamed, or replaced by similar options. The differences between the ImageReady menu bar and its Photoshop counterpart include the following:

MENU	ADDS
ImageReady (Mac OS X)	Preferences submenu contains different options (see Section 26.5)
File	Export Original, Save Optimized related commands (see Section 29.6), Output Settings (see 29.10), Update HTML, Preview In (see Section 27.5), and Jump To (see Section 26.6)
Edit	Paste In Place (same as Paste Into), Copy HTML Code, Copy Foreground Color As HTML, Arrange Layers, Align Layers To Document, Distribute Layers
Image	Duplicate Optimized (see Section 29.6), Variables (see Section 27.4), Apply Data Set, Preview Document (see Section 27.4), Master Palette
Layer	Layer Options (same as Layer Properties), New Layer Based Image Map Area (see Section 28.1), Match (see Section 28.6), Propagate Changes (see Section 28.6), Group/Ungroup Layers, Set Layer Position, Lock Layers, Link Layers, Select Linked Layers, Reverse Layers
Slices	Available only in ImageReady (see Section 29.1)
Select	Create Selections From Slices, Create Slice From Selection (see Section 29.1), Create Image Map From Selection dialog (see Section 29.1), Delete Channel
Filter	Last Filter
View	Preview (see Section 27.5), Show Optimized (see Section 27.5), Resize Window To Fit, Create Guides (same as New Guide), Hide Optimization Info (see Section 27.5)
Window	Animation (see Section 28.2), Color Table (see Section 29.4), Image Map (see Section 28.1), Optimize (see Section 29.3), Slice (see Section 29.1), Table (see Section 27.3), Web Content (see Section 24.4)
Help	ImageReady Help (same as Photoshop Help)

➡ 29.1 Slicing Your
     Interface

➡ 29.2 Working with
     Slices

Select All User Slices
⌘ Shift A
Ctrl Shift A

———

You can adjust the key-
board shortcuts for
undo/redo in the
ImageReady prefer-
ences (see Section 26.5).

The Slices Menu

ImageReady also includes the Slices menu that collects commands used to create and edit slices in the canvas.

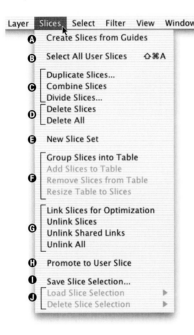

Ⓐ Turns guide lines into slices.

Ⓑ Chooses all slices that you have specifically cre-
    ated as opposed to auto slices created by
    ImageReady as space fillers.

Ⓒ Creates new slices based on existing slice(s)

Ⓓ Removes selected slice(s) or all slices, replacing
    them with rectangular auto slices.

Ⓔ Creates a new set of slices—accessible in the
    Web Content palette—that can be shown or
    hidden.

Ⓕ Sets how slices should be laid out using tables in
    the HTML code.

Ⓖ Commands to link and unlink selected slices,
    allowing optimization settings to be applied to
    all slices in the set when one of them is selected.

Ⓗ Turns the selected auto slice(s) into user slice(s).

Ⓘ Dialog allowing you to save one or more slices in
    a selection set that you can then quickly load.

Ⓙ Submenus listing saved slice selection sets to be
    either loaded (selected) or deleted.

ADDING "PREVIEW IN" BROWSERS

You can preview your web design in a web browser using either Photoshop's Save For
Web dialog or directly in ImageReady. Both programs will use the same list of browsers
for you to choose from, and you can edit that list.

To add or delete a preview browser or change the default browser, choose File > Preview
In > Edit Browser List. In the dialog, you will see a list of browsers that ImageReady has
located on your computer and buttons to add browsers that ImageReady missed, delete a
browser, or set the selected browser as the default used by the button in the Toolbox.

26.3 ImageReady Tools

ImageReady includes a more limited toolset than Photoshop, but the tools you will need for most web tasks are here with the same single-letter keyboard shortcuts. However, there are a few important differences in how Photoshop deals with tools in ImageReady. ImageReady does not include tool preset options (or any of the preset options found in Photoshop), so you cannot save the options you set for a particular tool. Also, ImageReady's brush tools use preset brush tips and shapes rather than the robust brush engine in Photoshop. This is more like the brushes used in Photoshop 6 than in more recent versions.

Many of the tools in ImageReady are identical to their Photoshop counterparts: Move, Magic Wand, Crop, Hand, Zoom, Foreground/Background Color, and Screen Modes.

Some tools that are separate in Photoshop are grouped into single toolsets in ImageReady.

ImageReady allows you to "tear off" a toolset from the Toolbox, creating a floating palette of that toolset. Click a toolset, and then click the arrow pointing down at the bottom of the toolset.

➡ 28.1 Creating
       Image Maps

➡ 29.1 Slicing Your
       Interface

Selection tools
Ⓜ

Move tool
Ⓥ

Slice tool
Ⓚ

Slice Select tool
Ⓞ

Image Map toolset
Ⓟ

Image Map Select tool
Ⓙ

Eraser tools
Ⓔ

Paint tools
Ⓑ

Type tool
Ⓣ

Shape tools
Ⓤ

Tab Shape tool
Ⓡ

Crop tool
Ⓒ

Eyedropper tool
Ⓘ

Hand tool
Ⓗ

ImageReady's painting tools allow you to choose preset brush tips and sizes, but do not allow you to directly edit these. You can, however, create custom brushes in Photoshop and import these into ImageReady.

26.3   ImageReady Tools *(continued)*

➠ 29.2 Working with
    Slices

Zoom tool
[Z]

Marquee tool
[M]

**Switch foreground and
background colors**
[X]

**Use default fore-
ground and back-
ground colors**
[D]

**Toggle Image Map
Visibility**
[A]

Toggle Slice Visibility
[Q]

Preview Document
[Y]

**Preview In Default
Browser**
[⌘][Option][P]
[Ctrl][Alt][P]

Toggle Screen Mode
[F]

Jump to Photoshop
[Shift][⌘][M]
[Shift][Ctrl][M]

———

To open the Toolbox,
choose Window >
Tools.

———

The default browser
for the Preview In
Keyboard shortcut will
be the last browser
chosen in the Preview
In submenu or Toolbox
drop-down.

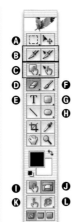

Ⓐ Selection tools Collects all selection tools (Marquee, Lasso, Magic Wand) and adds a rounded rectangle marquee that allows you to set the corner radius for a rectangular selection.

Ⓑ Slice tools The Slice and Slice Select tools are identical to those in Photoshop.

Ⓒ Image Map tools Toolset specific to ImageReady for creating image maps.

Ⓓ Eraser tools Does not include Background Eraser.

Ⓔ Type tool Only includes Horizontal Type tool, but type orientation can still be changed in the tool options bar.

Ⓕ Paint tools Collects many paint tools (Brush, Pencil, Clone Stamp, and Paint Bucket).

Ⓖ Basic Shape tools Basic shape tools allow you to draw shape layers and filled regions as in Photoshop.

Ⓗ Tab Shape tools Tab shape tools are tailored for certain interface widgets.

Ⓘ Toggle Image Map Click to show or hide image-map hot-spot boundaries in the canvas.

Ⓙ Toggle Slices Click to show or hide the slice lines in the canvas.

Ⓚ Preview Mode Click to turn on preview mode in the canvas, allowing you to test rollovers and optimization settings.

Ⓛ Preview In Browser Click to preview the document with current slices, image maps, rollovers, animations, optimization, and other output settings in the indicated browser. Click menu to choose an alternate browser in which to preview.

Ⓜ Jump To Photoshop Send document to Photoshop for editing.

ImageReady includes the Image Map toolset, not available in Photoshop. You use these tools to draw rectangular, circular, or free-form polygon shapes to use as hot spots in the canvas. In addition, the Image Map selection tool allows you to choose and edit the shapes of hot spots created with the other tools.

The Image Map toolset includes a rectangular, circular, and free-form polygon tool in addition to a selection tool for editing image-map shapes.

26.4   ImageReady Palettes

Palettes in ImageReady work almost exactly like palettes in Photoshop. You access them through the Window menu, you can dock them together either as a group or as palette windows, and you can save and restore their positions by choosing Window > Workspace. However, there are a few important differences, notably that ImageReady does not have the Palette Well.

Some ImageReady palettes include a diamond-shaped icon in the tab to the left of the palette name. Clicking this tab cycles through several views of the palette displaying different information and options.All fields include drop-downs to choose values from or to use a slider.

The ImageReady Info and Color palettes display a reduced set of modes—modes appropriate to web graphic work. The Layers and History palettes omit a few Photoshop features (such as the Adjustment/Fill layers drop-down and snapshots, respectively). The ImageReady Layers palette adds animation controls and the Unify buttons. The Styles palette records the styles of multiple rollover states. Otherwise, you will find palettes substantially the same as their Photoshop equivalents.

In addition to the palettes that are similar to those in Photoshop, ImageReady includes seven additional palettes. Some of these palettes (such as the Image Map tool) are used with ImageReady-specific tools, while others (such as Color Table) present options found in Photoshop but in a different formats.

PALETTE	DESCRIPTION	SEE ALSO
Animation	Add and edit animation frames in the selected layer.	Sections 28.2 and 28.3
Color Table	Adjust the colors in an indexed color table used with GIF or PNG-8 optimization settings. Similar to the Photoshop Indexed Color Table dialog.	Section 29.3
Image Map	Add information to image-map hot spots.	Section 28.1
Optimize	Set optimization options for an image or a slice.	Section 29.3
Slice	Add information to a slice.	Section 29.2
Table	Create tables for layout.	Section 27.3
Web Content	Add and edit rollover states to a slice or an image-map hot spot.	Sections 28.4 and 28.5

➡ 8.12 Changing the Indexed Color Table

➡ 15.2 Applying Effects and Styles

➡ 28.3 Editing Animations

➡ 28.5 Editing Rollovers

➡ 28.6 Editing Layers for Animations and Rollovers

Show/hide everything but the document windows
[T]

Show/hide all palettes
[Shift] [T]

26.5 ImageReady Preferences

⇒ 5 Presets and Preferences

⇒ 12.4 Selecting Colors with the Color Picker

Although there is some overlap with the Photoshop preferences, ImageReady includes a different set of preferences. ImageReady includes preferences for slices, image maps, and optimization. You access the ImageReady Preferences submenu through either the ImageReady menu (Mac OS X) or the Edit menu (Windows).

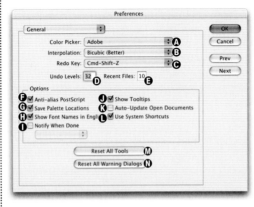

Ⓐ Choose whether you want to use the Photoshop Color Picker or your operating system color picker.

Ⓑ Choose a default interpolation method. ImageReady allows you to choose between Nearest Neighbor and Bicubic (recommended).

Ⓒ Choose the keyboard shortcut for Edit > Undo/Redo.

Ⓓ Enter the number of undo levels available. More undo levels require more memory and may slow down your system.

Ⓔ Enter the number of options to include in the Recent Files submenu in the File menu.

Ⓕ Check to automatically anti-alias PostScript graphics pasted into an ImageReady file.

Ⓖ Check to preserve palette locations after quitting ImageReady. Otherwise, palettes will reset to default locations.

Ⓗ Check if you want fonts that do not display in standard characters to use standard characters in font lists.

Ⓘ Check if you want to play an alert after ImageReady finishes a command. Choose the alert from the drop-down below.

Ⓙ Check if you want Tool Tips to appear when the mouse cursor is over an object in the interface.

Ⓚ Check if you want to open documents in ImageReady but edit them in another application (such as Photoshop) and then automatically update them when reentering ImageReady.

Ⓛ (Mac OS X only) Check to use system keyboard shortcuts if they conflict with ImageReady shortcuts. For example, Command-H will hide ImageReady rather than hiding slices, guides, and other extras in the canvas.

Ⓜ Click to reset all tools to their default values.

Ⓝ Click to reset all warnings so that they will appear even if disabled.

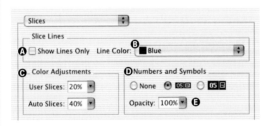

Ⓐ Check to show slice lines without the icons in the top-left corner.

Ⓑ Choose the color of slice lines.

Ⓒ Use the slider or enter a percentage value (1 through 100) for how much the color should dim when a user or auto slice is not selected.

Ⓓ Choose the size in which symbols should appear.

Ⓔ Use the slider or enter a percentage value (1 through 100) for the opacity of symbols.

26.5 ImageReady Preferences *(continued)*

General Preferences dialog
⌘ K
Ctrl K

To delete preferences, hold down while starting ImageReady
Option Shift ⌘
Alt Shift Ctrl

Ⓐ Check to show only a borderline around an image-map hot spot. If unchecked, the interior of the hot spot will be dimmed.

Ⓑ Check to show a bounding box around the image map.

Ⓒ Choose the color to use for hot-spot borders.

Ⓓ Use the slider or enter a percentage value (1 through 100) for the amount of interior dimming (see A).

In addition to the Guide and Grid controls found in Photoshop, ImageReady also includes Smart Guides, which only appear when an object's center is snapping to a particular guide. You can set the horizontal and vertical position of Smart Guides as well as their color.

In the top panel, choose the default optimization settings for new images or slices. You can use the previous settings, allow ImageReady to choose GIF or JPEG, or use an optimization preset that you choose from the drop-down. In the bottom panels, choose the default optimization settings to be used in the preview panes of the 2-Up and 4-Up previews. You can choose Original (uncompressed), Current (settings in the Optimize palette), Auto (allows ImageReady to determine best method), or one of the preset optimization settings.

26.6 ImageReady with Photoshop, GoLive, and Other Applications

Jump To Photoshop
[Shift][⌘] [M]
[Shift][Ctrl] [M]

———

When you move a document to another application, Adobe products refer to this action as a jump to the new application.

———

When jumping to Photoshop, all slices, layers, and guides will be preserved. In addition, rollovers, animations, and image maps will still be saved in the file, but will not be editable in Photoshop.

———

If you make changes to an image in Image-Ready that will affect the HTML, use the Edit > Update HTML… command to update your files.

ImageReady allows you to create and output images graphics for viewing on the Web, including the creation of the HTML code needed to display the web page. You can create, build, and deploy an entire website using only ImageReady. However, ImageReady has limitations both as an image-editing program and as a web-development tool. This is why Adobe created ImageReady to work closely with Photoshop to add more advanced image-editing capabilities and with GoLive to add more advanced web-development tools. But even if you are not using Photoshop or GoLive, you can select alternate image-editing and web-development software to work with ImageReady.

- To **jump the document to Photoshop,** click the Jump To button at the bottom of the Toolbox or choose File > Jump To > Adobe Photoshop. If not already running, Photoshop will open. The image will still be open in ImageReady, but grayed out to indicate that you are working on it in another program. You can jump back from Photoshop to ImageReady using the Jump To ImageReady button at the bottom of the Photoshop Toolbox or the File > Jump To > Adobe ImageReady command, or you can simply return to ImageReady using your operating system. Regardless of how you jump, changes made in other applications are applied to the image.

- To **jump the document to GoLive,** choose File > Jump To > Adobe GoLive. Follow the steps in Section 29.6 for saving the optimized website. After you click Save, the new website will open in GoLive. To edit any of the images while in GoLive, simply double-click the image in the GoLive document window to open it.

- To **jump the document to an alternate image-editing program** (such as Macromedia Fireworks), choose File > Jump To > Other Graphics Editor… Browse to find the program you want to use on your hard drive, and click Open. If you have not saved all changes to the image, you will be prompted to do so. The image will then open in the alternate image-editing software. Changes made in this program will be automatically reflected in the ImageReady version if you checked the Auto-Update Files option in the General Preferences.

- To **jump the document to an alternate web-development program** (such as Macromedia Dreamweaver), choose File > Jump To > Other HTML Editor… Follow the steps in Section 29.6 for saving the optimized website. After you click Save, the new website opens in the selected web-development software.

CHAPTER 27

Designing for the Web

WEB DESIGNS OFTEN START life as screen comps, static versions of the web pages that include all the elements that will be used to create the final interface. You can create these designs using both ImageReady and Photoshop, using the Jump feature to move the design back and forth between the two programs. However, ImageReady was developed with web design's unique needs in mind.

In this chapter, you will learn how to start a web page in either Photoshop or ImageReady, how to consider color while designing, and how to take advantage of several ImageReady features to create web pages.

27.1   Web Design Basics

New File dialog
⌘ N
Ctrl N

Open File dialog
⌘ O
Ctrl O

Show/Hide Extras
⌘ Ctrl H
Ctrl Shift H

Designing a website using either Photoshop or ImageReady begins by starting a new document (in either program) with dimensions that match the screen size you want for your web page or web element (more on web elements in the next chapter). You will then establish the structure of the page using a layout grid to define areas for specific uses as columns and rows. This is especially useful when designing using HTML tables; the grid helps align design elements and leads to a cleaner design that's easier to output to tables.

Starting a New Web Page Design

You can create a new web page in Photoshop or in ImageReady by choosing File **>**New… Enter a name for the new file, select a preset size or enter the dimensions directly, and then select a background (White, Background Color, or Transparent). If you are using Photoshop, be sure that the resolution is set to 72 dpi, that the mode is set to RGB, and set your units to pixels.

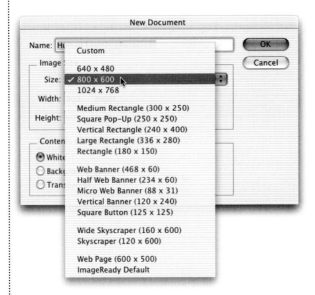

The ImageReady New Document dialog is slightly different from the Photoshop version. Since ImageReady is Web only, it automatically uses 72 dpi for the resolution, pixels for units, and RGB for the color mode. In addition, it includes several preset page sizes for Half Web Banner, Micro Web Banner, and Web Page, which is the default web page size on monitors set to 800 × 600 when system chrome is taken into account.

27.1 Web Design Basics *(continued)*

Creating a Layout Grid

To set guides in ImageReady or Photoshop, simply drag from the ruler (see Section 7.5). ImageReady, however, adds an option that you can use to add guides in a regular grid pattern. To create a grid of guidelines in ImageReady, choose View > Create Guides…, and set the options in the Create Guides dialog.

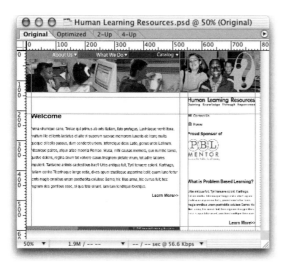

A layout grid defines the areas of the web page. The line on the far left defines the width of a web page displayed in a monitor set to a resolution of 800 × 600 when interface chrome is taken into account.

A Check to add horizontal guidelines.

B Check to add vertical guidelines.

C Enter a value for the number of evenly spaced guidelines. The value must be between 0 and half the image width or height minus 1. (For example, an image that is 640 pixels wide can have a maximum value of 319 for horizontal guides.)

D Enter a value for the number of pixels between each guide. The value must be between 2 and the image's width or height minus 1.

(For example, an image that is 480 pixels tall can have a maximum value of 479 for the vertical guides.)

E Enter a value for the position of the guide from the top or left side of the image.

F Check to clear all guides currently in the image.

G Check to preview the new guides in the canvas.

➡ 8.2 Understanding Image Modes

➡ 26.5 ImageReady Preferences

Show/Hide Guides

⌘ [;]
Ctrl [;]

Lock Guides

⌘ Option [;]
Ctrl Alt [;]

Most of today's monitors display at 96 dpi, although some older Mac monitors use 72 dpi. However, both web and TV designs are created at 72 dpi.

The canvas size you choose should reflect the screen size that people viewing your web page are likely to use. Most web surfers today use monitors set to a resolution of 800 × 600. However, if your audience is likely to be using older systems, set the canvas to 640 × 480.

You will be creating your designs in Photoshop so they should look consistent from browser to browser. Nevertheless, it is important to test in the actual browser environment to make sure that your designs looks as good as possible. See Section 27.5 for more details on previewing in a browser.

27.2   Web Color Basics

The painter Georges Seurat developed the technique of Pointillism. He placed small dots of paint from his palette onto the canvas close together in order to create the illusion of a continuous image. Computer screens work a lot like that, placing dots of color on the screen.

If you create an image on a machine that has thousands of colors in its palette and then display that image on a machine with only 256 colors in its palette, any colors in the image not in the palette of 256 will either be replaced by a closely matching color or dithered by trying to mix colors on the screen visually.

The number of colors that a computer screen can display depends on many factors, and obviously the more colors your monitor can display, the better your image will look. However, with web design, how the image looks on your computer is not necessarily how it will look on the computer being used by your website's visitor. Several factors affect the final colors:

Monitor The exact size and resolution of the monitor affects the final appearance of a graphic. Generally, monitors display in 8-bit (256 colors), 16-bit (approximately 65,000 colors), or 24-bit (approximately 17 million colors).

Operating system Different operating systems use different color look-up tables (CLUTs) that define the basic colors available. This consideration is especially important for older computers that can display only at 8-bit. In addition, different operating systems have different gamma values that define how dark the midtones of colors in a graphic are displayed.

Graphic format The graphic format you choose can limit the number of colors that can be recorded for an image. For example, you can use only 256 colors with the GIF format.

Photoshop can help you overcome many of these limitations to ensure that what you see is what they get.

Color Table

A color table is an indexed list of colors in an image used with the GIF and PNG-8 formats. These lists can have a maximum of 256 color values and a minimum of 2 color values. While you are working on your design, you need not worry about the exact color table; however, when you optimize your image, the color table plays a crucial role if you are using GIF or PNG-8 formats. See Section 29.7 for more details on using the color table to optimize GIF and PNG-8 images.

Dithering

Dithering uses two or more colors placed closely together in an attempt to fool the eye into seeing a single color. The dithered image has noticeable dots rather than smooth tones.

27.2 Web Color Basics *(continued)*

A graphic can be dithered in two ways:

By the browser If the operating system does not have a particular color in its CLUT that is used in a graphic, the browser attempts to simulate the color through dithering. Allowing the browser to dither graphics rarely produces seamless colors, tends to make the image look grainy, and can greatly degrade the quality of the image, especially anti-aliased text. However, this generally happens only on 8-bit computers.

In Photoshop or ImageReady You can manually dither graphics in Photoshop if you are using GIF, PNG-8, or WBMP file formats to optimize your image. When you dither manually, you can control the amount of dithering if the image is likely to be displayed on an 8-bit monitor or if there are too many colors in the image to be properly displayed using the available 256 colors in GIF and PNG-8 or the two colors in WBMP.

It is obviously preferable to set the amount of dithering in Photoshop or ImageReady rather than leaving it up to the operating system, and you do so while optimizing your image (see Section 29.3).

Using Web-Safe Colors

Web-safe colors are the set of 216 colors that older Mac and Windows computers share in their CLUTs and that display, more or less, the same across these two platforms. Should you limit yourself to these colors? Sticking to Web-safe colors slightly reduces your file size, and the colors were especially important in the 1990s when most web surfers were using computers with only 256 colors. However, the majority of computers today display thousands or even millions of colors without the need to dither them. To ensure the best results without dithering, use only the Web-safe colors when you are working with graphics that contain a lot of flat areas of a single color. You can set colors to be Web-safe in two ways:

While designing Generally if you want to use Web-safe colors, use them from the beginning of your design. To make sure that you are using the right colors, load one of the Web-Safe Color Swatch preset lists into the Swatches palette, which you can select from the bottom of the palette menu.

While optimizing Once you are ready to optimize your website for output, several settings on the Optimize and Color Table palettes let you force colors to be Web-safe (see Section 29.4).

Forcing colors to be Web-safe while optimizing takes some skill and practice to do so without degrading the quality of your image. Any anti-aliasing, gradients, opacity changes, effects filters, or adjustments will likely introduce non–Web-safe colors into your image. Start a design using browser-safe colors, and then adjust your colors during optimization. The idea is not to get *every* color in the color table to be Web-safe, but to get the large areas of color to be Web-safe.

➡ 8.1 Image Color Basics

Although the terms seem interchangeable, *CLUT* refers to the operating system's color table, and *color table* refers to an image.

The Visibone2 Color Swatch preset is generally the best for web design work. For more details on Web-safe colors, visit the Visibone website (www.visibone.com).

27.2 Web Color Basics *(continued)*

———

Adjusting the gamma
changes the actual
pixel values of your
web design to compen-
sate. Choosing View >
Preview adjusts only
the appearance on your
monitor; it does not
change the image
itself.

———

The Mac uses a gamma
value of 1.8;
Windows uses a darker
value of 2.2. Although,
both Mac and PC users
can adjust their Gamma
settings, we recom-
mend that Mac users
switch to 2.2 when
doing Web or video
design.

Adjusting Gamma with ImageReady

If you are designing for the Web, you must consider the gamma settings of the monitors
being used by the website viewer. Most web surfers run the Windows operating system. If
you are designing web pages using the Mac, your images will appear slightly lighter on your
monitor than on a Windows machine. However, use this feature with caution since it will permanently alter the appearance of your image. Generally, if you are worried about gamma, you
will want to work in the Gamma Preview mode rather than altering the image.

The same image shown in
Windows gamma (left) and
Mac gamma (right).

To adjust for gamma settings, ImageReady lets you perform a special color correction to
adjust the image for gamma values. To adjust gamma values, choose Image > Adjustments >
Gamma, set your options in the Gamma dialog, and click OK.

Ⓐ Use the slider or enter a value (0.1 through 9.99) to change the gamma value for the image from
its current value. This does not set the absolute gamma value for the image; it only adjusts the
current gamma level.

Ⓑ Convert gamma to Macintosh Click to automatically adjust the image if it is currently using a
Windows gamma and you want to switch it to a Mac gamma.

Ⓒ Convert gamma to Windows Click to automatically adjust the image if it is currently using a Mac
gamma and you want to switch it to a Windows gamma.

27.3 Creating Table-Based Layouts

Many websites rely on tables to create a consistent layout that accurately reflects the design they create in Photoshop and ImageReady. Both Photoshop and ImageReady allow you to output the HTML table code along with the images, setting this in the output options (see Section 29.5). ImageReady also allows you to define how tables are set up directly in the image using slices to define different table data cells. These slices are turned into tables nested within the main table of the image. Using the Tables palette, you can then set attributes about the table, including the cell padding, cell spacing, and border.

1 Using the Slice tool , group slices together to be output as part of a single table, select two or more slices, and then do one of the following:

   ■ Click the Group Slice Into Table button ▓ at the bottom of the Web Content palette.

   ■ Choose Slices > Group Slices Into Table.

   ■ In the Slice palette, change the slice type from Image to Table.

   ■ If one or more of the select slices is a part of an existing table, choose Slices > Add Slices To Table. All slices selected, but not part of the table, are added to the table.

2 Select a table in the document to edit by doing one of the following:

   ■ In the document, select the Table icon ▓ in a slice or any slice that is a part of that table with the Slice Select tool ▓.

   ■ In the Web Content palette, select the table directly by clicking its name.

3 In the Table palette, set the output options for the table:

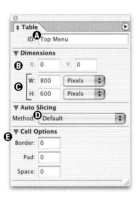

Ⓐ Table ID Enter a label that defines a unique ID for the table.

Ⓑ X and Y Position Enter the position of the table from the left (X) and top (Y) of the screen.

Ⓒ Width and Height Enter the width (W) and height (H) to be used by the table in either pixels or as a percentage of the browser window's dimensions.

Ⓓ Auto Slicing Method Choose how automatic slices should be output: the Default, As Columns (rowspans), or Forced As Columns (colspan).

Ⓔ Cell Options Enter values for the cell padding, cell spacing, and border to be used in the table.

➡ 29.1 Slicing Your Interface

➡ 29.2 Working with Slices

Show/Hide Extras

[Ctrl] [H]

[⌘] [H]

———

Although many web-sites still use tables for web layout, web designers are rapidly converting to CSS (Cascading Style Sheets) for today's web designs.

———

Although HTML allows you to nest tables inside tables to as many levels as you like, with ImageReady you can nest only one level down.

———

ImageReady will automatically create a user slice to fill the table where needed.

➡ 29.10 Specifying
Output
Options

Choosing Slices > Delete All also deletes all tables as well as slices.

ImageReady automatically generates spacer cells (called spacer.gif) if required by the design to render the image properly in certain browsers. A yellow warning icon shows in the Web Content palette next to the table's header.

If you want to select the outermost table in a document, you must use the Slice Select tool.

4 To delete tables you've nested inside a slice (effectively ungrouping them), choose the table you want to delete (see step 2 earlier), and then do one of the following:

- Choose Delete Slice from the Slice or Web Content palette menus. This deletes the table and the slice.

- Choose Slices > Delete Slice.

- Choose Slices > Remove Slices From Table. This will not delete an entire table, but only the selected slices.

5 Choose whether you want to delete just the table (Table Only) or the table and the slices (Table And Contents).

COLOR SETTINGS FOR THE WEB

Remember, you can set a color profile for the image to help overcome color differences between your computer and the end user's computer. Browsers that understand color profiles will use these settings. ImageReady does not allow you to set the color profile, but you can jump the image to Photoshop and add the color profile (see Section 8.7) and then jump back to ImageReady. To preview the color settings in ImageReady, choose View > Preview > Use Embedded Color Profile.

27.4 Creating Data-Driven Graphics

Websites often require dozens, hundreds, or even thousands of similar, but slightly different graphics to be created based on the same template. For example, if you are creating an online toy catalog, you might have photographs of hundreds of toys that need names, prices, or other details about the toy applied to them. Further, the toy might go on sale. This would not only change the price, but might require a special sale item graphic. Rather than creating a separate graphic for each instance, you can easily set up your Photoshop graphics to interact with a database. Don't worry if you are not a database pro. ImageReady allows you to set up images as data-driven templates that you can then use with an existing database to customize the graphics or to set variables manually to create the image iterations.

Defining Variables

Variables define how particular layers in the image can be changed. You can set three variables to control the visibility or content for any layer in a Photoshop document (.psd), depending on whether it is a Paint layer or a Text layer. (Other layer types cannot use variables.)

Ⓐ Visibility Lets you show or hide a layer between iterations.

Ⓑ Pixel Replacement (Bitmap layers only) Lets you replace the image in the layer with another image in a separate file.

Ⓒ Text Replacement (Text layers only) Lets you replace a string of text.

These variables require a specific name that should reflect the name of the variables defined in the database being used. After you set the variables for a layer or layers, you can use Adobe GoLive and Adobe AlterCast to bind a database to this file. Save the file as a template using the PSD format, and then follow instructions in GoLive to place the image and bind the variables using dynamic links.

You set variables for a layer in the Define panel of the Variables dialog. To set variables for a layer, follow these steps:

1 Select the layer for which you want to set variables in the Layers palette.

2 Choose Image > Variables > Define, or choose Variables from the Layers palette menu.

3 In the Variables dialog, set the variable types being used—Visibility or Pixel Replacement—and enter a variable name for each.

4 If you are working with bitmap layers using pixel replacement, you can also set Pixel Replacement options, which allows you to specify how an image should be treated if it is not the same size as the area defined by the original image (called the bounding box).

More than likely, you will want to give a unique name to the variables used by each layer; you cannot independently control values for variables in different layers if they are using the same variable name.

If you are not setting up the database yourself, make sure you consult with your database administrator and agree to the variable names to be used.

27.4 Creating Data-Driven Graphics *(continued)*

Variables cannot be set for the Background layer.

Think of each data set as an iteration of the image.

5 After you set the options, select another layer to set variables for it, click Next to set options for the data sets being used, or click OK to return to the image.

After you set up variables for one or more layers, you are ready to set up data sets that define variables for different image iterations.

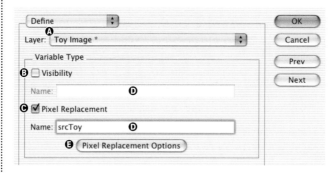

Ⓐ Choose from a list of layers in the image to define variables for that layer. An asterisk next to the name indicates that variables are set in that layer.

Ⓑ Apply Visibility variable Check to use a Visibility variable with this layer.

Ⓒ Apply Pixel Replacement/Text Replacement variable Check to use a Pixel Replacement variable with this layer.(This will read Text Replacement if a Text layer is being used.)

Ⓓ Variable names If the appropriate variable type is checked, enter the name of the variable being used by the database.

Ⓔ If this is a bitmap layer, click this button to open the Pixel Replacement options, which allow you to specify how an image will be treated if it is not the same dimensions as the original image it is replacing (see the next illustration).

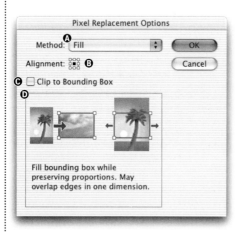

Ⓐ Placement Method Choose a method for how the new image should be placed into the area of the bounding box: Fit (resizes to fit height), Fill (resizes to fit width), As Is (crops to center of image), Conform (stretches image to fit width and height).

Ⓑ Bounding Box Alignment Click one of the white squares to set how the replacement image should be aligned in the bounding-box.

Ⓒ Clip to Bounding Box Check to use the bounding box to crop the replacement image.

Ⓓ Preview Displays a preview for how the selected method will affect a replacement image.

Working with Data Sets

You can manually create data sets to control iterations of the image using the variables you have set. This allows you to create different versions of the image, assigning different values to the variables and saving that version as a data set. This option can be time-consuming, though, and is mainly intended for use if there will only be a few iterations of an image.

27.4 Creating Data-Driven Graphics *(continued)*

To set up data sets for an image, follow these steps:

1 Choose Image > Variables > Data Sets or choose Variables from the Layers palette menu. You will see the variables defined for this image listed at the bottom of the window. If the Variables dialog is open, simply click the Next button. You must have at least one variable defined to create a data set.

2 Click the New Data Set button to start your first data set, and enter a name for the data set. The name should be something that helps you remember what content is loaded for this iteration of the image.

3 Choose a variable name from the Name menu or from the variable list, and then set its value.

- If this is a Visibility variable, choose either Visible or Invisible.

- If this is a Pixel Replacement variable, click the Choose… (Mac) or Browse… (Windows) button and select the graphic file to use with this iteration.

- If this is a Text Replacement variable, enter the text to be used with this iteration.

4 Repeat step 3 for each variable, and then repeat steps 2 and 3 to create a data set for each iteration. Click OK when you are finished.

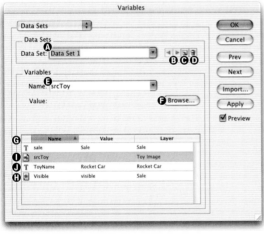

You can preview how the different data sets will affect the image (see Section 27.5).

Ⓐ New Data Set Name Displays the current data set. Click to choose a different data set from the drop-down.

Ⓑ Change Data Sets Click to move forward or backward between data sets.

Ⓒ New Data Set Click to create a new data set for this image.

Ⓓ Delete Data Set Click to delete the current data set.

Ⓔ Variable Name Choose a variable name from the drop-down.

Ⓕ Variable Value Click to set the value for the selected variable. For Pixel Replacement, this will be a link to a file. For Visibility, this will be two radio buttons for Visible or Invisible.

Ⓖ Variable list Displays the currently selected variable. Click to select a different variable to make changes above. Click a header to sort variables by that column.

Ⓗ Visibility variable Indicates a Visibility variable.

Ⓘ Text Replacement Indicates a Text Replacement variable.

Ⓙ Pixel Replacement variable Indicates Pixel Replacement variable.

Ⓚ Import Click to load a saved data set file to apply to the image.

Ⓛ Apply Click to apply the current setting for variables to the image.

27.5   Previewing Your Design

➡ 10.12 Storing Ver-
sions with
Layer Comps

Show original version

You cannot edit the
image while it is in
Preview mode.

Slices set to No Image
will not appear in the
ImageReady Preview
mode. Instead, the
background color
is used.

Often while you are working on an image, you will want to know how it will look when it hits the Web. Of course, many variables separate the original image you are working on and the way it might finally look to a website visitor. ImageReady provides several tools that allow you to preview the image and simulate a variety of conditions to help you make the best choices while designing.

Previewing in the Canvas

ImageReady allows you to preview your work directly in the ImageReady canvas as if it were a limited web browser.

- To preview the image in the ImageReady document window, choose Image > Preview Document or click the Preview Document button in the Toolbox. The image in the canvas will now act like a live web page, allowing you to view animations, rollovers, and image maps, although links will be inactive.

- To preview different iterations of this image using different data sets while in Preview mode, choose a data set from the drop-down in the tool options bar, or click the forward and back arrows to cycle through the list. As you cycle through the data set list, the image in the canvas changes to reflect the variable values set for that data set.

With ImageReady in Preview mode, the tool options bar allows you to select different data sets in which to preview the image.

- To end the preview, choose Image > Preview Document, click the Preview Document button in the Toolbox, or click the Cancel button . In addition, if you attempt to edit the image, ImageReady alerts you that you cannot edit the image in Preview mode and asks if you want to stop previewing.

Previewing Optimization Settings

You can view the image uncompressed (original), or you can preview the optimization settings in one of three optimized views (optimized, 2-Up, or 4-Up) by clicking one of the tabs in the top-left corner of the document window:

Original Shows the original uncompressed image.

Optimized Shows the image with compression settings.

2-Up and 4-Up View Shows two or four views of the image side by side in separate panes. You can choose to show the original version in one view and/or various optimized versions in the other panes, allowing you to compare how the optimizations settings affect the image.

27.5 Previewing Your Design *(continued)*

A Choose one of the tabs to select an optimization view.

B **View panes** Click anywhere in the pane to select it. The selected pane will have a black box around it. You can set the optimization settings for the images in the selected pane or select slices in that pane to optimize.

C **Optimization information** Displays the settings used to optimize the image and the estimated download time.

D **Regeneration warning** Indicates that the view has not been regenerated based on current optimization settings. Click to regenerate the view.

When optimization settings are changed, the image will need to be *regenerated* to reflect the changes.

- To regenerate the image automatically after every optimization, choose Auto Regenerate in the Optimize palette menu. However, this can slow you down if you are applying a lot of optimization settings at once. Choose Auto Regenerate again to turn it off.

- To manually regenerate an optimized image, choose Regenerate from the Optimize palette menu or click the Regeneration Warning button ⚠.

➡ 26.1   ImageReady Document Windows

➡ 29.3 Optimizing Images

Cycle to next optimization view mode
Shift ⌘ Y
Shift Ctrl Y

The Optimization setting preview tabs are also available in Photoshop's Save For Web dialog.

The Browser preview list can be torn off the palette like other tools, allowing you to keep a palette of buttons for one-click access to preview in any browser.

27.5   Previewing Your Design (continued)

➡ 29.6   Setting
Optimiza-
tion Options

➡ 29.10 Specifying
Output
Options

Preview in browser
⌘ Option P
Ctrl Alt P

———

When previewing in a browser, you can choose to include the code generated by ImageReady presented underneath the content. To turn this option on and off, choose File > Preview In > Include Source On Page.

———

Layer Comps allow you to preview different iterations of your web page without having to selectively turn layers on and off. See Section 10.12 for more details.

You can also set the optimized views to preview as if they were using browser dithering or a particular operating system's CLUT:

- To simulate how browser dithering may affect your image, with the canvas open in one of the optimization views, choose View > Preview > Browser Dither. The image will appear dithered regardless of your monitor settings and the dithering options set for the file format.

- To simulate how the image will look using either the Macintosh, Windows, or embedded color profile, choose View >Preview and then one of the settings: Uncompressed Color, Standard Macintosh Color, Standard Windows Color, or Use Embedded Color Profile.

Previewing in a Browser

You can open the image in a web browser to preview how it will look when output. ImageReady will use the current output options to generate an HTML page and place the image slices into this framework.

- To quickly preview the image in a browser, click the Browser Preview button in the Toolbox. To choose a different browser, click and hold the button and choose a browser from the drop-down.

- To preview the image in a browser, choose File > Preview In, choose a browser or choose Other…, and then browse to an application. This browser will not be added to this list or to the list in the Toolbox, but will be used as the browser for the Browser Preview button until another browser is selected.

- To edit the list of browsers you can choose from and set the default browser that is displayed in the Toolbox, choose File > Preview In > Edit Browser List.

The Edit Browser List dialog allows you to add/remove a single browser or have ImageReady find all the browsers on your hard drive. You can also set the default browser that shows in the Toolbox and is accessed by pressing Command/Ctrl Option/Alt P.

27.6   Creating Web Photo Galleries

If you are not a web design pro, but still need to create an attractive portfolio of your photographs, illustrations, or any images that you are creating, Photoshop includes a wizard that you can use to quickly set up web pages to present a catalog of your work. After you select a folder of images and set a few options, Photoshop outputs an entire website, including an index page with thumbnails of all the images and pages to display full-size versions of the images. You can choose from a variety of preset templates, or, if you are feeling more adventurous, you can edit existing templates or create your own customized templates.

➡ 4.8   File Browser

Ⓐ **Banner** You can customize titles, names, e-mail addresses, and even color schemes.

Ⓑ **Large Image** You can set the display size of the image in your preferences.

Ⓒ **Thumbnails** You can click smaller iconic versions of images to display the large-image version.

27.6   Creating Web Photo Galleries *(continued)*

➡ 6.5   Managing Images with the File Browser

To set up a web photo gallery, follow these steps:

1 Prepare the photos you want to use by doing one of the following:

■ Collect all the photos you want to use for the gallery into a single folder. You can place this folder anywhere on your hard drive or even on any drive that your computer can access over a network (although this may slow down the process).

■ In the Photoshop File Browser (choose Window > File Browser), choose all the images you want to include by Shift-clicking each.

2 In Photoshop, choose File > Automate > Web Photo Gallery.

3 In the Web Photo Gallery dialog, choose the style you want to use, enter your e-mail address if you want to receive feedback, choose the folder with the images, and choose where you want the new web pages to be created.

4 Once you enter the basic information, you can customize the site using the website options. All these settings are optional or can be simply left at their default values. Options that are grayed out are either not available or cannot be changed for the selected layout style.

Banner Options for the top banner in the page including your name, contact info, date, and the font and font size you want to use. The site name is used in the browser's title bar.

General Options for how the HTML code should be created. If you are unfamiliar with HTML, it is safe to leave the defaults, although you might want to include metadata for copyright purposes.

Large Images Options for how the large image should be displayed, including image quality, image dimensions, file size, and titles presented with the image.

Thumbnails Options for how thumbnails should be displayed, including dimensions, how many rows and columns to present them in, and titles presented with the image.

Custom Colors Options for background, text, link, and banner colors.

Security Options for specifying how custom text, filenames, copyright information, descriptions, credits, and titles are displayed. You can set the font, size, color, opacity, position, and rotation for each. In addition, the Custom Text option allows you to enter a message for display.

5 Once you have set your options, click OK. Photoshop begins to create your new website. You should see the files being opened, resized, and then saved. How long this takes depends on the number of images you are processing.

Once finished, you can see what your final product will look like by loading the page `index.html` into a web browser. If you are satisfied with the results, you can upload the files to a web server using any common FTP (File Transfer Protocol) software and invite people to your online gallery.

27.6   Creating Web Photo Galleries *(continued)*

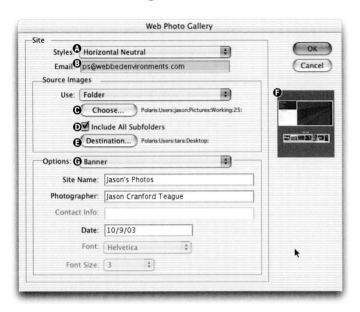

➡ 18.1 Applying Actions

➡ 27.7 Customizing Web Photo Gallery Templates

The Photo Gallery Wizard is available only from within Photoshop, not within ImageReady.

Ⓐ **Layout Styles**   Choose from a variety of layouts. This list will also include any styles that you create yourself as long as they are placed in the Adobe Photoshop CS/Presets/Presets/Web Photo Gallery folder (see the section "Customizing Photo Gallery Style Templates").

Ⓑ **Contact Email (optional)**   Enter an e-mail address (optional) to be used to receive feedback from viewers.

Ⓒ **Source**   Use the drop-down to specify whether you are using a source folder or using Selected Images From File Browser (see step 1). If you are using a folder, click Choose/Browse and specify the folder with your images.

Ⓓ **Include Subfolders in Processing**   Check to use folders within the source location. If this check box is cleared, only image files at the first level within the folder are used.

Ⓔ **Destination for Web Files**   Click to specify where the files and folders used to create the website are saved. You might want to create a new folder for these files.

Ⓕ **Layout Preview**   Shows a small thumbnail for the currently selected layout style (see A).

Ⓖ **Web Site Options**   Choose between different option panels that allow you to specify a variety of custom settings for your website.

27.7   Customizing Web Photo Gallery Templates

➡ 18.1 Applying
         Actions

The Photo Gallery Wiz-
ard is available only
from within Photoshop,
not within ImageReady.

Although the Web Photo Gallery offers several templates, you might want to interject
your own personal design into your gallery. To do this, you will need to copy and then
modify an existing template located in the Adobe Photoshop CS/Presets/Presets/Web
Photo Gallery folder. Editing the design, though, requires some knowledge of basic
HTML, so this is not for everyone.

Use a text editor (such as Notepad or SimpleText) or an HTML editor (such as
Dreamweaver) to edit the tokens (variables used in the HTML code to define where
certain attributes are used) in the following files:

Caption.htm Defines how the caption below each large image is displayed.

FrameSet.htm Defines the grid structure layout of a gallery created using frames.

IndexPage.htm Defines the grid structure layout of a gallery *not* using frames.

SubPage.htm Defines the layout of gallery pages with large images.

Thumbnail.htm Defines the layout of the thumbnail area of gallery pages.

You can rename the folder containing these files to whatever you want, but keep the filenames the same. Customized styles will appear using the folder name you chose in the
Layout Style list as long as you keep the folder in the Web Photo Galleries folder.

REMEMBERING THE WEB-SAFE COLORS

It's actually not that hard to remember all 216 Web-safe colors, not by name of course,
but either on the RGB or hexadecimal scales. Both scales use a list of three separate
values. The first value tells the computer how much red to mix in the color, the second
is green, and the third is blue. To be browser-safe, use RGB values of 0, 51, 102, 153,
204, and 255 (0 is no color while 255 is pure color) or hexadecimal values of 00, 33, 66,
99, CC, and FF (00 is no color while FF is pure color) in any combination in the three
slots. Therefore, 153 0 102 is the same as 990066 and produces a reddish purple.

CHAPTER 28

Designing Web Elements

YOU CAN CREATE AN entire web page comp in Photoshop and ImageReady, slice it up, output the slices to create the basic layout of your web page, and *then* use a program such as GoLive to add links, image maps, and other interactivity. However, ImageReady provides several tools that allow you to design for interactivity at the same time you are creating your graphic design and then output all the code you need to take your site directly to the Web.

Several common website elements require more than the simple graphic design in Photoshop to create them. In ImageReady, you can create multiple states for a button to use with JavaScript rollovers, create animations to add movement to your web page, create image maps to use large graphics for navigation, and create seamless backgrounds to add texture to your web page.

- 28.1 **Creating image maps**
- 28.2 **Creating animations**
- 28.3 **Editing animations**
- 28.4 **Creating rollovers**
- 28.5 **Editing rollovers**
- 28.6 **Editing layers for animations and rollovers**
- 28.7 **Creating seamless backgrounds**

PHOTOSHOP WORKSPACE

UNIVERSAL TASKS

PHOTO AND VIDEO TASKS

PRINT TASKS

WEB TASKS

28.1   Creating Image Maps

Using image maps is a common way to add large navigation graphics to a web page. For example, when creating a web page that shows the dates of a nationwide concert tour, you might want to allow visitors to click an area on a map of the United States to see concerts in that area. Using an image map, you can set hot spots (clickable areas of the image map) that link to pages displaying dates for that region of the country. ImageReady not only allows you to prepare the graphic for use as an image map, but also define the hot spots. If you output the image with HTML code, ImageReady uses the defined hot spots to automatically create the code for the image map in the web page.

ImageReady allows you to create image map hot spots in two ways:

Tool-based You can use the Image Map tool to draw hot spots on the image as circles, rectangles, or free-form polygon shapes.

Layer-based You can specify that the content of a layer is used to define the area of the hot spot. The hot spot will always readjust based on the content of the layer.

Adding Tool-Based Hot Spots

You create hot spots as rectangles, circles, or polygons. Polygons allow you to draw a free-form shape with as many sides as you want. To add a hot spot to the image for use in the image map, follow these steps in ImageReady, repeating them to create as many hot spots as you need:

1 Choose the Rectangle Image Map tool ⬚, Circular Image Map tool ⬚, or Polygon Image Map tool ⬚.

2 Set your preference for the tool in the tool options bar: First specify whether you want to create a fixed-size shape, and then enter the dimensions of the rectangle or the radius of the circle. The Polygon Image Map tool does not have any options.

3 Place your mouse cursor in the top-left corner of where you want the image map hot spot to begin.

■ For the Rectangular and Circular Image Map tools, click and drag to draw the desired shape.

■ For the Polygon Image Map tool, click to set the first anchor point, and then click the next point in the polygon. Repeat around the area for which you want to create a hot spot. When you are finished, either click the first anchor point, or, to close the hot spot with a straight line from the current anchor point, double-click or Command/Ctrl-click.

4 In the Image Map palette (Window > Image Map), enter optional information about this hot spot to help Photoshop generate the image map's HTML code. Show and hide the hot spot areas in the image by clicking the Toggle Image Map Visibility button ⬚ in the Toolbox.

28.1 Creating Image Maps *(continued)*

You can now save this image map as part of your optimized website (see Chapter 29).

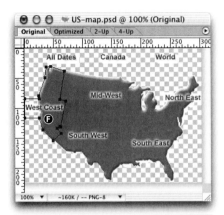

A **Area Name** Enter a name to be used to identify the hot spot.

B **URL** Enter a web address (either global or local) for the hot spot.

C **Link Target** Enter the name of the frame or window in which you want this link to appear. Four default options let you target the link to a new (_blank) window, to the same window or frame (_self), or to the frame's frameset (_parent) or to replace the entire frameset with the new page (_top) If the link appears in the same frame or window, you can also leave this blank.

D **Alt Text** Enter alternate text that is displayed if the image cannot be viewed. Adding this text is important to ensure that your website is accessible to all visitors.

E **Dimensions** If the hot spot is a rectangle or a circle, this area will be used to display and change the position and dimensions of the shape. If the hot spot is layer-based, this area allows you to choose the shape used for the hot spot.

F **Hot Spot** Selected hot spot in the image map.

If the hot spot is a rectangle, you can enter the position and dimensions directly in the Image Map palette. If the hot spot is a circle, you can enter the position and the radius.

➡ 10.11 Aligning and Distributing Layers

Image Map tool
[P]

———

Layer-based hot spots are edited when their content is changed. To change the layer-based hot spot's options, click the layer in the Layers palette and then make changes in the Image Map palette.

———

To change a layer-based hot spot into a tool-based hot spot, choose the layer in the Layers palette and then choose Promote Layer Based Image Map Area in the Image Map palette.

28.1   Creating Image Maps *(continued)*

➡ 27.5 Previewing
          Your Design

Cycle image map tools
[Shift] [P]

———

You can adjust how image maps are displayed in ImageReady's Image Maps preferences (see Section 26.5).

———

If the layer you are using for a layer-based slice is irregularly shaped, you will probably want to use Polygon and then set the quality as high or as low as necessary to get a good fit.

Editing Tool-Based Hot Spots

Hot spots that you create using the Image Map tools (not layer-based hot spots) behave a lot like layers in that they can be stacked, aligned, and distributed. When stacked, one hot spot will be over or under another hot spot. You can use the Image Map Select tool to not only move and reshape the hot spot, but also to restack, align, and distribute hot spots.

To begin editing an image map, choose the Image Map Select tool 🖑. In the canvas, click the hot spot you want to edit to select it and do the following:

- To **show or hide the image map**, click the Toggle Image Map Visibility button 🖑 in the Toolbox or choose View > Show > Image Maps.

- To **change or add information** about the hot spot, open the Image Map palette (Window > Image Map) and enter the information.

- To **change the stacking order** of this hot spot in relation to other hot spots in the image map, click an icon in the tool options bar or choose these options from the Image Map palette's menu:

🗇	Move to top
🗇	Move up one level
🗇	Move down one level
🗇	Move to bottom

- To **move** the hot spot, with the Image Map Select tool click and drag it within the canvas.

- To **adjust the shape** of a hot spot, click and drag an anchor point. The Map Select Tool cursor pointer will turn from black to white when it is over an anchor point.

- To **align** hot spots, Shift-click two or more hot spots and then click one of the alignment buttons in the tool options bar, or choose these options from the Image Map palette's menu. These options work just like the layer alignment options discussed in Section 10.11.

- To **distribute** hot spots, Shift-click three or more hot spots and then click one of the distribution buttons in the tool options bar, or choose these options from the Image Map palette's menu.

- To **delete** the hot spot, press Delete/Backspace, or choose Delete Image Map Area from the Image Map palette's menu.

- To **duplicate** the hot spot shape, Option/Alt-click and drag, or choose Duplicate Image Map Area from the Image Map palette's menu.

28.1   Creating Image Maps *(continued)*

Adding Layer-Based Hot Spots

One of the easiest ways to create hot spots for an image map is to use existing layers to define them. This allows you to use the existing layer structure of the image, which may already be split along the needed lines, to quickly generate your image map. To use a slice to define a hot spot in the image map, follow these steps:

1 Choose the layer you want to use as an image map hot spot (see Section 8.2). If the layer does not have transparent pixels, the hot spot will fill the entire canvas.

2 Choose Layer **>** New Layer Based Image Map Area. This option is also available in the layer's contextual menu. (Control/right-click the layer name in the Layers palette.) The layer will now have an image map tool icon next to the title.

Enter information about the hot spot in the Image Map palette (Window **>** Image Map). You will also want to choose the shape used to define the hot spot: Rectangular, Circular, or Polygon.

You can now save this image map as part of your optimized website (see Chapter 29).

Choose the shape being used to define the hot spot for the layer. If you choose Polygon, you also need to enter the quality used to define the polygon shape around the edges.

➡ 29.10 Specifying Output Options

Toggle image maps visibility

Ⓐ

Using the higher quality setting with layer-based slices in Polygon mode requires more data to create and creates slightly larger file sizes.

The Web Content palette (Windows **>** Web Content) also displays all the image map areas that you can hide and show just like layers in the Layers palette. Ctrl/right-click an image map area thumbnail icon to open a contextual menu with options to select, duplicate, or delete the hot spot.

ANIMATION AND ROLLOVER THUMBNAILS

You can set the size of the thumbnails displayed in the Animation and Web Content palette using the Palette Options dialog accessed through the palette menu. With frames and states, it is especially important to display the thumbnails as large as possible because they show how the image appears for that frame or state.

28.2　Creating Animations

➡ 27.5 Previewing
　　　 Your Design

Always add and edit
frames with the canvas
in Original View mode.
Although you can view
frames in any of the
optimization views,
the editing options
are limited.

Traditional animations are created using individual animation frames: still images that are part of a sequence. Displaying these images in rapid succession (each cell is displayed for a fraction of a second) creates the illusion of movement. The GIF format allows web designers to create simple animations, and ImageReady provides the tools to quickly create GIF animations from scratch or use existing images and layers to put an animation together. With ImageReady, you can assign a delay time to each frame, use the Tween command to quickly generate new frames, and specify looping for the animation.

Although animations are used in close conjunction with the Layers palette, all the action is in the Animation palette. To open it, choose Window > Animation. This palette is always horizontal, displaying the animation frames across the screen.

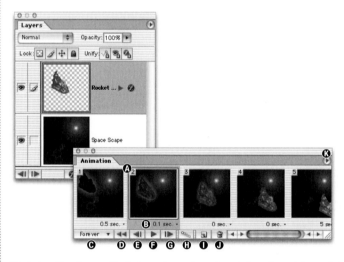

ⓐ Animation frame Each frame is numbered, and the selected frame is highlighted.

ⓑ Frame Delay Choose the amount of delay for this frame.

ⓒ Looping Options Choose a looping option for the animation.

ⓓ First Frame Click to jump to the first frame.

ⓔ Previous Frame Click to jump to the previous frame. This control also appears in the Layers palette.

ⓕ Play/Stop Click to play the animation in the canvas. Click again to stop the animation.

ⓖ Next Frame Click to jump to the next frame. This control also appears in the Layers palette.

ⓗ Tween Select two consecutive frames by Shift-clicking and click to open the Tween dialog.

ⓘ Duplicate Frame Click to duplicate the selected frame.

ⓙ Delete Frame Click to delete the selected frame.

ⓚ Animation palette menu Options for creating and editing animations.

28.2 Creating Animations *(continued)*

Starting an Animation and Adding Frames

All images start with an initial frame that represents the starting appearance of the animation. Every time you add a new frame, ImageReady duplicates the currently selected frame, allowing you to make changes to the image for that frame. To add a frame to an animation, follow these steps:

1 Set up your image the way you want it to appear in the first frame of the animation. To add a new layer every time you create a frame, choose Create Layer For Each New Frame from the Animation palette menu. This is especially useful if you must add a new visual element to each frame.

2 In the Animation palette (Window > Animation), click the Duplicate Frame button or choose New Frame from the palette's menu. This adds the second frame to the Animation palette, which will be selected.

3 Make changes to the image as desired. This can include moving layers, adding additional effects, changing effect settings, and showing or hiding layers. You can now edit the layers for this frame (see Section 28.4).

4 Repeat steps 2 and 3 to create as many animation frames as desired.

5 Click the Play button to preview the animation in the canvas.

Left: The first frame.
Right: In the second frame, the rocket ship has moved across the canvas.

Tweening Frames

Tweening allows you to set the beginning and ending conditions of an animation and then have ImageReady fill in the spaces, adding frames to create a seamless animation. For example, if you want to move an object across the canvas in a straight line, you can simply set the object to its initial position in the first frame and to its final position in the last frame and then tween the two frames. ImageReady calculates the position of the object in intervening frames to make it look as if the object is moving from one spot to the next. To tween frames, follow these steps:

1 In the Animation palette (Window > Animation), select the first frame you want to use in your tween animation.

➡ 28.6 Editing Layers for Animations and Rollovers

You can flatten an animation into individual layers (each new layer a composite of the original layers) by selecting Flatten Frames Into Layers from the Animation palette menu. The original layers are preserved, but hidden.

28.2 Creating Animations *(continued)*

➡ 29.10 Specifying
      Output
      Options

You can convert the layers in a file into frames by selecting Make Frames From Layers in the Animation palette menu.

You can have as many frames as you want in an animation—limited only by your computer's memory—but remember that every frame is a distinct image and adds to the overall download time for the image.

2 Click the Duplicate Frame button in the Animation palette to add the final frame for the tween animation. This creates two identical frames.

3 With the final frame selected, make changes to the image to set up how you want the animation to end. These changes can include the following:

Position Move objects in the canvas.

Opacity Change either the layer or the fill opacity, allowing you to fade an object in or out.

Effects Change the settings for effects applied to the layer.

4 Select frames to be tweened in the Animation palette:

■ To animate between two adjacent frames, select the first and last frame for the tween by Shift-clicking them.

■ To animate from a frame to a copy of the previous or first frame, select the frame to use as the first frame.

5 Click the Tween button ▨ in the Animation palette.

6 Set the options in the Tween dialog, and then click OK. Frames will be added to the animation between the two frames used.

You can now save this image map as part of your optimized website (see Chapter 29).

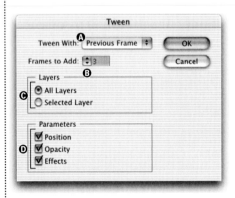

Ⓐ Tween With Choose the frames to tween. If you select a single frame, specify whether you want to animate to a copy of the previous frame or to a copy of the first frame in the animation. If you select two frames, this option is set to Selection.

Ⓑ Number of frames to Add Enter a value (1 through 100) for the number of frames to use to animate between this frame and the Tween With frame.

Ⓒ Specify layers to tween Specify whether to animate changes in all frames in the image or only the select layer. If you are animating only a single layer, you can reduce your file size somewhat by using only the Selected Layer option.

Ⓓ Specify parameters to change Check which parameters should be animated between the first and last frame.

28.3   Editing Animations

You can edit an entire animation or individual frames in a variety of ways:

- To set the **loop** for how many times the animation should play, choose an option from the Looping Options menu in the lower-left corner of the Animation palette: Once, Forever, or Other... If you select Other, enter a value for the number of times to loop, and click OK.

- To **edit** the content of a frame, click the frame to select it, and then make changes in the canvas and Layers palette (see Section 28.5).

- To **re-tween** the frames between two frames, select the range of frames and click the Tween button ![tween icon]. The frames between the first and last frame in the range will be replaced with the new tween.

- To **move** a frame, click and drag it to the desired position. To move multiple frames, Shift-click the frames to select them, and then drag them to the desired position. If you drag multiple discontiguous frames, they will be placed contiguously.

- To **reverse** the order of contiguous frames, select the frames and choose Reverse Frames in the Animation palette menu.

- To **delete** one or more frames, select the frame(s) and drag them to the trashcan icon ![trash icon] or choose Delete Frame(s) from the palette menu. You can also choose frames, click the trashcan icon, and click OK.

- To **delete the animation**, choose Delete Animation from the Animation palette menu.

Setting Playback Options

The delay time determines how long a frame in an animation pauses before proceeding to the next frame; the disposal method specifies what happens to the frame image after it is played. To set the delay or disposal method for one or more frames, either select a single frame or Shift-click to select multiple frames, and then do the following:

- To set the **delay** for how long the frame paused before proceeding to the next frame, choose a delay time or choose No Delay from the Frame Delay menu under each frame in the Animations palette.

- To set the **disposal** method for a frame, Control/right-click the frame's thumbnail and select a method:

    Automatic Frames are removed after display only if the next frame contains a transparency. This method generally produces the best results.

    Do Not Dispose Frames are not removed after displaying. New frames are placed on top, but previous frames show through in transparent areas of the current frame. Places an icon ![icon] next to the animation thumbnail.

    Restore To Background Always removes frames after display. Places an icon ![icon] next to the animation thumbnail.

➡ 27.5 Previewing Your Design

➡ 28.6 Editing Layers for Animations and Rollovers

If you are using the Redundant Pixel Removal Optimization option, you will want to choose Automatic disposal.

The actual speed at which the animation plays on the web page depends on the processor speed of the visitor's computer. So, just because it plays smoothly on your high-end dual processor G5 Mac does not mean it will play smoothly on an old x86 machine. Try to test on older machines if possible, and always keep your audience in mind.

———

The delay time for frames will not be accurate when previewing in the canvas. You will need to preview in a browser (see Section 27.5) to get an accurate idea of how the animation will display.

———

You can open a GIF animation in Photoshop, but you cannot view or edit individual frames. However, the frames will stay intact.

Using the Do Not Dispose method, each frame of the animation is displayed and remains.

Optimizing Animations

Optimization allows you to reduce the file size of an image, thus speeding its transmission across the Internet. Although most of the optimization in ImageReady is done in the Optimize palette, GIF animation has specific options that you can turn on or off while working. Choose Optimize Animation… from the Animation palette menu, and check the desired options:

Bounding Box Crops each frame to the area that has changed from the preceding frame. This creates smaller files and is generally recommended. However, some GIF-editing programs might not be able to open these files.

Redundant Pixel Removal Makes transparent all pixels in a frame that are unchanged from the preceding frame. This option is the default and is recommended. For this to work, the Transparency option in the Optimize palette must be selected, and the frame disposal method must be set to Automatic.

You can now save this animation as part of your optimized website (see Chapter 29).

DESIGNING BUTTONS

One common interface element that you will need to design is a button. More important, you will need to create attractive buttons that maintain a consistent look. Using Style Presets with the Shape tool is a quick way to create uniform buttons.

28.4   Creating Rollovers

Rollovers use JavaScript to tell a graphic to change when a certain condition is triggered through an action by the user to show a different state of the image. For example, placing the mouse pointer over an image triggers the Over state. ImageReady has six built-in states that roughly correspond to JavaScript events. In addition, you can enter your own custom states if you are using your own custom JavaScript code or development programs such as GoLive and Dreamweaver.

➡ 27.5 Previewing Your Design

➡ 28.5 Editing Rollovers

Animations applied to rollovers in the Normal state start playing as soon as the page loads.

The Web Content palette replaces the more specific Rollovers palette that was available in Photoshop 7.

(Home)   (Home)   (Home)   The Normal, Over, and Down states

Rollover States

STATE	DESCRIPTION
Normal	The default state used when the image initially loads. Unless otherwise indicated, all other states revert to the Normal state.
Over	Triggered when the mouse cursor is over the area without the mouse button pressed and persists until the mouse cursor moves out of the area.
Down	Triggered when the mouse cursor is over the area with the mouse button pressed and persists until the mouse button is released or the mouse cursor is moved out of the area.
Selected	Triggered after the area is clicked and persists until another area is clicked using the Selected state.
Click	Triggered after the area is clicked and persists until the mouse cursor moves out of the area.
Out	Triggered when mouse cursor moves out of the area if you do not want to revert to Normal.
Up	Triggered when the mouse button is released if you do not want to revert to Normal.
Custom	Triggered when using your own custom JavaScript code. This is useful if you are not using the Adobe-defined states. For example, Dreamweaver includes the OverWhileDown state, which allows you to specify how the rollover should look if it is rolled over while selected.
None	Saves the state for later use, but is not output

Although rollovers are used in close conjunction with the Layers palette, you add rollover states in the Web Content palette. To open it, choose Window > Web Content.

Starting a Rollover and Adding States

Rollovers in ImageReady are added to slices or to image map hot spots. You can then adjust the appearance of the image's layers for the various states you want in your web design. However, rather than slicing the interface yourself, ImageReady can automatically create a slice based on the shape of a particular layer that will adjust to the size of the pixels in the layer.

1   Add slices or an image map to the canvas. To add slices, do one of the following:

■   To manually add slices to the canvas, use the Slice tool [✎].

■   To add a rollover state associated with a layer, choose the layer and click the Create Layer-Based Rollover button [※] at the bottom of the Web Content palette. The new slice will appear in the Web Content palette with the Over state default.

2   Once you have slices or image maps in the image, add rollover states. Select the slice or image map you want to add a rollover to in the Web Content palette or in the canvas. (If you do not see the slices, click the Toggle Image Maps Visibility button [🖑] or the Toggle Slices Visibility button [▱] in the Toolbox.)

➠ **28.6** Editing Layers for Animations and Rollovers

➠ **29.1** Slicing Your Interface

Although you create most of the rollover animation in the Animations palette, you can use the Web Content palette to display, add, delete, copy, and paste frames using that palette's menu.

3 In the Web Content palette, either click the New Rollover State Button [⬛] or choose New Rollover State from the palette menu. ImageReady adds the next logical state to the slice or image map hot spot: Over, Down, Selected, Out, Up, Click, None. You can now edit the layers in the image to set the appearance for this rollover state.

4 Now that the rollover is set up, make changes to the position, visibility, text, effects, and opacity to create the rollover for the selected state.

You can now save your rollovers as part of your optimized website (see Chapter 29).

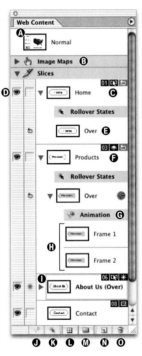

Ⓐ **Normal state** The default appearance for the rollovers in the image.

Ⓑ **Image map** Indicates a rollover using an image map.

Ⓒ **Slice-based rollover** A rollover that is a collection of rollover states.

Ⓓ **Show/Hide Slice** Click to hide the slice. This will not hide the slice's content, but simply disables the slice and all its Rollover states.

Ⓔ **Rollover state** The Over state associated with the rollover.

Ⓕ **Layer-based rollover** Icon indicates that this rollover is using a layer-based slice.

Ⓖ **Animation** Icon indicates that this rollover state uses an animation.

Ⓗ **Animation Frames** Frames used for animation associated with rollover state.

Ⓘ **Selected Slice** Indicates that this slice currently contains the selected state.

Ⓙ **Add Animation** Frame Click to add an animation frame to the selected rollover state.

Ⓚ **Create Layer**-Based Rollover Click to turn the selected layer into a slice with the Over rollover.

Ⓛ Group Slice Into Table Click to add the selected slice to a table (see Section 27.3).

Ⓜ New Slice Set Click to add the currently selected slice to a new folder (set) of slices. This is useful for organizing slices for different uses.

Ⓝ New Rollover State Click to add a rollover state to the selected rollover.

Ⓞ Delete Slice Click to delete the selected slice and its rollover.

Having a Single Event Trigger Multiple Changes

Although the rollover states are set up to reflect the changes within that slice, you can also set the slice to change the appearance of other slices in the interface. ImageReady refers to this as Remote Control Of Slices, which gives you the power to have a single event (for example, the rollover of a button) to trigger changes in multiple locations (for example, the button can glow, and a text description of what the button does can appear elsewhere on the screen).

28.4   Creating Rollovers *(continued)*

To use one slice to remotely control another slice, select the controlling slice, and then click the Remote Slice toggle (located to the right of the Show/Hide toggle) for each slice you want triggered from the control slice. You can also use the lasso next to the selected slice to connect to a remote slice in the canvas.

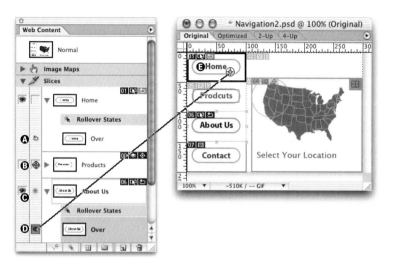

A State Contains Remotes Indicates that this rollover state affects remote slices.

B Slice Controlled by Remote Click to set this slice as a remote slice for the selected slice. This slice will be shown when the selected layer is triggered.

C Slice with Current State Indicates that this slice3 contains the currently selected (active) slice that is being edited.

D Lasso Click and drag to the slice in the canvas that you want to control by remote using the selected slice.

E Selected Slice This slice is the trigger to show all slices that are remote to it.

Adding an Animation to a Rollover

Rollover states can also use GIF animations that you create using a combination of the Web Content palette and the Animations palette. To create an animated rollover state, select the state you want to add animation to in the Web Content palette. Click the Add Animation Frame button ⌗ at the bottom of the Web Content palette, or choose New Animation Frame from the palette's menu. If you do not see this button, open the Palette Options dialog and make sure Include Animation Frames is checked. A new frame will be added to the selected state. You can now follow the instructions in Section 28.2 for creating an animation using the Animations palette.

➠ 29.10 Specifying
        Output
        Options

Toggle slices visibility
Q

If you do not see all the options discussed in the Web Content palette, open the Palette Options dialog and make sure Include Slices And Image Maps and Include Animation Frames are checked.

Naming the rollover states becomes especially important when it's time to output the image, because you can have ImageReady automatically use the state name as part of the filename to help identify it.

28.5 Editing Rollovers

Toggle slices visibility
Ⓠ

The Animation and
Web Content palettes
use their own separate
Clipboard when copy-
ing and pasting. Copy-
ing frames or rollover
states will not replace
the contents of the
ImageReady Clipboard
and vice versa.

After you add rollover states to a slice, you can edit the rollovers in a variety of ways:

- To **change a rollover's state**, Control/right-click its state and select a state from the contextual menu, double-click the rollover's state, or choose Rollover State Options… from the palette menu to select a state in a dialog. If you choose Custom, type the name of the state, or select a custom state previously used from the drop-down. If you choose Selected, specify whether you want this to be used as the default state when the web page is loaded.

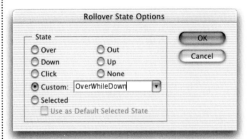

Choose a rollover state, or use Custom and enter the name of your custom rollover state.

- To **move** a rollover to a different slice or image map, click and drag the state to another rollover. This will not move the images used by the rollover state. Instead, the moved rollover state will use the images in the layers available to the rollover to which it has been moved.

- To **delete** a rollover state, select the state and click the trashcan icon 🗑 or choose Delete Rollover State from the palette's menu. To delete the entire rollover (including all states), choose Delete Rollover from the palette's menu

- To **copy** a rollover state, choose Copy Rollover State from the palette's menu. The state is now in a special rollover state Clipboard.

- To **paste** the layers of the copied rollover state, select a rollover state and choose Paste Rollover State from the palette's menu. This will not paste the images used by the rollover state. Instead, the pasted rollover state will use the images in the layers avail-able to the rollover in which it has been pasted.

- To **duplicate** a rollover state, select the state and choose Duplicate Rollover State from the palette's menu, or drag the state to the New Rollover State button 🔲 . The duplicated state will appear immediately beneath the original.

28.5 Editing Rollovers *(continued)*

Applying Rollover Style Presets

As with Photoshop, preset styles can be applied in ImageReady to any layer using the Styles palette (see Section 4.17). However, the ImageReady styles have one distinct advantage over their Photoshop counterpart: they also store the styles of rollover states. These special rollover styles appear side by side with other styles in the palette, but include a black triangle in the upper-left corner of the thumbnail. When you apply one of these styles to a layer, it automatically applies the styles for all the states that it has recorded. If the layer it is being applied to was not already a rollover, it is automatically turned into a layer-based rollover viewable in the Web Content palette.

The ImageReady Styles palette includes styles with one or more states bundled into them, indicated by the black triangle in the thumbnail.

- To **add a style to a layer**, select the layer in the Layers palette and click the style in the Styles palette, or drag the thumbnail of the style directly to the layer in the canvas.

- To **add a Style Preset based on the styles applied to an existing layer-based slice**, select the rollover in the Web Content palette, and then click the New Style button in the ImageReady Style palette or choose New Style from the Style palette's menu. In the dialog, type the name of the style, set the style options (make sure that Include Rollover States is checked), and click OK.

➡ 28.6 Editing Lay-
ers for Ani-
mations and
Rollovers

➡ 29.10 Specifying
Output
Options

If you change the state of a rollover to a state that already exists for that rollover, the original state will be changed to None.

VECTOR VERSUS BITMAP ANIMATION

GIF animations are a tried-and-true method for adding movement to your web pages, but they are severely limited in what they can do. Worse, the longer and more complex they become, the larger the file size and, thus, the longer the download time. This is because GIF animation relies on bitmap images to create the movement. Vector animation, on the other hand, allows you to create complex and interactive animations that will generally download far more quickly than GIF animations. The most common vector format for the web is Flash, but the new SVG (Scalable Vector Format) is a standard from the World Wide Web consortium that is slowly catching on.

28.6   Editing Layers for Animations and Rollovers

➡ 27.5 Previewing
      Your Design

Match
⌘ M
Ctrl M

Although both rollovers and animations have their own palettes, both rely on the Layers palette and the canvas to control the action of a state or a frame. Think of a rollover state or a frame as a unique version of the image that you can flip through or between using the Animation or Web Content palette. For example, when a particular frame in an animation is selected, you are viewing the image as it will appear when that frame is showing.

Changes to specific states and frames Changes made to the layer's opacity, fill opacity, blending mode, visibility, position, and style affect only the selected rollover state or frame.

Changes to all states and frames Changes made using the painting and editing tools, adjustments, filters, type, and transformations will be applied to all states and frames in which the affected layer exists.

Unifying Layers for Rollover States or Animation Frames

You use the unify buttons in the Layers palette to specify whether position, visibility, and/or style changes to a layer that would normally only be state- or frame-specific should be applied across all states in a rollover and all frames in an animation. To unify a layer's states or frames, select the layer in the Layers palette and click one of these buttons:

ICON	TYPE	DESCRIPTION
	Unify Layer Position	Changes to this layer's position will be applied to all states and frames.
	Unify Layer Visibility	Changes to this layer's visibility will be applied to all states and frames.
	Unify Layer Style	You will be asked whether to match all styles in this layer to the existing states and frames. Click Match to continue. Changes to this layer's styles, including opacity and blending mode, will be applied to all states and frames.

The visibility and styles of the Home Type layer are unified. The icon for the last unification button applied to a layer is displayed next to its name.

28.6 Editing Layers for Animations and Rollovers *(continued)*

Matching Layers Across Rollover States or Animation Frames

Matching allows you to apply the attributes of a layer in one state or frame to all the other states or frames using that same layer. For example, if you change the style of a layer in a particular animation frame and then want that layer's style change applied to all other animation frames, you can use the Match command. To match layers, follow these steps:

1 Select the state (in the Web Content palette) or frame (in the Animation palette) you want to apply to other states or frames. Then select the layer (in the Layers palette) that you want to match. (The layer must be a part of the rollover or animation selected.)

2 Choose Match… from the Layers menu or from the Layers palette menu.

3 In the Match dialog, specify whether to apply attributes from the selected state or frame to all frames in the current animation, to the rollover states in the currently selected slice or image map, or to all rollover states in the image that contains the selected layer.

4 Check the attributes you want to apply from the selected layer and click OK. All the relevant states or frames will be changed to match the attributes of the selected layer.

You can also use warping text to create a rollover or an animation, although not all the features are available.

Changes made to the Normal state or Frame 1 change all states or frames in which the affected layers exist. However, you can turn this feature off for animations by clearing the Propagate Frame 1 Changes option in the Layers palette menu.

BACKGROUND STATIC

You can include animations in a background image. Use this technique sparingly, but it can produce some remarkable results. A favorite is to create random static animation turning a web page into a TV tuned to a dead channel.

To do this, simply create an image in Photoshop with three to five layers, apply the Noise filter to each (Filter > Noise > Add Noise…) using uniform monochromatic noise, and apply a very slight Gaussian blur (Filter > Blur > Gaussian Blur). Then, move the whole thing over to ImageReady using the Jump command, and, in the Animation palette, use the Make Frames From Layers command in the palette's menu to create the static animation.

28.7   Creating Seamless Backgrounds

➠ 12.14 Using the Pattern Maker

➠ 14.1 Filter Basics

Reapply the last filter using the same settings
⌘ F
Ctrl F

Reapply the last filter using the dialog
⌘ Option F
Ctrl Alt F

———

Generally, you want to produce low-contrast backgrounds with a color that highly contrasts the foreground color you will be using for your text.

———

Backgrounds do not have to tile across the entire page. CSS (Cascading Style Sheets) allows you to set a background to tile once, horizontally only, or vertically only.

You can tile images into the background of a web page to add a lot of decoration and texture with a small graphic. ImageReady provides a special filter that allows you to blend the edges of an image to produce a smooth seamless background.

1 Open the image you want to use as the basis for your background and remove all slices (Slices > Delete All).

2 Choose Filter > Other > Tile Maker, choose a tiling method, and click OK:

Blending Edges Blurs the edges of the tile together to make a seamless tile. Enter a value (1 through 20) for the width to blend (larger values blend better but might distort the image), and check whether the image should resize to fill the tile (otherwise a black border is used at the edges).

Kaleidoscope Flips the image horizontally and vertically to create an abstract pattern.

3 To preview how the tile will look as a background, choose File > Output Settings > Background…, choose Background for the View option, and click OK. Now click the Preview In Browser button 🖐 to place the tile in a temporary web page.

Original tile

Blending Edges

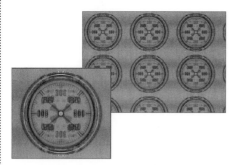

Kaleidoscope

CHAPTER 29

Outputting for the Web

BOTH PHOTOSHOP AND IMAGEREADY are set up to help you quickly optimize and save your web design to turn it into a web page. Although both programs include roughly equivalent capabilities to that end, they are implemented differently. Whereas image optimization is an integral part of the ImageReady interface, Photoshop places all optimization tools in a separate dialog, the use of which is the first step in saving the image. To begin optimizing and saving an interface, you slice it into pieces that can have separate optimization options and that can be saved as separate files.

29.1　Slicing Your Interface

➡ 3.8　Slice Tool

➡ 7.5　Using Rulers, Guides, Grids, and Snap

Slice tool
K

Slice Select tool (ImageReady)
O

If you designate a slice as being text, you may simply want to add text for placement only (FPO) and then edit the text in GoLive, Dreamweaver, or a text-editing program.

You use slices to split your image into specific regions to which you can then apply different optimization and rollover options. More important, when you save your image for the Web, you can have Photoshop or ImageReady save each slice as an individual file, which you will then reassemble using HTML as a web page. Every slice in the canvas is identified by small icons in the top-left corner of the slice that specify the number of the slice, identify the type of slice, and specify whether the layer is linked together with other slices to use common optimization settings. Slice icons are generally blue. If the slices are linked, however, they are automatically assigned a unique color code, a different one for each linked set. If a slice is an auto slice, the slice icons appear grayed out.

ICON	TYPE	DESCRIPTION
01	Slice Number	Each slice is given a unique number.
▨	User Slice With Image	Slice defined using the Slice tool.
⊗	User Slice With No Image	Slice will not be used as an image in the final output. You can add HTML text using the Slice palette.
▦	Layer-Based Slice	Slice defined based on the content of a specific layer.
01	Auto Slice	Slice created to fill areas not occupied by user, rollover, layer-based, or no image slices. All auto slices are linked and grayed out.
⅀	Linked Slice	Slice is linked to other slices. The same optimization settings are applied to slices in a linked set. Slices in the same linked set are color coded.
▦	Active Slice	Indicates that the slice contains the selected (active) rollover state.
⬁	Rollover Slice	Slice includes rollover information that can be viewed in the Rollover palette.
▦	Slice Is In Table	Indicates that the slice is a part of a table used for layout.
▦	Slice Is Remote Trigger	Indicates that the slice is a part of a rollover that triggers changes in other slices.
◈	Slice Is Remote Target	Indicates that the slice is triggered remotely by another slice.

29.1 Slicing Your Interface (continued)

Adding User Slices

You can draw slices directly into the canvas in either Photoshop or ImageReady using the Slice tool. To add slices to the canvas, choose the Slice tool from the Toolbox. As soon as the tool is active, existing slices are automatically displayed on the canvas. Next, set the style for the slice in the tool options bar:

Normal Allows you to create a free-form rectangular shape.

Fixed Aspect Ratio Allows you to constrain the height-to-width ratio. Enter values (1 through 999) for the *relative* width and height in the fields to the right.

Fixed Size Allows you to set the dimensions of the slice numerically. Enter values (1 through 999) for the width and height in the fields to the right.

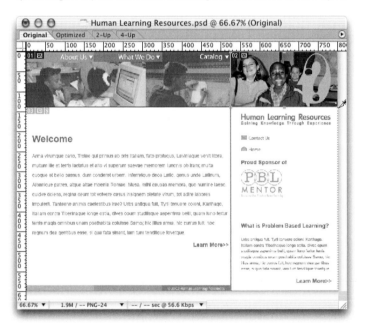

Finally, click and drag from one corner of the area you want to slice, Shift-drag to constrain the slice shape to a square, or Option/Alt-drag to draw the slice from the center. You can do this as many times as you want to create slices. Here, the first slice is being added to the web interface around the company logo in the top-right corner. Notice that the rest of the interface is using auto slices.

➡ 26.2 ImageReady Menus

➡ 26.4 ImageReady Palettes

Switch between slice tools (ImageReady; reverts after release)
⌘
Ctrl

Draw slice from center
Option drag

Alt drag

———

Slice appearance, including line styles, colors, numbers, and symbols, is set in the Slice preferences (see Section 26.5).

29.1 Slicing Your Interface *(continued)*

➡ 26.5 ImageReady
Preferences

➡ 28.4 Creating
Rollovers

Draw square slice
Shift drag

**Draw square slice
from center**
Shift Option drag
Shift Alt drag

———

Although you cannot select multiple slices in the Photoshop canvas, you can select multiple slices when using Photoshop's Save For Web feature (see Section 29.5).

Generating Slices

In addition to drawing slices directly in the canvas, you can use other tools (guides and selections) and features (layers) to generate slices automatically. To generate slices, do one of the following:

To generate slices based on guides in the canvas, first add and adjust guides as needed. In Photoshop, choose the Slice tool ✎ from the Toolbox and click the Slices From Guides button in the tool options bar. In ImageReady, choose Slices > Create Slices From Guides. Existing slices will be deleted.

To generate slices based on a selection (ImageReady only), make the selection in the canvas using one of the marquee tools and then choose Select > Create Slice From Selection. If the selection is not rectangular or if the edges are feathered, the slice will be made from the maximum width and height needed to encompass the entire selection.

To generate a slice based on a layer's content, choose the layer in the Layers palette and then choose Layer > New Layer Based Slice. A layer that is used to create a slice will have the Slice icon ✎ next to its name in the Layers palette. The dimensions of the slice will adjust if the content of the layer is edited or changed.

To generate a slice with a rollover (ImageReady only), choose the layer in the Layers palette and then click the Layer-based Rollover button 🔲 at the bottom of the Rollovers palette.

Setting Slice Options

One of the most powerful features of slicing the image is that you can specify information about the image contained in the slice that will be used to generate the filenames and HTML code used to create the web page. You can also define areas in the design that will not be graphics in the final web page and even enter text and/or HTML code to use in those areas.

To access the slice options, choose the Select Slice tool 🔲 , and then do one of the following:

- In Photoshop, double-click a slice in the canvas to open the Slice Options dialog. Set the options and click OK when you are finished.

- In ImageReady, with the Slice palette open (Window > Slice), select a single slice to enter information just for that slice, or select multiple slices to enter information that will be used for all the selected slices.

Although their formats are slightly different, both the Slice Options dialog and Slice palette contain most of the same options.

29.1 Slicing Your Interface *(continued)*

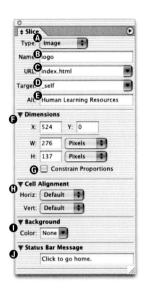

A **Slice Type** Choose Image, No Image, or Table for the slice type. Image slices are output as graphics, and No Image slices are output as empty areas that can contain HTML text.

B **Slice Name** Enter a name for the slice that will be used when naming files during export.

C **URL** If this slice is a hypertext link, enter the URL for the link or choose a previously entered URL from the drop-down.

D **Link Target** If this slice is a hypertext link, you can enter the name of a window or a frame to target or choose from a list of previously entered or standard target names.

E **Alternate Text** Enter an alternative text message to use if the image does not load or for Tool Tips. Adding the Alt message also ensures that your website is fully accessible.

F **Position and Dimensions** Enter the X and Y coordinates and width and height of the slice. You can also choose to use absolute pixels or a percentage for the width and height.

G **Constrain Width and Height** (ImageReady only) Check to link width and height so that changing one will change the other in proportion.

H **Cell Alignment** (ImageReady only) Choose how content within a cell should be horizontally and vertically aligned when output to HTML.

I **Background Color** Choose the background color for the slice. In Photoshop, select the background type (None, White, Black, Matte, or Other). If you select other, you choose the background color using the Photoshop Color Picker.

J **Status Bar Message** If this is a hypertext link, enter a message to appear in the browser's status bar when the mouse cursor is over the image.

If the slice is not an image, the dialog and palette will change slightly, presenting different options for the slice:

A **Text Field** Enter HTML text and HTML tags (if B is checked) that will be displayed in this area of the design in place of the image.

B **Text Is HTML** (ImageReady only) Check if you want HTML tags in the Text field to be interpreted as HTML. If this option is unchecked, HTML tags will be displayed as text on the page.

➡ 29.2 Working with Slices

Toggle slice's visibility (ImageReady)
Q

––––

If snap is turned on (see Section 7.5), slices will be aligned to the edges of guides, grids, and other slices.

––––

If you set the options for an auto slice, it is automatically changed to a user slice.

29.2   Working with Slices

Slice tool
[K]

**Slice Select tool
(ImageReady)**
[O]

**Switch between slice
tools (ImageReady;
reverts after release)**
[⌘]
[Ctrl]

**Toggle slices visibility
(ImageReady)**
[Q]

———

You cannot change the
stacking order of auto
slices.

———

When you delete a user
slice or a layer-based
slice, auto slices are
used to fill the vacated
space.

To specify information about, edit, or optimize a slice, you need to select it. With Photoshop, you can select and edit only one slice at a time in the canvas, although you can select multiple slices in the Save For Web dialog. With ImageReady, you can select multiple slices to edit simultaneously. In addition, slices are incredibly useful when you are optimizing your image or carving it up for output to HTML, but slice lines can be a distraction while you are editing your document.

To show or hide the slices, choose View > Show > Slices or View > Show > Auto Slices. In ImageReady, you can also click the Toggle Slices Visibility button 🖱 in the Toolbox or click the Hide Auto Slices button in the tool options bar.

To select a slice, choose the Select Slice tool 🔧 and click any slice in the canvas (including auto slices). In ImageReady, you can also select slices in the Rollovers palette.

To select multiple slices (ImageReady only), choose the Select Slice tool 🔧 and Shift-click as many slices in the canvas (including auto slices) as desired. You can also select multiple slices in the Rollovers palette by Shift-clicking.

To save a selection of slices (ImageReady only), select one or more slices in the canvas, choose Slices > Save Slice Selection, enter a name for the saved selection, and click OK. This saved selection will now be available in this document.

To load a selection of slices (ImageReady only), choose Slices > Load Slice Selection, and then choose one of the previously saved slice selections from the submenu.

To delete a selection of slices (ImageReady only), choose Slices > Delete Slice Selection, and then choose one of the previously saved slice selections from the submenu. The saved selection will be deleted, but the slices will not be deleted.

To convert an auto slice to a user slice, select the auto slice in the canvas using the Select Slice tool 🔧 from the Toolbox. In Photoshop, click the Promote To User Slice button in the tool options bar. In ImageReady, choose Slices > Promote To User-Slices.

To move slices, click and drag within the boundary of one of the selected slices. Auto slices will be added or reshaped to adjust for the slices' new positions. If you move the slice over other slice types, they will be stacked underneath the slice or slices being moved.

To resize slices, click and drag any of the sides or corners of any of the selected slices. Auto slices will be added or reshaped to adjust for the slices' new dimensions. If you resize the slice over other layer types, they will be stacked underneath the resized slice. If you select multiple slices in ImageReady, they will adjust to each other's resizing and not overlap.

To divide a slice, in Photoshop click the Divide Slice button in the tool options bar. In ImageReady, choose Divide Slice(s) from the Slices menu or Slice palette menu. Set the options for how you want the slice divided and then click OK.

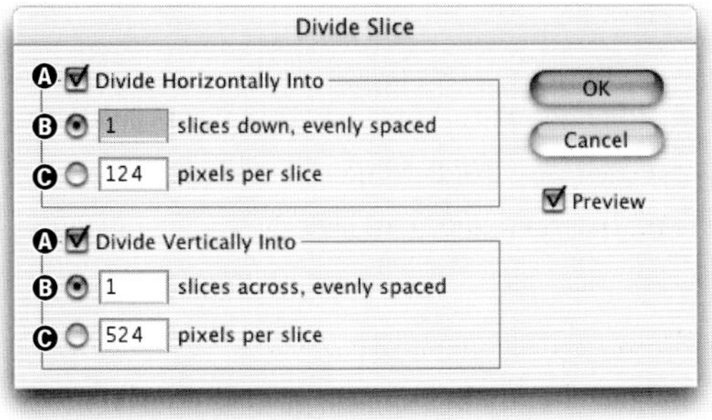

A **Divide Slice** Check to split the slice horizontally and/or vertically.

B **Evenly Space Slices** Choose to divide the slice evenly into the number of slices entered in the field to the right.

C **Pixels per Slice** Choose to divide the slice, with each new slice having a maximum width and height entered in the field to the right.

To copy and paste slices (ImageReady only), choose Copy Slice from the Slice palette menu, and then choose Paste Slice from the Slice palette menu. The copy will appear on top of the original. You can also paste the slice into another image open in ImageReady.

To combine slices (ImageReady only), choose Slices > Combine Slices. The slices will be combined into a rectangle user slice with dimensions to encompass all selected slices even if that means overlapping other slices. You cannot combine layer-based slices.

To duplicate slices, Option/Alt-drag the slice. In ImageReady, you can also choose Duplicate Slice(s) from the Slices or Slice palette menu, set your options, and click OK.

Check whether to also duplicate the Rollover states associated with the slice, duplicate layers associated with layer-based slices, and specify where to position the duplicate slices in relation to the original slice.

To change the stacking order of slices, click the Move To Top 🖹 , Move Up One Level 🖹 , Move Down One Level 🖹 , or Move To Bottom 🖹 button in the options bar. In ImageReady, you can also choose these options from the Slice palette's menu or the Slices > Arrange submenu. Stacking order is important for determining the order of rollovers.

To align slices (ImageReady only), Shift-click hot spots, then click one of the alignment buttons in the options bar or choose from the Slices > Align submenu.

To distribute slices (ImageReady only), Shift-click three or more slices, then click one of the distribution buttons in the options bar or choose from the Slices > Distribute submenu.

To delete slices, press Delete/Backspace or (ImageReady only) choose Delete Slice(s) from the Slices palette menu or the Slices menu. You cannot delete auto slices.

To delete all slices, (Photoshop) View > Clear Slices or (ImageReady) Slices > Delete All.

To lock all slices (Photoshop only), preventing any changes from being made, choose View > Lock Slices. Choose this option again to unlock the slices.

Sidebar:

➡ 26.4 ImageReady Palettes

➡ 26.5 ImageReady Preferences

➡ 29.1 Slicing Your Interface

Draw slice from center
[Option] drag

[Alt] drag

Draw square slice
[Shift] drag

Draw square slice from center
[Shift] [Option] drag

[Shift] [Alt] drag

Aligning and distributing slices is a good way to eliminate surplus auto slices and produce leaner files.

Saved slice groups are especially useful when you are outputting the image (see Section 29.11), allowing you to quickly choose to output only that group of slices.

Vertical margin tabs:

PHOTOSHOP WORKSPACE

UNIVERSAL TASKS

PHOTO AND VIDEO TASKS

PRINT TASKS

WEB TASKS

29.3   Optimizing Images

Save Optimized As...
(ImageReady)
Shift Option ⌘ S
Shift Alt Ctrl S

Save Optimized
(ImageReady)
Option ⌘ S
Alt Ctrl S

Save For
Web...(Photoshop)
Shift Option ⌘ S
Shift Alt Ctrl S

———

You can also create droplets in Photoshop using the Actions. See Section 18.4 for more details.

———

When a slice is *not* selected during optimization, its content's color will appear dimmed. This does not affect the final appearance of the graphics.

———

Remember that if you are in a 2-up or 4-up optimization view, you can use the Hand tool to move the viewable area of the canvas.

———

The Unlink Slice option is also available in the ImageReady Slice palette menu.

The key to optimizing images for the Web is to balance the need to reduce the file size against the need to produce high-quality attractive images. This can take some practice and experimentation, but fortunately both ImageReady and Photoshop provide tools to help you preview the effects of compression and quickly make changes before you commit to any particular compression scheme. In addition, you can compress different slices in the image using different options and use masks to vary the amount of compression over an entire image.

Applying and Previewing Optimization Settings

You can apply compression to an entire image, to an individual slice, or to multiple slices to reduce the file size and thus speed transmission of graphics over the Internet. Compression settings are added to optimized images. You can optimize images in the ImageReady canvas or by using the Photoshop Save For Web dialog.

To apply optimization settings to a slice, select one or more slices in the canvas, and then choose either a preset compression with preset options or a compression method. You can then set the options for the compression method as described in later sections in this chapter.

To preview the optimized version of the image, choose one of the tabs at the top of the ImageReady canvas or in the Photoshop Save For Web dialog: Optimized, 2-up, or 4-up. Both 2-up and 4-up present multiple panel views of the image, allowing you to optimize each in each view to compare the quality and size of different possible optimization settings. Select one of the views to apply optimization settings by clicking anywhere in that panel and then clicking a slice in that panel.

To update an optimized preview based on new optimization settings (ImageReady only), choose Regenerate from the Optimize palette menu. Previews that have not been updated will display a warning icon ⚠ in the bottom-right corner of the preview. Click this icon to regenerate the preview.

To automatically update optimized views when settings change (ImageReady only), choose Auto Regenerate in the Optimize palette menu. This command can be useful if you are making a few small changes, but can be time-consuming if you are making several changes at once.

Linking Slices to Optimize

To save time, you can link slices that will be using the same optimization settings. When one slice in the linked set is selected, changes to its optimization options affect all slices in the set. Linked images have the Link icon 〉 in the top-left corner of the slice, and slices in a linked set are color coded.

To link slices, use the Select Slice tool 🖾 to select two or more slices in the canvas, and then choose Link Slices from the Slices menu (ImageReady) or Setting menu (Photoshop).

29.3 Optimizing Images *(continued)*

To unlink slices, choose a slice in a set using the Select Slice tool , and then choose Unlink Slice (unlinks just the selected slice) or Unlink All (removes all links in the document) from the Slices menu (ImageReady) or the Select menu (Photoshop's Save For Web dialog). In ImageReady, you can also choose Slices > Unlink Set (unlinks all slices in the same set).

Saving and Loading Optimization Settings

After you fine-tune your settings, you can save them in a variety of ways for later use:

To save optimization settings, choose Save Settings in the Optimize palette menu (ImageReady) or Settings menu (Photoshop). Enter a name for the settings and save them in the Presets/Optimized Settings folder inside the Photoshop program folder. The new settings will appear in the Optimization Presets drop-down.

To create a droplet based on the optimization settings shown (ImageReady only), click the Droplet button , enter a name for the droplet, browse to the location where you want to save the droplet, and click Save. Images or folders of images dragged onto the Droplet icon will be optimized using the saved settings.

A droplet to convert images to GIF format using a 128-color, selective palette with dithering

Optimize to a Specific File Size

Rather than optimizing an image or a slice yourself, you can have ImageReady or Photoshop automatically optimize based on the file size you want. This method is not perfect, and there are obviously limits. You can nevertheless often achieve smaller files this way or even use this as a starting point and then modify the automatic settings to improve the image quality.

To optimize, select one ore more slices and choose Optimize To File Size in the Optimize palette (ImageReady) or Save For Web Settings menu (Photoshop), choose your options, and then click OK. If you select Total Of All Slices, optimization might take several seconds.

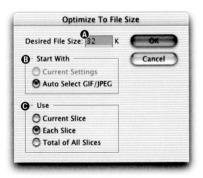

Ⓐ Desired File Size Enter a value for the final size of the slice or image after compression.

Ⓑ Start with Optimization Choose whether you want to start the compression using the current settings or allow ImageReady/Photoshop to choose whether to use GIF or JPEG format.

Ⓒ Slice to Use for Optimization Choose whether to base the optimization setting on the current slice settings, each slice individually, or the total of all slices in the image.

➡ 29.6 Setting Optimization Options

➡ 29.7 Optimizing with GIF or PNG-8 Compression

➡ 29.8 Optimizing with JPEG Compression

➡ 29.9 Optimizing with PNG-24 or WBMP Compression

Toggle optimization views (ImageReady only)
⌘ Y
Ctrl Y

Toggle gamma optimization views (ImageReady only)
Option ⌘ Y
Alt Ctrl Y

Toggle dither optimization views (ImageReady only)
Shift ⌘ Y
Shift Ctrl Y

———

The advantage of using ImageReady over Photoshop for optimization is that you can set your optimization options while working to test how they will affect the final piece, which may affect your design decisions.

———

If you do not save optimization settings in the Presets/Optimized Settings folder, you can still load them, but they will not appear in the palette's menu.

———

Once deleted, an optimization setting is gone forever, so think carefully before clicking OK.

29.4   Optimizing Images in ImageReady

Save Optimized As...
Shift Option ⌘ S
Shift Alt Ctrl S

Save Optimized
Option ⌘ S
Alt Ctrl S

Toggle optimization views
⌘ Y
Ctrl Y

Toggle gamma optimization views
Option ⌘ Y
Alt Ctrl Y

Toggle dither optimization views
Shift ⌘ Y
Shift Ctrl Y

———

When a slice is not selected during optimization, its content's color will appear dimmed. This does not affect the final appearance of the graphics.

———

Both Photoshop and ImageReady allow you to optimize images for the Web in real time so that you can see the results before saving.

You optimize in ImageReady during design, using the Optimize palette. This palette contains all the optimization settings, allowing you to preview optimization in the canvas while choosing the format (GIF, JPEG, PNG, WBMP) and individual optimization options. You can set the format and optimizations options for the entire document at once or select one or more slices to apply individual optimization settings for each area. If you do not see the Optimize palette, choose Window > Optimize.

A **Preview Tabs** Click to view a single optimized version of the image, two optimized versions side by side, or four versions.

B **Original Version** Displays an uncompressed version of the web page.

C **Optimized Version** Displays a version of the web page based on the optimization settings.

D **Update Alert** An Alert icon appears if the version showing in the preview has not been updated based on the current optimization settings.

E **Optimization Settings** Options for compressing images for display on the Web. See later sections in this chapter for details on each option.

F **Optimization Presets** Choose a compression method with preset options for the file format and optimization settings. You can still customize the options as desired.

G **File Format** Choose a compression method. The last settings for the method will be used.

H **Droplet** Click to save the current settings as a droplet. You can then drag and drop image files onto the icon to automatically create an optimized version of the file based on the settings.

29.5 Optimizing Images in Photoshop

You optimize in Photoshop while saving the image using the Save For Web dialog. This dialog not only contains all the optimization settings (such as the ImageReady Optimize palette), but also serves as a minicanvas with tools for working with individual slices created in the main Photoshop canvas. You can set the format and optimizations options for the entire document at once or select one or more slices to apply individual optimization settings for each area. To access the Save For Web dialog, choose File **>** Save For Web... You can then make changes and click Save to output the files or click Done to save your settings in their current state and return to Photoshop.

A **Tools** This limited toolset includes the Hand, Slice Select, Zoom, and Eyedropper tools.

B **Selected Color** Displays the current color selected by the Eyedropper tool.

C **Toggle Slice Display** Click to show or hide slices in the display.

D **Magnification** Enter or choose the magnification for the image(s) in the display.

E **Preview Menu** Choose viewing options for the preview area, including Browser Dither, Hide/Show Auto Slices, preview color palette, and predicted download times based on connection speed.

F **Preview Area** Displays the image in its original format or optimized or in 2-up, 4-up optimized views.

G **Color Values** Displays various color values for the pixel the cursor is currently over in the display area.

➥ 29.3 Optimizing Images

➥ 29.6 Setting Optimization Options

➥ 29.7 Optimizing with GIF or PNG-8 Compression

Save For Web...
Shift Option ⌘ S
Shift Alt Ctrl S

When a slice is not selected during optimization, its content's color will appear dimmed. This does not affect the final appearance of the graphics.

Both Photoshop and ImageReady allow you to optimize images for the Web in real time so that you can see the results before saving.

The advantage of using ImageReady over Photoshop for optimization is that you can set your optimization options while working to test how they will affect the final piece, which may affect your design decisions.

Remember that if you are in a 2-up or 4-up optimization view, you can use the Hand tool to move the viewable area of the canvas.

➡ 29.8 Optimizing with JPEG Compression

➡ 29.9 Optimizing with PNG-24 or WBMP Compression

———

The Unlink Slice option is also available in the ImageReady Slice palette menu.

———

If you do not save optimization settings in the Presets/Optimized Settings folder, you can still load them, but they will not appear in the palette's menu.

———

Once deleted, an optimization setting is gone forever, so think carefully before clicking OK.

ⓗ Browser Preview Click to preview the image in a browser (indicated by the browser's icon) or choose a different browser from the drop-down.

ⓘ Save Click to proceed to save the optimized image.

ⓙ Cancel Click to return to the canvas without preserving optimization settings.

ⓚ Done Click to return to the canvas and preserve the optimization settings.

ⓛ Optimization Settings Options for compressing images for display on the Web. See later sections in this chapter for details on each option.

ⓜ Optimization Presets Choose a compression method with preset options for the file format and optimization settings. You can still customize the options as desired.

ⓝ File Format Choose a compression method. The last settings for the method will be used.

ⓞ Color Table Click to view and edit the colors used if the image or slice is using the GIF or PNG-8 file format.

ⓟ Image Size Click to view and change the image dimensions. Enter a new width and/or height, enter a percentage to scale the image up or down, choose the quality used to resize, and click Apply. This resizes the image for this saved version and leaves the original version unchanged.

29.6 Setting Optimization Options

All images headed to the Web from Photoshop and ImageReady must be saved in one of three formats: GIF, PNG (8 or 24), or JPEG. In addition, you can save graphics that will be viewed on devices with black-and-white screens (such as mobile phones) in WBMP format. These formats take the file information and use various compression schemes to squeeze the file size down to make transmission of the files faster. All these formats are *lossy* formats in that the compression invariably leads to a little or a lot of loss in image quality. Each format is addressed in one of the following sections.

Weighted Optimization with Masks

You use masks to selectively protect areas of the image while editing (see Chapter 11). You can also use masks to selectively optimize parts of the image, allowing you to retain high quality in some regions while applying maximum compression to others. This weighted optimization allows you to control the amount of certain compression options applied:

JPEG Quality Applies higher JPEG compression to darker areas of mask and lower quality.

GIF Lossiness Applies higher GIF compression to darker areas of the mask and lower quality.

Dithering Applies greater amounts of dithering to lighter areas of the mask.

Color Reduction Applies greater amounts of color reduction to darker areas of the mask. (Quality settings are not available.)

To use weighted optimization with an option, click the Optimize button to the right of an option in the Optimize palette. In the Modify Settings dialog, set the masks to use for the weighted optimization and then set the quality options for how the option should be treated by layers for optimization.

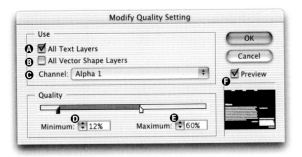

Ⓐ **Use All Text Layers** Check to use all text layers in the image as masks (see Section 17.1). This helps preserve text quality.

Ⓑ **Use All Vector Shape Layers** Check to use the vector masks in all shape layers (see Section 11.6).

Ⓒ **Use Channels** Choose an alpha channel to use as a mask (see Section 8.7).

Ⓓ **Minimum Quality** Use the slider (the black tab) or enter a value (1% through 100%) to set the minimum quality for areas that are completely unmasked.

Ⓔ **Maximum Quality** Use the slider (the white tab) or enter a value (1% through 100%) to set the maximum quality for the masked area.

Ⓕ **Mask Preview** Displays a thumbnail of masked regions in an image. White represents masked areas and will be the highest quality. Black represents unmasked areas that will receive the maximum compression. Gray areas will receive compression on a linear scale.

➡ 6.2 File Formats

➡ 11.1 Mask Basics

Optimized As...
(ImageReady)
[Shift] [Option] [⌘] [S]
[Shift] [Alt] [Ctrl] [S]

Save For Web...
(Photoshop)
[Shift] [Option] [⌘] [S]
[Shift] [Alt] [Ctrl] [S]

Toggle optimization views (ImageReady only)
[⌘] [Y]
[Ctrl] [Y]

Toggle gamma optimization views (ImageReady only)
[Option] [⌘] [Y]
[Alt] [Ctrl] [Y]

Toggle dither optimization views (ImageReady only)
[Shift] [⌘] [Y]
[Shift] [Ctrl] [Y]

Although the PNG format is supported by most browsers, the alpha-channel feature for PNG-24 is currently supported only in Internet Explorer 5 for the Mac.

Although WBMP format is currently useful, both cell phones and PDAs are swiftly migrating to color screens that may soon render this format obsolete.

Using the diffusion dither with any file format may cause noticeable seams between the edges of different slices.

29.7   Optimizing with GIF or PNG-8 Compression

Save Optimized (ImageReady)

`Option` `⌘` `S`

`Alt` `Ctrl` `S`

Save Optimized As... (ImageReady)

`Shift` `Option` `⌘` `S`

`Shift` `Alt` `Ctrl` `S`

Save For Web...(Photoshop)

`Shift` `Option` `⌘` `S`

`Shift` `Alt` `Ctrl` `S`

GIF format supports animation while PNG does not.

PNG-24 Supports transparencies using alpha-channels allowing you to have sem-transparent images and drop shadows.

Using the diffusion dither in adjacent slices may cause noticeable seams to appear across slice boundaries. To overcome this, link the styles and then apply the diffusion dither.

The color table is not accessible in Image-Ready if Auto Regenerate is turned off.

Using the diffusion dither in adjacent slices may cause noticeable seams to appear across slice boundaries. To overcome this, link the styles and then apply the diffusion dither.

Both GIF and PNG formats work well for compressing images that have large areas of solid color. GIF format is the undisputed king of web graphic formats and is supported in every graphic-capable browser. PNG, on the other hand, is a newer format that is not as widely supported, but is supported in most of today's browsers.

Both formats work by reducing the number of colors in the image's color table to 256 or fewer. In addition, both allow you to specify a particular color in the image as transparent. Background colors in the web page will show through transparent images.

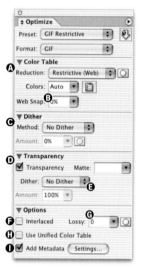

ⓐ Color Reduction Method Specify how colors in the color table should be eliminated from the color table (see the next subsection) in order to preserve the best image quality. Then choose the number of colors used for the image's color table. Fewer colors will create smaller files, but reduce image quality. You can also click the Palette button next to the Color option to open the Color Table palette to review colors being used in the image.

ⓑ Web Snap Use the slider or enter a percentage value to set the level at which colors are forced to be Web-safe.

ⓒ Dithering Method Choose the dithering method (see Section 27.2) you want to apply to the image. Then use the slider or enter a percentage for the amount of dithering allowed.

ⓓ Transparency Method Check to preserve transparent regions in the flattened image as transparent pixels in the final web graphic, and then choose the color to be used behind semi-transparent pixels in the image. This color should be the same color you are using for the background color in the web page. If you select transparent and do not select a matte color, semitransparent regions will be either full opaque (above 50% opacity) or fully transparent (below 50% opacity).

ⓔ Transparency Dithering Method If Transparency is checked, choose how partially transparent pixels should be dithered. Then use the slider or enter a percentage for the amount of dithering allowed. Allows you to create transparent areas that will better integrate with different colored backgrounds.

ⓕ Interlaced Check to use the interlacing method with the image so that it begins displaying before the file finishes downloading. For visitors with slower Internet connections, interlaced graphics may seem to load faster, but the file size is actually slightly larger. This option is located in the top-right corner of the palette for PNG-8. This feature is not generally recommended.

ⓖ Lossy Compression (GIF only) Use the slider or enter a percentage value (0 to 100) for the amount of compression used at the loss of image quality. The larger the value, the smaller the file, but the lower the image quality.

ⓗ Use Unified Color Table (ImageReady only) Check to use the same color table for all rollover states in this slice.

ⓘ Add MetaData (ImageReady only) Check to include metadata set for the image when exporting the optimized file. You can also click the Settings button to open the MetaData panel in the Output Settings dialog.

29.7 Optimizing with GIF or PNG-8 Compression *(continued)*

Refining the Color Table to Optimize

The color table displays all the colors currently used in the optimized version of an image or a slice using the GIF or PNG-8 file format. Generally, this table is controlled by the optimization settings. However, an additional way to further refine the optimization of GIF and PNG-8 images is to edit their color table manually.

The color table is in the Color Table palette in ImageReady (Window > Color Table) or the Color tab in the bottom right of the Save For Web dialog in Photoshop.

To sort the color table, choose one of the sorting options from the palette/tab menu: Unsorted, Hue (color value), Luminance (recommended), Popularity (most used in image).

To select colors, click a color square or choose one of the selection options from the palette/tab menu: All Colors, All Web Safe Colors, All Non-Web Safe Colors.

To save a color table, choose Save Color Table… from the palette/tab menu, enter a filename making sure to preserve the .act extension, and click Save.

To load a color table, choose Load Color Table… from the palette/tab menu, choose a file with the .act extension, and click Open. The new table will replace the previous table.

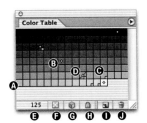

Ⓐ Color Square Click to select. Shift-click to select multiple colors. Double-click to use the Color Picker to change this color. Selected colors are surrounded by a white box.

Ⓑ Web-Safe Color A white diamond indicates the color is Web-safe.

Ⓒ Locked Color A white square indicates the color is locked.

Ⓓ Shifted Color A line through the color with a diamond indicates that one or more colors have been shifted to this Web-safe color.

Ⓔ Number of Colors in Table Displays the number of colors in the table.

Ⓕ Set to Transparent Click to make selected colors transparent. Click again to revert to color.

Ⓖ Set to Web-Safe Click to shift color(s) to closest Web-safe equivalents. Click again to shift back.

Ⓗ Lock Color Click to lock color(s), preventing them from being dropped during color reduction. Click again to unlock.

Ⓘ Add Color Click to add color selected by the Eyedropper to the color table. This allows you to select a color from the original version of the image to add into an optimized version.

Ⓙ Delete Color Click to delete the selected color(s) from the table.

➡ 29.6 Setting Optimization Options

➡ 29.10 Specifying Output Options

Toggle optimization views (ImageReady only)
⌘ Y
Ctrl Y

Toggle gamma optimization views (ImageReady only)
Option ⌘ Y
Alt Ctrl Y

Toggle dither optimization views (ImageReady only)
Shift ⌘ Y
Shift Ctrl Y

———

Although the PNG format is supported by most browsers, the alpha-channel feature for PNG-24 is currently supported only in Internet Explorer 5 for the Mac.

———

You cannot use the Lossy option in the GIF format with the Interlaced, Noise, or Pattern Dither options.

———

Using the diffusion dither with any file format may cause noticeable seams between the edges of different slices.

29.8   Optimizing with JPEG Compression

➡ 6.2   File Formats

➡ 8.6   Converting between Color Profiles and Devices

➡ 29.6   Setting Optimization Options

JPEG format works best for images with a lot of colors that require smooth tone transitions, such as photographs or images with subtle gradients. Setting JPEG compression requires you to set the level of compression as a numeric value, which determines how much information is removed from the image. Lower values produce higher compression (and thus smaller file sizes) but create square artifacts in the image that decrease its sharpness and quality.

Save Optimized (ImageReady)

[Option] [⌘] [S]
[Alt] [Ctrl] [S]

Save Optimized As... (ImageReady)

[Shift] [Option] [⌘] [S]
[Shift] [Alt] [Ctrl] [S]

Save For Web...(Photoshop)

[Shift] [Option] [⌘] [S]
[Shift] [Alt] [Ctrl] [S]

Toggle optimization views (ImageReady only)

[⌘] [Y]
[Ctrl] [Y]

Toggle gamma optimization views (ImageReady only)

[Option] [⌘] [Y]
[Alt] [Ctrl] [Y]

Toggle dither optimization views (ImageReady only)

[Shift] [⌘] [Y]
[Shift] [Ctrl] [Y]

Using the diffusion dither in adjacent slices may cause noticeable seams to appear across slice boundaries. To overcome this, link the styles and then apply the diffusion dither.

Using the diffusion dither with any file format may cause noticeable seams between the edges of different slices.

An image compressed using a JPEG value of 20. Notice the rectangular distortion artifacts.

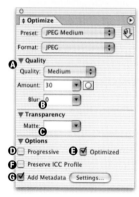

Ⓐ Quality Settings Select a quality setting from the drop-down, which changes the Quality value to the right. You can also use the slider or enter a numeric value (0 to 100) directly for the quality value. Low-quality values—30 or less—produce smaller file sizes but significantly reduce the image quality. You will need to experiment with quality levels to find the one that produces the smallest file size without diminishing the image quality too greatly.

Ⓑ Correction Blur Use the slider or enter a value (0 to 2) to set the amount of Gaussian Blur applied to the image to help offset the square artifacts produced by JPEG compression and producing smaller file sizes.

Ⓒ Transparency Matte Choose the color to be used behind semi-transparent pixels in the image. This color should be the same color you are using for the background color in the web page.

Ⓓ Progressive Download Check to use the progressive method with the image so that it begins displaying before the file finishes downloading. Progressive JPEG images require more RAM to display and are not supported in some older browsers. This feature is not generally recommended.

Ⓔ Optimized Format Check to use the enhanced JPEG format to automatically produce slightly smaller file sizes.

Ⓕ Include ICC Profile Check to include the ICC (International Color Consortium) profile set when specifying your color profile. This profile will be used by some browsers to ensure color consistency.

Ⓖ Add MetaData (ImageReady only) Check to include metadata set for the image when exporting the optimized file. You can also click the Settings button to open the MetaData panel in the Output Settings dialog.

29.9 Optimizing with PNG-24 or WBMP Compression

Two of the newest image formats are PNG-24, which provides gradual transparency instead of all-or-nothing opacity, and the WBMP black-and-white format for mobile devices.

Optimizing with PNG-24 Compression

You can use PNG-24 to compress both images with large areas of flat color or photographs. However, using PNG-24 tends to produce larger file sizes than other compression formats. Its great advantage, though, is that unlike the JPEG, GIF, and PNG-8 formats in which all pixels are either transparent or opaque, PNG-24 allows you to include as many as 256 levels of transparency in a single image. This allows you to place the image on any background without having to worry about the matte color set when you saved the image. The down side, though, is that many common browsers (such as Internet Explorer for Windows) do not support transparency with the PNG-24 format. To preserve the transparent pixels in the image, check the Transparency option.

The options for the PNG-24 format allow you to set the image to use the interlace method. You can also set the image to use transparency (transparent regions will be transparent on the web page) or to use a matte color behind transparent regions.

Optimizing with WBMP Compression

WBMP format is a black-and-white (no grayscale) format that is commonly used on mobile devices such as cell phones and PDAs. Although mobile devices with black-and-white screens can display images saved in color, these images are still translated into black and white, and the full color file still has to download. With WBMP you can control the quality of the image and significantly reduce its file size by eliminating color information. WBMP format has a limited number of settings that allow you to add and control dithering in the image.

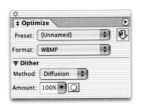

The options with the WBMP format allow you to choose the type of dithering applied to the black-and-white image and the amount of dither applied.

Save Optimized (ImageReady)
Option ⌘ S
Alt Ctrl S

Save Optimized As... (ImageReady)
Shift Option ⌘ S
Shift Alt Ctrl S

Save For Web...(Photoshop)
Shift Option ⌘ S
Shift Alt Ctrl S

Toggle optimization views (ImageReady only)
⌘ Y
Ctrl Y

Toggle gamma optimization views (ImageReady only)
Option ⌘ Y
Alt Ctrl Y

Toggle dither optimization views (ImageReady only)
Shift ⌘ Y
Shift Ctrl Y

Although the PNG format is supported by most browsers, the alpha-channel feature for PNG-24 is currently supported only in Internet Explorer 5 for the Mac.

29.10 Specifying Output Options

⇒ 28.1 Creating Image Maps

HTML output settings (ImageReady)
[Option][Shift][⌘] [H]
[Alt][Shift][Ctrl] [H]

HTML panel
[⌘] [1]
[Ctrl] [1]

Many web pages today use tables for layout, but CSS creates faster-loading layouts that are easier to adjust.

If you are using ImageReady or Photoshop to create the HTML that you will be using to create the web page based on the image you are outputting, you will need to set the HTML, Image Map, and Slice Output settings.

Output options are generally accessed from the same dialog associated with the Save Optimized dialog by choosing Custom from the Settings drop-down (see Section 29.11). However, you can also set the options directly in ImageReady, choosing File > Output Options and then choosing one of the submenu options.

HTML Output Options

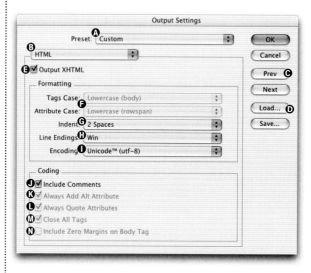

Ⓐ Setting Presets Choose a preset output setting.

Ⓑ Output Options Choose the output setting category.

Ⓒ Prev/Next Options panel Click to open the next or previous settings category.

Ⓓ Load/Save Settings Click to load or save settings using the .iros extension.

Ⓔ Output as XHTML Check if you want the code to be compliant with the XHTML Transitional standard. Generally, this is a good idea, although it may cause some problems with dynamic code.

Ⓕ Tag/Attribute Case Choose the case used for HTML tags and tag attributes. Due to changes in HTML standards, all lowercase is recommended.

Ⓖ Code Indent Choose how to indent the code: using tabs, none for no indenting, or using spaces (2 or 5 spaces is recommended).

Ⓗ Line Endings Choose how to treat line breaks in the code: Mac, Win, or Unix. Win for Windows is recommended.

Ⓘ Text Encoding Choose how text is encoded. For international use, utf-8 is recommended.

Ⓙ Include Comments Check if you want Photoshop to include comments about the generated code. Recommended.

Ⓚ Alt Attribute Check if you want to add the Alt attribute to all images. Recommended.

Ⓛ Quote Attributes Check if you want attribute values in quotes. Recommended.

Ⓜ Close All Tags Check to include a closing tag for all tag sets. Recommended.

Ⓝ Zero Margins Check to include attributes that will set the web-page margins to 0. Otherwise, the browser will set its default margin. This is not recommended if you are using CSS for layout.

29.10 Specifying Output Options (continued)

Saving HTML Files (ImageReady)

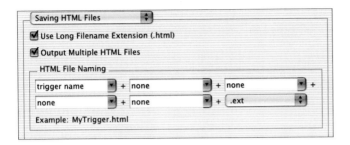

Choose how HTML files should be named during output. Generally, you will want to use the long file-name extension, but you won't want to output multiple HTML files unless you are using a single comp for multiple pages in a site. If you are outputting multiple files, you also need to specify how the files should be named.

➡ 28.4 Creating Rollovers

➡ 28.7 Creating Seamless Backgrounds

Saving HTML Files panel
⌘ 2
Ctrl 2

Slices panel
⌘ 3
Ctrl 3

————

Photoshop and ImageReady cannot generate server-side image maps for images that contain slices.

Slice Output Options

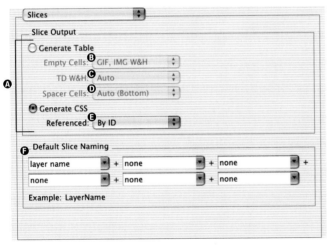

Ⓐ Tables or CSS Choose whether you want to use tables or CSS to lay out the page.

Ⓑ Empty Table Cells Choose the method for filling empty table cells: using a GIF image with width and height set in the image (recommended), using a GIF image with width and height set in the table, or using the NoWrap tag (not recommended).

Ⓒ Table Cell Width and Height Choose how to add width and height attributes to table data tags: Auto (recommended), Always, or Never.

Ⓓ Table Spacer Cells Choose how to add one row and one column empty cells around the layout table to space out nonaligned slices: Auto (recommended), Never, or Always. You can also specify that Auto and Always be placed at the bottom of the table.

Ⓔ Element Reference Choose how to generate CSS layers for layout: using the ID tag (recommended), placing the CSS code directly in the HTML tag, or using classes.

Ⓕ Naming the Slices Choose how to name slices automatically when added to the document. You can enter text directly in a field or choose a variable such as the document name, layer name, slice number, and date from the drop-downs.

Backgrounds panel
⌘ 5
Ctrl 5

Saving Files panel
⌘ 6
Ctrl 6

———

Almost all browsers support client-side mage maps. However, if you need to use server-side image maps for some reason, contact your Internet Service Provider (ISP) to determine whether they use NCSA or CERN specifications.

Saving File Output Options

Unlike the other output options, which are primarily used to output the HTML code used to create the web pages, the File Saving options allow you to specify how image files are automatically named when output.

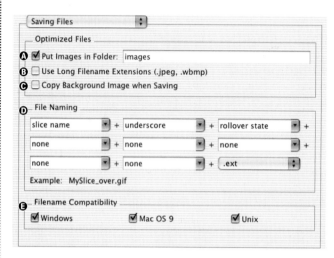

Ⓐ **Where to place images** Check to place the images in a specific folder. Enter the name of the folder to the right. If the folder does not already exist in that location, Photoshop or ImageReady will create it.

Ⓑ **Long Filename Extensions** Check to use four-letter filename extensions.

Ⓒ **Copy Background Image** Check to add a copy of the background image (specified in the Background options panel) to the folder when saving.

Ⓓ **File Naming** Choose how slices should be automatically named when added to the document. You can enter text directly in a field or choose a variable from the drop-down such as the document name, layer name, slice name/number, trigger name/number, rollover state, and date or a symbol such as a hyphen, an underscore, or a space. Some of these will only be used if the document contains slices or rollovers.

Ⓔ **Operating System Filename Compatibility** Check options for which operating systems the filename needs to be compatible. This will limit the length of the filename and prevent certain characters from being used to ensure that the filename will work in the operating system.

29.10   Specifying Output Options *(continued)*

Image Map Output Options (ImageReady)

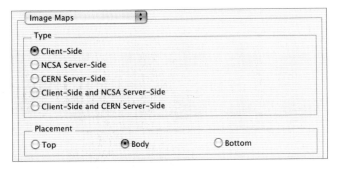

Choose how to code the image maps: as client-side (recommended) with the code embedded in the HTML, as server-side (NCSA or CERN) with the code generated as a separate file, or as a combination. If you are using client-side, specify where the image map code should be placed in the HTML. Body is recommended to keep the code with the image source tag.

Metadata panel
⌘ 7
Ctrl 7

Image Maps panel
⌘ 4
Ctrl 4

———

Some servers do not allow spaces in file-names, so using them is not recommended. Use underscores instead.

———

Often you need to output your web designs to show to clients. ImageReady allows you to quickly save a version of the file in a variety of standard formats using the File > Export > Original Document... command. This works much like saving the file (see Section 6.10), but does not preserve slices or compression settings. It automatically flattens the image and allows you to choose from only a limited list of file formats.

Background Output Options

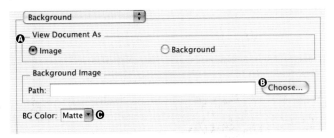

ⓐ Document Type
Choose whether this is a foreground image (Image) or a background image to be tiled in the background of a web page.

ⓑ Background Location
If this is a foreground image, choose a file to use as the background image on the web page. Either enter the path to the file directly, or click Choose to browse to and select the image. This image will not show up in the document canvas but will be used when the image is previewed (see Section 27.5).

ⓒ Background Color Matte Choose a color from the drop-down to use as the background color on the web page. This will not show up in the document window but will be used when the image is previewed (see Section 27.5).

MetaData Output Options (ImageReady)

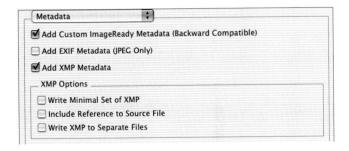

Check options to include certain data about the image that is not used specifically for display purposes. This will increase the file size, but allows you to better track the image.

29.11   Saving Your Website

**Save Optimized As...
(ImageReady)**
[Shift] [Option] [⌘] [S]
[Shift] [Alt] [Ctrl] [S]

**Save Optimized
(ImageReady)**
[Option] [⌘] [S]
[Alt] [Ctrl] [S]

**Save For
Web...(Photoshop)**
[Shift] [Option] [⌘] [S]
[Shift] [Alt] [Ctrl] [S]

———

After you save the file
the first time, in
ImageReady you can
quickly update the
code and or images
(depending on the set-
tings from the last save)
by choosing File > Save
Optimized.

———

You cannot save output
settings that you set
while saving the opti-
mized file. You can only
save your settings in
ImageReady while edit-
ing using the Output
Settings command.

Regardless of whether you optimized your images using the Optimize palette in ImageReady or chose File > Save For Web in Photoshop, the rest of the process for saving the website graphics is identical in both programs.

1 Set output options as needed.

2 If you are using Photoshop, choose File > Save For Web...

3 Set optimization options for the entire document or individual slices.

4 If you are using the 2-up or 4-up view, choose the version you want to use by clicking it, and then do one of the following:

  ■ In ImageReady, choose File > Save Optimized As...

  ■ In Photoshop, click the Save button in the Save For Web dialog.

5 In the Save Optimized As dialog, set your options and then click Save. Outputting the files might take a few seconds.

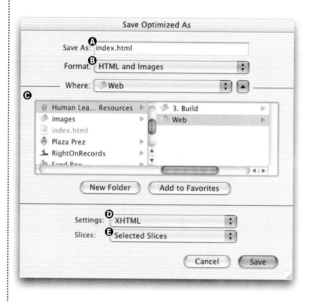

Ⓐ Output Filename Enter a filename. If you are saving HTML (see B), this will be used as the name of the HTML file and the .html extension should be preserved. If you are saving a single image only (no slices), this name will be used as the filename. If you are saving images only *with* slices, this name is ignored.

Ⓑ Ouput Format Choose what you are saving: HTML Only generates the HTML file needed to create the web page based on the settings you have made, Images Only saves the artwork needed to create the web page, HTML and Images saves both.

Ⓒ Save Location Browse to the folder in which you want to save the files. Remember, if you checked Put Images In Folder in your output options, a folder will be created with that name (unless it already exists in that location), and all sliced images will be placed there.

Ⓓ Output Settings Choose the output settings to use while saving. You can choose from the list of presaved settings or set the options by choosing Custom...

Ⓔ Slices to Save Choose whether you want to save all slices in the image, slices selected in the can-vas (ImageReady only), or Save For Web dialog (Photoshop). In ImageReady, if you saved any slice groups, you can choose those to output only the slices in that saved group.

Appendix: What's New in Photoshop CS and ImageReady CS

When deciding whether to upgrade from one version of a program to another, the first step is to consider whether the new features are worth the cost of upgrading. Photoshop CS offers several new features that make it an excellent upgrade for illustrators (layer comps), web designers (exporting layers to files), photographers (the Match Color adjustment), and filmmakers (edit images with nonsquare pixels). Of course, a new tool, a new feature, or an improvement is only valuable if you are going to use it. Following are some lists of the most important and noticeable changes from Photoshop 7 to Photoshop CS, with a brief description and a note about where in this book you can find more information.

New Features

FEATURES	DESCRIPTION	WHERE TO LEARN MORE
Camera Raw	Formerly a separate plug-in, the Camera Raw functionality is now directly integrated into Photoshop CS for opening files directly from supported digital cameras.	19.2 Working with Camera Raw Files
Customized Help menu	Add How To pages to the Help menu for in-house training.	2.11 Help Menu
Customized keyboard shortcuts	Set a keyboard shortcut for any menu command.	5.2 Setting Keyboard Shortcuts
Edit nonsquare pixels for video	Create and edit images using video pixel-aspect ratios.	20.1 Digital Video Basics
Histogram palette	Formerly a dialog, the image histogram is now in its own palette for handy reference while making image adjustments.	4.9 Histogram Palette
Layer Comps palette	Create different configurations of your work to keep several iterations in a single file.	4.12 Layer Comps Palette
Panoramic views	Use a wizard to combine two or more images into a seamless panorama.	19.9 Creating Panoramic Views
Printing to online services	Use a wizard to send files to print bureaus over the Internet directly from within Photoshop.	25.9 Printing and Online Services
Version Cue	Share files with other users over a network while maintaining version control using Web DAV.	18.10 Using Version Cue
Web Photo Galleries	Use a wizard to quickly set up a gallery/portfolio of images for display on the Web.	27.6 Creating Web Photo Galleries

New Commands and Tools

COMMAND/TOOLS	DESCRIPTION	WHERE TO LEARN MORE
Color Matching adjustment	Match color palettes between different images or layers in the same image	22.8 Matching Color Palettes between Images
Color Replace tool	Quickly remove red-eye or change any color in the canvas with this brush tool	3.9 Restoration Tools
Filter Gallery	Apply multiple filters to the image through a single dialog	14.3 Applying Multiple Filters with the Filter Gallery
Lens Blur filter	Simulate depth-of-field blurring normally done with a camera lens	14.4 Adding a Motion or Depth-of-Field Effect
Photo Filters adjustment	Simulate color filters added to a camera lens	22.11 Colorizing Images with PhotoFilters
Shadow/Highlight adjustment	Adjust tones in shadows and highlights while maintaining image quality	22.12 Quickly Correcting Shadows and Highlights
Viewing for video	View the image in different pixel-aspect ratios to simulate how the image will appear on a video monitor	20.3 Viewing for Video

Enhancements

ENHANCEMENT	DESCRIPTION	WHERE TO LEARN MORE
Brushes palette	Brush options can be locked when switching between different brush Presets to preserve the options, allowing you to combine options between different brushes.	4.4 Brushes Palette
File Browser	Radically redesigned to allow you to not only browse for image files but manage them as well.	4.8 File Browser
Full 16-bit editing	All core Photoshop features are now available for use in 16-bit editing mode, allowing higher-quality images.	8.3 Editing in 8-bit or 16-bit Modes
History tracking	Keep a log of your projects while working to track time spent for customers.	4.10 History Palette
Nested layer sets	Layer sets can now be nested within layer sets up to five levels deep.	10.7 Managing Layers and Layer Sets
Preset video layouts	Images can be started using standard video dimensions and include title-safe and action-safe guides.	20.2 Starting a New Image for Video
Text on a path	Text can be flowed along vector paths created with the Pen tool.	17.9 Creating Text on a Path

ImageReady Changes

ENHANCEMENT	DESCRIPTION	WHERE TO LEARN MORE
Output in XHTML and CSS	Create web pages using the latest web standards.	29.10 Specifying Output Options
Remote actions	Trigger image changes for one or more elements from a single-user action.	28.4 Creating Rollovers
Smart Guides	Guides appear to help you align objects while working and then disappear when no longer needed.	27.1 Web Design Basics
Tab and Pill Rectangle tools	Quickly create attractive buttons and tabs for website navigation.	28.4 Creating Rollovers
Table palette	Define the table structure to be used when creating HTML to lay out the design.	27.3 Creating Table-Based Layouts
Web Content palette	Control the nature of image maps and rollovers from a single palette.	26.4 ImageReady Palettes

Glossary

action A script that, when executed, performs a single operation or a sequence of operations in Photoshop. Photoshop comes with several prerecorded actions, or you can record your own actions and save them. You access actions from the Actions palette. See *4.3 Actions Palette*.

adaptive palette An indexed color table calculated to favor the most common colors in a particular image. Using an adaptive palette for creating GIF or PNG images maintains higher quality while reducing the overall file size of the image. See *8.11 Converting to Indexed Color Mode*.

Adjustment A command or special layer type used to adjust the appearance of a single layer (command) or of all layers underneath (layer). Adjustment commands are applied directly to a layer's content. Adjustment layers can be re-edited at any time to change the appearance. See *22.1 Adjustment Basics*.

alpha channel A type of layer created in the Channels palette that records the opacity of areas of the image using grayscale values to create an invisible "onion skin" mask over the image. See *8.7 Using Color in Channels*.

anti-alias A method used by computers to "smooth" the jagged edges of graphics and text objects on the computer screen by adding semi-transparent pixels along the object's edge. Anti-aliasing gives the illusion of increasing the object's resolution for screen display. See *17.1 Type Basics*.

artifact An imperfection in an image often caused by over compression, over manipulation, or a loss of color information. One of the most common examples of artifacts is the squarelike splotches in an overly compressed JPEG image. See *29.6 Setting Optimization Options*.

background color One of two selected colors, which is used for the color of background elements. For example, the background color is used to fill areas deleted from the *background layer*. The default background color is white. See *12.1 Color, Gradient, and Pattern Basics*.

Background layer A special layer type that appears behind all other layers in an image. This layer cannot be moved and deleting from it will fill the deleted area with the *background color*, but it can be hidden or completely removed, in which case *transparency* is used. See *10.2 The Background Layer*.

banding A noticeable color change in graduated tonal images. An unattractive artifact, banding occurs when too few colors are included in the image's color table. See *12.8 Creating and Editing Gradients*.

Bezier curves A system used to control the curvature of lines created mathematically for *vector* rather than *bitmap* graphics. The curves are controlled using a system of anchor points, direction handles, and handlebars. See *16.1 Path Basics*.

bit A binary digit. Computers use bits to store information. Each bit can have a value of either 1 or 0. A series of bits make up a byte, and a byte stores specific information such as a letter or a color. For example, images contain pixels, and each pixel has a specific color. The computer stores each pixel's color information as a series (byte) of bits that define the color value. See *8.1 Image Color Basics*.

bit depth The number of bits of color information devoted to a single pixel. There are two types of bit depth: image and monitor. The higher the bit depth value for an image, the more colors the image has in its color palette. For example, an 8-bit RGB image can contain as many as 256 colors. The monitor's bit depth is the number of colors that the monitor will display. This is set as an operating system preference as either 256 colors (8-bit), thousands of colors (16-bit), or millions of colors (32-bit). The number of colors a monitor can display is specific to the computer system. See *27.1 Web Design Basics*.

bitmap image An image made out of pixels, or dots of light, arrayed in a square grid. Each pixel has an associated color and transparency value. The human eye perceives the combination of these pixels as a contiguous image. See *8.1 Image Color Basics*.

Bitmap mode A Photoshop image mode that records all pixels in the image as either black or white. See *8.9 Converting to Bitmap Mode*.

black point The *level* at which pixels in an image are black. Tones in the image are adjusted from that point so that there is a smooth transition with minimal *colorcasts*. You can adjust the black point, *gray point*, and *white point* in both the Levels and Curves dialogs. See *22.3 Adjusting Color Levels Using Curves*.

blending mode The method used to combine the information of pixels when using image-editing operations or painting. See *Color Section: Blending Modes*.

brightness The measurement of the relative lightness or darkness of a pixel using a scale from 0 (black) to 255 (white) or sometimes as a percentage from 0 (black) to 100 (white). See *22.6 Adjusting Brightness and Contrast*.

brush A brush defines the shape, size (diameter), angle, roundness, hardness, and spacing. These options define the general nature of how the brush's stroke will appear. See *13.2 Selecting and Adjusting Brushes*.

burning A technique used in the darkroom to darken areas of an image by increasing the exposure in that area. Photoshop simulates this technique, using the Burn tool, by lowering the *brightness* of pixels. The opposite of burning is *dodging*. See *19.12 Dodging and Burning Images*.

canvas The editable region of the image displayed in the document window. See *1.3 The Document Window*.

channel Channels determine the combinations of colors used to create an image. The number of channels depends on the image's mode. For example, an RGB image contains three color channels—red, green, and blue—in addition to a composite channel of all three channels (which is generally the channel you work on). You can manipulate or draw on any of these channels. You can also hide a channel, eliminating that color from the image. The Channels palette can also include one or more alpha channels or spot colors used in an image. See *4.5 Channels Palette*.

chroma See *saturation*.

CMYK (cyan, magenta, yellow, black) The four ink colors used in *process color* printing. See *24.5 Preparing for Four-Color Printing*.

colorcast A sharp change in color between areas in an image sometimes produced when using *adjustments* or conditional blending. See *21.4 Conditional Blending*.

color depth See *bit depth*.

color mode The method used to record color values in an image. Each color mode has a unique color *gamut* that restricts the colors that can be recorded. Also referred to as the image mode. See *8.8 Converting between Image Modes*.

color model The method used to generate colors used in an image. The *color mode* of an image does not restrict the color model used to generate a color, but some colors generated may fall outside the color mode's *gamut*. See *12.1 Color, Gradient, and Pattern Basics*.

color table A list of color values used in a particular image file. Generally, the greater the number of colors in an image's color table, the clearer the image appears. Also referred to as a color lookup table (CLUT) or color palette. See *27.2 Web Color Basics*.

compression method File format and options used to reduce the size of a saved image file. Virtually all file formats use some form of compression to reduce file size. Some compression methods are lossless and do not degrade the apparent image quality; others are lossy and can more substantially reduce the file size but also degrade the image quality. Compression can be set either at the time the file is saved or when the image is being *optimized*. See *29.3 Optimizing Images*.

de-interlacing See *Interlacing (Video)*.

dither A method used in graphics to place two or more colors close together to create the illusion of a single color. See *27.2 Web Color Basics*.

dodging A technique used in the darkroom to lighten areas of an image by limiting the exposure in that area. Photoshop simulates this technique, using the Dodge tool, by increasing the *brightness* of pixels. The opposite of dodging is *burning*. See *19.12 Dodging and Burning Images*.

dots per inch (dpi)/dots per centimeter (dpc) A measure of the *resolution* of a particular image based on the number of dots in a given linear inch or centimeter of the printed image. The higher the number of dots, the higher the resolution and the sharper the image will be when printed. However, the higher the resolution, the larger the image's file size. See *7.3 Setting the Image Size*.

droplet An *action* that is saved as a file independent of Photoshop. Images can be dragged and dropped onto a droplet to have the actions automatically performed to it. See *18.4 Creating Droplets*.

effects Vector-based styles that can be applied to a layer, but, unlike *filters*, can then be changed as desired. See *15.2 Applying Effects and Styles*.

emulsion The photosensitive side of a piece of film or photographic paper. When printing to film or photographic paper, Photoshop needs to know whether this side is up or down. See *23.1 Print Basics*.

EXIF Information generally recorded by an image captured using a digital camera. The information includes date and time the picture was taken, resolution, ISO speed rating, f/stop, compression, and exposure time. Photoshop can display this information in the File Info dialog. See *6.5 Managing Images with the File Browser*.

feather The gradual opacity transition from the edge to the interior of an image eliminating hard edges and *colorcasts*. Feathering, however, is different from *anti-aliasing*, which applies semitransparent pixels in order to create the appearance of smooth edges. See *9.1 Selection Basics*.

filters Bitmap-based styles that can be applied to a layer but, unlike *effects*, cannot be changed once applied. See *14.1 Filter Basics*.

foreground color One of two selected colors, which is used for the color for foreground elements. For example, this color is used when painting with a *brush*. The default foreground color is black. See *12.1 Colors, Gradient, and Pattern Basics*.

gamma The measurement of the relative contrast and saturation for a computer monitor. Gamma values generally range from 1.0 to 2.8, but can range from 0.1 to 9.99. Gamma values are generally set by the operating system, with Macintosh computers using a default value of 1.8 and Windows computers using a value of 2.2. See *27.2 Web Color Basics*.

gamut The range of colors that a particular *color mode* can produce. Colors that cannot be produced by a particular color mode are said to be "out of gamut." See *5.7 Transparency & Gamut Preferences*.

gray point The *level* at which pixels in an image are 50% gray. Tones in the image are adjusted from that point so that there is a smooth transition with minimal *colorcasts*. You can adjust the *black point*, gray poin*t*, and *white point* in both the Levels and Curves dialogs. See *22.3 Adjusting Color Levels Using Curves*.

grayscale An image that records the *brightness* of pixels using only 8 bits in which any pixel can be one of 256 shades of gray. See *8.8 Converting between Image Modes*.

halftone image The output of an image using printing screens that break down the image into a series of dots of various sizes. Resolution for a halftone image is measured in *lines per inch* (lpi)

and depends on the printer's capabilities. When an image is sent to the printer, Photoshop communicates with the printer to automatically convert the pixel-based image to halftone dots. See *24.5 Preparing for Four-Color Printing*.

highlights An option that isolates the lightest parts of an image for editing separately from *midtones* or *shadows*. See *22.16 Using Color Variations*.

histogram A graph displaying the number of pixels in an image for a given input *level*. The histogram is useful for ensuring that the image maintains a uniform tonal range to produce the highest quality image and can be viewed separately in the Histogram dialog or as a part of the Levels dialog. See *4.9 Histogram Palette*.

History state Each action performed on an image in the canvas is recorded in the History palette as a History state. You can move back and forth between History states in the History palette. History state is often simply referred to as *state*, which should not be confused with *rollover state*. See *7.7 Changing Your Mind*.

hot spot The area of a hypertext link within an image map. See *28.1 Creating Image Maps*.

image cache Memory used to store fully rendered versions of the image at different magnifications. Higher values for the image cache accelerates image redrawing, but requires additional memory. See *5.11 Memory & Image Cache Preferences*.

Indexed Color An image mode used to reduce the color palette for a specific image to 256 or fewer colors. Although this can lead to some image quality loss, it generally significantly reduces the file size. There are several indexed color palette types (exact, system, web, uniform, perceptual, adaptive, and custom), each with its own benefits. See *8.11 Converting to Indexed Color Mode*.

Interlacing (Video) A method used in NTSC video to compress the image signal by creating two fields for every image. When importing NTSC video images as stills into Photoshop, you will need to de-interlace the image using the de-interlace filter. See *20.5 De-interlacing Video Stills*.

Interlacing (Web) A technique set during image *optimization* used by the GIF and PNG-8 formats to progressively display the image. See *29.6 Setting Optimization Options*.

interpolation Techniques used by Photoshop when *resizing* or *resampling* an image. See *7.3 Setting the Image Size*.

jitter Variations in the *brush* stroke that simulate the random oscillations that might occur while painting with a physical brush. See *13.1 Brush Basics*.

kerning The adjustment of space between two specific letters, as opposed to *tracking,* which sets the spacing on both sides of one or more letters. See *17.1 Type Basics*.

layer An isolated collection of image content that can be edited separately from other content in the image. Layers are controlled using the Layers palette. See *10.1 Layer Basics*.

layer mask A bitmap *mask* created by an *alpha channel* applied to a specific layer. See *11.2 Adding Layer Masks*.

leading The spacing between two lines of text in a paragraph. See *17.1 Type Basics*.

levels A measurement of the color or brightness values (0 to 255) in an image generally displayed

in a *histogram.* The levels in an image can be adjusted in the Levels dialog. See *22.2 Adjusting Tonal Range Using Levels*.

lines per inch (lpi)/lines per centimeter (lpc) A measurement of the *resolution* when printing using *halftones*. See *24.5 Preparing for Four-Color Printing*.

lossless compression Techniques used to reduce the size of an image file while saving without loss of image quality. These techniques are not as effective at reducing file size as *lossy compression* techniques, which reduce the file size but also degrade the image quality. See *25.4 Saving as Photoshop PDF*.

lossy compression Techniques used to reduce the size of an image file while saving that result in the loss of image quality. These techniques are more effective at reducing file sizes than *lossless compression* techniques, which reduce the file size but do not degrade the image quality. See *29.3 Optimizing Images*.

luminosity See *brightness*.

mask An element used to isolate parts of a layer preventing it from being edited. *Quick masks* and *type masks* are used to create selections, while *layer masks* and *vector masks* can be used to hide parts of a layer. See *11.1 Mask Basics*.

matte color The color used to turn the semitransparent pixels at the edges of an image fully opaque. This is needed when saving an image that cannot preserve semitransparent colors, such as GIF and PNG-8, so that the edges will integrate with the background color. See *29.6 Setting Optimization Options*.

midtone An option that isolates the midtonal range of an image for editing separately from *highlights* or *shadows*. See *22.16 Using Color Variations*.

NTSC (North American Television Standards Committee) system A video standard used in North America and South America and a few Asian countries. See *20.1 Digital Video Basics*.

optimization Options used to set the *compression method* used to reduce an image's file size for display on the Web. Web compression methods are all *lossy compression*. See *29.3 Optimizing Images*.

paint Used either as a noun meaning any color or pattern that is applied with a *brush* or as a verb referring to the action of painting. See *13.1 Brush Basics*.

painting tools Any tool in Photoshop that uses a *brush* to add *paint* to the *canvas*. See *13.1 Brush Basics*.

PAL (Phase Alternating Line) system A video standard used in Western Europe (including the U.K.), Australia, and most of the world. See *20.1 Digital Video Basics*.

PANTONE A popular brand of spot color inks. The PANTONE Matching System (PMS) is a catalog of inks that are referred to by specific numeric values that can be accessed in Photoshop through the Custom Color Picker. See *12.1 Color, Gradient, and Pattern Basics*.

path A vector object used to mathematically define a line or a shape. Paths are created using anchor points and *Bezier curves* to set their shape. See *16.1 Path Basics*.

pixel (picture element) An individual square of colored light that can be edited in a *bitmap image*. See *27.1 Web Design Basics*.

pixels per inch (ppi)/ pixels per centimeter (ppc) A measurement of *resolution* on computer monitors or scanned images based on the number of pixels in a linear inch or centimeter of the image. See *7.3 Setting the Image Size*.

plug-in An add-on mini-application or filter that adds functionality to Photoshop. See *14.1 Filter Basics*.

process color printing The four-color printing process using *CMYK* inks. See *24.5 Preparing for Four-Color Printing*.

proof colors A control that allows you to preview the image simulating a variety of reproduction processes without having to convert the image to that color work space. See *25.5 Creating Color Proofs*.

Quick mask A type of *mask* used to create and edit selections using *painting tools*. See *9.4 Creating Free-Form Selections*.

raster image See *bitmap image*.

rasterize The process of converting a *vector image* into a *bitmap image*. See *10.10 Rasterizing Vector Layers*.

resample To *resize*, *transform*, or change an image's *resolution*. When an image is resampled down, image information is discarded and cannot be brought back. When an image is resampled up, information is added through *interpolation*. See *5.4 General Preferences*.

resize To change the image's dimensions. This may or may not change the image's resolution, depending on how resizing is performed. See *7.3 Setting the Image Size*.

resolution The measurement of the number of units that occupy a given linear area of an image. Resolution is often measured as a ratio between the number of pixels, dots, or lines per inch or centimeter in the image. See *7.3 Setting the Image Size*.

RIP (raster image processor) Software or device used by a computer, a PostScript printer, or an image setter that rasterizes vector data for output. See *24.1 Preparing to Print*.

rollover A web-page behavior used to change a graphic's appearance when the page visitor interacts with the graphic using the mouse pointer. Each rollover has a corresponding image *state*. See *28.4 Creating Rollovers*.

rollover state A particular action in a *rollover*. Rollover state is often referred to as simply a *state*, but should not be confused with a *History state*. See *28.4 Creating Rollovers*.

saturation A color's intensity as measured by the difference in the color values used to create the color. Colors with low saturation, or chroma, have close color values rendering the color gray. See *22.7 Adjusting Hue, Saturation, and Lightness*.

screen angles The angles at which screens used to create a *halftone image* are placed when printing. See *24.4 Preparing Spot Color and Duotone Images*.

screen frequency The density of dots in a screen used to create halftone images, most often measured in *lines per inch (lpi)/lines per centimeter (lpc)*. See *24.4 Preparing Spot Color and Duotone Images*..

SECAM (Sequential Color and Memory) system A video standard used in some European and Asian countries. See *20.1 Digital Video Basics*.

shadow Option that isolates the darkest parts of an image for editing separately from *highlights* or *midtones*. See *22.16 Using Color Variations*.

slice Individual pieces of an image cut out of the full image to be used to create a final web page using HTML. Individual slices in an image can be *optimized* separately for output. See *29.2 Working with Slices*.

spot color Solid ink colors used in a print job. Spot colors can be used in addition to black or *process colors* to preserve a "pure" color that will appear more vibrant than if it was created using process inks. Each spot color requires its own channel in the Channels palette and plate for printing but is *color mode* independent. See *24.4 Preparing Spot Color and Duotone Images*.

state (History) See *History state*.

state (rollover) See *rollover state*.

stroke A line applied to the border of a selection, a path, or the edges of the content of a layer. See *15.13 Applying the Stroke Effect*.

tracking The adjustment in spacing on both sides of one or more letters, as opposed to *kerning* which adjusts only the spacing between two specific letters. See *17.1 Type Basics*.

transparency Areas in a layer that contain no pixels, allowing pixels from layers underneath to show through. If there is no *background layer* and there are no pixels in the image on any layers in a given area, the transparency pattern will show through. See *5.7 Transparency & Gamut Preferences*.

trap A technique used when preparing images for *process color printing* that helps reduce the number of unwanted gaps that sometimes appear when printing using *halftone* screens by adding overlapping areas of color. See *24.1 Preparing to Print*.

type mask A type of *mask* used to create and edit selections using type tools. See *17.1 Type Basics*.

value See *brightness*.

vector mask A vector-based *mask* created using *paths* applied to a specific layer. See *11.6 Adding Vector Masks*.

Web-safe colors The 216 colors (based on an 8-bit color palette) that the Macintosh and Windows operating systems share in common in their color palette. Web browsers on older computers display only a maximum of 256 colors, and the 216 browsers-safe colors always display on these machines with little or no change from machine to machine. See *27.2 Web Color Basics*.

white point The *level* at which pixels in an image are white. Tones in the image are adjusted from that point so that there is a smooth transition with minimal *colorcasts*. You can adjust the *black point*, *gray point*, and white point in both the Levels and Curves dialogs. See *22.3 Adjusting Color Levels Using Curves*.

XMP (Extensible Metadata Platform) The format used for file information embedded in an image file by Photoshop. XMP is an open standard based on XML. See *6.5 Managing Images with the File Browser*.

Index

Note to the Reader: Throughout this index **boldfaced** page numbers indicate primary discussions of a topic.

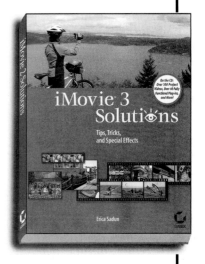
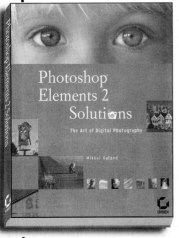

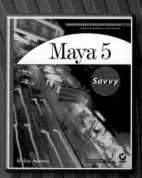